DISCARD

D1065290

Volunteers

Philanthropic and Nonprofit Studies
Dwight F. Burlingame and David C. Hammack, editors

Volunteers

A Social Profile

Marc A. Musick
and John Wilson

Indiana University Press
Bloomington and Indianapolis

This book is a publication of

Indiana University Press
601 North Morton Street
Bloomington, IN 47404-3797 USA

http://iupress.indiana.edu

Telephone orders	800-842-6796
Fax orders	812-855-7931
Orders by e-mail	iuporder@indiana.edu

The paper used in this publication meets the minimum requirements of
American National Standard for Information Sciences—Permanence of
Paper for Printed Library Materials, ANSI Z39.48-1984.

Manufactured in the United States of America

Library of Congress Cataloging-in-Publication Data

Musick, Marc A.
    Volunteers : a social profile / Marc A. Musick and John Wilson.
        p. cm.—(Philanthropic and nonprofit studies)
    Includes bibliographical references and index.
    ISBN 978-0-253-34929-3 (cloth)
 1. Voluntarism. 2. Volunteers. I. Wilson, John, 1942- II. Title.
    HN49.V64M87 2007
    302'.14—dc22
                                                           2007005798

1 2 3 4 5 13 12 11 10 09 08

Contents

Preface

This book combines what we believe to be the best of the most recent research on volunteers with additional research of our own on most of the topics covered. We explain the order of treatment in the introductory chapter, but after chapter 2, in which we cover some basic issues concerning definition and measurement, it is not necessary to read the chapters in any particular order. In the case of our own analyses, we report some results in the form of figures and tables in the text, but most of the empirical documentation for our arguments is contained in over one hundred tables that are not published in the book itself but are available in PDF form (http://www.iupress.indiana .edu/catalog/product_info.php?products_id=41769) for consultation by readers interested in looking at the analyses in more detail. We refer to these tables by number in the text within brackets [—]. In the appendix we describe the data sets on which we rely for our own analyses.

Acknowledgments

We gratefully acknowledge receipt of a University Cooperative Society Subvention Grant awarded by the University of Texas at Austin to help make publication of this book possible. We also wish to thank the RGK Center for Philanthropy and Community Service at the University of Texas at Austin for their generous support of this research.

Volunteers

Part 1.

An Introduction to Volunteering

In chapter 1 we describe and explain the recent upsurge of interest in volunteering. For a number of reasons, volunteer work has received increased scrutiny in recent years, much of it driven by public concern that volunteerism should be encouraged in the face of forces that threaten to undermine it. Increased funding for research in this area has been a boon to social scientists, providing abundant survey data on rates of volunteering in the population, socio-demographic differences in volunteerism, and detailed information on the hours volunteers contribute and the kinds of activities to which they contribute them. These same data also allow new insights into the consequences of doing volunteer work for the volunteer. In chapter 2 we tackle the difficult issue of properly defining volunteer work, paying particular attention to its relationship with social activism and caring for relatives and friends. Having defined the term, we then discuss various ways of measuring volunteer work in social surveys and anticipate some of the ways we will be using these measurements for data analysis later in the book. We conclude this chapter with a discussion of how to categorize the various types of volunteer work people do and how to use these categories to obtain a clearer picture of who does what kind of volunteer work.

1

The Importance of Studying Volunteering

Volunteering is a form of altruistic behavior. Its goal is to provide help to others, a group, an organization, a cause, or the community at large, without expectation of material reward. Sociological attempts to understand altruistic behavior are almost as old as the discipline itself. Indeed, Auguste Comte, the man who coined the term "sociology" in the middle of the nineteenth century, also invented the term "altruism" because, in societies increasingly given over to the pursuit of self-interest and material rewards, acts of selflessness were a puzzle. The rise of individualism ("egoism") created the problem of altruism. However, the systematic empirical study of volunteerism is relatively new, in part because the volunteer role has only recently become fully institutionalized and in part because of a tendency to marginalize volunteer work as a leisure time pursuit. Although volunteers are widely admired because they give their time freely to help others, their work is devalued precisely because it is given away. If a job were really worth doing, someone would be paid to do it.

Growing Interest in Volunteering

After several decades of neglect, an upsurge of interest in volunteering has occurred in recent years. Governments have assumed greater responsibility for mobilizing volunteer labor; surveys have been conducted to measure the extent and distribution of volunteerism; scholarly publications on the topic and professional associations devoted to the study and development of the non-profit sector in general and volunteering in particular have multiplied. There are a number of reasons for this.

First, after a period of time during which advocates of the welfare state anticipated the demise of charitable works as a means of providing social services, it is becoming more and more apparent that volunteer labor will *always* be necessary to help government agencies achieve their goals. The expansion of government in the twentieth century has not made volunteers redundant. Instead, politicians from both the left and the right have become advocates of volunteerism. For those positioned on the political right the economic crises of the 1970s called for a reduction in public expenditures, greater freedom for market forces, and the promotion of self-sufficiency and individual initiative. President Reagan complained that Americans had allowed government to take away services that used to be provided, and provided better, by private philanthropy. Prime Minister Thatcher expressed her belief that the volunteer movement was the true heart of social welfare provision and that the statutory services should be funded only to fill in the gaps left by private philanthropy. For those positioned on the political left, support for voluntarism came mainly in the form of encouraging grassroots civic participation, decentralization of power, and greater self-determination, especially for the under-privileged in society. Despite their differences as to why volunteers were needed, both parties agreed that more needed to be known about the volunteer labor force. For example, in many Western democracies governments have been pressured to supply quality end-of-life care at a level they cannot afford. Hospice programs have become an increasingly popular method of providing end-of-life care, but in the United States but more than three-quarters of the people who currently work in hospice programs are volunteers (Black and Kovacs 1999:479). Many other non-profit organizations and many government agencies now rely heavily on volunteer labor to achieve their goals. Volunteer labor has thus become an important instrument of public policy in many capitalist countries. This helps explain why, in 2002, after many years of neglect the U.S. government, through the Corporation for National and Community Service, began sponsoring annual surveys of volunteerism administered by the U.S. Bureau of Labor as a special supplement to the annual Current Population Survey (CPS). In this book we draw frequently on the data gathered in these surveys.

The growth of identity politics is a second reason why interest in volunteerism has grown in recent years. Identity politics focuses on issues of descent and claims to political power and social recognition based on group identities. As an expression of post-materialist values, this kind of politics signals a shift from issues of distribution to those of identity: it does not follow traditional class alignments. Identity issues have spawned a wide range of groups that draw heavily on volunteer labor but defy conventional theories of volunteering. It is impossible to account for this kind of volunteerism in terms of a "cost-benefit" analysis because the volunteer work is itself an expression of identity and is intrinsically rewarding. As a result of the rise of identity politics, a new demand for volunteer labor has arisen in areas (e.g., gay rights, Latino rights) to replace those that are declining (e.g., union organizer, fraternity officer).

A third reason for the upsurge of interest in volunteering is growing concern, best articulated in Robert Putnam's *Bowling Alone* (2000), that old models of civic engagement and associational life are strained by new forms of social diversity and by economic and technological changes that threaten to undermine "civil society" and weaken democratic political structures. Volunteers help counter this threat: they contribute directly to the democratic process during and in between political campaigns; many political offices at the local level are unpaid and rely on volunteers to fill them. Volunteerism also supports democracy indirectly, by helping create the "social capital"—an interlocking network of social relationships—upon which much of the social activism of a democratic society depends. Volunteerism can also temper the impersonalism of an increasingly bureaucratized life by getting people personally involved in their community and providing face-to-face services and the commercialism of an increasingly commodified society by offering services that are not contingent on the ability to pay. To the degree that people become concerned about the population becoming more privatized and deserting the "public square" they will also be concerned about the future supply of volunteer labor.

A fourth stimulus to studies of volunteering has been recent efforts to rethink the nature of work, or productive labor, in modern societies. Under the influence of feminist scholars, the idea of what counts as "productive" labor has been broadened to include household chores, child care, and care for elderly kin, as well as informal and formal help provided to relative strangers. A similar impetus comes from gerontologists interested in the continued productivity of an expanding elderly population whose post-retirement life can last as long as the years they spent on the job: volunteer work is one way to age "successfully." The study of volunteering is thus absorbed within a broader investigation of how work is being restructured and re-defined in capitalist societies. Typical of this approach is that adopted by Tilly and Tilly (1998:32) in their book on the varieties of work under capitalism. They point out that most work in capitalist societies is performed in the labor market, where it is commodified (i.e., remunerated). Household labor is production within households that is consumed by members of the same household. Volunteer work is "unpaid effort provided to parties to whom the worker owes no contractual, familial, or friendship obligation." As we noted above, the steady focus of social scientists on paid work and domestic labor has tended to overshadow the subject of volunteer work, which has sometimes been devalued precisely because it is unpaid. More recently, however, efforts have been made to integrate all studies of work in to the same conceptual framework. It is worth noting at this point that, by treating volunteering as "unpaid productive labor," we change the way we think about volunteering, from it being a gift of time to being simply work that is unpaid. It is therefore an activity that could be explained by using more or less the same theories as are used to explain participation in the conventional labor force, theories that refer to the resources individuals command.

A final reason why interest in volunteering has increased recently is the non-profit sector demand for science-based information on volunteers to be used for more effective recruitment and retention methods. The non-profit sector has transformed itself from the somewhat informal and inchoate world of philanthropy and charities to a more rationalized world where non-profit organizations model themselves on business corporations or government agencies. Non-profits confront much the same kind of organizational and operational problems as those faced by businesses and state bureaucracies. What does social science have to say about where to find people who are willing to volunteer and how best to recruit them? What do sociological studies tell us about the kinds of volunteer work people prefer to do? How can people today be persuaded to fit volunteer work into their increasingly busy lives? How can people surrounded by economic incentives and materialistic values be motivated to volunteer when pecuniary and other material rewards are unavailable? Given the difficulty of recruiting new volunteers, how can volunteers be persuaded to continue making their contribution? How is the volunteer role best incorporated into an organization in which paid staff exercise authority? In short, can the research findings of social scientists help practitioners better recruit, train, motivate, and retain volunteers in a non-profit sector rapidly taking on the rational properties of other sectors?

Outline of the Book

The book begins at a logical starting point: the definition of volunteer work. As we shall see, this is not such a simple matter as it might appear. Thereafter, the general outline of the book broadly follows the volunteer process as described by Snyder and Omoto (1992:219). The first stage (parts 2 and 3) involves the antecedents of volunteerism and addresses the issue of who volunteers and why. The second stage (parts 4 and 5) concerns the experiences of volunteers and those they work with and how these experiences are socially organized. The third stage (part 6) focuses on the consequences of volunteerism and looks at the changes in attitudes, knowledge, and behavior that occur in people when they undertake volunteer work.

We approach the study of the antecedents of volunteer work from the same perspective as that adopted by Brady et al. (1995:271) when they suggest reasons why more people do not get involved in civic life: "because they can't, because they don't want to, or because nobody asked." In other words, people cannot volunteer if they lack the individual resources needed, they will not volunteer if they are not disposed, or motivated, to do so, and they are unlikely to volunteer if nobody asks them to do so or, in what amounts to the same thing, they do not move in the social circles where doing volunteer work is common and expected.

We have arranged our discussion of the antecedents of volunteering with this categorization in mind, although we alter the order in which these topics are discussed. We start with a discussion of theories that invoke micro-level variables to explain volunteering. These variables describe attributes of individuals. We begin our discussion of attributes with theories that focus on people's state of mind as they contemplate volunteering (part 2). The common thread in these theories is people's subjective states: how they interpret the volunteer act and imagine themselves doing it. The discussion of micro-level variables continues with a review of theories that have in common the idea that people do not volunteer "because they can't": in other words, they lack the resources necessary (part 3). This section of the book reviews, and seeks to add to, the research on the influence of "human capital" on volunteering, namely, resources such as a good education, a well-paying job, plentiful free time, and good health. As a conclusion to this section on micro-level variables we discuss the influence of gender and race on volunteering. We leave the discussion of these "master statuses" (so called because their influence is universal) until last to enable us to see whether any influence of race and gender on volunteering is attributable to subjective dispositions or to variation in individual resources. For example, race differences in volunteering might actually be the result of differences in educational achievement between racial groups.

Part 4 of the book focuses on the social context of volunteering, describing the role of macro-level variables. We interpret the term "social context" broadly to embrace all variables that refer to the relationships people have with others. Social relationships alter the kinds of expectations placed upon us by others, our sense of obligation. They also limit our ability to volunteer even if we have the desire and the resources to do so. We begin by describing how volunteer work is influenced by the family life course. As we pass through life, our family relationships and obligations change, and these changes have a major influence on our volunteer work. We move on to a discussion of how extra-household social relationships, such as friendships and memberships in social clubs, influence volunteerism. We follow this with a chapter on one important reason why social context makes a difference: the influence of being asked to volunteer. We then draw back to look at the influence of neighborhood characteristics on volunteering. Expanding our horizon still further, we next look at cross-national differences in volunteering. We then compare historical periods by looking at the evidence on trends in volunteering.

It is important to note that social context can have an effect on behavior quite independent of the effect of individual-level variables. For example, we might be more likely to volunteer if we are doing well in school and getting good grades. But we might also be more likely to volunteer if we attend a school that organizes and supports community service. In this case, the social context is conducive to volunteering. Indeed, it might even boost the chances of volunteering of students who are not doing well in class. We assume that structural variables precede the act of volunteering and therefore cause it. For example, women living in households where there are school age children might, for that reason, take up volunteering. As we shall point out, however, it is quite possible that, for some women, the decision to devote a lot of their time to volunteering and the decision to have lots of children are made simultaneously.

We have thus laid out the thinking behind the arrangement of topics for the discussion of who volunteers and suggested some of the ways in which the various topics are related to each other. The important thing to remember is that, because we cannot talk about all things at once, we are forced to create an artificial separation between factors that are, in real life, interconnected. As we make our way through all these theories and variables, we will have many occasions to remark on the interconnectedness of variables and in many cases we analyze these interconnections. For example, we consider whether the influence of a micro-level variable, such as education, is moderated or changed by a macro-level variable, such as social networks. We are also aware of the fact that many of the studies we describe and many of our own analyses are cross-sectional. Volunteering and the "antecedent" variable are actually measured at the same time. This means that we have no way of knowing which comes first. For example, we find an association between volunteering and self-esteem: this could mean that people with high self-esteem volunteer more, or it could mean that volunteering boosts self-esteem. Even stable individual attributes, such as race and gender, can be affected by volunteering. For example, if doing volunteer work on behalf of a women's shelter changes your ideas about gender roles, you have changed your ideas about what it means to be a man or a woman. And although we have indicated some of the ways the variables are related to each other, the important thing to bear in mind is that they are all interrelated. For example, the more education we get the more trusting we tend to become, but trusting people probably do better in school and people who do well in school are more likely to volunteer. This makes the pathway from education to volunteering very complicated.

In part 5 we describe the research on performing the volunteer role. In the first chapter in this section we draw on survey data to describe and explain who does what kind of volunteer task. We are particularly interested in whether there is job segregation among volunteers—whether certain volunteer jobs are allocated to particular groups of people. In the second chapter in this section we draw mainly on ethnographic studies of volunteers in organizations. Most people volunteer in connection with an organization. Indeed, many surveys specify that the gift of time be made to an organization. Many organizations rely heavily on volunteer labor. How is the management of unpaid work different from the management of paid work? In the absence of pay, what incentives can organizations offer volunteers to encourage them to sign up and remain loyal? How committed are volunteers to their work and what determines their loyalty? How important is it that volunteer tasks meet the needs of the volunteer? How do organizations handle the relation between volunteers and paid staff? How do organizations manage the relation between volunteers and clients?

In part 6, we turn our attention to the consequences of volunteering for the volunteer. Many people believe that volunteering is good for them. What is the evidence to support this assertion? We examine the three kinds of consequences that have received the bulk of research attention. Chapter 20 discusses the research on volunteering and citizenship. We interpret the term "citizenship" very broadly to include not only attitudes and actions conventionally thought of as "citizen-like," such as voting, but also, in the second half of this chapter, social conformity. For example, is there any evidence that volunteering keeps young people "out of trouble"? According to social surveys, some people volunteer because they want to gain useful job skills, get their foot in the door of an organization where they would like to work for pay, or to make business contacts as a result of their volunteer work. Chapter 21 looks at the evidence on whether volunteers benefit from their volunteer work as far as jobs and wages are concerned. Finally, social surveys indicate that many people say they "feel better" as a result of their volunteer work. Chapter 21 also discusses the research on the effect of volunteering on health. Is there any evidence that volunteers enjoy better mental health than non-volunteers? What about physical health? Is there any evidence that volunteers experience fewer health problems and disabilities? Do volunteers tend to live longer than non-volunteers even when we take other factors that might contribute to their longevity into account?

In this book we rely heavily on data gathered by survey researchers. Much can be learned from these data about the characteristics of volunteers. However, all survey research relegates to the background the role of organizations and social institutions in shaping people's opinions and attitudes. In our case, we provide little information on how people's perceptions of volunteer work and their suitability for it, or their moral imperative to undertake it, are shaped by non-profit organizations and the voluntary sector in general. In real life, the relationship between the volunteer (supply) and the volunteer opportunity (demand) is an interactive one. Unfortunately, survey research treats individual characteristics as preconditions of volunteer work, as if the potential were fixed and known in advance. Interaction with a volunteer organization, or with volunteers working for it, or people who have been helped by it, can alter the way people think about themselves, changing, perhaps, an individual to a collective identity. Meeting a gay activist can turn a gay man from a villain to a victim. Nevertheless, survey research has added immeasurably to our knowledge of volunteers and the work they do. The profile of the volunteer can be drawn with considerable confidence on the basis of the data provided by these surveys with the help of appropriate analytical methods.

2

What Is Volunteering?

In this chapter we will interrogate the meaning of terms such as "volunteer" and "volunteerism." Besides the more obvious forms of one-on-one help, volunteering has been used to refer to mutual aid, as when a group of people work together to achieve a common goal, such as digging a well; organizational participation and self-governance, as when people contribute time to maintaining an organization, such as a religious congregation or a trade union branch; and campaigning and advocacy, as when people contribute their time out of a desire for social change and social justice, such as advocacy on behalf of people with disabilities. As we shall see, it is often quite difficult to decide whether an activity is volunteer work or not. Although the term "volunteer" is a familiar part of everyday language in Western cultures, we cannot be sure it indicates a distinct sphere of social practice in a way that is useful for scientific purposes. From a scientific point of view, concepts should be both internally consistent and clearly demarcate the phenomenon we want to study from others like it. They should group together actions that belong together and are distinguishable from similar but theoretically different actions. Where does volunteerism end and similar activities such as participating in a voluntary association, social activism, and caring for an elderly relative begin? Do we want to consider helping one's elderly neighbor clear snow from her driveway a volunteer act? We also want the term to be internally consistent. Should we treat mentoring teenagers, serving as a guide at the state museum, and preparing posters for the upcoming anti-abortion rally as the same kind of behavior?

Most social scientists—and most of the general public—are realists. They believe that volunteerism does, in fact, possess a self-evident essence. They believe there are clear and identifiable behaviors "out there" that can be described straightforwardly using terms such as "volunteer" and "volunteerism" and that all these behaviors have something in common. Once they are so described and measured, they can be explained through the use of conventional social science methods. Although this might seem to be a simple and straightforward solution to the definitional problem, it largely sidesteps the theoretically problematic status of the nature of volunteering. For example, economists think of volunteer work as unpaid productive labor, in part because it is easier to measure it with empirical indicators. But this tells us nothing about the diverse meanings of volunteer work, nor does it explain why productive labor is, in this case, unpaid. We need to remain open to the possibility that volunteerism is defined, in part, by its motivation.[1]

As part of its 2001 celebration of "The Year of the Volunteer," the United Nations issued a "toolkit" for people planning surveys to gather information on volunteers. Three criteria were used to identify volunteer behavior: it is not undertaken for financial gain; it is undertaken of one's own free will; it brings benefits to a third party as well as to the people who volunteer (Dingle 2001:11). But even with (or especially with) this rather simple definition, a number of caveats were issued. It was allowed that volunteers *can* be reimbursed (perhaps for expenses), but the amount should not exceed the market value of the work. It was acknowledged that people often volunteer as a result of peer pressure or a feeling of social obligation, but this is not the same as being *required* to do the work or being forced to do the work as a matter of need. Beneficiaries of volunteer work, it was allowed, *can* include friends, neighbors, and complete strangers as well as more abstract causes such as "the environment" or "the arts."

We begin this chapter by drawing a distinction between joining a voluntary association and volunteering. Membership in a voluntary association, especially where the membership is described as "active," can resemble volunteerism and is often associated with it, but it is not the same as volunteering. Then we will consider attempts to derive a social science definition of volunteerism from how that term is used and understood in everyday language. We will see that many people think of volunteers as providing help to others at some cost to themselves. We will consider how helpful it is to think of volunteer work being costly when people's ideas of cost can vary so widely. We will then discuss whether obligation is an essential part of volunteering, followed by a discussion of whether volunteer work is distinctive in its motivation. The bulk of the chapter is devoted to comparing the meaning of volunteering with two cognate sociological categories, social activism and caring. We will argue that there is more overlap between volunteerism and social activism than is ordinarily recognized by social scientists and that little is to be gained by treating them as distinct phenomena. We will argue that, although caring and volunteering are cognate activities in that one is the provision of help informally and the other the provision of help formally, this distinction between informal and formal is a crucial one. We will also argue against the position that volunteering is simply a formalized method of caring. We will conclude with a discussion of some of the hidden biases of particular ways of thinking about volunteer work.

Membership versus Volunteering

Although membership (or even "participation") in voluntary associations and volunteerism are associated, they are not the same thing (Cutler and Danigelis 1993:150). Indeed, it could be said that people who belong to a voluntary association and limit their involvement to simply attending meetings or otherwise drawing on the benefits of being a member (e.g., playing a tennis game at the tennis club, reading the newsletter) are quintessential "free-loaders" because they consume the "public goods" created by other members of the organization without contributing to their production. Even attending a meeting or rally sponsored or organized by a voluntary association is a questionable measure of volunteerism because behind the stage were people who actually planned, organized, and raised the funds necessary for the event. Surveys that go no further than simply asking if people are "active" members of a voluntary association are not therefore providing much information on volunteer work (Hooghe 2003b:54).

Given the fact that volunteering is often defined as unpaid work *for an organization,* there is bound to be considerable overlap between membership in voluntary associations and volunteering. The World Values Survey data from 1990–1993 shows that the countries with the highest rate of voluntary association memberships are also the countries with the highest rate of people doing "unpaid work for" an organization. Iceland, the Netherlands, and the United States have the highest membership rates and the highest volunteer rates. Nevertheless, in most cases, the volunteer rate (people doing unpaid work for an organization) is about half the membership rate (Torcal and Montero 1999:172). And many people volunteer who are not members of a voluntary association at all. You do not have to belong to a voluntary association to teach people to read, drive them to the hospital for their doctor's appointments, or answer the telephones during the fund-raising campaign of the local public radio station. Later on in the book we will look at the relation between voluntary association memberships and volunteer work. We will find that joiners tend to be volunteers, but we will also find that by no means do all joiners volunteer. Indeed, anybody who has done volunteer work for a voluntary organization will be painfully aware that a small minority of members does much of the work.

The Net-Cost Definition of Volunteering

Having established that volunteer work is different from mere membership, even active membership, in a voluntary association, we are better positioned to define volunteer work in more general terms. When people think of a volunteer, they almost always imagine someone who is making a *sacrifice* to help another person, an organization, or a cause. In other words, they tend to think of volunteer work in terms of rewards and costs, as demonstrated in a remarkable series of studies in which respondents were asked to classify a range of behaviors according to how closely they approximated their idea of volunteerism. The first study used content analysis of writings on volunteering to arrive at a "synthesized" definition of volunteer work with four components. According to this definition, a volunteer act is voluntary, un-rewarded, organized, and of benefit to strangers. To see how well these components reflected popular understandings of what it means to be a volunteer, a list of twenty-one questionnaire items, each describing a particular act, was developed. Respondents were asked to rate each item on a scale of 1 = definitely a volunteer to 5 = not a volunteer. The item receiving the lowest mean score was "An adult who offers his or her time to be a Big Brother or Big Sister." The item receiving the highest mean score was "An accountant charged with embezzling who accepts a sentence of 250 hours of community service in lieu of prosecution." There was widespread agreement on these ratings (Cnaan et al. 1996). Evidently, people think of human behavior largely in utilitarian terms, assuming that an activity will not take place unless rewards exceed costs. Volunteering is defined as behavior that violates this rule. The more seriously the rule is violated, the more confidently people assign the behavior to the volunteer category "the individual incurring higher net-cost is likely to be perceived as 'more' of a volunteer than someone with a lower net-cost" (Miejs et al. 2003:20).[2]

The net-cost approach assumes that volunteers provide a service for which they do not get material rewards or, if they do, their costs exceed these rewards. It does not rule out any possibility of volunteers obtaining material benefits, such as job skills or business contacts. Almost all (93%) of the volunteers surveyed in the 1997 United Kingdom National Survey of Volunteering saw nothing wrong with people obtaining qualifications (e.g., first aid skills) as a result of their voluntary activity. Not surprisingly, young people (18–24) were twice as likely as older people to approve of this (Smith 1998:104). As we shall see later, the issue is one of motives. If people volunteer *only* because they want to improve their job skills then it is considered too utilitarian, too calculating, to be considered a real gift of time. Selflessness is therefore an important component of the lay definition of volunteering. We should put the interests of the other person or the group ahead of our own. Although surveys show that volunteers are uncomfortable with the idea of getting paid for what they do, the payment of volunteers is not an anachronism (Frey and Goette 1999:2).[3]

In the United States it is deemed acceptable for volunteers to have their out-of-pocket expenses, such as travel and meals, defrayed, or they can claim these donations as charitable gifts on their income tax returns. AmeriCorps, one of the best-known volunteer programs in the United States, pays its workers.[4] In return for one year of service volunteers are awarded an education scholarship, the amount being doubled for two years of service. Significantly, the reward here is not cash, which would have been symbolically inappropriate, but credit toward something deemed good by the wider society. At the other end of the life course, Foster Grandparents are also paid a stipend. The justification in this case is that older people should be encouraged to volunteer to have a more productive and rewarding life of retirement but they, more than younger people, will be deterred by lack of economic resources. In the United Kingdom, the non-profit organization Age Concern recruits volunteers to act as "Good Neighbors" to look after a number of elderly people in their neighborhood. As with the Foster Grandparents program, the organization assumes that the financial cost of volunteering is an impediment and that stipends can help overcome it.

Stipends for volunteering are rare. Few non-profit agencies and voluntary associations can afford to offer this inducement. There are also ethical and psychological reasons for not offering stipends. In the eyes of many, volunteer work is an opportunity to express values of compassion and the like and it would not be ethical to allow volunteers to profit materially from their work. In addition, volunteer work becomes less attractive if material incentives are attached to it. This is explained by a number of social psychological experiments showing that people who are paid to perform a task they did previously for its own sake tend to reduce their effort. "External" rewards undermine intrinsic motivation.[5]

What about benefits other than material rewards? Do these exclude the activity from the volunteer category? Unfortunately, none of the fifty items shown to the respondents in the surveys described earlier allow respondents to indicate they receive psychic benefits from volunteering and we do not know whether someone who admitted to seeking them would be defined as a less than "pure" volunteer (Miejs et al. 2003). And yet volunteers frequently acknowledge the psychic benefits they receive from volunteering. A focus group study in which participants were already volunteering found that for some volunteers "the intrinsic rewards were so great that they described their participation in voluntary activity as a 'selfish' exercise" (Flick et al. 2002:51). Admittedly, non-volunteers, who do not share the "taste" for volunteering, might not be so quick to see these kinds of benefits. Interestingly, some of the younger volunteers in the focus groups described their work as "less honorable" because they believe they benefited from it, even if these rewards were intrinsic.

Finally, we should note that "interests" narrowly defined often play some role in volunteer work. We are more likely to become environmental activists if our backyards are being polluted than we would if our backyards were not threatened. The threat raises the chances we will get involved, although it is by no means a sufficient condition. A study of participation in block organizations set up to help residents find ways to revitalize their neighborhoods found that activists had lived in the community longer and had more children living at home than residents who did not get involved (Wandersman et al. 1987:542). Activists were more likely to define their neighborhood as having problems than non-activists. In short, residents with a greater "stake" in their neighborhood and who were more aware of the need for community action were more likely to volunteer. When Illinois residents were asked in 2000 what it would take to get them more involved in volunteer activities, the most frequently mentioned factor was more free time (25%), but a sizeable minority (18%) said they would get more involved if they were personally affected by the outcome, if their neighborhood was affected by development, if their jobs demanded some action, or if they would personally benefit from the activity (Profile 2001). In all these cases, volunteers stood to benefit from the work, but this did not disqualify them from volunteer status because they were pursuing a collective good that others would enjoy even if they contributed none of their time. Volunteers often, therefore, pay a premium price for any benefits they reap and, because there are others who will benefit even though they do nothing, interests alone cannot be a sufficient explanation for their behavior.

Using Motives to Define Volunteering

The net-cost approach tries to be objective about the definition of volunteering. It should be possible for a third party to look at the "volunteer" activities and decide whether the costs exceed the benefits, in which case the designation is appropriate. This is congruent with the utilitarian approach, according to which volunteer work is unpaid productive labor. From a utilitarian perspective there is no need to ask what the work means to the volunteer. Volunteering is simply work done outside the home and outside the job market in an organizational setting, performed during the time left over from housework, child care, and paid work. It is not really a form of leisure because leisure time pursuits tend to be abandoned once they no longer provide intrinsic gratification, whereas people will continue volunteering even though it is sometimes unpleasant. From the utilitarian perspective, volunteering cannot be defined by its motivation. Motives might explain volunteer work but they do not define it.

Other social scientists, however, believe that motivation is intrinsic to a definition of volunteer work. It is not simply "unpaid labor" but unpaid labor that is appropriately motivated. This is already intimated in the earlier discussion about the role of benefits in defining volunteering, where benefits are allowed so long as they are not the primary reason for doing the work.[6] Thus, although there is agreement that people can benefit from their volunteer work, they must not volunteer *for the purpose of* gaining those benefits. They would, presumably, continue to volunteer even if those benefits disappeared. In a focus group convened to discuss the duties of citizenship, a majority of members agreed that volunteering was a good example of virtuous behavior. The group members then debated whether it was possible to judge an act as virtuous without considering the underlying motive. One woman said, "In order to classify someone as good—good citizen, good person—you've got to look at their motives" (Conover et al. 1993:161). If people are properly motivated, any benefits they might earn as a side effect of their volunteer work are tolerated. For example, serving on the board of trustees of a cultural institution is a prized symbol of social status in many communities. Often membership on the board is conditional on donating a large sum of money to the institution. But the suspicion that a person is donating this money *in order to* get a place on the board is enough to blackball him. "You have to demonstrate . . . that your heart is in the right place" (Ostrower 2002:28).

In the public mind, then, volunteer work is not simply unpaid labor but unpaid labor performed for the correct reason. "Good works" are inspired by virtues such as generosity, love, gratitude, loyalty, courage, compassion, and a desire for justice (Martin 1994:31; Wuthnow 1995:175). Purity of motivation becomes the template against which individual acts are compared and volunteer status is denied to those motivated primarily by self-interest (Campbell and Wood 1999:44). Non-profit agencies reflect this view, that "real" volunteers have the right motives and respond to the right incentives. For example, emergency squads resist the use of financial incentives (such as tax credits, health benefits, or assistance with continuing education) to attract new volunteers because they worry recruits attracted by an incentive program would not be committed in the same way as "pure" volunteers (Thompson 1993a). The core members of the search and rescue organization studied by Lois (2003:68) denied themselves the reward even of prestige in the community: "one technique of self-denial was to wear pagers on a belt but to turn them in toward the body so that the search and rescue emblem was not visible. By downplaying their group affiliation, members signaled to others that they were not motivated by self-gain."[7]

In summary, a sound argument can be made that motives help define volunteer work and that volunteer work cannot simply be defined as "unpaid labor." But it is no simple matter to agree on the appropriate motivation for volunteer work, and this has persuaded most social scientists to treat motives as exogenous to volunteer work. They do not constitute volunteer work, but they can help explain it. In chapter 4 we will discuss various approaches to the relation between volunteerism and motives.

Volunteering and Social Activism

To a considerable degree the study of volunteerism has developed independently of the study of social activism. Volunteerism has been most closely associated with studies of voluntary associations and non-profit organizations, while social activism has been most closely associated with studies of social movements. They have developed as somewhat distinct fields of social science investigation, as if they referred to totally different social phenomena, each requiring its own conceptualization and theorization. In this section we will consider the meaning of volunteerism as distinct from social activism. We will then discuss some of the similarities between the meanings of the two terms.

Differences

Volunteering and activism are typically contrasted using phrases such as "palliation versus prevention," or "short-term versus long-term solutions to social problems." Volunteering targets people; activism targets structures. Activists care "about solutions that would not depend so completely on each individual's personal feelings of generosity and personal ability to donate money, space, and time but on solutions that would be built into official institutions" (Eliasoph 1998:175). The activist changes while the volunteer maintains: "Some types of participation are aimed at fostering cooperation (especially volunteering), others at raising hell" (Uslaner and Decker 2001:183). The activist mans the barricades, marches and demonstrates, boycotts, strikes, signs petitions, and occupies buildings; volunteer work is a "mopping up" activity, "dealing with the unfortunate social externalities of a formal economic system which expresses its imperfections harshly and inequitably in the lives of ordinary people" (Milroy and Wismer 1994:74). The activist fights to create and secure funding for shelters, counseling services, health centers, and the like, while the volunteer helps run the places once they are established. A literacy tutor who becomes convinced the illiteracy of those he is mentoring is due to racism might continue to teach writing but might also look for ways to get involved in improving education facilities in minority neighborhoods and thus become an activist. On the other hand, a volunteer might choose to "fight" AIDS as a friendly visitor to people dying of AIDS although he is aware of political campaigns organized to improve the treatment of AIDS patients in which he could become an activist (Chambre 1995:124).[8]

This distinction between changing social conditions and providing services is part of the vernacular language of politics. In *Volunteerism and the Status of Women: A Position Paper* issued by the Women and Volunteerism Task Force of the National Organization of Women, "change-directed" volunteerism (of which the organization approved) was distinguished from "service-oriented" volunteerism, which "seeks to complement insufficiently funded social services with non-paid labor in order to alleviate social ills. In addition it blunts the pressure for a more equal distribution of the nation's wealth, by muting the unrest which threatens the economic privileges and power of the well-to-do" (quoted in Gold 1979:21). The organization disapproved of "service-oriented" volunteerism. A distinction between volunteering and activism is also implied—and abetted—by the way in which governments treat voluntary organizations, at least in the United States, where tax exempt status is granted only to those organizations that refrain from lobbying, issuing propaganda, electioneering, or engaging in any other partisan political activity.

There is much to be said for making these distinctions. Making the coffee after Sunday morning worship service is surely different from knocking on doors in a voter registration drive in the segregated South in the 1960s. We do not think of volunteers when we hear of people being threatened, beaten, jailed, suspended from school or college, fired from their jobs, or having crosses burned on their lawn. The same distinction can be drawn between different types of organizations. Some organizations provide social services; others see their mission as political or social change, their goal being to bring people together into an organization that can exert power.

Empirical evidence suggests that this distinction between volunteerism and activism is real to many people, that they are aware of differences and choose between them. Poppendieck (1998:274) believes that some people adopt the identity of volunteer and reject the identity of activist because being a volunteer gives them more satisfaction: "Preparing a meal with a group of other people and serving it is fun; writing to your representative is work." People are drawn to volunteer work because of the opportunity to provide a direct service. They can actually see somebody's hunger satisfied. Although these same people might recognize that joblessness and homelessness are the ultimate causes of that person's hunger, they are not as interested in the kind of work aimed at ending unemployment or providing low-cost housing. Some AIDS volunteers see their work as primarily targeted at individuals, trying to encourage more "safe sex" or helping the sick and needy. They make an effort to show that their volunteer work is *not* a political act or statement. They are involved for purely humanitarian reasons, as if AIDS were simply another disease and as if gays are not the only people to get it. They are simply responding to people in crisis. They do not see themselves as involved in a struggle for gay rights. Many decide to volunteer because a friend or acquaintance has AIDS. In contrast, other volunteers emphasize the needs of the gay community. To them, the AIDS epidemic—and the government's failure to fight it with more resources—is an attack on the community of political proportions and requires political action to deal with. They are more disposed to describe their work in the language of activism. For these "gay politicos," volunteering is a natural extension of their overall political beliefs. Their involvement in the AIDS issue is a political statement, if only as a way to express their solidarity with the gay community (Kayal 1993:124).

As people turn their attention away from serving individuals and focus on broader issues of social justice and exploitation their "vision expands" (Wuthnow 1991:253). They become aware of the extent of the problem they face or the root causes of the suffering they are trying to alleviate. Vela-McConnell (1999:173) describes "Brad," a volunteer at a homeless shelter who, as a result of his involvement, became more aware of the structural reasons for homelessness and hunger:

> They say we have enough food to feed the world three times over or something like that, and yet some people can't afford to eat anything. There's something in the very structure and if we tried it so long one way, why wouldn't we at least try it another way because it is *not* working this way.[9]

For some volunteers, the shift to activism happens when they redefine what they are doing. For example, women who began with the idea of volunteering in a rape crisis center as service provision came to believe that rape had deeper causes and broadened their vision, although they continued doing the same work (Abrahams 1996:774). People who move from volunteering to activism define commitment in a different way. They no longer think of it in terms of time but in terms of personal investment: commitment means you are willing to "put yourself on the line."

The case for drawing a distinction between volunteerism and social activism is buttressed if they attract different types of people. One author found that the typical volunteer was middle aged and married with children, whereas the typical activist was more likely to be younger, single, and childless (Whittier 1997:767). In the National Longitudinal Survey of Labor Market Experience women were asked whether they had done any "unpaid volunteer work in the past year." They were also asked whether they had done "any volunteer work to change social conditions," a type of work we would define as social activism. The volunteers who were *also* activists had higher family incomes, more years of education, and were more likely to be members of a racial minority than the volunteers who were not activists (Caputo 1997). Although the profile of the volunteer was therefore different from the profile of the activist, thus supporting the idea that the activities are somewhat different, the activists were actually higher class than the volunteers, doubtless a reflection of the general tendency of middle class people to be more involved in politics.[10]

Similarities

Despite these arguments that volunteer work is different from social activism, an equally persuasive case can be made that they are very similar activities and that "most activists are volunteers" (Ellis and Noyes 1990:8). First, the volunteer concept includes advocacy, which is a form of service that is very close to social activism. Advocacy organizations seek to affect the outcomes of public or private decisions on issues that affect the fortunes of the organization's clients or broader constituencies. Their goal is to direct or create social change by influencing public policy or corporate practices. In 1982, the President's Task Force on Private Sector Initiatives defined volunteering as "the voluntary giving of time and talents to deliver services or perform tasks with no direct financial compensation expected" and specifically included "advocacy for causes, groups, or individuals" as examples of such work (Thoits and Hewitt 2001:115). Advocacy groups comprise about a quarter of all non-profit organizations (Wuthnow 1998:122). Indeed, the advocacy role of the non-profit sector may be "more important to the nation's social health than the service function the sector also performs" (Salamon 2002:10). Volunteers can advocate in any number of ways: they can work to identify problems that have been neglected by government agencies and the media; they can develop and promote new positions and policy alternatives; and they can help fund and staff research organizations and foundations dealing with problems such as environmental protection, medical research, or immigration.

A second reason why the two concepts overlap in meaning is that the same activity can be interpreted as one or the other, depending on the social context and the motives and interests of the volunteer. As far as social context is concerned, the absence of large scale social and political movements at the end of the twentieth century made the idea of volunteering for the homeless, or for people with AIDS, or for battered women "about the most 'radical' thing a person can do" (Wagner 2000:169). In a relatively non-contentious environment, volunteer work stands in for political action. As far as individual motivations and interests are concerned, the same activity can be interpreted in several different ways. For example, some see acting as an ombudsman in nursing facilities for the aged as helping elderly residents deal with their day-to-day problems of living; others see the same job as one of advocacy and acting to protect the rights of the aged (Keith 2003:25). In another example, rape crisis counselors challenge sexism at both individual and collective levels. They provide resources to help individual rape victims while also fighting sexual assault as a social practice and sexism in general. In the early days of fighting HIV/AIDS—and still to a large extent today—syringe-exchange programs were illegal, an underground operation. Although volunteers were providing a service in making available new syringes to drug addicts, "the volunteers enacted their exchange as a form of civil disobedience" against the unjust laws forbidding the practice (Kelley et al. 2005:367).

The argument that volunteerism is about the personal and activism is about the political is undermined whenever the boundary between the personal and the political becomes blurred. For example, community-based AIDS organizations engage in

> street level prevention efforts (distribution of condoms, dental dams, and safer-sex information); support services for people living with HIV (treatment issues, emotional support); assistance with related social problems (immigration, housing, health care, substance abuse, food, etc.); promotion of positive images of

lesbians and gay men . . . ; and efforts to shape public policy and public opinion around AIDS through education, lobbying, and protest. (Stockdill 2001:214)

Is this volunteerism or activism? It is clearly intended to empower people affected by HIV/AIDS and to promote their self-worth and dignity, but it is also intended to improve the standard of living of people affected by HIV/AIDS by, for example, changing housing policies.[11] The same shading of meaning is found in a subject interviewed by Vela-McConnell (1999:173), who describes how working at a homeless shelter has alerted him to the structural reasons why people are homeless: "there's something in the very structure" that needs repair. This man sees his activities as private and personal, helping the homeless on an interpersonal basis, *and* public and impersonal, helping to do something about homelessness by raising awareness of its roots in unemployment. This perspective on volunteering indicates how hard it is to draw the distinction between private and public and how misleading it might be to draw a sharp distinction between volunteering and activism. For many people, their volunteering is a political act.[12]

A third reason why the distinction between volunteerism and activism is misleading has to do with the claim that volunteerism is all about service motivated by compassion, whereas activism is all about advocacy motivated by justice. According to this distinction, people become social activists when they are angered by the unfair treatment of others and want to do something about it. Activism is issue-oriented. This description certainly fits many prominent examples of social activism. Admittedly there are many forms of volunteerism, such as being a docent at an art museum, that are not inspired by outrage at how others have been treated. However, the justice motive does not separate activists from volunteers. Much of what we conventionally call volunteering is inspired by a commitment to a cause. A man who volunteers to protect women entering an abortion clinic from protestors stationed outside may be interested less in the individual women than he is in the cause of civil rights. Similarly, if a woman offers to help out at a battered women's shelter, the chances are quite good that, besides the individual help she might be able to provide to the patrons of the shelter, she is inspired by a sense of injustice. She feels that not only are individual women being abused but that all women are victimized by "the patriarchal system." A person who volunteers is not necessarily blind to the need for more structural changes. Freedman (1999:173) quotes a volunteer as saying that he believes his local school system needs "more systemic kinds of changes" but "[i]n the meantime, we'll take the one-to-one approach." Conversely, just because people think of themselves as volunteers does not mean they are driven by compassion. There is nothing in the *nature* of volunteer work that makes it compassionate. "Being emotional is thus a label, a construct. It is not just an internal state" (Groves 2001:228). People do not necessarily volunteer *because* they are impelled by emotion. The emotional tone of volunteer work emerges as the result of the volunteers' interaction with each other, with the people they are trying to help, and with the public at large. The lesson is that we should be careful about using an emotion—such as compassion—to define volunteering because the characterization of volunteerism as tinged with emotion is socially constructed.

In summary, rather than thinking of volunteer work and social activism as two separate activities, it might be better to think of activism as a sub-type of volunteering distinguishable by a number of characteristics. Not only does it demand *collective* action, it is intended to achieve a *collective* good. The perceived need for collective action calls for the adoption of some kind of collectivist orientation and therefore some kind of group identity is more important in the case of activism than volunteering. A slightly different version of this argument is that activism and volunteerism are both forms of altruism. Altruism is any voluntary, intentional act designed to benefit other persons from which there is no expectation of reward. There are different kinds of altruism. Political altruism would be any act performed by a group on behalf of another group where the goal is social change or a redefinition of power relations. "Activists" is what we call people who engage in political altruism. "Volunteering" is not a form of political altruism because it lacks an "explicit political aim" (Passy 2001:7). In this book we will use an expansive definition of volunteering that includes forms of what many social scientists would define as social activism because we believe that more is to be gained from stressing the overlap in meaning between the two concepts than is lost by blurring the boundary between them.[13]

Volunteering and Caring

As one kind of unpaid work, volunteering overlaps in meaning with terms such as "helping" and "caring." What is the relation between these concepts?

Informal Helping

Volunteer work is conventionally defined as being performed on behalf of or in connection with an organization. The organization will define the volunteer role, specify volunteer tasks, set schedules, screen new recruits, train them and manage them, and, if necessary, dismiss them. Volunteer work is a form of bureaucratized help, not to be confused with informal helping, which is unpaid service people provide on a more casual basis, outside of any organizational context, to someone in need.[14] The Independent Sector surveys, upon which we rely heavily in this book, treat helping others (such as running an elderly neighbor to the drugstore) as one type of volunteer work. One problem with including informal helping as a form of volunteering is that it is all too easily confused with a generalized exchange network or cycle of reciprocity, as in the exchange of services between neighbors and friends. It does not seem appropriate to consider mothers exchanging babysitting services as volunteers. *We therefore do not include this category of helping in our studies.*

Care Work

Care work is normally associated with kin relations. It denotes face-to-face help provided to an individual toward whom one feels some kind of social responsibility: "visiting, managing household tasks, providing transportation, and the direct provision of personal care" (Farkas and Himes 1997:S180). Ellis and Noyes (1990:5) refer to these as "basic responsibilities"—help that is necessary, unavoidable, required, and generally expected. There are three ways of distinguishing volunteering from care work. First, caring is usually an outgrowth of already existing social relationships and it is usually quite diffused. Often the caregiver is living with the care receiver and is "on call" all the time. Volunteering, on the other hand, is quite specific, in the sense that the reach of the obligations entailed is strictly controlled and the recipients of help are not necessarily known to or related to the volunteer. Second, the caregiver is likely to think of the role as an inescapable responsibility (Rozario et al. 2004:436). Care work implies strong obligations, primarily to one's relatives, fictive kin, or other members of the household. In contrast, volunteering is "non-obligatory" (Dekker and Halman 2003:1). For most people volunteer work is something we choose to do.[15] For this reason, those who volunteer in connection with their job, their school curriculum requirements, or some family duty are less likely to be considered true volunteers (Miejs et al. 2003:20). Indeed, according to one feminist writer, volunteer work is more acceptable precisely when the work is done by choice (Adair 1997:25). Third, caring carries with it strong expressive components. The emotional tie between the caregiver and the person being cared for is inseparable from the task. Taking care of your elderly parents yourself is very different from paying an aide to do it for you. In contrast, volunteering can be quite instrumental, devoid of emotional or expressive overtones: it is simply unpaid productive labor. It matters not who performs the work as long as it gets done. In summary, the distinction between care work and volunteering does seem to be a useful one, and it has some degree of external validity.

We find quite persuasive the arguments that caring and volunteering are distinct activities. However, we must be careful not to exaggerate the differences between them. First, although volunteer work is one way we choose to spend our leisure time it can also be seen as a duty, something we believe we owe to our community or to a group or organization to which we belong. This sense of duty moves volunteer work much closer to care work, the difference being that the obligation is owed to a larger social entity rather than to specific others. Members of an organization (e.g., religious congregation) may well feel under strong pressure to "take their turn" helping out with organizational events. The upper class women interviewed by Daniels (1988) treated their volunteer work as a serious social obligation. They did not want to be thought of as simply occupying their leisure time with socializing. In Japan, volunteering in connection with the PTA is regarded as part of a mother's duty toward her child (Nakano 2000:103).[16] In short, volunteer work is not always freely chosen. "Voluntary" is not a synonym for "willing." Many people volunteer grudgingly out of a sense of duty or obligation to others they would prefer to avoid. Whether or not the volunteer work is a felt obligation and whether meeting that obligation is pleasurable or not pleasurable is an empirical matter: "it must be determined whether volunteers feel they are engaging in enjoyable and satisfying activity that they have had the option to accept or reject on their own terms" (Stebbins 2004:4).

In summary, although there are differences between care work and volunteer work we should be careful not to exaggerate these differences and remain sensitive to the fact that the same activity might well fall into either category, depending on the way the activity is framed by the volunteer and the context in which it takes place. We would not go so far as Wuthnow (1995), however, who defines volunteer work as the institutionalization of kindness, as if it is simply for formalization of the care work that goes on between family members. While this approach correctly emphasizes the virtuous aspect of volunteer work as "the habitual practice of courage and compassion" (Wuthnow 1995:9), it draws volunteer work too close to care work, an association that encourages us to think of volunteerism as aimed primarily at mitigation or palliation, an identification we have already rejected.

Conclusion

Deciding what should count as volunteer work turns out to be much more difficult than it might at first appear. Words such as "volunteering" are folk concepts as well as scientific concepts. They are used by, and have meaning for, people going about their everyday life. Often their meaning is contested. People do not agree on what should count as volunteering. Sometimes they use words like "volunteering" as labels to pin on people and their actions in order to denigrate them; at other times, these same words are used to indicate approval. One solution to the definitional problem is to redefine the meaning of work because volunteering is, after all, unpaid work. "What constitutes an activity as work, as opposed to something else such as leisure, is not whether it is paid but whether it involves the provision of a service to others or the production of goods for the consumption of others" (Taylor 2004:38). To be classified as one rather than the other, the donor and beneficiary must have the appropriate relation to each other, the help provided must be of an appropriate kind, the occasion of helping must be proper, and so on. For most of us, our lives consist of doing a number of different types of work, depending on how organized they are, whether they are performed in the public or private sphere, and whether they are paid. What we normally think of as a job, as when we ask people what they do for a living, is formally organized, located in the public sphere, and is paid. Diagonally opposed to this is work that is informal, private, and unpaid (e.g., taking care of a relative). What is normally considered volunteer work is formal, public, and unpaid, such as providing legal advice to a non-profit group free of charge. "Providing legal advice" can, of course, be located in many other domains. We might be doing this for our parents. Edging into the public sphere, we might provide it on an informal basis to a neighbor or work colleague. If we are very busy, we might do all of these "jobs" simultaneously. This means that tasks, such as preparing a legal document, are not *essentially* volunteering. It all depends on the social context in which they are performed. There are situations in which this task would be considered altruistic and others where it would not (Cnaan et al. 1996).

As we have already noted, in this book we will assume a quite expansive definition of volunteerism that reaches over into social activism: "volunteer work includes not only the unpaid provision of services directly to others in need, but also political activism and community representation on boards of various agencies" (Thoits and Hewitt 2001:116). However, we will not include in the definition tasks such as child care or informal and casual helping such as dog sitting for one's neighbor. This is because volunteering is "organized voluntary activity focused on problem solving and helping others" (Jenkins et al. 2003:1) and the fact it is organized is important. Our strategy is to build theories and conduct analyses that will be, in principle, applicable to both kinds of activity.

Measuring Volunteer Work

Definition is a precondition of measurement. Once we have come to some conceptual agreement as to what volunteering is we must try to measure it if we want to gather survey data on it. In this section we will describe a number of approaches to the measurement of volunteering, several of which we will use throughout the book, and we will also comment on some of the problems associated with measuring volunteer work. As we shall see, how much volunteering we see in the social world has a lot to do with how it is measured.

Time-Span

When asking survey respondents to tell us about their volunteer work, it stands to reason that the longer we give our respondents to have volunteered the more of them will have done so. The Independent Sector survey of 2001 found that 27.5 percent of Americans had volunteered in the past month but

44.2 percent had volunteered in the last year (Toppe et al. 2002:37). This is the reason why survey estimates of volunteering are usually higher than estimates derived from time diaries. The surveys typically ask if the respondent has volunteered at any time during the past month or the past twelve months. The span of time covered by time diaries is much shorter.[17] This is not to suggest that time diaries under-estimate or more conventional surveys over-estimate the volunteer rate. They simply capture different ways of volunteering. If most of the volunteer population is made up of people who volunteer all the time, then the time diary and the survey rates will converge. If the volunteer population contains many people who volunteer only sporadically (although they might contribute many hours), then the two figures will diverge.

The Volunteer Rate and Volunteer Hours

Researchers want to know not only whether or not a person volunteers but also how many hours he or she contributes. The rate of volunteering in a population or a sub-group of the population does not necessarily correlate with how many hours a week or year members of that population contribute. For example, in our own analysis of the Independent Sector data we found that women are more likely to volunteer than men but, among volunteers, men contribute more hours than women. Similarly, African Americans are less likely to volunteer than Whites but, if they do volunteer, they contribute more hours. Then there are groups who are more likely to volunteer but contribute no more hours than other groups. Middle aged people, college graduates, frequent church attenders, parents, and home owners are more likely to volunteer but they contribute no more hours than volunteers from different social backgrounds. As we consider the various antecedents of volunteering we need to specify carefully whether we are explaining the rate of volunteering or the number of hours volunteered.

Concentration

Computing the rate of volunteering for a population or the average number of hours contributed tells us nothing about the distribution of volunteer effort in a population. One thing we would like to know is how evenly the burden of volunteer work is spread across all volunteers. We analyzed the Independent Sector data to see if volunteers share volunteer work evenly among themselves. We found this was far from the case. A tiny minority (3.5% of Americans, or 10 percent of the volunteers) contributed 39 percent of all the hours volunteered and just below 8 percent (or 25% of all volunteers) contributed 68 percent of all hours worked. The volunteer effort in Canada is also quite concentrated. A mere 7 percent of all Canadians (one-quarter of the 26.7% of Canadians who volunteer) provided 73 percent of the total volunteers hours contributed in 2000. This is similar to the skewed distribution reported in 1997 (Hall et al. 2001:32). More remarkably, perhaps, in 1997 half of all Canadian volunteers contributed only 8 percent of the volunteer hours (McClintock 2000:12).

These data indicate that populations normally contain a few people who do an enormous amount of the volunteer work. Each population could be said to express a ratio of highly committed to less committed volunteers. If, for example, high commitment is defined as six or more hours a week, a certain proportion of volunteers will meet this criterion, while the rest will fall below it. Using a measure of high commitment volunteers we can also see how highly concentrated the volunteer work is in any particular domain. For example, Lyons and Hocking (2000:47) calculated the high commitment volunteer concentration rate for eleven different volunteer domains or "fields." The fields of arts and culture, environment and animal welfare, and foreign and international activities relied most heavily on the input of a few highly committed people. In other fields, such as sports and recreation, education and youth development and business, and professional associations and unions, the volunteer effort was more widely distributed.

Another way of measuring the distribution of volunteer work in a population is to ask which groups in the population contribute the greatest *proportion* of the time given. This is different from measuring the rate of volunteering or the average number of hours contributed. For example, we used the Independent Sector data to compare the percentage of each group in the sample with the percentage of total hours volunteered contributed by each group. [1] The result is a measure of the ratio of hours to sample segment. For example, women make up 52 percent of the sample and contribute 55 percent of the hours: the ratio is 1.05. Men make up 48 percent of the sample and contribute 45 percent of the hours: the ratio is .94.[18]

Regular and Occasional Volunteering

Just as we can ask how volunteering is distributed across a population, we can also ask how volunteering is distributed across the life of an individual. Simply asking people whether they volunteer or even how many hours they volunteer does not tell us much about how their contributions are structured across time. Two people could cite the same number of hours but work very different volunteer schedules.[19] Obviously, many more people volunteer sporadically than volunteer regularly. This would not be captured if we simply ask whether they volunteered at all in the previous year. A British survey showed that about half of those who had volunteered in the previous month had been active for fewer than fifty days throughout the year—probably once a week—and a quarter of all volunteers had been active for no more than five days in the preceding year (Goddard 1994:12). Those who volunteered only occasionally did not make up for this by contributing more hours when they were active. They reported the same number of hours per day.[20]

The Timing of Volunteer Work

Measures of the rate of volunteering or average hours contributed in the course of a year tell us nothing about *when* people volunteer. Are there peaks and valleys in the demand for and supply of volunteer workers? Is there a vacation time for volunteers? Data from the British General Household Survey of 1992 enable us to plot fluctuations in volunteering across the calendar year because the process of data gathering lasted twelve months and the month of the interview was noted. Respondents were asked if they had volunteered at any time in the past month. Volunteer activity peaked in April and again in July and December and was at its lowest in February and March, but in fact the rate of participation did not change much over the course of a year. More hours were volunteered in the summer than in the winter (Holloway et al. 2002). Time diary data, which typically records activities over a twenty-four-hour period, can tell us how volunteer work is scheduled over the course of a week. In the United Kingdom, volunteer work is most likely to take place on a Saturday or a Sunday (Ruston 2003:6). This, of course, reflects the fact that most of us are busy at work during the week and the popularity of volunteer work for sports and church activities, both of which are more likely to take place on the weekend. Knowing when people volunteer is as important as knowing how much they volunteer if we want to understand how volunteer work meshes with other social obligations. For example, older volunteers are more likely to volunteer in mid-week than middle aged volunteers because they are more likely to be retired (Almeida et al. 2001:148).

Range of Volunteering and the Dispersion of Hours

Just like paid workers, volunteers can have one job or multiple jobs. Some devote their volunteer time to a single organization, while others contribute time to more than one activity. In this book we refer to the number of different volunteer activities as the *range* of volunteering. According to the 2005 Current Population Survey (CPS) special supplement on volunteering, 69.6 percent of Americans aged 16 or above who volunteered contributed their time to only one organization, 18.9 percent to two organizations, 7.0 percent to three, 2.4 percent to four and 1.7 percent to five or more (U.S. Bureau of Labor Statistics 2005). As we shall see later in the book, some groups in the population volunteer for a wider range of volunteer activities than others. For example, 16.5 percent of college graduates volunteer for three or more activities compared to 3.2 percent of high school dropouts.

By combining the number of hours volunteered and the number of different volunteer activities to which those hours were contributed, it is possible to measure the *dispersion* of hours. Does the respondent focus all his or her volunteer contributions on one activity or spread them across several? We measured dispersion in the Independent Sector data by creating two variables: the first sorts the respondents into those who volunteered for less than ten hours a month per activity and those who volunteered for ten or more per activity; the second divides the respondents into those who volunteered for one activity and those who volunteered for two or more. Cross-tabulating these variables yielded four types of volunteering. A quarter of the respondents were intensely committed to volunteer work: they were active in two or more areas and worked ten or more hours a month in each of these areas. The largest group (33%) volunteered for just one organization but contributed more than ten hours a month to that organization. The next largest group (30%) volunteered for just one organization but contributed less than ten hours a month to that organization. Members of a fourth group (20%) spread their efforts over more than one activity but contributed less than ten hours to each organization. The modal form of volunteering among Americans is therefore to concentrate on one activity, but we should not ignore the group of volunteers who contribute quite a lot of their time to more than one organization. For these people, volunteer work seems to be a vocation. [2]

The Validity of Survey Responses

An important measurement issue in the social research on volunteering is the validity and reliability of responses to social surveys. This is an issue with surveys of all kinds and is not unique to studies of volunteerism, but there are reasons to believe that measuring the quantity of volunteer work through social surveys poses especially difficult problems. Volunteering is not a primary social role for most people, even for those who do volunteer. Its referent is vague: what do people think when they hear this word? Its boundaries are unclear: do people count time spent preparing for and driving to their volunteer assignment? It is hardly surprising that estimates of volunteering tend to fluctuate from survey to survey much more than estimates of rather similar activities, such as voting. This has led social scientists to pay special attention to the reliability of measures of volunteering. Reliability means that repeated uses of a measure produce identical results. One way to test reliability is to repeat surveys on different populations or at different times, but we cannot rule out the possibility that any variations we find are the result of real differences between populations or changes over time. To avoid this problem, Keeter et al. (2003:14) asked the same questions on volunteering in three surveys administered within a short span of time. They asked, "Have you ever spent time participating in any community service or volunteer activity, or haven't you had time to do this? By volunteer activity, I mean actually working in some way to help others for no pay." They found that in the spring 2002 survey 22 percent of 18- to 29-year-olds said they had volunteered, with 23 percent and 25 percent from the fall 2002 surveys saying that they had done so. This would suggest that the measurement is quite a reliable one because it is unlikely major changes in volunteerism would have occurred in that time. But using panel data they came to a more sobering conclusion. They asked a sample of New Jersey residents if they had "ever worked together informally with someone or some group to solve a problem in the community where you live?" They found that only 62 percent of the respondents provided the same reply when they were asked the same question three months later. By contrast, 92 percent gave consistent answers on whether they had voted in the 2000 general election.

Accuracy of Recall

Problems with recall might be one reason for these inconsistent responses. Social surveys that require the respondent to report activities over the past week, month, or year are subject to errors caused by respondents' faulty memories. The further back the respondent is expected to remember the more suspect recall becomes. It is most likely to result in under-reporting. Surveys that ask for volunteer hours per year tend to yield lower estimates *per unit of time* than surveys that ask for volunteer hours in the past month or week. It has been suggested that asking respondents to recall hours volunteered over the past twelve months is suspect because they are likely to overlook minor episodes of volunteer work and that "asking about volunteer service in smaller units, such as hours per week or month, helps to aid recall" (Steinberg et al. 2002:500).[21]

One problem with this method is that respondents are first asked if they volunteered and then asked to name the organizations for which they volunteered. Toppe (2005) believes this leads to an undercount of the number of volunteers because the first question allows too many people to define themselves as not being volunteers simply because they define the term more narrowly than the researchers. It would be preferable, he argues, if respondents were simply given a list of volunteer activities and asked to say whether or they volunteered for any of them in the past twelve months. A special survey of American youth aged between 11 and 19 conducted in 2005 adopted this method, although a truncated list of only four volunteer activities was provided. The volunteer rate for the 16- to 18-year-old group in the 2005 survey was much higher than the volunteer rate for the 16- to 18-year-old group in the 2004 CPS survey (Grimm et al. 2005:15).[22]

Positive Response Bias

Memory loss leads to under-reporting of volunteer work, but response bias can lead to inflated claims. In a society where helping others is honored and esteemed, people might be tempted to exaggerate how helpful they are. Indeed, agreeing to be interviewed itself is a form of volunteerism, and for this reason volunteers are almost certainly over-represented in social surveys. The rate of volunteer work among teenagers can easily be over-estimated due to social desirability bias, to which they are more inclined than adults. In one survey, 20 percent of those who said they were volunteers were unable to describe the activity they had engaged in *during the past month* even though they were provided a list of types of activities to jog their memories (Niemi et al. 2000:52).

Keeter et al. (2003:9) have proposed one method of avoiding the "social desirability bias." By first asking if the respondent has *ever* done volunteer work they allow the respondent to "get credit" for having done so, however long ago it might have occurred, but they follow this up with a further probe about whether this work was done in the past twelve months. A further refinement is to ask those who indicated they had volunteered in the past twelve months whether they did so on a "regular basis, or just once in a while." Their own survey found that 40 percent of the American adults interviewed had never volunteered, about a quarter (26.7%) had volunteered at some time in their lives but not in the past twelve months, and about a third (32.6%) had volunteered in the past twelve months. Of those who reported having volunteered in the past twelve months 22.7 percent had done so on a regular basis. By asking the screener question whether the respondent had ever volunteered, some of those who like to think of themselves as volunteers, and to appear so to others, can answer in the affirmative, but not sully the responses as far as recent, and more reliably reported, volunteer work is concerned

Context

People's responses to questionnaires are biased by the context in which the questions on volunteering occur. In the Independent Sector surveys, close to half the respondents said they had volunteered in the past twelve months (51% in 1990, 48% in 1992, 44% in 1994, 46% in 1996, and 50% in 1999). Is this the true rate of volunteering? A prominent scholar believes it is inflated by the surveys' special attention to charitable activities (Wuthnow 1995:25). The most recent Current Population Survey reports a much lower proportion (27.4%) of Americans aged 16 or more as having volunteered in the last year (U.S. Bureau of Labor Statistics 2005).

The measurement of volunteering used in the various data sets we analyze in this book can be found in the appendix. Although the measurement of volunteering contained in the CPS is extremely detailed with respect to the time-span during which volunteering occurred (respondents are asked how many weeks they volunteered in the last year for each organization they mention, how many hours per week, and how many hours in the last year), the survey is flawed, for our purposes at least, because no questions on religion are asked, and religion is such a vital contributor to volunteerism. As we note above, there are also problems with the way in which CPS respondents are not given a list of possible volunteer activities from which to choose, which possibly underestimates the rate. Hence our primary reliance on the Independent Sector surveys.

The accurate measurement of volunteering in social surveys continues to be a problem. Respondents are being asked questions about how they spent their time over the past twelve months and, despite the prompts they are given, the activity about which they are being asked is rather vaguely defined and the likelihood of an accurate account of the number of hours spent on it is rather low. Under-reporting is likely because such activities can often be overlooked or the time spent on them under-reported, but a counterbalancing over-reporting is suspected because doing volunteer work is a positive thing. Aside from these problems of validity and reliability, problems are created by the different ways in which volunteer work can be measured. We can set out to measure the rate of "any" volunteering in the population; the hours volunteered per day, week, month, or year; the number of different activities volunteered for; the timing of the volunteer work across the year, week, or day; the average volunteer hours; the dispersion of volunteer hours; or the concentration of volunteer hours in particular population groups. In this book, space limitations mean we will focus mainly on any volunteer at all during the past year, average hours (per month in the case of the Independent Sector data), and range of activities.

Domains of Volunteering

A glance at any local newspaper is sufficient to remind us that volunteers contribute their time to a wide variety of causes. The same volunteer activity (e.g., fund-raising) can take place in many different organizational settings—a school, religious congregation, environmental group, animal shelter, women's health clinic, and so on. The volunteer labor market is therefore segmented in much the same way as the paid labor market is divided into different sectors or "fields." Perhaps the only similarity between a middle aged female who visits shut-in elderly because they are fellow members of a religious congregation and a young male who makes fund-raising telephone calls for a wildlife protection group is that they both give their time for nothing. Distinguishing volunteer work by the setting in which it occurs is potentially very important. Different types of volunteer work will call for different resources, attract different population groups, appeal to different motives, speak to different interests, and have different consequences for the volunteer. In this book we will use the word "domain" as a somewhat neutral term to refer to the types of volunteer work social surveys have distinguished.

The taxonomy of volunteer work is in its infancy. In the absence of any social science guidelines, survey researchers tend to use ad hoc categories to classify volunteer work: some categories refer to the people being served (e.g., "youth," "elderly"); some to the type of organization in connection with which the work takes place (e.g., "professional association," "church"); and some to the cause being served (e.g., "the environment," "welfare," "civic"). As a result, the list of domains varies from one survey to another: the Independent Sector, General Social Survey, and Census Bureau use fifteen categories and the World Values Survey uses fourteen categories, but the categories are not the same. To complicate matters, as the methods of surveying volunteer work have improved, the list of organizations for which respondents *could* volunteer has been extended in order to jog their memories.

In an effort to develop a more systematic basis for the classification of volunteer work, Salamon and Anheier (1996) classified organizations in the non-profit sector as if they clustered into different "industries" depending on the product or service they generate. The result is twelve "fields of nonprofit activity," some of which are subdivided. These are: Culture (including recreation), Education (including literacy), Health, Social Services (including emergency aid), Environment (including animal protection), Development (including neighborhood organizations), Civic and Advocacy (including political), Philanthropy (including fund-raising), International, Religious, Business and Professional, and Unions, plus "Other." These domains were used in the most recent Canadian survey of volunteering (Hall et al. 2001:40), but the Independent Sector survey, on which we rely principally, uses a different taxonomy and the recent Current Population Survey Special Supplement on Volunteering uses its own classification.[23]

Lack of agreement about domain definition poses serious problems when trying to compare the results across surveys. And without standard classifications, comparisons between societies are virtually impossible because the conceptual space is not the same. For example, the most frequently mentioned domain of volunteer activity in the United States is religious, whereas in Canada this domain accounts for only 14 percent of the mentions. The highest fraction (23%) of Canadian volunteers is active in the domain of "arts, culture and recreation" (Hall et al. 2001:40). But this comparison makes little sense unless we know that Americans and Canadians chose from the same array of volunteer options.

The same problems occur when we try to plot trends across time. Inconsistent classifications mean that later surveys do not replicate earlier surveys, making it impossible to detect changes in what people volunteer for. If successive cross-sectional surveys change their classification of volunteer work, it becomes difficult to study period effects. For example, rates of volunteering might be high for political organizations during times of political upheaval and this will show up in surveys conducted at the time, but we cannot compare those surveys with more recent surveys unless the same classification is used. Inconsistent definitions also render it more difficult to track individual changes. If panel studies change their classification of volunteer work during the course of the study it becomes impossible to see if people change their volunteer preferences over the course of their lives.

Inconsistent classifications also pose problems for those trying to explain volunteer behavior. Although it might be possible to explain volunteer work in the aggregate, it is not possible to replicate studies of particular volunteer activities. Without consistent classifications it becomes difficult to associate particular groups of people with particular domains of volunteering. For example, volunteers tend to be better educated than non-volunteers, but it is common sense that the influence of education varies by activity. A college degree might well improve our chances of being asked to serving on the art museum's board of trustees, but it will probably have little effect on our chances of coaching Little League baseball. Another example is occupation. Some types of volunteering are probably more closely connected to one's job than others. Volunteer work, such as helping out at the union hall or writing the newsletter of the local chapter of a professional association or trade association, is likely to be more closely associated with the kind of job we have than is helping out at a food distribution center or teaching Bible study. Another example is religion. How often we attend church makes a difference to whether or not we volunteer in connection with our church but not, perhaps, in connection with a civic organization. In summary, conventional models of volunteer work that lump all kinds of volunteering together to simply measure "volunteer hours," or use a "range" measure of volunteering summing the number of different volunteer activities, miss much valuable information. The models are incorrectly specified because their dependent variable is not internally coherent. In the process, the precise effect of predictor variables on volunteering is underestimated. But without some agreement as to what these different volunteer activities are, and why they are different, the prospect of making advances in this area remains uncertain.

Part 2.

Subjective Dispositions

In part 2 we describe the association between individual perceptions and volunteering. We have borrowed from Moen (1997:133) the term "subjective dispositions" to describe the phenomena discussed in the chapters in this section. It is an umbrella term that covers a wide variety of concepts—personality traits such as empathy, motives, values, attitudes—that have one thing in common: they all refer to the way people interpret themselves and the world around them. It assumes we cannot understand human behavior entirely from the "outside" by looking at people's objective attributes or their social position; we have to know something about what is going on in their minds.

The subjective component of human behavior covers a wide array of phenomena, some of them more fixed and stable than others. In part 2, the chapters are ordered in such a way that we begin with psychological characteristics believed to be most enduring, in the sense that they will influence behavior regardless of changes in social situation or circumstance. We then move gradually to subjective dispositions that are believed to more malleable, subject to change as the result of alterations in life circumstance or in reaction to social events and experiences. Thus we begin with the idea of personality traits, a concept referring to behavior patterns that are relatively inflexible. We then move to a discussion of motives in which we explore the idea that volunteering must be explained, at least partially, by understanding people's intentions or goals. According to the functionalist theory we examine, these goals are finite in number but enduring and therefore to some degree transcend particular times and places. In the chapter that follows, we look at the influence of values, norms, and attitudes on volunteering. The topics in this chapter are themselves ordered on a dimension of durability. Values are fairly deep-seated and abstract evaluative ideas acquired during the course of socialization that change slowly if they change at all. Norms are the rules by which values can be actualized. These rules for living are somewhat more malleable than values in the sense that situations and circumstances can lead people to ignore or re-interpret them. Finally, we discuss the influence of attitudes on behavior. Attitudes are evaluative ideas directed toward particular objects. These ideas must have a certain level of durability to qualify as attitudes at all (e.g., our attitudes about affirmative action do not change from day to day), but they are more malleable than values or norms.

As we describe these various subjective dispositions and trace their link to volunteering we will have occasion to observe on numerous occasions that the meaning of these concepts and the role they play in theory is much debated in the social sciences. Even the existence of personality traits, for the example, is contested by some social scientists. Many sociologists are uncomfortable with the idea that motives compel us to behave in certain ways. They assign to motives a different role in the explanation of volunteering. And we will have many occasions to observe that the precise link between subjective dispositions and actual behavior can be obscure. Many social scientists, for example, are skeptical of the idea that our values have much to do with our actual behavior. People can say they are in favor of equal rights but find a practical reason to discriminate against others on the basis of their race when hiring new employees. Nevertheless, social science must pay attention to the subject component in any study of human behavior. As a species, human beings are unique in attributing meaning to their behavior and the behavior of others around them. They make their choices based on these meanings. It makes sense to believe that a person, however well endowed with the resources necessary to volunteer (e.g., free time), might nevertheless decline to do so if she believes the work would be ineffective in dealing with the problem or if she does not trust volunteer agencies to conduct themselves responsibly.

3

Personality

A personality trait is a disposition to act in a certain way, regardless of the situation. For example, a behavior pattern, such as being gregarious, that manifests itself across different social settings and relationships and is durable over the life course is a personality trait (Penner et al. 2005:374). Personality differences are likely to play some role in determining who volunteers simply because of the voluntary nature of the activity. This is because personality differences tend to be submerged in situations where certain kinds of social behavior are demanded as, for example, in a military "boot camp," but they emerge in situations where there are few external demands on an actor to behave in a certain way (Penner 2002:451). Whether personality traits are the result of genes or socialization, their theoretical appeal lies in their stability. Knowing something about an individual's personality enables us to anticipate how he or she will react to situations, such as being asked to volunteer.

The structure of the personality is multi-layered. Higher-order and more general personality traits each contain several lower-order, more specific behavioral tendencies. Personality psychologists refer to the higher-order traits as the "Big Five": extroversion, neuroticism, conscientiousness, agreeableness, and openness to experience. There is less agreement about the component, lower-level, specific traits. This is important, because the Big Five describe very general dimensions of individual difference and are unlikely to be associated with specific behaviors, whereas the lower-order traits should be better predictors of actual behavior.

Once the Big Five traits are unpacked into their lower-order components it is easy to see why some social scientists believe that volunteers have different personalities. Extroversion means lack of social inhibition, assertiveness and self-confidence in social situations, and a high energy level. Neuroticism encompasses the tendency to see the world as distressing or threatening, low self-esteem, low self-efficacy, and a weak sense of mastery. Conscientious individuals are attentive, persistent, orderly, careful, and responsible. Agreeableness means being cooperative, considerate, empathic, generous, trusting, and kind. Openness to experience, "the most debated and least understood of the Big Five traits" means a tendency to seek stimulation and explore new environments, being creative, aesthetically sensitive, and insightful (Caspi et al. 2005:459). Volunteers are likely to score high on extroversion, conscientiousness, agreeableness, and openness, and low on neuroticism.

In what follows we will survey the evidence linking personality traits to volunteering.[1] We include in this survey not only studies specifically drawing on personality theory but also those that have invoked personality concepts to explain volunteerism in an ad hoc way. We therefore include in this chapter research on the influence of self-efficacy and trust because they are considered lower-order personality traits in the psychological literature. (Neurotic people have low self-esteem and low self-efficacy. Agreeable people are empathic and trusting.)[2] We begin with studies using a number of personality trait measures to explain volunteerism. These studies do not necessarily confine themselves to the Big Five. We will then discuss studies testing for the effect of specific personality traits, such as empathy and self-efficacy. Where appropriate we supplement these studies with analyses of data from the Independent Sector surveys.

Elshaug and Metzer (2001) compared three groups of people on various personality measures. The first was a group of volunteers preparing food for a Meals on Wheels program. The second group consisted of paid food preparers employed in various hotels and cafeterias. Volunteer firefighters made up the third group. The participants completed a battery of questions intended to measure personality traits such as neuroticism, extroversion, openness, agreeableness, and conscientiousness. There were no personality differences between the two groups of volunteers, but both groups were different from the paid food preparers in being more extroverted (particularly being warm and expressive of warm emotions) and more agreeable (particularly being more trusting and more altruistic). There was no association between personality measures and length of volunteer service. This study seems to support the theory that volunteers have different personalities, but it is just as important for what the researchers did *not* find: volunteers were no more gregarious, assertive, open, or conscientious than the paid workers, and no less neurotic.

Carlo et al. (2005) examined the association between personality and volunteering among small samples of college students in the United States. Nineteen percent of the students were currently volunteering and 90 percent had volunteered at some point in their lives. Personality traits were assessed using a version of the Big Five Inventory. The only trait not correlated with volunteer behavior was neuroticism. Agreeableness had the strongest correlation, followed by extroversion. However, in multivariate analysis, only agreeableness was related to volunteering. The authors note that one facet of agreeableness is being compliant with respect to others and, as we shall see in chapter 13, being asked is an important stimulus to volunteering.

Bekkers (2005) compared non-volunteers with religious volunteers, volunteers for secular organizations, and (because the data were gathered in the Netherlands) volunteers for "pillarized" associations; that is, secular organizations split along religious lines (political parties, women's organizations, workers' unions, and schools). Compared to non-volunteers, religious volunteers were less open to experience ("openness"), less able to take the perspective of the other, but more empathic and somewhat more extroverted. After controls for religion and socio-economic resources, only extroversion remained associated with volunteering for religious organizations. Compared to non-volunteers, volunteers for pillarized associations were less neurotic and more empathic. After controls, only empathy was associated with volunteering. None of the personality characteristics were associated with secular volunteering. Once again, this study provides only weak evidence that personality matters when it comes to volunteering.

One of the most systematic studies of the association between personality traits and volunteering used data from MIDUS, a large-scale nationally representative survey of Americans, conducted in 1995. Six personality traits were measured in the survey: agency, agreeableness, extroversion, conscientiousness, openness to experience, and neuroticism. (This is the "Big Five" with agency broken out of the extrovert trait.) Volunteers scored higher on agency—a composite of self-confident, forceful, assertive, outspoken, and dominant; communion (agreeableness)—a composite of warm, caring, softhearted, and sympathetic; and conscientiousness—a composite of responsible, hard-working, and careful. However, none of these traits had a *direct* effect on the number of hours volunteered per month. Rather, all three were positively related to generativity, and generativity was positively related to volunteering. Generativity (which we will discuss in the next chapter) is a multifaceted psychosocial construct measuring people's concern for the welfare of the next generation and, more broadly, for the well-being of others. According to this study, then, personality traits do influence volunteering but mainly by helping shape a self-perception of oneself as a helpful and caring (generative) person (Rossi 2001c:296).

Amato (1990) looked at the influence of a number of personality traits on a variety of helping behaviors. His index of "formal planned helping" activities included, but was not confined to, volunteer behavior. Personality variables included adherence to a norm of social responsibility; empathy, interpersonal trust, mastery, efficacy, and a measure of the extent to which the respondent tended to see other people as largely responsible for the problems they faced. Two samples were drawn, one of undergraduate students and one of non-students contacted by the students. Among the non-students personality traits were unrelated to any kind of formal planned helping. Among the students, only the variables measuring adherence to the norm of social responsibility and efficacy were related to volunteering. Formal planned helping was much more strongly related to frequency of interaction with family, the number of friends nearby, the number of neighbors known, the number of club and organizational meetings attended, and frequency of church attendance. In short, this study provided no support for the theory that personality makes a difference to volunteering. Sociological differences rather than personality differences explained volunteering—although the measure of volunteering and the sample used was less than ideal.

Four of the behavioral dispositions identified by personality psychologists have received attention from other social scientists, particularly social psychologists.[3] Here we will briefly review the research on the influence of extroversion, empathy, trust, and self-efficacy on volunteering.

Extroversion

Doing volunteer work takes us out in to the public sphere where we interact with relative strangers—other volunteers, paid staff, and clients. People who are comfortable, even take pleasure in, interacting with a wide range of people are probably more likely to find volunteer work attractive. An opportunity to test this hypothesis is provided by the Americans' Changing Lives (ACL) data set, which contains a number of questions intended to measure whether respondents are extroverted or introverted.[4] Respondents who scored high on the extroversion index were more likely to volunteer (Herzog and Morgan 1993).[5] We extended this analysis of the ACL data in three ways. We included all respondents in the sample rather than confining the study to those 55 years of age and over. We added a test for the effects of neuroticism, measured by such items as, "Are you a worrier?" and "Would you call yourself a nervous person?" Third, while the earlier studies used cross-sectional data we estimated the influence of extroversion and neuroticism, measured in 1986, on the range of volunteer activities in 1989, controlling for the range in 1986, and on whether the respondent volunteered at all in 1989, controlling for whether he or she volunteered in 1986. This method allowed us to see if personality brought about a change in volunteering between the two waves of data collection. Our results replicated the earlier finding that volunteers tend to be more extroverted than nonvolunteers, but neuroticism had no influence on volunteering. [3]

Empathy

One of the lower-order components included in the agreeableness personality trait is empathy. Empathizing means recognizing what another person may be feeling or thinking and responding to those feelings with an appropriate emotion of one's own. The empathic person is quick to feel the same kind of emotions as the other person, enabling him or her to have a much better grasp of the experience from the standpoint of the other. "We have stepped in their shoes—engaged in role taking—in order to see and experience the world as *they* do" (Vela-McConnell 1999:39). Empathic people characteristically respond to, rather than ignore, others' problematic situations, and "may exhibit altruistic, prosocial behaviors that reflect and encourage social competence" (Schieman and Turner 2001:381). Most researchers "agree that empathic arousal is fundamental to many kinds of helping" (Penner et al. 2005:368).

The Independent Sector survey does not contain a conventional measure of empathy (e.g., "I am usually aware of the feelings of other people"). However, by factor analyzing a list of questions asked in the 1992 survey we created a proxy measure of this personality trait.[6] This measure includes not only empathy but also a sense of responsibility to help others. Psychologists agree that empathy must be accompanied by a feeling of responsibility for the welfare of others in order to motivate volunteer work. We must not only be able to put ourselves in the place of others and feel what they are feeling, but we must also be *concerned* about those others (Eisenberg 1992:44). Prior to factor analysis, the items were coded so that a high score indicated empathy, while a low score indicated self-concern. Women were more empathic, as were whites (as opposed to all other racial groups), the college-educated, frequent church attenders, and mainline and evangelical Protestants (compared to those with no religious affiliation). Controlling for these variables, volunteers were more empathic than non-volunteers. [4] The Independent Sector repeated the first item on our list ("We all have a right to concern ourselves with our own goals first and foremost, rather than with the problems of other people") in their 1996 and 1999 surveys. We therefore pooled the data from 1992, 1996, and 1999 and regressed volunteerism on this item. Volunteers were more likely than non-volunteers to reject the notion that we have the right to concern ourselves with our own problems. The more strongly they disagreed, the more activities they volunteered for. In short, there is quite convincing evidence that volunteers are more empathic people than non-volunteers.

Trust

Personality psychologists think of trust as a component of the agreeableness trait. The trust concept is very important in the social sciences but, like many others, its precise meaning is contested. The trust about which economists write is "strategic" trust. It describes our expectations about how specific people will behave. Trust develops in the context of exchange relationships. Other social scientists think about trust as a value. It is a statement about how people *should* behave. It is not the result of experience: even if people let you down, you are expected to behave as if they could be trusted. "The Golden Rule does *not* demand that you do unto others as they do unto you. Instead, you do unto others *as you would have them* do unto you" (Uslaner 2002a:23). According to this argument, trust is not based on reciprocity but on shared moral values and identities. We bestow trust on people like us: people who we believe share our values and beliefs; people who are members of the same moral community. Furthermore, we tend to feel responsible for people we trust. We feel especially bad if those people experience difficulties not of their own making (Uslaner 2002a:2). This values-based approach to trust attributes this disposition less to contemporary experiences—as in the economic argument—than it does to socialization. "If a person has trusting parents, can influence family decisions, determine his own friends, and feels free to disagree with his parents, he will have a strong probability of becoming a truster" (Uslaner 2001:110). Parents who are trusting and tolerant act as role models for their children who, in turn, show more trust in others.

Theorizing trust as the outcome of socialization is undoubtedly a more sociological way of thinking about the phenomenon, but it also changes the meaning of the concept closer to a behavioral disposition. We do not re-think our position on trust in every new situation or relationship. If we learn to be trusting in early life we are likely to continue to be a trusting person even if we occasionally experience disappointment by having our trust in others betrayed.[7] This kind of stability suggests that trust is not too reactive to changes in life experiences and social situations but is, instead, a trait that stays with us over the course of our lives. Uslaner (2006:8), a proponent of the socialization argument, acknowledges that generalized trust is largely stable throughout one's life (a "stable predisposition"), citing as evidence the fact that three-quarters of the participants in the 1972–1974–1976 American National Election Study panel study responded in the same way to the generalized trust question each time they were asked. Trusting people are not only likely to exhibit this trait over the course of their lives; they are more likely to *generalize* their trust. For example, in one Canadian survey, respondents were asked the standard personal trust question ("Most people can be trusted"). They were also asked how much they trusted their neighbors, members of their local community, members of the province in which they lived, and members of their racial or ethnic group. Trust scores were highly correlated. Respondents who trusted one referent tended to trust the others, supporting the notion that this item is measuring a general disposition to trust others (Veenstra 2000).

Being a trusting person makes it easier to volunteer (Brady et al. 1999:162; Wood 1997:601). It is difficult to work cooperatively with others if we do not trust them to pull their weight. Trust therefore helps overcome the free rider problem. We are more likely to volunteer to clean up our neighborhood if we trust our neighbors not to shirk their responsibility to do likewise. Trust also helps overcome barriers between helpers and helped. We are more likely to agree to help others if we think they deserve it, really need it, and appreciate it—that their appeal for help is genuine. For example, we are more likely to wash dishes in the soup kitchen if we trust that members of the public come to the kitchen only if they are truly hungry and in real need. Trust helps foster reciprocity: we are quicker to offer help if we trust others to return the favor should we ever need help ourselves. For example, we are more likely to help an elderly person if we trust that people from the next generation will help us when we become infirm. In this respect, trust plays the same role in gift exchange as it does in currency exchange. Volunteer work is a donation of time that does not require an immediate or specific return. Instead, the volunteer gets symbolic credit that he or she can cash in later. Finally, research has shown that a trusting person has a more benign attitude toward the world. If we do good things for others, good things will happen to us. A trusting person has faith in the basic decency and civility of others (Wilkinson and Bittman 2003:7).

In recent years, social scientists have paid a lot of attention to the influence of trust on social participation of all kinds. The World Values Survey (WVS) provides an opportunity to examine the association between volunteering and trust in a number of different countries. The trust question is, "Generally speaking, would you say that most people can be trusted or that you can't be too careful in dealing with people?" Volunteering is measured by asking respondents if they had done "unpaid work" for a voluntary association in the past year. According to the WVS, volunteers are more trusting people, regardless of any socio-economic differences, a finding that is robust across all countries included in the survey (Anheier and Kendall 2002:344). Crucially, simply belonging to a voluntary association, without doing any work for it, is not associated with trust at all (Stolle and Rochon 1999:203; Whiteley 1999). In an analysis of data from a 1996 survey including both Canadians and Americans, Smidt (1999) found that trust was positively associated with volunteering, regardless of education and frequency of church attendance. Dekker (2004) analyzed data from the "Civil Society and Volunteering" survey conducted in the Netherlands in 1996–1997. He found a positive association between social trust and regular volunteering. Finally, we note a 1998 study of Norwegians that found those who were volunteering more than an hour a week were more trusting than those who contributed few hours or not at all. However, the trait had a stronger effect on volunteer range than volunteer hours, suggesting that trust has its strongest effect on getting people initially involved in volunteer work than the intensity of their commitment once they start volunteering (Wollebaek and Selles 2003a:74).

While these studies support the theory that trust encourages volunteering, others suggest caution in drawing this conclusion. Dekker and van den Broek (1996:139) analyzed 1991 WVS data from the United States, Great Britain, West Germany, Italy, and Mexico. They found that trust and volunteering were associated only in Great Britain and West Germany. Uslaner (2002b:242) used the WVS data to compare Canada and the United States. Canadians were more trusting than Americans but this did not lead to higher volunteer rates in Canada because the association between volunteering and trust was weaker in Canada than in the United States. He attributed this to the fact that interpersonal trust is more important in individualistic societies such as the United States.[8]

Faced with these mixed results, we analyzed the data from the Independent Sector surveys of 1996 and 1999, using the standard question, "Generally speaking, would you say that most people can be trusted or that you can't be too careful in dealing with people?" We found that volunteers were indeed more trusting than non-volunteers, regardless of age, race, education, income, or frequency of church attendance. We then asked whether being a trusting person mediated the effect of other attributes on volunteering. For example, do well-educated people volunteer more because they are more trusting? Surprisingly, we found that trust had no mediating effect. [5] For example, although frequent churchgoers are more trusting, this is not the reason they are more likely to volunteer. Although highly educated people are more trusting, this is not the reason they volunteer. Although the affluent are more trusting, this is not the reason they volunteer. One reason for the failure to find any mediating effect might well be that the socio-demographic and religious variables explain little of the variation in interpersonal trust. This supports the argument that trust is a personality trait that is going to influence volunteerism regardless of social situation. We will return to this issue in the conclusion to this section.

Trust and Domains of Volunteering

If we think of trust as a psychological resource, then the question arises as to whether it is equally useful for all types of volunteer work. One intriguing possibility is that trusting people are more likely to volunteer for those types of activities that involve providing services to others in need but less likely to volunteer for activities that involve confrontation with authorities or working to change the system. For example, an American study found that trust and volunteering were positively associated only in the case of volunteering in connection with churches and schools (Kohut 1997:44). An additional analysis of the same data sorted civic activities into a "civic engagement" cluster and a "government engagement" cluster. The former consisted of volunteering in connection with voluntary associations: in this case volunteers were more trusting. The latter consisted of activities such as working for a political candidate or campaign, contacting a public official, and attending a political meeting: in this case the volunteers were *less* trusting. In short, politically oriented volunteering seemed to be motivated by lack of trust; service-oriented volunteering was motivated by trust in others (Greenberg 2001).

We examined the Independent Sector data to see if the influence of trust varied by domain of volunteering. We aggregated some of the types to obtain sufficiently large cell sizes. We preserved religious volunteering as a separate domain. We grouped arts, culture, and education into one category. Another category was health and human services volunteering. A fourth category was recreation and youth development. An advocacy category included environment, political, public society benefit, foundations, international, and work-related volunteering. We found that trust had its strongest effect on volunteering in the education, arts, and culture category, followed by advocacy volunteering. The effect of trust on recreation and youth development was only half as strong as its effect on volunteering in connection with schools or the arts. [6] These results do not replicate those of Greenberg (2001), perhaps because we have no equivalent of the politically oriented volunteering category, but it remains a puzzle as to why trusting people would be more readily drawn toward some types of volunteer work than others.

Self-Efficacy

Political scientists often refer to efficacy to explain variations in civic engagement. They reason that people are more likely to be politically active if they believe they can make a difference, which is the essential component of self-efficacy. They are less likely to undertake any project if they have little confidence their efforts will bear fruit. It is an old adage that you have to "believe in yourself" in order to succeed. Personality psychologists treat self-efficacy as a sub-component of the neurotic personality trait. Self-efficacy is important because it changes the calculus of the costs and benefits of volunteer work. Efficacious people are less likely to think they are "wasting their time." They set themselves more realistic goals; or at least the goals they articulate are more realistic. They believe they can make a difference and that they *do* make a difference. They believe their volunteer work enhances the quality of life in the community and provides tangible benefits in the form of helping people or maintaining institutions such as schools. Efficacy is similar to mastery, also a lower-order personality trait included within neuroticism. Mastery measures the degree to which people feel in control of their own fate. A person who scores high in mastery would certainly disagree with this standard questionnaire item: "I often feel I am being pushed around in life." A masterful person feels he or she has self-control rather than being controlled by external events.

Efficacy and mastery help move empathy and responsibility to action. A person who is not actively engaged in his or her community might justify this inaction in the same way as the focus group member who told researchers,

> I don't make a significant difference. I think about that a lot. No one person can make a real significant difference unless that person is blessed with that type of energy. (Profile of Illinois 2001)

People will be put off volunteering if they are easily discouraged by others refusing to help or by the failure to achieve immediate, tangible results. A survey of Illinois residents asked them which of a number of reasons prevented them from being more involved in their community. Twenty-six percent said they did not know enough about the issues; 13 percent said they did not have the needed skills; and 12 percent said they did not think it would make any difference (Profile of Illinois 2001). These respondents are saying they do not get involved because they lack faith in their ability to make much of a contribution. Respondents in the survey who were engaged in their community were very different. They were more likely to express the view that individuals can make a difference to the quality of life in their community and that people like them can affect what their local government does.

A 1992 survey of Philadelphians measured self-efficacy by asking, "Overall, how much impact do you think people like you can have in making your community a better place to live?" Just over a quarter (28%) of the sample believed they could have a "big impact." Were volunteers even more likely to express this view? The results were mixed, depending on the volunteer domain. Among those volunteering for religious groups, 36 percent said they thought they could have a big impact, compared to 28 percent of those volunteering to help the poor, elderly, and homeless, 24 percent of those volunteering for community groups, and 23 percent of those volunteering for youth development groups or for schools and tutoring programs (Kohut 1997:39). These are small differences—and we should note that only zero-order effects are reported: there are no controls for socio-economic or demographic variables. These factors are controlled for in a number of multivariate studies of self-efficacy and volunteering. Herzog and Morgan (1993) used two items from the ACL survey to measure efficacy: "I take a positive attitude toward myself" and "I can do just about anything I set my mind to do." At the zero-order level, efficacy had a positive effect on the chances of volunteering, but after controls for socio-economic differences, the efficacy effect disappeared, due to the positive association between efficacy and socio-economic status. This study was restricted to respondents 55 years of age or older, but Thoits and Hewitt (2001:124) found the same result in the whole ACL sample. Mastery was positively correlated with volunteering at the zero-order level, but the effect went away once controls for socio-demographics were imposed. Thus it seems as if the relation between self-efficacy or mastery and volunteering might be spurious: higher socio-economic status people score higher on these indexes *and* they are more likely to volunteer.

To further investigate the effect of self-efficacy on volunteering we turned to the Independent Sector data, using a question included in the 1992, 1996, and 1999 surveys: "It is in my power to do things that improve the welfare of others." Women and frequent churchgoers were more likely to agree with this statement while the elderly were less likely. Controlling for these factors, volunteers were more likely to express confidence in their ability to help others, and the more hours they volunteered and the more organizations they volunteered for, the more confident they were. [7] Further analysis of the Independent Sector data showed that self-efficacy partially explains the positive effect of education and income on volunteering. It therefore has both direct and indirect effects.[9]

We noted earlier that self-efficacy is more influential when it is combined with a felt obligation to help others. People are more likely to volunteer when they believe they ought to do something *and* they can do something: they are both willing and able. We were able to test this hypothesis using a factor analysis of the 1992 Independent Sector survey items on attitudes, during which we uncovered a latent factor comprised of the following items:[10]

"I feel a moral duty to help people who suffer." (.584)
"It is in my power to do things that improve the welfare of others." (.804)
"It we all volunteer time and effort, social problems like poverty and hopelessness can be overcome." (.725)

This latent factor combines responsibility (the first item) with efficacy. Prior to factor analysis we coded the items so that a high score indicated greater efficacy. Volunteers scored higher on this factor than non-volunteers, even after controls for the socio-demographic variables. [4] In summary, although our measures of self-efficacy do not exactly correspond to those used by personality psychologists, they are close enough to gauge the extent to which people have confidence in their own powers to achieve their goals. The latent factor we uncovered adds a valuable component of felt obligation to this personality trait. Together, they support the argument that volunteers feel more efficacious than non-volunteers.

Before we leave the topic of self-efficacy, we should note that personality traits are only one of a number of factors associated with volunteering. Personality psychologists do not claim that personality traits work in isolation from other individual attributes but rather combine with them. This raises the question of whether a trait like self-efficacy has a stronger influence on volunteering for some groups in the population than others. For example, among people who might otherwise stand little chance of volunteering or even being asked to volunteer, a personality trait such as self-efficacy would have special value. This issue is addressed in a study of college students who were asked if they were currently doing "off campus volunteer work of a charitable or helping nature" (Serow et al. 1990:161). They were also asked their opinion of how effective "average citizens" are in solving social problems. As expected, students with high efficacy scores were more likely to be volunteering, but this effect was confined to those whose mothers held graduate degrees. In other words, only students from comparatively comfortable backgrounds connected feelings of efficacy with volunteer work. There was no compensation effect: students from less privileged backgrounds did not get an extra "boost" from feeling efficacious.

To replicate this study we used data from the Independent Sector surveys, using the efficacy index described above. Controlling for socio-demographic and religious variables, we estimated a model including interaction terms for educational achievement and scores on the efficacy scale. [8] The positive effect of self-efficacy was stronger for people with limited education. In short, our findings indicated a compensation effect for the personality trait, rather than the enhancing effect found in the study described in the previous paragraph. Since our analysis is based on a representative sample of the American adult population and uses the respondent's own education as a component of the interaction term, it is probably more reliable, but this is clearly an issue that deserves further study.

The Prosocial Personality

Both the studies we have reviewed and our own analyses indicate quite clearly that personality traits help differentiate volunteers from non-volunteers. Certain traits are consistently associated with volunteering. This raises the question of whether there is a prosocial personality type—a bundle of traits that distinguishes volunteers from non-volunteers. A noted personality psychologist believes there is. It consists of two dimensions:

> The first we call other-oriented empathy which appears to primarily concern prosocial thoughts and feelings. People who score high on this factor are empathetic and feel responsibility and concern for the welfare of others. The second dimension is called Helpfulness, which appears to concern prosocial actions— frequently engaging in helpful actions and an absence of self-oriented reactions to others' distress. (Penner 2004:600)

In a study of AIDS volunteers, both empathy and helpfulness predicted how committed volunteers were. Volunteers with more prosocial personalities were less likely to drop out over the eight-month duration of the study. In another study (of volunteers at a homeless shelter) people with prosocial personalities were again more strongly committed: that is, they served longer (Penner 2002). It is not clear at this time, however, whether this prosocial concept can help distinguish volunteers from non-volunteers.

Conclusion

Most of us know people who always seem to be ready to help others, to listen to other people's concerns sympathetically, to assume more than their "fair share" of the work of any group to which they belong, anxious to "do their part," while others seem self-centered, unsympathetic, skeptical of the value of service to others, and more than ready to stand back and let others do the work. It is also plausible that, rather than being a reflection of any single personality trait, helpfulness is a bundle of traits. For example, Hart et al. (2006:640) conclude that "individuals who are typically positive in mood, able to regulate emotions, frequently experience sympathy, and are effective in interactions with others are more likely to become involved in community service." Some go even further and suggest that volunteers probably have prosocial personalities. It is easy to imagine the prosocial person stepping forward when the group needs someone to do the dirty work of keeping the group going.

These arguments notwithstanding, there is considerable debate about whether or not there are any behavioral dispositions that are stable enough to qualify as traits (Ardelt 2000). This is important because, if dispositions such as trust are deemed unstable, they hardly qualify as traits at all. As we noted earlier, economists believe trust is based on rational calculations using past transactions as a guide. If we are repeatedly "let down" by other people we change our mind and become less trusting. Some sociologists, pointing to the way in which trust varies by education, income, family relationships, church-going, and even neighborhood, also reject the notion that there is anything permanent about it (Wuthnow 1998:199). It is hardly surprising that those who enjoy financial and social security have more benign attitudes toward their fellow human beings while the dispossessed or more marginal groups in society lack trust in others (Kohut 1997:24–25; Smith 1997:189).

We contend that social variations in personality traits do not deny the existence of durable predispositions to act in certain ways. It is well known, for example, that women score higher than men on agreeableness and conscientiousness. It is well known that better-educated adults are more open to new experiences (Rossi 2001c:272). In the case of the most disputed of the traits we describe—trust—we feel justified in treating it as a stable disposition because the survey question used to measure it asks about trust in "other people" or "people in general." This open-ended question is tapping a general disposition, focusing on no particular object. This is different from asking about trust in particular people, groups, or social institutions, such as the mass media. This version of trust is actually a measure of confidence; it gauges the extent to which we think these institutions are capable of doing the job for which they were designed. Such evaluations resemble attitudes more than personality traits. These attitudes can change.[11]

Virtually all of the authors we have cited recognized how difficult it is to determine causal priority in the relation between trust and volunteering. The general approach to the relation between trust and social participation is to treat them as reciprocally related. Trust encourages volunteering. At the same time, volunteering encourages trust because most volunteering takes place in the context of voluntary organizations that "implicitly provide guidelines on whom to trust, whom not to trust, and in which circumstances" (Anheier and Kendall 2002:349). For personality psychologists the problem with this argument is that, if a personality trait can be influenced by a social practice such as volunteering, then it is not quite as stable as they maintain. The longitudinal structure of the ACL makes it possible to perform a limited test of the hypothesis that "personality" is the result, rather than the cause, of volunteering by using the measure of mastery. As we noted above, mastery had no influence on changes in volunteering between 1986 and 1989, but volunteering did have a positive effect on changes in mastery between 1986 and 1989. Based on the results of this single study, mastery is the effect of volunteering rather than its cause. This issue needs to be examined more thoroughly, using three waves of data to better estimate reciprocal effects and more measures of personality traits.

The most open-minded way to approach the study of personality and volunteering is to assume that both personality and social situation are important. The question then becomes how much of the variation in volunteering is due to "situation" and how much is due to personality. If apparent personality differences disappear when differences in social situation are controlled, then we should be skeptical of the claim that there are durable trait differences. Recall that we found that trust did not mediate the effect of other variables on volunteering. For example, although highly educated people are more trusting, this was not the reason they volunteered. We believe one reason why trust does not mediate the effect of socio-demographic (or religious) variables is that these variables explain very little of the variation in interpersonal trust. Using the Independent Sector data from 1996 and 1999 we constructed a sociological profile of trusting Americans. The measure of trust in the survey was the standard question, "Generally speaking, would you say that most people can be trusted or that you can't be too careful in dealing with people?" We coded this item so that a high score indicated more trust. We were able to construct a profile of the most trusting Americans: they were middle aged, well educated, affluent, and frequent churchgoers. African Americans were less trusting than any other racial group. But there were no gender, parental, marital, or employment status differences in trust, and the variance explained by the model was very small ($r^2 = 0.09$). [9] Although there is some social structural variation in trust between persons, as most personality psychologists would readily admit, this variation does not help us explain why some people are more trusting than others, leaving personality traits as an attractive alternative explanation. Although most sociologists have either ignored personality traits in their analyses of volunteering or denied their existence, it would seem that this is a misguided strategy. As we have suggested earlier, not only might personality traits add to our ability to explain volunteering, they might also interact with sociological variables, such as social class, to help further refine the profile of the volunteer. Although there are undoubtedly reciprocal effects between personality traits and volunteering (traits are not impervious to change) it would be foolish to deny causal status to personality characteristics and to deny the stability of these characteristics: "The person-situation debate, concerning whether consistencies in individuals' behavior are pervasive or broad enough to be meaningfully described in terms of personality traits, can at least be declared about 98% over" (Funder 2001:199).

4

Motives

The most obvious way to explain why people volunteer is to ask them their reasons for doing so. Indeed, a complete explanation of any kind of human behavior must refer to intentions, reasons, or motives. If we want to leave any room at all for human agency in how we think about social action, we must allow our subjects to envisage the results of what they hope to achieve, along with the means of attaining them. This is what motivates them to act. In this chapter we will review, and make a contribution to, the research on the link between motives and volunteering. As with personality, the motives concept has proved to be a troublesome one for social scientists. Much of this chapter is taken up with a discussion of the functional theory of motives. This theory is based on the assumption that all persons have the same basic psychological needs. Particular forms of behavior can be accounted for by referring to these needs. The theory assumes that needs (or the motivation to meet those needs) are universal. All people have these needs although they do not necessarily choose the same means for satisfying them.

After our review of this theory of motivation and the research that has used it, we will describe some other motivational theories of volunteering. We will then consider more sociological theories of motivation that take a rather different approach to the subject. Sociologists do not deny the existence of motives but most of them would disagree with the psychological interpretation of their role in social life. First, they believe that motives should refer to specific outcomes, such as being generous to our grandparents, not broad dispositions, such as benevolence, because being motivated means having an image of the desired result and working toward its achievement. Second, they are skeptical of using people's reasons for their actions as an explanation of those actions because these reasons can be feigned, mixed, unacknowledged, or even unconscious. Third, even if we acknowledge that actors are motivated this does not mean their accounts of their motives are sufficient to explain their actions. Knowing what an actor wants to do is only the beginning of explaining what they are doing, not the end. As Parsons (1949:217) wrote long ago, "the treatment of the concrete differences of behavior as direct manifestations of differences of ultimate motivation alone is clearly illegitimate in that it fails to take account of the institutional factor." In short, motives are never *sufficient* explanations for human conduct. It is always necessary to take "external influences" into account (Sills 1957:83).

In this chapter, we take the view that sociological and psychological perspectives on motivation are not necessarily opposed to each other. First, by looking at the kinds of resources people have, or where they are located in the social structure, sociologists can do quite a good job of explaining how people come to volunteer but not why; motive theory does quite a good job of explaining why people decide to volunteer but not how they get the opportunity to do so in the first place. For example, one reason why motives are not a sufficient explanation for volunteering is that being asked is so important. Anything that increases the chances of being asked, such as social contacts, will therefore play a crucial intermediary role. Even highly motivated people are unlikely to volunteer unless they are asked, and people with little motivation to volunteer might agree to do so if they are constantly badgered by friends to give some of their time. Second, while motivation theory might teach us that people have certain needs (e.g., avoiding loneliness), we need to know something about the social structure to explain why these needs are met by volunteering. Third, while motivation theorists might be correct in thinking there are a finite number of motivations that drive human beings, we need to know something about the social structure to explain why certain motives are more important for some people than others.

In chapter 2 we discussed the way in which people tend to define volunteering in motivational terms: only if actions are properly motivated are they considered instances of volunteerism. People consistently rank volunteer activities based on the "purity" of their motivation. Truly selfless acts, undertaken with no expectation of reward, receive the most credit (Cnaan et al. 1996:375; Midlarsky and Kahana 1994:38). A focus group study of how people perceive the duties of citizenship found that a majority agreed that volunteering was a good example of virtuous behavior, although not necessarily a strict requirement for citizenship status. Members got into a discussion of whether it was possible to judge an act as virtuous without considering the underlying motive. "One woman said, 'In order to classify someone as good—good citizen, good person—you've got to look at their motives'" (Conover et al. 1993:161).

Early studies of volunteer motivations simply asked people why they volunteered and treated whatever reason they gave as the cause of their behavior. This is unsatisfactory because the motive is "contained" in the end and makes little sense outside the context of that action. It contributes little to our understanding to hear a woman "explain" her contribution to a neighborhood clean-up campaign by saying how much she desires a clean neighborhood. Earlier studies were flawed in another way. All too often, information was gathered only from volunteers. In the social sciences, this is referred to as "selecting on the dependent variable" because data are gathered only on those who volunteer and those who do not volunteer are ignored. With no comparison group of people who have chosen not to volunteer we cannot be sure that motivation is making any difference at all. The non-volunteers might well have the same needs and be similarly motivated. For example, in the Canadian National Survey of Giving, Volunteering and Participating (2000) volunteers were asked whether they agreed or disagreed with seven possible reasons for being a volunteer. Almost all volunteers (95%) agreed they volunteered to help a cause they believe in (Hall et al. 2001:43). However, we cannot attribute any causal significance to this measurement because we do not know whether there are people who also believed in a cause (e.g., animal protection) who did not volunteer.

Functional Theory of Motives

The best-known and most sophisticated psychological theory of volunteer motivations takes a functional approach. Functional analysis is concerned with the reasons and purposes that underlie and generate beliefs and actions. People act when they think a particular activity will serve important psychological functions for them. According to this theory, individuals initiate volunteer behavior if they believe it will serve one or more psychological needs (Snyder et al. 2000). The empirical research problem consists of identifying what these needs are and seeing if people's desire to reach function-specific goals explains why they volunteer.

The Volunteer Functions Inventory (VFI), with its six separate motivations for volunteering, formalizes ideas found in much of the psychological writing on why people volunteer. As we noted earlier, the problem with the earlier research on motivations for volunteering was the unsystematic nature of the list of possible motivations. A review of the earlier research literature on volunteer motivations found reference to altruistic, ideological, material, status, social relationships, leisure time, and personal growth motivations (Fischer and Schaffer 1993). A 1982 "Volunteer Needs Profile" included reference to the need for experience, feelings of social responsibility, the need for social contact, responding to the expectations of others, the need for social approval, expectation of future rewards, and the need to achieve (Schondel and Boehm 2000). Not only were these lists ad hoc, they often asked respondents to *rank order* the motivations as if some must be more important than others. As we shall see, not only is the VFI presented as being exhaustive of all possible motivations and replicable across studies, it also avoids the problem of ranking by asking respondents to rate the importance to them of each need. Empirically, all motives could be rated important.

According to the functional theory of motivation, the same act can serve different functions for different people. The reason for performing the act is more important than the act itself. It is not possible for an outside observer to look at an act and decide what need it is intended to meet. This can be illustrated by looking at the results of a study of fifty-three active and fifty-three inactive ombudsmen serving in nursing facilities for the elderly who were asked their motivation for volunteering. Although they were all doing the same job, they gave various reasons for doing it. The largest group of ombudsmen were motivated by justice concerns: they wanted to help protect the rights of the elderly, who they considered defenseless. Some of the volunteers (28%) wanted to give something back to their community, while another group (20%) volunteered because a loved one had benefited from being in a nursing facility. Only 5 percent mentioned volunteering because they felt compassion for the elderly, probably because the job of the ombudsman was not to provide care but to help protect rights. Seven percent of the ombudsmen volunteered because they were attracted to a job in which they could use and develop their work skills. The role of the ombudsman was thus open to many interpretations and had the potential to meet many different needs. Some stressed the advocacy aspect of the role; some wanted to be mediators; some were educators; and a few were there as friendly visitors providing emotional support to the elderly who needed it (Nathanson and Eggleston 1993).

As the VFI has been developed and tested in empirical studies, six motivations have emerged as consistently associated with volunteer work. We should note that the same volunteer activity could help meet several different needs.

Values

By working to achieve desired goals, or values, people remain true to an ideal conception of themselves. This is what people mean when they say they volunteer because "I can do something for a cause that is important to me." Nearly all Canadian volunteers (95%) gave this as one reason for doing volunteer work (Hall et al. 2001:43). More than two-thirds (69%) of the teenagers surveyed by Wuthnow (1995:75) said they volunteered because "I want to give of myself for the benefit of others." Value-oriented motives were mentioned by most of the volunteers contacted in a survey of Illinois residents in 2001. Nearly all (93%) said they wanted to make their community a better place; 65 percent said they were doing it because everyone should be involved; 50 percent wanted a chance to influence government policy; and 35 percent mentioned the principles of their religious faith (Profile of Illinois 2001). People who say they volunteer because they want to "reduce world hunger" or "change government policies affecting hunger" are motivated by values. It also includes any expression of "altruism," as when concern for other people's welfare prompts a person to volunteer. It includes people who volunteer because they "care about the community," whether this is a place (e.g., neighborhood) or a social category (e.g., the gay community). As noted above, value motivation can also mean that the volunteer act is itself a value statement. A certain way of treating other people helps a person act out her values. By her own conduct she expresses her values. Teske (1997:125) calls this the "pursuit of objective meaning." It is imaginable, for example, that the goals toward which we feel impelled by values motivation (e.g., eradicating hunger) could be achieved by means other than volunteer labor. The important thing is that the individual has internalized certain values, wishes to see them actualized, and takes pleasure in acting in such a way as to realize these values.

Enhancement

The second function volunteerism serves is to offer learning experiences about different people, places, skills, or oneself as, for example, when a person says, "Volunteering lets me learn things through direct, hands-on experience." A person who volunteers to help people with AIDS in order to learn more about the disease, how it spreads, and how it is being dealt with would fall into this category. So would a woman with arthritis who volunteers to help others cope with the pain of arthritis, if she wants to learn more about the pain and how to manage it (Barlow and Hainsworth 2001:211), or a person who volunteers to serve in an underdeveloped country to learn more about other cultures and other peoples. Some of the upper class women interviewed by Daniels (1988:181) seemed to have been motivated to volunteer by a desire to meet people from across class and race boundaries, and spoke proudly of the wide range of acquaintances and contacts they had developed as a result of their community service. Volunteer work can also enhance experience by its physical and mental challenges—the adrenaline rush of participating in search and rescue efforts, the excitement of fighting fires, the fear and apprehension associated with many protest activities. Kelley et al. (2005:373) believe that one of the primary motives for people to volunteer for a needle-exchange program was that being "on the street" was "tinged with danger."

> I kind of like the fact that it was kind of illegal, it makes me feel a little daring. So that fills my need of being like on the cutting edge or something. I've definitely noticed that that's something I kind of feel now, like "ha-ha," doing something in defiance.

Social

The social function is the need to fit in and get along with members of groups important to us. This motivation seems to be behind a lot of volunteer activity. In one study, eight out of ten volunteers said they volunteered because it gave them the chance to be with people whose company they enjoyed and 74 percent said it gave them the chance to be with people who shared their ideals (Profile of Illinois 2001). Volunteers at community centers in Canada designed to provide safe places for children and "a variety of nutrition, play, family home visiting, drop-in, educational, cultural, and social action programs" in poorer neighborhoods spoke of the centers as a place for visiting, talking, socializing and "feeling part of it all." "I enjoy it. I don't have much of a social life . . . Plus, I feel like, you know, on the same level as everybody else" (Reitsma-Street et al. 2000:659). Each center was a site of respectful inclusion and acceptance, not only for the clients but also the volunteers. Social motivations are foremost in an account given by a contributor to *Good Housekeeping* magazine describing an organization called "Single Volunteers." The premise of this organization is that volunteer work is a good place to meet like-minded people and perhaps find someone to marry. One local chapter of the organization spent a weekend clearing brush in a state-owned public park.

> We worked hard all day, and then stayed up until three in the morning, talking. When it was time to go, nobody wanted to leave. People said they hadn't had that sense of togetherness for a long time. I mean, how many adults get to have a slumber party? (Penney 1998 227:27)

Nine out of ten EMS volunteers said intra-squad friendships were "a strong or moderate" motivation for them; two-thirds were motivated by a desire to belong to a cohesive group (Thompson 1993a). Perhaps we should not be surprised that EMS volunteers should attach so much importance to social bonding as a reason for volunteering given the nature of their work. Nor should we be surprised that volunteers at a homeless shelter attributed more importance to this motivation than a comparison group of volunteers at an animal shelter (Ferrari et al. 1999:46). Poppendieck (1998:176) interviewed elderly people who volunteered to act as "gleaners" following behind agricultural workers to pick the rejected fruit and vegetables for food banks.

> After I retired, I started looking for something to be active at and volunteer at . . . I've been doing this about three years, since I retired. I do it at least three days a week. I come out every morning. It's like physical exercise and, besides, it's helping other people. I kind of enjoy it . . . seeing the people and talking and that kind of thing.

Multiple motivations are apparent in this quotation: the desire to help people in need; the desire to keep fit and healthy; and the desire to get out of the house and meet people.

Social motivation is expressed in volunteering to win the social approval, or meet the expectations, of people important to us. If a volunteer says, "People I am close to want me to volunteer," she is socially motivated. Bowen et al. (2000) found that the desire for social approval was the second most highly rated motivation for volunteering, almost as important as values. A hospice volunteer told Robert Coles (1993:80): "For me, it's a place where I feel myself needed and where I can live up to the expectations of others." Volunteering is also a way to express one's solidarity with a group, as when a volunteer says, "To make society run, you have to put in your time" (Becker and Dhingra 2001:328). This kind of motivation is often found where peer counseling is an important feature of volunteer work. Adair (1997:24) quotes the coordinator of the Birth Control and Unplanned Pregnancy Program at the Women's Health Clinic in Winnipeg as saying that former clients of the program often come back as volunteers: "They put a different perspective on it and are able to say 'this happened to me.'" Solidarity is also expressed in choosing to volunteer if we have been affected by or benefited from the service we now choose to provide. In volunteering, we share our knowledge, sensitivity, skills, and concern with others similarly afflicted. Nearly two-thirds of Canadian volunteers said they had been personally affected by the cause for which they were working (Hall et al. 2001:43). Half the volunteers working as ombudsmen in long-term care facilities had prior family or personal involvement in long-term care (Nelson et al. 2004:117). Chambre (1995:123) found that most of the small group of AIDS volunteers she interviewed either had close relatives who were gay or had been injection drug users or had close relatives or friends with a history of drug use.

Career

The fourth motive for volunteering is to obtain career-related benefits, such as work skills or business contacts. Abrahams (1996:773) found that some of the women volunteering at a rape crisis center were considering a career in counseling. Community involvement, for one woman, meant doing accounting work and was her chance of "keeping a foot in the door" until the day she returned full-time to the labor force (Abrahams 1996:784). In Pearce's (1993:35) study of volunteer workers "the Chapter chairwoman of the volunteer-staffed family planning clinic and the coordinator of the poverty relief agency were professionals (nurse and social worker respectively) keeping active in their professions through their volunteer work while raising small children." Also included under this heading would be people who volunteer because it is a requirement or obligation attached to a job or club or association membership.

In social surveys, an example of this motivation would be, "Volunteering allows me to explore different career options." Surveys typically find that only a small minority of people look upon volunteer work chiefly as a means of improving job prospects, but considering how uncomfortable people are with the idea that volunteers could materially benefit from their service, the proportion is quite high, especially in certain subgroups in the population. Young people are most likely to volunteer for this reason, especially if they have yet to enter the labor force.[1] Young adults are more likely to see volunteer work as a substitute for paid work, something they can do to occupy their time usefully and gain skills until they get a job.[2] But this motivation is not confined to younger people. It is also important for older people without jobs.[3]

Although some might feel uncomfortable citing work-related motivations for volunteering, it is quite common for schools, colleges, and volunteer agencies to tout this as a reason for doing volunteer work. Indeed, some non-profit organizations specifically use volunteer work to train unemployed people for paid jobs. In the 1980s, a number of community development organizations were established in the United States with support from philanthropic foundations, mainly in low-income neighborhoods, their purpose being to encourage and support local community activism and promote activities such as affordable housing, teen mentoring, and women's shelters. Another part of their mission was to act as a substitute for job training programs the community did not otherwise provide. Their stated goal was to "take the volunteers to another level—find a job and leave us" (Gittell et al. 2000).

In the United States, where competition for places in colleges and universities can be quite fierce, the practice of volunteering while in high school in order to improve one's chances of being offered admission is apparently a widespread form of "resume-padding." Many high school students have come to believe that "service" is necessary for any type of college admission, especially the more selective institutions. The more young people begin to think that their life chances are tied to a college degree from a selective institution and that their chance of being admitted to such an institution is influenced by doing volunteer work while in high school, the more "inflated" the volunteer rate of teenagers becomes. As we shall see in chapter 10, a survey conducted in 2005 estimated the volunteer rate of Americans aged between 12 and 18 at 55 percent, more than one and a half times the adult rate of 29 percent (Grimm et al. 2005:2). In interviews with seventy high school students in the United States, Friedland and Morimoto (2005:10) found that many were volunteering "at high levels," motivated by "the perception that voluntary and civic activity is necessary to get into any college, and the better the college (or, more precisely, the higher the perception of the college in the status system) the more volunteerism was necessary." This could be why "college bound" high school students are more likely to volunteer than those who are not planning to attend college. The 2005 survey cited above also found that 43 percent of students reporting a grade average of B+ or higher were involved in community service as part of a school activity, compared to 26 percent of those with a grade average of C or lower.

Protective

The fifth function volunteerism may serve is called "protective" because it has to do with enabling people to deal with inner conflicts, feelings of incompetence, uncertainties about social identity, emotional needs, and the like. For example: "Volunteering is a good escape from my own troubles"; "Volunteering helps me work through my own personal problems." Here volunteering can be seen as a form of coping, as when gay men volunteer to help people with AIDS as a way of dealing with their own fear of the disease (Chambre 1995:123) or women volunteer to work at a rape crisis center to heal from their own experience of being raped (Abrahams 1996:773). Blackstone (2004:356) found that many women volunteering for the Komen Breast Cancer Foundation were doing so as a way of connecting with other women who shared the same experience of breast cancer diagnosis. AIDS activists surveyed by Jennings and Anderson (2003:190) worked a lot harder as volunteers if someone close to them had contracted AIDS. Most of them gay, they were afraid not only for themselves but for the wider gay community. The death of partners, sons, brothers, and friends also incited feelings of anger and frustration, and a desire to do something about the problem. Not all AIDS volunteers are gay, of course, but while straight volunteers expressed a values motivation, gay volunteers were more likely to talk about learning about the disease and how to cope with it (Simon et al. 2000). An emergency squad volunteer interviewed by Wuthnow (1991:25) admitted that, "I don't feel I have self-worth unless I'm helping people, so I'm really justifying my existence by helping somebody else." One woman told Daniels (1988:56),

> I was deeply unhappy in my first marriage. Jane . . . said ". . . you should consider the League of Women Voters." And I did. I just ate it up.

A volunteer at a well woman's clinic told Merrell (2000:34),

> I'd done a lot of part-time jobs when the children were small and then I'd stayed at home for a while. And then when you have trouble say like in a marriage, it really knocks you for six, that sort of thing. Well then where you go out into the world again and you do different things and then you find, like for instance, running the group and when it's successful, you think "Oh well yes I can do that you know" . . . . it's amazing people don't always realize what they are capable of, do they?

Some of the volunteers working in charity (thrift) shops in England surveyed by Horne and Maddrell (2002:81) cited therapeutic reasons for doing so, a way of recovering from mental and physical illness, drug abuse, or the loss of a loved one. Another expression of the protective motivation is the desire to "feel useful" in a world where being productive is highly valued and being unproductive, or useless, is stigmatized. Older people frequently cite this motivation for volunteering (Barlow and Hainsworth 2001; Okun et al. 1998:619; Warburton et al. 2001:598). According to one volunteer in the Foster Grandparent program for children in hospital, "It wasn't a hard decision—you just see the need. You can't be here an hour that you don't see those children need you, and you know you need something besides sitting at home" (Freedman 1999:77).[4]

Understanding

The sixth function refers to volunteerism as a means of personal growth and ego-enhancement (Snyder et al. 2000:371). For example: "Volunteering makes me feel important"; "Volunteering allows me to gain a new perspective on things." Fifty-nine percent of Canadian volunteers give "exploring one's own strengths" as a reason for volunteering (Hall et al. 2001:43). One woman told Daniels (1988:56), "In volunteering, I gained personal esteem. I found out I could do something. I could get some self-identity and some confidence." But almost as many (64%) drew on another framework to suggest another reason: "It makes me feel good about myself when I care for others" (Wuthnow 1995:75). One volunteer at a well woman's clinic told Merrell (2000:35), "Quite often it was the only thing I'd done at all during the week where you actually felt at the end of 3 or 4 hours that you'd accomplished something. You got an immediate feedback." A volunteer at a community center in Canada spoke of being a better mother as a result of her work. "Because you're getting your confidence, your children can learn from that. You're speaking your mind, and they learn that they can do it too" (Reitsma-Street et al. 2000:660). Another expressed pride in being able to learn new skills in middle age. Many changed from feeling "like I have nothing to offer" to realizing that there were many tasks at which they were quite accomplished. Personal growth is also behind the motivation to volunteer in order to realize a chosen identity: "If I am to become more Christ-like, I must serve" (Becker and Dhingra 2001:328). Abrahams (1996:776) describes a middle class professional Latina who got involved in volunteer work in order to get closer to her ethnic identity and learn more about it. This is similar to people who volunteer "to meet people with similar interests." They are using volunteer work to identify and build a community of others to which they can belong.

How Useful Is the VFI in Distinguishing Volunteers?

Do motives help us explain why some people volunteer and others do not? To answer this question we review the studies that have used the VFI, or some version of it, in empirical research. The important issue is whether volunteers rate these motivations more highly than non-volunteers. They are not linked to volunteer work by definition: all of the functions can be served by behaviors other than volunteering. Nor is motivation the only antecedent of volunteering. What happens when we control for these other antecedents?

One study, using a nationally representative sample of Americans, found that volunteers rated *all* VFI motivations higher than non-volunteers. The study asked respondents to rate the importance of twenty reasons for volunteering. Volunteers indicated the importance of each reason for why they were volunteering, while non-volunteers indicated how important each reason would be to them *were* they to volunteer. Factor analysis was used to see if the responses to the twenty questions clustered in a manner that reflected the six functions of volunteerism identified in the inventory. A six-factor structure emerged in both the volunteer and non-volunteer samples. Volunteers ranked all motivations higher than non-volunteers, with the exception of career motivations, which the non-volunteers saw as more important. The survey also asked volunteers how long they had been volunteering. The more experienced volunteers attached greater importance to values, enhancement, social, and protective motivations while the less experienced attached more importance to career and understanding motivations. Motives were also related to frequency of volunteering: people who volunteered often attached more importance to values and enhancement motivations; the more importance they attached to career motivations, the less often they volunteered. The inventory even helped predict what type of volunteer work people do. For example, working on behalf of the environment was less popular among people motivated by career concerns and more popular among people motivated by understanding motives. Social motivation encouraged people to volunteer in connection with a religious organization but was not associated in any way with volunteering in connection with adult recreation or the arts (Clary et al. 1996:494).[5]

The VFI has proven its usefulness in a number of other applications where motives are linked to actual volunteer behavior. Beginning with the recruitment of volunteers, the inventory can be used to predict who is most likely to respond to calls for volunteers. This line of investigation is important because simply asking people who are currently volunteering why they volunteer may simply yield justifications for the activity that have been generated on a post hoc basis. It is also important from the standpoint of recruiters: appeals from volunteer agencies that directly address the individual's motives are likely to be more persuasive. In an experiment involving college students, Clary et al. (1994) found that participants shown a recruitment message that matched in content a motivation of great importance to them were more likely to find the message appealing and more likely to express an intention to volunteer in the future. In another experiment Clary et al. (1998) showed students a number of different brochures each highlighting one of the six functions of volunteerism. The students, who had earlier rated their motivation for volunteering, found a brochure more appealing if it matched their motivation. The conclusion is warranted that appeals for new volunteers will work best if they are couched in terms that speak directly to an individual's needs at the time. For example, college students might have stronger needs for career enhancement activities; elderly people might have stronger needs for social engagement or ego-enhancement activities.

In our own analysis of the Independent Sector survey data we obtained results very similar to those reported earlier. Volunteers attached more importance to feeling needed, compassion, the respect of others, gaining new perspectives, and solving one's own problems. The only motivation non-volunteers rated as more important than volunteers was making new contacts.[6] [10]

Other Approaches to Volunteer Motivations

The functional theory is by no means the only motivational theory of volunteering. In the next section we will review some the other approaches that have also invoked motives as an explanation for volunteering.

How Many Motives Are There?

Many social scientists believe that the influence of motivation on volunteering is an important topic, but not all of them agree there are six motivations. For example, a factor analysis of responses to motivation questions in a 1987 Canadian study arrived at a three-factor solution. The "self-interest" motivation included a desire to meet people, learn, accomplish something, make employment contacts, use skills, use spare time, and benefit to self. The "obligation" motivation included references to religious beliefs, obligation to one's heritage, a desire to give to community, or obligation to an organization. The "altruism" motivation included a desire to help others or help a cause (Chappell 1999:13). Other scholars believe there are only two motivations—selfish and altruistic (Frisch and Gerrard 1981; Latting 1990). When Hwang et al. (2005) factor analyzed the WVS data on reasons for volunteering for Canada and the United States they arrived at a two-factor solution: one factor measured "altruistic" motives for volunteering (e.g., compassion for those in need) and the other measured "self-oriented" motives for volunteering (e.g., for social reasons, to meet people). These factors were positively related.[7]

At the other end of the spectrum are scholars who agree that motivations are interrelated (a person rating one motivation high is likely to rate another high) but it is unlikely they form into clusters in this way. Consequently, any attempt to categorize motives or find some latent factor underlying a cluster of motives is misguided (Okun et al. 1998:613). Instead, they argue, social researchers should give people specific goals with which to associate their volunteer work. This list of goals is infinite. Typical of this kind of study is Okun's (1994) exploration of motivations for volunteering among people 60 years of age or older. In the survey he uses, respondents were asked why they volunteered. The most frequently mentioned reason was to help others (83%), followed by a desire to be useful (65%), moral responsibility (51%), social obligation (28%), companionship (24%), occupy spare time (14%), combat loneliness (15%), learn new skills (14%), alleviate boredom (13%), and guilt (35%). Although the list of possible reasons is infinite, the average respondent mentioned only three. Because this study used only volunteers it is not possible to compare them with non-volunteers, but the authors found no relation between the number of motives mentioned and how frequently people volunteered: only the need to feel useful and sense of moral obligation predicted frequency of volunteering, no doubt a reflection of the advanced age of the respondents in the survey.[8] This study therefore provides some support to the general argument that motives are important, but its method of conceptualizing motives, far removed from the idea of there being an "inventory" of relevant motives, distinguishes it from the earlier studies. Psychologists who do not take the functional approach to motivation are less inclined to think there is a finite list of reasons for doing anything.

Batson's Four Motive Theory

A rather different psychological approach to motivations for volunteering is associated with the work of Daniel Batson, who has written extensively on altruism. He sees motives as "goal-directed forces induced by threats or opportunities related to one's values" (Batson et al. 2002:430). Motives are not dispositions, which we think of as fixed, but states of mind that can change depending on the context. Batson thus distinguishes his approach from the functional theory of motivation, with its assumption that there is a fixed and finite range of motivations tied to specific psychological needs. In Batson's view, the list of potential motives is endless.

Batson distinguished four "classes" of motivation for involvement in community improvement. Surprisingly, he includes *egoism* as one class of motives. In this case, the ultimate goal is to increase one's own welfare. Self-benefits include material well-being, social recognition, praise, and avoiding guilt and shame. However, benefiting others can result as an unintended consequence from actions impelled by this motive. Or a person might help others as an intermediary step to achieving a more distant self-interested goal. Admittedly, this kind of motivation is not an enduring basis for volunteer work:

> the student whose ultimate goal is to volunteer at a local nursing home to add community service to her resume is not likely to last. Her goal has been reached the first time she enters the building. (Batson et al. 2002:435)

The problem with using volunteer work as an instrument to reach some further self-interested objective is that, should another instrument offer itself as a more efficient way of furthering self-interest, volunteer work will be abandoned in favor of it.

In the case of *altruism* the goal is to increase the welfare of another person. Altruistic behaviors, in Batson's view, are driven primarily by emotion, sparked by empathy and compassion. Empathy for those less fortunate than oneself is certainly a frequent motivator of volunteer work and volunteers can probably be recruited by framing an issue as one of compassion (e.g., the plight of the homeless, or animals in a shelter). Batson does not believe, however, that empathy is a very reliable motivator of volunteer work. It is difficult to feel empathy for complete strangers and neither empathy nor compassion explain why someone would volunteer to help an anti-pollution campaign.

A more surprising class of motivation is *collectivism*. Batson believes we can be motivated to volunteer in order to increase the welfare of a group. It is certainly true that people are more likely to volunteer on behalf of a group if they identify with that group. The volunteer for Habitat for Humanity whose ultimate goal is to ease the plight of the poor displays this kind of motivation, but it is unclear whether this comprises a distinct class of motivations.

In *principlism* the motivation is to uphold some moral principle. The volunteer who invokes ideas like duty and justice is motivated by principle. This is a common mobilizing force in advocacy volunteering. It also appears in the case of people feeling that they should not "free ride" but do their "fair share"—for example, volunteering to help maintain the buildings and grounds of the local church they attend. Without implying that we always behave morally, Batson is arguing that volunteering is often motivated by an appeal to morality—it is simply something we feel we *ought* to do. This motivation overlaps with the values motivation of the VFI.

Generativity

Generativity is a concept originally developed by the psychologist Eric Erickson to describe the concern some people display for the welfare of the next generation and, more generally, for the welfare of the wider community. The Loyola Generativity Scale has been developed to measure individual differences in generativity, which we include in this section because it is described as an "inner drive, need, or motive that is experienced in adulthood as an especially compelling desire or want" (McAdams et al. 1998:10). It measures the extent to which adults feel they are sought out for advice, that other people need them, that they have made a unique contribution to society, and that they have had a good influence on the lives of many people.[9] Rossi (2001a:116) used a generativity scale in her analysis of the MIDUS data. Volunteers scored higher on generativity than non-volunteers. Notably, generativity predicted volunteering for a wide range of activities, including health-related, school or youth-oriented work, work for a political organization, and any other type of service for an organization or charity.

Hart et al. (2001:210) used the Loyola Generativity Scale in their study of "social involvement" of American adults aged between 34 and 65, expecting to find that generativity would be "an important motivational force" in activities such as volunteering. Of the several measures of social involvement they use, their index of political participation comes closest to being a measure of volunteerism because it includes as one of its four components working for a political party or campaign. They found that generativity predicted political involvement only for the African Americans in the sample: there was no effect for Whites. The fact that the measure used in this study taps political advocacy more than service volunteering might explain its failure to predict volunteering among Whites.[10]

The Political Economy of Motivation

Thus far we have discussed motivation from a psychological perspective. Economists—and many political scientists—also refer to motives when discussing volunteerism. From the viewpoint of economists, prospective volunteers seek out, or are attracted by, incentives or inducements offered by voluntary organizations. Motives therefore play a crucial role in their theory of volunteering because it explains how volunteer organizations solve the "free rider" problem—the tendency for people who stand to benefit from volunteer work to stand back and let others do it. In the economic model, motives become "interests" to which appeal can be made by offering the right incentives. Different incentives appeal to different interests. For example, people who have an interest in enriching their social life will respond to incentives that offer them frequent interaction with other persons. To a greater degree than psychologists, economists stress the importance of the provision of incentives by organizations. Motives alone will not trigger volunteer behavior. Motives have to be appropriately harnessed by the volunteer organization by matching incentives to motivations. The psychological approach often lacks this structural dimension, treating volunteer work as if it took place in a social vacuum.

Political scientists tend to define motives as having an interest in "issues that animate political participation" because they focus largely on volunteer work intended to affect government (Burns et al. 2001:120). In the language of political science, volunteers are said to be "motivated by a concern for" a particular issue (Burns et al. 2001:125). This is similar to the idea, particularly evident in the world of grassroots activism, that grievances help mobilize volunteers. People living in neighborhoods affected by pollution are more likely to volunteer for a clean-up campaign than people living in clean neighborhoods. Political scientists agree with functional psychologists that interest in an issue (e.g., abortion) need not be the only motivating factor behind volunteerism. For example, Schlozman et al. (1995:277), in discussing the "benefits" of volunteering, describe how they asked respondents to "recollect their motivations for getting involved"—as if anticipated benefits and motivation are the same. They identified four kinds of "benefit": material benefits "such as jobs, career advancement, or help with a personal or family problem"; social gratifications such as enjoyment of working with others; civic gratifications "such as satisfying a sense of duty or a desire to contribute to the welfare of the community"; and "the desire to influence collective policy." The similarity here to the VFI is quite apparent.

Sociological Approaches to Motivation

The sociological treatment of motives is different from the psychological. Indeed, many sociologists express skepticism that motives are of much use in explaining patterns of social behavior. They reject the idea that motives are springs of action, refusing to believe there are any identifiable drives, needs, or impulses that can be linked to specific actions. They either dismiss altogether the idea that motives explain volunteering (Smith 1982:28) or radically re-interpret the meaning of the concept so that it plays an entirely different role in the theory of volunteering.

Speaking generally, there are a number of reasons to be skeptical of motivations as an explanation for social behavior. Most obviously, people's declarations of motives are notoriously unreliable. In the United States, a culture of benevolence encourages us to use moral rhetoric to mask instrumental motives. We claim we are volunteering because we feel compassion although we are volunteering to improve our job prospects. In Daniels's (1988) study of upper class women volunteers, few were ready to acknowledge social climbing as their motive, although they were more than willing to attribute this motive to others, a tendency also noted by Sills (1957:95). Conversely, because we live in an acquisitive society, we often use instrumental rhetoric to mask non-instrumental motives. In a self-regarding culture, people are reluctant to admit they are doing something without concern for their own welfare. They feel social pressure to avoid taking too much credit for their "selfless" actions. Notice how people are more likely to say, "I *just* wanted to help" than "I wanted to help" (Wuthnow 1991:76). Notice, also, that, in order not to appear too saintly, they discover personal benefits in their volunteer work. For example, while it is true that volunteers like to say how much they benefit from serving others, Wuthnow (1991:95) believes this is merely "reciprocity talk" in which volunteers articulate their need to "complete the transaction" by indicating how much they enjoy the work so that a balance is restored to the relationship. A volunteer at a well woman's clinic told Merrell (2000:33), "So that's a big reason why I stay, because I'm not just giving, I'm getting and I think perhaps that is the key, that as volunteers we are giving and I know I am giving and if I didn't have that, I didn't enjoy the positive feelings and you know, the joy from the work, then I wouldn't stay." Notice that sociologists are not saying that "motive talk" is irrelevant to the study of volunteering. It is simply that they assign motives a different role. The most important difference is that the psychological approach locates motives within the individual rather than in social structures and processes. Sociologists believe this focus on inner states is misdirected: "let us break with the common assumption that intentions—or, worse yet, reasons given by the participants after the fact—explain social processes" (Tilly 2001:41).

Sociologists do not deny the existence of motives (or "motive talk"), nor do they dismiss entirely the idea that motive talk plays some role in the volunteer process, and yet they are uncomfortable with the psychological theory of motivation. How is this seeming contradiction resolved? According to sociologists, motives are not "subjective 'springs' of action lying in the psychic structure or organism of the individual" (Gerth and Mills 1953:114). They do not lie about in the mental closet gathering dust until the time comes to "apply" them to a decision that needs to be made. On the other hand, actions have no meaning without some motivational interpretation being given to them. The true function of motive talk, therefore, "is to persuade others to accept our act, to urge them to respond to it as we expect them to, and to make them believe that our act springs from 'good intention'" (Gerth and Mills 1953:115). In other words, we use motive talk to make (good) sense of our actions. Stating the motive establishes the act for what it is (Blum and McHugh 1971). For example, this act is murder (i.e., deliberate killing) because we can attribute it to jealousy. This act is suicide because we can attribute it to despair. To cast an act as "suicide" we need to think of it as an act of desperation. The death is not "suicide" at all until we have invoked the right motive. Motives therefore help make the act what it is. The motive "contains" the act. It is not surprising, then, that volunteers have little difficulty telling researchers why they volunteer. They are ready to give an account of their actions.

This does not mean motives are without causal significance. Sometimes, anticipations of acceptable justification will control conduct ("If I did this, what would they say? How would I explain it?"). Whether or not we perform an act might well depend on whether we think we can give a reasonable or socially acceptable explanation for it. And by winning social acceptance for us, motive attribution can strengthen our will to act. Also, while we perform many acts without having a really clear idea of what we are doing, if we *can* attribute a motive to it it has more meaning to us and we are more likely to sustain it over a long period of time. This argument throws an entirely new light on what we see when we read the answers to survey questions asking respondents to explain why they are volunteering. We are not asking them what caused them to volunteer but how they account for their volunteer behavior, how they wish to be seen by others: "Descriptions of motives are thus stories that show how one thing leads to another" (Wuthnow 1995:79).

Sociologists agree with psychologists that the same act can have several different motives behind it, but from the sociological perspective this simply means the same act can have several different justifications. Sociologists believe the actor chooses whichever motive appears to be most persuasive *depending on the social situation.* By treating volunteer motives as the expression of pre-existing needs, psychologists deny that volunteering is a stream of action with a history, directed by actors defining goals and objects of action as they unfold over time. Rather than preceding action, as psychologists claim, motives are attributed in a socially contingent way, as action unfolds. Social *interaction* therefore determines when talk about specific motives is appropriate, which motives are relevant, and which are irrelevant. This points to a problem with asking people their motives for volunteering as if they preceded the volunteer act. The actual experience of volunteering often leads to such radical changes in attitudes toward the activity that the original goals are forgotten or the volunteer becomes unable to separate her initial reasons for volunteering from the reasons that make sense to her now. Vela-McConnell (1999:13) describes how he initially agreed to volunteer at a shelter for battered women and their children because he wanted to meet people and the people working at the shelter seemed like the kind of people he would like to get to know:

> However, my worldview began to change because of my experiences as a volunteer. Through my volunteer work, I was made more aware of domestic abuse—and not just the simple facts but the everyday, lived realities of those suffering from abuse . . . While I had originally become involved in order to meet people, I soon became committed to volunteering out of a sense of responsibility to the people I served.

Actors are constantly defining and re-defining their motives as they interact with others. This is illustrated by the case of the animal rights activists cited chapter 2 when we were discussing the difference between volunteerism and activism. Opponents, by accusing animal rights activists of sentimentality, sought to devalue their work by classifying it as care work and thereby blunting its political impact. This was a special problem for female activists, whose volunteer work was prone to be negated by this framing device. They did not want to be seen as motivated by compassion, for political reasons. In consequence, they develop a frame for their actions emphasizing rights and justice over compassion and care. It would be wrong to think of these labels being definitions of motivation for acting. Rather they are strategies chosen for political reasons (Groves 1995).

Recall that the VFI is based on the assumption that all individuals have certain definable needs and it is these needs that actions address. When people give their reasons for volunteering, they are referring to these needs. From the sociological point of view, motives do not refer in any direct way to the needs of individuals. Instead, they are components of an ideology, worldview, or framework of understanding. These are all words for those systems of beliefs and values that give meaning to our world. They sit at the back of our minds functioning to make our behavior and that of others around us more meaningful. The way in which a framework of understanding gives people reasons to care is illustrated in Wuthnow's (1995) analysis of teenage volunteers. He explains how young people must be given reasons to care about the welfare of others in order to find the work meaningful and sustain it. These reasons are embedded in "languages" or "frameworks" they learn from their parents, other role models, peers, and institutions such as schools and churches. Wuthnow (1995:66) gives four examples of frameworks of understanding that are frequently drawn on for motivations to account for volunteer work. Humanitarianism combines a feeling of compassion or sympathy with a value that attaches importance to helping those toward whom one feels compassion. One of the most important values of this framework is the equality of people and the importance of tolerance and connectedness. A happiness framework is more ego-focused on the intrinsic and extrinsic rewards of volunteering wherein helping others is important but it should provide satisfaction to the giver as well. A reciprocity framework emphasizes the importance of "giving something back," giving in anticipation of needing help oneself, or "passing on" the help received by helping someone else. The definition of being in a position fortunate enough to have something to give back is highly subjective. This framework also includes volunteering motivated by a sense of injustice or unequal treatment and wanting to make the world a better place. Finally, the self-realization framework emphasizes the role of volunteer work in enabling people to realize their full potential.

Each framework calls forth, defines, and legitimates its own set of motives. Each provides its own "vocabulary" for talking about motives. Notice that Wuthnow's frameworks are quite similar to the "functions" identified in the VFI. The difference is that, while the VFI assumes these motivations refer to a fixed number of individual needs, Wuthnow assumes that motives make sense only in the context of particular institutions, each with its own language. If we live in a community where a particular language is not spoken, we are unlikely to account for our volunteer work with motives drawn from that language. The sociological question thus becomes: why are *these* motives acceptable in *this* context?

Sociologists do not deny that intentions play a role in human behavior. Indeed, if we want to explain a specific action or pattern of action, we must refer to intentions and reasons for doing it. But, for the sociologist, the question, "What was their intention in volunteering?" is usually a prelude to other questions like, "Why does one group of people have one motivation and another group of people have another motivation?" In short, sociologists believe that motives are socially determined rather than fixed attributes of individuals. They believe that social surveys showing that the reasons people give for volunteering vary systematically across social groups indicate that a social location, such as social class position, determines motives rather than individual needs. For example, a 1997 survey of volunteering in the United Kingdom asked respondents to indicate which, if any, of a list of reasons explained why they were volunteering. They were permitted to mention more than one motivation. The proportion mentioning each reason was as follows:

I offered to help—48%
Someone asked me to help—47%
Interests or needs of family or friends—45%
Personal needs—42%
I wanted to improve things, help people—35%
To help meet community needs—26%
I wanted to meet people, make friends—25%
I had time to spare—21%
I'm good at it—15%
I thought it would give me a chance to learn new skills—15%
Connected to my job—11%

Broadly speaking, these motivations can be divided into those that primarily address the respondent's own needs and interests and those that speak to the needs and interests of others. Comparing the raw percentages (unadjusted for socio-economic and religious differences) there are social differences in the likelihood of a specific motivation being mentioned by the respondent. Men were more likely than women to mention their own needs and interests and women were more likely than men to mention the needs and interests of others. Older people were more likely to mention their own needs and interests, community need, wanting to meet people, having time to spare, and being good at it. They were less likely to mention a connection with one's job, and having the chance to learn new skills. Those in the lower income brackets were more likely to mention having time to spare, and wanting to meet new people. They were less likely to mention a connection with a job or a community need (Smith 1998:64). Another survey, this time in Canada, also found that motives vary systematically by social position. Career motivations were more likely to be cited by lower income, lower education, younger, female, and less religious respondents. Social obligation was more likely to be cited by lower income, low education, older, married, and religious respondents. Value motivations were more likely to be cited by women and religious respondents (Chappell and Prince 1997). Although we have only zero-order results from these two studies, *it is quite evident that motivation is not distributed randomly across human populations.* These structural variations in the likelihood of mentioning a motive are something of a challenge to psychological theories of volunteer motivation, according to which volunteerism speaks to universal individual needs.

In order to explore the problem of the social determination of motives further we analyzed data from the Independent Sector survey.[11] Our intention is to see if motive talk is socially structured. Are people in different social categories more or less likely to say that a particular motive was, or would be, important to them as volunteers?

Gender

A number of surveys suggest that men and women volunteer for different reasons.[12] Analyzing the Independent Sector data, we found that women generally rate all motivations as more important than men, with the exception of making new contacts for one's business. [11]

Race

The association between race and motivation for volunteering is an unexplored area.[13] Our analysis of the Independent Sector data showed that Hispanics rated all the volunteer motivations more highly than Whites and Non-Hispanic Blacks rated all the volunteer motivations more highly than Whites with the exception of compassion, where there was no racial or ethnic difference. The widest race/ethnic difference was found in the career motivation: Hispanics and African Americans are much more likely than Whites to attach importance to this motivation. [11] Minority groups are thus more strongly motivated to volunteer but actually volunteer at a lower rate, suggesting there are structural barriers to their participation. They are also more likely to have instrumental reasons for volunteering, suggesting they use it as a means of acquiring human capital necessary for getting a job.

Age

Previous studies have shown that motivations for volunteering change over the life course (Sundeen and Raskoff 1995). "As people move through the life course they attach different meanings to the volunteer role" (Omoto et al. 2000:182). Aging means changing social agendas. In their early adult years, people are primarily interested in making social connections and establishing interpersonal relationships. In middle age they are mainly interested in finding a sense of purpose and making a commitment to society. As they grow older, people become less future-oriented, focusing more on the present, which in turn leads to a shift in priorities. Goals related to knowledge-seeking and preparation for a future life decline in importance and goals related to emotional gratification and strengthening social ties become more important.[14]

In our analysis of the Independent Sector data, we compared the youngest age group (16–24) with all other age groups. We found no motive more important for older people. Indeed, in four cases—social, career, protective, and understanding—the importance of the motive declined with age. There were no age differences in enhancement and values motivation. [11] This provides partial confirmation of the earlier studies in that the importance of career motivations declined, but there is no indication that other motivations become more important.

Education

Education has the potential to change our outlook on the world and therefore the way we think about volunteers and volunteer work. The relation between education and motivation for volunteering has not been explored, but it is likely that more schooling means people will be more self-confident, more secure, more knowledgeable about social issues, more aware of social problems and ways of tackling them, and so on, all attributes that could influence why they volunteer. In the Independent Sector sample, the more education people had the more likely they were to say that volunteering would be a way to gain a new perspective—an enhancement motivation. [11] Highly educated people were less likely to say they were motivated to volunteer in order to feel needed, gain the respect of others, or deal with their own personal problems, indicating the greater self-confidence a good education bestows. This finding suggests that the motivation of more highly educated people tends toward more value-oriented and more structural reasons for volunteering rather than those addressing individual needs of either the client or the volunteer.[15]

When we looked specifically at the non-volunteers, we found that respondents with some college education (but not beyond) were more likely to say they would volunteer in order to deal with their own personal problems. This suggests that college dropouts who are not volunteering could be recruited on the grounds it would provide a partial substitute for their formal education. When asked why they had *not* volunteered, high school dropouts were less likely to give lack of time as a reason for not volunteering, more likely to give poor health, more likely to say they lack the personal resources (e.g., lack necessary skills, no transportation) and social resources (e.g., no one asked me, don't know how to become involved). Compared to advanced degree holders, they were more likely to say they are not interested in volunteering or that people should be paid for their work. [12]

Income

Poorer people are more likely than rich people to think about volunteering as a means of dealing with their personal problems, which are no doubt more profound. It is the inclination of poor people to focus on concrete, immediate needs and help provided on a person-to-person basis. We found that, the more people earn, the less important to them was feeling needed, compassion, and dealing with their own personal problems. [11] Putting these results together with those for education paints a picture of lower class people as less likely to be motivated to volunteer by the desire to bring about social change and more inclined to volunteer as a way of coping with problems they face in life.

Employment Status

Earlier, we pointed out that career motivations are likely to be rated as more important by people who are preparing for or looking for jobs. They see volunteer work as a stepping-stone to regular employment. We can test this hypothesis by looking at differences in motivation by employment status. Presumably, people who already have jobs would not rate this motivation highly. The Independent Sector data contain information on employment status (self-employed full-time, self-employed part-time, employed full-time, employed part-time, not in the labor force). Using respondents not in the labor force as our comparison group, we found little evidence that people not in the labor force were more likely to attach importance to career motivations. The Independent Sector survey does not, however, distinguish between people who are unemployed (i.e., looking for a job) and people who are not in the labor force (e.g., homemaker). Self-employed part-time workers did rate enhancement, values, career, and understanding motives more highly than those not in the labor force, suggesting that these might be people who have chosen to work part-time in order to be able to explore these benefits of volunteer work. We also found that full-time self-employed workers rated as more important volunteering in order to make new business contacts, which makes sense in light of their economic interests. [11]

Marital and Parental Status

Being single is sometimes the result of and sometimes the cause of personal problems such as difficulty getting along with others. Single people tend to have poorer mental health than married people. This would suggest that single people who volunteer might well do so for reasons very different from married people. Okun et al. (1998:619) found that single people were more likely than married people to say they volunteered for "protective" reasons; "volunteering helps me work through my own personal problems." It is also plausible that single people are more likely to volunteer as a means of meeting new people—a social motivation. However, we found only one difference in our analysis of the Independent Sector data. Compared to married people, those who were divorced or separated attached more importance to protective motivations, such as volunteering to help deal with their own personal problems. Interestingly, single people (i.e., those who had never married) rated this motivation no higher than married people, suggesting that the status of the divorced or separated person is more stressful.

As we shall see in chapter 10, parents are more likely to volunteer than adults without children. This tendency is usually attributed to the needs of the child, the volunteer role being an extension of the parental role. We found that parents attached more importance than the childless to feeling needed, to making new contacts to help them in their business or career, and to gaining a new perspective on things. [11] These differences suggest a number of possibilities. The parental role can be quite isolating, especially for women, and volunteer work can help connect them to social relationships outside the home, hence the allusion to feeling needed. This motivation also suggests that parents volunteer in connection with needs their children make them aware of, such as unsafe streets, inadequate schools, and poor recreational facilities. Children also draw parents out into the community, especially schools. Hence they become more aware of community problems and gain a new perspective on things. It is also likely that parents volunteer (e.g., for sports coaching) in order to be close to their children and learn more about them.

Religion

Religious beliefs are often treated as a component of the values motivation, which is one reason for thinking that religious people attach more importance to the values motivation. But the main reason why this motivation would be rated as important is that churches preach the virtue of compassion. Churches are less likely to emphasize the more instrumental motivations, such as those included in the career category. Bowen (1999:21) examined religious differences in motivation for volunteering. Dividing the population into "inactive" (never or rarely attend church) and "active" (weekly or at least once a month), he found no differences in motivation by level of religious activity, with the exception that the religiously active were slightly less likely to endorse the motivation of volunteering in order to improve job opportunities and more likely to say they volunteer in order to fulfill religious obligations. We partially replicated this finding: frequent churchgoing increased the importance of *all* the motivations in the Independent Sector battery with the exception of making new business contacts. [11] It would be wrong, then, to think of church attendance teaching people only values-based reasons for volunteering. For example, frequent churchgoers attach more importance to social motivation—they are more likely to agree that volunteering is an important activity to the people they respect. They are more likely to say that they gain a new perspective on things and help dealing with their own personal problems by volunteering.

Frequent churchgoers volunteer more than non-religious people, regardless of their religious faith or denomination. However, each denomination tends to interpret benevolence in its own way. Each has its own framework of understanding and therefore its own "vocabulary of motives." Members of evangelical churches frame their volunteer work in largely spiritual terms: "If I am to become more Christ-like, I must serve." Members of liberal Protestant denominations, on the other hand, think of volunteer work mainly in terms of contributing to society: "we have an obligation to help others as citizens" (Becker and Dhingra 2001:328). The first is more redolent of enhancement motivations: volunteering makes you a better person. The second is redolent of values motivation: volunteering makes the world a better place in which to live. Using the Independent Sector data we compared the responses of members of various denominational groups with those who said they had no religious affiliation, controlling for frequency of church attendance. [11] Interestingly, a minority religious group, the Jews, attached the most importance to feeling needed, followed by mainline and liberal Protestants. Catholics attached no more importance to this motivation than the unaffiliated. Although the teachings of compassion are prominent in all the faiths and denominations, only mainline Protestants attached more importance to this values motivation than the unaffiliated. Compared to the unaffiliated, only Protestants attributed more importance to volunteering to earn the respect of others and gaining a new perspective on things. There were no denominational differences in the importance of making business contacts or solving one's own problems. In short, even controlling for frequency of church attendance, religious affiliation does make *some* difference to "motive talk." Conspicuously, Catholics do not seem to invoke motives for volunteering any different from those who have no religious affiliation; and only in the case of volunteering out of a desire to feel needed do people of Jewish faith stand out from the unaffiliated. The vocabulary of motives for volunteering seems to be primarily the language of Protestantism, and principally its more mainstream and liberal components.

Domain

In the preceding discussion we focused on how motivation for volunteering varies across social groups. We treated volunteer work as if it were all the same. In chapter 2 we described the enormous variation in types or domains of volunteer work. We cannot separate our thinking about the motivation for volunteer work from our thinking about what that volunteer work entails. Serving as a docent in an art gallery is very different from acting as a "buddy" for AIDS patients. Even volunteering to help AIDS patients can mean doing quite different kinds of work and if the work is different, people might have different reasons for doing it. For example, one study found that AIDS volunteers who chose to be "buddies" were motivated by values, whereas those who chose to work in other capacities, such as staffing the telephone or doing office work, were motivated by protective needs: they were volunteering as a means of coping with their personal anxieties and fears about AIDS and death. They wanted to help, but not to get too close to the actual AIDS patients (Snyder and Omoto 1992:229). In a study of elderly people volunteering to help fellow arthritis sufferers deal with their pain, researchers found they rarely invoked values motives for their face-to-face work. They were more likely to say they volunteer because they want to be useful to others or give some purpose to their lives; that is, to give enhancement motives (Barlow and Hainsworth 2001:213).

We turned to the Independent Sector data to see if the association between motives and volunteering varied by domain. We estimated the mean levels of agreement with a reason for volunteering by volunteer area, adjusted for socio-economic, demographic, and religious differences. [13] We used the motive questions described above and used as domain a grouping of volunteer work into advocacy, education, human services, youth development, and religion. We compared the ratings given by people volunteering in connection with their church with the ratings given by people volunteering in the other four domains. As we might expect, volunteering because of compassion for others (values motivation) was more highly rated by religious volunteers than any other kind of volunteer, except those working in the area of human services where person-to-person care features prominently. Religious volunteers were less likely to rate as important volunteering in order to enhance one's career than volunteers doing advocacy and education-related work, a reflection of the fact that advocacy and education-related volunteer work is more likely to demand and encourage job-related skills. Religious volunteers were also less likely to say they were volunteering because others expect it (social motivation), at least compared with people volunteering in connection with education. This might well reflect the community pressure felt by people, particularly parents, to get involved in their schools. Interestingly, religious volunteers were less likely to rate gaining a new perspective on things (understanding motivation), at least compared to human services volunteers, suggesting that, outside the church, human service volunteering is partly driven by a humanistic desire to learn more about one's fellow human beings by caring for them. Finally, protective motivation was rated as more important by volunteers working in connection with a church, at least compared to those working in connection with education or youth development. This might indicate that churches use volunteer work as a way for members to enrich their spiritual life and as a way of dealing with their religious doubts and uncertainties.[16]

Conclusion

In this chapter, we have reviewed the research on the association between motives and volunteering and added some analyses of our own. Comparing Independent Sector respondents who volunteered in the last year with those who did not volunteer, the volunteers consistently rate the VFI motivations as more important, the one exception being career motivations. [10] That is, motives do help discriminate between volunteers and non-volunteers. We argued that discovering these differences is only the beginning of analysis of this problem. The deeper question is why people give particular reasons for doing volunteer work. We found a number of differences, depending on gender, race, socio-economic status, family status, religion, and the domain in which the volunteer work takes place. Although the debate about the theoretical status of motives is bound to continue, whatever they are measuring, they are significant and should not be ignored.

This is not to say, by any means, that motivations are sufficient to explain volunteer behavior. The volunteer act is over-determined by a multitude of factors, only one of which is motivation. If we rely too heavily on motives to explain volunteer behavior we overlook the fact that volunteering is broadly patterned, following socio-economic, gender, racial, and other contours in the human population (Thoits and Hewitt 2001:118). On the other hand, the research reported in this chapter cautions us against ignoring motives altogether. Whether we endorse the psychological or the sociological approach, motives play a role in mobilizing volunteer service. Micro and macro processes establish parameters for each other. Motives need a macro-link because the actualization of goals, even their recognition as goals, is limited by social structures. Social structures need a micro-link because structures that ignore or suppress motivations will not endure.

5

Values, Norms, and Attitudes

Volunteer work has been called "an agreeable obligation" (Stebbins 2004:4). This seeming oxymoron neatly captures the fact that volunteer work is *both* voluntary, in the sense of being something we do only so long as it is agreeable to us (unlike doing household chores) *and* a social obligation in that we are taught it is proper to be concerned about the welfare of others and that we should make time to help others in need. This is not true of many other ways we spend our leisure time, such as playing poker or watching television. In this chapter we discuss the influence of these ideas about what is good and proper on individual volunteer behavior.

It is an important sociological principle that human behavior is governed by normative patterns that define what are felt to be, in the given society, proper, legitimate, or expected modes of action or social relationship. These patterns are supported by common moral sentiments. Conformity with them is not a matter of expediency but of moral duty. Some actions are socially acceptable and approved of while others are reprehensible and disapproved or even directly prohibited. Stable social interaction is possible only if, within limits, people do the right thing at the right time in the right place. At the most specific level these patterns consist of role expectations, spelling out what people in specific positions are expected to do in relation to other role players.[1] At the most general level these patterns consist of values and norms. Sociologists assume that action is teleologically oriented to the attainment of goals (value-oriented) and to conformity with the regulatory rules (norms) by which those goals should be achieved.

In chapter 4, we explored the way in which values figure in the functional theory of motivation. By working to achieve desired goals, people remain true to a conception of themselves. In this chapter we will discuss values from a more sociological perspective. Values provide the broadest guides to social behavior, as when we declare freedom, justice, compassion, or democracy as values. Values belong to society, but individuals vary in the degree to which they support them or have "internalized" them to the point where they consider them beyond question. Survey research can capture the extent to which individuals subscribe to the values prevalent in a society and it is possible to see if this influences volunteer behavior. Value-oriented behavior is often confused with personality trait-based behavior, but the two are not the same: "Traits are enduring dispositions; values are enduring goals" (Hitlin and Piliavin 2004:361). Personality is more fixed than values in that we have more cognitive control over our values; we can "re-think" them.

Because they are so general, values cannot serve as guides to specific behavior and must therefore be supplemented by norms, which are socially determined and legitimated rules for achieving the broad goals articulated in value statements. Once again, norms belong to society: they are rules upon which societies more or less agree. But individuals will vary in the extent to which they know, pay heed to, and derive rewards from conforming to a society's norms. Thus, there are individual variations in attitudes toward norms (e.g., affirmative action hiring programs) and normative behavior (e.g., not cheating on one's income tax returns). These individual variations can be detected by survey researchers and, insofar as they might have a bearing on volunteer behavior, their influence can be measured.

In this chapter, we deal with values first because they are more abstract than norms, which are specific to situations and subject to interpretation in the light of social circumstances. The third topic with which we deal is attitudes. An attitude is an evaluation of a specific object (e.g., attitudes toward specific social groups, types of people, social institutions, or social practices). Attitudes are not only more specific than values or norms they are also more flexible. Values imply norms and attitudes. We endorse norms and we adopt attitudes toward objects because we have internalized certain values. For example, if we value generosity and compassion we are more likely to endorse the norm that people in need should be helped and because we endorse this norm we are less likely to adopt negative attitudes toward the homeless and more likely to have positive attitudes toward those who help them.

Values

Volunteer work can either be a means to the achievement of certain desired end states or a means for people to "act out" their values. Values are standards by which things are compared as more or less correct, more or less good, more or less honorable. At the most general level, values speak to rather abstract and general ideas, such as individual freedom of choice and action. At a more specific level, values pertain to issues, such as hunger, poverty, racism, homelessness, drug abuse, abortion, and the like. When people say they volunteer for this or that because "it is the right thing to do" they are invoking values. They do not expect us to ask *why* it is the right thing to do. Values do not exist in isolation but cluster in ideologies or worldviews, such as "liberal" and "conservative." We tend to become emotionally attached to the values we endorse strongly. The conservatives who volunteer to join picket lines outside abortion clinics care deeply about the right to life. Our values not only influence whether we volunteer, they also steer us in the direction of specific activities and organizations. For example, nearly half (48%) of the volunteers for Bread for the World (BFW), a membership-based lobby group promoting anti-hunger legislation, rate themselves as liberal or extremely liberal (Cohn et al. 1993:120).

In the opinion of many scholars, organizations will recruit volunteers only if they appeal to their values and beliefs (Hunt et al. 1994:191). Material incentives will never be enough because volunteers are guided primarily by their conscience, their sense of right and wrong (Cohn et al. 1993:128). Volunteers do, therefore, have a "stake" or interest in their volunteer work, but it is not material but ideal. Workers volunteer to help run their trade union not only because it will help improve their working conditions but also because they believe in unionism. Parents volunteer for the PTA not only because their children will benefit but also because they believe in quality public education. Men coach Little League not only because they have sons or daughters who play baseball but also because they believe organized sports build character. Mothers help out at a child care center not only because their children are enrolled but also because they value certain child-rearing practices. Home owners are more likely to join a neighborhood association not only to protect real estate values but also because they care about a certain quality of life in their community. Gay men volunteer for AIDS organizations not only because they want to help people like themselves but also because they believe the needs of minority groups should not be neglected. Values can also be an *obstacle* to volunteering. For example, conservative Protestants are unlikely to volunteer to help AIDS victims because of their commitment to traditional family values (Omoto and Snyder 1993). Kelley et al. (2005:370) found that the majority (60.7%) of volunteers working in a needle-exchange program to fight the spread of HIV/AIDS had no religious affiliation.

Values help explain why people think that volunteering is the best way to solve a problem. For example, certain values speak to the human need for dignity and self-respect. In light of these values, the morally correct way to deliver a service is to provide it for nothing because it is the only way the recipient's dignity can remain intact. Informed by values, volunteer work becomes intrinsically rewarding, aside from its efficiency in feeding, clothing, and sheltering people. For many people, the need to "do something" is as strong as the need to "get something done." This is why people sometimes choose rather inefficient ways of reaching their goals. Why would a high-priced lawyer contribute time to Habitat for Humanity? The simplest answer is that he values housing for low-income people, but this does not account for the formal inefficiency of his efforts. It is not rational for a lawyer to spend eight hours of his time helping build houses for low-income people when his legal services are valued at $200 an hour. It would be more rational if he billed extra hours of legal work and paid a skilled carpenter to do the house building for him. But when the lawyer picks up his hammer rather than his pen he is not interested in being efficient so much as he is in actualizing his values. In light of his values, his actions make perfect sense. If he regarded building the house as simply a productive activity, its value would not change if a substitute performed the work in his stead. But building the house is an expressive activity for him; its consummatory value would be diminished if a builder were hired to do the job. Furthermore, hiring a builder to do the job with the lawyer's money would reduce the activity to an economic exchange, which would injure the dignity of the low-income person for whom the house is being built: it becomes a "handout." It is highly significant that Habitat for Humanity requires its clients to help build the houses intended for them. The lawyer has learned that help that takes the form of a personal gift of time is more valuable to him *and* his client. Indeed, in becoming part of a social relationship, the help has become priceless. Volunteers for a Parent League group running concessions for school athletic events for the purposes of raising money for the school display the same kind of values-based logic:

> What is remarkable about this emphasis on fund-raising is that, for most volunteers, it would have been much easier and cheaper to pitch in money from their own pockets than to spend that enormous amount of time, money and effort on fund-raisers and the elaborate equipment they required. But just chipping in money would have missed their point . . . Fund-raising really seemed to be "doing something." (Eliasoph 2003:203)

Values give us the strength to volunteer even if few people around us seem willing to do their share. Values also help explain why some volunteers are more committed to their work than others. A comparison of active and inactive trade union volunteers found that the inactive volunteers were more likely to say they had been coerced into joining the union because of closed shop rules. They were also more likely to have joined the union for its individual benefits. The active volunteers expressed stronger support for values of unionism and collective action generally (Fosh 1981:73). This is strikingly similar to volunteering as a form of "witnessing" found in religious circles, where service means offering oneself to others as an example: "one bears a message and hopes that it will, in time, be understood and accepted" (Coles 1993:6).

In the opinion of many sociologists, values are notoriously poor predictors of actual behavior. Values are, by definition, abstract statements that do not specify actual behaviors. For example, many different forms of social behavior can be justified by invoking the value of "freedom." Values are better predictors of human behavior when they refer to specific acts as desirable or undesirable. If the "right to life" is tied specifically to opposition to abortion and steps that can be taken to oppose abortion it becomes a more reliable predictor of behavior. It is not surprising, then, that surveys show a better fit between values and behavior if the values refer specifically to the behavior in question. Thus we find that volunteers for church-related activities rate religious values more highly than those who do not volunteer, but those religious values do not predict secular volunteering (Cnaan et al. 1993:37; Hodgkinson et al. 1990).

In the section that follows, we will first discuss the connection between four sets of values and volunteering. We will then see if there is a connection between valuing volunteering itself and actually doing volunteer work.

Humanitarianism and Volunteering

Humanitarianism is a set of values rather than one particular value. It "combines a feeling of compassion or sympathy with a value that attaches importance to helping those toward whom one feels compassion" (Wuthnow 1995:66). As a moral obligation, humanitarianism requires that we treat all people equally, redress inequities, and help those who are suffering or in need of help. People often refer to humanitarian values to explain why they volunteer: "They realize 'needs'; feel 'responsibility'; have 'dedicated themselves'; express 'concern'; care 'what happens to people in the community'; are guided by 'a warm and sincere desire to right human wrongs'; and give 'their time and effort, and skills . . . to help make their communities better places to live in'" (Sills 1957:82). One group of researchers looked at volunteering among business executives. They found that managers who were primarily achievement-oriented were more likely to place company welfare—and their own careers—over community welfare. In contrast, executives who expressed humanitarian values endorsed community involvement "whether or not it would enhance one's career" (Christenson et al. 1988:823). Analyzing data from the American Values Survey (1989), Wuthnow (2004:125) looked at the relation between the importance people attached to helping people in need and having engaged in charity or social service activity. The odds of having volunteered in the past year were more than four times greater among those who said helping people in need is absolutely essential than among those who said it is less important. Those who believe helping people is absolutely essential also contributed more hours.

Materialism and Volunteering

In capitalist societies volunteers are often admired as people, but their work is devalued. We tend to assume that if a job is really worth doing, it will be paid for. This bespeaks a potential conflict between materialism and volunteerism. Volunteerism is motivated by a concern for others; materialism is motivated by a concern for oneself. In a highly materialistic society devoted to the pursuit of economic gain, working for nothing is devalued, even stigmatized. Volunteers speak of being looked down upon simply because they volunteer: "people call us mugs for working for no money" (Campbell and Wood 1999:44). Because volunteers give something valuable away (their time) without expectation of return they violate two of the most basic axioms of capitalist cultures: that time being scarce, it should not be wasted; and that, since our responsibility is, first and foremost, to look out for ourselves, time should not be wasted on others. As volunteers, people operate in a moral economy, where the rules of exchange are dictated by values, social relationships, and group identities, and the currency is gifts. But as paid employees, or as consumers, they operate in a market economy where the rules of exchange are dictated by the calculations of profit, and the currency is money. To a large degree these economies are at odds with one another. In the moral economy, actions are driven by values, the desire for justice, feelings of compassion, and social obligation. In the cash economy, actions are driven by self-interest, where interest is usually defined in terms of material comfort. In one respect, a market economy expects, even requires, us to be selfish, to "look out for ourselves." Individuals are assumed to want to maximize their possession of "goods the having of which is in one's interests" (Teske 1997:131). Well-being would therefore be measured primarily by economic wealth, but other measures would include the power and prestige wealth can buy. It does not include, however, self-interest in the psychological sense, where actions are guided by a desire for self-fulfillment, or self-esteem. There is less likelihood that this second kind of "self-interest" would clash with volunteerism.

Materialism is an attachment or devotion to objects at the expense of attachment or devotion to persons. It connotes selfishness, "an individualistic emphasis on self-interest that devalues the community and the need to care about others" (Wuthnow 1994a:179). For example, people who buy their children gifts rather than spending "quality time" with them are materialists. People who place earning money above all other life activities, or who choose jobs on the basis of their material rewards, are materialists. It seems unlikely that a person who subscribes to materialist values would have the time or inclination to spend much time helping others. Survey evidence seems to confirm this: materialists are less likely to volunteer (Uslaner 2002b:241).[2] These findings are not too surprising. Many volunteers pride themselves on being abstemious, free of the temptations of the flesh. Volunteer work gives them a "free space" uncontaminated by "materialism, greed, affluence, advertising or simply the world of business" (Wuthnow 1991:271). For example, Habitat for Humanity volunteers typically blame the chronic shortage of volunteers on a widespread addiction to materialism: too many people have bought into consumer culture and equate being more with having more (Baggett 2001:105). Japanese volunteers, especially those who had made a "career" out of it, "expressed a sense of distance from mainstream society, criticizing its emphasis on materialism and individual success, and emphasizing alternative values such as community, caring for others and learning for its own sake" (Nakano 2000:99).[3]

Individualism and Volunteering

Like materialism, individualism would appear to present a direct challenge to the values of volunteerism. We normally expect self-interest to run counter to group interest. It is difficult to reconcile an intense commitment to personal autonomy with a strong concern for the welfare of others. In chapter 3, we discovered that volunteers tend to be more empathic than non-volunteers. The survey evidence seems to support the notion that individualists are less likely to volunteer. In a U.S. survey, volunteers attributed less importance than non-volunteers to "being able to do what you want to do" (Wuthnow 1994a:346). Compared to non-volunteers, Canadian volunteers are more "other-directed": their world view "is notably (a) rather more universalistic or cosmopolitan than particularistic, (b) inclusive, (c) trusting, and (d) more prosocial than individualistic" (Reed and Selbee 2003:97). The more Canadians care about other people and the greater the responsibility they feel for helping the needy, the more hours they volunteer.

Some commentators view the rise of individualism with alarm because it threatens to stifle the volunteer spirit. But the society most committed to the values of individualism, the United States, is also the society with the highest volunteer rate. How can this be explained? Wuthnow's (1991:22) interviews with volunteers provide an answer to this question by showing that intense commitment to self-realization is not incompatible with altruism. Volunteering has become one way Americans obtain personal fulfillment, by providing them with a clear sense of identity. Volunteering is a way of showing inner strength, self-confidence, and ability to interact with others comfortably. In highly individualistic societies volunteer work has therefore become a means of expressing one's individuality. Eliasoph (2003:202) was surprised at how little community there was in volunteer activities and how much room there was for the pursuit of individual interests.

As a volunteer myself, I had difficulty finding a niche that was not simply working alone on a pre-designed project. I often asked what I could do to help: I could drive around town alone delivering hot meals to the elderly, meet an "at risk" child once a week to give support, supervise the playground before school, provide a "safe house" for kids who were in trouble, go to a street fair to sell raffle tickets for a volunteer group; maybe another volunteer would show up, but if not, I could do it by myself . . . Volunteers did not think of themselves as doing good as a group, but as individuals.

In short, the rise of individualism does not seem to be a major threat to volunteerism because people are learning to modify volunteer work to suit individualistic needs.

There is another reason why individualism does not necessarily pose a threat to volunteerism. In the United States, individualism has meant "not the individual's independence from other individuals, but his and their freedom from governmental restraint" (Schlesinger 1944:1). This is why one of the most vocal proponents of the value of individualism—Ronald Reagan—could also be one of the most ardent advocates of volunteerism. Indeed, according to this logic, individualists should be most supportive of volunteerism because it is a way to limit the reach of government into their private lives.

Religious Values and Volunteering

Given the moral component in volunteering, it is not surprising that the connection between religious values and volunteering has attracted a lot of attention. By teaching altruistic values and encouraging prosocial behavior, religions elevate the importance of caring for others to a position of importance (Fischer and Schaffer 1993:60; Wuthnow 1994a:47). A Canadian told researchers that she volunteered "because Christ did so much for me and because that's what he's told us to do and to use our gifts . . . with other people and so . . . working in the community and helping other people has come really out of my Christian background and my faith" (Pancer and Pratt 1999:48). In some countries, such as the United States, the association between religion and volunteering is so strong that helping the needy is seen as a religious virtue, as if secularists do not share this value (Ammerman 1997:366). Helping others has thus become one of the most important ways Americans demonstrate they are religious: their faith is expressed in ameliorating suffering. Living a largely secular life in other domains, American churchgoers make their volunteer work an avocation.

In this section we will review the research on the link between religion and volunteering and add some analyses of our own. We do not have direct measures of religious values. Instead, we use religious affiliation as a proxy measure of religious values on the assumption that people join specific denominations because of the values they espouse. In our own analyses we control for frequency of church attendance, a topic we address specifically in chapter 14. This section thus asks whether affiliation alone is enough to create differences in volunteering, regardless of frequency of church attendance. We begin by looking at simple affiliation, regardless of faith or denomination, compared to not belonging to a church at all. We then look at differences between religious faiths, mainly in the United States, where this means the distinction between Protestant, Catholic, Jew, and other religions. We then look at denominational differences within Protestantism.

Religious Affiliation

Although we cannot be sure what people mean when they reply to a survey question about their religious affiliation, if religion makes any difference at all to volunteering we would assume that those who claim no affiliation at all would be less likely to volunteer. A 2000 Canadian survey found that people who reported a religious affiliation were more likely to volunteer than those with no affiliation (Lam 2002:415). De Hart (2001:94) analyzed 1996 survey data from the Netherlands. A third of the sample had volunteered in the past year. Whereas about half of the Calvinists, half of the members of the Dutch Reformed Church, and 41 percent of the Roman Catholics had volunteered, only a quarter of the unaffiliated had volunteered.[4] Comparing Jews in the United States with a denominational affiliation with unaffiliated ethnic Jews, Lazerwitz and Harrison (1979:662) found the affiliated were more likely to be "active in general voluntary associations," especially if they belonged to a more liberal denomination. Heinz and Schnorr (2001:603) found that a large proportion of American lawyers volunteer on a regular basis but the rate was even higher among those with a religious affiliation.

Interfaith Differences

In countries like the United States, most people claim an affiliation with a church and the really interesting question is whether the church they choose to affiliate with makes any difference to their chances of volunteering. For many years, the United States was a predominantly Protestant country, but the waves of immigration that brought Irish, Italian, and Hispanic immigrants have increased the Catholic presence in the population. This has importance consequences for volunteerism if Catholics volunteer at a lower rate than Protestants. Most of the studies in this area show that Protestants *are* more likely to volunteer than Catholics or Jews (Chambre 1987:73; Greeley 1997; Hoge et al. 1998; Ladd 1999:72; Lam 2002:413; Wilson and Janoski 1995).[5]

Wuthnow (2004:54) found that, compared to mainline Protestants, members of Catholic congregations were less likely to say that their church sponsored day care programs and homeless shelters, but they were more likely to sponsor tutoring programs. There was no interfaith difference in the likelihood of sponsoring a food pantry or kitchen. In a survey of U.S. congregations, Chaves et al. (2002:119) found that Catholic congregations were substantially more likely to organize or encourage volunteer work than mainline

Protestant congregations—if volunteer work consisted of holding a group meeting or class to organize or encourage people to do volunteer work. But once the definition of volunteering was broadened to cover sponsoring or participating in food programs and housing programs mainline Protestants come out ahead. Mainline Protestant congregations were also more likely to have "hosted a representative of a social service organization as a visiting speaker" and to have "sponsored or participated in a mentoring program." One reason for the Protestant-Catholic difference might be the way churches are organized in the two faiths. The congregational form of religious organization favored by most Protestant denominations nurtures horizontal relations of interaction between congregants, which, in turn, increases members' chances of being asked to volunteer. Protestant congregations are also more democratic and have more committees on which laypeople are expected to serve. They also tend to be smaller than Catholic parishes (Coleman 2003:36).[6]

Denominational Differences

In the United States, mainline Protestant denominations (e.g., Lutheran, Methodist) have been deeply involved in civic affairs from the nation's founding. Indeed, for many years they virtually constituted the civil society. In the nineteenth century, guided by a theology emphasizing progressive social betterment through public campaigns and legislation, they helped found many benevolent associations, such as the YMCA. In contrast, evangelical Protestant churches, which emerged at the beginning of the twentieth century, emphasized individual piety as the path to social betterment. Most of their "volunteer" work was targeted at improving the spiritual lives of their members and whomever they could convert to their cause.

This denominational divide persists to this day. In the National Congregations Study (1998), Chaves (2004:53) found that congregations associated with evangelical denominations were less likely to sponsor social service programs than congregations affiliated with more liberal denominations or Catholic parishes.[7] Using the members' perception of their congregation's theological orientation, Wuthnow (2004:56) found the same pattern. Congregations defined as theologically conservative were less likely than more moderate or liberal congregations to sponsor counseling programs, meetings for alcoholics, and ministry to AIDS victims. No denominational differences were found in ministry to prisoners, programs for job seekers, distributing food to the poor, shelter for the homeless, tutoring programs, or day care programs. However, the more liberal the congregation, the more service programs it sponsored. These differences were net of congregation size or rural/urban location.[8]

In the United States, denominational differences are inflected with racial differences. Some of the largest of the mainline Protestant denominations (e.g., Baptist, Methodist) have parallel and independent White and African American organizations. Depending on their race, Protestants regard volunteering differently. The Black church has adopted a "social gospel" orientation, encouraging members to be concerned about conditions in this life. The kind of volunteering encouraged by the teachings of the Black Protestant church focuses on community building and political participation. In the White church "social consciousness is preached more from the tradition of the Christian gospel of service—acting for others—rather than a tradition of 'God helps those who help themselves'" (Secret et al. 1990:92). Using a survey in which respondents were asked if their congregations sponsored a variety of service activities (food pantry or kitchen, day care program, homeless shelter, tutoring program), Wuthnow (2004:54) found that Black Protestants were less likely than mainline Protestants (their largely White counterparts) to sponsor counseling programs, meetings for alcoholics, ministry to AIDS victims, ministry to prisoners, programs for job seekers, distributing food to the poor, shelter for the homeless, or day care programs. Only tutoring programs were unaffected by race. These differences were net of congregation size or rural/urban location. Chaves (2004:54) also found that predominantly African American congregations offered fewer social services than predominantly white congregations, although they did sponsor a wider *range* of programs and were more likely to offer opportunities to volunteer in the areas of job training, substance abuse prevention, and employment assistance. This picture might surprise those who assume that, because the church plays a more pivotal role as a social institution in the Black community, it would therefore mobilize more volunteer work. In comparison to their often-wealthier White counterparts, Black churches rank comparatively low when it comes to offering programs for which church members can volunteer.

Institutional differences between denominations such as these lead us to anticipate finding that denominational affiliation makes a difference to the likelihood of volunteering. A study of Canadians grouped "inactive" affiliates (i.e., those who never attend their church) with those professing no religion at all and then compared this group with Canadians belonging to various religious denominations. Mainline Protestants were almost twice as likely to volunteer as Roman Catholics, although the Catholics who did volunteer donated about the same amount of time as mainline Protestants. Conservative Protestants volunteered at the same rate (58%) as mainline Protestants but contributed many more hours—200 hours a year per volunteer compared to 160 among mainline Protestants (Bowen 1999:16). We analyzed the Independent Sector data to see if similar differences exist in the U.S. population. These are shown in Figure 1.

Compared to those with no affiliation at all, liberal Protestants were the most likely to volunteer, followed by mainline Protestants. Catholics and Jews were no more likely to volunteer than unaffiliated Americans. Evangelical Protestants were *less* likely to volunteer than the non-affiliated. Controlling for socio-demographic differences and frequency of church attendance, liberal Protestants were still more likely to volunteer than the unaffiliated and evan-

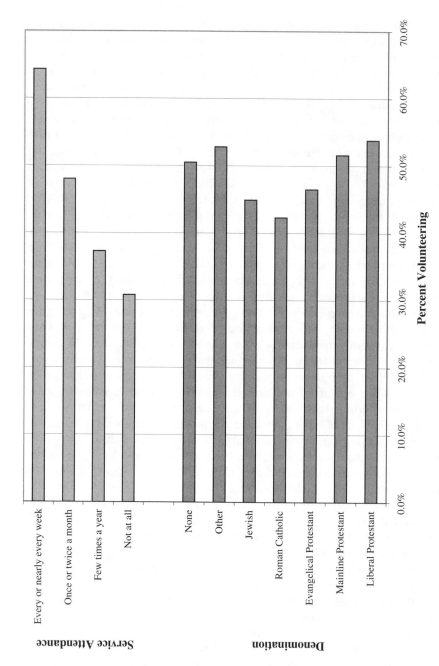

Figure 1. Adjusted percentages volunteering by religious denomination and service attendance.

gelical Protestants remained less likely. There was still no difference between Jews and the non-affiliated. However, Catholics were now much *less* likely to volunteer than the non-affiliated and mainline Protestants were no different than the non-affiliated. *Thus, denominational affiliation, by itself, does make some difference to the likelihood of volunteering, chiefly in that evangelical Protestants and Catholics are less likely to volunteer and liberal Protestants are more likely.* Among those who volunteered, however, evangelical Protestants contributed more hours than the non-affiliated. There were no other denominational differences in the intensity of volunteering. [15]

In the foregoing analysis, we did not delve into the issue of what people are volunteering for. The relatively low rate of volunteering among evangelicals has sparked some debate because it conflicts with values that support volunteerism in the Protestant tradition, and it is surprising in view of the fact that evangelicals are well known for contributing a lot of their time to their church. The conventional argument runs as follows. Evangelicals are inclined to adopt an "us versus them" outlook on the world, are less trusting of others, and tend to retreat into their own religious community. Because of their belief that "religious-transformative assistance . . . will encourage personal responsibility, pride and social rehabilitation" they do contribute a lot of their time to providing help to others but this help is directed mainly at fellow church members. In addition, their congregations are high maintenance organizations that consume a lot of their adherents' free time, channeling their energies inward (Cnaan et al. 1999:9). For these reasons, they cut back on their outreach activities (Becker and Dhingra 2001:329). In contrast, members of liberal Protestant groups are more heterogeneous and more trusting of strangers, and a greater proportion of their service work reaches out into the community "beyond their own faith community to work with others and to help people in need who are different from themselves" (Uslaner 2002b:240). As a result, evangelicals tend to be less civically engaged in the wider community than other Protestants or even Catholics. Regardless of educational level, the odds of an evangelical belonging to at least one secular voluntary association is about 20 percent lower than a Catholic and about 50 percent less than a mainline Protestant (Wuthnow 1999:338). Evangelicals are busy people, but most of their work focuses on the many needs of their church. When church members in five different American denominations were asked, "How many hours, if any, during the last month have you given volunteer time at your church to teach, lead, serve on a committee, or help with some program, event or task?" the most hours were reported by the more conservative denominations (Baptists and Assemblies of God) and the fewest by Catholics (Hoge et al. 1998:475). But the evangelical hours of service were devoted to helping people like themselves. Wuthnow (1999:342) interviewed "Gary Rush," who is an evangelical:

His Sundays and evenings are taken up with church activities to the point that he has little time to be involved in anything outside the church. More important, he regards the church as a place unlike any other. Almost all of his close friends belong to the church, and he values the fellowship with them as a kind of utopian experience . . . He does not aggressively proselytize his neighbors, but he believes the community can only be served one person at a time. Thus he prefers to work with the few individuals who come to the church seeking help, rather than cooperating with other organizations, because he can tailor his responses to the particular needs of these individuals.

The more often Gary goes to church the more he focuses all his volunteer work on maintaining the church (e.g., helping with Sunday school programs) and helping its members (e.g., visiting shut-ins). His evangelical beliefs reinforce the view that members of the church are special and the world beyond the church is something to be treated with caution. And the more committed he becomes the more likely is he to focus all his volunteer work on the church itself. This is in sharp contrast to members of mainstream Protestant denominations that intersect in many ways with secular non-profit organizations in the community. They are likely to get involved in the many inter-denominational coalitions and alliances formed to help deal with community problems. Catholic congregations occupy a mid-point between these two contrasts.

It should come as no surprise, therefore, to learn that evangelicals rank at the top of denominational groups most likely to have volunteered *for their church,* but when it comes to volunteering outside the church only African American Protestants do less. Catholics divide their efforts evenly, and Jews are more likely to volunteer for secular than for Jewish activities (Wuthnow 2002:386). As with Gary Rush, the more evangelicals get involved in their church, the less time they have for other kinds of volunteering. Campbell (2004) demonstrates this in an analysis of data from the Citizen Participation Study (1995). He constructs an index of "political engagement" consisting of contacting public officials, belonging to a community board, and working on an electoral campaign. This index is therefore both broader than volunteering because it includes non-volunteer items and narrower than volunteering in general because it measures only time given to local political activities. Nevertheless, the results of the study are of interest because the author also measured time spent on church activities each week (in addition to attendance at worship services). The evangelicals spent by far the most time on church activities—2.3 hours a week on average, compared to 1 hour for Protestants and 0.86 hours for Catholics. In the sample as a whole, the time spent on church activities was positively related to political engagement, but it was negative for evangelicals. The more time they spent on church matters, the more disengaged they were. Wilson and Janoski (1995:149) also found that the more time evangelicals spent in church, the less secular volunteer work they did.[9]

In light of the fact that Americans are sometimes accused of wearing their religious affiliations lightly, these findings clearly indicate that denominations matter as far as volunteering is concerned. Protestants no doubt agree with one another on the virtue of helping the needy, but they define need, who should be helped, and how they should be helped in very different ways. Liberal and evangelical Protestants agree that needy people should be helped but evangelicals are more likely to say that they care because their religion teaches them to care, while liberals look on volunteering as a path to self-improvement and social betterment. For conservatives, volunteering is the kind of sacrifice their religious beliefs expect them to make, a time of testing and trial that makes sense in light of their rejection of materialism (Wuthnow 1991:133). Liberal Protestants, on the other hand, regard their volunteer work as a civic duty and an opportunity for self-betterment (Becker and Dhingra 2001:330).

These liberal-conservative differences within the Protestant faith are interesting in light of the growing popularity of evangelical churches. They seem to run counter to the evidence that, after many years of avoiding civic engagement, evangelicals have become more active in the public square. The answer to this conundrum can be found by looking more closely at what counts as volunteer work "inside" as opposed to "outside" the church. Evangelicals are accused of concentrating all their volunteer energies on strictly religious needs and ignoring the needs of the wider community, whereas liberal and mainline Protestants are more willing to try to tackle these needs. But evangelicals would not necessarily accept this distinction between what is inside the church and what is outside the church. They would consider many of their volunteer activities as being community-targeted. For example, Wuthnow (1999:355) cites the case of an evangelical who volunteered to serve on a committee to supervise a "Sunshine Fund" intended to help the pastor provide food and clothing to people in need, whether or not they were members of the church. Conversely, much of the volunteer work mainstream Protestants do is targeted mainly at raising funds for their congregation or organizing activities mainly intended for its members. The difference is that evangelicals are much more likely than liberal or mainstream Protestants to see their church as the pathway to volunteer work, or the gateway through which clients come to receive help. A survey of opinions about faith-based social services found that, given the choice between religious, secular non-profit, and government approaches to tackling various social problems evangelical Protestants most often chose the religious strategy. They believe faith-based efforts are the best means of feeding the homeless, counseling prisoners, mentoring youth, controlling teen pregnancy, managing drug addiction, and providing child care, but mainline Protestants preferred secular non-profit approaches to mentoring, teen pregnancy, addiction, and child care (Pew Research Center 2001:7). Evangelicals are therefore more inclined to blur the line between service work and evangelism. Indeed, their volunteer work is frequently a thinly disguised missionary enterprise. For example, the International Union of Gospel Missions, an evangelical group serving the homeless, stresses personal contacts between church members and homeless people "which are predicated upon Christian teachings and transformational experiences. Providers and volunteers pray and read the Bible with clients, while providing quality care that ranges from basic needs of food, clothing, and shelter to permanent housing and drug and alcohol rehabilitation" (Cnaan et al. 1999:161). This is in line with evangelicals' more conservative outlook on social issues. It would therefore be wrong to paint evangelicals as so insular and self-centered that they contribute little to the volunteer labor supply. Not only is much of their "religious" volunteering directed at social service programs, they still contribute more hours to secular organizations than either active Catholics or the religiously inactive (Bowen 1999:18). Catholics, on the other hand, tend to volunteer at a relatively low rate and most of the volunteer time they do contribute goes to secular agencies (Bowen 1999:43).

In summary, there are denominational differences in the proclivity to volunteer in the United States. They are not large, but they are consistent, and they are not attributable to the socio-economic differences that exist between the denominations or to different churchgoing habits. To some extent, this is a matter of where people choose to direct their volunteer energies and how they interpret the volunteer work they do. For evangelicals, the line between sacred and secular, the line between mission and charity, is blurred. Compared to mainline Protestants they volunteer less for clearly secular activities, such as those focused on environmental or peace issues. They are less likely to be active in some areas, such as campaigns for civil rights for minorities, but more likely to be active in others, such as right to life campaigns. While they might lag behind other Protestants, they are ahead of Catholics, who consistently record the lowest rate of volunteering once socio-demographic differences are controlled. We do not yet have a clear understanding why this Protestant-Catholic difference exists. It might have something to do with the more voluntaristic organization of Protestant congregations that themselves provide so many more volunteer opportunities. This is, of course, a structural characteristic, a difference in how religion is practiced, and we will return to this issue in a later chapter. But as far as values are concerned, it might have something to do with a more communal perspective among Catholics, less individualistic while being just as humanitarian, but favoring collective, structural, and perhaps government solutions to social problems.

Valuing Volunteer Work

As noted above, the more specifically a value addresses a particular form of behavior, the stronger the association between the two. Expressing support for the value of benevolence does not predict volunteer behavior as well as expressing support for the value of doing volunteer work. Thus, volunteers value more highly than non-volunteers working to improve their communities, helping the less fortunate, providing personal charity, and doing something to help their country and society (Flanagan et al. 1999:149; Sundeen 1992). A survey (1996) of Canadians and Americans found that respondents were more likely to volunteer for both secular and religious causes if they agreed it was important for people to get involved in their community (Uslaner 2002b:247). In 1991, American teenagers were asked about their personal goals in life and also about their volunteer activity in the previous twelve months. The likelihood of volunteering overall was higher among those who attached importance to giving time through volunteer work to charitable and religious organizations. The connection between values and volunteering was even more apparent when the authors of the study examined different types of volunteer work separately. Religious goals (i.e., "making a strong commitment to your religion or your spiritual life") were positively associated with volunteering in connection only with religious organizations; they were negatively associated with environmental volunteering. Civic values (e.g., "making the world a better place") were positively associated with volunteering in connection with health, education, environment, and the arts, but no other form of volunteering. Material values (e.g., "making a lot of money"), on the other hand, were negatively associated with all types of volunteering (Sundeen and Raskoff 1995:346). The value most strongly and consistently linked to volunteer behavior was "Giving time through volunteer work to charitable and religious organizations." This is hardly surprising. Abstract values can be actualized in many different ways. For example, the belief that one should be generous to others might make us feel obligated to volunteer, but could equally well make us feel obligated to donate money instead. Specific values leave less room for interpretation.

We cannot tell from these studies whether support for these values is confounded with other attributes, such as religiosity or social class. Nor can we tell whether the values are a cause or simply a result of volunteering. To solve this problem we turned to the Americans' Changing Lives survey, in which respondents were asked if they agreed that "Life is not worth living if one cannot contribute to the well-being of other people." Nearly two-thirds (62%) of the sample strongly agreed with this statement and a further 26 percent agreed "somewhat." To help determine causal effects we used a logistic regression model to estimate the influence of this value in 1986 on volunteering in 1989, net of the level of volunteering in 1986. [16] The results were positive and significant. Once again, despite the skepticism expressed by some sociologists that values are meaningless when it comes to predicting behavior, we find that values do matter.

Norms

Norms are rules of conduct specifying what should and should not be done in specific situations. "Norms are situation based: values are transitional" (Hitlin and Piliavin 2004:361). Norms are implied by values. For example, a value that places family ties above all others implies a norm against adultery. Norms are external to us, in two senses. In one sense, "normative" means what is typical or customary. We feel obliged to do something if all others around us are doing it, especially if they are important to us. This explains the commonly held notion that we should donate as much money to charity as people with whom we compare ourselves. In the second sense, normative means social expectations. We are more likely to do something if we believe people important to us expect us to do it, whether or not they are doing it themselves. For example, upper class women are expected to perform services for those less fortunate than themselves because it is one way in which people in their status group demonstrate their superiority. Another example of social expectations is found in the business world: managers who report their company expected them to get involved are more likely to do so (Christenson et al. 1988:818).[10] Normative pressures are evident in the following quotation from a hospital volunteer:

> The hospital was my first [volunteer experience] . . . it was my teacher. It was grade six, I think it was, and . . . we'd talk and stuff and there was a group of my friends and she [the teacher] said you know, this would be great for you guys to do this, so then . . . I went and applied and got in and started volunteering there. (Pancer and Pratt 1999:48)

The "warm glow" volunteers experience as a reward for their sacrifice comes not from the client (often there is no client) but from the approval of others for their generous acts. As one volunteer put it,

> Obviously people like to be liked and thought of as kind. People would say, "Young Mrs. B, she's a good soul." It's nice when people say things like that about you. (Campbell and Wood 1999:122)

Although social conformity relies to some degree on overt social pressure and social sanctions, norms are often internalized. We do something because we know it is the right thing to do, not because we will "look bad" if we deviate.

In a culture of benevolence where values of compassion, charity, stewardship, and justice are emphasized, rules are necessary to show people how to behave in accordance with these values. In this section we will discuss the influence of three norms on volunteering: the norm of generalized reciprocity, the norm of justice, and the norm of social responsibility.

Norm of Generalized Reciprocity

A norm of generalized reciprocity states that a person should provide a service to others, or act for the benefit of others, in the generalized expectation that this kindness will be returned at some undefined time by some unspecified person, in case of a future need. It is different from a norm of particularized reciprocity where people help one another on the understanding that they might need the same kind of help from that person tomorrow. A norm that enjoins actors to reciprocate favors in a generalized way encourages formal volunteering because the "clients" are rarely in a position to return the favor, nor does the volunteer necessarily need the client's help. For example, a woman who prepares meals for homeless people does not expect those people to cook meals for her. A norm of generalized reciprocity explains why people are not deterred by the prospect of others "free riding" on their volunteer work: they believe they should give their share, regardless of how many others are contributing. Simpson (1996:21) describes how volunteer firefighters are expected to respond to calls for assistance without questioning whether those in need of assistance deserve it or would ever be in a position to return the favor: "All who live in the territory, formalized as the fire district, are considered part of a moral community, and entitled to a claim on whatever aid the community is organized to provide."

When people say they volunteer in order to "give something back" to their community they are invoking the norm of reciprocity: "Helping others is a way of paying debts for the good things I have received" (Wuthnow 1995:75). Giving something back applies not to an individual but to the community of which that individual is a member. The norm is there for the community. This is what happens when school and college alumni volunteer for their alma mater, when people volunteer because they "want to do their share," and when people volunteer to keep the minutes of the meeting of a tennis club although they no longer play, or agree to help out with the scout group long after their children have left it. Beyond Welfare, founded in 1997, is a non-profit organization whose mission is to help people on welfare or in poverty to work toward economic self-sufficiency. The organization sets up "partnerships" between middle class volunteers and "clients" trying to make it off welfare. Many volunteers for this organization are motivated by their desire to pay for the privileges they enjoyed growing up in middle or upper middle class backgrounds. "I have been blessed with a lot . . . I feel a need to help people that aren't as fortunate as myself" (Bloom and Kilgore 2003:437). Similarly, middle class Black women who volunteer to mentor young and poor Black mothers as part of the "Birthing Project" want to give something back to the community now that they are upwardly mobile (McDonald 1997:783).

In some cases, the volunteer is returning a favor he or she has received in the past, not to the donor of the original favor, but to generalized others who might be in need of similar services. Many who volunteer to help people affected by HIV/AIDS were once clients themselves (Stockdill 2003:218). When arthritis sufferers volunteer to offer pain management courses because they have taken such a course themselves and benefited from it, they are hoping to "return the favor" (Barlow and Hainsworth 2001:205). The same desire to pay back is expressed by those who offer to help the elderly because, when they were working full-time and could not care for their elderly relatives, others did: it is now time to return the favor (Keith 2003:34). The same rule is being invoked when people say they help the elderly because they owe something to the older generation. "When I heard about the [ombudsman] program, it occurred to me that this would be a way to give back a small portion of their [the elderly] hard work in developing our community" (Keith 2003:21). Recovered alcoholics reciprocate by volunteering for Alcoholics Anonymous. Some people volunteer for the homeless "out of acknowledgement of their own economic vulnerability and gratitude for the good fortune of having homes" (Allahyari 2000:110). Adults volunteer to help with youth organizations such as the Boy Scouts and Girl Guides because they were members when they were younger and want to help maintain the organization (Bussell and Forbes 2002:249). As one volunteer put it, "I was a Scout leader—my boys were in the Scouts and I wanted to give back something to the movement because they had gained from it—self-sufficiency, adventure" (Campbell and Wood 1999:123). Daniels (1988:70) gives many examples of volunteering as a cycle of generalized exchange:

> One woman became active in mental health organizations in memory of a schizophrenic sister. Another did public relations and made movies for the heart association because she herself had had open-heart surgery. Another organized a rehabilitation society after her recovery from a crippling disease. A reformed alcoholic created county and state services to combat alcoholism. One woman who had been raised in an orphanage became a leading light in improving the lot of orphans and dependent children more generally.

One in five of the volunteers for the National Foundation for Infantile Paralysis signed up because they had personal experience with the disease and had received help dealing with it: they had either had it themselves or knew someone close to them who had contracted it (Sills 1957:86). Volunteering gave these "polio veterans" a chance to discharge an obligation: "When you accept help you always feel that you'd like to repay" (Sills 1957:91). The norm of generalized reciprocity also motivates volunteering in anticipation of needing help in the future. Anticipated need probably helps explains why hospice volunteers tend to be older than the general population (Field and Johnson 1993:1627).

Eckstein (2001:841) shows how residents of a Boston neighborhood responded to requests for volunteer help because of their respect for community norms: " 'We believe in community helping,' noted a man who spent long hours at the Boys and Girls Club as a child. 'At the Club we first learned to give beyond our family.' " So committed were members of the neighborhood to the spirit of giving they occasionally volunteered for group-sponsored causes that were at odds with their private views. Nothing could more clearly indicate the power of social norms over individual preferences. Community groups engaged in a complex round of reciprocity whereby they offered their members as volunteers for activities of other groups (e.g., fund-raising) in anticipation of reciprocity some time in the future. They were noticeably reluctant to offer help to groups outside the community, a gesture that would weaken the community's own chain of reciprocity. Such norms of generalized reciprocity are more firmly institutionalized in communities that are relatively stable and homogenous. In the Boston case, community norms of mutual assistance rested on a foundation of racial, ethnic, and class homogeneity. The community was predominantly blue-collar Catholic in its composition and had very low residential turnover. Shared economic circumstances meant that voluntary groups had many needs in common. The low turnover rate, the class and ethnic solidarity, the somewhat insular nature of the community, the overlapping social institutions (e.g., schools and churches) made it much easier for people with relatively low amounts of human capital (education, income, occupational status) to volunteer frequently or give a lot of their time. This is a striking manifestation of the power of social norms: they elevated the volunteer rate of a population normally disinclined to do volunteer work.

Norm of Justice

Once our immediate self-interests are taken care of, our behavior tends to be guided by our sense of fairness and justice (Blau 1964:230). Fairness or justice is a social norm prescribing just treatment as a moral principle. We disapprove of people who treat others unfairly and we feel anger and resentment if we are treated unjustly. Many who write about volunteerism frame it as a form of "charity" or prosocial conduct. The implication is that people volunteer because they empathize with the plight of others and want to help them, which is certainly the case. But volunteering also includes working on behalf of others because we feel bitter, resentful, or angry. This is especially true where justice issues are paramount. Where people feel an injustice has been done to them, the group they belong to, or a group they identify with, they are more likely to feel they have to do something about it, such as volunteering their time for a cause that promises to help them.

In volunteering influenced by justice norms, the motivating force is identification with an unjustly subordinated group, opposition to that injustice, and recognition of the need for collective action to end it (Mansbridge 2001:240). Thinking about volunteering in these terms, it is easier for us to see how many people get drawn into helping others because the problem they are dealing with has come close to them and they believe that solving the problem is a justice issue. For example, after a drunken driver killed her daughter, Candy Lightner organized Mothers Against Drunk Driving, her purpose being to re-write the laws to control the kind of behavior that led to the loss of her daughter. Frequently, the norm invoked in such cases is equal treatment or ensuring that people get what they deserve or are entitled to (including punishment).[11]

Norm of Social Responsibility

The norm of social responsibility is very similar to the norm of general-ized reciprocity, but there is no sense of exchange or return. It requires us to place the community's well-being before our own personal interest. Pancer and Pratt (1999:38) believe that a norm of social responsibility helps explain volunteering "if someone feels a sense of connection to those outside her or his family and friends [or] . . . an obligation to help those in the community, nation or society at large who are in need."[12] In 1984, the General Social Sur-vey asked Americans whether, as citizens, they regarded doing volunteer work as their responsibility. Nearly one in three (31.3%) responded that it was a "very important" obligation, and a further 56.1 percent said it was "somewhat important." Just over two-thirds of American adults surveyed in 1995 agreed that it is very important for people to get involved in their com-munity by volunteering their time. African Americans (83%) were more likely to think so than Whites (66%) or Hispanics (51%). Eight out of ten said it was important for young people to learn the value of community ser-vice and 58 percent thought that community service should be a graduation requirement (Wirthlin Group 1995a).

When people are asked what makes a good citizen, they often invoke the norm of social responsibility. A good citizen is socially responsible. Volun-teers are more likely to mention this criterion than non-volunteers. In a series of focus group studies conducted in Illinois in 2000, most group members agreed that good citizens are people who look out for their neighbors and who are aware of the goings-on in their community, but the more civically engaged members were more likely to say that good citizens should do some-thing to help their community, otherwise they had no right, as citizens, to complain about it. The volunteers in the groups treated the norm of social re-sponsibility even more seriously. They believed citizens were under an obliga-tion to find out what was going on in their community and to do something about it rather than sitting back and letting things happen (Profile of Illinois 2001). An accompanying survey of a random sample of residents of the state found that the civically engaged were more likely to agree that every person should give some time for the good of his or her community (Profile of Illinois 2001).

When asked why they volunteer, people will often refer to a social obli-gation to help others in need or speak of their "civic duty" to care for the community (Hodgkinson and Weitzman 1996:243; Verba et al. 1995:272; Wuthnow 1991). Those who believe it is important to get involved in one's community are more likely to volunteer, although the effect is stronger for secular than religious causes (Uslaner 2002b:247). A 1988 survey of a ran-dom sample of adult Americans asked respondents how seriously they took their responsibility to volunteer to help other people. Those who said they took it very seriously were more likely to have volunteered in the past twelve months. The effect was confined to non-profit non-sectarian forms of volunteering in general and volunteering for the arts and civic, social, or fraternal volunteering (Sundeen 1992). Another survey, focusing on middle aged Americans, measured the norm of social responsibility by a four-item scale designed to assess how obliged respondents feel to help others at cost to themselves (e.g., being willing to pay more for health insurance to help the uninsured, volunteering time or giving money to a cause you support). The higher they scored on this scale the more hours they volunteered each month (Rossi 2001c:296).[13] A 1994 survey of eleven European countries asked respondents whether they agreed or disagreed with the following statement: "Everyone has a moral responsibility to do unpaid work at some time in their life." Overall, half of the respondents agreed, but 60 percent of the volunteers agreed compared to 44 percent of the non-volunteers (Gaskin and Smith 1997:61). The authors conclude that prosocial attitudes are particularly likely to translate into action if norms are present to support the action. Reed and Selbee (2003:97) used a ninety-item battery of questions put to a random sample of Canadians to see if they could construct a volunteer profile. Volunteers were more likely than non-volunteers to believe that "individuals have a responsibility to support and contribute to the common good, regardless of the responsibilities for supporting the common good that may be delegated to organizations or institutions such as churches or governments" and "in the necessity of active personal involvement in contributing to the common good over and above the standard obligations of citizenship such as paying taxes." Liu and Besser (2003) analyzed data taken from a random survey of Iowa residents, focusing on respondents aged 65 or more. The survey included a battery of questions they used to construct a "norm of collective action" index.[14] The more strongly respondents supported this norm the higher their level of "involvement in local improvement activities and events" (Liu and Besser (2003:352).[15] Respondents in a 1996–1997 survey conducted in the Netherlands were asked if they agreed with the statement that everybody should do voluntary work at times. Volunteers were more likely to agree with this statement than non-volunteers ($r = .24$, $p < 0.01$) (Dekker 2004). In summary, norms do seem to make a difference to volunteering. At least we know that volunteers are more likely to invoke and express support for norms of generalized reciprocity, justice, and social responsibility.[16]

Attitudes

Attitudes are favorable or unfavorable evaluations of an object. "Values focus on ideals; attitudes are applied to more concrete social objects" (Hitlin and Piliavin 2004:361). While attitudes are subject to change and are heavily influenced by social context, they provide a way of translating values and norms into specific views on particular issues and act as a guide to conduct with regard to those objects. For example, the rule against adultery, if endorsed, would imply certain attitudes toward people who engage in it and the circumstances, if any, under which it might be excused.

A survey of middle managers found attitudes (e.g., "I have more important things to do than getting involved in community affairs") and volunteer behavior to be highly correlated (Christenson et al. 1988:818). Here the connection seems obvious. But the link between attitudes and behavior is not always so strong. A study comparing environmental activists in Ontario, Canada, and the state of Michigan in the United States with a random sample of the population in those two regions found that the activists scored higher on a set of items designed to measure attitudes toward growth, such as, "The earth is like a spaceship with only limited room and resources" (Steger et al. 1989:250). However, the attitudinal differences between volunteers and nonvolunteers were quite small. Had the attitude items measured people's views on the appropriateness and usefulness of environmental activism for tackling problems caused by economic growth, the differences might have been larger. We took this lesson to heart in our own investigation of the relation between attitudes and volunteering in the Independent Sector data.

For a number of years (1992, 1994, 1996, and 1999) the Independent Sector survey asked respondents about their attitudes toward charitable organizations. Most of these questions were directed at the issue of whether Americans were discouraged from contributing money to charitable organizations because they did not think they were necessary, effective, honestly managed, and so on. However, some of the items in this battery of questions have more general relevance to volunteering. People are less likely to volunteer for organizations if they regard them as ineffective, corrupt, no longer necessary, or unlikely to make good use of their time. Respondents were asked to indicate whether they agreed with a number of statements about charitable organizations. We coded the responses such that a high score indicated a favorable attitude and we factor analyzed the responses to these items. The result was a two-factor solution. One factor measured respondents' opinions about the need for charitable organizations.[17] Women, Non-Hispanic Blacks, middle- and upper-income people, and frequent church attenders had the most positive attitudes toward charitable organizations. Controlling for these differences, volunteers had a more positive attitude toward charitable organizations than non-volunteers. [17] The second factor measured the respondents' level of trust in charitable organizations.[18] Women were more trusting of charitable organizations than men, as were the more highly educated, singles, middle-income earners, renters, and frequent church attenders. Retired people were less trusting than full-time workers, the only employment difference. Controlling for these differences, volunteers were more trusting of charitable organizations than non-volunteers. [17]

In summary, attitudes toward charitable organizations do seem to make some difference. One reason people do not volunteer is that they have negative attitudes toward non-profit organizations, seeing them as either unnecessary or untrustworthy.

Confidence in Charitable Institutions

The Independent Sector surveys provide another opportunity to measure the association between attitudes and volunteering because they ask respondents about their level of confidence in specific charitable organizations. The most trusted charitable institutions were youth, religious, educational, and human services. The least trusted were international, public benefit (e.g., civil rights organizations), and federal organizations such as the United Way. This is almost certainly a reflection of how close the organization is to the daily life of the respondent. Once again, we factor analyzed the responses. [18] They grouped into three factors (i.e., a positive attitude toward one institution in the group was highly correlated with a positive attitude toward another institution in the group). The first was comprised of private educational institutions, from elementary to collegiate. The second was comprised of health, religion, and human services. The third contained all the rest (environment, public/social benefit, youth and adult recreation, arts and culture, foundations, charitable appeals, and international).

We first examined which groups in the population had the most confidence in each of the clusters of charitable institutions. Confidence in education-type organizations was higher among Hispanics than any other racial group, and was higher among married people, frequent church attenders, the young, the better educated, and the more affluent. Confidence in health, religion, and human services non-profits was higher among women, minority groups, and frequent church attenders, and lower among the middle aged and self-employed full-time. Confidence in the remaining cluster of charitable organizations was higher among women, the young, minority groups, renters, frequent church attenders, and the more highly educated and affluent.

Confidence in charitable institutions in the United States is thus not randomly distributed across the population. Members of racial and ethnic minority groups display more confidence in charitable institutions, as do women—with the exception of education, where there is no gender difference. Frequent churchgoers also express more confidence, as do members of higher socio-economic groups—with the exception of human service organizations. There would appear to be a class difference here: human services organizations, which are more likely to target the needs of the poor and dispossessed, are more trusted by them; educational institutions, which serve the needs of the upwardly mobile, are more trusted by people who have benefited from them. This could reflect either familiarity with the institution or a positive attitude toward the institution based on its mandate.

Confidence in Charitable Institutions and Volunteering

Having discovered structured differences in attitudes toward charitable organizations, we looked at the data to see if attitudes were associated with volunteering. [19] We found that people who have confidence in charitable organizations are more likely to have volunteered in the past twelve months even after controlling for socio-demographic and religious variables. Looking at the types of charitable organization one by one, only confidence in international organizations was unrelated to volunteering. However, when we estimated the effect of confidence in one charitable institution while controlling for the effect of confidence in any of the others, the results changed. Now only confidence in higher education, youth development, and private foundations was associated with volunteering. To some extent, then, *the association between volunteering and confidence in charitable organizations has less to do with attitudes toward a particular type of charitable organization than it has to do with a disposition to trust charitable institutions in general.* With cross-sectional data we cannot tell whether the attitudes precede and help determine volunteer work or are the result of being a volunteer.

Self-Esteem

We include a discussion of the influence of self-esteem on volunteering in this chapter because it is an attitude toward an object "even though the holder of the attitude and the object toward which the attitude is held—the self—are the same" (Rosenberg et al. 1995:142). Self-esteem refers most generally to an individual's positive evaluation of the self. Individuals with high self-esteem see themselves as effective and competent. Generally speaking, people with high self-esteem are more likely to "initiate and pursue desired lines of action" (Thoits and Hewitt 2001:118). Items such as "I take a positive attitude toward myself" and "At times I think I am no good at all" are typically used to measure self-esteem. High self-esteem is frequently linked to academic and occupational achievement. It is highly likely that it also plays a role in unpaid labor such as volunteering because it cuts the (psychic) costs of being a volunteer. An analysis of the ACL data confirms this. Controlling for level of volunteering in 1986, the researchers found that the higher the self-esteem of the person in 1986, the more hours that person volunteered in 1989. The link between self-esteem and volunteering was membership in voluntary organizations: people with high self-esteem are more likely to be "joiners" and their membership leads to more volunteering (Thoits and Hewitt 2001:118).

Conclusion

Sociologists generally agree that values, norms, and attitudes are important components of social action. Values are the most general statements of legitimate ends that guide action. This does not mean that societies have perfectly integrated systems of values, nor does it mean that individuals are incapable of holding conflicting values. "As a society we pay lip service to altruistic values, but these values must be seen in the context of our other pursuits, the majority of which focus on ourselves rather than others" (Wuthnow 1991:11). We are quite capable of valuing one thing and doing another or of finding room within our value system for behaviors in which we wish to indulge. For example, teenage volunteers are no less likely than non-volunteers are to say that having a nice home, furnishings, and clothes is one of the top goals in life. People inspired by religious teachings to help the needy want more out of life, rather than less. "Unwilling to abandon their interest in work and money, but wanting to be altruistic as well, they want it all" (Wuthnow 1994a:253).

Whereas values describe desirable goals, norms specify the means, or the rules for achieving the goal. Neither values nor norms are *sufficient* to explain particular courses of action. Pacifist values might inspire a person to oppose war and social norms might indicate some form of non-violent action to achieve this goal, but no specific action is predicted at this level of generality. Non-violent action has to be organized and efforts have to be mobilized. Because values and norms are necessary but not sufficient components of social action we should not be surprised if, by themselves, they explain a limited amount of the variation in volunteering. If values alone were sufficient to guarantee a supply of volunteers, non-profit agencies would not have such a difficult time recruiting and retaining volunteers. Although many people espouse opinions expressing support for volunteer work and endorse values of voluntarism and charity, only a few typically act on the basis of these beliefs: "the mere existence of a given value in society can seldom if ever by and of itself ensure that the behavior required by the value will actually take place" (Sills 1957:37).

Values and norms do not predict volunteering very reliably because they are quite malleable, open to interpretation and negotiation. We are not "hard-wired" with culture. Values and norms do not lie deeply embedded in our consciousness making certain actions imperative. "What is in operation is a practical sense of *where* to talk about 'values'; of which 'values' are supposed to be relevant where; and of where 'values' are basically irrelevant" (Eliasoph 1998:19). As we saw in chapter 4, values are part of an ideology or larger framework of meaning. Their function might be less as an antecedent of volunteering and more of an aid to understanding what kind of reasons and motivations volunteers find appealing (Dekker and Halman 2003:77). Thus, even when we find an association between values and volunteering in cross-sectional analyses, we cannot assume that the values preceded the volunteer work; the work may have encouraged us to change our values (Sundeen and Raskoff 1995:354).

Values, by definition, transcend social situations, and therefore the association between values and *volunteering in general* is likely to be rather weak.

Volunteer work assumes many forms, each inspired by a different set of values. Although we might volunteer at an abortion clinic because we value freedom of choice, we are not for that reason more likely to volunteer for any other causes. Although religious teachings might inspire us to volunteer at a soup kitchen, they might prohibit our volunteering to help AIDS patients. Because values are so general, they are interpreted in different ways depending on the social situation. A 1996 survey of Canadians and Americans asked if they favored the free market over government as a way of dealing with social problems. Respondents living in the United States were more likely to volunteer for secular causes if they expressed support for the value of free enterprise, whereas respondents living in Canada were *less* likely to volunteer if they espoused this value (Uslaner 2002b:247). In other words, the association between values and volunteering was moderated by social context. In the United States, government is seen as bad, something volunteerism replaces; in Canada, government is seen as good, something volunteerism complements.

Norms provide us with rules to live by, but even more than values, they are negotiable. Identity theory helps explain why. Volunteer work is not impelled by abstract ideas of what people *ought* to do ("The world would be a better place if everybody volunteered"). Volunteering is not merely the result of being taught the right rules. There is no absolute moral standard for volunteering. For social norms to operate, people have to think they apply to them. If people do not think of themselves as volunteers, or potential volunteers, norms that enjoin volunteer work will be unknown, dismissed as irrelevant, or simply ignored.

The connection between attitudes and behavior is also acknowledged to be weak (Schuman and Johnson 1976:168). For this reason, some scholars dismiss the "values and attitudes" model of volunteering (Thoits and Hewitt 2001:118). However, it would be premature to reject this approach to explaining volunteering. Three general rules of investigation seem to apply in this area. The first is that multiple item measures of attitudes are more stable and reliable than single item measures. The second is that attitudinal and behavioral variables should be measured at the same level of specificity. Thus pro-environment attitudes do not predict volunteering very well, nor do attitudes toward environmental organizations. However, attitudes about the usefulness of volunteer work in this area, or favorable attitudes toward people who work on behalf of environmental organizations, are better predictors. Third, attitudes toward behavior or action are better predictors of behavior than attitudes toward objects. Anti-war sentiment does not predict participating in a peace march in Washington. However, attitudes about the efficacy or importance of peace marches as a way of ensuring peace do a better job.

It is all the more striking, in light of these criticisms, that volunteers do have different attitudes toward charitable organizations and toward themselves than non-volunteers. This relationship is reciprocal. For example, attitudes toward abortion might prompt an individual to join the picket line outside an abortion clinic, but the attitudes are strengthened (or weakened) by the experience. One of the most difficult issues in studying the relation between confidence in charitable institutions and volunteering is sorting out this cause and effect relationship. "Assuming most organizations fulfill their missions and make good use of volunteer time, confidence felt by volunteers in charitable institutions should rise" (Bowman 2004:254). Role identity theory helps explain these reciprocal effects: as people continue to volunteer, commitment to the organization increases and, as commitment increases, self-concept changes. Once the volunteer role becomes part of their identity, people strive to bring their behavior in line with this identity (Penner and Finkelstein 1998:526). With cross-sectional data it is quite difficult to estimate these reciprocal effects, but Bowman (2004:266) used a simultaneous-equation bivariate probit model to overcome this difficulty. He observed a lower rate of volunteering within the group of respondents with low confidence in charitable institutions, but he also observed that volunteering increased confidence in them. The effect of confidence on volunteering was stronger than the reverse effect of volunteering on confidence. This study is a striking affirmation of the lesson to be learned from this entire chapter: subjective dispositions do matter.

In concluding this section of the book on subjective dispositions, we reaffirm that volunteering is over-determined. Many factors help explain why somebody volunteers. As we shall see, explanations must be multi-dimensional and multi-layered. This point can be illustrated by two examples of the multi-dimensional approach. Cohn et al. (2003:315–316) argue that four sets of factors determine whether "members" of voluntary organizations become "volunteers" or active members. The first is ideological conviction, or the extent to which individual members share the values and goals of the organization. The second is organization, or structures that allow (or require) members to interact frequently to facilitate friendships and emotional bonds between members. Leaving the organization becomes a matter of leaving one's friends, perhaps letting them down. Without structures (e.g., local chapters) to facilitate social interaction, monitoring becomes more difficult and individuals are less accountable for their input and commitment. The third is legitimacy. Members are more committed the more they support their leaders and are willing to support their decisions. This means having a structure that allows leadership to be assigned on a basis that seems reasonable and legitimate to members. Finally, good communication between staff and volunteers and between volunteers is highly important. Active members of BFW (i.e., those who helped with lobbying by calling congressmen, trying to recruit new members, and so on) were more ideological (i.e., more likely to believe that world hunger problems are the result of high levels of military spending, the practices of multinational corporations, and corruption among third world elites) than inactive members. They were more likely than inactive members to have close friends who were also members of BFW and to belong to a local branch of the organization.

They were more trusting of the officials of the organization and supported their decisions. Simply having the "right" values and attitudes was necessary but not sufficient to mobilize members to actually perform volunteer work.

In another study, Park and Smith (2000:273) suggest four possible ways in which religion and volunteering are related: religiosity, or behaviors and attitudes toward religion (a measure of religious identity); socialization, or the sense of belonging to a particular religious tradition or group (a measure of affiliation); social networks, or the degree of access to other religious adherents; and religious socialization, or exposure to religious values and behaviors during one's formative years. They conducted a study of church-related volunteering that had taken place "at some point in the past two years" among Protestants who attended church frequently. They found that religious socialization made some difference: respondents whose parents were mainline Protestants were more likely to have volunteered. However, the respondent's own religious affiliation (i.e., "liberal," "evangelical," "mainline Protestant," "other Protestant," and "charismatic") made *no* difference. Nor did religious salience—or strength of religious identity—make any difference. These cultural measures of religion paled in comparison with more structural effects. Social networks were important. Respondents who numbered many Christians among their family and friends were more likely to volunteer. Participation in church activities (e.g., potluck suppers, choir practice) was by far the strongest predictor of volunteering. The same was true of volunteering for work not connected to the church. Participation in church activities had a strong positive effect on secular volunteering, while frequency of church attendance had a negative effect. Thus, within this Protestant sample of frequent church attenders (a significant limitation), neither religious identification nor affiliation played any role in volunteering once social network measures were controlled. Once again, we see that values are a necessary but not a sufficient condition for volunteering. Whether we think of culture and structure as additive or acting in some kind of combination, the research of Park and Smith (2000) indicates that the influence of religion on volunteering is attributable to both cultural and structural mechanisms with, perhaps, the structural links being the more discriminating: the religious community itself (i.e., the congregation), or the social ties that congregational life foster, is the mechanism that connects the culture of religion and volunteering. In this respect, a religious congregation functions much like any other non-profit organization. It institutionalizes the volunteer role and provides a community—part bureaucracy and part family—that fosters philanthropy. However, there is, in all likelihood, a qualitative difference in this regard. Thus, while the Mormon ward promotes volunteer work in its notion of the "calling," this call comes not from the local bishop but from God. Beliefs must play some part in giving religious organizations a special role in encouraging volunteer work. We will return to this issue of organization later in the book.

Part 3.

Individual Resources

In part 3 we discuss the influence of individual resources on volunteering. We use this term to describe a cluster of factors that are all objective attributes of individuals having in common the property that they can be used as resources for doing volunteer work. Unlike the subjective dispositions discussed in part 2, these resources do not refer to what is going in people's minds but to characteristics of individuals that can be measured objectively. Of course, we often have to rely on the individual for information on his or her objective characteristics, as when we ask about hourly wages, but in principle this information could be gleaned from a third party, such as the employer. In this respect, the issues covered in part 3 are no different from those that would be covered in a study of why people move from one job to another: we would be interested in their education, age, health, or current income. However, it might seem strange to describe these factors as resources in the context of a behavior that is conventionally believed to spring from an inner desire to do good to others. Acts of generosity are commonly believed to have their wellspring in values, beliefs, norms, and a host of intra-individual factors such as personality, but this perspective overlooks the important point that volunteer service is *work*. For too long work has been thought of as *only* that is done for pay, but this is not the proper definition of work. What makes an activity work "as opposed to something else, such as leisure, is not whether it is paid but whether it involves the provision of a service to others or the production of goods for the consumption of others" (Taylor 2004:38). By focusing only on work for pay, we overlook a host of other productive activities, such as child care, housework, and other services provided free, which we hardly think of as work at all. The same thing happens with volunteering. It is a gift, but it is also a form of work: unpaid labor that produces something of value. By thinking of volunteering not only as a gift but as unpaid labor we shift the emphasis from the motivation behind the act to its productive aspects. Like any other form of labor, unpaid labor consumes resources, using up energy, time, and often money and other material goods. And, like any other kind of labor, volunteer work demands certain skills that some people have and others lack.

The more we think of volunteer work as labor, just another form of productive activity, the more we think of the resources necessary to perform it. Resources are inherently scarce, and people must decide where and when to use them. A woman who works for pay full-time and spends many hours in addition looking after her children and cleaning house will have little time left over to do much else, let alone take on additional work as a volunteer. For people who lack the confidence, schooling, or social contacts, it is extra burdensome to be asked to organize and run a fund-raising campaign or meet with elected officials to discuss changing their spending priorities. The resources required to do volunteer work are unevenly distributed in the population. Not everyone has what it takes to organize a meeting, edit a newsletter, pay membership fees, march on a picket line, counsel abused women, mentor youth, or rescue lost climbers. Only those with the necessary skills will think of volunteering, or be asked to volunteer. Organizations looking to hire volunteers are likely to seek people who they believe will be the most productive and the least troublesome to manage and motivate. Like any other organization, they prefer to recruit the most highly qualified applicants.

The argument that volunteering demands resources that are unevenly distributed in the population implies that resource-poor people are at a disadvantage as far as getting volunteer jobs is concerned. This flies in the face of the reality that demand for volunteers clearly outstrips the supply in the voluntary sector. It would seem that volunteer jobs are available for as many people as want them, regardless of the resources they possess. It also flies in the face of the reality that philanthropic work is, by definition, something people do of their own volition. Deciding to volunteer depends on our wants and desires, not what we can bring to the table. Despite these objections, there are a number of reasons to pay attention to individual resources when explaining volunteer behavior.

First, there are always vacancies in the regular labor force that people are not able, or do not choose, to fill. The volunteer labor force is no different. Second, volunteer work calls for various kinds of skills and aptitudes, in the same way that regular work does. Not all people have these skills. Individual resources therefore also refer to *competence*. For example, we are more likely to agree to help out at a nursing facility for the aged if we have some experience taking care of elderly relatives, if we think we have the social skills necessary to relate to older people, or if we have a job, such as nursing or social work, that has prepared us for the tasks we are likely to be given. Being asked to help out during a political campaign might draw more on experience with office work or clerical duties. Being accepted into a volunteer search and rescue team is conditional on proving we have physical skills, such as skiing or climbing. A third reason why it makes sense to think in terms of resources for volunteering is that the way we get regular jobs and the way we get volunteer jobs are quite similar. The beginning of a search for a regular job is often unplanned, just as we stumble upon opportunities to volunteer. Many jobs, both paid and unpaid, become available to us on casual occasions (at church, work, on the athletic field) but these "casual" encounters are structurally determined. For example, women might be less likely to be asked to volunteer at work and more likely than men to be asked at school. Finally, the fact that volunteer work is voluntarily undertaken does not rule out the possibility that opportunities to volunteer are limited by lack of resources. After all, voting, while an obligation of every citizen, is purely voluntary. This does not mean election turnout is randomly distributed: citizens with automobiles are more likely to vote than citizens without them. Many efforts are made to encourage people to vote, just as many efforts are made to get people to volunteer, but shortage of resources will always be a problem. In neither instance can we assume that these efforts to mobilize people will be randomly directed or randomly effective. This is especially true of volunteer work, which demands more commitment and sacrifice than voting. The fact is that most people are never asked to volunteer. "Moreover, inclusion in a recruitment network is not a random process but is highly structured by several characteristics that are also related to activity" (Verba et al. 1995:134). In short, the sociological issue with respect to entry into the volunteer labor force is the same as it is with respect to entry into the paid labor force. How is the market for labor socially structured? "It is the institutional setting . . . that places certain opportunities in people's path, rules out certain possibilities, and nudges someone to choose certain options rather than others" (Wuthnow 1995:31).

In summary, an adequate theory of volunteering must focus on individual differences in the enabling resources. Enabling resources are those that are useful, or required, for performing volunteer work. As we shall see, this primarily means education in modern societies, but income, occupation, free time, and health should also be treated as individual resources.

Rational Choice Theory

People normally look to husband their resources, "spending" them only if they think they will get some kind of profitable return for them. Given the same rewards, volunteering is more attractive to the resource-rich to than the resource-poor. If volunteer work demands money, the rich will find it easier to do; if it demands knowledge and "civic skills," the well educated will be less challenged by it; if it requires heavy lifting, the physically healthy will find it more tolerable; it if is very time consuming, those with "time on their hands" will find it easier to bear the burden. In other words, the resource-rich are more likely to "profit" from doing volunteer work.

The theory that underlies the resource approach to volunteering is therefore rational choice theory. It assumes that rational actors would not contribute services to others unless they received something in exchange and profited by the transaction: "for an individual to undertake any volunteering activity the benefits must be greater than the costs incurred for that activity" (Handy et al. 2000:48).

Unlike the theories described in chapter 3, rational choice theory makes no reference to motive other than self-interest. It assumes that all humans must be selfish to some degree in order to survive (Smith 1982). For example, Vaillancourt (1994:814) believes that, despite appearances to the contrary, volunteers are not making a sacrifice by donating their time "since all activities, *by definition,* must be a source of private benefits" (our emphasis). It then becomes a matter of finding the individual benefits in seemingly selfless acts and finding out how they outweigh the costs involved. Benefits include not only private material benefits, such as increased work skills, but also private intangible benefits, such as the "warm glow" helping others provides. As one volunteer put it,

> A part of it [motivation to volunteer] goes back to self-esteem and looking back at the good you've contributed and feeling better about yourself . . . and saying "I've done something that's mattered" . . . . The reward is this feeling like I've made a difference in my community not just to myself and the kids but [to] our community. (Basok et al. 2002:2)

The rewards of volunteering also include public benefits, such as believing that the rate of teenage pregnancy will fall as a result of one's work in a counseling center. Public benefits might be thought of as "altruistic benefits" because the individual has placed a positive weight on the other's welfare in her utility function. Such a person would be willing to give up some of her own consumption in return for an increase in the other's consumption (Rose-Ackerman 1996:713). According to this logic, there will be a "payoff" to volunteering. For example, if people volunteer for the local fire department they help lower their own property taxes.

There is much to be said for the rational choice theory of volunteering. Actors clearly do weigh costs and benefits when they consider taking up volunteer work. Excessive costs discourage people from volunteering. "Even when my principles tell me I ought to act collectively and I identify deeply with a particular group, I am less likely to act if I conclude that my actions are not likely to have a positive effect or that a small positive effect will be offset by major personal costs" (Mansbridge 2001:249). Nakano (2000:98) describes the consequences of being a "professional volunteer" in Japan, a person who has devoted most of his life to volunteer work:

> The price he paid for devoting himself to civic life was the middle-class ideal of home ownership and self-respect and satisfaction in its attainment. The cost

of his civic life was measurable in money and accompanying achievements that he did not earn.

It is more difficult to recruit volunteers to do jobs that are demanding or to make long-term commitments. The recruit will be thinking, How much cost am I going to bear? This includes the individual's assessment of how the authorities will respond to his or her volunteer activities, some of which might involve violating the law or disturbing the peace. Some kinds of volunteer work require us to "invest" heavily in the role by undergoing extensive training, and we like to think this investment will pay off.

Assessing costs can be quite subjective. They include anxieties, uncertainties, and concerns about failure to perform the volunteer role adequately. They include the social stigma attached to being associated with certain kinds of people (e.g., AIDS patients, drug addicts, homeless people). In addition to the fear of contracting the disease, AIDS volunteers find that others stigmatize them and avoid them because of prejudicial attitudes toward the people they are trying to help: "active volunteers often suggest that many of their associates respond differently to them after learning about their involvement as volunteers" (Snyder and Omoto 1992:216). A one-year follow-up of AIDS volunteers found that those who had quit said that their work had taken up too much of their time and it caused them to feel embarrassed, stigmatized, or uncomfortable. Even the cost of time spent on volunteering is subjective because it is determined by the value placed on other uses of that time (e.g., time foregone from work, from being with family members, from other leisure time pursuits). Social obligations also impose costs. Many older people, having retired from a life of having to get up and go to work or take care of the children or both, welcome a life, not of laziness, but of work they can pick and choose. Thus, in a comparison of elderly volunteers and non-volunteers, those who had chosen not to volunteer did not feel they had less time or were busier than the volunteers but they were more likely to think that volunteer work would tie them down (Warburton et al. 2001:598). The cost in this case was not the amount of time but the *commitment* of time. Many kinds of volunteering impose emotional costs. An ethnographic study of the Home Start program in the United Kingdom exposed the psychological burden imposed by the work of giving emotional and practical support to mothers having difficulty coping with their children:

> You get emotionally involved, you hear things you don't ever want to hear . . . sleep-losing things. I worry sometimes into the night, for example, once about alleged sexual abuse of a child. I was aghast, and I felt powerless. (Bagilhole 1996:197)

Volunteer agencies are painfully aware that they will not attract enough volunteers or keep them long if they impose too many demands on them. To offset the costs of volunteering, they offer incentives. On rare occasions economic incentives are used: "[l]ow income older people are more likely [than richer] to be interested in the [stipended] Senior Companion" program (Caro and Bass 1995:90). But more often rewards take the form of recognition. Volunteers are more likely to drop out if their work goes unrecognized (Field and Johnson 1993:1629).

There is, therefore, no necessary antithesis between volunteering and self-interest. Indeed, Martin (1994:127) argues that a certain measure of self-interest is often necessary: "Vulnerable to discouragement and burnout, volunteers do well to combine their altruistic desires with a sense that their own good is interwoven with helping others." Included among these rewards are "solidary benefits," the pleasure of socializing with staff, other volunteers, and clients, to whom emotional attachments may be formed (Wuthnow 1998:149). As we shall see in a later chapter, there is a lot of evidence that one of the benefits of volunteering is making friends. People who volunteer for the purpose of making new friends find this benefit especially rewarding (Leighley 1996). Volunteer work can also provide the kinds of rewards we normally associate with good quality jobs and that many people might not be able to get through their day jobs. For example, people who volunteer as emergency squad technicians, as firefighters, and as search and rescue volunteers get excitement and thrills their dull and routine jobs conspicuously lack (Gora and Nemerowicz 1985:40). Simpson (1996:21) found that firemen relished the risk of fighting fires. Novitiates were advised never to drive the truck because that role would not be as exciting as actually fighting the fire. It is also evident that some people volunteer in order to increase their stock of human capital. They volunteer to acquire, or refresh, job-related skills or they hope their unpaid work will lead to a paid job. Volunteering thus becomes an investment in the future, similar to on-the-job training or taking an adult education course. This probably accounts for much of the volunteer work performed by teenagers and young adults. It also probably explains why some homemakers volunteer and why people who have newly moved into a community volunteer (Schram and Dunsing 1981:374). Elite philanthropic organizations have a "payoff" in the form of helping volunteers (mostly women) create new, socially desired friendships and prestigious associations they can list on their volunteer or business resumes. Kendall (2002:46) observed that, for most women who volunteer for elite philanthropic organizations, service is its own reward, but many of those same women find alluring the social recognition such organizations can provide: "recognition for oneself or one's children is a crucial motivating factor behind the women's hard work and continued involvement." In addition, volunteers often benefit directly from their work. As Wuthnow (2004:106) notes, "a large share of the volunteering that occurs in the United States is devoted to running churches, youth programs, and neighborhood associations in which volunteers themselves are the prime beneficiaries."

In summary, while it is unwise to reduce all volunteer work to a utilitarian calculus, the evidence does seem to suggest that, for the average person, ability to pay the cost of doing the work is an important consideration, as are the rewards to be gained from doing it. Of course, we seldom know for sure what those rewards are (we cannot tautologically assume there must be rewards otherwise the behavior would not occur) but we can infer costs by looking at the kinds of resources volunteer work demands and seeing how many of those resources people possess.

6

Socio-Economic Resources

In this chapter we analyze the influence of socio-economic resources on the probabilities of volunteering. As we noted in chapter 1, the significance of these resources for volunteering becomes more apparent if we think of volunteering as unpaid labor that, like other forms of labor, expends resources. Indeed, the imposition of cost is one of the defining features of volunteer work. Those who can more easily afford these costs are more likely to volunteer, and volunteer more hours.

Education

We begin this analysis of the influence of individual resources on volunteering with education because it is the most consistent, and often the strongest, predictor of volunteering. A number of reasons have been given as to why volunteers are more educated than non-volunteers (Brady et al. 1995:285; Cohn et al. 1993:125; Downton and Wehr 1997:22; Eisenberg 1992:50; Herzog and Morgan 1993:137; Nie et al. 1996:45; Rosenthal et al. 1998:480). More schooling encourages more cosmopolitan attitudes, fosters empathy with the less fortunate, and builds self-confidence. It improves cognitive functioning, informing people about the world around them, raising consciousness of social problems, encouraging people to be more analytical and more critical about social conditions, and teaching them how groups and organizations are governed and operated. Poorly educated people are more likely to say they do not volunteer because they do not know how, whereas highly educated people are more likely to say they lack the time (Lasby 2004:10). [12] The more education people have the more extensive and heterogeneous are their social networks, which increases the chances they will be asked to volunteer. Aside from expanding social networks, educational qualifications, such as degrees and titles, are a form of credentialing, signaling one's capabilities to do volunteer work.

We will now review the research on the association between education and volunteering, following this with some analyses of our own using data from the Independent Sector surveys.

High School

In chapter 10 we will discuss the influence of family background on volunteering among youth. We will find that youths from higher socio-economic status families are more likely to volunteer. In this section, we are interested in finding out if students who do well academically are also more likely to volunteer, regardless of the socio-economic status of their parents. A number of studies have shown that academic performance and participation in all manner of extra-curricular activities go together and there is no reason this should not also apply to volunteer work. One study asked U.S. teenagers if they had done any volunteer work in the previous twelve months for any of seven different types of organization (e.g., health organization, education organization).[1] The volunteers had higher grade point averages than the non-volunteers. Volunteers with higher grade point average also contributed more hours. The difference in grade point average between volunteers and non-volunteers in this study was small, and the positive effect of academic achievement was confined to volunteering in connection with schools and youth development (e.g., Boy Scouts) (Sundeen and Raskoff 1994:394) but a larger study, of U.S. students in grades six through twelve, uncovered the same pattern of association. Among those who had received "mostly" A grades the volunteer rate was 33 percent, compared to 16 percent among those who had received mostly D or F grades (Nolin et al. 1997:8).[2] Of course, we cannot be sure from these statistics whether grades are causing volunteer activities or vice versa nor can we be sure that the kinds of students who volunteer are not simply also the kind of students who get good grades.

College

After graduating high school, many students enter college. Going to college is by itself a mark of educational achievement. Is there any difference in the rate of volunteering among young people according to whether they attended college? One study surveyed young people before they entered college (age 17 or 18) and again when they left college (age 22 or 23). The study then compared changes in volunteering among this group with the changes in volunteering among young people in the same age cohort who did not attend college. The young people who attended college were more likely to be volunteering at age 17 or 18 than those who did not. In other words, college-bound (and more academically proficient) high school seniors were already more likely to be volunteering. When the young people were re-interviewed after college graduation, the gap between the college and non-college group had widened, but only in the case of volunteering in connection with a civic organization. No effect was discernible in the case of sports, social, or religious volunteering (Egerton 2002). Based on this study, attending college does not, by itself, increase the chances of volunteering, at least immediately after finishing college.

As far as differences in academic performance within the college population are concerned, the evidence is somewhat mixed. Because there is not much room for variation in academic performance within the college student population, we should not expect very large correlations between academic performance and volunteering while in college. Nevertheless, one study did find that verbal (but not math) scores on college entrance examinations predicted volunteering two years after graduating college. Students with the lowest SAT verbal scores donated just over one hour to community service while those with the highest scores donated more than twelve hours. In this case, verbal aptitude, not overall intelligence, fostered community service. However, neither the respondent's college grade point average nor the academic rank of the college attended (according to *U.S. News & World Report*) made any difference to volunteerism two years after graduation (Nie and Hillygus 2001).

Standardized tests and grade point average measure cognitive ability. They do not measure the other kinds of influences college education can have on students. Going to college can change the way students look at the world around them, depending somewhat on the kind of curriculum students choose to follow. Nie and Hillygus (2001) found that, regardless of race and parents' level of education, American college students who selected a social science curriculum committed more hours to community service after college than those who majored in business. This is partly the result of self-selection into a particular major and partly the result of socialization while in it: young people interested in politics, social issues, and community service select and find more interesting a social science curriculum, and the social science curriculum reinforces a predisposition to community work that is already there.

In summary, education and volunteering become associated quite early in life. High school students who are doing well in class are more likely to also do volunteer work. Most of these academic achievers are likely to go to college, but the one study to compare those who go to college and those who do not found only limited evidence that college itself made much difference. Schools are probably creating a climate where academic achievement and doing community service can be easily coupled. Once the student graduates high school, he or she is allowed much more freedom and is less subject to social pressures to be "all-rounded." The influence of college seems to consist mainly of steering people in the direction of volunteer work through the choice of curriculum rather than differences in cognitive ability. Although studies of the adult population show that college graduates volunteer at higher rates than high school graduates, this difference does not appear immediately. Education therefore has a "sleeper effect." As we shall see, young adulthood is a low point in volunteering over the life course, and the positive effects of education are not felt until people reach middle age, when the pressure to volunteer intensifies, mainly as a result of parenting responsibilities.

Adults

As noted above, few findings are as robust as that which shows a positive association between years of schooling and adult volunteering. In the United Kingdom, 43 percent of degree holders volunteered in the past year, compared to 29 percent of those who left school at age 16. Thirty-six percent of volunteers had attended college or earned a degree, compared to 18 percent of non-volunteers (Goddard 1994:9).[3] In Canada, 23 percent of those with just a high school diploma were volunteers, compared to 39 percent of college graduates (Lasby 2004:3). According to a survey conducted in the United States in 2003, only 22 percent of Americans with just a high school diploma were volunteers, compared to 34 percent of those with some college experience and 46 percent of college graduates. The more education Americans receive, the more hours they volunteer and the wider the range of activities in which they get involved (U.S. Bureau of Labor Statistics 2003:2). All social groups benefit from having more education: the positive influence of education is approximately the same for men and women, whites and African Americans, singles and married people, those working and those not working, and both recent immigrants and long-established citizens (Boraas 2003:5).

Our analysis of the Independent Sector data replicated these findings. Although college-educated Americans comprised only a fifth of the sample, they contributed 40 percent of the hours. [1] Education had a positive effect on the likelihood of having volunteered in the past twelve months, the number of volunteer domains, and the number of hours volunteered in the past month. [20, 21] Although more highly educated people donate more money to charity, regardless of their income, they do not substitute giving money for volunteering. They contribute more hours *and* donate more money. [22] The positive influence of education is found in many other countries. According to the World Values Survey, education is positively associated with volunteering overall, for service-type volunteering, activist-type volunteering, and even religious volunteering.[4] [23]

Education and Domain

Earlier, we argued that education is a resource for volunteer work because it means we are better informed about social issues, know more about governance and how groups and organizations work, and have developed the necessary "civic skills" demanded in many kinds of volunteer work. But in this section we argue that this kind of resource is better suited to some kinds of volunteer work than others. In the United States, for example, graduating college almost doubles the chances of volunteering for an environmental organization but it reduces the chances of volunteering for a religious organization (U.S. Bureau of Labor Statistics 2003). Analyzing data from the Citizen Participation Survey, Norris (1996:478) found education to be positively related to political campaign work but unrelated to "informal" community work. A study asked Boston area residents if they had volunteered to help with a political campaign. Age, gender, health, number of children in the home, number of hours worked, number of years living in the community, and home ownership had no effect on the likelihood of being a political volunteer: only level of education (and level of interest in government affairs) made a difference (Burr et al. 2002:101). Volunteers for Bread for the World are expected to communicate frequently with their congressmen to urge the passage of hunger alleviation legislation. Not surprisingly, more highly educated people are over-represented among these volunteers (Cohn et al. 1993:117). Dealing with highly stigmatized populations, such as AIDS victims, is also more common among highly educated people (Omoto and Snyder 1993). Education has an especially strong influence on volunteering in connection with instrumental groups, such as professional associations, and groups that benefit from volunteers having the cultural capital that goes along with advanced education, such as culture and arts groups (Shapiro 1984:74).

Education, whether it is in the form of higher cognitive abilities, organizational skills, or a more structural awareness of the roots of social problems, can be of little help when it comes to doing some kinds of volunteer work and occasionally it can be something of a barrier. For example, where volunteer work consists mainly of accompanying patients on outings, offering companionship, providing support to patients and families in waiting rooms, shopping and doing errands, and taking patients from one facility to another, as it does in the case of hospital volunteers, more highly educated people might avoid this kind of menial, person-to-person work and people with limited education might feel more comfortable doing it because it relies on "people skills." Handy and Srinivasan (2004) found that, whereas just over half (55%) of all volunteers in Ontario, Canada, had earned some kind of post-secondary certificate, diploma, or university degree, only 34 percent of hospital volunteers in the province had done so. In the United States, volunteer firefighters, and public safety volunteers in general, tend to be less educated than the general population (Thompson 1993a; U.S. Bureau of Labor Statistics 2003).

These studies imply that the positive influence of education varies by domain. We tested this hypothesis using the Independent Sector data. As far as volunteer range was concerned, where the variable is measuring how many different activities the respondent volunteered for, education had a positive effect on all domains. [25] As far as volunteer hours were concerned, education made a difference only to youth development: those with a high school diploma contributed an average of fourteen hours in the past month, compared to eight and a half hours for respondents with advanced degrees. [24] This probably reflects the inclusion of sports and recreation in this category. Education thus has a more consistent influence on how many different activities Americans get involved in than it has on how intensely they get involved, as measured by hours contributed.

Moderating Effects

We treat education as a resource that lowers the costs of doing volunteer work. It does so by increasing self-confidence, teaching organizational skills, expanding social networks, and raising the prospects of being asked. But social scientists know that resources such as education do not necessarily "count" the same for all members of the population. In the conventional labor market, for example, minority groups might have to earn extra education credits to obtain the same rewards as members of the majority group. Individual resources are also only *potentially* useful for doing volunteer work. Unless the individual is placed in a position to make use of those resources, they will be useless. In this section we investigate whether the influence of education on volunteering is moderated by two measures of minority status—race and gender—and one measure of structural opportunity—life course stage.

Gender

Theoretically, gender has the potential to moderate the influence of education on volunteering for two reasons. The first is that volunteering is considered primarily as women's work. This would mean that women need fewer "qualifications" to volunteer because of their non-educational resources and therefore the influence of education is weaker for women than men. The second argument is that the "credentialing" function of formal education works better for men because their qualifications are treated more seriously, are generalized to other domains more readily, and therefore "count" for more when it comes to volunteer work. Both arguments suggest that women's volunteering is less influenced by education than men's. Two studies support this argument by showing that education has a stronger effect on men's volunteering than women's (Caiazza and Hartmann 2001:14; Schlozman et al.

1995). But another study, of membership in an environmental group, giving money to an environmental group, and taking part in a demonstration or protest, found that education had a stronger influence on women than men (Barkan 2004:926). The 2002 Current Population Survey (CPS) on volunteering also found that education had a stronger influence on women than men (U.S. Bureau of Labor Statistics 2002). In light of these contradictory findings, we used the Independent Sector data to test for the interaction between gender and education. Controlling for other socio-demographic variables and religiosity, we found no interaction effect at all: education had the same effect on women and men. [26]

Race

In an earlier study we looked at racial differences in the effect of education on volunteering (Musick et al. 2000:1556). We hypothesized that the benefits of education are blunted in the case of African Americans because of prejudice against them: their education is discounted. In that study, we divided respondents into African Americans and Whites, excluding those who did not fit into these categories because of the relatively small sample size in the survey we used (ACL). We estimated the effect of education on volunteer hours, controlling for income, health, religion, and social participation. Our hypothesis was confirmed: education was positively related to volunteer hours for Whites but had no effect on the hours contributed by African Americans.

Age

Earlier in this chapter, in our examination of the association between educational achievement and volunteering among high school and college students, we speculated that education might have a "sleeper effect" on volunteering. Because young adults have very low volunteer rates, the positive effect of education is suppressed until people reach middle age, when the social pressure to volunteer is stronger and educational credentials begin to signify volunteer potential. We tested this hypothesis using the Independent Sector survey data. [27] The hypothesis was confirmed: the positive effect of education was strongest among Americans aged between 40 and 59. This suggests that education is a form of "capital" that can be "banked" for a while and called upon when social relationships and other social obligations begin to increase the pressure to volunteer.

Mediating Effects

We use the term "mediating effects" to describe the mechanisms linking education and volunteering. They describe the pathway by which people get from what they learn in school and college to volunteer work. Earlier in the chapter, we suggested what some of these mechanisms might be. We argued that education changes the way people think about themselves and about volunteering. It also changes the scope and quality of their social relationships with other people. In this section we look at the role of attitudes, social networks, and being asked to volunteer.

Subjective Dispositions

One theory why educated people are more likely to volunteer is that they have different subjective dispositions. Educated people are more likely to have attitudes considered conducive to volunteering. They are empathic, efficacious, more likely to feel they have a duty to help others, and less likely to think they have the right to concern themselves with their own goals first and foremost, rather than with the problems of other people. [28] More important, these attitudes account for some of the educational differences in volunteer rates. In addition, the more education Americans receive, the more trusting of other people they are. This also accounts for some of the educational difference between volunteers and non-volunteers. [9]

Social Participation

Another explanation for the link between education and volunteering uses network theory. More education means more extensive social networks. Numerous studies have shown that highly educated people tend to be "joiners." The Independent Sector data confirm this: education has a positive effect on membership in service groups, college groups, civic associations, school groups, professional associations, voluntary associations, religious groups, and political groups. It has no effect on membership in fraternal orders, veterans groups, or labor unions. [29] More highly educated people also meet with friends and neighbors more frequently, a measure of informal social interaction. We found that social participation (as measured by the number of organizational memberships and informal social interaction) partly explains why highly educated people are more likely to volunteer. [20] Taken together, memberships and informal social interaction account for about half the effect of education on volunteering, most of this being attributable to differences in the number of organizational memberships. [30]

Recruitment

Extensive social networks certainly increase exposure to opportunities to volunteer, and for this reason increase the chances we will be asked to volunteer. We will take up the whole issue of volunteer recruitment in chapter 13, but here we are interested only in whether recruitment accounts for some of the association between volunteering and education. Earlier, we suggested that educational credentials make people more attractive targets for volunteer recruiters. The Independent Sector data show that people at the bottom of the educational ladder are more likely to say they do not volunteer because they do not know how to get involved, no one has asked them, and no organization has contacted them. [12] We found that more highly educated people are indeed more likely to be asked to volunteer, providing tentative support for the "ability signaling" theory. [31] Just under a quarter (24%) of high school dropouts were asked to volunteer in the past year, compared to 68 percent of those with advanced degrees.[5] When we added a variable measuring whether the respondent had been asked to volunteer the educational gap narrowed considerably.[6] Compared to people with limited education, the more educated were likely to have been asked by a friend or co-worker and less likely to be asked by a family member. We also found that, the more education people have, the less likely they are to refuse if asked. [32]

The pathway from education to volunteering becomes a little clearer after this analysis of mediating effects. The more education we have the more memberships we have and the more memberships we have the more likely we are to be asked to volunteer, and getting asked to volunteer increases the likelihood we will do so. [33] However, this is not the only pathway from education to volunteering, because highly educated people are also more likely to volunteer than people with limited education, regardless of whether they have been asked.

Income

There are two ways of thinking about the association between income and volunteering. One is to assume that volunteer work imposes costs in the form wages foregone because of absence from paid work: the higher the wages, the higher the costs of volunteering. If actors are rational, the more they earn the less they will volunteer, which means that volunteer hours will be *inversely* related to wages (Romero 1986:31). Another way of thinking about income and volunteering is to treat volunteer work as unpaid productive activity that is costly to perform. Eighteen percent of Illinois residents said they were not more involved in their community because they could not afford the money it takes (Profile of Illinois 2001). When Canadians were asked why they were not volunteering, 30 percent of those earning less than $20,000 a year gave cost as a reason, compared to 10 percent of those earning over $100,000 (Lasby 2004:10). For people on low incomes, the incidental expenses of providing food and other services to people in need (e.g., taking a mentored youth to the zoo), decent clothing, or the costs of transportation can make all the difference between volunteering and not volunteering (Reitsma-Street et al. 2000:665). Even if volunteer work itself is not expensive, it is often channeled through voluntary organizations that expect their members to pay dues and incur other incidental expenses. Nor can we rule out "ability signaling" or status generalization as an explanation of the link between income and volunteering: status signals (e.g., cars, clothing, neighborhoods) associated with higher incomes mean wealthier people are more likely to be the target of recruiters. Finally, income affects interests. Wealthier people have a greater "stake" in a number of the issues that call for volunteer work, from safer neighborhoods to better schools. Volunteer work often brings with it the expectation that you give money as well, and this can be prohibitive for some people. A study of hospice volunteers found that most gave not only their time but also money by, for example, refusing to claim for travel expenses (Field and Johnson 1993:1632). People who volunteer for, or are selected to serve on, boards of trustees of cultural institutions must be able to donate considerable amounts of money to the institution as a prerequisite to being asked. Failure to contribute can be grounds for being asked to leave the board (Ostrower 2002:5). Some kinds of volunteer work, such as lesbian and gay activism, place people at risk of arrest. The costs of being arrested, including raising bail money and missing work, "weight more heavily on working-class and poor people" (Stockdill 2001:212). These arguments imply a *positive* relation between income and volunteering: the more we earn, the more we volunteer.

With only a few limited exceptions, studies of the association between income and volunteering support the second argument outlined above: income and volunteering are positively related (Day and Devlin 1996:47; Menchik and Weisbrod 1987; Smith 1998:29).[7] Although income does have a positive influence on the chances of volunteering, when it comes to how intensively people get involved in their volunteer work, income operates rather differently. Freeman (1997:S152) found a negative relation between wages and volunteer hours among those who were employed. Gallagher (1994b:36) found that income had a positive effect on the number of groups to which elderly people belong, but no effect on the number of hours volunteered overall. Woolley (1998:15) found a curvilinear relation between income and number of hours volunteered: Canadians earning between $20,000 and $39,000 contributed the most hours while more wealthy people contributed no more hours than people on low incomes. These three studies lend somewhat more support to the opportunity cost theory: people earning higher wages are more reluctant to take time off work to volunteer.

The Independent Sector surveys did not gather information on individual income but the income of the household in which the respondent lives. At the zero-order level, household income was positively related to the rate of volunteering. [34] A third (34%) of respondents living in households earning less than $25,000 volunteered in the past year, compared to 63 percent of respondents living in households earning $75,000 or more. Income was also positively related to the number of different domains in which respondents volunteered, and to the number of hours volunteered. Compared to those in the lowest income bracket, middle-income earners ($50,000 to $75,000) volunteered the most hours. People living in households with an income of less than $25,000 made up 38 percent of the sample but contributed only 23 percent of the hours. [1]

Having established that income and volunteering are correlated, we will spend the rest of this section exploring some of the reasons why. In the process, we will also control for a number of socio-demographic and religious variables to better isolate the influence of family income on volunteering.[8]

Social Participation

It is a sociological truism that richer people belong to more voluntary associations, in part because they can better afford the expenses of doing so. This might help explain why they volunteer more. Informal social interaction (casual meetings with friends and neighbors) is less affected by income: the very poorest do not interact informally as much as other income groups, but there is no difference among those other groups. [35] The Independent Sector data confirm that household income and number of memberships are positively related. There are a few exceptions to this rule. People in the middle-income category are the most likely to belong to fraternal orders, political groups, and labor unions; but income has no effect on membership in veterans groups, or on membership in religious groups, at least until the highest income bracket. [29]. As we shall see in chapter 13, people are more likely to volunteer if they are asked, and people in the highest income bracket are more likely to be asked [36]: 32 percent of those with family incomes less than $25,000 had been asked to volunteer in the past year, compared to 60 percent of those with family incomes of $75,000 or more. [37]

In chapter 11 we will show that volunteers tend to belong to more voluntary associations than non-volunteers. Combining this information with our knowledge of the connection between income and being asked, we can envisage a number of different "pathways" from income to volunteering. The first is a direct route. Regardless of memberships and being asked, high-income people are more likely to volunteer. The second is a pathway through memberships to volunteering. Income has a positive effect on memberships that, in turn, has a positive effect on volunteering, regardless of having been recruited. The third is a pathway through being recruited. Regardless of number of memberships, higher income people are more likely to be asked to volunteer, and this explains their higher rate. Finally, it is possible that a pathway exists through memberships and being asked, to volunteering. High-income people are more likely to be members of associations and, for this reason, are more likely to be recruited and, for this reason, they are more likely to volunteer. As complicated as this sounds, it is still a highly simplified representation of all the possible relationships involved, but nevertheless we analyzed the Independent Sector data to see if we could untangle this relationship.

We first estimated a model regressing volunteering in the past year on household income, controlling for all the usual socio-demographic and religious variables. As we expected, income was positively related to volunteering. We then entered a variable measuring memberships. Virtually all the income difference disappeared. We then entered being asked into the model. As shown in Table 1, the income effect became totally insignificant.

Table 1. Estimated Net Effects of Demographics, Association Membership, and Being Asked on Any Volunteering.[1,2]

	Model 1	Model 2	Model 3	Model 4
Demographics				
Female	.25***	.32***	.14*	.20***
Race: Black (a)	−.57***	−.44***	−.44***	−.34***
Hispanic	−.37***	−.26**	−.28**	−.20+
Other race	−.75***	−.60***	−.64***	−.52**
Age: 25–34 years (b)	−.02	.00	−.03	−.02
35–49 years	.11	.05	.10	.07
50–64 years	−.07	−.16	−.05	−.13
65+ years	−.25+	−.36**	−.06	−.15
Socioeconomic Status				
Education: High school (c)	.43***	.39***	.33***	.31***
Some college	1.00***	.79***	.75***	.60***
College graduate	1.47***	1.04***	1.14***	.84***
Post-college	1.85***	1.23***	1.43***	.94***
Income: $25,000–$49,999 (d)	.25***	.14*	.12+	.04
$50,000–$74,999	.30***	.09	.14	−.02
$75,000+	.32***	.05	.09	−.12
Owns home	.18**	.16**	−.01	−.02
Employment Status (e)				
Self-employed full-time	.36***	.29**	.34**	.26*
Self-employed part-time	.59***	.48**	.46*	.42*
Other-employed full-time	−.02	−.05	.01	−.01
Other-employed part-time	.43***	.35***	.37***	.32**
Retired	−.15	−.24*	−.26*	−.31*
Family Status				
Marital Status: Single (f)	.01	.03	−.03	−.02
Divorced/separated	−.04	−.08	−.17	−.19+
Widowed	−.16	−.09	−.20+	−.14
Have kids	.26***	.25***	.18**	.18*
Other Factors				
Religious Service attendance	.55***	.54***	.49***	.48***
Membership number	—	.69***	—	.52***
Asked to Volunteer	—	—	2.67***	2.54***
Intercept	−2.79***	−2.87***	−3.35***	−3.38***
R^2	.20	.26	.40	.42

Notes:

[1] Unstandardized logistic regression coefficients are shown.

[2] Reference categories: (a) Non-Hispanic White; (b) <25 years; (c) <High School; (d) <$25,000; (e) Unemployed; (f) Married.

$p < .05$; ** $p < .01$; *** $p < .001$

In short, income does not exert a direct effect on volunteering. Although it is true that memberships increase volunteering in part by increasing the chances of being asked, they also have a direct effect on volunteering independent of being asked. Income thus generates two partially overlapping links to volunteer work.

If both income and memberships increase the chance of being recruited, the question arises as to whether simply adding more memberships to income will increase the chances even more. Or do more memberships become less significant in the recruitment process as people's earnings increase? Is the relation between income and memberships additive or multiplicative? If it is multiplicative do memberships enhance the power of income or substitute for it? We tested this hypothesis by creating an interaction term for income and memberships to predict being asked. We found that the more memberships people had, the weaker the influence of income on being asked. Income and memberships were, to some degree, acting as substitutes for each other. [38] Low-income people can improve their chances of being recruited by joining a voluntary association—or we can encourage more low-income people to volunteer by inducing them to join a voluntary association.

Finally, we examined the hypothesis that the effect of income on volunteering varies by level of memberships and being asked. [39]. That is, the effect of income does not simply "pass through" memberships and being asked but is changed, or modified, by them. Using interaction terms for income and memberships and income and being asked, we found that, as the number of memberships increased, the positive effect of income decreased, suggesting that memberships were being substituted for income. Perhaps people who are not joiners can "buy" their way into the volunteer role. People who are joiners need less money because they have other, social, resources. In the case of being asked, we found that the positive effect of being asked was stronger for people in the highest income bracket. Targeting a high-income person is more efficient than asking a low-income person.

Moderating Effects of Domain

We noted above that it can be quite expensive to serve as a volunteer on the board of some philanthropic organizations because one is expected to donate handsomely to the cause. This raises the question whether income is more important as a resource for some domains of volunteering than others. Voluntary organizations that rely heavily on financial support from members make it more difficult for poorer people to join and volunteer. Conversely, some voluntary organizations are founded precisely to discount the significance of income in our daily lives. Long-term peace activists, many of whom have advanced degrees, deliberately choose to live "a simple material life as a central feature of their peace careers" (Downton and Wehr 1997:11). Their incomes are much lower than those normally earned by well-educated people. This connection between income and domains of volunteering has rarely been studied. Raskoff and Sundeen (1995) found that income was positively associated only with health and education-related volunteering and had no influence on religious volunteering. In a United Kingdom survey, income was positively related to volunteering in the domains of children's education, sports, religion, and health and social welfare, but poorer people were more likely than rich people to volunteer to help the elderly (Smith 1998:49).

Looking at the Independent Sector data, we found the positive effect of income on volunteering to be fairly consistent across all domains of volunteering. [40] Poor people were always the least likely to volunteer, except in the area of foundations (e.g., breast cancer) where there was no income effect, and public benefit, where income began to make a positive difference only after family income exceeded $75,000. The most common pattern was for people in the middle-income category to volunteer at the highest rate. Volunteering for human services, religion, recreation and the environment are middle class activities: middle-income people are the most likely to volunteer in these areas, followed by the rich.

Moderating Effects of Race and Gender

The reason we should expect racial differences in the effect of income on volunteering is that minority groups are forced to draw on different kinds of resources to enable their community activities than do members of majority groups, amongst whom the standard sorting criteria of education, occupation, and income are most likely to be used to find and recruit volunteers. In an earlier study, we tested this idea using data from the ACL, splitting the sample into Whites and African American respondents and estimating Tobit regression models to see if education and income had the same effect on hours volunteered in the two communities (Musick et al. 2000). Education and income had a positive effect on the number of hours volunteered by Whites. However, these variables had no effect on the volunteer hours of African Americans, for whom frequency of church attendance was a much more powerful predictor of volunteerism.

Given the salience of the volunteer role to women and the fact that households typically rely less on the woman's than the man's earnings, we might expect income to have less influence on volunteering among women than men. However, the evidence on the interaction of gender and income on volunteering is decidedly mixed[9] and in our own analysis of the Independent Sector data we found no interaction effect for gender: income had the same positive effect on men and women.

In light of the fact that volunteer work is a gift of time, not money, it is rather surprising that it has much effect on volunteering at all, especially after controlling for education, gender, race, age, and hours worked for pay. However, we found positive effects for income, at least as far as the chances of having done any volunteer work is concerned, and using a measure of family income. We cannot conclude from these findings that the opportunity cost theory of income and volunteering is wrong because we do not have information on individual income in the Independent Sector data set. It is still possible that volunteer contributions (measured by number of hours) drop off as people begin to earn large salaries: their time simply becomes too valuable. On the other hand, it is questionable whether loss of pay is indeed an opportunity cost of volunteering. It is implausible that the only way working people can find the time to volunteer is by giving up time for paid employment.

Volunteering and Donating Money: Substitutes or Complements?

Prosocial behavior includes donating money as well as giving time. By studying only the association between household income and volunteering we ignore the fact that there are other ways for people to act on their altruistic impulses. Some people might not give much time because they give a lot of money and some people might give a lot of time because they cannot afford to give much money. From a rational choice perspective, money and time can be substituted for each other. Some people say they are not volunteering because they are already giving money, especially if they are older, working full-time, and earning good wages (Lasby 2004:10). Rational choice theory also predicts that the substitution effect varies by level of income. As hourly wages rise, people are more likely to substitute money donations for volunteering because the hours spent volunteering impose higher opportunity costs, whereas the marginal cost of each additional dollar donated is lower: it makes more sense to replace hours volunteered with money donations. Conversely, workers on low wages can ill-afford to make cash donations, but their time is relatively cheap. It makes more sense for them to make their contribution in the form of labor than money. An alternative theory is that time and money are not substitutes at all but instead complement each other: as one increases so does the other. This complementarity theory is intuitively plausible for two reasons: first, some volunteering requires that dues be paid or donations made and it therefore stands to reason they would be associated; second, giving time and money are separate but related indicators of an underlying factor, such as altruism, meaning that a person disposed to volunteer will also respond to appeals for charitable donations.

An analysis of Dutch data largely supports the complementarity theory. Volunteers were more likely to give money than non-volunteers, they gave more often, they gave larger amounts of money, and they gave more as a fraction of their income than non-volunteers. Not surprisingly, the volunteers mainly contributed to charities in the sector in which they were active as volunteers. Multivariate analysis, in which variables that might influence both volunteering and giving were controlled, revealed that only giving something, not the amount, or fraction of income given, was positively related to volunteering. In other words, there is considerable overlap between giving and volunteering, but this is mainly because they are both forms of prosocial behavior stemming from the same set of social factors such as church attendance, income, employment status, and the like (Bekkers 2002).

The Independent Sector data provide information on both donating money and giving time. We use this information to see if giving and volunteering are substitutes or complements. As noted earlier in this chapter, information on donating time is gathered from individuals but the information on giving money pertains to the household. Thus, when we say that, for example, women are more likely to give money than men and to give larger amounts of money, we mean that women reside in households that give more money than the households men reside in. But for the sake of brevity we will refer to the individual. Apart from the gender difference just noted, the primary variable of interest is family income because we would expect more affluent households to donate more money. This is what we find: respondents living in households with incomes over $75,000 a year give four times as much as respondents living in households with less than $25,000 a year in income. Our profile of the person most likely to make donations controls for gender and family income. Givers were older, more highly educated, self-employed working full-time, professional and managerial workers, working in the non-profit sector, married, with children, home owners, frequent churchgoers, and White. [41] Overall, the profile of the respondent who lives in a giving household is quite similar to the profile of a respondent who volunteers.[10]

Given how similar givers and volunteers are, there is little indication that people substitute charitable donations for volunteer work.[11] We confirmed this with further analysis of the Independent Sector data. We regressed volunteering on the odds of giving money in the past year and (among givers only) on the amount of money given, controlling for all our demographic and religious variables. [42] We found a strong positive association between giving money and volunteering. Donating money had about the same effect on volunteering as a post-college education. Of course, when we say "effect" we cannot be sure that giving comes first and volunteering is a consequence. In all likelihood, the relationship between giving and volunteering is reciprocal. Interestingly, the effect of income on volunteering disappeared when we entered the donating variable into the model, suggesting that donating money mediates the effect of income on volunteering. Giving money acts as a conduit to volunteering for upper income people: without it they would be no more likely to volunteer than lower income people.

The ready association between donating money and volunteering suggests there are four types of household in America. In the first (5% of our sample), the respondent volunteers but the household does not give any money. In the second (29%), the household gives but the respondent does not volunteer. In the third (42%), the respondent volunteers and the household gives money. In the fourth (24%), the respondent does not volunteer and the household does not give money. Evidently, it is uncommon for people to volunteer if they do not already give money. Using multinomial regression analysis, we compared the people who neither volunteered nor gave with people in the other three categories. [43] Since we are already familiar with the altruists (those who both give and volunteer) and the uninvolved (those who do neither), the individuals of principal interest were those who volunteer without giving and those who give without volunteering. It is in these two groups we see some evidence of substitution. We found that, compared to those who neither volunteered nor donated, older, childless, single respondents working full-time or not in the labor force with higher incomes and rarely attending church were more likely to *substitute giving for volunteering*. These seem to be the less well-integrated individuals, albeit with higher incomes: if they choose to be altruistic at all, they will opt to give money rather than their time. Compared to those who neither volunteered nor gave, the White, younger, better-educated, low-income, self-employed respondents who were married with children and attended church frequently *substituted volunteering for giving*. These are better-integrated individuals with the freedom and resources necessary to spend time working for others: if they choose to be altruistic at all they will opt for giving their time rather than their money. [41, 44]

Occupation

Penner (2004:649) maintains that the positive effect of income on volunteering has nothing to do with money at all. People with higher incomes are simply less likely to be hourly employees and enjoy more freedom to take time off from their jobs to volunteer. This is a familiar argument and warrants serious consideration. In chapter 7 we will focus on the issue of whether hours spent working for pay limit the number of hours spent volunteering, but Penner is pointing to a rather different issue, which is that some jobs offer more autonomy and self-direction than others, which makes it easier to volunteer. Jobs at the top of the occupational ladder possess a number of desirable attributes in addition to their large salaries, one of which is that people are allowed more discretion over how to manage their time. In this section we will review the evidence bearing on the hypothesis that occupational status influences volunteering.

In modern industrial economies our station in life is largely determined by the kind of job we have. It helps determine how much leisure time we have and how we spend it (Pavalko 1988:296). Sociologists detected a link between occupation and volunteering many years ago. They noticed that volunteerism was more common among "the business class." In their 1925 study of Muncie, Indiana, Lynd and Lynd (1929:460) observed that "the social calling of the certain working class housewives is still not uncommonly 'visiting the sick and needy'," whereas "the more impersonal group methods of giving are . . . diffusing more rapidly among the business class." This is not to say that working class people never volunteered (many would have been active in their churches, fraternal orders, and trade unions) but upper and middle class people, especially women, took upon themselves the responsibility of being community housekeepers. Sociological studies conducted in the 1950s almost always found that middle class people—small business owners, junior managers, self-employed workers, and white-collar workers—volunteered at the highest rate. The most famous depiction of the "business class" during this era, William Whyte's (1957:163) study of "the organization man," described how junior corporate executives, anxious to establish themselves as leadership material, were expected to volunteer, despite the fact that few of them seemed to enjoy it. Other members of the middle class were also more likely to volunteer than blue-collar workers or service workers, especially if their jobs depended on building local networks and a reputation in the community, such as realtors, storeowners, insurance agents, stockbrokers, and bankers (Vidich and Bensman 1960:55). Professionals in the community were also eager to volunteer because they otherwise lacked opportunities to advertise and promote their services. For self-employed lawyers, volunteering was a socially approved method of getting to be known by other members of the community. A "successful attorney" rationalized his volunteer work in this way:

> Professional and business men must look after their own interests, and it would be ridiculous not to recognize this. Insurance men, for example, are certainly interested in publicity, yet it would be unfair to say they are not also interested in the cause. It works both ways. For example, I took it for advertisement purposes. Here in Fabric Town, they have used every new lawyer for drives. It's well known that we work every new lawyer to death in the town, because it is good business. (Sills 1957:92)

In addition, most lawyers, accountants, doctors, and other professionals belonged to associations that required or encouraged members to do volunteer work, as in the pro bono activities expected of lawyers. Many other professionals worked in non-profit settings (e.g., hospitals, churches, colleges, museums) that relied heavily on volunteer labor and where opportunities for volunteer work were abundant.

Although the era of the conformist organization man seems to have passed, business executives continue to feel pressure to volunteer in their community. About two-thirds of the middle-level managers surveyed in the 1980s said their company expected them to participate in community affairs, and just over seven out of ten were currently volunteering, averaging between two and three activities each (Christenson et al. 1988:817). The many economic upheavals of the 1980s and 1990s, as companies downsized, exported jobs abroad, fired white-collar workers, and abandoned communities, encouraged companies to be even more vigorous in promoting volunteer work. There is a certain irony in the fact that Sam Walton, founder of a company alleged to have contributed to the decline of community life, required his managers to join organizations such as the Elks, the Chamber of Commerce, and religious congregations (Zukin 2004:82). These direct pressures to volunteer, however, can be only part of the reason why people in middle class jobs volunteer more because the volunteer rate is extremely high in occupations, such as teaching, where this pressure does not exist. After a review of the more recent data on occupation and volunteering we will consider some of the other reasons why the "long arm of the job" reaches into the world of volunteers.

Almost all social surveys find that professionals and managers volunteer more than blue-collar workers, with white-collar workers somewhere in the middle. This association between occupational status and volunteering is fairly robust, being found in many different surveys in several different countries.[12] Analyzing the data from the 2003 CPS supplement on volunteering, we found that the rate of volunteering in the United States ranged from a high of 57 percent among lawyers and judges and 52 percent among secondary school teachers, to a low of 25 percent among sales workers and 20 percent among construction workers, with managers (45%) and clerical workers (38%) in between. These are, however, zero-order relationships and, as we saw earlier in this chapter, education is positively related to volunteering and this might account for some or all of the difference in volunteering by occupational status.[13] In an earlier study, we looked at the association between occupational status and volunteering in the United States (Wilson and Musick 1997b). Initially, we found blue-collar workers volunteered for fewer activities than professional, managerial, or sales and clerical workers, but after we controlled for education, the difference between blue-collar workers and sales and clerical workers disappeared, although professionals and managers continued to volunteer at a higher rate. Analyzing the Independent Sector data, we found that professionals comprise a quarter of all the employed people in the sample but contribute 40 percent of the hours volunteered by employed people. Managers and clerical workers contribute roughly in proportion to their numbers in the employed population. Blue-collar workers comprise 43 percent of the employed sample but contribute only a quarter of the volunteer hours. [1] When we controlled for the usual socio-demographic and religious variables we found a linear effect of occupational status: *the higher the status, the higher the rate of volunteering*. Only in the religious domain was occupational status unrelated to the likelihood of volunteering. [45]

Job Quality and Volunteering

We mentioned a number of reasons why occupational status and volunteering might be related. For example, managers and professionals volunteer more because their careers might well depend on it. But this is not the only reason why volunteering is more common in these occupational groups. Managers and professionals do different kinds of work than clerical and manual workers. Sociologists have long been interested in these differences and their consequences for life outside the workplace. Most agree that there is "spillover" from paid work to non-work roles (Staines 1980) in which the more agreeable traits of the higher status occupations lead to leisure time pursuits that are more active, creative, and rewarding.[14]

More recently, the argument has been put forward that higher status jobs encourage volunteering because they are more likely to teach "civic skills" such as being able to write letters, plan meetings, give speeches and presentations, and make strategic decisions. The theory is that civic skills learned and used on the job are directly transferable to many forms of civic engagement, such as working on a political campaign, lobbying, participating in a protest or demonstration, doing informal community work, serving on a board or leadership committee, and helping out with a political organization (Verba et al. 1995). If this is true, occupations act as a powerful sorting mechanism because high status jobs "provide more by way of participation-enhancing experiences than do lower-level jobs" (Schlozman et al. 1999:37). This explanation of the link between job and volunteering does not refer to self-interest, as does the argument that managers volunteer because they are pressured to do so, nor to social psychological factors, such as efficacy, but to individual resources: professionals and managers simply have more of the individual attributes volunteer work demands and it is thus less costly for them to do it.

Studies linking higher occupational status with civic skills do not, by themselves, establish that it is the quality of the job that provides these skills. Do managers and professionals acquire more civic skills on their job because those jobs provide more autonomy and self-direction? In an earlier study, we took data from two panels of Americans' Changing Lives (1986 and 1989) to test this hypothesis. We constructed a volunteer index for both years. Respondents were asked whether they volunteered for any of the following types of organization: religious, school, political or labor, elderly, other. The index summed the total, thus providing a range of 0–5 for each year. We measured self-direction on the job using the *Dictionary of Occupational Titles* to rate occupations on a number of characteristics: freedom from supervision, lack of routinization, and the substantive complexity of the job. By regressing 1989 volunteer level on 1986 volunteer level and 1986 self-direction we were able to determine the effect of 1986 occupation on 1989 volunteering net of 1986 volunteer level and thus be fairly confident that occupation is "causing" volunteering rather than the other way around. The results confirmed the importance of self-direction on the job. The more self-direction respondents enjoyed on the job, the more volunteer activities they were involved in. Strikingly, this was true regardless of their occupation, the sector in which they worked, or their level of education (Wilson and Musick 1997b:264). Of course, we could not tell from this analysis alone whether self-directed jobs taught people more civic skills because the ACL did not measure them. We then turned to the Citizen Participation Survey conducted by Verba et al. (1995). That survey did not measure self-direction on the job, but it did include proxy measures. The first asked respondents to estimate the amount of education required for their job. The second asked them how much on-the-job training was required for their job. Both measures were highly correlated with self-direction. The survey also asked respondents if they had been "active" in voluntary associations. We treated this as a proxy of volunteer work. Our analysis revealed a positive association between the proxy measure of self-direction and the proxy measure of volunteering, thus partially replicating the analysis of the ACL data. We then entered the measure of civic skills into the model, whereupon the effect of the proxy measure of self-direction on volunteering became weaker, indicating that self-direction has a positive effect on volunteering because it enhances civic skills (Wilson and Musick 1997b:267).[15]

Social Networks and Being Recruited as Mediators

Another theory to help explain the positive association between occupational status and volunteering is that people with high status jobs, such as professionals and managers, belong to more voluntary associations and have more extensive social networks. They do more volunteer work because they are more socially integrated. Our analysis of the Independent Sector data refuted this notion. Higher status people are indeed more socially integrated—they belong to more voluntary associations and they do spend more time in many kinds of informal social interaction—but this does not explain why they volunteer more. [46] Simply having more extensive social networks does not give professionals and managers any kind of advantage when it comes to volunteering. What does make a difference is being recruited—and high status workers are more likely than low status workers to be asked by someone to volunteer their time. Recruitment accounted for close to half the volunteer gap between managers and blue-collar workers and about a fifth of the gap between professionals and blue-collar workers. [47] This analysis does not close the door on the issue of occupation, networks, and volunteering because the measure of social networks in the Independent Sector survey is far from adequate. Perhaps a more accurate measure would reveal a more definitive role for social networks.

Job Satisfaction and Volunteering

Professional and managerial jobs are more intrinsically rewarding and, as a result, job satisfaction tends to be higher among people who fill them (Pavalko 1988:208). Job satisfaction might therefore be the link between occupational status and volunteering. People who are satisfied with their jobs might well have a more positive outlook on the world and a greater disposition to volunteer to help others in need. An alternative theory is that people who are dissatisfied with their job look elsewhere for the satisfactions rewarding work is supposed to provide. They choose volunteer work as a compensation for having an unsatisfactory job.

Although the link between occupational status and job satisfaction is fairly well established, we know much less about the link between job satisfaction and volunteering. Occasionally, studies find that people find rewards in their volunteer work they are denied in their everyday job. For example, emergency squad volunteers liked their work precisely because it was voluntary and not something they *had* to do. They enjoyed the relative freedom from "the boss" and the fact they were entrusted with serious responsibilities. In some respects, their volunteer work was a surrogate form of upward mobility. More of the blue-collar volunteers thought of themselves as professionals when executing their emergency squad duties than did volunteers who actually were professionals (Gora and Nemerowicz 1985:88). Through their service, they were able to take pride in their work, which was denied them in their real job. It is not clear how much we can generalize from this one study. The MIDUS data showed that job satisfaction had no influence on volunteering for men. However, the women in the sample volunteered more hours if they were dissatisfied with their job (Rossi 2001e:454). Like the EMS volunteers, they may have been looking to volunteer work to provide them with satisfaction their job denied them. We explored this issue further by analyzing the ACL data from 1986. We found a positive relation between job satisfaction and volunteering, thus contradicting the Rossi findings, but the relationship was very weak, and it disappeared when we introduced a control for life satisfaction, which was much more strongly associated with volunteering. [48] This analysis casts some doubt on the theory that job satisfaction, in particular, has any influence on volunteering. One does not need to be satisfied with one's job to feel like volunteering, merely satisfied with life in general.

Occupational Status and Volunteer Domain

Up this point, we have focused on whether or not people in different occupations volunteer at all, largely ignoring what people volunteer for. But few people decide to volunteer in general; rather, they decide to volunteer for a particular organization or cause. These volunteer choices might well be influenced by the kind of job they have. A number of studies have demonstrated class differences in volunteer preferences. Members of the upper class favor ameliorative volunteer projects devoted mainly to community preservation and individual welfare, largely working within the system, without defining problems as having a structural foundation or calling for radical social change. Their goal is more likely to be one of solving community problems by fund-raising and donating time and money to local programs and agencies. This is quite apparent in a study of members of "The International Association of Women" (a pseudonym for the Junior League), an American organization intended to develop its members' potential for community service and leadership (Markham and Bonjean 1995). The membership was definitely WASP: only 2 percent of the members belonged to a racial minority and only 2 percent were Jewish. Only 1 percent had not gone to college and household incomes were far above average. The few women who were employed had prestigious jobs. For the homemakers, their social class was determined by the high status jobs of their husbands. Members were asked to rate the importance of a number of problems in their communities. Three issues, involving children and education, were rated as the most important, with adolescent issues, criminal justice, and substance abuse following close behind. Ranked low in importance were issues such as citizens' involvement in politics, urban revitalization, race and ethnic relations, adult mental health, aging, and the environment. Social problems requiring political action and social re-structuring or increases in government spending and higher taxes received scant attention. The women showed remarkably strong consensus on the definition and salience of these issues. Socialization by the organization accounted for some of this consensus but it was more likely the result of careful selection of new members. Women did not choose, nor were they selected, to volunteer for this organization unless their ideas about the volunteer role and the function of volunteerism in the community coincided with an upper class ideology of community housekeeping. Their elite status imposed a strong obligation to volunteer but within a strictly limited set of philanthropic activities. They avoided the "hands-on" type of volunteer work providing services directly to the needy and focused instead on making this service possible for others to provide by fund-raising or on volunteer work, such as fostering the arts, intended to "civilize" the life of the community. Their superior status made them uncomfortable with acting in a serving role. Working in a thrift shop was allowed only because the client was a customer and not necessarily a needy person (Daniels 1988:221).

Two other studies also suggest that occupational status makes a difference to the kind of volunteer work people do. In the United Kingdom, professional and managerial workers were more likely than any other occupational group to work through formal groups to take political actions, but the "petty bourgeoisie" (self-employed artisans, shopkeepers, small businessmen) were far less likely. As "individualists" they preferred person-to-person service provision, especially helping people improve themselves (Parry et al. 1992:218). Wuthnow (1998:106) describes middle class suburbanites as being drawn more toward service provision than social activism: "they are capable of insulating themselves from serious social problems, and they are reluctant to favor social programs that might benefit others at expense to themselves—they are generally in favor of cutting welfare, public expenditures, food stamps and legal aid."

Even within the same profession, occupational rank determines the kind of work volunteers do. Heinz and Schnorr (2001:610) describe two lawyers, both busy volunteers, but occupying very different rungs on the ladder of advancement within the profession.

The two respondents reporting the most extensive participation in voluntary associations were both white, male, senior partners in major downtown firms, and both had high incomes. One was 59 years old, the other was 65. Both were Episcopalians. One did undergraduate work at the University of Chicago and then law school at Yale, while the other went to Yale first and then the University of Michigan Law School. Both did corporate litigation. One reported activity in the Episcopal Church, the Republican National Committee, three country clubs, two traditional, downtown "men's clubs," the boards of two private secondary schools, and the board of a major museum (of which he had formerly been the chairman). The other reported activity in the Democratic Party of Cook County, five downtown social clubs, his law school's alumni association, two civic organizations, and four major cultural and arts institutions. These are, of course, quite exceptional cases. Another respondent with a high level of activity presents a different profile: a solo practitioner with a relatively low income, age 46, he attended De Paul Law School, represented individuals and a few small businesses, and did primarily criminal defense, consumer bankruptcy, landlord-tenant, probate, and "general family practice." He reported activity as an officer of an independent political organization, an adviser to a Hispanic community group, past president of the local Kiwanis club, a member of the local public school council, a member of a school reform organization, and a member of a Methodist congregation. Another example is a practitioner in a small firm, age 43, who attended Chicago Kent Law School, had a moderate income, and reported doing a mixture of personal and business litigation, including criminal defense, probate, some personal injury plaintiffs' work, and residential real estate transactions. He said that 25 percent of his clients were businesses and that 90 percent of those businesses were small. His activities were in his parish of the Catholic Church, the Holy Name Society (of which he had been an officer), the Democratic Party ward organization, the nominating committee of his children's parochial school, an organization assisting the disabled, and the Irish Fellowship Club. While the character of the patterns of participation of these respondents differ, all of them had unusually high levels of activity.

Unfortunately, it is not possible to examine the association between occupational status and type of volunteer work in this amount of detail with survey data, but by sorting the types of activity listed in the Independent Sector surveys into five domains, it is possible to see if the positive effect of being a professional or manager is robust across all types of volunteering. [45] The domains are advocacy (environment, political, public benefit, foundation, international, and work-related); education (arts and education); human services (health, social services); youth development (recreation, youth development); and religion. Professionals and managers are more likely to volunteer than blue-collar workers *only* in advocacy, education, and human services. (The occupational effect was strongest in educational volunteering, even though we control for education.) Clerical workers were more likely to volunteer than blue-collar workers *only* in education, human services, and youth development. Occupational status made no difference to the odds of volunteering for religion. Clearly, occupational status functions as a resource for some kinds of volunteering much better than others.

Sector

The differential influence of occupational status, depending on domain, is a subject that deserves much more exploration. Whatever advantage high occupational status gives, it does not "count" in many cases. We cannot leave the subject of occupational status, however, without discussing the role played by sector in shaping the volunteer labor supply. Sector is a measure of where occupations are located in the economy. The same occupation can be located in very different economic environments: a physician serving in the military is working under very different conditions from a physician working for a drug company, and both are different from a physician working alone in a private practice who is, essentially, self-employed. By sector we mean whether the job is located in the public sector (national, regional, or local), the non-profit sector, or the private sector. Self-employed workers are treated as a separate category.

Public Sector

Public sector workers are likely to volunteer more than private sector workers, regardless of their occupation, for a number of reasons. Public servants have different ideas about the duties of citizenship, different values and interests. They are more skeptical of the efficiency and effectiveness of market solutions to social problems (Macy 1988:347). They place a high priority on helping others and being useful to society (Norris 2004:18), and they attach more importance to humanitarian values, express stronger support for social equality, and are more tolerant (Brewer 2003). Whereas private sector workers tend to be motivated by extrinsic factors, such as money, public sector workers tend to be motivated by intrinsic factors, such as providing a service or helping others (Cacioppe and Mock 1984). In short, whether it is a result of self-selection or socialization on the job, public sector workers have different values and attitudes from private sector workers, differences that potentially affect their level and manner of civic engagement.

Cultural differences are not the only reason to expect public sector workers to volunteer more than private sector workers. Public sector workers belong to more civic groups and are more engaged in those groups (Brewer 2003; Reinarman 1987). Many work in areas, such as education, health care, employment assistance and re-training, welfare, public safety, and the like, where individual needs for assistance—and the inability of either state or market to meet these needs—is impressed upon them daily. Their agencies often work in conjunction with non-profit organizations and religious congregations that rely heavily on volunteer labor to meet their obligations. Quite aside from any differences in values, a woman who works as a social worker in the local juvenile justice system is more aware of volunteer opportunities than a man who repairs automobiles for a living.[16]

Non-profit Sector

Although some of the studies cited above group non-profit and public sector workers together, or ignore the non-profit sector altogether, it is quite an important part of modern industrial economies and appears to be growing. In 2001, 12.5 million Americans were employed in the non-profit sector, comprising 9.5 percent of the total labor force in the United States (Independent Sector Nonprofit Almanac). More people worked for a non-profit organization than for the federal and state governments combined. Non-profit sector workers express strong support for altruistic values and are, by virtue of their jobs, exposed to many more opportunities to volunteer than workers in similar occupations in the private sector. According to one survey, half of the non-profit sector workers had volunteered in the previous twelve months, compared to 36 percent of the public sector workers and 20 percent of the private sector workers (Wuthnow 1994b).

Self-Employment

People who work for themselves often have jobs identical to those who work for someone else, such as plumber, physician, beautician, or tax accountant. But economists and sociologists usually treat self-employed people as a different "class of worker" because the context in which they perform those jobs is so different. Being their own boss, they have more control over their work schedules. Thompson (1993a) found that a disproportionate number of the EMS volunteers he surveyed were self-employed. He attributed this partly to their flexible schedules.[17]

In the 2002 CPS special supplement on volunteering, non-profit sector workers contributed the most hours a year (68) followed by state government workers (55), local government workers (55), federal government workers (54), the self-employed (53), and private sector workers (28). Non-profit sector workers contribute more time because they are more likely to volunteer in the first place. Among volunteers, it was federal employees who contributed the most hours (161), followed by non-profit sector workers (148), self-employed (139), state government (135), local government (127), and private sector workers (109). The pattern is clear: private sector workers not only are less likely to volunteer, they contribute fewer hours if they do so. In an extended analysis of these data, Rotolo and Wilson (2006b), found that non-profit sector workers are the most likely to volunteer and volunteer the most hours, followed by local government workers, state government workers, the self-employed, federal employees, and private sector workers.[18] The sector differences did not vary significantly by domain of volunteering.

We also analyzed the Independent Sector data to examine the relation between sector and volunteering. Compared to the private sector, the highest rate of volunteering occurred in the non-profit sector, followed by the public sector and self-employment. Among employed respondents, non-profit workers comprised 7 percent of the sample but contributed 14 percent of the hours. Public sector workers comprised 15 percent of the sample but contributed 23 percent of the hours. Conversely, private sector workers contributed 52 percent of the hours, despite comprising 66 percent of the employed respondents in the sample. [1] These sector differences remained after we controlled for socio-demographic and religious variables: compared to private sector workers, non-profit sector workers were the most likely to volunteer, followed by public sector workers and the self-employed. [45] This pattern of results, consistent across two studies using different social surveys, clearly indicates that non-profit workers, who often accept lower wages in order to work in the sector, do not treat this as a substitute for volunteering. Likewise, public sector workers, who are in some respects already public servants, do not rest on their laurels but instead also volunteer their time to serve the common good.

Sector, Recruitment, and Volunteering

The argument that public and non-profit sector jobs encourage volunteering rests partly on the premise that private sector workers are less likely to be recruited. If this were true, more public and non-profit sector workers should say they had been asked to volunteer than workers in other sectors. We tested this theory using the Independent Sector data. Being recruited partly mediated sector effects in the case of public and non-profit sector workers and the effect of being self-employed disappeared altogether with being asked in the model. [47] In short, sector determines the structure of opportunities to volunteer, principally by increasing the likelihood of being recruited for volunteer work.

Occupation and Sector Combined

The insight provided by sector theory is that jobs vary in their nature (and consequences) depending on the context in which they are performed. Thus far we have treated occupation and sector as if they were separate pathways to volunteer work, but by combining occupation and sector we get a more accurate picture of the influence of each on volunteering. Jobs do not exist independent of the sector in which they are located, while sectors are made up of different kinds of jobs (e.g., there are more professionals in the public sector than the private sector). Thus, while professionals in general might volunteer more than blue-collar workers we do not know if professionals in the private sector are inhibited from volunteering by the for-profit nature of the sector in which they work. In an earlier study we compared blue-collar workers in the private sector (who volunteered for the fewest activities) with other occupation-sector combinations, controlling for education. The data we used do not separate non-profit workers from public sector workers and we cannot therefore make this distinction but, compared to private sector blue-collar workers, professionals in the public sector (including school teachers) volunteered the most, followed by self-employed managers, private sector managers, public sector managers, private sector professionals, and sales and clerical workers in the public sector (Wilson and Musick 1997b:264). There were no other differences. The influence of occupation therefore proved to be fairly robust across sectors, although sector did make *some* difference within occupation, as with the fact that professionals in the public sector volunteer for a wider range of activities than professionals in the other sectors.

We repeated the analysis described in the preceding paragraph, using the Independent Sector data. On this occasion we were able to isolate non-profit sector workers. Once again, we compared all other occupation-sector combinations with blue-collar workers in the private sector, who volunteered for the fewest activities. The self-employed professionals volunteer for the broadest range of activities, followed by non-profit clerical workers, public sector managers, non-profit professionals, public sector professionals, self-employed managers, and private sector managers. Despite the addition of the non-profit sector to this analysis, the broad pattern of results is the same as that found in our earlier study, in that professionals and managers volunteer for more activities. Sector does not disturb this major fault line. However, there are some instances where sector has made a difference; for example, by increasing the incidence of volunteering of clerical workers in the non-profit sector. [49] In short, we believe that both sector and occupational status make a difference to volunteering, although they seem to do so additively—each contributing to part of the explanation. There is little evidence of a multiplicative relation between them whereby one variable amplifies the effect of the other.

In conclusion, the "long arm of the job" has fascinated sociologists for many years. Despite the tendency to think of volunteer work as a leisure time pursuit it is profoundly affected by the way people earn their living. Certain jobs instill self-confidence, teach civic skills, encourage prosocial values, act as status markers (recall the description of the two lawyers), and often bring with them strong normative pressures to be active in the community. Such jobs are conducive to volunteer work and can be contrasted with occupations in which jobs are typically tedious, boring, insecure, and in which work discourages active leisure time pursuits and encourages a focus on the short-term needs of the immediate family. As a result, volunteers are not randomly distributed across the occupational spectrum. Volunteering remains a largely middle class pursuit, if middle class is measured by belonging to the professional and managerial ranks, and this is not due to the superior educational credentials of workers in those ranks. Some of this difference is probably due to the skills people need to have and acquire in the performance of jobs in those occupational categories and some of it has to do with the social integration of professionals and managers in the organizational life of their communities.

7

Time and Health

In this chapter we review the arguments that free time and good health are resources that make it easier for people to volunteer or, to put this somewhat differently, lack of free time and poor health increase the costs of volunteering.

Free Time and Volunteering

It is natural to suppose that people are more likely to volunteer if they have free time available. In this section of the chapter we will look at how paid work time influences time spent volunteering. We will then look at the influence of other time commitments on volunteering, such as housework. People commonly cite shortage of time as a reason for not volunteering. For most adults, what they do for a living is their primary role in life, rivaled only by family responsibilities; the volunteer role is secondary. Few of us can afford to put volunteering ahead of earning a living. When people are asked, "What are the biggest barriers to your being more involved in your local community?" they most often cite lack of time. In one study, 30 percent blamed long work hours, odd work shifts, and frequent work-related travel for their failure to volunteer (Profile of Illinois 2001). Over half (58%) of respondents in a United Kingdom survey who were not volunteering said they did not have the time (Smith 1998:140). Three-quarters of Canadians surveyed gave lack of time as the main reason for not volunteering more (Hall et al. 1998:37). Even retirees, who might be expected to have more time to volunteer, cite lack of time as one reason for not volunteering and for not volunteering more—although for people in this age group, health concerns and family obligations are also important (Bass and Caro 2001:44).

Of course, citing lack of time might simply be a convenient excuse for not volunteering, but it is significant that people who are most likely to be short of time are the most likely to give this reason. The Canadians most likely to say they cannot volunteer because they lack the time are young to middle aged adults working full-time (Hall et al. 2001:15). Almost twice as many employed Americans wish they had more time to volunteer than unemployed and retired persons (Kohut 1997:12). When we looked at the reasons for not volunteering during the previous twelve months given by respondents in the Independent Sector surveys we found that full-time workers were almost twice as likely to mention lack of time as those without jobs. [52] The time squeeze theory, whereby work time squeezes out volunteer time, is even more convincing when data can be cited showing that volunteers who try to combine volunteer work with paid work feel more pressured. Goss (1999:393) found that volunteers feel more "hassled" than non-volunteers. A Canadian survey found that volunteers were more likely than non-volunteers to say their work hours are too demanding (Gomez and Gunderson 2003). In short, there is abundant evidence that most people see volunteer work as demanding a commitment of time from them and that some feel less able to make this commitment than others. People who try to combine jobs and volunteer work are also more likely to report time pressures than people who have jobs and do not volunteer or people who volunteer and do not have jobs.

It is one thing to say that people who, by objective standards, have less free time are more likely to give shortage of time as an excuse for not volunteering and another to predict that shortage of time actually leads people to cut back on their volunteer hours. Having a paid job might well impose extra time demands on us, but it also takes us out into the community, expanding our circle of acquaintances and thereby increasing the chances of us learning about volunteer opportunities or being asked to do volunteer work. A 2000 survey of Illinois residents found that 38 percent of the employees worked at companies that sponsored a community project for which they were encouraged to volunteer; 28 percent worked at companies that gave incentives or recognition to employees who volunteer; and a quarter worked at companies that gave money to the organizations for which they volunteered (Profile of Illinois 2001). A focus group member described how he had been recruited at work: "Well, actually the deputy chief came up to me and asked me if I wanted to volunteer for [the Citizens Police Academy] or if I would put the time into it, so I did it" (Profile 2001).[1]

Even if we are not pressured to volunteer by our work colleagues, there are other reasons to be skeptical of the idea that holding down a job makes it more difficult for us to volunteer. People's time can be elastic if they are sufficiently motivated to take on a number of tasks. The relationship between work hours and free time is not zero-sum. For every additional hour of paid work, only half an hour of free time is surrendered, and "even less as the estimated workweek goes beyond 50 hours" (Robinson and Godbey 1997:194). Another reason to be skeptical of the time squeeze theory is suggested by the old adage: "if you need a volunteer ask a busy person." Volunteers might well simply be highly active people who happen to have lots of energy and good time-management skills. It is not necessary for them to choose between working for pay and volunteering because they find a way to fit both activities into their day. This could explain why teenagers who have part-time jobs while in school are *more* likely to volunteer than those without a job (Ladd 1999:74; Sundeen and Raskoff 1994:394). It is difficult to believe this behavior is the result of recruitment in the workplace, considering the kinds of jobs teenagers usually get while in school. It is more likely to indicate that some students like to be busy and find ways to achieve this goal despite the time pressures involved. In summary, whereas the time squeeze theory predicts that work hours and volunteer hours are inversely related—as the former go up, the latter go down—a social integration theory predicts a positive relationship—people with jobs volunteer more than people without them.

In this section we review the evidence on the relation between work hours and volunteer hours and add some analyses of our own. The social integration theory receives considerable support from one of the most consistent of the findings in the research on volunteer work, which is that part-time employees volunteer at a higher rate than people without jobs (Johnson et al. 2004:61; Robinson and Godbey 1997:174; Vaillancourt 1994:820). In the 2000 Canadian survey on volunteering, a third of part-time workers volunteered, compared to 27 percent of full-time workers, a quarter of unemployed workers, and 24 percent of those not in the labor force (retirees, homemakers, students) (Lasby 2004:3). The 2005 Current Population Survey (CPS) of volunteering found that 38.2 percent of part-time workers had volunteered in the past twelve months, compared to 29.8 percent of full-time workers, and 24.4 percent of those not in the labor force (U.S. Bureau of Labor Statistics 2005:2).[2]

People with jobs are thus more likely to volunteer, especially if those jobs are part-time. But this tells us nothing about the influence of work hours on the number of hours contributed to volunteer work. The 2005 CPS survey found that the median hours volunteered by part-time workers was fifty-one, compared to forty-five for full-time workers and sixty-two for those not in the labor force (U.S. Bureau of Labor Statistics 2005). In short, part-time workers might well be the most likely to volunteer (i.e., they volunteer at the highest rate) but they do not necessarily contribute the most hours, which are donated by people with the most free time.[3]

Up this point we have reported only bivariate associations between work hours and volunteering. This does not take into consideration the fact that work hours are correlated with other factors that also influence volunteering, such as education, marital and parental status, and physical health. In a multivariate study of Canadian data with controls for these variables, full-time workers volunteered at a *lower* rate than those not in the labor force (Ravanera et al. 2002). Oesterle et al. (2004:1140) report similar results: each additional month spent working full-time lowers the odds of volunteering by 4 percent.[4]

The multivariate studies thus indicate that full-time work is an impediment to volunteering, and thereby support the time squeeze theory, but they do not distinguish between working the standard forty-hour week and working overtime, which, as we shall see, is an important distinction to make. In an earlier study we found that, among those who worked forty hours a week or more, the relation between work hours and volunteer hours was positive— the more hours they worked the more they volunteered (Wilson and Musick 1997b). The tendency for people who spend fifty or sixty hours a week at work to volunteer more than people who work the standard forty-hour week contradicts the time squeeze theory. Freeman (1997:S156), an economist, attributes this to differences in taste, ability, and energy between people who work the standard work week and people who regularly work longer hours, but he presents no evidence to support this assertion. More plausible explanations are that the business and occupational pressures to volunteer we described above weigh most heavily on workers, such as business executives and lawyers, who traditionally work long hours. Jobs that demand long hours also compensate by permitting the flexible scheduling of work, whereas the full-time worker, punching in a regular forty hours a week, has a job that is closely supervised, tightly scheduled, and physically demanding. In short, to some degree, the effect of work hours is an artifact of unmeasured attributes of the jobs that correspond with work hours.

Our analysis of the Independent Sector data largely confirms the results of previous studies (these data do not permit us to study extended-time workers). The rate of volunteering in the past month ranged from 26 percent among retirees and 29 percent among those not working to 37 percent among full-time employees and 45 percent among part-time employees and self-employed full-time workers, to a high of 50 percent among self-employed part-time workers. However, as above, we found no zero-order difference in the range of different volunteer activities or the mean number of hours volunteered in the past month. In our multivariate analysis we controlled for socio-demographic variables and church attendance, looking at the effect of work hours on the rate, range, and hours of volunteering. We used as our comparison group those not reporting any work hours at all and we controlled for retirement status. The pattern for *rate* and *range* was exactly the same as the zero-order effects: part-time workers (both self-employed and employees) and self-employed full-time workers were more likely to volunteer than those not in the labor force. Full-time employees had the same volunteer rate and range as those not working: apparently, some work is good, but too much work is bad. The pattern for hours volunteered during the past month (among those who volunteered during the past month) was different. [21] Part-time workers donated no more hours than people without jobs. Full-time workers did, however, contribute fewer hours than people not in the labor force. In summary, having a job increases the likelihood we will do *some* volunteer work but the number of hours we work for pay determines how much of that volunteer work we do. In this respect, work hours are a deterrent to volunteering, because part-time workers contribute more hours than full-time workers. One reason is that part-time workers are more likely to be asked to volunteer, perhaps because the recruiter knows they have more time to spare. [20, 21] Part-time workers are ideally placed to do volunteer work: they have a job and are therefore more socially integrated than the unemployed or housewives, but their job does not demand so much of their time that they cannot respond to invitations to volunteer. It is worth repeating that our analysis of the Independent Sector data cannot distinguish between people who work the standard workweek and those who regularly put in longer hours, and therefore it provides only a partial picture of the relationship.

Unemployment

People who report zero work hours can do so for two main reasons. The first is that they are not in the labor force and have no wish to enter it, they have some impediment that prevents them from working, they are retired, or they are in school or college full-time. Another reason is they are unemployed. In social surveys, people currently without a job but actively searching for one are considered unemployed. We discovered earlier that people without jobs are less likely to volunteer but contribute more hours if they do. The question naturally arises as to whether this is equally true of these people who have made a decision not to be part of the labor force and the unemployed, who would like to join it. Unemployed people might volunteer less because their job search time prevents committing to volunteer work, or they might be constrained by government regulations concerning unemployment benefits.[5] Another reason why unemployed people might be discouraged from volunteering is that being without a job is a stigmatized status and damaging to self-esteem. Joblessness, especially for a long period of time, can be a very dispiriting and socially isolating experience. Unemployment also tends to encourage social isolation. Not only does the person not meet with workmates on the job, he or she is likely to lose touch with those people outside the workplace. Unemployment also means a loss of income and makes it more difficult to travel and pay the expenses of belonging to clubs and associations for which volunteer work might be expected. In a United Kingdom survey the unemployed were more likely to say they were not volunteering because no one had asked them or they lacked information, transportation, or money to pay expenses (Goddard 1994:7). Unemployed Canadians are more likely to say they do not volunteer because it costs too much (Lasby 2004:10).

An alternative theory is that unemployed people find volunteer work especially attractive. They are searching for new jobs and might therefore have an additional incentive to maintain or improve job skills or obtain access to paying jobs by volunteering on a temporary basis, getting a foot in the door. As one unemployed person told Australian researchers, "When I started [volunteering] I was hoping for some casual work but now I am enjoying it and look forward to going every week" (Flick et al. 2002:61). Volunteering can also be a way of coping with being out of a job. For many people who have been working all their lives becoming unemployed means their life has little structure, there is not much to occupy their days. Another unemployed Australian told the researchers:

> I was bored witless at home and to me volunteer work was really meals on wheels . . . . . . It was really about stimulation from my standpoint. (Flick 2002:61)

For other people, losing their jobs is a mixed blessing. While it does mean a loss of income it also brings free time to do what they always wanted to do. McDonald (1997:23) describes the attitude of unemployed working class women in England to their volunteer work: "For them, voluntary working was not a bourgeois pastime of 'good works' for the poor and needy, but rather stemmed from experience of caring for families which, now their families placed fewer demands on them and employment had ceased, became translated into care for others." In some respects, unemployed people are like retirees. They feel the loss of a regular, productive job and they are looking for something to replace it, if only temporarily. A woman who had been laid off at age 56 and unable to get another job told McDonald (1996:23),

> My son says "why can't you relax, Mum, and just retire?" But it's difficult when you've been busy bringing up a family and working full-time. Your whole nature is geared up to the pressure of working. I need something to occupy my time.

Undoubtedly, some unemployed people volunteer in order to make social contacts, gain new job skills, build up resumes, all in preparation for a return to the labor force, but they also volunteer to structure their time, maintain social contacts, and buttress their self-esteem. One unemployed volunteer told McDonald (1996:26),

> This isn't a job. A job is paid employment. I don't mind doing this and getting nothing for it. It's better than sitting on me backside at home. You're helping people. It's personal satisfaction. Doing something right. So it's work experience and it's good for a reference.

Survey data from the United Kingdom show that unemployed people have the lowest volunteer rates, especially men, and the longer they have been unemployed the less likely are they to volunteer (Goddard 1994:7; Haezewindt 2002:23; Smith 1998:334). In Canada the volunteer rate for employed people in 2000 was 28 percent, compared to 25 percent among the unemployed (Hall et al. 2001:34). The 2003 CPS special supplement on volunteering showed that 26.7 percent of the unemployed in the United States had volunteered in the past year, compared to 31.2 percent of the employed and 24.6 percent of those not in the labor force. If the unemployed do volunteer, their extra free time would suggest that they could contribute more hours than people with jobs, but the evidence is somewhat mixed. In the United States, unemployed volunteers contribute the same number of hours a year as employed volunteers (U.S. Bureau of Labor Statistics 2003:2). In Holland and Australia, unemployed volunteers contribute more time than employed volunteers (Australian Bureau of Statistics 2002; De Hart and Dekker 1999:86), while in Canada they contribute less time (Hall et al. 2001:34; Woolley 1998:25).

Women are more likely than men to volunteer if unemployed: a third of unemployed American women volunteered in 2002, compared to a fifth of the unemployed men (U.S. Bureau of Labor Statistics 2003:2).[6] In the 2000 Canadian National Survey of Giving, Volunteering and Participating, while 25.3 percent of the total sample had volunteered in the previous year, only 19.7 percent of the unemployed males but 30.4 percent of the unemployed females had volunteered (Ravanera et al. 2002). In Australia, unemployed females volunteer at a rate of 34 percent, compared to 22 percent for unemployed males (Australian Bureau of Statistics 2002). The reasons for this gender difference are not clear at this time. Women might be more ready to see volunteer work as an alternative career and they might spend less time searching for other jobs. Men might feel more stigmatized by unemployment and are less willing to take on unpaid jobs as a substitute.

In light of these analyses, we should be careful when using labor force status to predict volunteer behavior. The conventional distinction between full-time and part-time work is clearly useful, but working zero hours can mean quite different things depending on whether the respondent would like to return to the labor force and whether the respondent is male or female.

Work Hours and Volunteer Domain

Up to this point, we have disregarded the fact that there are many types of volunteer work and that organizations structure their volunteer commitments in very different ways. Many volunteer opportunities are explicitly connected to workplace or professional issues, and people outside the labor force cannot take advantage of them or have no interest in doing so. Having a job also changes people's interests in political and social issues, which in turn alters their volunteer preferences. Burns et al. (2001:323) found that, among college-educated, married women with school age children, those who had jobs were more likely to be involved in community politics than women without jobs, but when it came to working for the PTA or any other kind of organization focused on children, homemakers were more active than women with jobs. Free time, in this case, was inflected by the choices these women had made about the kind of life they wanted to lead. As far as commitments are concerned, voluntary agencies that schedule their activities during the working day will have difficulty attracting full-time workers, especially those who have to clock in and clock out. For example, working full-time could have a more damaging impact on volunteering as a teacher's assistant in a school, which takes place during the day, than volunteering for a parent-teacher organization, which holds meetings in the evening (Schneider and Coleman 1996:97).

We explored the idea that the influence of work hours varies by volunteer domain in the Independent Sector data. We compared full-time and part-time workers to respondents who were not working for pay, because they were unemployed, a student, or a homemaker.[7] We estimated the effect of work hours on thirteen different areas. Recall that, overall, employed people are more likely to have volunteered in the past twelve months than people without jobs. Of those with jobs, the full-time workers were the least likely to have volunteered (i.e., they were similar to those not working). Looking at volunteering by domain, we found that full-time workers were the most likely to have volunteered for a work-related organization, otherwise they were less likely to have volunteered than other respondents, including those not employed at all. The coefficients for employment status by domain in our logistic regression models were not always significant, probably because of the small cell sizes resulting from our disaggregating the volunteer work into thirteen different categories, but full-time workers were nevertheless significantly less likely than those without jobs to volunteer in the areas of the environment, public benefit (this includes fire and rescue squads), and foundations. For the other types the coefficient for full-time work was always negative, although not significant. In other words, the reason why full-time workers volunteer more than people without jobs is that they are more likely to volunteer on behalf of a trade union or professional association. This positive effect is masking the fact that they are actually less likely to volunteer in most other areas. The positive effect of working part-time, on the other hand is much more straightforward and much more robust in the sense that it is found in most domains of volunteering. Only in the areas of health, public benefit, political organizations, and foundations are part-time workers not more likely to volunteer than those who have zero working hours. [40]

The Structure of Work and Volunteer Time Demands

Paid work and volunteer work are both scheduled activities. Not all leisure time hours are equally useful or pleasurable because how we spend our free time depends on what other people are doing. For example, having free time when others are at work is not as valuable as having free time when others have free time. Having free time when you choose it rather than having free time when it is granted to you is more rewarding, and useful. The same could be said of volunteer hours. They are not all equally demanding. Consider two people who volunteer the same amount of time over the course of a year, one intermittently, the other regularly. Let both of them accept a new job that demands 50 percent more hours of paid work from them. It is obvious who will be most affected by this change. The influence of paid work hours therefore depends on how volunteer work is structured.[8] Volunteers also differ in how they allocate their time to volunteer work and this, too, moderates the influence of work hours. The volunteer population can be divided into two groups: regular volunteers commit a steady supply of hours throughout the year; episodic volunteers commit their hours once a year. For example, Allahyari (2000) distinguished between "committed" volunteers and "holiday" volunteers. The latter volunteered only on special occasions, such as Christmas and Thanksgiving, while the former volunteered on a regular basis all the year round. A simple measure of volunteer hours does not capture this crucial distinction and the result is that we obscure the true relation between work hours and volunteer hours. In light of recent changes in volunteering in favor of more episodic schedules, this topic deserves more attention from scholars.

Turning to the scheduling and timing of paid work, it is unrealistic to think that people calculate the marginal effect of one extra hour of paid work on their leisure time pursuits as if they can clearly see that adding one more hour of paid work inevitably means subtracting one hour of volunteer work. Working for pay has fixed costs, resulting from travel to work, clothing, day care, and the like. Deciding whether to take a job at all is very different from deciding how many hours to work on that job. For this reason, it is probably more correct to say that paid work hours have less effect on how many hours people volunteer than they do on *when* they volunteer and what they volunteer for. Almeida et al. (2001:148) show that elderly volunteers are more likely than younger people to volunteer mid-week rather than weekends. Data from the UK 2000 Time Use Survey show that unemployed people who volunteer contribute more hours than employed people who volunteer, but this difference disappears at the weekend (Ruston 2003:6). People with flexible work schedules volunteer at a higher rate, as do those who work schedules that give them time off during the day: Canadians working a split shift (i.e., split between early morning and the end of the day) are more likely to volunteer than those working the regular day shift. Canadians working rotating shifts, on the other hand, are the least likely of all workers to volunteer (Soo and Gong-Soog 1998). Japanese workers with no fixed work schedule, making their free time somewhat unpredictable, volunteered at a lower rate than part-time workers, although they were still more likely to volunteer than full-time workers (Statistics Bureau 2002). Surprisingly, flextime does not increase the likelihood of volunteering, but people who perform their paid work at home are much more likely to volunteer than those working a regular shift (Gomez and Gunderson 2003), and self-employed people (who have considerable control over when they work) are more likely to volunteer than people who work for someone else (Freeman 1997:S156; Thompson 1993a, 1993b). In short, some measure of control over one's work schedule, or a work schedule that permits breaks in the work day, is conducive to volunteer work, especially where this work entails some kind of long-term commitment (Negrey 1993:111).

Other Time Demands

Jobs are not the only demand on scarce time resources. The important question is not how much time people spend at work, but how many hours of free time they have. For example, taking a job means spending time getting to work that could otherwise be spent volunteering. During the typical five-day week, the average American spends two hours getting to and from the job. This is twice the number of hours a week the average American volunteers. Putnam (2000:213) estimates that for each additional ten minutes Americans spend commuting they cut their involvement in community affairs by 10 percent. In this respect, suburban sprawl and traffic congestion are real threats to civic life.[9]

Whether or not people have jobs to go to, they will experience many other demands on their time. When non-volunteers report they are "too busy" to volunteer, they might not be referring to their jobs at all, but to the caring responsibilities they have in addition to their job (Gallagher 1994a:575). It is unusual for social surveys of volunteering to gather data on other uses of time. One notable exception is a study using data from a 1995 Time Budget survey in the Netherlands. For the men in the study, the more free time they had the more they volunteered. Men with over sixty hours of free time (the part of the week remaining after deducting for all commitments for work, education, household care, sleeping, meals, and other personal care) volunteered three times as many hours a week as those who had less than forty hours of free time a week. Time spent informally socializing was curvilinearly related to volunteer time: too little or too much time spent socializing reduced volunteer time. The same was true for time spent watching television and reading newspapers and reading in general. In all these forms of mass media consumption, moderate amounts were the most conducive to volunteering. In the case of Dutch women the overall amount of free time had less impact. The more time women spent informally socializing the less volunteer work they did. Television viewing was unrelated to volunteering among women. Reading newspapers and reading in general had a positive effect on volunteer hours (De Hart and Dekker 1999:90–91).

Unfortunately, this study reports only zero-order effects: there are no controls for possible spuriousness. For example, the positive relation between newspaper readership and volunteering might be due to both being associated with education. In addition, the percentage differences were often quite small and possibly due to chance. Furthermore, studies conducted in the United States and the United Kingdom failed to uncover any relationship between free time and volunteer time (Robinson and Godbey 1997:194; Ruston 2003). It seems that free time *in general* is not a particularly good predictor of volunteer time. It is more likely that people juggle how they allocate their time across specific activities. This would mean that volunteer time is more contingent on variations in other specific time demands. We will now examine two of these demands: giving help informally and providing care for relatives.

Informal Helping

Formal volunteering and informal helping (running errands for neighbors, baby-sitting for relatives not in the household, visiting a work colleague in hospital) are often contrasted as two different ways of providing care for others outside the household, as if people must choose between them. If this were the case, people would cut back on their volunteer time if they began to devote more time to informal helping. An alternative theory is that one activity leads to the other because the friends and contacts we make helping others informally draw us into volunteer work and become a major reason for continuing to volunteer. If this were the case, formal and informal helping would complement each other. It is also possible that both kinds of helping behavior result from some third factor, such as being extroverted or empathic, in which case they should go together, but not in the causal way implied by the second theory.

Most social surveys indicate that formal and informal helping are positively related. The UK 2000 Time Use Survey looked at three ways of occupying free time: socializing, informally helping others, and volunteering. On average, the British spent four minutes a day volunteering, a rather small fraction of the five hours and twenty-six minutes of free time they enjoyed each day, but volunteers were slightly more likely than non-volunteers to help others informally (Ruston 2003:6). In the United States, Gallagher (1994a:575) found that volunteers spent more time helping friends than non-volunteers.[10] A Canadian study found that the more informal help senior citizens provided the more likely they were to volunteer (Jones 1999:12).[11] A study of older Europeans (aged 50 years or more) found that people who were providing help informally were more likely to be volunteering also than those who had provided no help (Erlinghagen and Hank 2006:572). In this study, countries that reported high levels of volunteering (e.g., Denmark, Sweden) also reported high levels of giving informal help and the countries that reported low levels of volunteering also reported low levels of informal help.

The Independent Sector surveys include in their list of possible volunteer activities an "informal-alone" option. This is a valid measure of informal helping. Forty percent of those who had done volunteer work in the past year had also helped informally, compared to only 6 percent of those who did not volunteer, a statistically significant difference that did not change much when we altered the time period to the past month or the past week or when controls were imposed for socio-demographic variables, family status, and church attendance. [54] The more areas in which the respondent volunteered, the more likely was he or she to have helped informally.[12] In order to explore the association between informal helping and formal volunteering further we regressed informal helping on formal volunteering, with all the usual controls imposed. No matter whether we defined formal volunteering as a binary measure or number of domains (range), the effect on informal helping was positive, regardless of whether the time period was the past week, the past month, or the past year. [54] We then regressed hours spent informal helping on hours spent formal volunteering, a more rigorous test of whether the activities are complements or substitutes. [56] Hours of formal volunteering were positively associated with hours of informal helping, whether the time period was the last month or the last year. When we changed the time period to the last week, however, we found a curvilinear relation between the two methods of helping: the more time people spent helping others informally, the more time they spent volunteering, but only up to a point, after which the time spent informally helping forced the respondent to cut back on volunteer hours. [57] See Figure 2.

One explanation for this might be that the hours spent volunteering and hours spent helping in the past week are more accurately remembered and the real relation between them is revealed more precisely. Another explanation might be that people who report having volunteered and helped in the very recent past are indicating a high level of commitment (or obligation) to both kinds of unpaid work, which forces some compromises upon them as to where they allocate their time.

Caring for Relatives

Americans are living longer and are likely to have longer periods of disability in old age. Family members are more likely than ever before to be called upon to provide care for an elderly relative. The consequences of these trends for volunteerism are unclear at present because the research does not

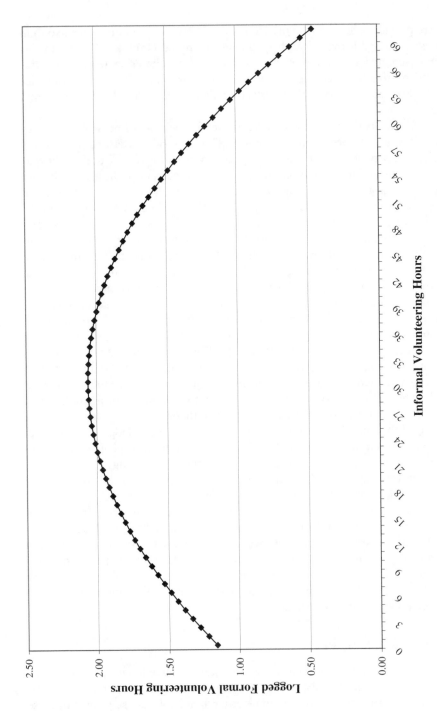

Figure 2. Estimated net effect of informal volunteering on formal volunteering.

indicate clearly that people have to choose between these two activities. One theory is that the care-giving role competes with the volunteer role for the time and attention of family members. People with multiple primary roles, such as parenting or looking after an aged parent, feel more "time crunch" than other role occupants (Roxburgh 2002:126). When asked to identify the biggest obstacles to them becoming more involved in their community, a sample of Illinois residents placed work demands at the top of the list, but family responsibilities came second. Respondents indicated they wanted to spend more time with their families or that they were too busy participating in activities with their families or that they were prevented from volunteering by having to care for a relative (Profile of Illinois 2001). A competing theory is that "caring persons" are both more likely to volunteer and to spend time caring for relatives: "Women who have the time and the inclination to volunteer may be similarly inclined toward contributing their time and talents to caring for their ill or infirm kin" (Robison et al. 1995: S369).

In her analysis of the MIDUS data, Rossi (2001c:295) found that volunteering and care-giving time were positively related, although the correlation was weak ($r = .07$). In fact, caregiving influenced volunteering only if the recipient of the care was a child: "the more time adults spend counseling and advising their own children, the more time they devote to volunteer service in the community" (Rossi 2001d:340). Furthermore, the positive effect was entirely confined to youth-related volunteer work, and the effect in that case was much stronger for adults between 24 and 40 than older adults. In all likelihood, volunteer work has been integrated into the parents' concept of what it means to care for their children. A subsequent analysis of the same data set showed that the null effect of caregiving reported by Rossi is a function of her failure to distinguish the target of the caregiving and her failure to analyze men and women separately. Men giving care are no more or less likely to volunteer than men not providing care. In the case of women, only giving care to the elderly reduces the likelihood of doing care work (Taniguchi 2006).

A sub-sample of the Americans' Changing Lives (ACL) survey aged 50 years or more at baseline (1986) was analyzed by Burr et al. (2005) to see if time spent giving care to others reduced volunteer time. Caregiving was measured by a question on help given to friends or relatives who were having trouble taking care of themselves. About one-fifth of the sample (21.3%) reported providing some such care in the past twelve months and 38.4 percent had volunteered. More of the volunteers than non-volunteers were caring for others and they spent more hours on care work than non-volunteers. The respondents who spent the most time on care work volunteered the most. In short, there is no evidence that care-giving time stands in the way of volunteer time. The authors found, however, that the target of care work makes a difference. Caregivers of non-relatives are more likely to volunteer than caregivers of relatives. For example, someone who spends a lot of time caring for a spouse is no more or less likely to volunteer than someone who does no care work at all. This suggests an explanation for why caregiving and volunteering are linked. Giving care to non-relatives exposes the caregiver to more opportunities to volunteer. Indeed, when the authors controlled for whether the respondent had been asked to volunteer the effect of the care-giving variables disappeared. Although we cannot be sure that caregivers are simply more likely to be asked, this does suggest that caregivers to non-relatives are more likely to volunteer than those not providing care or providing care to relatives because they become embedded in wider social networks, which exposes them to recruiting drives by those seeking new volunteers.

The most complete study of the effect of caregiving on volunteering uses data from the 1997 Australian Time Use Survey. It is complete because several kinds of time use are recorded and their separate effects on volunteering are estimated. Expenditures of time on five categories of activity were recorded: housework, volunteering for the community, providing informal support to non-household family and friends, employment, and child care. Volunteering was defined as time spent on any activity that a respondent reported performing for the community. Neither informal helping hours nor hours spent taking care of children had any effect on volunteer hours (Hook 2004:102).[13] Another analysis of the same data, using all the adults in the survey, found that providing care and assistance within the household was associated with below average times spent on volunteering activities. In contrast, caring for someone outside the household was associated with above average time spent volunteering (Wilkinson and Bittman 2003:15).

Time diary data from Canada suggests that the association between time spent volunteering and time spent giving care to children varies by gender and the age of the children. When the children were under six, mothers spent 3.0 hours on child care if they were volunteering and 3.2 hours a day if they were not volunteering. The implication is that women must choose between volunteering and taking care of children. Fathers with children under six, on the other hand, averaged 1.6 hours a day on child care whether they volunteered or not. Their time commitment to child care was so small it had little effect on their volunteer work. When the children entered school, the picture changed. Now, the more time mothers spent on child care the more likely they were to volunteer; and the same was true of fathers. Child care had changed from being a deterrent to volunteering to encouraging it, and this change was particularly obvious in the case of women (Jones 2001:73).

In short, although it is probably true that volunteering is difficult for people who spend many hours a day taking care of a spouse or an elderly relative, outside of these extreme cases, caring for relatives either has no effect on volunteer hours or, in the case of school age children, it has a positive effect. The variable effects of children are more fully dealt with in our section on the life course, but it is worth noting in this context that the presence of school age children in the household increases the likelihood of volunteering compared to having no children, especially among women, whereas preschool children decrease the likelihood of volunteering. Preschool children simply take up more of their mother's time than school age children. Caring for people outside the household, however, seems to have a positive effect on volunteering.

Housework

Besides caring for family members, the major household responsibility most of us face is cleaning and maintaining the house or apartment and its surroundings. Although studies of housework show that the time allotted to it is very flexible—and has been declining over time—it nevertheless has the potential to limit the amount of time we could spend volunteering. Hook (2004:112) found that the more hours Australians spend doing housework, the less time they spend doing volunteer work. A Dutch study found that men cut back on their volunteer time if they spend more time on household and family care tasks, whereas women volunteer more as they spend more time on household and family tasks (De Hart and Dekker 1999:89).[14] In one study conducted in the United States, time spent on housework had a positive effect on volunteer hours for both employed women and men, although the effect was stronger for women. This pattern is rather difficult to explain. Rossi (2001e:454) speculates that "time invested in domestic maintenance may function as an index of commitment to the personal care and pleasures of others at home, which is then generalized to include concern for the welfare of more distant members of the community." Although she confined her analysis to employed married adults, she does not control for hours spent on paid work, which is surely going to play some part in determining how much people volunteer. It could be that women who spend more hours on housework are part-time workers, who are also more likely to volunteer.

The research on the effects of other forms of unpaid work on volunteer labor is in its infancy, which probably explains the inconsistent results from one study to another. In the case of informal helping outside the household, the research strongly suggests a reciprocal relationship. Informal helping leads to volunteering, which in turn increases the likelihood of providing informal help. But the influence of caring for relatives is somewhat more obscure. In chapter 10 we will return to the influence of children on parents' volunteering, but the pattern seems to be that preschool children are a deterrent to volunteering but school age children encourage it, especially for women. Neither the influence of caring for spouses nor for elderly relatives is clear at this time. This is due, in part, to the fact that most of the studies reviewed above do not control for the respondent's paid work hours or, in the case of married respondents, the work hours of the spouse.

We also need to know more about *how* volunteer work and other forms of unpaid work are related. The volunteer role is typically regarded as secondary to the primary roles of work and family. This means that child care and caring for other family members are probably given priority. Volunteer work is fitted around these strong obligations. Housework is a slightly different matter. It is a chore family members need to get done, but it is quite flexible, and it is possible that people decide how much housework to do after they have decided how much volunteer work to do. Women are the primary caregivers in our society, and for this reason, most of the studies of informal helping, caring, housework, and volunteering reviewed in this section focus on women, for whom the conflict of roles is most acute. Women show no signs of cutting back on formal helping because they are busy helping informally or providing care. These activities are either independent of each other or they positively reinforce each other. Women are fitting volunteering responsibilities around their caring responsibilities. Little (1997:2000) describes how, at especially busy times, such as annual fetes or during Christmas celebrations, women would set aside or ask others to take responsibility for their other unpaid work chores: "husbands and neighbors were frequently left babysitting and some 'non-essential' work around the home was put on hold." On a more routine basis, the women simply found ways to dovetail their volunteer work and their other caring responsibilities, fitting volunteer tasks around school hours or organizing meetings and other activities at times that would not interfere with their care work. Time is quite elastic for women.

Health and Volunteering

In the rest of this chapter we will review briefly the research on health as a resource for volunteering. Our assumption is that poor health raises the cost of doing volunteer work. We will postpone our discussion of the reciprocal relation between health and volunteering until chapter 21.

In the context of labor market studies, good health is treated as a form of human capital, a resource that can increase monetary and other rewards (Schram and Dunsing 1981:373). Health is much like income and education (with which it is associated) in being an individual attribute or resource: "a volunteer who does not have good health must expend a much larger portion of his or her available energy on volunteering tasks than otherwise would be required" (Fischer and Schaffer 1993:24). As we have already seen, people most often cite lack of time as the main reason why they are not volunteering, but health concerns or physical abilities are also mentioned often. Asked to identify the "biggest barriers" to being more involved in their local community, 15 percent of the respondents to a survey of Illinois residents cited poor health or they said they felt "too old" to participate (Profile of Illinois 2001). Health problems probably account for some of the socio-demographic differences in volunteering. They are more likely to be cited as an obstacle to volunteering by older people, widows or widowers, high school dropouts, people not in the labor force, and low wage earners (Lasby 2004:9). In the Independent Sector surveys, only 9.5 percent of those not volunteering gave poor health as a reason, but if we look at specific segments of the population we see that this can be a significant obstacle. For example, 26 percent of Americans aged 65 or more gave this as a reason for not volunteering in the past year, compared to 4 percent of those under 26. The kinds of social groups we would expect to have more health problems are also more likely to give this as a reason for not volunteering: 14 percent of high school dropouts gave this as a reason compared to 4 percent of those with an advanced degree; 13 percent of those earning less than $25,000 gave this as a reason, compared to 2 percent of those earning $75,000 or more. The remarkable thing is that these class differences persisted even after controls for all the socio-demographic and religious variables. [52, 12]

Mental Health

As a persistent and substantial deviation from normal functioning, mental illness impairs the execution of social roles, such as volunteering. The term "mental health" covers a syndrome of symptoms of an individual's subjective well-being, including positive feelings about the self and life in general, a sense of purpose in life, and positive relations with other people. Perhaps the most familiar form of mental illness is depression. The symptoms of depression include a feeling of hopelessness, lack of energy, and negative perception of interpersonal relationships. This illness has attracted the attention of social scientists interested in volunteerism because it so obviously raises the cost of doing volunteer work. Gracia and Herrero (2003) surveyed a random sample of citizens of a major Spanish city, asking them about their degree of involvement in the community. Although the scale of participation is not a specific measure of volunteerism, it includes volunteer work as one of eleven items. (The coefficient alpha for the index was 0.83, indicating considerable covariance between the items.) The interesting feature of this study is that data were gathered twice, six months apart. It is therefore possible to estimate the effect of psychological distress on community participation in the second wave, net of the level in the first wave, thus creating a change score, and making it possible to see if level of distress in the first wave led to a decline in volunteering.[15] The more distressed respondents reported the steepest decline in community participation, a pattern that remained after controlling for gender, age, marital status, education, and income, and was fully equivalent across all socio-demographic groups. Depression also had a significant negative effect on volunteering among the sample of Americans studied by Thoits and Hewitt (2001). Using the 1986 and 1989 panels of the ACL survey, they estimated the effect of 1986 depression symptoms on 1989 volunteering, net of 1986 levels of volunteering. Depression had a negative influence on volunteering after controls for socio-economic status. Further investigation showed this to be the result of lower levels of social integration: more depressed people rarely attended church or the meetings of voluntary associations and for this reason were less likely to volunteer.

Physical Health: Subjective Assessments

A number of scholars have considered the influence of physical health on volunteering. Some use questions in which people were asked to rate their own health. Canadian data from both 1987 (Day and Devlin 1996:44) and 1997 show that self-rated health and volunteering are positively related: in the 1997 survey, 35.8 percent of those who rated their health as good had volunteered in the past year, compared to 27.4 percent among those who rated their health as fair and 22.8 percent of those who rated their health as poor (Reed and Selbee 2000a:50). Interestingly, however, self-rated health made little difference to the number of hours contributed: Canadians in poor health volunteered an average of 146.4 hours a year; in fair health, 149.3 hours a year; and in good health, 149.6 hours a year (Reed and Selbee 2000a:52).[16] A study of Australians aged between 49 and 87 found that those who rated their health as good were more likely to be volunteering (Warburton et al. 1998:239). In the United States, most of the research on the relationship between self-rated health and volunteering has focused on the elderly population, presumably on the assumption that failing health will be a major impediment to volunteer work in this population. Chambre (1987) found a strong positive relation between volunteering and perceived health among a sample of Americans 65 years of age and older.[17] Hunter and Linn (1980) compared volunteers aged 65 or more at a Veterans Administration hospital with a random sample of older people living in nearby retirement homes who were not volunteering. The volunteers reported fewer somatic complaints (e.g., headaches, dizziness), they were less anxious, less depressed, and had a stronger will to live. Overall, the more satisfied people were with their lives, the more likely they were to volunteer. Choi (2003) used data from the Asset and Health Dynamics among the Oldest Old survey to investigate the influence of health on Americans aged 70 years or older. Overall, 13 percent had volunteered in the past year. Just over a third (36%) of the volunteers reported their health as good, compared to 22 percent of the non-volunteers, a statistically significant difference that held up after controls for gender, income, education, age, employment status, and religion. A 2004 study of elderly Europeans in ten countries found that the volunteer rate among those who rated their health as "good or better" was double that of those who rated their health as "fair or worse" (Erlinghagen and Hank 2006:575).

Physical Health: Objective Assessments

Another approach to gauging physical health is to ask respondents not how they rate their health overall but to report specific capabilities and illnesses. Once again, most of the research in this area has focused on older populations. Functional health is measured by the ability to perform basic motor acts, such as bathe, climb stairs, or walk. Chronic illness is measured by whether the respondent suffers from an ailment such as rheumatism or hypertension. Focusing on Americans 55 years old or older, Herzog and Morgan (1993:130) found that respondents who reported a great deal of functional impairment were only half as likely to volunteer as those who reported no or little functional impairment. However, health status was not related to number of hours volunteered. In a study of an even older group of Americans (aged 70–79 years) the "high functioning" elderly were four times more likely to volunteer than "low functioning" elderly (Glass et al. 1995).[18] In an earlier analysis of the ACL data we found that 10 percent of the sample reported having at least one functional impairment: among volunteers for religious organizations the rate was 8 percent; among volunteers for secular organizations the rate was 10 percent; and among non-volunteers the rate was 13 percent. These differences are not large and were not adjusted for other factors, but they are statistically significant. We found the same pattern with respect to chronic illness. The empirical range of chronic illnesses reported was 0–3. The mean for the sample as a whole was 0.14, for non-volunteers 0.17, for religious volunteers 0.11, and for secular volunteers 0.12. Once again, these differences are not large and were not adjusted for other variables, but they are statistically significant (Wilson and Musick 2003:265).[19]

Finally, we should note the possibility that health is more of an independent influence on volunteering in some populations than others. In one study we conducted, we found that health status had a stronger effect on the volunteer hours of Black Americans than White Americans. The explanation is that health is more strongly correlated with income, education, and voluntary association membership among Whites than it is among Blacks. Controlling for these factors in our analysis eliminated the health effect for Whites but not for Blacks (Musick et al. 2000:1556).

Conclusion

In this chapter we have discussed the contribution of two resources—time and health—to volunteering. Both are important. Other demands on people's time do limit how much volunteer work they do and they do more volunteer work if they are healthier. The relation between free time and volunteer time turns out to be quite complicated and a number of issues remain unresolved. First, we should not assume that all people count paid work hours the same. Long work hours are not necessarily perceived as an impediment to volunteering. A lot depends on people's freedom to choose when they work. For example, part-time workers typically volunteer more than full-time workers, but not all do so. In an intriguing but incomplete analysis (because only women are concerned), Putnam (2000:201) shows that part-time workers volunteer more hours than full-time workers, especially if they are working part-time *voluntarily* rather than as a result of not being able to get a full-time job. Women who work full-time by necessity are even less likely to volunteer than part-time workers if they choose to work full-time. Women who work part-time by choice might well be doing so to make room for volunteer work. Second, we should treat neither paid nor unpaid work as activities to be measured by a continuous variable, such as hours and minutes, because neither can really be measured by hours spent on the job. Both are "lumpy" in the sense that taking a job or becoming a volunteer commits us to a certain "lump" of hours, not just one or two extra hours. In the case of paid work this means, for example, that we commit to a certain number of hours commuting to work each week and, of course, it means that we commit to a certain block of hours. Few of us can add or subtract an hour to accommodate other demands on our time. In the case of volunteer work we have more flexibility, but we still typically commit to a certain number of hours per week. Although they are not numerous, they are nevertheless an obligation we might be reluctant to assume. As part of a research project on the civic engagement on the residents of Illinois seven focus groups were conducted in seven locations. In three of the groups, members were selected to be highly engaged in civic activities; in four the participants were screened to make sure that they had not been involved in group activities and did not consider themselves active in their community. All were employed either full- or part-time. Members of the civically engaged groups tended to be older, have children, be married, have completed college, and attend church at least once a month. The unengaged were more likely to be single, childless, have only high school or some college education, and attend church infrequently. The unengaged members of the focus groups were concerned about lack of time, but group discussion suggested that this masked a genuine fear of involvement. They were unsure about what the volunteer activity would entail; the level of commitment required and the skills and talents necessary. "The project needs a beginning and an end. And it's not going to be five times as many hours of commitment as they tell you when you originally say, yeah, I could do this" (Profile of Illinois 2001). In short, people are concerned as much with the commitment of time as they are with the amount of time.

A second set of issues has to do with the nature of the volunteer work. First, we have demonstrated the value of distinguishing between the rate of volunteering and hours volunteered. Taking a job can actually have a positive effect on the chances of us volunteering at all but can have a negative effect on how many hours we contribute. Thus, homemakers might be less likely to volunteer but they "compensate" for this by contributing more hours and thus might well end up donating more total hours than people with jobs. Second, the type of volunteer work involved might well moderate the relation between free time and volunteering. People who volunteer their time in the form of specific tasks, such as helping out at the soup kitchen, are offering hands-on solutions to local, community problems, often on a face-to-face basis. It is relatively easy for them to measure their contributions in units of time and, indeed, their assignments are often measured in hours. People who think of themselves as activists, however, do not calculate their effort in measures of time simply because the problems with which they deal are so difficult and intractable. When activists think about all the social problems they would like to solve, "there would not be enough volunteers to right all the wrongs, and still the problem would not be addressed at its roots" (Eliasoph 1998:242). The infinite nature of social problems makes activists reluctant to think in terms of time expenditures. In short, the assumption that we all calculate trade offs between different kinds of work in the same way does not hold up under empirical scrutiny. Third, although we naturally think that people calculate the cost of volunteering in terms of the paid work time they sacrifice, we should not assume they make this calculation independent of how much they want to do volunteer work, as if volunteering has some kind preconceived value. In fact, the value of paid time is partly a function of how important volunteering is to people. Time is a sociological phenomenon: we *feel* busy; we *make* time. The chances are, the more enthusiastic we are about our volunteer work, the more we believe our volunteer work is of value and will be effective, the more we discount other uses of our time, including working for pay, and the more likely are we to think we have time for it (Passy and Giugni 2001:132). Time-consuming volunteer tasks that are pleasant are less "costly" than unpleasant tasks that take little time at all. In a 1992 survey, teenagers were asked if they could imagine themselves doing a number of tasks. They found it much easier to see "themselves helping with a school program to warn about drugs than feeding a handicapped person, [or] working with an elderly person than helping an AIDS patient" (Wuthnow 1995:279). The second choice was more distasteful and threatening than the first, not more time consuming. It is not accurate to treat all volunteer hours as equally demanding. People will "find time" for tasks they enjoy; they will be "too busy" to perform unpleasant tasks.

A third set of issues has to do with the causal relationship between volunteer time and other time demands. We have assumed that paid work and care work are primary roles and volunteer work is a secondary role. But this is not always true. The relationship between paid work and volunteer work can take many forms. Little (1997) interviewed women living and volunteering in a rural part of England. Some women were volunteering as a substitute for paid work, which they would prefer to have but could not get. They believed fewer women would volunteer if good employment opportunities were available. But a number of women seemed to give priority to the volunteer role. They admitted it would be difficult for them to take on a full-time job given their volunteer commitments. Many of these women gave as a reason for doing part-time work that they wanted to preserve time for doing volunteer work.

The influence of health on volunteering seems to be somewhat more straightforward. Good health is a resource without which many productive activities could not be performed. Mental disorders, such as depression, pose a major obstacle to making any kind of commitment to regular service. Functional impairments and chronic illnesses likewise raise the costs of doing volunteer work. Both physical health and mental health vary by socio-economic status. Some of the apparent effect of health is undoubtedly due to these social class differences. But the better studies control for this possibility and health effects remain. Some of the health effects are mediated by social integration—healthier people seem to socialize more and are for this reason more likely to be recruited. Finally, as we indicated at the beginning of the section on health and volunteering, this relationship must be analyzed carefully because it is equally likely that people enjoy better health *because* they volunteer. We will return to this subject in chapter 21.

8

Gender

In our approach to gender and volunteering we side with Gerstel (2000:468), who rejects essentialist arguments that women do most of the nurturing and caring work in most societies because women are "naturally" more caring than men or because women are somehow morally superior to men. Instead, we find two other arguments more compelling because they have more sociology in them. The first acknowledges that females are more disposed, or feel more obliged, to care than males: women consistently rate themselves (and are rated by others) as more empathic and altruistic than men (Greeno and Maccoby 1993:195). But this is the result of socialization, not genes. Of course, the extent to which children are exposed to traditional gender ideologies varies, as does the extent to which this socialization determines adult behavior, as we shall see. The second argument is more structural. Women do most of the care work because, in a patriarchal society, women are required to do most of society's "dirty work." Subjective dispositions have little to do with this tendency. Although variations in employment temper these obligations, women are expected to "take care of" those in need, whether this care work is formally organized or not. "From extended nursing of an ailing mother to cooking an occasional meal for a bereaved friend to volunteering for a local church soup kitchen, it is women, across race and class, who have provided a disproportionate share of care" (Gerstel and Gallagher 1994:519).

We do not subscribe to the view that gender will inevitably shape volunteer attitudes and practices, no matter what. This is partly because the volunteer role is not a primary role, unlike family and work roles. Primary roles, such as caring for young children, are deeply imprinted with gender ideology because they are so important. Volunteer work is a more ephemeral role, clearly secondary to these other more important roles. Thus, while it is true that women do most of the unpaid household labor in modern societies, it is not inevitable that they do most of the volunteer work. Indeed, Hakim (1996:46) has asserted, "The idea that women are unique in doing a substantial volume of the voluntary work has no basis in reality." She draws this conclusion on the basis of surveys in the United Kingdom showing not only virtually no difference between men and women in the proportion who volunteer but also that men donate more hours than women (seventeen per month compared to fifteen per month). This suggests that, despite the female stereotype of the volunteer described below, volunteer work might not be as gendered as other forms of unpaid work such as child care, elder care, or housework and house maintenance.

In this chapter we will find out whether the indisputable influence of gender on care work is also found in volunteer work. Our approach will be to see if there are differences between men and women with respect to motives, attitudes, and perspectives on volunteering that might lead them to volunteer at different rates. This is the socialization argument. We then consider the argument that gender differences in volunteering are a result of differences in the structural position of men and women. If this is true, once these differences in structural position are controlled, gender effects should disappear. For example, if education encourages volunteering and men are more highly educated than women, any positive effect of being female will be suppressed by their educational disadvantage.

Gender and the Volunteer Role

Looking back to the beginning of the twentieth century, the historian Scott (1991:21) observed a "nearly universal assumption that women were responsible for community welfare." At that time, middle class ideas about appropriate roles for men and women expected men to achieve self-realization through public, productive, and independent action, while women were expected to find self-fulfillment in service to others, primarily in the household but secondarily (for women who had servants to do household chores) through activities promoting community welfare (Daniels 1988:8). Volunteer work, bearing the stigma of being unpaid, was assigned to the female sphere. It fulfilled cultural expectations that women should be compassionate and nurturing. In turn, philanthropic work contributed to the definition of gender roles: becoming a woman included learning how to volunteer. In order to perform this function, volunteer work had to be appropriately characterized. The organization skills required, the sheer drudgery of the work, the fortitude and courage demanded by volunteer work, were downplayed. Instead, the activity was defined primarily as a pastime, a form of leisure or consumption. These ideas remained current among the upper middle class women interviewed by Daniels (1988:9) in the 1970s:

> Much of the work that women volunteers do is seen as part of leisure activity. Some of their own comments suggest that they may accept this view. They say, for example, that they do the work because they enjoy it, not because they have to. Or they regard the expenses of volunteering as part of something they *like* to do and therefore part of their amusement rather than a work expense.

Historically, volunteer work has reproduced gender ideologies in another way. By volunteering, women could enter the public arena without calling into question their femininity. Their public work was approved so long as it could be seen as "an accepted extension of their defined roles as wives and mothers" (Scott 1991:24). Their presence in civil society was thus depicted as another form of mothering, taking care of the moral rather than the utilitarian side of life. "Not only did they sew and knit for the poor just as they did for their own families, they also behaved as good mothers were supposed to: rewarding virtue, attempting to cure bad habits, and concentrating special attention upon children and women, precisely as they did at home" (Scott 1991:15). In this respect, volunteer work, because of its close association with women, acquired the non-political connotation it still has today.

This is not to deny that some women were active as volunteers in nineteenth-century social movements, often occupying leadership positions. Through a host of social movements women were able to exercise collectively an influence they lacked individually, gaining compensation for their exclusion from political parties, the legal profession, Congress, the military, the ministry, and the business elite. They also learned valuable political skills and knowledge. But these early social activists comprised a tiny proportion of women, principally the daughters of substantial farmers and plantation owners and wives of professional men (Scott 1991:80), and the movements they organized and populated focused primarily on moral reform, taking social problems such as prostitution, gambling, intemperance, even slavery and women's rights, and casting them as moral issues on which women could speak with authority.

The volunteer role was thus gendered in its institutionalization, made possible by the wives of upper and middle class men withdrawing from the labor force. It became a mark of superior social status for women to abstain from work even if they had obtained the educational credentials that would fit them for it. Instead, they were expected to channel their energies into their home and into community housekeeping. They served their husbands by doing good works. For example, physicians' wives were allowed to "get their hands dirty" doing clerical work, such as stuffing envelopes, for the hospital auxiliary but it would not have been socially acceptable for them to take a job as a secretary (Stephan 1991:227). An older Canadian woman interviewed by Meadows (1996:173) recalled how,

> [O]ver where my husband worked he said they were desperate for people to volunteer, and that would be a good thing for me to do. And of course it didn't pay and all and besides I was the wife of the head of the place and of course everything was rosy. So I started off with one of the volunteer organizations, delivering goods and yakking to the men and I found I loved it.

She went on to describe her circle of friends:

> Quite a few of them were university graduates and their husbands said they could do all the volunteer work you like and you can do Junior League or anything else but you can't take pay. We just accepted it.

This did not apply to working class women, most of whom were obliged to have full-time jobs, take in boarders, or do occasional work, such as sewing clothes, to supplement the household income. They provided extra-household help informally. The ideology that legitimated the traditional male breadwinner family thus helped gender the volunteer role. As late as the 1970s, a survey found that wives were more likely to volunteer if their husbands disapproved of them having a job (Schram and Dunsing 1981:376).

Despite several decades of progress in the achievement of civil rights for women, they are still "expected to care for the personal and emotional needs of others, to deliver routine forms of personal service, and, more generally, to facilitate the progress of others toward their goals" (Eagly and Crowley 1986:284). More than men, they are expected to put care responsibilities ahead of other life activities. It is therefore easier for women to imagine making volunteer work a "career" than it is for men. Extended over the life course, volunteer work can substitute for paid employment for women more than for men, for whom the work role is primary (Stephan 1991). Despite the increase in dual-earner families, most married women still believe they are the "secondary earners" in the family. They do not treat their income as essential to the survival of the household and are likely to forego income in favor of child rearing and educational activities and to have intermittent work histories. Voluntary work fits neatly into this conjugal role (Hakim 1996:70).

Feminist Criticisms of Volunteerism

The cutbacks in government services instigated by the Reagan and Thatcher administrations in the United States and Britain were coupled with calls for volunteers to step up and do the work formerly performed by fired public sector workers. Some commentators expressed alarm at this development because of the pressure exerted on women in particular to help deliver a whole range of human services. There was talk of a "semi-invisible welfare state" consisting of "women volunteers providing free care at the frontline of service delivery" (Bagilhole 1996:202). These debates are reminiscent of those that took place during the 1970s, when feminists launched an attack on volunteerism as "one of the oldest, most subtle, most complicated ways in which women have been disengaged from the economy with their own eager cooperation" (Gold 1971:384). They depicted volunteer work as nothing but the extension of domestic service outside the home: "From a feminist and/or progressive unionist point of view, voluntarism is clearly exploitative—in its implications that social justice for all classes can be achieved through the moral 'service' of some who are expendable, albeit out of choice" (Gold 1971:393). Betty Friedan included a criticism of volunteerism in her 1963 influential best seller, *Feminine Mystique*. The housewife's "feeling of emptiness" could not be assuaged by the "endless whirl of worthwhile community activities" (quote in Murray 2003:149). To Friedan, access to real jobs—careers—was blocked by volunteer work. Community work was part of the feminine mystique, a way for women to "fill time" in a ladylike way. In 1973, the National Organization for Women passed a resolution condemning volunteering as an extension of unpaid housework that reinforced women's low self-image. Later historians have sought to challenge the view that the volunteer work of women in the 1950s was quite so meaningless and disempowering and, indeed, by the end of the decade, NOW had changed its bylaws to remove the prohibition against service volunteering (Ellis and Noyes 1990:266), but questions surrounding the association between volunteerism and women's roles remain (Murray 2003).

In the opinion of contemporary feminists, volunteer work continues to be gendered, but in a more subtle way, by influencing the kind of volunteer work men and women do. When men assent to undertake volunteer work it tends to be in the public domain. "Public domain characteristics include primarily civic, industrial, professional, organizational, public, community, extra-domestic, bureaucratic, and formally rationalized dimensions; private domain characteristics are familial, intimate, informal, personal, nurturant or preservative, and household related" (Brown and Ferguson 1995:160). Men's work on behalf of the community is thus an extension of their authority in the workplace. It is seen as more rational and "civic." In contrast, any work women do outside the household on behalf of others in the community is characterized as an extension of their expertise and authority in the private domain. It connotes volunteer work on behalf of people in need. In the context of this ideology, women find it more difficult than men to play the role of the advocate or social activist, where these terms denote public action to influence legislative, judicial, political, or mass media institutions.

These differences are illustrated in a study of women helping fight toxic hazards in their community. Although opinion polls show that women care more about the environment than men, they are less active in national environmentalist movements such as the Sierra Club. And yet they are more likely than men to participate in local actions, such as getting involved in groups fighting the dumping of toxic waste in specific locations. Most are house-wives, typically from working class and lower middle class backgrounds, be-cause these are the neighborhoods adjacent to which most of the dumping takes place, and many became active after seeing their own children become ill (Brown and Ferguson 1995:148). Although they are barely visible in the leadership ranks of larger environmental movements, women rapidly ascend to leadership positions in local groups. This is partly because they choose to describe themselves not as civil rights activists but as guardians of morality: corporations are targeted not because they have violated the rights of citizens but because they have violated a moral imperative of caring and responsibil-ity for the next generation. At the core of women's involvement in the toxic waste campaign are reproductive concerns: "Women are particularly con-cerned with the reproductive hazards they face and with the impact on child-hood health of familial exposure to toxic wastes" (Brown and Ferguson 1995:162). This case could be multiplied many times. It is an instance of a general pattern whereby the volunteer work of women is described using tra-ditional terms of nurturance, caring, and moral concern and in which women have a harder time than men being accepted as actors on the public stage. Women are not entirely absent from the public domain; they are very active in many kinds of political volunteering and social activism. But for women more than men, volunteer work is associated with parental roles or caring roles more generally.[1]

Socialization

In a well-known book, Gilligan (1982) argued that women differ from men in their adoption of an ethic of care and responsibility for others. Men, in contrast, tend to think in abstract terms, emphasizing justice concerns and individual rights. The implication is not that women are more likely to vol-unteer than men but that they express their ethic of caring in different ways and in different social contexts. Survey research using large random samples show that girls have more prosocial attitudes than boys. In a 1995 study of adolescents in seven European countries, girls were more likely than boys to feel compassion or concern for the well-being of others, regardless of their social class or level of religiosity (Flanagan et al. 1998:461). Girls were more likely than boys to say that their families emphasized an ethic of social re-sponsibility in their upbringing (Flanagan et al. 1998:463). In the United States, adolescent girls (67%) are more likely than boys (53%) to believe it is important for young people to learn the value of community service. Girls are also more likely to believe that community service should be a graduation re-quirement (Wirthlin Group 1995b:15). Girls are more likely than boys to ex-hibit altruistic feelings and empathy and to feel guilty when they have not been compassionate. Peer group support for volunteer work is stronger for girls than boys. A study conducted in England found that 20 percent of the schoolgirls (14–16 years old) were regular volunteers compared to only 8 percent of the boys: the boys were ridiculed if they volunteered (Roker et al. 1999b). Even the stigma attached to volunteering among teenagers is gendered: for boys, volunteering is a sign of softness; for girls it is a sign of adopting an adult role too soon (Wuthnow 1995:160). It remains an open question, however, as to whether these differences reflect deep-seated traits, as implied by Gilligan's argument.[2] Most sociologists would argue that boys and girls are different because of the way they are socialized. Learning to accept responsibility for care is part of learning to be a woman.

The Meaning of Volunteering

Earlier, we suggested that the volunteer role might mean different things to men and women. Men take a more instrumental approach to their volunteer work. This can mean a number of things. First, for women, doing care work is part of their understanding of themselves as persons, "whereas young men are more likely to associate caring with the accomplishment of specific tasks" such as raising funds for a particular campaign (Wuthnow 1995:152). Second, while women are more likely to regard caring as an expression of their selfhood, "men are more likely to associate caring with the specific roles they play" such as volunteering at their children's school once they become fathers or volunteering at work once they reach a certain occupational level (Wuthnow 1995:166). Third, men are opportunistic about volunteer work—they respond to requests to volunteer if it suits their needs and fits their schedule—whereas women engage in what Rossi (2001c:303) calls "compulsory altruism." Women's volunteer roles are not so much choices as fates. Their volunteer work is hardly "voluntary" at all but is, instead, the discharging of a duty "shaped by the institution of motherhood and the motherhood mandate" (Prentice and Ferguson 2000:119). For example, mothers who volunteer at day care centers do so in order to make them more "caring places" for their children—the simulation of home in a public setting. Fourth, women are more likely than men "to emphasize expressive motives, such as feeling needed, feeling compassion toward people in need, and gaining enjoyment" (Wuthnow 1995:168). This difference in instrumentality crops up in an Australian survey of teenagers and young adults that found males who were unhappy with their jobs volunteered more than those who were content with their jobs, but among the females satisfaction with job was unrelated to volunteering. Males were more likely to volunteer if they were unhappy with their future prospects, whereas females were more likely to volunteer if they were happy with those prospects. In short, for females, volunteering seemed to be independent of their work or work intentions, but for males volunteering was instrumental, tied more closely to how they felt about their jobs

(Brown et al. 2003:12). Fifth, men rely more on specific rewards for doing volunteer work than women. In a study of homeless shelter volunteers women ranked as the most positive experience "gaining in awareness and understanding," while men ranked "guest attitude and appreciation" as the most rewarding aspect. Twenty percent of the men but only 5 percent of the women mentioned fulfilling a need as a positive experience. The men adopted a more instrumental attitude toward their volunteer work. The men at the shelter certainly did "nurturing" work, providing direct assistance to "guests," but tended to rationalize their involvement instrumentally. Conversely, the women were quite capable of taking on many of the more instrumental roles normally performed by men but tended to define these roles in social and emotional terms (Anderson and Osmus 1988). The same volunteer role could therefore be interpreted in different ways depending on the gender of the volunteer.

Writing at the height of the feminist movement Gold (1971:384) declared, "until recently 'volunteer' was synonymous with 'woman.' " In the intervening years many changes have occurred in gender relations, not the least of which is the movement of many more middle class women into the labor force. More recently, even mothers of young children have been taking on full-time jobs. Not only have the traditional ideas about gender domains changed, but women have experienced a time squeeze that many believe has undermined this stereotype: women no longer bear the brunt of the burden of doing community service work, and women have become much more active in advocacy and political movements. In this section we will review the results of surveys to measure the extent of gender differences in volunteering. Because we believe ideas about the activities appropriate for men and women are learned, we will begin by looking at the evidence concerning young people and then move on to the study of adults. Another reason for this sequence is that gender differences in volunteering might well change over the life course as men and women take on work and family responsibilities. We will then look at surveys to see if men and women volunteer for different kinds of volunteer work.

Adolescents

Earlier, we described how teenage boys are more likely than teenage girls to disparage peers who do volunteer work. Teenage girls express stronger support for prosocial values than teenage boys. The evidence is somewhat mixed on whether this results in differences in volunteering. Looking back, adult males and females are equally likely to say they did volunteer work in their youth (Toppe et al. 2002:93). A 1991 survey asked American teenagers if they had done any volunteer work in the previous twelve months: there was no gender difference (Wuthnow 1995:162). Other studies, however, point to gender differences, although they are typically quite small. A survey of sixth through twelfth graders in the United States found that girls were more likely to be currently volunteering than boys (Nolin et al. 1997:36).[3] Just over half the girls (53%) volunteered compared to 45 percent of the boys. A 2005 survey of a random sample of American youth aged between 12 and 18 found that 58 percent of the girls had volunteered in the past year, compared with 49 percent of the boys. The girls were also more committed to the volunteer role: they were more likely than boys to be regular volunteers, whereas the boys were slightly more likely than girls to be episodic volunteers (Grimm et al. 2005). Monitoring the Future, an annual survey of high school seniors in the United States, shows a consistent but quite small gender difference in volunteering. Averaging the five years between 1990 and 1994, 64.8 percent of the males but 73.1 percent of the females had volunteered (http://nces.ed.giv.pubs98). In 2001 the same survey found that 38.8 percent of the females but only 28.2 percent of the males had volunteered at least once or twice a month in the previous year (Fox et al. 2005:84). A 2001 survey of U.S. college freshman also found gender differences in volunteering. Freshmen were asked how many hours they had spent doing volunteer work in their senior year in high school. More of the males (36.4%) than females (24.1%) said they had not volunteered at all. They were also asked if they planned to volunteer while in college. In 1990, 10.9 percent of the males and 22.1 percent of the females planned to volunteer. By 2001, the number of freshmen planning to volunteer in college had risen but the gender difference remained much the same: 14.9 percent of the males and 31.3 percent of the females (Astin et al. 2002).

Longitudinal studies suggest that the gender gap widens as people make the transition to adulthood. In a cohort of high school students in St. Paul, Minnesota, who were followed for some years after graduation, there were no gender differences while the students were in high school but when they became adults many of the males stopped volunteering and some of the females started volunteering, thus creating a gap between them (Oesterle et al. 2004:1143). Another study, also based on longitudinal data and a more representative sample, provides a slightly different picture. In the National Education Longitudinal Study of 1988, respondents were first asked about their volunteer work in 1992, when they were high school seniors. Information on volunteer work was gathered again in 1994 and 2000. In this study, girls were much more likely (50% to 38%) to volunteer than boys in high school. Two years after having graduated high school, this gender difference had disappeared. However, by 2000, when the respondents were aged 26, the male rate had dropped to 29 percent and the female rate to 37 percent, restoring the female advantage. As men and women entered adulthood and began to assume adult responsibilities, gender differences reappeared (Planty and Regnier 2003:4).

Adults

Adult women are more likely than adult men to value helping others (Wilson and Musick 1997a). Women score higher than men on a measure of "communion"—being helpful, warm, caring, and sympathetic—whereas men score more highly than women on "agency"—being forceful, assertive, and outspoken (Rossi 2001c:272). In addition, many people see volunteer work as part of the woman's domain. Burns et al (1997:378) found that "compared with husbands, wives were more likely to report being able to give time to voluntary activities—charitable, political, or social—without consultation [with their spouse]." This was true regardless of whether the wife worked full-time, part-time, or did not work for pay at all. While men might feel the same pressure to be charitable and philanthropic as women, "it is more likely to be pressure to make financial contributions than to serve as volunteers; recruiters often assume that men's roles as primary breadwinners preclude their serving as volunteers" (Rossi 2001c:304).

Despite these differences in attitudes, a review of the survey data on volunteering in different countries suggests caution when generalizing about the influence of gender on volunteering. In some countries (United States, United Kingdom), women are more likely to volunteer than men but men contribute more hours than women. In some countries (e.g., Australia), women are more likely to volunteer than men *and* they contribute more hours (Australian Bureau of Statistics 2002). In some countries (e.g., Canada), there is no gender difference in the overall rate of volunteering but men contribute more hours than women (Boraas 2003:4; Goddard 1994:15; Reed and Selbee 2000a:37). When all European countries are grouped together no gender differences are evident, but this is because females volunteer less than males in some countries, such as Sweden, and more than males in others, such as Great Britain (Gaskin and Smith 1997:29). In Japan, women are slightly more likely to volunteer than men (Statistics Bureau 2002). These gender differences in the rate of volunteering are typically small and they do not really give much support to the idea that volunteering is women's work.

Up to this point we have described studies reporting only zero-order level relationships. No controls are imposed for important socio-demographic variables and some of the gender differences reported above might be spurious. For example, in Canada, men and women are equally likely to volunteer, but once socio-demographic differences are controlled women have a greater probability of volunteering than men (Ravanera et al. 2002:5). We therefore turned to the Independent Sector data to perform a multivariate analysis of this problem. Prior to adjustments for other characteristics, women were more likely to volunteer and volunteered for more areas than men. There was no difference in the number of hours volunteered among those who had done volunteer work in the last month. Controlling for socio-demographic characteristics, the gender effect on any volunteering and volunteer areas became more pronounced. In other words, the characteristics were suppressing the gender effect: women would volunteer even more than men if they had the same socio-demographic characteristics. Volunteer hours remained unaffected. When we added church attendance to the model, the gender gap narrowed. Women volunteer more than men because they attend church more frequently. Volunteer hours remained unaffected. [58] American women are therefore slightly more likely to volunteer than men, in part because they attend church more frequently, and they would volunteer even more than men if they possessed the same socio-economic resources as men. However, these differences in religiosity and socio-economic status did not alter the fact that men and women volunteer the same number of hours, if they volunteer at all.[4]

Husbands and Wives

One of the major life transitions adults undergo is to get married. Families provide a "micro-environment" in which to observe gender differences in volunteering because spouses need to sort out who is responsible for doing what kinds of work. Many of the tasks of maintaining the household and taking care of children are divided between husband and wife. The question naturally arises as to whether the same gendered division of labor occurs with respect to volunteer work. Burns et al. (1997:378) gathered data from 273 married respondents: 179 married women and 94 of their husbands. They were asked about help they had provided in the last month on an informal basis (i.e., to non-kin or friends) and on a formal basis (i.e., hours spent volunteering). Husbands belonged to more groups than their wives, but there were no spousal differences in the number of hours volunteered. In a much more extensive analysis of nearly twenty thousand married couples, Rotolo and Wilson (2006a) found that 27 percent of the husbands had done some volunteer work in the past twelve months, compared to 35 percent of the wives, although there was no gender difference in the number of hours donated among those who did volunteer.

Gender Differences by Domain

Earlier, we mentioned the possibility that men and women are drawn to different kinds of volunteer work because they have been socialized into different ideas about what it means to care for, and about, others. The ethic of care articulated by men sounds different from the ethic of care articulated by women. Women express their altruism in terms of care and nurturance, whereas men express their altruism in terms of justice and being fair. This has less to do with essential gender differences than with the social situations in which men and women find themselves. Women take responsibility for the detailed, day-to-day care of kin and friends, where the provision of help is in many cases expected by the recipient (e.g., an aged parent). Men's "care work" is less focused on interpersonal relationships and is more likely to be impersonal and public. A man might explain his care work as an attempt to "make the world a better place," while women are more likely to refer to others who need (or expect) their help (Gerstel 2000:477).

> Women . . . act based on the issues that are most prominent in their lives. Abortion, education, and children's issues are all policy areas that women are more likely to confront directly based on gender roles and expectations. For disadvantaged women, basic human needs, social issues, and crime all directly touch the "private" family well being that women are traditionally responsible for. In contrast, men's gender roles focus on "public" sector issues and are reflected in their interest in taxes and other fiscal issues. (Caiazza and Hartmann 2001:6)

If this is true, men will be more likely than women to volunteer in connection with political and advocacy activities, and women will be more likely than men to volunteer for human service delivery and for activities linked to family roles, such as those associated with children, youth, and the elderly. It is well known that some areas of volunteer work have become the "preserve" of one gender. Volunteer fire and rescue departments are overwhelmingly male (Perkins 1988; Simpson 1996; Thompson 1993b, 1995). Hospice volunteers are almost all women.[5] In the United Kingdom, charity or thrift shops, where women typically comprise more than 80 percent of the volunteers, are defined as feminine spaces by both shoppers and volunteers (Horne and Maddrell 2002:77).[6]

To be sure, these are selected examples, and surveys of the general population rarely find such extreme differences in volunteer activity by gender. This is mainly because the categories used in surveys to identify different volunteer areas are so broad they embrace a wide variety of organizations offering a wide variety of services. Nevertheless, a pattern of gender differentiation by domain is discernible. For example, a 1991 survey asked American teenagers if they had done any volunteer work in the previous twelve months for any of seven different domains of volunteer work (e.g., health, education). Girls were more likely than boys to volunteer for health and education organizations. Boys were more likely than girls to volunteer for environmental groups (Wuthnow 1995:162).[7] A 1985 survey of adult Americans (18+) found that women were more likely to volunteer than men but only in the areas of health, education, religion, and fund-raising (Sundeen 1990:490). A random sample of Iowa residents was asked about their participation in church and non-church groups. Men were more likely than women to participate in non-church groups, women more likely than men to volunteer in church-related groups (Liu et al. 1998:443). In their study of married couples in the United States, Rotolo and Wilson (2006a) found that wives were more likely than their husbands to volunteer for religious, youth, culture and arts, and health-related organizations, whereas husbands were more likely than wives to volunteer for sports and civic organizations. Smith (1998:46) reports gender difference in "fields of interest" for the United Kingdom. Women were more likely than men to volunteer for children's education and religious activities; men were more likely than women to volunteer for sports and hobby organizations. In Australia, men were more likely than women to volunteer in connection with sports and recreational associations, business or professional associations and unions, and emergency services (Australian Bureau of Statistics 2002). In Japan women were more likely than men to volunteer for health, helping the elderly, the handicapped, children, environmental conservation, and disaster relief; men were more likely than women to volunteer for sports, culture and the arts, and public safety (Statistics Bureau 2002). A 1994 survey of eleven European countries found significant gender differences in only three domains: 36 percent of men but only 20 percent of women volunteered in connection with sports; 20 percent of women but only 16 percent of men volunteered in connection with social services; and 16 percent of women but only 9 percent of men volunteered in connection with schools (Gaskin and Smith 1997:35; Hofer 1999:121; Hooghe 2001:166).

It is difficult to summarize the results of these surveys because no consistent method of categorizing volunteer work is used, but some tentative generalizations can be made. First, the relatively modest gender differences in volunteering *in general* conceal conflicting tendencies at the level of particular volunteer activities. Men are more likely than women to volunteer in connection with public safety (or emergency services), sports, work-related activities, and, with somewhat less certainty, political or advocacy groups. Women are more likely than men to volunteer in connection with their church, schools, and for human services work in general (helping the ill, the elderly, the poor, and the hungry). Although these differences are quite small, they offset each other to give a slightly misleading picture at the level of overall volunteering. Second, in many areas of volunteer work there are no discernible gender differences: we should not be too hasty in assuming that a gender pattern found in one area is going to be found in others.

Most of the results reported above are zero-order effects. They do not control for factors, such as education and income, with which gender is frequently associated. We cannot be sure that even these minor differences indicate real gender effects until we control for these other factors. In order to isolate gender effects we turned to the World Values Survey (WVS) and the Independent Sector data. We sorted the volunteer activities in the WVS survey into "service," "activism," and "religion." [59] In the service category we placed social services, education, youth work, sports and recreation, and health organizations. In the religion category we placed just one organization, the church. In the activism category we placed labor unions, political groups, local community action groups, third world development organizations, conservation and animal rights organizations, professional associations, women's groups, and peace movements. On the basis of the research described earlier, we expected women to prefer service and church-related volunteering and men to prefer activism, but this is not what we found at all. Women were much *less* likely than men to volunteer to provide a service, and slightly *more* likely to volunteer as activists. There was no gender difference in the likelihood of volunteering in connection with religion. One probable reason why women were not more active than men in the "service" category is the inclusion of the sports and recreation type of volunteering in that category, which is a popular form of volunteering in Europe and which men tend to dominate. Another possible reason is that the activism category includes groups we would expect women to be more interested in than men (e.g., women's groups). Finer distinctions, not possible with this data set, are necessary to test accurately for gender effects on domain of volunteering. In our analysis of the Independent Sector data, men were over-represented in sports and work-related volunteering. Women were more likely than men to volunteer for human services, education, and religion, as well as arts and culture. There were no gender differences in volunteering for political, environmental, or public benefit activities.[8] [40] This is a somewhat clearer pattern of gender influence on choice of volunteer work than that found in the WVS data, but this might have as much to do with the way the domains are aggregated as it does with real differences in gender preferences in volunteer activity. Nevertheless, gender does matter: even after controls for the factors that might render this influence spurious men and women prefer, or are allocated to, different types of volunteer work.

Why the Gender Difference?

Both our own studies and those of other social scientists indicate that women are slightly more likely to volunteer than men, although they volunteer no more hours than men. These results certainly do not support the contention that volunteer is synonymous with woman but they do leave something to be explained. Why are women more likely to volunteer in most areas than men? In this section we will review some of the answers to this question that have been proposed.

Culture

An Australian female volunteer told researchers, "Men aren't interested in volunteering. They would rather play bowls and have a few drinks with mates" (Flick 2002:74). This attitude reflects a common stereotype that men prefer not to volunteer and suggests there might be cultural reasons for the gender difference we have found. It is well known that men and women approach the subject of social relationships in different ways, and this could help explain why they volunteer at different rates. In a general summary of the research on the topic of values and gender, Beutel and Marini (1995) conclude that female relationships to others are characterized by greater emotional intimacy, self-disclosure, and supportiveness, whereas male relationships emphasize mutual involvement in activities, impersonal gregariousness, and camaraderie; females exhibit a greater desire to be agreeable, to diffuse group tension and display group solidarity, whereas men engage in more task-oriented behaviors (giving suggestions, directions), are more competitive, and are less averse to disagreements; women are more likely than men to aspire to jobs that require social skills and call for emotional support, jobs that require helping others, and jobs that do not involve competition with other workers. They also found that people believe that women are kinder, more compassionate, and better able to devote themselves to the welfare of others; women are more likely than men to overlook differences between themselves and others and to have a sense of responsibility toward the underprivileged; and women are more adept than men at playing roles calling for empathy, moral reasoning, and taking the role of the other. To determine the empirical validity of these assumptions, they examined gender differences in values among respondents to the Monitoring the Future survey, a repeated cross-sectional survey of U.S. high school seniors. They used data from 1977, 1982, 1987, and 1991. They took five items from the survey and constructed a variable they call "compassion."[9] Females were more compassionate. Controlling for religiosity (church attendance frequency and importance of religion) did not eliminate this gender difference, although it did reduce it. In short, women are more compassionate than men and part of the reason is they are more religious.

The same data also showed that males and females look for different things in jobs. High school seniors were asked to rate the importance to them of a number of job characteristics. Two could be considered "altruistic rewards": "a job that gives you an opportunity to be directly helpful to others" and "a job that is worthwhile to society" (Marini et al. 1996:54). The researchers compared male and female ratings of the importance of these job attributes across four waves of the survey. Having a job that was helpful to others was rated very important by 58 percent of the females and 36 percent of the males. Being worthwhile to society was rated as very important by 51 percent of the females and 39 percent of the males. These gender differences persisted even after controls for race, parents' education, mother's employment, and religion. Other studies confirm these gender differences in values. A large 2001 survey of college freshman in the United States asked students whether they thought it was important to help others in difficulty: 60 percent of the males but 80 percent of the females thought it was important (Astin et al. 2002). The National Citizen Engagement Survey (2002) found that women expressed stronger support for prosocial norms than men. Fifty-one percent of the women (aged 15–25) agreed that "my responsibility is to make things better," compared to 43 percent of the men (Jenkins 2005:9).

Stating value positions is one thing; acting on the basis of those values is another. We cannot be sure these cultural differences translate into behavior. For example, Rossi (2001c:292) found that, although women were more compassionate than men, this did not explain why they were more likely to volunteer. We looked at the data from the Independent Sector surveys to see

Table 2. Estimated Net Effects of Personal Attitude
Indices and Controls on Any Volunteering.[1,2]

	Model 1	Model 2
Female	.25*	.08
Empathy	—	.64***
Pro-social	—	.88***
Intercept	−3.13***	−7.28***
R^2	.25	.28

Notes:
  [1] Unstandardized logistic regression coefficients are shown.
  [2] Models are adjusted for race, age, education, income, home ownership, work status, marital status, parental status, and religious service attendance.
  $p < .05$; ** $p < .01$; *** $p < .001$

if cultural differences could help explain gender differences in volunteering. We found that, regardless of religious and socio-economic and demographic differences, women were more empathic and more prosocial than men.[10] [28] To see if these dispositions helped explain the gender difference in volunteering we regressed gender on volunteering and then entered two variables measuring empathy and prosocial sentiments into the model.

As shown in Table 2, *the effect of gender on volunteering became insignificant when we entered these subjective dispositions into our model.* This result provides solid support for the theory that women are more likely to volunteer than men because of cultural differences.

We also examined gender differences in attitudes toward charitable institutions. One question in the Independent Sector survey measured the respondent's opinion about the need for charitable organizations and another measured the respondent's level of confidence in charitable organizations.[11] Women scored slightly higher on both measures. Because people who had more positive attitudes toward charitable institutions were more likely to volunteer, this partially explains the gender difference. Women volunteer more than men because they have more favorable attitudes toward charitable organizations. [51] This finding also supports a cultural theory of gender differences in volunteering.

Structure

From the perspective of structural theory, cultural differences between men and women are either secondary to, or can only operate within, the confines of structural differences between them. It does not matter how much women would like to volunteer or feel some responsibility to do so, if they lack the resources or the opportunities they are less likely to do so. We will deal with the influence of marital and parental status on volunteering in chapter 10, and we have already discussed the influence of employment status, or work hours, on volunteering. Here we will focus on explaining gender variations in volunteering as a result of differences between men and women in work and family roles.

Employment Status

Historically, volunteer work has operated as an *alternative* career for women outside the domain of paid employment. In the past, many women volunteered as a substitute for paid employment when norms concerning women's work outside the home made it difficult or when the jobs available to women were unpleasant and poorly paid. Volunteer work was an acceptable form of public life for women, especially for those belonging to the middle class. In this respect, volunteer work has always functioned as a source of autonomy and independence for women in their marriage. A female volunteer at a well woman's clinic told Merrell (2000:34), "It's an important part of my life. It's made me, part of me a single person in my own right, because when I started with (the clinic) I wasn't as independent as I am now and it's given me strength to be independent." Thus, despite the feminist criticisms of volunteerism we noted earlier, volunteer work can be empowering for women in marriages that are otherwise patriarchal (Abrahams 1996:783).[12] For other women, volunteer work is clearly a compensation for the low-quality jobs to which their gender has assigned them. Abrahams (1996:782) quotes one 66-year-old woman as saying,

> I don't know how other women feel, but I sure know how I feel, because of my age I've always had better jobs and more fun as a volunteer than I ever had in any paid work I ever did . . . I'm absolutely sure for me that what I volunteer for is always more important than what I get paid for.

Women are more likely than men to regard their volunteer work as an alternative to paid employment. For example, female emergency squad volunteers are less likely than their male counterparts to have a full-time job. For the women, being a volunteer *is* their job; for men it is an extension of their job (Gora and Nemerowicz 1985:13).[13]

Work Hours

In chapter 7 we looked at the influence of work hours on volunteering. The stereotype of the volunteer as a woman is partly based on the assumption that women, especially married women, have more free time than men because they are less likely to be in the labor force. There has been much speculation in recent years that the increasing labor force participation of women will eliminate gender differences in volunteering because women will no longer have the extra time to devote to volunteer work. As we pointed out earlier, the relation between work hours and volunteering is far from simple, and it is by no means clear that work hours have anything to do with gender differences in volunteering.

It is no secret that many voluntary associations and non-profit organizations are experiencing increasing difficulty getting women to volunteer, suggesting that their rate of volunteering might well fall to the level of men as they enter the labor force in increasing numbers. For example, members of the Junior League (a woman's organization) were surveyed in 1975 and again in 1992. In 1975, 16 percent were employed full-time, 17 percent were employed part-time, and the rest were homemakers. By 1992, nearly half (47%) of members were employed full-time and a further 20 percent were employed part-time. The employment rate of members had doubled in seventeen years. In response, the organization began scheduling more meetings in the evening, relaxed the volunteer work requirements for maintaining membership, and gave members more choice over when to do their volunteer work (Markham and Bonjean 1996). The movement of women into the labor force had also re-allocated volunteer labor within the organization so that it was not so widely dispersed among members. In 1975, members without jobs volunteered 39 percent more hours than members with jobs, but by 1992 this difference had shrunk to 30 percent. The negative impact of being employed on volunteer hours seemed to have declined in the seventeen-year span, but appearances can be deceiving. In fact, a few "super-volunteers" who were not employed had turned Junior League work into an avocation, occupying virtually all their time. In 1975, the 11 percent of members who volunteered ten hours a week or more contributed 31 percent of all the hours devoted to the organization. In 1992 these super-volunteers comprised only 9 percent of the membership but contributed 34 percent of the hours volunteered. The organization had thus adjusted to the increased labor force participation of women by concentrating more of the work in the hands of the minority of members without paid jobs (Markham and Bonjean 1996:707).

This study suggests that women volunteer less if they take a job and implies that any increase in the number of hours women work compared to the hours that men work will lessen the gap in volunteer hours between them, but survey data are needed to test this hypothesis. Using data from the Independent Sector surveys, we first analyzed the differences in work hours between men and women. Men were more likely to be in the labor force than women, and if women were working outside the home they were more likely than men to be working part-time. [60] When we looked to see if employment status mediates the link between gender and volunteering we found that *work hours did not explain the gender gap in volunteering.* [61] Women were spending less time working outside the home, but this was not the reason they were more likely to volunteer. We repeated this analysis using the Current Population Survey (CPS) data. The gender coefficient changed very little when we controlled for work hours. [62]

In chapter 7 we noted that increased work hours do not necessarily lead to a cutback in volunteer hours and it should therefore not come as a surprise that women who enter the labor force are not, for that reason, less likely to volunteer. Sociologists believe that women's time is more elastic than men's and we should not transfer our thinking about how the work hours of men affect their leisure time to our thinking about how the work hours of women affect their leisure pastimes. The multi-tasking environment in which women operate means they have been socialized to find the time to do many different things, perhaps simultaneously. This would mean that time spent on one task does not detract from time spent on another task—at least as much as it does for men. Two studies lend support to this theory. The first was a study of Israeli volunteers (aged 54–75), which found that men were more likely to say that their wife would have to find a way to accommodate their commitment to volunteer work to other demands on their time than women were to say their husbands needed to make this accommodation. This pattern of expectations continues even after people retire: women are still expected to find a way to continue to do volunteer work, regardless of other demands on their time from their families (Kulik 2002). The other study sampled residents of Ohio. In this sample men and women were equally likely to volunteer but, whereas men who volunteered were significantly less time pressured than other men, female volunteers were *more* time pressured than other women— and they reported more time pressure than men who volunteered. Why would male volunteers feel less time pressure than female volunteers? The answer is to be found in the kind of volunteer work they did. Men's volunteer activities were much more likely to involve sports-related organizations and hobby and special interest groups. These clearly had less impact on men's time than the volunteer work of women, which was more likely to include school-related activities, job-related associations, and working on behalf of civic and service clubs. Women's volunteer work consisted of mundane tasks, such as taking one's turn at a child's day care center or providing baked goods for a bake sale to raise money for a school trip, that were simply extensions of traditional female roles (Roxburgh 2002:140). The men's volunteer work was more discretionary and thus more subject to the influence of other time demands. They could drop their volunteer work if those other demands became too pressing. Women were different: they had to find time for volunteer work, even if other time demands increased. In short, if women need to accommodate other time demands in this way rather than giving in to them, then any extra time they spend on housework or child care is unlikely to help explain any gender differences in volunteering.[14]

Occupational Status

The idea that volunteerism is an alternative career for women is based on the assumption that women are less likely to be in the labor force. The men simply do not have the time to do the volunteer work. But if women do have a job, they are less likely than men to have the kind of professional or managerial job associated with volunteering. The implication is that women would volunteer even more than men if they had the same jobs as men.[15] We turned to the CPS data to explore this issue further, confining our analysis to respondents who had a job so that we could measure their occupational status. We first determined the proportion female in each occupational category: managers 42.5 percent, professionals 57.9 percent, clerical and sales workers 63.7 percent, and blue-collar workers 15.6 percent. We then estimated a model containing a gender variable and the usual socio-demographic controls, followed by a model containing the occupational status variable, using blue-collar workers as the contrast category. The gap between males and females narrowed as a result of the inclusion of the occupational status variable, indicating that women volunteered more than men partly because of their superior occupational status. A glance at the gender distributions within the occupational categories given above indicates why this is so: *women volunteer more than men, in part, because they are less likely to have a blue-collar job, an occupational category in which the rate of volunteering is the lowest.*

Social Networks

In chapter 12 we will describe how social networks help mobilize volunteers. The more people we know, and the more different people we know, the more likely we are to be asked to volunteer, and to volunteer. If there are gender differences in the size of social networks, this might explain some of the gender difference in volunteering. For example, Verba et al. (1995) explained the gender gap in civic engagement by showing that women were excluded from the recruitment networks in which men were involved. We looked at the Independent Sector data to see if social networks had anything to do with gender differences in volunteering. [63] We used two measures of social networks: number of voluntary association memberships and informal social interaction.[16] After determining that men have more memberships than women but there are no gender differences in informal social interaction, we entered these variables separately to distinguish their effects. After controlling number of memberships, the gender coefficient increased in size, indicating that lack of social network connections is inhibiting female volunteerism. Entering informal social interaction into the model made no further difference to the gender coefficient, confirming that voluntary association memberships partially explain the gender gap. *Women would volunteer even more than men if they belonged to as many voluntary associations as they do.* We also looked at the role of church attendance. Women attend church more frequently than men and they are also more likely to volunteer. By controlling for church attendance, we cut the gender effect almost in half. *One of the reasons why women volunteer more than men is that they attend church more frequently.* [20] As far as social networks are concerned, then, voluntary association memberships and church attendance seem to counterbalance each other: women have fewer resources of one kind, but more of the other. We also used the Independent Sector data to see if women volunteer more than men because they are more likely to be asked. Regardless of socio-demographic and religious differences, women were more likely than men to be asked to volunteer. After controlling for being asked, the gender effect on volunteering was greatly reduced. [64] *Women volunteer more than men because they are more likely to be asked to do so.* Interestingly, this is true even though they belong to fewer voluntary associations.

Moderating Effects

In the introduction to the book we argued that master statuses, such as gender, social class, age, and race, do not exist and operate in a social vacuum but intersect with each other, moderating and changing the way each behaves. This means we must pay careful attention to statuses, such as race, that might moderate the influence of gender on volunteering.

Race

Each gender is comprised of different racial and ethnic groups. This raises the possibility that race moderates the gender effect on volunteering. For example, a recent survey asked American teenagers to rate the importance of giving time through volunteer work to charitable, religious, or community organizations; making financial contributions to charitable, religious, or community organizations; making the world a better place; and doing things for people. White girls expressed stronger support for these prosocial values than White boys, but there were no gender differences among African American teenagers (Beutel and Johnson 2004). There are two hypotheses with respect to the potential moderating effect of race on gender. The first is that minority groups have a stronger need for solidarity, and social divisions tend to be attenuated by this need: class, age, and gender differences in civic engagement will be less pronounced in minority communities. The second is that gender differences are more pronounced in the African American community because, historically, women have been expected to shoulder more of the burden of community service than men (Hall-Russell and Kasberg 1997:29). According to this second theory, the gender ideology according to which women are more likely to do volunteer work than men is more pronounced in the Black community. Black women are made to feel a special responsibility to "hold the Black community together" (McDonald 1997:776). They are motivated by empathy for other Black women *and* African American norms of solidarity, responsibility, and accountability. McDonald (1997:776) refers to this combination of motives as "normative empathy." It finds expression especially among middle class Black women who want to help their less fortunate "sisters." Landry (2000:65) offers a slightly different argument: race moderates the gender effect on the *type* of volunteer work people do. For white women, volunteer work has been seen as an extension of their house-keeping role. Women's involvement in early social reform movements had to be justified on these grounds, and the "cult of domesticity" that legitimated women's exclusion from the workforce and "public" life in general allowed women to be active in their communities only if this was seen as an extension of their role as wives assisting their husbands or mothers taking care of their children. Black women, on the other hand, not only engaged in "charity" work but also "racial uplift" on behalf of the Black community as a whole. Black women, more than white women, tried to combine the three roles of family, work, and community activist (Landry 2000:72).

Analyses of this problem using survey data have yielded mixed results. The CPS data show that the gender gap is wider among Whites than non-Whites (Boraas 2003:4). Another study, using data from the Citizen Partici-pation Survey (1995), confirmed this, finding that in the sample as a whole men were *more* likely to volunteer than women (the volunteer measure is tilted toward political activities), but in the Black community the rates were virtually the same (Burns et al. 2001:299). Another study, of California resi-dents, drew finer distinctions within the non-White population. Although women in general were slightly more likely to volunteer than men this was not the case in the Asian American community, where there was no gender difference. The authors of the study speculate that this might be due to more extensive family obligations among Asian Americans (Ramakrishnan and Baldassare 2004:78). We used the Independent Sector data to test the hy-pothesis that gender differences in volunteering are more pronounced among Whites than African Americans. *The only statistically significant finding was that the gender gap in the number of areas for which people volunteer was smaller in the case of African Americans. Race made no difference to the gender effect on the chances of volunteering at all or the number of hours volunteered.* [65] We can therefore support neither the argument that soli-darity brings men and women together to do volunteer work nor the argu-ment that Black women are singled out as especially responsible for doing volunteer work.

Age

In chapters 10 and 11 we analyze volunteering changes over the life course. We will describe an American pattern whereby the volunteer rate is relatively high among people aged between 16 and 24 because a high pro-portion of them are in school or college where, in many cases, community service is either encouraged or required; the rate declines as people enter early adulthood (25–34) when many people are single, geographically mobile, and childless; it peaks in middle age, largely in response to the needs of school age children; and it declines subsequently as people pass through the empty nest phase, retire from their jobs, and begin to encounter the debilitating consequences of old age. Age variations in volunteering have a lot to do with changes in marital and parental status. Insofar as gender affects how marital and parental roles are performed, we should expect the influence of these roles on volunteering to differ by gender. Because women are primarily responsible for taking care of children, we would expect gender differences to be more pronounced in mid-life, when a larger proportion of volunteer work is focused on children's needs. This is exactly what the survey data show. In the United States, the gender gap gets wider in middle age (Boraas 2003:4). In later life, a higher proportion of volunteers are female, but this is because women outlive men: they actually have an equal tendency to volunteer (Chambre 1987:59). In middle age, women volunteer at a rate twelve percentage points higher than men, but among those aged 65 and over, the difference has shrunk to 1 percent (U.S. Bureau of Labor Statistics 2003).[17] The same pattern is found in the United Kingdom: overall, men and women are equally likely to say they had volunteered within the past three years, but in the 30–49 age group, women are more likely than men (Coulthard et al. 2002:7). A 2002 survey of Australians found that the gender difference in volunteer rates peaked in the 35–44 age category (Australian Bureau of Stastistics 2002).

We analyzed the CPS data to test for this age-gender effect. The results are shown in Figure 3. The percentages reported are adjusted for other sociodemographic variables. For the population as a whole the rate of volunteering is initially higher in the 16–24 age category largely because of high school and college encouragement of community service work. It falls in the 25–34 age category, to rise again in the two middle age categories, after which a decline begins, interrupted by the immediate post-retirement period. Comparing the rate for men and women, the volunteer rate is higher for women at all ages. The low rate of volunteering in early adulthood is principally attributable to reluctance of men to volunteer. Overall, the "bulge" in volunteering that occurs in mid-life, when most men and women have children of school age, is more pronounced for women than men. *The gender gap in volunteering does therefore vary across the life course, mainly in association with the child-rearing phase of life.*

Education

In chapter 6 we described how volunteer work has traditionally been a middle class activity. Working class people have tended to provide help more informally. These class differences intersect with gender such that the gender gap widens higher up the social ladder. According to the CPS data from 2002, the more schooling respondents had received the wider the gap between the volunteer rate of men and women (Boraas 2003:4). We tested the

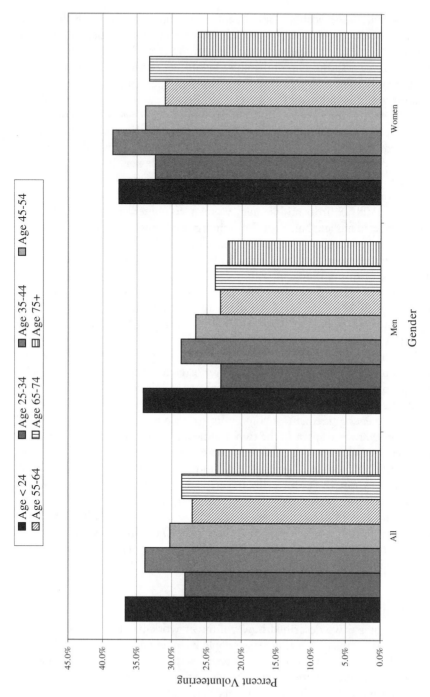

Figure 3. Adjusted mean levels of any volunteering by age category and gender.

interaction hypothesis with data from the Independent Sector, using education as a measure of social class. We found no overall interaction effect, but we did see effects in two domains. The positive effect of being female was stronger among those who had earned a high school diploma (versus dropping out of high school) in the case of educational and religious volunteering. [26] In short, education does not moderate the effect of gender on volunteering: women are more likely to volunteer than men, regardless of their social class.

Conclusion

In the United States, women are more likely to volunteer than men, they volunteer in more areas, but they do not volunteer more hours. The rather small gender difference is partially attributable to cultural factors (e.g., empathy), differences in social practices (e.g., church attendance), and the demands of other roles (e.g., mothers volunteering for their children). Women would volunteer even more than men if they joined voluntary associations at the same rate. The gender effect varies somewhat with race and age but not social class. Women and men choose different activities for which to volunteer, but the differences are small and both men and women volunteer in all domains. This is not to deny there are "gender enclaves" such as emergency squad work, which is predominantly male, and hospice volunteering, which is predominantly female. In the United States, these gender differences are fairly robust across surveys and they are independent of other possibly confounding factors, but reports on volunteering in social surveys are probably biased in favor of men and therefore the gap might be wider than it appears: men tend to over-interpret their behavior as altruistic while women under-interpret it (Midlarsky and Kahana 1994:227).[18] In Europe, the popularity of sports and recreation volunteering and the smaller number of people volunteering in connection with churches results in men being slightly more likely to volunteer than women.

In chapter 17 we will take up the question of whether the future supply of volunteer labor is threatened by the fact that more and more women are working outside the home. Based on the results described in this chapter it seems unlikely that the pool of volunteer labor will be seriously affected by this change. This is partly because women manage to find the time to do the volunteer work they consider necessary and partly due to the fact that voluntary associations and non-profits find different ways to use volunteer labor. Nevertheless, just because women find the time to do volunteer work does not mean they do it willingly or without hassles. Some volunteer tasks are difficult to fit into the "double shift" of working mothers and not all organizations (or spouses) have made the adjustment necessary. We described how the Junior League has re-structured the organization of volunteer work to accommodate the increasing number of members who are working mothers.

But the voluntary sector as a whole has still not adjusted adequately to the changing role of women and has not adopted "women friendly practices."

> No one asks volunteers, do you need childcare? They'll ask you what your food preferences are if you're going to a conference, but they won't ask you, say if you serve on a board, do you need accommodation because of children, e.g., an earlier meeting time? They don't ask you if you need hotel accommodation with a play area or supervised childcare services, etc., or, for example, offer women charitable receipts for childcare expenses. (Mailloux et al. 2002:12)

In the nineteenth century, volunteer work was one way in which women could leave the confines of the domestic sphere and enter the public domain. Although these spheres are no longer so rigidly separated and although women today find it easier to act on the public stage, they still find it expedient to legitimate their volunteer work by invoking family responsibilities. The emphasis has, however, changed. Whereas earlier women would have turned political issues into domestic issues they are now more likely to turn domestic issues in political issues. Women who volunteer to help out in day care centers are good examples. Many of these day care centers, while nominally private, obtain funding in various forms from public agencies and must conform to state mandates. To this degree they are public agencies. But the women who become involved in these day care centers as volunteers do so primarily because they are concerned about the quality of care their own children are receiving while they are at work. Their volunteer work is both domestic and public at the same time. It is even subject to public regulation: in some provinces in Canada parental involvement is a requirement of having one's child attend the center (Prentice and Ferguson 2000:1214). In short, women are not inevitably consigned to private, face-to-face volunteering by gender ideology. Women undertake a lot of community activism. This could be defined easily as public work, but the home—and by extension, the street and the neighborhood—is regarded as primarily the sphere of the woman rather than of the man. "Consequently, when a rent increase or a deterioration in service impinges on the home, it is usually the woman's task to deal with it since it lies within their sphere" (Lawson and Barton 1990:48). The line between private and public is transgressed.

9

Race

Social scientists regard race not as a biological phenomenon but as a socially constructed reality in which groups are ordered in a hierarchy based on real or alleged physical characteristics. These characteristics are then used to classify people into dominant and subordinate groups. Members of an ethnic group share cultural characteristics such as language or religion, and its members are believed to have a common origin. Ethnic groups are also ranked—as in the social distinction between English and Irish White Americans. While some social scientists would prefer to abandon the term "race" altogether in favor of "ethnicity" because the latter term avoids any hint of biological determinism and because the so-called racial groups (e.g., "Blacks") differ so much in terms of their ethnicity (e.g., language, religion, country of origin) that it makes little sense to think of them as a single (racial) group, others want to preserve the distinction to refer to the superior power of the racial designation, with its imputation of biological superiority and inferiority and its ability to naturalize relations of domination and super-ordination. For example, it is easier for Italian Americans to avoid or escape social stigma by Whites of English descent than it is African Americans. In addition, racialization is a common form of oppression. For example, many Anglos socially construct Hispanics as a distinctive and inferior racial group, using physical characteristics to code this (ethnic) minority group as inferior.

Although there are many racial and ethnic groups in the United States, the dominant relation is a hierarchical one based on White-on-Black oppression, dating from the days of slavery. But Hispanics and Asian Americans are playing increasingly prominent roles in American society, the Hispanics being closer in social standing to African Americans, the Asian Americans being closer in social standing to Whites. The Hispanic population in the United States is comprised of those who describe their origin or descent as Mexican, Puerto Rican, or Cuban or who say they are from other Caribbean or Latin American countries or from Spain. The sociological significance of these identities is that race and ethnicity continue to be major determinants of people's "life chances" in the United States. They influence access to education, jobs, housing, health care, political office, and sundry other aspects of contemporary living. Differential access to these resources is bound to have some effect on the volunteer rates of different racial and ethnic groups, which we will investigate in this chapter. But there is also a possibility that racial and ethnic identities influence volunteering over and above these factors because of socio-cultural differences between them.

Social scientists have long been interested in racial and ethnic differences in civic engagement. Their thinking has been guided by a number of theories. One theory is that minority group status alienates people from "the system" and discourages involvement in civic life. Another theory argues the opposite. The very exclusion of minority groups from mainstream economic and social life compels them to establish their own social institutions in which leadership positions are available and for which volunteer labor is needed. A third theory also predicts higher rates of civic engagement, arguing that members of minority groups have a strong vested interest in acting collectively to defend their economic and social position. Minority status interest in "defending the race" creates a demand for volunteer labor in the Black community that is not present to the same degree among Whites. For example, given their status in society and their greater consciousness of race issues, it is hardly surprising that Blacks are more likely to participate in ethnic/cultural organizations than Whites (Stoll 2001:548). According to this argument, not only are Blacks more likely to be active on behalf of their community than Whites, but also race will trump the interests of class. In the White community the middle class might do most of the volunteer work but in the Black community the interests of solidarity overcome class divisions. In the Black community, professionals, such as teachers, lawyers, and ministers, seem to feel even more of a responsibility to become active in their community than White members of this occupational group.[1]

Black women in the Delta who work in helping professions find themselves in a unique position as leaders in their own communities. They have the benefit of knowing the economic and political landscape where they live and are savvy about how to get things done; they may be trusted by both the poor and the powerful. They have a sense of obligation to their community as members of the middle class relatively unfettered by the white elite, and they have a kind of 'self-interest' in making this community a better place for their own children. (Duncan et al. 1999:155)

Racial solidarity means that Blacks who have "made it" feel a strong obligation to those who have been left behind. They are motivated to "give something back." In the words of an African American volunteer,

> There are some expectations among the people that I know and have known that black people will take care of each other, just because they're black. It's like the perception we have about blood relatives. You never put a blood relative out on the street. It's extremely taboo. (Smith et al. 1999:21)

This is not an abstract sense of generalized reciprocity, which is just as common among Whites, but instead is tied to the survival of the community and its members. Blacks are expected to help out because they are Black. "The African American community as a whole expects more from its own people than from the larger white community . . . and when my friends work for AIDS organizations and such they expect me to give 'cause they know me" (Smith et al. 1999:15). An African American told Smith et al. (1999:18),

> My parents definitely taught by example, and their teaching was: "You serve the black community." My father and both grandparents were attorneys and they served the black community where I grew up and I know they took cases *pro bono*. That's just what you do, and you don't say no to people 'cause you want to make more money and you give by being leaders in the community and speaking in the community for or against different things that are going on and also if at all possible you put your kids through school. That's giving back.

Volunteering is therefore one way for members of minority groups to express their solidarity with other members of the group. A 60-year-old African American male with a graduate degree describes his civic activity:

> I donate 10 percent of my income to charity and do a lot of volunteer work. I lecture, I'm in One Hundred African-American Men, I mentor African-American MBA students, and I serve on many boards. I used to coach and advise kids: I was even a scoutmaster once. (Hall-Russell and Kasberg 1997:24)

Despite the accumulation of ethnographic and anecdotal evidence on racial differences in volunteering, social scientists have only recently begun study these differences systematically. The civil rights movements of the 1960s and 1970s sparked considerable interest in racial differences in political participation, including volunteer work on behalf of political campaigns, issues, and organizations. Numerous studies found that Blacks were more active politically than Whites, once differences in socio-economic status were controlled. Blacks were said to be compensating for their exclusion from conventional avenues of social advancement by "over-participating" in voluntary associations (Guterbock and London 1983). It is unclear how much these findings generalize to volunteering today because Blacks had a strong vested interest in the civil rights campaigns of the time and, in any case, what might be true of volunteering in connection with political organizations might not be true of volunteering in connection with other kinds of voluntary associations and non-profit organizations.

Volunteer Differences by Racial and Ethnic Group

We are thus presented with two competing theories as to the relation between minority status and volunteering. One predicts that racial minority groups will volunteer less, in large part because they lack the individual and social resources necessary and have become disillusioned with civic life. The other predicts that minority groups volunteer at the same or even higher rate than the majority group because the voluntary sector is a place for them to find alternative sources of status and power and a way for them to express their solidarity with and help other members of a beleaguered group. In this section we will look at a number of social surveys to see if either of these theories is valid.

Youth Volunteering

Relatively little is known about racial/ethnic differences in volunteering early in the life course. A study of 14- to 16-year-old children in England found that Whites were almost twice as likely as to volunteer as the (mainly Asian) ethnic minority children in the study, some of whom expressed fears of racism if they became involved (Roker et al. 1999b). A recent survey of American youth aged between 11 and 19 found that 56 percent of the Whites had volunteered in the past year, compared to 53 percent of the Asian Americans, 47 percent of the African Americans, and 31 percent of the Native American Indians (Grimm et al. 2005). A 2001 study of American high school seniors, however, found that 34.7 percent of White Americans had volunteered "at least once or twice a month" in the previous year compared to 36.1 percent of Blacks. On the other hand, more Blacks (27.4%) had never volunteered than Whites (20.5%). Whites were more likely than Blacks to volunteer "a few times a year" (Fox et al. 2005:84). Unfortunately, it is not possible to determine from these reports how much of the difference is due to race or ethnicity and how much is due to the socio-economic differences between racial and ethnic groups.

Adult Volunteering

Judging by the results cited above, Black youth are less likely to volunteer than White youth but we do not know how persistent these differences are. A study that followed the same American high school cohort in consecutive surveys found that the racial gap changed over time. Whites volunteered more than Blacks in high school, but two years after graduation the only racial or ethnic difference was a gap of seven percentage points between Whites and Hispanics. Six years later, the Blacks in the cohort were volunteering more than any other racial group (Planty and Regnier 2003:9). Most surveys, however, indicate that adult Whites volunteer more than Blacks. According to the 2003 Current Population Survey (CPS) survey, the rate of volunteering among Whites was considerably higher (30.6%) than among Blacks (20.0%), Asian Americans (18.7%), and Hispanics (15.7%) (U.S. Bureau of Labor Statistics 2003). Among volunteers, Blacks and Whites averaged the same number of hours per year, with Hispanics and Asian Americans contributing fewer hours. Using the same CPS data on a sub-sample of California residents, Ramakrishnan and Baldassare (2004:58) found that, although Whites accounted for only about half the population, they contributed about three-quarters of the volunteer hours donated by the state's residents. Blacks contributed volunteer work in proportion to their representation in the population. Both Hispanics and Asian Americans were under-represented: Latinos accounted for more than one in four adult residents but for only 14 percent of all volunteer hours; Asian Americans account for 12 percent of the adult resident population in California but only 7 percent of volunteer hours.[2]

The population of the United Kingdom is more racially homogeneous than that of the United States, but racial and ethnic minorities nevertheless comprise a significant portion of the population. The Home Office Citizenship Survey found that Blacks (42%) were slightly *more* likely to have volunteered than Whites (39%), with Asian (35%) reporting the lowest rate. Black women were the most likely to volunteer (45%) and Asian women the least (32%) (Prime et al. 2002:4).

In our own bivariate analysis of the Independent Sector data Blacks volunteered at a lower rate than Whites but, among volunteers, Blacks contributed more hours. There was no difference in hours volunteered between Whites and other racial groups.[3] [53] Using the CPS data set we were able to distinguish more racial or ethnic groups but we could not control for frequency of church attendance. At the zero order level, 30 percent of White Americans volunteered in the previous twelve months, compared to 20.0 percent of African Americans, 18.7 percent of Asian Americans, and 15.7 percent of Hispanics. Whites were more likely to have volunteered than any other racial group. However, among volunteers, African Americans contributed the most hours. We display the results of this analysis in Figure 4. These percentages and mean level of hours volunteered by those who volunteer are adjusted for socio-demographic differences.

Race and Domain

The different resources, culture, and interests of racial and ethnic groups suggest that they will be prefer, or have a greater need for, different types of

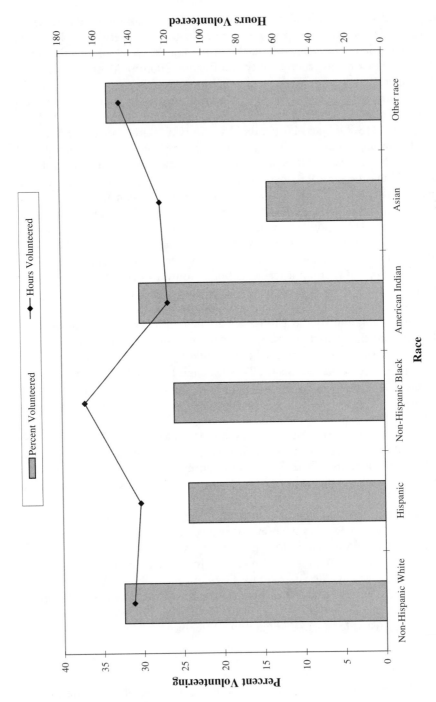

Figure 4. Mean levels of any volunteering and hours volunteered by race.

volunteer activity. As a result of social exclusion and economic deprivation minority groups give more priority to volunteer work devoted to defending the group from oppression by (for example) joining racial and ethnic associations, the delivery of needed social services, and meeting immediate, local needs, through neighborhood associations and community groups. Minority groups see little benefit in volunteering for groups concerned with non-local issues, such as environmental pollution or international aid, and their socio-economic position militates against volunteering for artistic and cultural activities. They also have less interest in professional and other economic associations because they are unlikely to have economic or social interests promoted by them, with the exception of labor unions.

Besides the influence of socio-political interests, Black volunteering is also affected by the role of the church in the Black community. The history of African Americans in the United States is one in which life has been centered on the church. Black civic life in the twentieth century was largely built on the foundation of the church and "the black church continues to be the primary institution through which blacks engage in philanthropy" (Hall-Russell and Krasberg 1997:22). Blacks are more likely than Anglos or Hispanics to say that religion is important to them, they give more hours to "church work" per week, and they are more likely to have served as a board member or officer in their church (Burns et al. 2001:284; Stoll 2001:548). Because Blacks have a stronger interest in, or preference for, volunteering in connection with the church, the influence of race on volunteering in this domain should be the reverse of that found in other areas: Blacks should volunteer more than Whites.

Finally, we might expect minority groups to be especially concerned with organizations and non-profits focusing on the needs of the poor because so many of their members live at or below the poverty line. The oppression African Americans face in the United States compels them to turn inward to their own community for many of the social services Whites do not need, can buy for themselves, or more easily obtain from the government. Several scholars have written that when Blacks volunteer they tend to focus more than Whites on the pressing needs in the Black community, such as efforts to deal with crime and provide human services (Ferree et al. 1998:17; Gallagher 1994b:76; Portney and Berry 1997:639; Sundeen 1992). The need for social service delivery is so strong that African Americans with the resources to perform high status volunteer work, such as fund-raising for a museum, donate their time instead to social service work. A Black woman with a graduate degree told Hall-Russell and Kasberg (1997:13),

> If you have been nurtured in a community by not only your family and friends, but also from the institutions in place in that community, you cannot simply turn your back once you have 'made it'. There are still children left in those neighborhoods that need role models just like you had.

Successful African Americans who turn their back on their community are referred to as "sell-outs" and are said to be "cashing in." The stronger demand for social service provision might help explain why elderly Blacks volunteer more hours than elderly Whites, since they are more likely to be surrounded by other elderly people in need of help (Fischer and Schaffer 1993; Gallagher 1994b:37; Glass et al. 1995). If Black communities have more social service needs than White communities, volunteering in this domain should also reverse that found in other areas, except religion: Blacks should volunteer more than Whites.

We used the Independent Sector data to see if there were racial differences in volunteering by domain, controlling for socio-demographic and religious differences. This data set only allows us to make meaningful distinctions between Whites, African Americans, and Hispanics. As far as religious volunteering was concerned, Blacks were more likely to volunteer in this domain than Whites, until church attendance was controlled, after which Whites volunteered more than Blacks. African Americans do volunteer more for their church, one reason being they attend church more often. As far as human services are concerned, Blacks volunteered less than Whites, and even more so when church attendance was controlled. Blacks were less likely to volunteer for political organizations than Whites. *In no domain other than religion did Blacks volunteer more than Whites.*

Hispanics are also a minority group in the United States, experiencing the same kind of social exclusion faced by African Americans. In addition, most of them belong to the Catholic church, which, as we learned in chapter 5, does not encourage volunteer work as much as Protestantism. Our analysis of the Independent Sector data showed that, like other minority groups, Hispanics volunteer less than Whites in the following areas: environmental causes, adult recreation, youth development, and health organizations. There were no differences between Hispanics and Whites in international, education, human services, public benefit, arts and culture, foundations, or political volunteering. But in no domain were Hispanics more likely to volunteer than Whites. [40]

In summary, the commonly held view that the church is the target of much of the volunteer work of African Americans is largely supported by these analyses but otherwise they are less likely to volunteer than Whites. The growing Hispanic population volunteers in no domain more than Whites, but in several domains they volunteer just as much once their socio-economic differences are eliminated. There is no evidence that either Hispanics or Non-Hispanic Blacks are especially drawn to human services volunteering or advocacy volunteering.

Explaining Racial Differences in Volunteering

In the United States, Whites are more likely to volunteer than other racial groups, although they contribute no more hours than African Americans. In this section we will review some of the theories that might help explain this racial difference.

Immigration

Racial and ethnic differences in the United States and other western societies are easily confounded with immigrant status because waves of immigration have been associated with particular racial and ethnic groups. Newly immigrant groups tend to start at the bottom of the social ladder. They are less familiar with social customs and civil practices and they usually face discrimination from established residents. For cultural reasons, recently arrived immigrants are likely to be unfamiliar with the volunteer role as it is practiced in the United States and other modern societies. A study of younger Canadians found that first-generation immigrants were more likely than long-established residents to give as a reason for not volunteering their ignorance of how to get involved (Tossutti 2003). Newly arrived immigrants do not speak the native language well and, as we shall see, this makes it more difficult for them to get involved in volunteer work. Newly arrived immigrants also tend to be socially isolated, their ties concentrated within their racial or ethnic community, and their social networks are correspondingly smaller. In consequence, they are more likely to be ignored or overlooked by volunteer recruiters.[4]

Survey data from several countries show that it takes a while for immigrants to begin volunteering. For example, a quarter of Canadians who entered the country thirty or more years ago volunteered in the past year, compared to 18 percent of newly arrived immigrants (Gomez and Gunderson 2003). This is not due to the inferior economic status of immigrants: the higher rate of volunteering among Canadians born in the country holds up even after controls for income, education, frequency of church attendance, health status, labor force participation, and marital and parental status (Ravanera et al. 2002). It is more likely to have something to do with language barriers: Canadians whose first language is not English are less likely to volunteer (Day and Devlin 1996:44). Immigrant status is also important in Australia, another country that has been the destination point for many emigrants and where immigrant status is tied to social status. A 2000 survey found that 34.3 percent of those born in Australia volunteered compared to 25.4 percent of those born outside the country (Australian Bureau of Statistics 2002). This difference is also probably due, in part, to language difficulties: Australians for whom English was not their primary language were less likely to volunteer (Brown et al. 2003:9). The significance of language (itself an indicator of broader cultural assimilation) is demonstrated in a special study of California residents showing that only about 10 percent of first generation non-citizens and 17 percent of the naturalized first generation immigrants volunteered in the previous year compared to 26 percent among second generation and 30 percent among those who were third generation or higher (Ramakrishnan and Baldassare 2004:60). English speakers were more likely to volunteer than Spanish speakers, after controlling for immigrant generation.[5]

Guided by this research, we analyzed the CPS data from 2003 to see if immigrant status explained some of the effect of race and ethnicity on volunteering. [66] First, we confirmed that the longer respondents had lived in the United States the more likely they were to volunteer, controlling for sociodemographic differences. Immigrant status did nothing to explain the volunteer gap between Whites and African Americans, but it did account for some of the difference between Whites and Hispanics and Whites and Asian Americans. Controlling for immigrant status also altered other racial or ethnic differences. At the zero order level, the gap between Whites and Hispanics was wider than that between Whites and Blacks. After we controlled for immigrant status, this pattern was reversed: now the gap between Whites and Blacks was wider than the gap between Whites and Hispanics. Immigrant status did a better job of explaining the difference between Whites and Hispanics than it did the difference between African Americans and Whites. We conclude that the more assimilated Hispanics become, the more they will begin to volunteer at the same rate as Whites. The same is not true for Blacks. We should note that immigrant status only partially mediates race and ethnic differences in volunteering. Even with year of entry into the United States controlled, Whites are still more likely to volunteer than Blacks, Hispanics, or Asian Americans.

Social Networks

As we shall see in chapter 12, social networks connect individuals to opportunities to volunteer. If there are racial differences in social networks, this might help explain racial differences in volunteering. A 1995 national survey asked American teenage volunteers how they had learned about the volunteer work they were currently doing. About a fifth of them learned through participation in an organization or group. White teenagers were more likely than non-White teenagers to have learned about volunteer opportunities in this way (Sundeen and Raskoff 2000:188). In an earlier study, we analyzed Americans' Changing Lives (ACL) data to see if social networks helped explain race differences in hours volunteered in the past year (Musick et al. 2000). Taking the standardized means of two variables we created an index of informal social interaction.[6] Formal social interaction was measured by two variables: frequency of attendance at voluntary association meetings and frequency of church attendance. Blacks had higher rates of informal social interaction, meeting attendance, and service attendance.[7] They were thus involved in a more complex web of social interactions than Whites. Informal social interaction, meeting attendance, and service attendance all increased the number of hours volunteered. Controlling for informal and formal social interaction widened the gap in volunteer rates between Blacks and Whites. In other words, *the tendency of African Americans to have higher rates of both formal and informal interaction compensated for their lack of individual resources (e.g., income, education) to bring the volunteer rates of the two races closer together.* Whites would volunteer even more than Blacks if their social networks were as extensive.

This is a surprising finding not because social networks encourage volunteering but because the networks of Blacks in the ACL survey were more extensive than those of Whites. We therefore partially replicated this study using data from the Independent Sector survey.[8] [20, 21, 53] Unlike the earlier study, Blacks belonged to fewer voluntary associations, although they did report higher levels of informal social interaction and church attendance. Before entering the social network variables in our model we determined that Whites were more likely to volunteer and volunteered in more areas than other racial or ethnic groups. Looking first at *any* volunteering, we discovered that Whites would volunteer even more than Blacks and Hispanics if they attended church as frequently as they do. On the other hand, it was also clear that Blacks and Hispanics do not volunteer as much as Whites partly because they belong to fewer voluntary associations. We found much the same pattern of results with respect to the number of volunteer activities reported by respondents. Minority groups thus gain from their religiosity but lose from their lack of other social networks. As far as number of hours volunteered is concerned, Blacks donated more hours than Whites (there were no other racial differences) but this had nothing to do with frequency of church attendance. On the other hand, Black volunteers would contribute even more hours than Whites if they belonged to the same number of voluntary associations.

Is Church Attendance More Important for African American Volunteering?

In the two analyses just described, we discover that church attendance helps explain some of the race difference in volunteering. People who attend church frequently are more likely to volunteer, and Blacks attend church more frequently than Whites. But historians have long maintained that the church is a *more* important social institution in the Black community than among Whites, the implication being that Blacks are more involved in their churches and that religion is more important to them.[9] As reported above, African Americans and Hispanics are less likely to volunteer than Whites, a gap that widens when we control for church attendance. In other words, both groups would volunteer even less than Whites than they do now were it not for the fact they attend church more often. This finding, however, does not quite answer the question whether the church is *more* important to Black volunteering than White.

The argument that the church is more salient to the civic life of Blacks has a long history. It points to the way in which minority communities have relied heavily on the church to mobilize service on behalf of the community. Blacks are believed to channel more of their philanthropic work through their churches because they feel more in control of them. "In the past, non-profit organizations that have sought to get African American support for their various campaigns have gone to the church. Many Blacks prefer to sponsor church programs because they are suspicious of other non-profit organizations" (Smith et al. 1999:25). In one recent survey Blacks were more likely than Whites to say their church had influenced their decision to volunteer (Ferree et al. 1998:76). If this line of argument is correct, frequency of church attendance should have a stronger effect on volunteering among Blacks than Whites. If, for example, the only volunteer activities available to Blacks are in connection with a church, then being an active member of that church is going to be a crucial determining factor. This suggests that the race *moderates* the positive influence of church attendance on volunteering.

There is another reason why church attendance might mobilize Black volunteers more effectively than Whites. Because of the way they are organized, African American churches involve more of their members in the kind of practices that foster volunteerism in the wider community. More intense involvement in the communal practices of their congregation teaches African Americans the kinds of skills they will need in the volunteer world. Verba et al. (1995:319) found that Blacks engage in more of the "civic acts" that teach civic skills (such as the ability to run a meeting) in church-related organizations than do Whites. Whites, on the other hand, engage in more civic acts than Blacks in secular organizations. When it comes to acquiring civic skills, Blacks get more out of church activities than Whites and Whites get more out of secular activities than Blacks.

In an earlier study, we compared the influence of church attendance on volunteering among Blacks and Whites. Frequency of church attendance had a much more powerful influence on Black than White volunteering.[10] Interestingly, the reverse was true of frequency of attendance at voluntary association meetings, which had a more powerful influence on White volunteering than Black volunteering (Musick et al. 2000:1556).[11] Church attendance has a stronger influence on Black volunteering than White volunteering because Black churches are greedier institutions than White churches, absorbing more of their members' volunteer time in congregational activities. The stronger effect of church attendance in the Black community would therefore be due to the fact that a lot of Black volunteering is for the church to which they belong. This becomes apparent when we compare the percentages of each race who volunteer for each of the five domains identified in the Americans' Changing Lives data set: education, elderly, political, religious, and "other." In the sample as a whole, Whites are about as likely to select church-related volunteer work as Blacks, but among those who volunteer for just one activity (and these comprise the majority of volunteers) Blacks are much more likely to select church-related work than Whites. *In other words, frequency of church attendance has a more powerful influence on the volunteer work of Blacks because that volunteer work is more likely to be connected with their church than is the case for Whites.* In summary, religious practices, such as attending church attendance, do seem to have a stronger effect on Black volunteering than White volunteering, but they mainly serve to mobilize volunteer in connection with the church.

Recruitment

One reason for looking at social networks and frequency of church attendance is that they increase the chances of being recruited to volunteer. Any evidence that minorities are less likely to be asked to volunteer indicates that discrimination is being practiced, especially if being asked is an important trigger event. Diaz et al. (2001) conjecture that Hispanics have lower volunteer rates than Anglos because they are less likely to be targeted by recruiters, but we can turn to survey data to resolve this issue. When non-volunteers are asked to say why they are not volunteering, 68 percent of Blacks explain they were not asked, compared to 44 percent of Whites (Ferree et al. 1998:64). Blacks are indeed less likely than Whites to be asked to volunteer (Hodgkinson 1995:44; Verba et al. 1995:151). The fact that White Americans are more likely to be asked to volunteer than African Americans is not entirely due to their higher levels of education and occupational status (Musick et al. 2000). *At every level of socio-economic achievement Blacks are less likely to be asked than Whites, and this accounts for some of the racial gap in volunteering.*[12] [67, 20]

This topic is worthy of much more study because it has to do with the question of whether or not there is a pattern of racial exclusion in the voluntary sector to equal that found in the employment sector. Whites volunteer more than minority groups because, in part, they are more likely to be recruited. The inferior resources of the Black population cannot entirely account for this pattern. However, it would be premature to conclude this is evidence of racial discrimination. The voluntary sector is somewhat racially segregated, and there are abundant volunteer opportunities for members of racial and ethnic minority groups within their own racial and ethnic communities.

Values

In part 2 of the book we discussed the role of subjective dispositions in volunteering, describing how personality traits, motives, values, norms, and attitudes influence how much people volunteer. If there are racial differences in subjective dispositions, they might help account for the racial gap in volunteering. Previous research does not lend much support to the theory that culture accounts for the racial differences. Blacks and Whites are not all that different as far as values relevant to volunteerism are concerned. Hughes (2001:193) constructed a measure of "altruism" using MIDUS data, defined as the felt degree of obligation toward helping others at one's own expense (e.g., collecting money for cancer research). There were no racial or ethnic differences in altruism. Even when racial differences in values have been found, they do not explain the gap in volunteering. In an earlier study, we found that Blacks were less likely than Whites to believe that helping others is important to living a good life, but this did not explain the racial difference, mainly because it was only weakly correlated with volunteering (Wilson and Musick 1997a).

Another way that culture could explain racial differences in volunteerism is by steering minority groups away from the palliative approach of providing service and toward structural solutions to social problems by legislative means. Blacks might simply be more skeptical of the effectiveness of volunteer work in dealing with the problems they face. It has been argued that volunteerism "connotes a form of privatized and individualized response to our human social problems" (Lisman 1998:16). Reliance on charity presumes that hunger, poverty, illiteracy, homelessness, and other social ills are rooted in individual shortcomings. This contrasts with the view that social problems have structural causes that must be tackled by social reform and political action. While Blacks and Whites are equally likely to attribute poverty to individualistic factors (Kluegel and Smith 1986:300), Blacks are more likely than Whites to believe that the government has an important role to play in funding and organizing programs for the poor (Sigelman and Welch 1994:142). Blacks are also more likely than Whites to believe that charitable organizations are doing work the government should really be doing (Ferree et al. 1998:77). These attitudinal differences might explain why fewer Blacks volunteer. Surveys show that people who believe that "the government has a basic responsibility to take care of people who can't take care of themselves" are less likely to volunteer than those who disagree with this statement: highly committed volunteers, those who volunteer four or more hours a week, feel very strongly that the work of alleviating social problems cannot be left to the government (Hodgkinson and Weitzman 1996:4–129). If Blacks believe governments, not individuals, should be tackling social problems, they might be less disposed to volunteer for this reason.

As we noted in part 2 of the book, the Independent Sector survey does not include questions on values but does include many measures of subjective dispositions, and we used some of these to explore differences between racial groups and to see if these differences accounted for the racial gap in volunteering. The question with the most direct bearing on values asked respondents if they felt they had a moral duty to help people who suffer. There were no racial differences in the responses to this question. We also used the measure of self-efficacy described in chapter 3: "It is in my power to do things that improve the welfare of others." Again, there were no racial differences. When we used the more extensive measure combining the feeling that we ought to help others less fortunate than ourselves with the belief what we could do something about it (see chapter 3). There were no Black-White differences on this index, but Hispanics were more prosocial than either of the other two groups. Finally, we used the measure of empathy developed in chapter 3: Whites scored higher on this index than Blacks or Hispanics. The important point, however, is that *none of these cultural differences accounted for race difference in volunteering.* [28, 68, 4] There is little evidence that racial and ethnic groups volunteer at different rates because they hold different values, have different perceptions of themselves, how to tackle social problems, or the effectiveness of volunteer work.

Trust

In chapter 3 we showed that trusting people are more likely to volunteer. One possible explanation for the racial difference in volunteering is that minority groups have good reason to be less trusting of others and this explains their lower rate of volunteering.[13] Minority groups do tend to be less trusting of others and of political institutions. Does this mean they are less likely to be active in their community and volunteer for voluntary organizations and non-profits? A study of the residents of Philadelphia and the surrounding suburbs found that Blacks had lower levels of interpersonal and institutional trust but trust was not related to volunteering and therefore did not help explain racial differences in volunteering (Kohut 1997). A survey of residents of Mobile, Alabama, in 1994 asked respondents how often they had worked to bring about change in the community. They were also asked to indicate their level of trust in the government of the city of Mobile, using a three-item battery of questions (e.g., "when government leaders here in the city of Mobile make statements to the people on television or in the newspapers, how often do you think they are telling the truth?"). The data showed that Blacks volunteered more often than Whites, controlling for age, gender, occupation, and education. They were also more trusting than Whites (Emig et al. 1996). In this case, because Blacks had higher trust than Whites, and because trust was positively related to volunteering for Blacks and not for Whites, it did help account for some of the racial difference, although the circumstances in this case (a study of one city, using as a dependent variable working to bring about change in the community, and measuring trust in local government officials) might make this rather unusual. Also, the cross-sectional data make it impossible to conclude that trust has positive consequences for volunteerism (at least among Blacks) because volunteering might increase the level of trust.

Drawing on the Independent Sector data we used a standard measure of generalized trust to look at the association between race, trust, and volunteering. The question was: "Generally speaking, would you say that most people can be trusted or that you can't be too careful in dealing with people?" Blacks were less trusting than Whites, but there was no difference between Hispanics and Whites. [9] *Lower levels of generalized trust did not significantly account for the racial gap in volunteering.* [5] We then used the items measuring confidence in charitable institutions to see if attitudes toward philanthropic organizations might account for the racial gap in volunteering. There were no racial differences in respondents' trust in charitable organizations, but Blacks were slightly more likely to see a need for charitable organizations than Whites. [69] However, controlling for these attitudes made no difference to the racial gap in volunteering. *Our conclusion is that the racial differences in generalized trust and in perceived need for charitable organizations do not explain why Whites volunteer more than Blacks and Hispanics.*

Social Class

Sociological debates about the significance of race in modern societies tend to focus on the issue of whether race has declined in importance relative to class, some arguing it has (Wilson 1980) and others contending that racism remains an important fact of life regardless of class (Willie 1978). The first group cite evidence showing that class is now a more reliable predictor of social mobility in the African American community and that Blacks are just as differentiated along class lines as Whites; the second group point to studies in a number of fields, such as housing, health care, and financial assets, showing that controlling for class does not eradicate race differences in life chances. If the first group of scholars is correct controlling for social class should get rid of any race effects on social participation in general and volunteering in particular; and this is indeed what most studies have found (Bobo and Gilliam 1990:382; Burns et al. 2001:299; Chambre 1987:77; Clary et al. 1996; Cutler and Danigelis 1993:155; Ellison and Gay 1989; Guterbock and London 1983; Kincade et al. 1996; Latting 1990:122; Romero 1986; Sundeen and Raskoff 1994:394; Wandersman et al. 1987; Woodard 1987:286; Wuthnow 1998:236). A few studies have found that Whites volunteer more than Blacks even after controls for socio-economic status (Glass et al. 1995; Raskoff and Sundeen 1995: Wilson and Musick 1997a).[14] Diverse results such as these make it difficult to conclude whether there really are race effects independent of social class. The studies differ widely in their definition of volunteering, their population samples, their control variables, and their methods of analysis. In what follows, our aim is to provide a surer foundation for drawing conclusions about the relation between social class, race, and volunteering by using a good measure of volunteering, a nationally representative sample of the population, and multivariate models suitable for the task in hand.

In an earlier study we used the ACL data to estimate the effect of race on volunteer hours, controlling for functional health, informal and formal social interaction, age, gender, church attendance, and marital and parental status (Musick et al. 2000). Initially, Whites had a 9 percent higher probability of being volunteers than Blacks and they contributed 5.13 more hours annually than Blacks if they did volunteer, but once we introduced educational and income variables into the model, the race difference disappeared. Using the Independent Sector data we estimated the effect of race on any volunteering in the past year, controlling for gender and age. Whites were more likely to have volunteered than any other racial or ethnic group. We then entered education and income variables into the model. The coefficients for Non-Hispanic Black and Hispanic were cut by a half and by two-thirds, respectively. In short, Whites volunteer more partly because they have more education and higher incomes. [70] We replicated this analysis using the 2003 CPS data. [71] The racial gap between Whites and other racial and ethnic groups narrowed once we controlled for education and income, the exception being the difference between Whites and Asian Americans, which became more pronounced. Asian Americans would volunteer even less than Whites if they did not have the same level of education and income. In short, two studies show that race continues to have an effect after controls for social class, and a third shows that race effects disappear once class is controlled for.

Social Class and Race Interaction

Up to this point we have discussed issues of race and class as if they operated independently of each other, but there is class stratification within races and racial stratification within classes (Omi and Winant 1986:34). A class is defined partly by the place and value it gives to racial differences, just as races are defined partly by their class composition. It follows that the effect of race on an outcome will be determined by which class fraction the actor belongs to, just as the effect of class depends on the actor's race. This raises the question whether the normal socio-demographic predictors of volunteering have the same effect on minority groups as they do on the majority group.

In this section we argue that White volunteering is more subject to class variation than Black volunteering. As we have seen, when it comes to resources for volunteering, religiosity counts more than class in the Black community.[15] The focal position of the church in the Black community suggests a further reason why the effect of class on volunteering should be weaker among Blacks than Whites: education and income do not translate into the same amount of status and prestige for Blacks as they do for Whites (Mirowsky and Ross 1989). Blacks looking to climb socially must turn, more so than Whites, to the church as a source of social status. In the church they can obtain positions of power and prestige denied them in mainstream organizations controlled by Whites.

In an earlier study we tested the theory that White volunteering is moderated by class differences more than Black volunteering, using data from the ACL. We found that education and income had positive effects on volunteering for Whites but not for Blacks (Wilson and Musick 1997b). Among Blacks, high-school dropouts were just as likely to volunteer as college graduates; and Blacks living below the poverty line were just as likely to volunteer as Blacks earning large salaries. Expectation states theory helps explain this pattern. Normally, people who have high status jobs (e.g., judge) are considered more competent in many settings outside the workplace and hence get generally better access to more powerful roles. This is why volunteer recruiters target people with educational credentials and other forms of human capital: they are judged to be more competent, even for jobs for which they have no training. However, this pattern of status generalization applies to Whites more than Blacks, whose educational attainment is discounted.

Conclusion

For a variety of reasons, racial and ethnic minority groups in the United States volunteer less than Whites, the one exception being that African Americans are more likely to volunteer in connection with their churches than are Whites. If they do decide to volunteer, however, African Americans contribute just as many hours as White Americans. Minority groups might be less likely to volunteer but this does not mean they provide no help to others. In subordinated groups help tends to be delivered more informally because their members lack the resources to provide assistance in a more organized fashion. When Americans 45 and older were asked if they did any "volunteering on your own to help your community or someone who was in need" more of the African Americans (41%) and Hispanics (41%) responded affirmatively than Whites (36%) or Asian Americans (32%) (Kutner and Love 2003). Sociologists believe that minority groups compensate for their limited economic resources by creating more intensive social support networks, characterized by frequent interaction, close affective bonds, and liberal exchanges of goods and services (Stack 1974). They prefer to provide aid on a personal basis, rather than through formal organizations.[16] This does not mean that minority groups ignore community needs, because informal assistance is defined as a community good. For example, African Americans define the family broadly to include "fictive kin" such as "cousins," "uncles" and "aunts" to whom they are not related by blood. They would not consider helping such people as volunteer work but the assistance reaches far beyond the household.[17]

The same pattern is found in other minority groups. Hispanic Americans emphasize the value of personal relationships, or making connections through people known personally. Trust in the individual is an important principle in the Hispanic community, and trust is most easily bestowed on

"the circle of those in whom you have *confianza*—family, *compadres*...
close friends, and friends of the family" (Royce and Rodriguez 1999:15).
Outside this circle, trust rapidly diminishes, making it difficult to mobilize
support for organizations and strangers served by those organizations. For
example, the Mexican American Legal Defense and Education Fund has a
more difficult time soliciting donations than the NAACP (Royce and Rodriguez 1999:15). Hispanics therefore tend to focus most of their giving on
the extended family, which often includes family members in their country of
origin. One Guatemalan told researchers: "Giving to strangers is laughable"
(Smith et al. 1999:50). Another said,

> When you are fortunate and receive something extra, it is luck and should be
> shared and enjoyed. [My parents] were generous when they could be and some-
> times when they could not. I don't remember many times when they gave some-
> thing for nothing. [Guatemalans] are not Americans and our manner of giving
> things is not comparable. To give something for nothing in our culture is only
> to be gullible, to have been tricked. (Smith et al. 1999:64)[18]

Members of the Asian community in the United States have an equally restricted notion of generalized reciprocity, as here expressed by a Japanese
American.

> We can't survive without helping each other. The only way people can survive is
> by helping each other . . . I think that the dominant white culture is strongly
> based on independence, while, I think this is true with other Asian cultures, but
> Japanese cultures is more based on interdependence and from that basic point
> the interpersonal relationship is so different, more of the "You scratch my back
> and I'll scratch your back" sort of thing going on and it is more accepted in the
> Asian cultures. (Smith et al. 1999:124)

Given these sentiments we might expect racial and ethnic minority
groups to exhibit higher rates of informal helping to "compensate" for their
lower level of volunteering. Indeed, the time spent helping informally might
well prevent them from spending much time volunteering formally. However,
in chapter 7 we demonstrated that people who spend time helping others informally tend to spend *more* time volunteering. One of the basic premises in
this argument therefore seems to be false. The activities do not compete with
each other. Chambre (1995:125) notes that some of the volunteers helping
out at a hospital where AIDS patients were being cared for had already been
informally visiting gay men with AIDS, some of them at home, and some of
them in other hospitals. They were doing this on their own initiative. Informal visiting sensitized them to the seriousness of the problem. They were also
more likely to be noticed and invited to formally volunteer. For Black and
Hispanic volunteers this was the most common route into volunteer work.
"For them, visiting the sick was an important and familiar activity but being

a 'volunteer' was less familiar and required a real invitation" (Chambre 1995:126).

In an earlier analysis, we looked at racial differences in providing help informally, holding volunteering constant (Musick and Wilson 1997a). We found no racial differences in the likelihood of providing informal help. However, we found that volunteers were more likely to offer informal help. Because Blacks were less likely to volunteer, they were less likely to provide informal help. We explored this issue further using the Independent Sector survey, which asks respondents if they had "volunteered" informally and alone in the past year. We first regressed informal volunteering on race, controlling for all the usual socio-demographic and religious variables. [72] Non-Hispanic Blacks were *less* likely than Whites to have provided informal help in the previous twelve months, as were Hispanics. Among those who provided any informal help at all, there were no Black-White differences in the number of hours spent helping, but Hispanics contributed more hours than Whites. The difference in informal helping persisted after we controlled for whether or not the respondent had volunteered in the previous twelve months. That is, regardless of how much volunteering they do, Blacks are still less likely to provide informal help than Whites. These two analyses of two different data sets contradict the argument that minority groups channel their altruistic impulses into more informal kinds of helping as a substitute for doing volunteer work.

In summary, the studies reported in the chapter confirm that there are racial and ethnic differences in the rate of volunteering that are only partly attributable to factors such as social class, social networks, values, trust, and the like. These remaining racial differences might well be attributable to discrimination, because minority group members are less likely to be invited to volunteer. The studies also indicate, however, that, once they enter the volunteer labor force African Americans contribute just as many hours as Whites. The race differences are such that they moderate the influence of social class on volunteering, although they do not appear to make much difference to the effect of gender. Finally, there is little evidence that Blacks compensate for their lower rate of volunteering by providing help more informally.

Part 4.

The Social Context of Volunteering

All of the theories we discussed so far treat the individual as the unit of analysis. They focus on intra-individual attributes such as personality traits or motivations, on the decision-making processes of individual rational actors, on identify formation and its consequences, or on the objective resources individuals possess that reduce the cost of volunteering. "The sociological analysis of altruism is dominated by the idea that it is a scarce resource unevenly distributed across individuals" (Healy 2004:4000). This level of analysis offers many valuable insights into volunteerism, but it obscures the fact that human beings are first and foremost social actors whose thinking and behavior are shaped by those around them. The capacity for altruistic action is structured and developed by the organizational and institutional environment. People are induced to volunteer by their social context, as well as by their individual dispositions and resources. What sociologists call social structure helps explain why employed people are more likely to volunteer than the unemployed, why married people with school age children are more likely to volunteer, why active church members, and people who are active members of all kinds of voluntary associations, are more likely to volunteer. Structure also helps explain why one spouse is more likely to volunteer if the other is doing so, why parents volunteer more than the childless, why middle aged people volunteer more than young adults. Structure helps explain why schools, voluntary associations, religious congregations, and neighborhoods influence volunteer behavior.

Social structure consists of "visible" social relationships, such as seeing our co-workers each day, or visiting the teachers in the school our children attend. It also consists of the social arrangements that influence our conduct even though we are barely aware of them. For example, by going to church each Sunday we increase our chances of being connected to volunteer opportunities both inside and outside the church because the church, as an institution, has alliances with other sacred and secular organizations. Structure has two faces: it both constrains and enables. Social relationships can prevent us from volunteering, as when we become parents of small children or we move into a neighborhood where we know few people or where there are few voluntary associations. Social relationships are also enabling, as when our children reach school age, giving us a little more spare time and drawing us into school activities, or when we join a civic organization, such as Kiwanis, Rotary, or the Junior League, where volunteer work is expected as a condition of membership. In the latter sense, social relationships are "social resources." This term describes the enabling factors that exist in the social environment of the actor. The more social resources we have, the more likely are we to reach our goals. Let's say we are motivated, even expected, to volunteer. That becomes our goal. However, we will not achieve our goal if we lack the social resources. For example, few people learn about volunteer opportunities through the mass media, and even if they do, they are rarely inspired to volunteer as a result (Brudney 1990:159). Personal invitations to volunteer are much more effective than impersonal appeals (Midlarsky and Kahana 1994:219). Knowing someone who is already active in the work for which you are being recruited is especially persuasive (McAdam and Paulsen 1993:644). In this respect, finding volunteer work is quite similar to finding a regular job. The contact you have with that other person, and that person's knowledge of volunteer opportunities, is a social resource. It does not belong to you so much as inhere in the relationship between you and that other person.

Social resources add richness and complexity to our explanation of volunteer behavior. They remind us that what matters for volunteering is not only what is going on in people's minds or how many individual resources they have but who they know and who they mix with on a routine basis. This fact is often obscured by social survey methods, which focus on the individual as the unit of analysis. Remember that social resources inhere in the relations *between* people rather than in the individual. As we shall see, people are more likely to volunteer if they are socially integrated; that is, if they have an extensive network of social ties that do not overlap much but connect them to new people. These networks furnish access to information, they provide social support, and they expose us to recruitment efforts.

Social resources play an especially important role when volunteering calls for collective action, such as a march, demonstration, or boycott. This is because they help overcome the "free rider" problem. If we interact frequently with other members of our social group or community we develop a sense of solidarity with them: their fate becomes linked to ours. This, in turn, makes it more likely we will respond to calls to volunteer on behalf of that group. We trust the other members not to sit back and let us do the work. Solidarity is measured, in part, by our expectations of getting support from other members of the group. This means that providing support for others is partially contingent on believing you can rely on getting support from them. In a 1992 survey, Philadelphians were asked how many people they could turn to for support when they needed it. Forty percent said they had many people they could turn to. Volunteers were twice as likely to say they had many people they could turn to (Kohut 1997:41). A 2000 survey of residents of Illinois asked them how much social support they thought they could count on. "Do you have someone outside your immediate family whom you can count on to help if you need it?" "Do you have friends or neighbors who count on you to help them when they need it?" "In the past month, have you helped a friend or neighbor?" Thirty-one percent of those who scored high on this index were heavily involved in civic life, compared to 6 percent of those who scored low (Profile of Illinois 2001). In a 2000 survey conducted in the United Kingdom, respondents were asked how many people they could turn to in a crisis. They were defined as having *low social support* if they had fewer than three people they could turn to in a crisis. They were also asked about their level of civic engagement. They were defined as being "not civically engaged" if they met three criteria: they were not involved in a local organization; they had not taken any action to solve a local problem in the last three years; and they did not feel any sense of civic engagement. (This last criterion was itself a composite of how well informed people felt about their community; whether they felt they, personally, could influence local decisions; and whether they felt that, by working together, people in their neighborhood could influence local decisions.) Twenty-seven of the civically unengaged were defined as receiving low social support, compared to 18 percent in the sample as a whole (Coulthard et al. 2002:5). Of course, volunteering increases the chances of having people you could to turn to in a crisis and therefore we must describe this as an *association* between having supportive people around you and volunteering.

10

The Life Course: The Early Stages

The life course concept refers to the way in which interwoven social institutions, such as the family, school, and work, shape individual lives over the course of time. From a life course perspective, age is an empty variable: age is simply an indicator of the stage of life a person has reached. The life course of most people in industrial societies consists of three major stages: an early part devoted to socialization and formal education or training; a middle part devoted to setting up a home, forming a family, and working to support it; and a third phase beginning when children leave home, passing through retirement, and ending in death. In this and the following chapter we will review the research on the influence of the life course on volunteering and supplement the existing research with our own analyses. We will first provide a broad overview of the association between the life course and volunteering, how volunteer preferences change with age, how volunteering at one stage of life is connected to volunteering at a later stage, and how volunteer preferences change over the life course. We will then return to follow the individual through the life course in more detail, beginning with volunteering in the teenage years, moving on to volunteering in young adulthood, and then dealing with how volunteering is affected by getting married and starting a family. Finally, we will describe what happens to volunteer work as we reach the third phase of our life, during and after retirement.

The Life Course and Volunteering

Looking at volunteer work from a life course perspective we are made instantly aware of the importance of "biographical availability" (McAdam 1986:70). In adolescence, the volunteer rate is actually higher than it is in early adulthood, at least in the United States, because schools, churches, and other youth-oriented institutions encourage or, in some cases, require community service of their young people. Young adults in their early 20s experience the time pressure of multiple commitments and engage vigorously in a wide variety of leisure time pursuits—a lifestyle not normally associated with doing volunteer work (De Hart and Dekker 1999:92).[1] They also have a high rate of new marriages, which is another reason they volunteer less. Stoker and Jennings (1995:427) found that young adults who were newly married were less civically engaged than unmarried young adults otherwise similar in personal circumstances and individual traits. Although marriage, in the long run, might increase the chances of volunteering, the likelihood is that it first introduces new demands and new priorities that divert the couple's attention from civic involvement.[2]

Once people reach early middle age, they begin to settle down: they have established a career or have a steady job, they have bought a house and put down roots in the community, they know more of their neighbors, they attend church more frequently, and they have children in local schools. It is among this group that the volunteer rate peaks. A subsequent decline in the rate of volunteering is mainly associated with the graduation of children from high school and the fact they are no longer involved in youth sports or other youth development activities such as the Boy Scouts. Volunteering does not seriously fall off until people reach old age, when infirmities, shortage of money, lack of transportation, and social isolation combine to make it more difficult to volunteer.

Up to this point we have discussed only the influence of life course stage on the likelihood of volunteering at all, but life course has a different effect on the intensity of commitment to volunteering. Goss (1999:389) found a bell-shaped curve in the rate of volunteering at all (high in middle age) but a different trajectory with respect to the number of times volunteered in the previous twelve months. The average number of times volunteered rose gradually from 18 years of age through to the 35–44 age group, remained flat until age65, after which time it began to rise again. The Current Population Survey (CPS) data from 2005 shows that, among volunteers, the number of hours volunteered per year is highest among those aged 65 or more, followed by those aged between 55 and 64. Volunteers aged between 16 and 34 contribute the fewest hours (U.S. Bureau of Labor Statistics 2005). In our analysis of the Independent Sector data we partially replicated these findings. [24] Although the mean hours volunteered in the last month reached its peak among the 35- to 49-year-olds, the 65 and over group were not very far behind; indeed, the difference was statistically insignificant. Although these results are slightly different the overall pattern is clear: the rate of volunteering is shaped like an inverted U but the number of hours contributed per volunteer is more linear, gradually rising as we age. Only when we reach the ranks of the "oldest old" do health problems force us to cut back on our volunteer work.

The Life Course and Volunteer Preferences

People's reasons for doing volunteer work change as they pass from one life stage to another. They develop different interests, have different needs, their social relationships change, and they acquire different resources. This is clearly evident in the social survey data on domains of volunteering. A 1994 study of eleven European countries found that sports and recreation volunteering was the most popular choice among young adults, while middle age people gave more of their time to schools, and older people focused on social service work (Gaskin and Smith 1997:36). The most popular form of volunteering among young Americans is in connection with youth development organizations, followed by civic and community groups and environmental organizations. They are less interested than are older people in working in connection with a church (Lopez 2004:6).[3] Although young people are less interested in more routine forms of advocacy volunteering, they turn out in greater numbers for the kind of "high risk activism" associated with protest movements. They are more available for this kind of work—their time is relatively plentiful, social obligations are few, and, for those in school or college, work commitments are flexible—but we cannot ignore the thrill and excitement of risky volunteering, which also appeals to young people. They are more likely than older people to take on high adrenalin work, such as search and rescue and emergency squad volunteering (Gora and Nemerowicz 1985:26).

The influence of primary roles—work and family—is evident in the volunteer preferences of middle aged people. A United Kingdom survey found that improving children's education and working with youth were the most popular volunteer areas in the 25–44 age group (Smith 1998:48). In later middle age, children have left home and volunteer interests turn away from youth-related issues. Using longitudinal data, Stoker and Jennings (2001:9) found that, as people approached their 50s, they turned away from youth development and school-related volunteering and became more interested in volunteering for organizations providing social services. Volunteering in connection with religious organizations, citizens' groups, and hobby groups, as well as caring for the elderly are all more popular among older people (Smith 1998:48).

In our analysis of the Independent Sector survey data we found that Americans of all ages volunteer for health, international, arts, and work-related organizations. [40] The older they were, the less interested they were in either youth or adult recreation, but the more interested they became in volunteering in connection with political organizations, at least until they reached retirement age. The middle aged, commonly seen as the most active, volunteered more than young adults in education, religion, public benefit, and political domains but less than young adults in adult recreation. In short, life course makes a difference to people's volunteer preferences. Broadly speaking, preferences change from a focus on sports and recreation among young volunteers, to political, youth development, and school-related volunteering in middle age, to religious, hobby, and social service interests among the elderly.

Volunteer Histories

Life course analysis invites us to think about volunteer work in the same way we think about paid employment: we start at the bottom, acquire experience and job skills, and, as a result, climb the job ladder until we (or most of us) reach a plateau, after which our job fortunes begin to decline. Of course, some people never enter the labor force and therefore have no job history at all. The same is true of volunteering. Some never enter the volunteer labor force at all. Others participate just once or twice but never again. Yet others seem to pursue a "career" in volunteering, moving from one volunteer opportunity to another. Social surveys take a snapshot of the population, telling us what it looks like at the instant the survey is conducted. Unless the respondent is asked about his or her past, the information in the survey arrests motion. For this reason, social surveys underreport the volunteer contributions individuals have made over the course of their lives. For example, Bowen et al. (2000) asked a sample of women aged between 50 and 80 about their volunteer work. Whereas less than half (40%) said they were currently volunteering, three-quarters of them had volunteered at some point in their lives. Robison et al. (1995:S365) analyzed data from a survey in which women who were first interviewed in 1956 were re-interviewed thirty years later. The women were asked to report the number of years since the first interview they had spent doing volunteer work. The average woman had spent just over a third of that time volunteering. What is interesting about this study is that three-quarters of the women (the same proportion as in the Bowen et al. study) had volunteered at some point in past thirty years and, although only a very small number of the women (8%) had volunteered for the entire thirty years, the most common pattern was intermittent participation in the volunteer labor force. Undoubtedly, some people follow the same trajectory of advancement in their volunteer work they and others follow in their paid work. Once they begin volunteering they are likely to continue to do so, because they acquire a taste for the work, they gain the necessary skills to lower the cost of future volunteering, and they acquire a reputation as someone willing to volunteer. Oesterle et al. (2004:1141) found they could reliably predict if a person was currently volunteering if they knew whether that person had volunteered in the previous year. Respondents were almost eight times more likely to volunteer in a given year if they had volunteered the year before. Prior volunteering will predict current volunteering even more reliably if it occurred recently. The longer ago the volunteer work was performed the less likely it is to predict current volunteering.[4]

Having given a broad overview of the way volunteer behavior changes across the life-span, we will now examine each of the life stages in detail, beginning with the teenage years, moving into young adulthood. In the next chapter we will describe volunteering in the middle age years of marital and parental life, concluding with volunteerism among the elderly.

Youth Volunteering

Teenagers are often portrayed as rather self-centered, preoccupied with material possessions, and uninterested in community affairs, political activities, or helping others. In addition, many of the voluntary associations that sponsor and organize volunteer work are relatively inhospitable to teenagers, the one major exception being the church. The teens would therefore appear to be a wasteland as far as volunteerism is concerned. But in the United States, at least, interest in volunteerism is quite high among teenagers. A special survey (discussed in chapter 2) of American youth aged 11–18 found that 55 percent had volunteered in the previous year (66% if they were given specific prompts concerning volunteer activities) (Toppe 2005:8).[5]

Youth volunteering bears the imprint of parental influence because young people are still living at home. Numerous studies have demonstrated the habit of volunteering tends to be passed from one generation to another.[6] The mother's volunteering is more influential than the father's, due partly to her greater efforts to integrate her children into her own activities and partly to the fact that she is more likely to volunteer for child-related activities than the father (Segal 1993:105; Wuthnow 1995:157).

Although the facts are clear that volunteering can be transmitted from generation to generation, the mechanisms that make this possible are by no means obvious. At the most general level, it is possible to distinguish two theories, each indicating a specific mechanism.

Socialization

Socialization theory focuses on the fact that the volunteer role has to be learned.[7] Young people are more likely to take up volunteering if they have been socialized into playing the role, by schools, churches, youth development organizations (e.g., Boy Scouts) and, above all, by their parents. Children raised in homes where they hear talk about local community issues or whose parents specifically emphasize the importance of community involvement are more likely to volunteer than children whose parents are silent on these issues (Center for Democracy and Citizenship 2002:42; Keeter et al. 2002a:30; Prudential Spirit of Community Youth Survey 1995). By teaching the right goals and values to their children—honesty, kindness, fairness, trustworthiness, sharing—parents inculcate a norm of social responsibility, which in turn encourages volunteering. Flanagan et al. (1998:465) analyzed the results of a seven-country survey in which adolescents were asked: "When you think about your life and your future, how important is it to you personally to (a) contribute to your country and (b) do something to improve your society?" In every country, teenagers whose parents emphasized the need to be attentive to others, especially those less fortunate than themselves, were more likely to have as a personal goal that they will contribute to their country and do something to improve their society. Not only did they *intend* to do something to improve their society, they were more likely to do something about it: "in all countries, family values of compassion and social responsibility were the most consistent correlates of teen involvement in service in their community" (Flanagan and Faison 2001:10).[8]

Parenting Styles

Family research has shown that a high level of parental support (e.g., affection, praise, encouragement) has a variety of positive outcomes among children and adolescents, such as psychological adjustment, academic achievement, high self-esteem, an internal locus of control, social competence, and "the exhibition of considerate and altruistic behavior" (Amato and Booth 1997:17). As far as encouraging volunteering is concerned, the style of parenting is as important as the substance (Pancer and Pratt 1999).[9] Clary and Miller (1986) interviewed volunteers aged 17–49 working at a telephone crisis-counseling agency and followed up these interviews to see if they completed their six-month commitment to contribute four hours a week of unpaid labor. They found that parents help determine completion in the following way. Those who reported having parents who gave examples in their own behavior of altruism *and* were more nurturing (e.g., were not afraid to show their feelings) were more likely to complete the six months.

Unfortunately, the longitudinal data needed to test the theory that parenting styles help determine whether children will eventually volunteer are scarce, but three studies have attempted to throw some light on the influence of the family *environment* on children's volunteering and these are of interest because of the possibility that children brought up in an environment that was supportive and cohesive and in which prosocial values were emphasized would be more likely to volunteer later. A study reported by Rosenthal et al. (1998) has been following a mainly middle and upper middle class group of Americans for twenty-one years. Data were gathered at 3, 12, and 24 months and 6, 9, 13, 18, and 21 years of age. During childhood the parents were asked questions intended to measure family cohesion and emphasis on moral and religious values. At age 18, the children were asked to describe their volunteer activities. Neither of the measures of *early* family environment had any effect on volunteering at age 18. The chances of volunteering were much more strongly influenced by family environment at the time the volunteer work was actually taking place. Another study, using NLSY data containing a series of items intended to assess the cognitive, social, and emotional resources available to the child in the home, found a positive correlation between family support in 1992 and voluntary service in 1994 (Hart et al. 1998:520). However, a re-analysis of these data found no difference between volunteers and non-volunteers in the amount of conflict they reported between their parents or the amount of emotional support they had received from them after a variable measuring level of joint child-parent activity was added to the model (Hart et al. 1999:380). In other words, it is far from clear that teaching values has much effect on children unless the parents exhibit behavior to their children consonant with those values, a subject to which we now turn.

Role Modeling

It is important that children see or hear about their parents' volunteer work because lessons in values are more persuasive if children have an example to follow (Bengtson and Roberts 1991). As one volunteer put it,

> My mother used to volunteer with the Catholic Church. So I always knew there was volunteering. . . . A lot of people just don't know about volunteering but I knew what my mother had done so I knew it was out there. (Flick et al. 2002:62)

In a few cases, children learn the volunteer role by serving as an apprentice to their parents. Parents supervise their children as they try on the volunteer role, making sure it is neither too trivial nor too demanding. In some areas, the parental influence is very plain to see: it is not unusual for fathers to pass their volunteer fire fighter jobs to their sons (Simpson 1996:22). In fairly closed communities (e.g., in rural areas), adult volunteers are under extra pressure to get their children involved in community activities to demonstrate their own commitment to the community, especially if they volunteer for any kind of leadership position (Chan and Elder 2001:24).

Dramatic recent evidence of the role modeling of volunteer work comes from a 2005 survey of American teenagers, which found that 78 percent of those whose parents volunteered were also volunteers themselves, compared to 48 percent of those whose parents were not volunteers. This study found that the more role models the teenager had the more likely was he or she to volunteer. For example, in cases where both parents and siblings volunteered, the volunteer rate was 86 percent compared to 38 percent where no other family members volunteered (Grimm et al. 2005:9). The role modeling effect was especially powerful in the case of regular volunteers—those who volunteered at least twelve weeks a year. Its influence on episodic volunteerism was weaker.

We used the Independent Sector data to measure the influence of parental volunteering on the respondent's likelihood of having volunteered in the past year. Just over a quarter of the respondents (25.4%) reported that both of their parents had been volunteers when they were being raised, 17.4 percent said only their mother had volunteered and 3.8 percent said only their father had volunteered. Respondents who reported that both their parents had volunteered were nearly three times as likely to be volunteers themselves as those who reported neither parent volunteering. The respondents whose mother had volunteered were nearly twice as likely. The influence of the father volunteering was weaker but still significant. [73]

There is some dispute among social scientists as to how specific role modeling must be to have the desired effect. Some believe parents need not be volunteers themselves but simply be generally active and helpful in their community.[10] All it takes, apparently, is for young people to see their parents helping non-family members. Rossi (2001c:291) believes the role modeling need only take the form of demonstrating social skills: "if parents are generally helpful, friendly, and sociable toward people outside the family, the probability is stronger that their children will be exposed to many family, friends, and kin and as a result will early on acquire social skills plus an interest in and ability to be helpful toward other people."

It is difficult to distinguish socialization from role modeling because they usually go together. Chan and Elder (2001) studied Iowa families to see if parents passed on values and practices to their children.[11] The children were asked if they were currently involved in "community activities," such as 4-H, church choir, volunteer work at a hospital, scouts, or recreational programs. The more clubs the parents belonged to, the more clubs their children belonged to. The degree of family commitment to volunteer work was also a positive factor. Compared to children with two uninvolved parents, youth belonging to families with only one socially active parent were no more likely to be involved in community activities. Having two socially involved parents who were non-leaders increased the odds of the child's social involvement about 2.5 times; having at least one parent serve as a leader increased the child's involvement 3.6 times, and having both parents serve as leaders increased the odds by five times. Furthermore, parents and children were more likely to volunteer *together* if at least one of the parents was a leader. Another analysis of the same data collapsed fourteen community activities into one composite measure because preliminary analysis of the data showed that the positive connection between parental involvement and child involvement did not differ by the type of activity. Intergenerational linkages were quite apparent. Tenth grade adolescents from high involvement families participated in 5.4 activities, compared to 4.9 among adolescents from low involvement families, a statistically significant difference. Children were especially likely to be involved if their parents served on a board or were committee members and even more likely if *both* parents occupied leadership roles. Because it is unlikely that having two parents occupy leadership roles increased the socialization level, this finding points us in the direction of a role model explanation. "Children who realize their parents care enough about communities to spend time and energy maintaining them are likely to model such behaviors" (Fletcher et al. 2000:44). Although these studies were limited to small towns and rural areas in a largely agricultural state and their results are therefore not generalizable to the rest of the American population, they do suggest that role modeling is more important than socialization in passing volunteerism from one generation to another.

Parental Influence Depends on the Type of Volunteer Work

Role modeling theory predicts that parents who volunteer are more likely to have children who volunteer, but it says nothing about which type of volunteer work is the most influential or what kind of volunteer work children are most likely to take up as a result of seeing their parents volunteer. For example, Wuthnow (1995:125) speculates that children are most likely to volunteer if their parents are volunteering in connection with their church because, of all voluntary associations, a religious congregation is the most likely to encourage the involvement of the entire family in its programs: churches are "family friendly" and provide many opportunities for children to see their parents volunteering and for parents and children to volunteer together.

The few studies of this topic suggest that paying attention to the type of volunteer activity is important. A cross-sectional study found that only children who were volunteering in connection with religious, health, or environmental organizations reported having parents who were volunteers (Sundeen and Raskoff 1994:392). (The parent's volunteer type was not recorded.)[12] McLellan and Youniss (2003:54) asked students in two Catholic schools in the Washington, D.C., area if they had done any social service volunteering. They found that students with parents involved in social service volunteering were nearly four times more likely to be volunteering than students with parents who did other kinds of volunteer work. Apparently, some role models are more persuasive than others. The authors go on to show a consistent and positive association between parent volunteer type and student volunteer type. That is, parents who volunteered for social service organizations were more likely to have children who volunteered for social service organizations than they were to have children who volunteered for tutoring, advocacy, or doing "functionary" work, such as filing or fund-raising.

Status Transmission

Socialization and role modeling are two explanations for the inheritance of volunteering. Status transmission is another. We already know that socio-economic status makes a difference to the likelihood of volunteering. Parents bestow not only values and lessons on their children; they also provide them with economic resources. This raises the possibility that it is the resources, not the lessons learned or the roles modeled, that encourage or enable the children to volunteer.

Status transmission theory argues that children follow their parents' example in volunteering because they inherit their parents' socio-economic status. Numerous studies have shown that family background, and specifically the socio-economic status of one's parents, influence volunteering (Brown 1999a; Child Trends DataBank 2003; Hart et al. 1998:519; Sundeen and Raskoff 1994:392; Youniss and Yates 1999). The direct effect takes this form: parents' status predicts their children's volunteerism regardless of education of the child. But parents' socio-economic status has both direct and indirect effects on children's volunteering. The indirect effect takes this form: higher status parents tend to have highly educated children who in turn are more likely to volunteer. For example, one study found that 58 percent of adolescents whose parents had at least a college degree were currently volunteering, compared to only 34 percent of children of parents lacking a college degree, *regardless of whether the parents were volunteers* (Nolin et al. 1997:23).[13]

There is another reason why coming from a well-to-do family encourages volunteering. Children from higher class backgrounds are more likely to come from stable households, where two parents are in residence. This kind of environment is conducive to the rearing of children who have prosocial values and attitudes. Lichter et al. (2002) used data from the 1996 panel of the NLSY to study about a thousand young people aged between 14 and 18 who were still in high school.[14] About a quarter of the teenagers had volunteered in the past year (outside of required community service). By using information obtained from mothers the researchers were able to estimate the influence of negative early life experiences on the chances of volunteering in connection with churches or mentoring youth. Boys raised by a single parent volunteer less than boys reared by two parents (there was no difference among girls). Girls living below the poverty line volunteered less than girls from more affluent households (there was no difference for boys).

For a number of reasons, then, children raised in higher status families volunteer more than children raised in lower status families. This creates a problem of interpreting the link between generations. Is it due to socialization or status transmission? Beck and Jennings (1982) set out to answer this question by using data from two waves of a panel study. Both children and parents were interviewed in 1965, when the children were high school seniors. Parents and children were questioned again in 1973, when the children were 26 years old.[15] The authors found that both pathways were used. The parents bestowed socio-economic resources on their children who then acquired resources of their own, enabling them to do more volunteer work. The second pathway saw higher status parents getting more involved in civic work and, in turn, encouraging their children to become involved also.

Another study used a special feature of the National Longitudinal Surveys of Labor Market Experience (NLS) to see if children inherit their parents' volunteer habits. The survey provides information from both mothers and daughters in many households included in the survey. Because the women were asked about their volunteer work it is possible to see if mothers who volunteer are more likely to have daughters who volunteer and to determine whether this is due to socio-economic advantages mothers pass on to their daughters or to the volunteer behavior of the mother, or both. The mother's volunteering had a positive effect on her daughter's baseline volunteering (i.e., her hours of volunteering at the start of the study) but had no effect on *growth* in volunteering over the course of the study (between 1978 and 1991). The probability of an increase in volunteering over the life course of the young women, on the other hand, was a positive function of the socioeconomic status of the household in which they were raised. In other words, mother's volunteering influenced the level at which the young women "began" volunteering but had no influence on the upward trajectory in hours volunteered thereafter. Instead, this upward trajectory was largely a function of the social class background of the women. It would seem, then, that mothers who volunteer act as *initiators* of their daughter's volunteer work, helping get their daughters involved, but they have little effect on the subsequent volunteer career of the daughter (Mustillo et al. 2004). Although the results of these studies are slightly different they are alike in confirming that both socialization and status transmission play a role in passing volunteering from one generation to another.

One reason to suspect that both theories are valid is that each helps explain the transmission of a particular type of volunteering. This hypothesis was tested in a study that divided volunteer work into self-oriented and community-oriented volunteering.[16] Self-oriented voluntary associations have as their primary purpose furthering the interests of their members. They rely on volunteer labor, but the incentive for doing that labor is that the members of the organization will reap the rewards. Examples of this type of association are business and professional associations, trade unions, and veterans' groups. Community-oriented associations, on the other hand, have as their goal protecting the community as a whole. They provide a service or product for outsiders or seek collective goods. Examples of this type are associations intended to provide care for children, the elderly or the sick, organizations devoted to neighborhood improvements, fraternal organizations, and service groups. Information on voluntary association activity was gathered from parents and children. The parent's level of activity in 1973 had a positive effect on their children's level of activity in 1982, but only in the case where parents were engaged in community-oriented volunteering. The picture was very different when the focus turned to socio-economic variables (i.e., the status transmission theory). Parents' socio-economic status in 1973 had a positive effect on their children's self-oriented volunteering in 1982, but no effect at all on their community-oriented volunteering. In short, community-oriented volunteering was almost entirely inherited through the socialization pathway: the role modeling of the parent had a powerful influence over his or her offspring, regardless of socio-economic status. Self-oriented volunteering, on the other hand, was inherited from parents indirectly. Parents make it possible for their children to acquire human capital that in turn makes volunteer work feasible. The parents' economic resources were devoted mostly to getting their children involved in self-oriented volunteer activities, but when it came to more community-oriented volunteerism parents contribute something else—their own "witness" as volunteers (Janoski and Wilson 1995).

Youth Volunteering and Peer Groups

Adolescents are highly susceptible to peer pressure and, although they certainly heed their parents, the desire to fit in with their own peers also influences their behavior. A study of pupils in two Catholic high schools demonstrates the power of peer pressure in this age group. Students were asked if they had done any voluntary community service during the preceding year that was not for school credit. The researchers then grouped the students into reputational peer group categories by asking students to rate the importance to their peer group of: being popular, working on a school publication; having a steady boyfriend or girlfriend, participating in school clubs; going to parties; and getting good grades. The peer group categories were: the school crowd (e.g., they endorse studying); the fun crowd (e.g., they endorse being popular); the all-around crowd (e.g., they rate all activities as important); and the disengaged crowd (e.g., they rate all the items as unimportant). Members of the school crowd were significantly more likely to be volunteering while members of the fun crowd were unlikely to have volunteered. This unique study of peer group pressures for and against volunteer work among youth is extremely valuable and should be replicated. While volunteerism is often portrayed as an individual choice guided by differences in personal background, relationships with peers is a more proximate cause of the decision to volunteer (Youniss et al. 2001). A more detailed analysis of the data showed that school children tend to select the same specific volunteer activities as their peers. For example, they were three times more likely to volunteer for social service organizations if members of their peer group were also doing so (McLellan and Youniss 2003).

Youth and Adult Volunteering

By volunteering early in life people acquire experience and skills that lay the groundwork for volunteering in later life. In many respects, middle aged volunteers are simply young volunteers who have aged. From a human development perspective, it is no surprise that adult volunteers are more likely to say they volunteered in youth. Volunteer work exposes young people to prosocial reference groups where they can learn to bond and connect with others and acquire a sense of collective identity concern for other people; it creates a sense of social solidarity, fighting the egotism typical of that age, teaching youth that their goals can be realized when the group's goals are achieved; it fosters trust in acquaintances and strangers; it encourages a positive view of humanity as fair, helpful, and trustworthy; it eases interaction with people outside one's immediate circle who come from somewhat different social backgrounds and, perhaps, have different views of the world (Flanagan 2003:257–258). We should therefore expect to find that, as people leave adolescence and enter adulthood, they take the habit of volunteering with them.

The Link between High School and College

For many Americans the transition from adolescence to adulthood occurs simultaneously with going off to college. Because colleges provide a supportive environment for volunteer work and because academically proficient students are more likely to volunteer, we can expect those who go to college to volunteer at a higher rate than those who enter the labor force at age 16 or 18. In 2002 the volunteer rate of Americans aged 16–24 who were enrolled in school or college was almost double that of those who were not enrolled in school or college (Boraas 2003:5). The gap in volunteering between those who attend college and those who go straight into the labor force on graduating from high school is even wider if college is a private one (Horn and Berktold 1998; Horn et al. 2002).

If we think about leaving high school and entering college as an important life transition, the trajectory of volunteering can take a number of directions at this point. Many will simply continue volunteering: students who volunteer in high school are indeed more likely to volunteer in college (Trudeau and Devlin 1996:1884). Others will quit volunteering once they enter college. A third group with no previous experience begins volunteering in college. A final group will not have volunteered in high school and will not do so in college. A study of American high school seniors who were re-interviewed two years after graduation tries to explain who is most likely to fall into which of these categories. The largest group of college students (39%) volunteered in neither high school nor college. Of those who were volunteering in college, 53 percent began in college and 47 percent continued doing volunteer work they began in high school. The students making the transition in and out of the volunteer labor force had quite distinct profiles. Those who quitted volunteer work when they entered college were no different from other college students in terms of socio-demographic characteristics, but they were less religious, had lower educational expectations, were less likely to be a member of a fraternity or sorority, and worked fewer hours a week for pay. They were more likely to have attended school where community service was required of all seniors and less likely to have attended school where community service was encouraged. Obviously, forcing a student to do volunteer work is not good for encouraging sustained volunteerism. The group going in the opposite direction, taking up volunteer work once they entered college, were no different in socio-demographic terms, but they were more religious, had higher educational expectations, and they were more likely to be members of fraternities, sororities, and other college groups. They were less likely to have attended a school that required community service and more likely to have attended a school that simply encouraged it. Interestingly, then, encouraging community service in high school had a positive effect, even on students who do not avail themselves of this opportunity. College students who continued volunteering during the transition (the most committed) were more likely to be female, higher socio-economic status, a youth group member in high school, had begun volunteering early, in 10th grade, and attended a school that encouraged community service. They were also more religious, had higher educational expectations, were more likely to belong to college student organizations, and watched less television (Marks and Jones 2004). These patterns are interesting and informative. There are personal characteristics such as religiosity, that encourage students to continue or take up volunteering in college and there are contextual factors, such as the degree to which the high school encouraged volunteer work that also have a positive effect on future volunteering. We will discuss the effect of school and community service requirements on volunteering in chapter 14.

Youth Volunteering and Early Adulthood

Looking beyond the college years and (for those who do not attend college) looking at the early adult years, the influence of youth volunteering is still visible. Just over two-thirds (67.3%) of the volunteers in the 2001 Independent Sector survey had volunteered as adolescents, compared to 49 percent of those not volunteering (Toppe et al. 2002:91). Damico et al. (1998) use data from the *National Longitudinal Study of the High School Class of 1972* to trace the long-term impact of high school activities on the civic participation of adult females. While in school they were asked whether they were active in a variety of extra-curricular activities and whether they were serving as "leader or officer" in a school organization. In 1976 and 1986 the women were asked once again if they were active members of a variety of voluntary associations. In 1972, all but 18 percent of the senior class were active in at least one school organization and a quarter were involved in four or more. The more active girls were more likely be to in the "academic" track than the general or vocational track, partly a result of their higher socio-economic status. The researchers then examined the influence of high school activity level on active participation in community groups four years later (1976) and fourteen years later (1986). The results were quite striking. As might be expected, level of education was a strong predictor of participation in both 1976 and 1986, but regardless of education, the level of high school activity had a positive effect on community participation in both 1976 and 1986. Indeed, the influence of high school activity on 1986 volunteering remained even after controlling for level of community participation in 1976 (Conway et al. 1996:430). Significantly, the respondent's level of community participation at age 32 depended quite a lot on whether the student had merely been a participant in or had chosen to lead the school activity. Simply being a member of a high school group or passively participating in the group either had no effect on later community participation or, as in the case of school sports, had a negative effect: athletes were less likely to be active participants at age 32. The positive influence of volunteering for leadership roles was more consistent: with the exception of government/media, all leadership activities (including sports) were positively related to community activism in 1986. These effects are quite striking, considering that the gap between first and second survey is fourteen years and that the effects are net of employment status, marital status, education, and presence of school age children in the household (Conway and Damico 2001).

Reaching further out into the life course, Astin et al. (1998) analyzed data from a national sample of former college students from whom data were collected when they were in their freshman year (1985), four years later (1989), and again nine years after matriculation (1994–1995). On each occasion respondents were asked if they had spent time volunteering in the past year. Thus, for the 1985 panel the respondents are being asked about their volunteer work during their senior year in high school, in the 1989 panel they are being asked about their volunteer work during their senior year in college. There was a modest correlation between the hours spent volunteering in high school and hours spent volunteering in college ($r = .18$) and between volunteering in college and volunteering four years later ($r = .16$). Even after controlling for hours per week spent volunteering during college, the frequency of volunteering in high school influenced hours spent volunteering nine years later. The habit of volunteering is quite persistent, for there is a direct effect of high school volunteering on adult volunteering regardless of whether the person volunteered in college, and the "total" effect of high school volunteering plus college volunteering is even stronger:

. . . among those who did no volunteer work during either high school or college, only 13% were spending one hour or more per week in volunteer work nine years after entering college. This figure more than triples, to 49%, among those who volunteered frequently during high school and averaged one or more hours of volunteer work during college. (Astin et al 1998:196)

TYPES OF VOLUNTEER WORK IN YOUTH AND ADULT VOLUNTEERING

In an earlier section we asked if the type of volunteer work done by parents makes any difference to the influence they have on their children. We can ask the same question of the children themselves: does the kind of volunteer activity in which they got involved as an adolescent make any difference to whether they will be volunteering as adults? Metz et al. (2003) asked students from a suburban middle class public school near Boston to say whether they intended to perform voluntary service after high school ("not very likely" to "definitely will"). They were also asked if they had done any volunteer service in the past year. Sixty-seven percent indicated they had done some kind of community service. They were then asked to describe that service and the authors coded their responses in to "social cause service" and "standard type of service." The first type placed students directly in contact with people in need or involved students in causes to improve or remedy an explicit social problem (e.g., working with the elderly in a nursing home, raising awareness to end racism). Standard types of service included tutoring or mentoring students in their school, coaching youth sports, or doing administrative work or manual labor. Social cause service participants had the strongest intentions of future volunteering, followed by standard service volunteers and non-serving students. Volunteering in high school therefore seemed to help build an identity as one who volunteers and is likely to respond to the call to volunteer but volunteer work that asked the person to work directly with the needy or to directly confront some social issue was the most effective in building this identity. Regrettably, we cannot tell from this study how much of this is due to the self-selection of the more "civic-oriented" students into social cause types of volunteering.

Conclusion

We have provided a lot of evidence in this section in support of the developmental approach to volunteering. Volunteering is passed from one generation to another and early volunteering plants the seeds for later volunteering. Other factors moderate this pattern of development: children raised in stable homes probably get an additional impetus from their parents; high school volunteers who go on to college are probably more likely to maintain the habit of volunteering. Nevertheless, traces of the influence of youth volunteering on adult volunteering can be found in middle age. Without longitudinal studies that extend our knowledge into late middle age and later life it is not possible at this time to say how long the influence of youthful volunteering is felt. Nevertheless, the longitudinal studies provide us with the most accurate picture of the development of volunteering over the life course.

One important issue that remains unresolved is separating the effects of youthful volunteering from other extra-curricular activities in which young people get involved. Some scholars are skeptical that volunteer work has anything special to contribute (Verba et al. 1995; Yates and Youniss 1998). Indeed, Andolina et al. (2003:275) believe that "participation in high school organizations provides a stronger connection to later civic engagement than does early volunteering or service learning experiences." Others disagree. For example, one study found that those who became active in school political groups were twice as likely to volunteer after school graduation as those who got involved in non-political groups. Merely getting involved in sports or religious groups had no long-term volunteering benefits (Keeter et al. 2002a:34).

Another issue has to do with how the association between youth volunteering and adult volunteering is interpreted. Does this mean that volunteer work has become a habit, something people learn early in life, much as they might an appreciation for an art form or is it simply a matter of people with a certain disposition to volunteer who are more likely to accept an invitation to contribute when they are young as well as when they are old? Brown (1999b:33) attempts to answer this question by looking at a number of attitudes about adult volunteering to see if the effect of youth volunteering on adult volunteering disappears. She divides the adult population into those with "good attitudes" and those with "bad attitudes." "Persons with good attitudes strongly agree or mostly agree with the statement: 'It is in my power to do things that improve the welfare of others,' and state as a major motivation either 'helping individuals meet their material needs' or 'enhancing the moral basis of society.' Persons with bad attitudes disagree with the first statement and report that the second and third statements' objectives provide no motivation." She finds that people with "good attitudes" and adequate income are almost five times more likely to have volunteered in the past year than people with bad attitudes. More important for our purposes here, she finds that, among those with bad attitudes and adequate income, having volunteered as a youth *makes no difference* to the likelihood of volunteering as an adult but it does make a difference among those with adequate income and good attitudes. In other words, youth volunteering makes little difference to adults who possess neither a sense of empowerment nor concern for others.[17]

11

The Life Course: The Later Stages

In this second chapter on the life course we describe the role of volunteering in the middle phase of life, which, for the vast majority of people, is marked by forming a family—getting married and raising children. In the concluding section of the chapter we will analyze the role of volunteering in later middle age and in elderly populations. Although it is becoming increasingly difficult to summarize neatly the successive phases of the family life cycle, most Americans get married in their 20s and subsequently have children, spending most of their 30s and 40s raising them. When children are very young, they inhibit their parents' ability to do much outside the household other than paid work. Once they reach school age, however, children act as a social magnet for their parents, drawing them into a wider range of extra-household activities, including volunteer work. As we have already noted, our relationship with other family members is chiefly responsible for the familiar inverted U-curve in volunteering over the life course. For most people, parental and marital statuses go together, but in the review and analysis described below, we need to pay attention to their separate effects.

Volunteering and Marriage

Sociological research has shown that married people have a stronger sense of well-being than single people: they are happier, have clearer sense of purpose in life, possess higher self-esteem, and feel more in charge of their own fate (Waite and Gallagher 2000:70). As we have seen in earlier chapters, these are all subjective dispositions that favor volunteering. In this review of the research on marital status and volunteering, we need to keep in mind several issues. First, there are a number of different ways of being not married: for example, Burns et al. (2001:319) found that merely being single did not necessary result in less volunteering; the formerly married (divorced and widowed) were the least likely to volunteer. Second, marital status is easily confounded with other statuses. The most obvious is parental status because the majority of parents are married, but single people also tend to be younger and have lower incomes and for this reason are less likely to volunteer. Third, we cannot assume that the effect of marriage is the same for all people. As we shall see, there are reasons to believe that getting married has a stronger effect on the volunteer behavior of some groups than others.

We analyzed the Independent Sector data to see if marital status makes any difference to the chances of having volunteered in the past twelve months, controlling for socio-demographic variables and, most importantly, parental status. [20] We contrasted being married with several forms of being unmarried: compared to being married, respondents who had been widowed were the least likely to volunteer (we control for age) followed by the never married and the divorced or separated. Significantly, when we controlled for frequency of church attendance, the positive effect of marital status went away. This would seem to suggest that married people are more likely to volunteer than single people because they attend church more frequently, but when we separated volunteer work into separate domains we found that marriage had a positive effect *only in the context of religious volunteering*. [74] The reason why church attendance seems to mediate the influence of marital status on all volunteering is that religious volunteering, which it does mediate, is so popular.

Judging by these analyses, marriage does not have much influence on volunteering in general, especially after differences in church attendance (and parental status) are controlled. While this might be true of the population as a whole it is still possible that marriage has a positive effect for some people, in certain social contexts. Although there is not much research on this issue there are a number of possibilities. First, marriages are notoriously gendered: each spouse has his or her own perspective on the marriage. This raises the possibility that conjugal roles work differently for husbands and wives. A 1987 Canadian survey show that single men do less volunteer work than married men while single women do *more* volunteer work than married women (Vaillancourt 1994:818). Analyzing Canadian data from 2000, Ravanera et al. (2002) found that separated or divorced men were *more* likely to volunteer than married men, the never-married, and men who had lost their spouses.[1] On the other hand, married women were no more or less likely to volunteer than those who had separated or divorced. It was the never-married women who had the highest volunteer rates and the widowed who had the lowest. The never-married women had possibly chosen a life of civic engagement and volunteering that prevented them from getting married.[2] Second, religious, racial, and ethnic groups define the institution of marriage differently and this might also temper the effects of marriage on volunteering. Where getting married does not mark a particularly significant change in status or social connections, or where the marital bond is ephemeral, it might not have much effect on volunteering. In more conservative communities where "family values" are emphasized, being married is a preferred status and being single or widowed, and particularly being separated or divorced, are stigmatized statuses, and stigmatized people might well be less likely to volunteer or asked to volunteer. A 1993 study of randomly sampled members of 625 congregations in the United States covering five denominations, found that marital status had no effect on the number of hours contributed to church work. The only exceptions to this generalization were the two most conservative denominations, the Assemblies of God and the Southern Baptists, where single members and married members had higher levels of volunteering than those separated, divorced, or widowed (Hoge et al. 1998:474). The implication is that these churches do not welcome volunteers who occupy these statuses, or people who occupy these statuses do not feel welcome.

Spousal Effects

Economists assume that volunteer work is costly because it consumes time. Households must decide how to allocate this chore across family members in the context of the other demands on their time (Freeman 1997; Schor 1991:161). For example, spending two or three hours a week at the soup kitchen takes time away from one's children, housework, and one's spouse. According to this *substitution* theory, the volunteer hours of husbands and wives vary inversely. A wife who volunteers for three or four hours a week increases the role overload of her husband because he must substitute for her around the house while she is away. Under these circumstances he has to cut back on his volunteer hours.

The alternative theory assumes that the volunteer work of the two spouses *complement* each other. For a number of reasons, married couples tend to behave alike: either they both volunteer or neither volunteers. First, people are strongly influenced by people with whom they are intimate, who they trust, and with whom they have frequent contact. Second, the conjugal bond makes joint volunteering possible, which eases the anxieties and insecurities associated with taking on the volunteer role. The Big Brother/Big Sister—a mentoring organization—recognizes this when it encourages married couples to volunteer together. Third, married couples tend to be jealous of each other's time. One spouse might "encourage" the other to volunteer in order to legitimate his or her own volunteer activities, as when husbands encourage their wives to join a ladies' auxiliary to their fraternal order. Conversely, a *lack* of interest in doing volunteer work on the part of one spouse will discourage the other spouse from volunteering. They resent their partner's commitment to volunteer work. This is particularly true of husbands: only 4.2 percent of the women in Gallagher's (1994b:136) survey thought they did too much volunteer work, but 19 percent of the husbands thought their wives did too much volunteer work. One British woman told researchers she eventually gave up being a scout leader because

> it took up all my time, and my husband felt it was unfair, me going off all the time. I used to get into terrible trouble. I would come home from work and say I was going to the Scouts and my husband would say "Oh you're not going out again, are you?" so for doing good one gets punished in a way. (Campbell and Wood 1999:126)

Another wife blamed her husband directly for the fact she did not volunteer as much as she liked: "I would do more for my church, it's important to me, but my husband is not interested, he is frightened of religion, it's just not relevant to him" (Campbell and Wood 1999:121). Fourth, spouses share many social relationships. Compared to men and women who are not married, they are more likely to have overlapping memberships in voluntary associations, attend the same church, live in the same neighborhood, have children attending the same schools, and share many economic interests and social concerns.

The research on spousal influences on volunteering largely supports the complementarity theory. Trade union members who are active in local branch affairs are more likely to have a spouse who is also active (Fosh 1981:58). Freeman (1997) found that 59 percent of the men married to women who were volunteers were volunteers themselves, compared to only 10 percent of the men married to women who were not volunteers. Seventy percent of the women married to men who volunteered were volunteers themselves, compared to only 16% of the women married to men who did not volunteer. Furthermore, respondents married to spouses who volunteered contributed more hours than respondents married to spouses who did not volunteer. Hook (2004) used time diary data kept by married couples in Australia to analyze the relation between paid work, housework, and volunteer work. She found a positive relation between the volunteer hours of husbands and wives.

Who Has the Most Influence?

There is little dispute among sociologists that women do most of the care work, even in modern societies. Wives and mothers are more likely to regard volunteer work as an obligation than husbands and fathers. If only one spouse volunteers it is more likely to be the wife than the husband (Wuthnow 1995:272). For this reason, women are likelier to "draw men in" to providing unpaid labor than vice versa (Gerstel and Gallagher 2001:208). When married couples were asked whether they could decide to undertake charity work without first checking with their spouses, 33 percent of the husbands said they would check with their wives first, compared to only 14 percent of the wives who said they would check with their husband first (Burns et al. 2001:188). The implication is clear: a husband looks to his wife for approval of volunteer work more than a wife looks to her husband. In an analysis of Current Population Survey (CPS) data from 2002 on nearly twenty thousand married couples in the United States, Rotolo and Wilson (2006a) show that the spouses have a reciprocal positive effect on each other's volunteer hours; that the influence is stronger when spouses are volunteering in the same domain; and that the influence of the wife is stronger than the influence of the husband. Interestingly, couples living together but not married (i.e., cohabiting) had *no* influence on each other's volunteer behavior.[3]

Volunteering with a Spouse

The studies reported above show us that spouses influence each other's volunteer behavior but they do not tell us whether spouses volunteer together, although this must have something to do with why husbands and wives are alike in their volunteer behavior. Only the Independent Sector asks whether or not the respondent volunteers with his or her spouse. We looked at the data for respondents who were both married and had volunteered some time in the past year (1992). A remarkably high proportion of these married volunteers had volunteered alongside their spouse (41.4%). Husbands were more likely to say they had volunteered with their spouse than wives. Whites were more likely to volunteer together than non-Whites. Surprisingly, the tendency to volunteer together did not increase with age: indeed, it tended to decline, although the beta coefficients for age were significant only at the < 0.10 level. Retirees also tended to volunteer together but again the beta coefficient was significant only at the < 0.10 level. As far as predicting which married couples would volunteer together was concerned, the only significant factor was church attendance: the more frequently married volunteers attended church, the more likely they were to volunteer with each other. [75]

Volunteering and Parental Status

Marital and parental statuses are highly correlated, which is simply another way of saying that most parents are married. We should not be surprised if they "cancel each other out" in multivariate models. For example, Selbee and Reed (2001:4) found that marriage had a positive effect on volunteering among the middle aged but a negative effect on volunteering among the young adults. This difference disappeared, however, once they controlled for children in the household. The negative effect of being married in the younger age group was actually the negative effect of having young children. However, in our analysis of the Independent Sector data we have found that both marital and parental status are related to volunteering. The parental effect is partially mediated by being asked. [20] Parents are more likely than the childless to be asked to volunteer, regardless of their marital status.

Becoming a parent is a major life transition. It is a time when many young adults finally "settle down." Lois (2003:58) found that her search and rescue volunteers, routinely engaging in highly risky activities and constantly on-call, often summoned for duty in the middle of the night, were disproportionately childless. However, much depends on the age of the child. Children in the household can both limit and encourage volunteer work on the part of their parents. Young children make it difficult for parents to volunteer, but school age children tend to draw them into volunteer work.[4] The impact of having children on one mother's level of volunteering is evident in the following quotation:

> I'm going to have to be less active certainly until the kids are a little older because I didn't have kids in order to go to meetings all the time . . . Also, I don't think I have quite as much energy as I did when I was twenty . . . I'm also committed to spending a lot of time with my kids. So it means that instead of writing a leaflet at night, I'm scrubbing the bathroom because there wasn't any time to do it during the day or preparing supper for the next day or else just bed because I'm so tired. (Klatch 2000:515)

When they reach school age, children reverse roles and begin to draw their parents into the wider community. Their volunteer work reflects "the demands that youth organizations and schools place on parents to serve as troop leaders, coaches, board members, and so forth; the fact that parents of young children may be setting down roots in the neighborhood and feel a greater stake in its future; and the fact that parents may step up church involvement as part of the child-rearing process" (Goss and Putnam 1998:5). Parents of school age children have a stake in maintaining organizations and activities that cater to their children and that, as individuals, they could not provide on their own, such as sports teams and scout troops.[5]

The presence of children of various ages in the household undoubtedly accounts, in part, for the shape of the trajectory of volunteering across the life course. Canadian data gathered in 1997 showed that the volunteer rate of people aged between 15 and 24 with children of their own was 16 percent, compared to 34 percent who were not parents. When parents are in their teens or early adulthood, their children are young: they are an impediment to volunteering. Once people reach middle age, however, their children are in school and the effect of parental status is reversed: parents volunteer more than people without children. The volunteer rate of parents aged between 44 and 55 is 49 percent, compared to 30 percent among those of that age who are childless (Jones 2001:71).[6] The finding that parents with young children volunteer fewer hours than those with older children is one of the most reliable in the sociological research on volunteering (Clain and Zech 1999;

Damico et al. 1998:20; Garcia and Marcuello 2002; Gora and Nemerowicz 1985:17; Goss and Putnam 1998:5; Hayghe 1991; Johnson et al. 2004:61; Menchik and Weisbrod 1987:177; Schlozman et al. 1994; Vaillancourt 1994; Wuthnow 1998:76).[7]

Having established that children influence their parents' volunteer contributions we next consider whether all parents are equally affected. For a number of reasons we believe that the influence of children is felt more by some parents than others. The first of these is work time. We have already described how full-time workers volunteer less than part-time workers and homemakers. A logical implication is that the negative effect of preschool children will be stronger and the positive effect of school age children will be weaker for full-time workers. Gender is another moderating factor. A gendered division of labor in the American household means that women are primarily responsible for taking care of children. A logical implication is that the negative effect of preschool children and the positive effect of school age children will be stronger for mothers than fathers. Finally, we will look at marital status because the time cost of having children is higher for single parents than married parents. A logical implication is that single people are even less likely to volunteer if they have preschool children and not as likely to volunteer if they have school age children.

Effect of Children Varies by Work Hours

Parents who work full-time find it much more difficult to volunteer if their children are very young than parents who are not in the labor force or work less than full-time.[8] For example, one study found that working mothers with young children have the lowest volunteer rate (Kohut 1997:43). To fully understand how work hours moderate the influence of children on parental volunteering it is necessary to create categories of work and parental status and estimate their influence on volunteering. A recent study found that, among mothers of children less than age 18 living in the household, homemakers were the most likely to volunteer and mothers employed full-time were the least (Rotolo and Wilson 2007). In other words, the women who responded most positively to having children in school were those with the most time to spare. Turning to the inhibiting effect of having preschool children, the study showed that, compared to homemakers with school age children, all mothers with preschool children volunteer less, but especially if they worked full-time. In other words, the demands imposed by having preschool children (compared to having school age children) were greater among women who work full-time. Likewise, compared to homemakers with school age children, all women with no children volunteered less, but especially if they worked full-time: that is, the positive effect of having school age children (over having none at all) was stronger in the case of homemakers than in the case of full-time working mothers. Looking at these patterns from the perspective of work, we see that women with part-time jobs were more likely to volunteer and they volunteered more hours than women working full-time, *but especially if they had school age children in the household.* Full-time work lowered the probability of volunteering and hours volunteered, *but less so for mothers with school age children.*

Effect of Children Varies by Gender

The influence of children on their parents' volunteering is likely to be felt most keenly by mothers, who bear most of the responsibility of looking after children. Thus, the negative effect of having small children in the house is stronger for mothers than fathers.[9] When children reach school age, they begin to draw their parents into volunteer work, much of it associated with youth-related activities or the schools their children are attending. However, this is much truer of mothers than fathers. For many mothers, volunteer involvement in children's activities is "just part of bringing up children" (Flick et al. 2002:58). One Australian focus group member told researchers: "The mothers who go and help at the preschool and the school and at the tuck-shop, canteens and that, they don't look at themselves as being volunteers . . . she would see her self as doing it for her child" (Flick et al. 2002:58). Mothers go out of their way to care for the people around them; fathers are more often described as people who simply enjoy being around other people. "Whereas mothers actually help their children or their children's friends, fathers are admired for being gregarious, liking to do things with people, liking to spend time together, or being someone with whom one can have a good time—indeed, dad is just a regular guy" (Wuthnow 1995:155). This could be interpreted simply as women extending their roles as mothers into the community, or disenchantment with the role of the full-time mother and a search for more variety and stimulation (Clary and Snyder 1991; Gallagher 1994b:131; Negrey 1993:93). Abrahams (1996:781) found that half of the Anglo women she interviewed began volunteer work when they had children and were taking time off from employment. The women spoke of their volunteer work as a (temporary) substitute for paid employment: "For me, my chosen vocation at this moment is to be a full-time mom and by being involved in a program like this, I get a lot of positive reinforcement for the choice that I've made." For these women volunteer work was a way to enhance the devalued status of motherhood.

Becoming a parent of a school age child is thus likely to have more impact on women than men. One survey asked parents if they had attended a general school meeting, a regularly scheduled parent-teacher conference, a school or class event, or volunteered in their child's school in the past year. Whereas four in ten of the parents had volunteered, only 15 percent of the fathers had done so, compared to 41 percent of the mothers. The mother was the only spouse to volunteer in 27.7 percent of the marriages, while the father was the only spouse to volunteer in 2.9 percent of the marriages. The responsibility of parenthood thus fell more heavily on the mother than the father. In the case of single parent families, the gender gap was narrower. Twenty-three percent of the single fathers volunteered compared to 28 percent of the single mothers. In other words, when men are the sole parent they assume some of the volunteer responsibilities they leave to their wives when they are married (Nord et al. 1997:103). Vaillancourt (1994:823) found that the presence of children 0–2 reduced the volunteer work of Canadian mothers but had no significant impact on that of men. Children of school age increased the volunteer work of both parents. Among Australians without dependent children the men were slightly more likely to do volunteer work than the women, but if dependent children were present the women were more likely to volunteer than men (Australian Bureau of Statistics 2002).

We analyzed the CPS data to see if the influence of children on volunteering varied by the gender of the parent. Both mothers and fathers are more likely to volunteer if their children are between 6 and 13 years of age. This is true for all volunteering and for volunteering for education-related and church-related organizations. We also found a significant gender interaction effect. Compared to parents of children aged 2 or under, parents of children between 6 and 13 years of age were much more likely to volunteer but mothers were especially likely to do so. This was true of all volunteering, volunteering for schools, and volunteering for the church. The influence of children aged 14–17 on educational volunteering was also stronger for mothers than fathers. Both mothers and fathers of children aged 2 or under were less likely to volunteer than the married couples who had no children at all, but the negative effect was stronger for mothers than fathers. In short, gender does seem to make a difference to the influence of children on volunteering: young children deter their mothers more than their fathers and school age children involve their mothers more in volunteer work than their fathers.

Effect of Children Varies by Marital Status

We noted above that marital and parental statuses are highly correlated, but not all parents are married and not all married couples have children. Single parents have less time to volunteer than married parents. Segal (1993:181) found that the number of children increases the chances of a parent volunteering more when there are two parents present. Burns et al. (2001:97) found that single parents reported the lowest rate of volunteering, while married people with no children reported the highest rate. Sundeen (1990) sorted respondents to a 1985 survey of adult Americans into: married/preschool child; married/school age child; married/no child; single/preschool; single/school age; and single/no child. Respondents were asked if they were currently volunteering. Compared to the single/no child group, married/preschool and married/school age child were more likely to have volunteered. For single parents, having children of any age neither increased nor decreased the chances of volunteering. Married people with no children were no more likely to volunteer than single people. Thus it seems that, although other studies have found that married people with preschool children volunteer less than married people with school age children, they still volunteer more than single people, whether those single people are parents or not. And, although studies often show that married people volunteer more than single people, they do not if they are childless.

We analyzed the CPS data to see if marital status moderates the influence of parental status on volunteering. As noted above, the age of children makes a difference to parental volunteering and we therefore took this variation into account also. The CPS data divides the ages of respondents' children into several ranges: 0–2, 3–5, 6–13, 14–17, and 18 or more. Because many parents have children in more than one of these age ranges, the CPS data also codes all possible combinations of children in these ranges below the age of 18. Earlier research on this issue has relied upon variables indicating whether parents have children in a certain age range, such as preschool or school aged. The problem with this approach is that it does not adequately capture the true heterogeneity of families. That is, some families have children in only one age range, but many families have children in multiple age ranges. How then do we capture the effect of having children in a given age range yet pay heed to the fact that parents may also have children in other age categories? Using the CPS data, we coded dichotomous variables for each of the child age ranges. At this point, our method is similar to that used by other researchers in the area. However, we also code several dichotomous variables indicating the number of child age categories present in the family. For example, a family with two children aged 9 and 10 would be coded as having only one child age category. In contrast, a family with two children, one aged 2 and another aged 10, would be coded as having two child age categories. Using these dichotomous variables as controls, we then estimated mean levels of volunteering for respondents with children in each of the age categories shown above.[10] Similarly, we estimated mean levels of volunteering for respondents without children to provide some baseline comparison. Given previous research on these issues, we computed means for all respondents and then split the sample by marital status to generate means for married and non-married respondents. Finally, we examined the mean scores for three types of volunteering: (a) any volunteering, (b) volunteering for religious organizations, and (c) volunteering for educational organizations.

Figure 5 describes the results of our analysis, showing the mean level of volunteering for parents of children in each of the age categories for all respondents and for single and married respondents and for all volunteering, volunteering in connection with schools, and volunteering in connection with religious organizations. The positive influence of school age children is obvious from this figure, *although it is stronger for married than single par-*

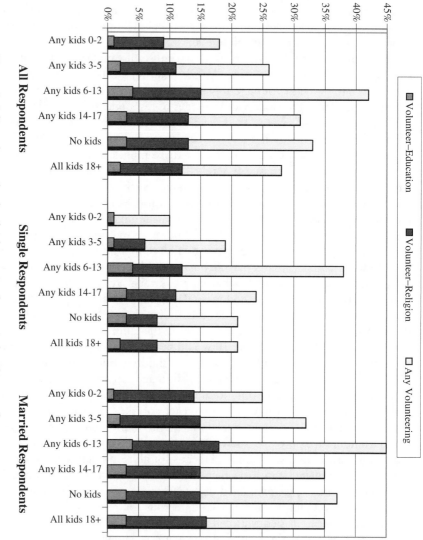

Figure 5. Adjusted mean levels of volunteering by marital and parental status.

ents. Similarly, the negative effect of having young children is consistent across all types of volunteering and both singles and married respondents, although it is *stronger for single than married people.* In short, marital status clearly moderates the influence of children on parental volunteering. The figure also reveals some other interesting patterns. Older children are not always a positive force when it comes to volunteering. In the case of married people only, the volunteer rate is slightly higher for those with no children than it is for those with teenagers in the household, although this difference is not found in the two sub-types we focus on in the figure. That is, married couples with teenagers will volunteer at the same rate as married people with no children if they are volunteering in connection with a school or church.

Effect of Children Varies by Domain

As we noted above, some kinds of volunteer work become more attractive when we have children, but others—those which are more time consuming, more risky or dangerous—will become less attractive. Parental status does not therefore encourage volunteering *in general.* Parents will be drawn toward, or be recruited for, activities that speak directly to their children's needs or toward activities that address community problems that might have an impact on their children's welfare, such as safe streets and parks, clean air and water, and drug-free neighborhoods. Having children diverts their attention away from advocacy volunteering and toward serving individual needs.[11]

Data from the 2002 CPS survey show that parents were more than twice as likely to volunteer for education and youth-oriented organizations as persons with no children. In contrast, volunteers with no children were about twice as likely as parents to volunteer for a social or community service organization such as a homeless shelter or senior citizen shelter (Boraas 2003:6).[12] Another study found that, with children in the home, parents are more likely to volunteer for community-oriented groups (where the benefits are collective) but less likely to volunteer for a more self-oriented organization, such as a professional association or a union (Janoski and Wilson 1995). Kohut (1997:43) found that mothers with children were more likely to volunteer than women without children, but especially for youth development programs, school and tutoring programs, religious organizations, and neighborhood or civic groups. Romero (1986) found that women volunteered more for child-related activities if they had children younger than 18 in the household but they were no more likely than childless women to volunteer for church and social welfare activities. Rossi (2001d:341) found that, while having children to care for increased how many hours a parent volunteered, it increased the hours donated to school or youth related activities the most. Carlin (2001:809), using time-diary records kept by married women, found much the same pattern:

Those with children volunteer at a higher rate than those without children. The difference is greater for volunteering to child and family organizations, but the difference is substantive and significant for all kinds of volunteering lumped together.

We confirmed this general pattern in our analysis of the Independent Sector data. [40] Children had a positive effect on education and youth development volunteering but a negative effect on volunteering for arts and politics.

Volunteering in Mid-Life: Conclusion

It is fitting that family statuses should have such a strong influence on volunteer behavior because, in so many ways, volunteer work is an extension of the care family members provide each other into the public sphere. Getting married and having children are major life transitions that alter in fundamental ways our priorities, obligations, resources, and social networks. Inevitably, they influence how much free time we have and how we choose to spend that free time. The manner in which these transitions influence volunteering demonstrates the significance of both individual resources and social networks, a major theme of this book. Regardless of whether they have children, married people go to church more frequently (or divorced, separated, and widowed people are more likely to stop going to church), and this partially explains why they are more likely to volunteer. In addition, married people with school age children get involved through the social networks their children help create. But we observed that the effect of this status is not confined to child-related volunteering, suggesting either that the social networks have diffuse influences on parents' volunteering or that when children start school their parents have more free time. We found that children connect their parents to volunteer opportunities: with children in the household people are more likely to be recruited to volunteer. Single parents, on the other hand, are so squeezed for time they have little left over for volunteer work. The fact that single parents have difficulty finding time to volunteer should be quite worrying to non-profit organizations because family structures are changing: the number of single mother families in the United States grew from three million in 1970 to 10 million in 2003 and the number of single father families grew from less than half a million to two million (Fields 2004). We also found that family roles are performed in the context of other productive roles, such as working for pay. The influence of family roles on the volunteer role is clearly moderated by these competing demands. Parents with school age children experience more difficulty getting involved in activities associated with their children's education if they are working full-time. This, too, should be a concern for non-profit organizations because the proportion of families where both parents work full-time is rising. Finally, we assume that family and work roles are primary and the volunteer role is secondary. Parents will fit their volunteer work around the primary demands of work and family. But we cannot assume that people decide how to allocate their time in such a linear fashion. It is quite likely that women especially make decisions about whether or not to work based on their desire to have children. Women first have children, then accommodate their work hours to meet the demands of parenthood, perhaps leaving the labor force or going part-time, and as a result have more time to volunteer. The family role "drives" the volunteer role because it has affected the work role.

Volunteering in Later Life

Americans have conflicting images of later life. On the one hand, it is seen as a phase of life when people can finally retire and enjoy the fruits of their labor. They are relatively free of social obligations and can do what they want. If they lacked the time to volunteer before, now is the time to begin. On the other hand, later life is associated with declining health and energy and living on lower incomes as well as shrinking social circles, all of which raise the cost of volunteering to the older person. In fact, neither of these images is correct, although each contains a grain of truth. "Data demonstrate that neither the stereotype that elders are frail and dependent nor the stereotype that they are affluent retirees seeking leisure is correct" (Morrow-Howell et al. 2001:289). The later part of life is not inevitably comprised of decrements. Many older persons have accumulated a lifetime of skills and knowledge with which to enrich their post-retirement life. Thanks to improved health and economic security retirement has emerged as a life stage in its own right, complete with its own culture, norms, activities, and lifestyles. Given these changes, and given the extended life span of people who have reached retirement age, it is possible that the elderly will volunteer just as much, perhaps even more, than they did when they were working and had heavy family responsibilities.

Many older people express a strong desire to maintain an independent and productive lifestyle in retirement and they attach more importance to volunteering than younger people. When asked "How important do you think it is for people to be involved in the community by volunteering their time for things like charitable, civic, cultural, environmental or political activities," just over two-thirds of Americans (67%) said it was very important, but the proportion rose steadily with age, from 50 percent in the under 30 group, to 65 percent in the 30–49 age group, to 75 percent in the 50 and over age group (Wirthlin Group 1995a:5). Gerontologists applaud this attitude. They believe the key to successful aging, defined as "positive interaction with others, a sense of purpose or meaning, and an attitude toward life as an opportunity for growth" is to remain active within the community and engage as much as possible in goal-directed, purposeful behavior (Fisher et al. 1998:44). Some gerontologists prefer the term "productive aging" because it counters the negative image of older people as dependent and unproductive members of society beset by health and financial problems. Volunteer work is an example of productive aging because it "produces socially valued goods and services, whether paid or not, or that develops the capacity to produce those goods and services" (Bass and Caro 2001:40). Describing volunteer work as producing socially valued goods avoids the connotation that it is simply a way for the elderly to pass the time or have a social life. Encouraging volunteer work among the elderly thus has to be understood in the context of the cultural framing of what it means to be elderly in a capitalist society, where feeling useful is an important source of self-esteem, and where the elderly are liable to be stigmatized as no longer being productive.

Prompted by beliefs that volunteering is good for the elderly and that the country could benefit from tapping this pool of labor, politicians have stepped up their efforts to mobilize the elderly for volunteer work. In the United States, organizations such as Foster Grandparents, the Retired and Senior Volunteer Program, and Senior Companions are government efforts to harness this labor supply. All are part of Senior Corps, which is administered by the Corporation for National and Community Service. Together, these programs engage more than two million elderly Americans in service to their communities each year. The Foster Grandparent Program began in 1965 as a national demonstration effort to show how low-income persons, aged 60 and over, have the maturity and experience to establish a personal relationship with children having either exceptional or special needs. The Senior Companion Program was set up by Title II of the Domestic Volunteer Service Act of 1973 to enable older persons to work with other older persons who might need their help. Foster Grandparents and Senior Companions receive a small stipend and modest health benefits. In the United Kingdom, the Home Office gave a grant-in-aid in 2001 to a non-profit called Experience Corps, the goal being to act as broker between potential volunteers aged 50 and over and the needs of charities and other organizations. In addition to these government or quasi-government organizations, non-profit organizations have sprung up to mobilize senior volunteering. One of the best known is the Retired and Senior Volunteers program, founded in the United States in 1969 with the intention of encouraging more seniors to do volunteer work using the skills they had acquired on their job. The R.S.V.P has been emulated in the United Kingdom and Australia.

At the beginning of this chapter we described the age profile of the volunteer labor force in the United States. According to the 2003 Current Population Survey Volunteer Supplement, the likelihood of having volunteered in the past year and the number of volunteer activities peaked among those aged between 40 and 45. As they age, people tend to contract their volunteer commitments; presumably to those activities they prefer most (Hendricks and Cutler 2004). Recall that in chapter 6 we demonstrated that both education and income have a positive influence on volunteering. Both factors can help explain why the volunteer rate declines in later life. To test this hypothesis, we estimated a model using the Independent Sector data in which we first entered the age variable (with controls for race and gender) and then entered the education variable. As a result, the likelihood of an elderly person volunteering (compared to the youngest age group) increased. Indeed, in the case of respondents aged between 74 and 81 the sign of the coefficient changed: no longer less likely to volunteer, they became more likely to volunteer than young people. This is almost certainly due to the lower levels of educational achievement of people born during the First World War. Entering the income variable separately we arrived at the same result: elderly people are less likely to volunteer because they have lower household incomes. [71] Although the rate and range of volunteering might decline in old age, the total hours volunteered among those volunteering continues to rise throughout the life span, beginning to decline only when individuals reached the age of 80. For example, volunteers aged 65 years or more contributed eighty-eight hours a year, compared to forty hours a year among young adult volunteers (16–24) (U.S. Bureau of Labor Statistics 2003).

Thus the overall pattern is for older people to become steadily less likely to volunteer and to volunteer for fewer organizations, but for the hours contributed by each volunteer to increase until he or she enters the ranks of the oldest old. This age profile is found in most industrialized societies for which we have volunteer data. Canadian data from 1997 data showed that 23 percent of seniors (65+) volunteered in the past year, compared to 31.4 percent overall. However, they contributed more hours per year than any other age group. In 1997 they averaged 202 hours compared with the next largest category at 160 hours for those aged 55–64 (Chappell 1999:10). The age differences can be striking: Canadians aged 65 and over volunteer 61 percent more hours a year than Canadians aged 15–24 (Woolley 1998:25). A 1997 UK survey found that the rate of volunteering peaked in middle age (45–54), but people 65 years of age and older volunteered the most hours per week (Smith 1998:27). Dutch people in the age range 55–74 are somewhat less likely to volunteer than those in the 35–54 age bracket, but if they do volunteer, they contribute more hours (De Hart and Dekker 1999:86). Older Australians are no more likely to volunteer than younger people but, if they do volunteer, they work longer hours (Warburton et al. 2001:587).

Volunteering and Retirement

The major life transition in later life is retirement. This "third phase" of life means that most people have a chance to allocate their time differently. As we have seen, older people do not have higher volunteer rates than people who are still working, but they contribute more hours. It is tempting to attribute these hours to the free time that retired people enjoy. But this confuses the aging process with the retirement process and they are not necessarily the same thing due to the wide variation in the timing of retirement. Just how easy it is to misinterpret the significance of retirement for volunteering can be seen by a study in which 20 percent of Americans who retired between 1986 and 1989 had quitted volunteering by 1989. Although this seems to be conclusive evidence that retirement causes people to quit volunteering, the rate for those who did *not* retire in that time period fell by almost the same amount and was actually steeper for those who were working full-time. The attrition probably had more to do with the aging process than with retirement itself (Mutchler et al. 2003).

People look forward to having more free time when they retire. Nearly half of all Americans believe a "life of leisure" is an important element of the ideal retirement life-style (Moen et al. 2000:249). But they do not necessarily mean a life of idleness. In the same survey just over a third (36%) saw volunteering as an important part of their life in retirement. Retired Americans do not lose their desire to be productive: "keeping busy and being active are central values" in capitalist societies (Chambre 1987:7). This norm helps explain why volunteer work figures so prominently in the retirement plans of many Americans: just over half of the retired Americans who were currently volunteering told researchers that, before they retired, they had anticipated that volunteering would be a "very important" part of their retirement (Peter D. Hart 2002:4). However, we should treat such statements with caution. Many retirement plans amount to little. In the study just cited, three in ten of the retirees who were not currently volunteering admitted to having made plans to do so after they retired (Peter D. Hart 2002:4). Respondents in a 2003 survey of currently employed 50- to 70-year-old Americans (the "Baby Boomer" generation) who had yet to retire were asked how prominently various activities figured in their plans for retirement: just over half (54%) said "spending more time with family and friends" and nearly half (48%) said that "a chance to relax" and "a chance to have more fun" featured prominently in their plans. Only 19 percent mentioned "doing volunteer or charity work," despite the fact that half of them were currently volunteering (Brown 2003:68). Close to three in ten had no plans to work after they retired. This group was asked to rate a list of reasons for not working: one in five said "a desire to volunteer" would be a major factor, but when they were asked to select *just one* major reason for not working in retirement only 2 percent selected a desire to volunteer (Brown 2003:38)

Although we should be skeptical of the intentions of people as they approach retirement, the important point is that most retirees are both capable of and willing to work. Their departure from the labor force is just as likely to be a response to age-based social norms, age discrimination in the workplace, or the availability of pension benefits that would be denied them if they earned a wage. Many retirees therefore look for substitutes for the productive roles they have given up as well as replacements for the social relationships they formed in the workplace. Senior volunteers are more likely to say they volunteer to stay busy and keep active, whereas younger volunteers are more likely to mention career development, self-discovery, and assistance in dealing with their own problems (Black and Kovacs 1999:281). In summary, this argument predicts that retirees are *more* likely to volunteer and, perhaps, volunteer more hours, than older people who have yet to retire.

The reverse of this argument is that volunteer work and paid work are complementary, not competing, activities. Recall that, in an earlier chapter, we observed that employment had a positive influence on volunteering. According to this theory, retirement is likely to lead to a decline in volunteering because people lose touch with many of those who might have kept them involved in volunteer work. Another reason to believe that retirees volunteer less is that they are looking for respite from the kinds of obligations volunteer work entails. Retirees believe they have "paid their dues." A third reason is that retirees do not necessarily think of themselves as having more free time than before they retired. Even people who cease working altogether after retirement do not think they have more free time (Chambre 1987:9). Indeed, older Australians (55+) surveyed in 1997 were *less* likely than younger Australians to say they had time to spare (Warburton and Crozier 2001). This is a reminder that we cannot simply assume that the time saved from work is "free time" waiting to be filled up with volunteer work.

One of these theories predicts that volunteer work will increase after retirement and the other predicts it will decrease. Continuity theory predicts there will be no change. Advocates of continuity theory believe both the preceding theories exaggerate the effects of retirement on the life-style of older people. Continuity theory postulates that, in adapting to aging, people attempt to preserve and maintain long-standing patterns of thought and behavior, relying on established strengths and skills. In this context, continuity does not mean the absence of change but change that is adaptive in ways that enable the individual to build on established strengths. By the time we reach middle age we will have spent many years developing a preference for, and competence in, certain kinds of activities. We will have developed certain kinds of role relations, friendships and social activities with which we feel comfortable. If aging, for whatever reason, causes us to cut back on our activities, we will drop first those with which we feel least comfortable and are least proficient at. If aging gives us more free time, we will expand former roles and social relationships rather than taking on new roles or forming new relationships. We "recycle" the roles of middle age for new uses in old age (Payne and Bull 1985:263). This does not necessarily mean the adaptation is always successful but simply that we look for continuity. Advocates of continuity theory believe that the "role loss" thought to occur in old age has been exaggerated. Retirees do not necessarily feel they are short of friends or social contacts. Elderly volunteers are no more likely than younger ones to take up volunteering *in order to* establish new connections. They *are* more likely than young people to cite as important the opportunity to help others, to accomplish something worthwhile, and belief in a cause. Alleviating loneliness is mentioned by very few (Moen et al. 2000).

The simplest way to decide whether retirement itself, rather than age, makes a difference to volunteering is to compare the volunteer rates of older people who are still in the labor force and people who have retired. Warburton et al. (1998:239) found no difference in the rate of volunteering between Australians aged between 50 and 80 who were working and those who were retired. Similarly, a study of elderly Europeans (aged 50 years or more) found no difference in the likelihood of volunteering between those who were working, those who were retired, and those who were not in the labor force (e.g., homemakers). In our own analysis of the Independent Sector data, we found that, compared to people not in the labor force, people with jobs were more likely to volunteer and retired people were less likely to volunteer. However, there was no difference among volunteers in the number of hours contributed. [20, 53] Retirement thus appears to lower the volunteer rate without having any effect on the number of hours contributed by those who do volunteer.

These simple cross-sectional comparisons can be deceiving, for a number of reasons. First, they do not take into account the argument of continuity theory according to which people do not fundamentally change their social activities when they retire. Simply comparing the volunteer rates of retired and non-retired elderly persons says little about the effect of retirement on volunteer activity because volunteer activity prior to retirement is not measured. The second reason cross-sectional comparisons can be misleading is that they lump all retirees together when in fact they are a very heterogeneous group. For example, retirement might well reduce the rate of volunteering overall but more so for those who take a full-time job after they have retired. We will deal with each of these issues in turn.

As far as continuity is concerned, we used longitudinal data from successive waves of the Americans' Changing Lives (ACL) to look at the effect of volunteering prior to retirement on what happened to volunteer hours after retirement.[13] We found that the more hours people volunteered before retirement the more likely they were to cut back on the number of hours volunteered after retirement. To some extent we must attribute this to a ceiling effect. Busy volunteers have "nowhere to go" in terms of hours contributed but down. However, the important point here is that there is no evidence here of people *increasing* their volunteer output once they retire.

As far as social heterogeneity among retirees is concerned, the chances of people continuing to volunteer after they retire are affected by when they retire, the kind of job they had before retirement, whether or not they choose to work in retirement, and how they think about their status as retirees. For example, one study of 50- to 70-year-olds compared "earners" and "work enthusiasts" (Brown 2003:62). Members of the first group (predominantly male) were likely to have retired early but without enough savings to support themselves. More of this group gave money or health benefits as a major reason for working in retirement and few of them planned to volunteer. The "work enthusiasts" intended to continue working in retirement without, however, identifying money as a major motivation for working in retirement. They had plans to volunteer when they retired. It is no coincidence that a disproportionately high number of the work enthusiasts were professionals and self-employed. Having a satisfying and rewarding job, they were more likely to imagine a retirement full of activity, including both volunteer and working for pay. Obviously, we have to pay attention to what people are retiring *from*. In chapter 6 we demonstrated occupational status and volunteering are associated and the question is whether this association continues after retirement. Herzog and Morgan (1993:140) believe that, after they have retired, "professionals are more attracted to work and work-like activities because they have had more positive work experiences, and they probably also have more satisfying and interesting experiences in the kinds of volunteer work that are available to them." Moen et al. (2000:90) agree that the prestige of one's pre-retirement job lingers on after retirement. A British study of older men shows how pre-retirement occupational status casts a shadow over retirement activities. The subjects of the study were men aged 65, who were shown an extensive list of organizations and asked to which groups they belonged.[14] Almost half (44%) of the men who previously had professional or managerial jobs were volunteering, compared to just one in seven of the manual workers. Controlling for health, household income, marital status, and age, professional and managerial and white-collar retirees were still more likely to volunteer than blue-collar retirees. In their retirement, working class men were more likely to get involved in social clubs intended to provide opportunities to enjoy leisure in the company of others (Perren et al. 2003). Middle class retirees probably felt a greater need to compensate for their loss of productive roles than their working class counterparts.

Unfortunately, these studies pay little heed to continuity theory and fail to acknowledge that volunteering after retirement is probably nothing but a continuation of the volunteering that went on before retirement. To explore this issue, we analyzed the American Changing Lives data from 1986 and 1989 to see if the prestige of the job prior to retirement made any difference to volunteering after retirement. Once we controlled for whether or not a person volunteered before retirement, pre-retirement job prestige had no effect on either the number of post-retirement volunteer activities or the number of hours volunteered. Studies that infer continuing effects of previous jobs on post-retirement activities based on cross-sectional data and that do not take into account previous levels of volunteering can be misleading.

The second form of heterogeneity is what people retire *to*. For many people, retirement does not mean the end of paid work. Indeed, many "retirees" end up working full-time, either by choice or necessity. This is an important source of social heterogeneity in the retiree population because we must assume that employment status has the same effect on volunteering after retirement as it has on volunteering before retirement. In other words, full-time work reduces the amount of free time retirees have for volunteering but part-time work can be socially integrative, helping a retired person avoid social isolation.

The research on the relation between labor force status and volunteering in retirement has produced mixed results. One study found that Canadians who returned to work after retiring were more likely to volunteer than those who fully retired (Jones 1999:10). Soo and Gong-Soog (1998) also found that the elderly who had fully retired were less likely to volunteer, and if they did volunteer, contributed fewer hours than those who had taken a post-retirement job. But we cannot afford to jump to any conclusions on the basis of these studies. It is quite likely that the relation between work and volunteering in retirement is spurious. Retirees who return to work are in better health than those who leave the labor force altogether, and they may also be younger. This might explain why Caro and Bass (1997) found no relation between rate of volunteering and employment status after they controlled for age, education, religious activity, and self-reported health. Going back to work was not "causing" these individuals to volunteer; rather, both were part of a general activity syndrome evident among seniors with more resources. A study of Australians, which found no connection between work and volunteering among retirees after suitable controls, also supports this argument (Warburton et al. 1998:239).

Once again, these studies do not control for whether respondents were volunteering before they retired. However, they do raise the question of whether employment status in retirement moderates the effect of pre-retirement volunteering on post-retirement volunteering. One study found that, among 55- to 74-year-old Americans, paid work had little impact on volunteering in later life *among those already volunteering*. Among those who were not volunteering before they retired, on the other hand, employment status did make a difference: those who fully retired or cut back their working hours in retirement were more likely to begin volunteering (Mutchler et al. 2003). Perhaps people who have not volunteered before look to this kind of work to fill up some of their newly acquired free time.

Volunteer Hours

Up to this point, we have been discussing the influence of retirement on the likelihood of volunteering at all, but we have already observed that, while the rate of volunteering eventually begins to decline with age, the number of hours contributed by each volunteer continues to rise until the ranks of the "oldest old" are reached. The number of hours contributed would seem to be much more a function of available time than the chances of volunteering at all. This raises the question of whether the fully retired volunteer more hours than people who take up new jobs in their retirement. One study found that, among volunteers, retirees who had returned to work contributed an average of twelve hours a month, compared to twenty-one hours a month among those volunteers who had not returned to work (Moen et al. 2000:86). Another study confirmed this negative relation between volunteer hours and employment among the elderly: the fully retired volunteer the most hours (Caro and Bass 1997). A 1997 UK survey found that the fully retired were less likely to have volunteered in the last twelve months than people in paid employment but they contributed more hours per week (4.6) than those in paid jobs (3.8) (Smith 1998:26).

Retirement not only encourages people to contribute more hours, it also re-schedules those hours. Retirees are more likely to volunteer during the weekday than younger people. They volunteer more hours during the week, but there are no age differences in the number of hours volunteered at the weekend (Almeida et al. 2001:148). Time budget data from the UK 2000 Time Use Survey shows that 16- to 24-year-olds averaged one minute of volunteering a day, 25- to 44-year-olds averaged two minutes, 45- to 64-year-olds averaged five minutes, and 65-year-olds averaged over eight minutes (Ruston 2003:13). However, there were no age differences in time spent volunteering at the weekends. And, although we have no survey or time diary data on this, older Americans tend to be shy of steady commitments to volunteer work. They much prefer flexibility in their volunteer assignments (Moen et al 2000:259). Unfortunately we do not have data on whether fully retired older people schedule their volunteer activities differently from retirees who have returned to work.

To explore further the influence of employment in retirement on hours volunteered (rather than the rate of volunteering) we analyzed data from three waves of the ACL data set: 1986, 1989, and 1991. Using information on retirement and employment status we created five categories and calculated the mean hours volunteered for each category, adjusted for gender, race, age, education, self-reported health, and frequency of church attendance. The categories were not retired and working full-time; not retired and working part-time; not retired and not in the labor force (mainly homemakers); retired and not working; retired and working (we collapsed part- and full-time because of small cell sizes). We used two measures of volunteer work: volunteer range (number of different domains in which the respondent volunteered) and volunteer hours. Throughout the three waves, full-time workers not retired contributed fewer hours than any group of retirees, whether they were working full-time, part-time or not working at all. We therefore focused on the contrast between full-time workers not yet retired and retirees, some of whom have returned to work and others not. Full-time workers not yet retired volunteer fewer hours than either of the two groups of retirees. This confirms that, after controls, older people who have fully retired volunteer the most hours, followed by older people who have retired but returned to work, followed by full-time workers who have not yet retired.

Timing of Retirement

Earlier we noted the wide disparity in the timing of retirement. Some people retire when they are relatively young while others postpone retirement as long as they can. If for no other reason, early retirement might be associated with more volunteering in later life because early retirees are younger and in better health. A contradictory argument is that early retirement is a sign of disaffection with work and work-like obligations or perhaps mental or physical health problems and, for these reasons, might be associated with lower rates of volunteering. Moen et al. (2000:85) found that people who retired "on time," when they were in their 60s and 70s, were more likely to volunteer than those who retired "early," when they were in their 50s. This might have something to do with people being tired of work of all kinds *and* commitments of all kinds and wanting to take a break from them while they are in good health. It might also be a function of the fact that people with meaningful and rewarding jobs are both more likely to postpone their retirement and volunteer. Early retirees might signal, by their early retirement, that they have unpleasant jobs, and these workers tend to have lower volunteer rates. This might have something to do with whether the retirement was voluntary or involuntary. Voluntary retirees are more likely to be volunteering than involuntary retirees. Involuntary retirees are also more likely to miss their jobs, and retirees who miss their jobs are less likely to volunteer (Chambre 1987:29). The topic of the influence of attitudes toward retirement and their influence on volunteering in retirement deserves more study.

Volunteering and the Stages of Retirement

Americans today can look forward to spending many years in retirement. This phase of life has its own stages. Some gerontologists believe that, when people initially retire they "take a break" from many other kinds of social obligations only to resume or take up volunteer work later. Caro and Bass (1997) have addressed this theme in a number of analyses. They found there was no difference in the rate of volunteering by years since last job: people who retired last year had the same volunteer rate as people who retired ten years ago. However, when respondents were asked whether they would consider doing volunteer work, those who had only recently stopped working were more likely to say they would. The longer they had been retired the less receptive people were to the idea of volunteering. This might have had something to do with declining health because only 18 percent of those who had recently stopped working reported health as a major obstacle to volunteering compared to 37 percent who had been out of the labor force for six years or more. However, it also suggests that the newly retired are especially anxious about taking on unpaid work immediately. But the picture gets complicated because the effect of having recently retired on willingness to volunteer was weaker among those who retired early. Apparently people who retire when in their 50s are more interested in finding new, paying jobs than finding volunteer work to do, and they are less eager to do volunteer work.

In another study, Moen and Fields (2002:35) found a slight tendency for newly retired Americans to take up volunteering. Comparing two panels of longitudinal data (1994, 1996) they asked who was more likely to have taken up volunteering in that time frame. Those who retired between 1994 and 1996 were more likely to have begun volunteering than either those who were already retired in 1994 or those who were still working for pay in 1996. The newly retired were also slightly less likely to stop volunteering between 1994 and 1996. This was especially true of women and those with low pre-retirement incomes. This transition analysis is useful because a simple, cross-sectional, comparison of the volunteer rates of retired and non-retired people in these same data (i.e., in 1994) showed no difference in volunteer rates between them. It belies the proposition that people "take a break" after they return only to take up volunteering later. Our own analysis of the 1986 panel of the ACL supports the analysis described above. Controlling for age, health status, and a number of other socio-demographic variables, we found the longer a person had been retired the *less* volunteer work they were doing.

Aging and Volunteer Domain

Older people have different interests than younger people and for this reason they join different kinds of voluntary associations. They are more likely to be members of fraternal, service, veterans, religious, and farm organizations. Younger people gravitate towards sports, youth, school, and professional organizations. Unions, hobby groups, school fraternity/sorority, nationality, and literary groups are age-neutral (Cutler and Danigelis 1993: 151). As far as volunteer work is concerned, older people favor volunteer activities where they can help on a one-to-one basis and see the fruits of their labor immediately. Not surprisingly, older people are also drawn to volunteer work that targets other older people. For example, Handy and Srinivasan (2004) conducted a survey of hospital volunteers in Ontario, Canada. The most commonly performed activities of these volunteers were accompanying patients on outings, providing companionship, providing support to patients and families in waiting rooms, shopping and doing errands, and taking patients from one facility to another. Nearly half (49%) were retired. Payne's (2001) study of New Zealand hospice volunteers found that 53 percent were 60 years old or older. Nelson et al. (2004:117) found that 64 percent of the volunteers working as ombudsmen in long-term care facilities were retired. Phillips et al. (2002b) studied forty-nine volunteers working in agencies providing home and community care services to the elderly and disabled. Sixty-nine percent were retired compared to only 12 percent among volunteers in the community as a whole. Besides helping other senior citizens, the elderly prefer volunteering in connection with religious organizations. Advocacy volunteering is less appealing to them (Peter D. Hart 2002:3). CPS data from 1989 showed that church-related volunteering was by far the most popular among the 55+ age group, followed by civic or political organizations, hospital or other health organizations, and social or welfare organizations (Soo and Gong-Soog 1998). In the 2003 CPS data, religious volunteering was the most popular choice among older people and it was in that area that age had its most positive influence. Age also positively influenced volunteering for social and community service organizations, health, civic, political, and professional organizations. However, people over 65 were less likely to volunteer for education or youth services, environmental or animal care organizations, and public safety organizations (U.S. Bureau of Labor Statistics 2003). In our analysis of the Independent Sector data we largely replicated these results: compared to respondents aged between 18 and 24, respondents aged 65 or more were more likely to volunteer for religious and political organizations and less likely to volunteer for schools, youth development, adult recreation, and environmental organizations. In the remaining seven areas the young were just as likely to volunteer as the elderly.

Reasons for Volunteering among the Elderly

A major life transition, such as retirement, changes the way we think about ourselves and the world around us. We develop different interests and acquire different needs and the motivation for volunteering changes correspondingly. Numerous studies have shown that elderly people give different reasons for volunteering. Compared to younger people, they are more motivated by religious beliefs and values; by social reasons having to do with seeking or being with friends; by a desire to keep busy, be productive, maintain faculties and skills; and to feel they are needed by others. They are less interested in volunteering in order to explore their own strengths (Horne and Maddrell 2002:81; Jones 1999:14; Keith 2003:21). Just over half (53%) of the Senior Corps volunteers surveyed were widows or widowers and 65 percent were living alone. Volunteers who were living alone reported higher improvement scores in overall quality of life as a result of their volunteer work, suggesting they benefited especially from the social side of their activities (Gartland 2001:34). Older people are also more likely to cite "keeping busy" as a reason to volunteer, and they are also more likely to say they volunteer because they have "time on their hands" (Fisher et al. 1998:48). A retiree told McDonald (1997:27),

> It gives me something to do. If I wasn't involved with the [charity] shop I'd go daft. I'd get depressed. I like taking part in things. If I didn't have this, I think I'd curl up in a chair and deteriorate.

One Australian focus group retiree who had lost his wife said he had taken up volunteering because "you get so bored with life, your home is empty so you look for something to do" (Flick et al. 2002:60). Another said he had taken up volunteering once he retired because he had not been satisfied with his paid job and wanted to do something productive that would give him more satisfaction. It is important to remember that older volunteers do not cite these as reasons for *taking up* volunteering because many of them already are. They do not change their level of volunteering much, but they do change their reasons.

Loss of Spouse

Role loss theory predicts that married people who experience the death of a spouse will look for ways to replace the marital role in their lives, perhaps by volunteering, but the picture is not quite so simple. As we mentioned earlier, there are three theories, or at least sets of expectations, about what happens to people as they age and experience role loss. "Activity" theory argues that as social roles become less available people replace lost roles with new ones in order to preserve their self-identity. "Disengagement" theory proposes that older people disengage from social activities as they lose roles. "Continuity" theory proposes that, in old age, people more or less continue whatever level of activity they enjoyed in middle age.

These theories have yet to be applied to the analysis of the relation between spousal loss and volunteering. Utz et al. (2002) looked at adults' level of social participation six months after the loss of their spouse, using data from the Changing Lives of Older Couples study.[15] Those who lost a spouse were compared to continuously married respondents. The researchers include baseline level of social participation in their analysis (i.e., before the loss of spouse). Baseline social participation was a strong predictor of social participation at the six-month follow-up period, giving support to the continuity theory. *Loss of the spouse had no effect on social participation at all.* One reason for this might be that the social integration of widows and widowers varies considerably depending on the nature of their relationship to their spouse. Some people's lives do not change that much because they were not dependent on their spouse and were immersed in other family relationships, neighboring, friendships, and more public forms of social engagement. For others, the death of the spouse severs most of the links they have to the world around them.

In our own analysis of the Independent Sector data we found that the widowed had the lowest volunteer rate (36%), compared to a rate of 51 percent for the married, 41 percent for the single (never married), and 43 percent for the divorced and separated. [76] Married people also volunteered for more types of organizations and widowed people volunteered for the fewest. However, there were no differences in the hours volunteered. Controlling for age and a number of other socio-demographic and religious attributes, the difference between married and widowed respondents disappeared—although this might have something to do with the relatively small number of widows in the sample. [77] Widows were less likely to volunteer for religious organizations than married people (as were other types of unmarried people), but otherwise widowhood made no difference.

One issue we are not able to tackle with the Independent Sector data is whether volunteer work by the spouse before he or she died makes any difference to the loss of that spouse. For some married couples, volunteering might well be a joint activity and this is disrupted by the death of one of them. Stoker and Jennings (1995:428) provide interesting information on the effect of widowhood. Although their findings pertain to an index only one part of which is volunteer work their findings are very suggestive. Their data set contains rare information on people who were widowed in young adulthood. They find that (among a sample that is mostly middle aged) widowhood has a negative effect on activity level *but only among those whose spouse's had been active.* Looking at the results of this small number of studies, it is difficult to predict the consequences of spousal loss for volunteering. Much seems to depend on the age at which the loss is experienced, the volunteer activity of the spouse who died, the type of volunteer work and, no doubt, the nature of the marital relationship.

Conclusion

Beginning in the 1980s, the contraction of social services combined with the prospects of more and more Americans enjoying a long and healthy retirement to focus the attention of policy makers on the role volunteer work could play in the elderly population. In addition, traditional sources of volunteer labor, such as housewives, began to dry up as more women worked full-time. The fact that older people could work during the daytime meant they could step into the shoes vacated by the housewife. These changes coincided with the emergence of a new outlook on aging stressing the productive potential of the older population. Gerontologists argued that, as many more people live longer lives, aging is not inevitably accompanied by frailty, dependence, and financial need. Many elderly people continue to live in their own homes, are well integrated into their community, and enjoy good health. Many continue to be economically productive, not only as paid employees, or self-employed entrepreneurs, but also as volunteers in many different kinds of organizations.

Continuity seems to be the predominant pattern for volunteering in later life: people tend to maintain the habits they had before retirement but they modify them in light of their new circumstances. If they volunteered in middle age, they volunteer in old age; if they did not volunteer in middle age, they are unlikely to take it up when they retire (Gallagher 1994b:135; Okun 1993:67).

Although some social scientists believe that senior citizens are assuming a larger proportion of the volunteer work performed in industrialized societies

(Putnam 2000), there is still considerable untapped potential in the older population. For every two seniors who volunteer, there is another willing and able to volunteer (Caro and Bass 1995:73–78). Nearly 40 percent of the 55- to 74-year-old Americans surveyed who were not volunteering said they would like to, and nearly half of those who were currently volunteering would like to do more (Mutchler et al. 2003:1288). Perhaps some of this eagerness to volunteer reflects social desirability bias: respondents feel they ought to express an interest in being charitable even if they are not volunteering currently. But it might also reflect real failure to recruit older people because of age bias, difficulties with transportation, and lack of recent experience with volunteer work. Of course, this does not mean older people would volunteer if they were actually asked. People who are not currently volunteering but respond in surveys that they might be willing to do so are more educated than those who say they would not be willing but less educated than those who are currently volunteering. Sociologically, they are mid-way between volunteers and non-volunteers. It is hard to predict how they would behave if the invitation were made.

In a subsequent chapter we will discuss the influence of volunteering on health. This subject comes up often in discussions of how to improve the quality of life of the elderly population. "Successful aging" is believed to include volunteer work. But it is uncertain whether the elderly need to be volunteers in order to age successfully or simply maintain a high level of social engagement. Being "productive" might not be as important as simply being connected. What is the difference between playing a round of golf with one's buddies everyday and volunteering, as far as mental health is concerned? What does meaningful involvement in social life mean? Does the activity have to be productive? Does it have to focus on other people rather than one's self? Is improving one's golf game an example of successful aging? We do not yet know the answers to these questions.

Finally, although we have occasionally commented on the meaning of retirement and its influence on volunteer work, much more research needs to be done on this topic. Although life course indicators (e.g., marriage, retirement) are usually treated as if they were objective indicators of life course phase, the life course has a social psychological dimension, expressed in the saying "you're as old as you feel." For example, non-volunteers among the elderly are more likely than volunteers to say they are too old to volunteer regardless of the level of their reported health (Warburton et al. 2001:600). If elders have internalized images of older life as one of passivity and inactivity they are less likely to be socially active. Retirement is, in many respects, a state of mind. For some retirees, their departure from the labor force is welcomed and permanent. They have no intention of returning to work. Other retirees are more ambivalent about their new status in life. They do not necessarily see themselves as no longer working. We do not know much about the effect of these attitudes on volunteering. One study of unmarried retired women ages 56–91 found that some of the "retirees" had returned to work. Of the retirees who had not returned to work, some had no desire to, while others were planning to return to the labor force. The latter group, those women who were planning to take a job, was more likely to be volunteering than women who had fully and finally retired. Volunteer work was probably functioning as a stepping-stone back to paid employment (Stephan 1991). More research needs to be conducted on how volunteer work, in all its varieties and meanings, fits into the subjective world of older people—how they regard the aging process, what their goals are for the rest of their life.

12

Social Resources

In this chapter we describe how social resources mobilize volunteer work. Individual-level resources (e.g., free time) provide only a partial explanation for volunteering. Resources embedded in relations between people are equally important. In this chapter we focus on three kinds of social resource. The first is informal social networks, by which we mean friendships and regular contacts with neighbors and kin residing outside the household. The second is formal social networks. By this we mean memberships in "secondary" associations, such as clubs, voluntary organizations, political parties, and religious congregations. The third is church attendance.

Some sociologists might use the term "social capital" to refer to the phenomena we describe in this chapter because it denotes resources embedded in relations between people, but we find ourselves in agreement with Furstenburg and Kaplan (2004:219) when they write,

> the idea of social capital, while attractive, is being used so promiscuously that it is on the verge of becoming quite useless in empirical research. Unlike its conceptual cousin, human capital, social capital has achieved no common definition, much less common measurement.

We do not wish to abandon the idea that social relations provide people with resources (e.g., information) they would otherwise lack, but we see no need to introduce into this discussion the idea of "capital" with all of its connotations of investments and returns.

Informal Social Networks

Informal social networks perform a dual role in the mobilization of volunteers. Their structural role is to create ties between people outside the household. The more social ties we have beyond our immediate circle of friends and family the more likely we are to meet people who are volunteering, have information about volunteering, expect us to volunteer, ask us to volunteer, and support (or condemn) our decision to volunteer. The larger our social network, the shorter the distance between a potential volunteer recruiter and us. The cultural role of networks is to socialize us into a particular way of looking at the world. In this case, the form of the network is less important than its content. Friends, acquaintances, co-workers, and the like influence how we think about social issues, how important those issues are to us, what we think about volunteer work in particular, and how we estimate our chances of being successful in our volunteer work (Passy and Giugni 2001:131). For example, the majority of AIDS activists interviewed by Stockdill (2003:28) were already immersed in political networks prior to doing AIDS work. Not only were they more likely to meet someone looking for volunteers to help AIDS patients, they were well educated about the importance of the work and the need for volunteers. Community organizers have long been aware of the importance of social networks and frequently use them as recruiting tools (Smock 2004:65). For example, people who volunteer for Habitat for Humanity rarely show up on their own but come "with their friends, families, classmates, and fellow members of their civic organization, church, of their workplace's community service group" (Baggett 2001:132).

The most immediate social network beyond the nexus of family relations consists of friendships. People who have more friends tend to volunteer more hours (Rossi 2001b:118). Friendships can be used as "side payments" to overcome the free rider problem: we volunteer because we do not want to let our friends down. One survey asked respondents how many people in the locality they knew personally. Among those who said they knew nobody the volunteer rate was 31 percent but among those who said they knew between twenty-one and thirty the rate was 50 percent (Smith 1998:38). Respondents in the Americans' Changing Lives survey were asked how frequently they had conversations or meetings with friends and acquaintances. The more frequent the contacts, the more hours they volunteered and the more volunteer organizations they worked for (Wilson and Musick 1997a:705).

In the 1996 and 1999 Independent Sector surveys respondents were asked: "Please tell me which answer comes closest to how often you do the following things": Spend a social evening with parents or other relatives; spend a social evening with someone who lives in your neighborhood; spend a social evening with friends who live outside the neighborhood; spend time, socially, with friends from work or professional organizations; spend time, socially, with friends from your church or synagogue; spend time, socially, with friends from voluntary or service organizations; spend time with friends participating in sports or recreation activities. Options given were every week or nearly every week; once or twice a month; only a few times a year; and not at all.[1] We analyzed these responses to see if this kind of "schmoozing" encouraged volunteering.

True enough, the more friends people had, the more likely they were to volunteer. [78] We then examined the net effect of each type of friendship network by entering them simultaneously into a regression model.[2] Spending time with friends from outside the neighborhood, from church, a voluntary association, and sports organization were all positively related to volunteering. On the other hand, the more informal kinds of socializing—with friends, family, neighbors, and co-workers, had no influence on volunteering.

It seems that friendships limited to one's immediate social circle have no positive influence on volunteering. The most likely reason why people with more friends are more likely to volunteer is that they are more likely to be asked. To test this hypothesis, we re-estimated the models, including a variable indicating whether the respondent had been recruited. The size of the coefficients for overall informal social interaction and interacting with church members diminished, indicating that people who spend more time with friends overall and people who spend more time with friends from church in particular are more likely to be recruited, and this is indeed one reason why they are more likely to volunteer. However, people who spent time with friends in voluntary associations or sports groups were not more likely to be asked to volunteer. Perhaps these friends mobilize volunteer work by volunteering with the respondent or supporting his or her decision to volunteer rather than by overt recruitment.

As a final step in the analysis of friendships and volunteering we examined the possibility that social class moderates the effect of friendships. If people form friendships with people much like themselves (which seems to be the case), then middle class people will have as friends other middle class people. This means that their social networks are more likely to contain other volunteers than the social networks of working class people. The logical consequence is that an increase in informal socializing has a stronger effect on the chances of a middle class person volunteering. We found that middle class people (as measured by education and income) do more "schmoozing" and they volunteer more. The positive effect of informal socializing on the *range* of volunteer activities was stronger for the more highly educated respondents and for those with higher earnings. This no doubt has something to do with the social class composition of the networks of people with whom middle class people socialize. However, there was no interaction effect in the case of volunteer hours or the odds of volunteering at all. [79]

In summary, people who interact frequently with friends do seem to volunteer more, but only if these friends are drawn from secondary associations rather than from their immediate social circle. In only one case, friends drawn from one's church, does being asked helped explain why friends are a positive influence. Lastly, middle class people "benefit" more from their social interactions, but only with respect to how many different volunteer activities they engage in and not the intensity of their volunteer commitment.

Voluntary Association Memberships

The Independent Sector data just analyzed show that spending time with friends from a voluntary association increases the number of voluntary activities in which people engage. This finding is hardly surprising in light of the role voluntary associations play in organizing volunteer work. Indeed, some might say that belonging to a voluntary association and volunteering are virtually the same thing or, at the very least, belonging to a voluntary association is a precondition for volunteering. Nevertheless, there are differences between being a member of a voluntary association (even an active one) and being a volunteer. A person might describe herself as "active" in her voluntary association if she is an assiduous consumer of the public goods the association provides (e.g., sporting events) but she plays no part in producing those events. In addition, there are many types of volunteer work that are not organized by voluntary associations. Non-profit organizations, such as hospitals, homeless shelters, and literacy councils, rely heavily on volunteers. One does not need to join these organizations to volunteer for them. In addition, many people volunteer to help public sector organizations that are not voluntary associations, such as schools, correctional facilities, parks, museums, and the like.

Reasons Why Memberships Encourage Volunteering

Why should membership in voluntary associations encourage volunteering? At one level, of course, the answer to this question is obvious. First, many of the surveys of volunteer work define volunteering as unpaid work *given to, or on behalf of, an organization.* Undoubtedly, many people will have a voluntary association in mind when answering this question. A 2000 survey of residents of Illinois asked them why they did not volunteer more. Seventeen percent said they "don't like to join groups" as if this were a requirement for doing volunteer work (Profile of Illinois 2001). Second, many respondents think of the unpaid work they do to maintain an organization when they think of volunteer work. Serving as treasurer of a hobby group is therefore volunteering. For many members, volunteering is a matter of "taking your turn" in doing the chores necessary to keep the organization going. In light of these first two reasons, the more organizations you belong to the more chances, or obligations, to volunteer you have. Third, associations provide information on volunteer opportunities. According to Wuthnow (1998:65), even garden clubs, which are organized primarily to serve self-interested purposes, can foster interest in volunteer work because they help inform members about community problems and make it easier to recruit for volunteer work. For example, one club mobilized its members to help "beautify" the grounds of one of the public buildings in its community. Fourth, voluntary associations help define the volunteer role. When people join voluntary associations they learn what it means to volunteer, how to set limits around the care they provide (Wuthnow 1991:201). Fifth, members of voluntary associations share information about each other, develop emotional bonds to other members and are, for this reason, more likely to do volunteer work on their behalf. For example, members of religious congregations are urged to visit members who have become "shut-ins." Sixth, voluntary associations make it easier to monitor how much people give to their community: the amount of effort people contribute to a cause can be more easily watched and sanctioned where they are fellow members of an organization. This is one reason why it is easier to surmount the "free rider" problem in smaller voluntary associations. Seventh, many voluntary associations such as college sororities and fraternities, civic groups, and fraternal orders have a service project requirement for becoming and remaining a member. At the elite level, volunteer organizations resemble closed organizations and membership is by selection or nomination. In many cases, being willing to do volunteer work (e.g., raising money for the arts in the community) is a condition of being a member. Eighth, voluntary associations create obligations (to the organization and its members) they can recognize and honor publicly. The volunteer's effort is rewarded not only by the client but also by one's fellow volunteers. The founder of the Atlanta Community Food Bank, in describing the volunteers who come to the bank to help with sorting food, noted that "they mostly come as groups, not individuals" (Poppendieck 1998:33). Voluntary associations in the community supplied teams of volunteers. Finally, membership in a voluntary association encourages people to feel efficacious, that their volunteer work is not a waste of time but has some chance of bringing about social and political change: "it increases perception of collective effectiveness, which in turn reinforces the perceived individual effectiveness" (Passy and Giugni 2001:142).

Volunteering and Memberships: Evidence from Surveys

There is no shortage of survey data showing that the more memberships people have the more likely are they to volunteer, although few of the older studies control for important confounding variables. Even among teenagers, "joiners" are also volunteers. A study of students in grades six through twelve found that 42 percent of the students who were involved in student government were volunteering regularly, compared to 22 percent of those not in student government. Thirty-one percent of those engaged in other school group activities were currently volunteering compared to 14 percent of those not involved (Nolin 1977:9).[3] Eighty-two percent of the adolescents in the NLSY who reported voluntary service in 1994 had been a member of a sports team or social club in 1992, compared to only 8 percent of those who were not involved with a sports team or club (Hart et al. 1998:520). Indeed, being a team or social club member was a better predictor of voluntary service in 1994 than family income, home environment, or academic ability. This does not mean these background factors are unimportant, because family income, ethnicity, home environment scores, and gender are associated with membership in teams and clubs. This pattern is repeated at the other end of the life course. In a study of elderly residents of Iowa, respondents (aged 65 or older) were asked how many local groups they belonged to. Answers to this question proved to be the strongest predictor of volunteering, of greater magnitude than education, family income, gender, and age combined (Liu and Besser 2003:359).

We looked at the association between voluntary association memberships and volunteering using data from the 1996 and 1999 Independent Sector surveys.[4] Respondents were asked, "Other than a church or synagogue, are you a member of an organization?" In 1996 only they were asked how *often* they participated in the activities of the organization.[5]

Number of Memberships

We look first at the number of memberships people have. If membership in a voluntary association provides a connection to volunteer work, do many memberships mean more volunteering? Respondents were allowed to list up to twelve memberships, but the mean number for the sample was less than one (0.91). We found that the more memberships people had the more likely they were to volunteer. [78]

Membership Type

Although people are more likely to volunteer the more memberships they have, most people belong to only one association if they belong to any at all. It is therefore important to isolate the effect of *particular* memberships on volunteering. To achieve this goal we performed logistic regression, using a dichotomous variable (membership/no membership), estimating a model with membership in each of the twelve types of organization as independent variables and volunteer work as the dependent variable. [78] The only types of membership *not* associated with doing volunteer work were fraternal orders and labor unions. The strongest positive associations were found in the case of school groups, religious groups, and the generic category "voluntary associations."

Memberships, Trust, and Volunteering

There has been much debate among social scientists as to whether people become more trusting as a result of joining voluntary associations. Some argue that voluntary associations are places where people of different social backgrounds meet and where routine interactions with a heterogeneous group of people build generalized trust. Others argue that voluntary associations build only particularized trust—in other members of the association—and do little to foster trust in people in general. We learned in chapter 3 that trust encourages volunteering. We tested the hypothesis that trust helps explain the effect of memberships on volunteering by first estimating a model regressing any volunteering on the number of memberships and then estimating another model including trust in other people.[6] The regression coefficient for number of memberships did not change, indicating that memberships and trust have independent effects on volunteering. [81] We then examined whether trust acts as a link between memberships and volunteering only for certain kinds of voluntary associations. [82] We first estimated the effect of membership type on volunteering and then entered the trust variable. In no case did the coefficient for the membership type change. In short, memberships do not promote volunteering because they increase trust. This suggests that people volunteer either because they are members of several voluntary associations or because they are trusting people.

We also tested for an interaction effect to see if memberships and trust were substitutes for each other (i.e., the positive effect of memberships might be stronger among less trusting people). As shown in Figure 6, we found the reverse to be true: the positive effect of memberships was stronger among people who were more trusting. Membership is a "resource" that is better exploited if we are more trusting.[7] An alternative interpretation of the same result is that trust has a stronger effect on volunteering among "joiners." Among people who belong to no voluntary associations an increase in trust has no effect on volunteering. Among those who belong to seven or more associations, more trust means more volunteering. The memberships are helping turn trust into action by offering opportunities to volunteer and, perhaps, increasing the chances of being recruited, a topic to which we will now turn.

Memberships, Being Asked, and Volunteering

Earlier, we suggested that one way to explain the positive effect of memberships on volunteering is that joining a voluntary association makes it more likely we will be recruited. Using the Independent Sector data, we estimated the effect of number of memberships on any volunteering in the past twelve months, number of volunteering areas, and number of hours volunteered. [80] We then re-estimated the model with being asked included. In the case of any volunteering and volunteering range, being asked accounted for some of the membership effect, but this was not the case with volunteer hours. This makes sense. Being asked influences whether or not we volunteer at all and how many different organizations we volunteer for, but not how committed we are to the work, which will depend more on individual resources such as free time and health.

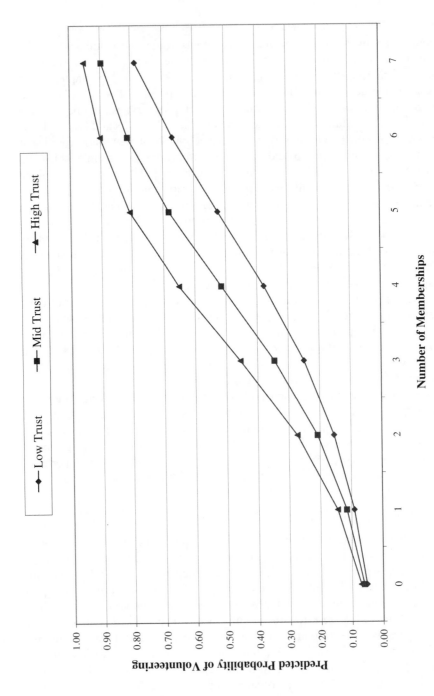

Figure 6. Predicted probabilities of any volunteering by trust and memberships.

But what if the *type* of membership alters the odds being asked to volunteer? We found that membership in fraternal orders, veterans' organizations, alumni organizations, and labor unions made no difference to the odds of being asked whereas membership did increase the chance of being asked if the respondent belonged to a political organizations, school group, service club, or "voluntary association." Having gathered this information on variation in rates of being asked by membership we were able to move to the final step of the analysis, to see what effect membership has after being asked is added to the control variables. [80] As expected, being asked weakened the membership effect: indeed, in the case of service clubs, civic organizations, religious organizations, and political organizations, membership became insignificant with the introduction of the recruitment variable. In other words, membership in these organizations is of significance to volunteering *only* because it increases the odds of being asked. In the case of the other memberships, however, unmeasured variables are contributing to the membership effect. Even after being asked is entered into the equation, memberships in school-related, professional, veterans, and generic "voluntary associations" are still positively associated with volunteering.

Membership Intensity and Volunteering

Some people have only nominal membership in voluntary associations. Their "participation" amounts to little more than paying their dues and reading the newsletter. Others participate more intensely, attending every meeting assiduously. If membership functions as a gateway to volunteering, it makes sense to expect that level of intensity would have something to do with it. To test this hypothesis we used data from the 1996 Independent Sector survey, the only occasion on which respondents were asked how often they attended meetings of the voluntary associations to which they belong.[8] If intense participation increases the chances of volunteering then the nominal members should be little different from the non-members. This is precisely what we found. [83] In all but two types (voluntary associations and veterans' organizations) nominal members are no more likely to volunteer than non-members. Finally, if people who attend meetings frequently are more likely to volunteer, one likely reason is that their attendance makes it more likely someone will ask them to volunteer.[9] Indeed, we found that this was the case: the more often respondents attended voluntary association meetings the more likely they were to be asked to volunteer and, having been recruited, they were more likely to volunteer. [83]

Social Resources as Mediators of Individual Resources

We have demonstrated that social resources (informal social networks and voluntary association memberships) have a positive influence on volunteering, but we have ignored the question of who has the most social resources. This is an important question because the answer to it will contribute to a better understanding of who volunteers. In this investigation, social resources become a mediating variable, one that connects and helps explain the relation between two other variables.[10]

We tested the hypothesis that social resources explain the link between individual attributes and volunteering using the data on memberships in the Independent Sector surveys. Memberships helped explain why Whites volunteer more than minorities, why the middle aged volunteer more than the elderly and the retired, why education is positively related to volunteering, why rich people volunteer more than poor people, and why the self-employed volunteer more than people not in the labor force. In all of these cases, social resources helped explain why one group volunteered more than another. We also found that the number of memberships *suppressed* the gender effect we reported in chapter 8. In other words, once we controlled for the fact that men have more memberships than women, they volunteered even less than women. Women would volunteer even more than men if they had the same number of memberships. [84]

Moderating Factors

In this section we consider the possibility that individual and social resources act jointly to encourage volunteering. We ask whether certain people volunteer more simply because they make better use of their social resources. For example, we could imagine situations where people are inhibited in their use of social resources by their lack of individual resources (e.g., free time). Specifically, we test the hypothesis that social resources are of greater benefit to higher status people. Not only do they have more social resources to begin with, they make better use of them. Our reasons for proposing this hypothesis are as follows. First, according to the homophily principle (like attracts like), friendship networks tend to be socially homogeneous (Blau 1977). Middle class people tend to have middle class friends; working class people tend to have working class friends. Because people in similar status situations reinforce each other's inclination to behave in a manner characteristic of those positions, having more friends increases the likelihood that one will conform to the norms of that status position (Laumann 1973:97). Middle class people are more likely than working class people to be surrounded by others for whom volunteer work is a social norm. An increase in social resources for a middle class person improves the chances of meeting a volunteer, or at least another person who subscribes to the volunteer norm. An increase in social resources does not have the same consequences for a working class person. The social resources of higher class people are also of superior quality to those of working class people. For example, higher status "joiners" are more likely to be a member of a committee or hold some kind of office in a voluntary association. Thus membership means something very different for higher status people and is a more potent influence on volunteering.

In an earlier study (Wilson and Musick 1998) we used four indicators of social resources to see if their influence on volunteering was stronger for middle class people than working class people. The first measured how many people the respondent felt he or she could call upon for help or advice. The second measured how many of these friends knew each other. (This is occasionally referred to as "network density.") The third measure was frequency of contact with friends either by telephoning or visiting. The fourth measure tapped formal interaction, using frequency of attendance at meetings and church services. For the dependent variables we used the range of different volunteer activities and the number of hours volunteered over the past year. Social class was measured by education, occupational prestige, household income, and the value of assets owned.

We found that more highly educated people made better use of all forms of social resources. That is, the positive effect of interacting with friends, having lots of friends, having more "open" networks of friends (few overlapping ties among those friends), and frequent attendance at meetings and services was stronger among the better educated. The same was true of income. And, in the case of assets, only number of friends was not moderated. When estimating the effect of occupational prestige, we restricted the analysis to those who were working or who had retired but where the last job was recorded. Once again, we found that social resources had a stronger effect on people with high occupational prestige, the one exception being network density. We then looked at hours volunteered. The results were very much the same, with the booster effect of education being consistent across all four measures of social resources. These results demonstrate impressively that individual and social resources do not simply add to each other, nor do they substitute for each other, but rather they *complement* each other. Although the results are more consistent when volunteer range instead of hours is used as a measure of volunteering, this makes sense: social connections influence how many different volunteer activities people engage in more than how many hours they contribute.[11]

Another possible moderator of the effect of social resources on volunteering is gender. Social networks represent a pathway to volunteering. There is some indication in previous research that women are more likely to use social contacts to get a volunteer job than men.[12] We analyzed the Independent Sector data to see if gender moderated the influence of social resources on volunteering. [85] We used three measures of social resources: frequency of church attendance, number of memberships, and informal social interaction. The effect of neither church attendance nor memberships varied by gender, but informal interaction benefited men more than women.

Religious Congregations as Voluntary Associations

More Americans belong to a religious congregation than any other voluntary association. If memberships encourage volunteering, then getting involved in a religious congregation should play a significant role. Just over a third (34%) of all American volunteers surveyed in 1992 said they became volunteers because they belonged to a religious congregation, by far the most commonly cited reason (Greeley 1997a). It is hardly surprising that membership in a religious congregation encourages volunteering because religious teachings typically stress the responsibility to do charitable works. In chapter 5 we demonstrated denominational differences in the rate of volunteering, suggesting that beliefs and values do matter. But joining and becoming active in a local congregation might well be enough to cultivate prosocial attitudes on their own because joining a community of worshippers means accepting a set of norms in which the needs of the group are placed before the needs of the individual (Cnaan 2002:275). Indeed, Becker and Dhingra (2001:329) believe that "[s]ocial networks, *rather than beliefs*, dominate as the mechanism leading to volunteering, and it is the social networks formed within congregations that make congregation members more likely to volunteer" (our emphasis).

We do not believe that congregational participation *replaces* belief as the explanation for the link between religion and volunteering. Rather, we maintain that social participation in the life of the church has an additional effect on volunteering and (as we shall demonstrate) it can enhance the effect of belief on volunteering. In this section we will analyze the influence of congregational participation on volunteering, by which we mean attendance at worship services and participation in congregational activities. Volunteering through the church is not only a rewarding form of personal participation, a way of making friends within a like-minded community, but it is also easier if friends made through the church encourage and support it (Hoge et al. 1998:480).

Church Attendance

Numerous studies have demonstrated that people who attend church services frequently are more likely to volunteer. Indeed, church attendance rivals education as a predictor of volunteering (Campbell and Yonish 2003:96). This is true of young people (Smith and Faris 2002:47) as well as the elderly (Herzog and Morgan 1993:137). The gap between frequent church attenders and non-attenders is sizeable. For example, just over half (52%) of Australians who had attended church in the past month had volunteered in the previous year, compared to 29 percent of the non-attenders (Australian Bureau of Statistics 2002). Forty percent of Canadians attending church on a weekly basis had volunteered in the past year, compared to 25 percent of the non-attenders. The average annual hours volunteered among those who never attended church was 148, compared to 202 for those who attended church weekly. Although those who attend church weekly comprised only 19 percent of the Canadian population, they contributed 35 percent of the total volunteer hours (McKeown et al. 2004:10). In the United States, 37 percent of the population attends church on a weekly basis, but this group contributes 59 percent of the hours. [1] Just over half (53%) of Americans attending church every, or nearly every, week volunteered in the past year, compared to 35 percent of those who attended church once or twice a month, 25 percent of those who attended a few times last year, and 19 percent of those who did not attend church at all. [86] As we showed in Figure 1 (chapter 5), regardless of socio-economic status, age, race, gender, and religious affiliation, the more often respondents attend church the more likely they are to volunteer. However, frequency of church attendance makes no difference to the number of hours volunteered in the past month. [15]

Church Attendance and Volunteer Domain

By far the most popular volunteer activity in the United States is work on behalf of a religious organization. It is hardly surprising, then, that frequent churchgoers feature prominently among the ranks of volunteers. The question is whether frequent churchgoing has a positive effect on *all* kinds of volunteer work. One study of American teenagers found that frequency of church attendance had a positive effect on volunteering, but most of this was attributable to the very strong effect of church attendance on religious volunteering: its effect on educational volunteering was negative (Sundeen and Raskoff 1994:395). While some studies find that frequency of church attendance is unrelated to some types of volunteering (McKeown et al. 2004) most find that its influence is pervasive, albeit stronger in some domains than others (Bowen 1999).[13] Analyzing the Independent Sector data, we found that church attendance had its most powerful effect on volunteering in connection with church, followed by youth development volunteering: it had only a weak effect on environmental volunteering and political volunteering. [40] In short, church attendance does encourage volunteering, but its influence is probably limited to the kinds of causes and missions that churches are most likely to sponsor.

Church Attendance and Denomination

Some scholars attach so much importance to church attendance they have concluded that the effect of religious affiliation is conditional upon it: "religious inclination makes very little difference unless one becomes involved in some kind of organized religious community" (Wuthnow 1991:156).[14] In chapter 5 we demonstrated that religious affiliation does have an effect on volunteering, regardless of frequency of church attendance, but this argument is worth examining in detail here. It implies that the relation between church attendance and religious affiliation is multiplicative rather than additive. Religious beliefs, however conducive to volunteering, must be energized and given practical direction and support through social involvement in the life of the church before they will mobilize volunteers. Conversely, church attendance will have little positive influence on volunteering if the teachings of the church do not encourage volunteer work. For example, one study found that the positive effect of church attendance on volunteering was stronger for mainline Protestants and Catholics than evangelicals (Wuthnow 1999). The significance of church attendance for volunteering is therefore contingent on the teachings of the church.

The combined effects of churchgoing and religious affiliation were analyzed in a study in which respondents were asked to rate their level of activity in religious organizations and how often they attended church services, measures combined to form an index of "church activism." They were also asked if they were doing volunteer work in the community. The level of church activism had a positive effect on volunteering only for liberal Protestants and Catholics. Among evangelical Protestants, volunteering was curvilinearly related to church activism: very frequent attenders were as unlikely to volunteer as the infrequent attenders. Conservative Protestant denominations discourage volunteer work among their more committed members because they are "high maintenance" organizations, demanding a lot from their members by way of church upkeep (Wilson and Janoski 1995). Frequent church attendance is not therefore always good for volunteering.

We tested the hypothesis that denomination moderates the effect of church attendance on volunteering using the Independent Sector survey data, comparing the influence of being unaffiliated with being affiliated with one of several groups of denominations. [15] Frequent churchgoers were more likely to volunteer but the effect was much stronger for those with a religious affiliation than those without one. Evangelical Protestants were more likely to volunteer than the unaffiliated, especially if they attended church often. In contrast, among Catholics, frequent churchgoers volunteered less than the unaffiliated. For Catholics then, frequent churchgoing discourages volunteering. This is congruent with Bowen's (1999:178) finding that frequent church attendance does not boost the volunteer rate of Catholics as much as it does Protestants: among frequent church attenders, Catholics volunteered only a quarter of the hours contributed by conservative Protestants.[15] Comparing denominations with one another rather than with those who do not have a religious affiliation we once again see that denomination moderates the effect of church attendance. Figure 7 is a bar chart showing the number of different areas of volunteering reported by members of different denominational groups, by frequency of church attendance. Among those who do not attend church, evangelicals hardly volunteer at all but among more frequent churchgoers they volunteer almost as much as mainline and liberal Protestants.

This study does not confirm the results reported in Wilson and Janoski (1995), which show frequent churchgoing evangelicals volunteering at low

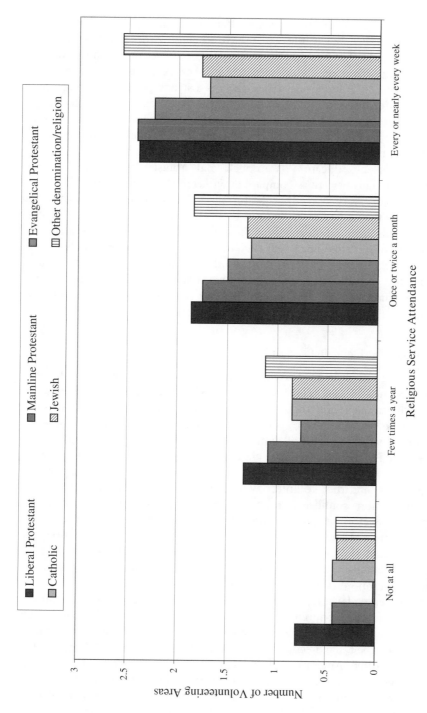

Figure 7. Estimated levels of volunteering over the past year by religious service attendance and denomination.

rates. This might result from using different measures of church attendance and volunteering, but it might also have something to do with what people are volunteering for. Perhaps the moderating influence of denominational affiliation depends on the volunteer activity. For example, when it comes to volunteering for religious activities, there is a strong positive relationship between church attendance and volunteering among evangelicals, even stronger than it is among mainline Protestants. Evangelical church attendance also increases the chances of volunteering for youth development. In the case of Catholics, church attendance has a positive effect on volunteering, but only in the area of education (Campbell and Yonish 2003:102; Wuthnow 1999:350). This pattern is compatible with the theory that evangelical congregations are very "greedy" institutions. They expect a lot of volunteer work from their members to support their various activities. Where volunteer work means working on behalf of the church, as it does among evangelicals, frequent church attendance will encourage it, but when more secular activities are included, as they are among mainline Protestants, the effect of church attendance is attenuated. This suggests we should use caution in referring to church attendance as a "social resource" for volunteering: it is a resource for some kinds of volunteer work but not for others.

Why Does Going to Church Frequently Encourage Volunteerism?

Having established that frequent churchgoing is a consistent predictor of volunteering, the task remains to explain why. There are three possible reasons why frequent churchgoers are more likely to volunteer. The first is that the more often people go to church the more likely are they to hear sermons teaching them the virtue of doing volunteer work (Wuthnow 2004:121).[16] Indeed, it is true that frequent churchgoers in the United States are more likely to believe they have a moral duty to help others, it is in their power to help others, and that volunteer work can overcome social problems. They also have more confidence in charitable institutions. We looked at the Independent Sector data to see if these beliefs and attitudes helped explain the positive effect of church attendance on volunteering, but we found no mediating effect at all. [28, 51] In short, "religious involvement and altruistic values work hand in hand, rather than one explaining away the effects of the other" (Wuthnow 2004:127).

Another explanation for the influence of church attendance on volunteering is that frequent churchgoers are more socially integrated. The more often Americans go to church the more voluntary associations they belong to, regardless of their socio-economic status, age, race, and parental status. And the more often Americans attend church, the more frequently they see friends, neighbors, and acquaintances.[17] [20] By including controls for number of memberships and informal social interaction in a regression model, we were able to cut the effect of church attendance by about a quarter. In short, it is true that frequent churchgoers volunteer more because they are more socially integrated into their communities.[18]

Another reason why frequent churchgoers are more likely to volunteer is that they are more likely to be recruited. The Independent Sector survey tells us who asked a person to volunteer. Not surprisingly, frequent churchgoers were more likely to say that a fellow church member had asked them, whereas they were no more likely than infrequent churchgoers to have been asked by a family member or colleague at work. [87] The more important point is that 58 percent of weekly churchgoers had been asked to volunteer, compared to 31 percent of those who never attend church, regardless of socio-economic and family status. [31] The greater likelihood of being recruited helped explain why frequent churchgoers volunteered for a wider range of activities, but it did not help explain whether the respondent volunteered at all. [21] This makes sense: volunteering for a variety of different activities is more contingent on being asked than devoting many hours to a single activity.

Religious Groups and Organizations

More than any other voluntary association, religious congregations aspire to be a community for their members that meets their need not only for spiritual sustenance but sociability as well. Besides worship services they offer myriad opportunities for social engagement, such as Bingo nights, choir practice, Bible study, support groups, and covenant groups. More than worship services, these activities enable the congregants to get to know each other better. It is highly likely that people who attend church often also get involved in these groups, but they are not the same thing by any means and it is important to assess the contribution of group activities in addition to church attendance. Unfortunately, survey data on church group activities *and* church attendance are quite rare. One study, of a random sample of Indiana residents, found that, whereas church attendance had no effect on secular volunteering, involvement in church groups had a positive effect (Jackson et al. 1995). Harris (1999:126) looked at the influence of church attendance on "collective action," defined as working with others to solve community problems. Once again, church attendance and collective action were not related, but people who were involved in church-related groups were more likely to have worked with others to solve community problems. This pattern was repeated in a study of Iowa residents.[19] Lam (2002:414) actually found a *negative* relation between church attendance and secular volunteering once she controlled for being a member of a church-related organization, working as a volunteer in such an organization, and being an officer in such an organization. A very similar finding resulted from another study of the effects of participation in church activities and church attendance on religious and secular volunteering. The respondents in this study were all churchgoing Protestants (i.e., they attended church at least two or three times a month) and are therefore by no means representative of the American population. Respondents were asked how often they participated in church activities such as Bible study, choir practice, potluck meals, and so on. They were also asked if they had volunteered for church-related and non-church-related activities in the last two years and how often they attended church in the last year. With church activities and church attendance in the same model, church attendance had no effect on church-related volunteering. However, church activities were positively related to this form of volunteering. When it came to secular volunteering, church activities were once again positively related to volunteering but now church attendance was negatively related. High levels of church attendance actually *reduced* the odds of this kind of volunteering (Park and Smith 2000).

These studies have in common the finding that participation in church group activities has a positive effect on volunteering and that church attendance does not have a positive effect once this participation is taken into account—or in some cases it has a negative effect. Most of the authors choose to interpret this finding as meaning that group participation is mediating the effect of church attendance on volunteering: frequent churchgoers volunteer more because they belong to more groups. Without longitudinal data, we cannot rule out another explanation: that, for unknown reason, some people are *both* more likely to attend church and get engaged in church groups and including both variables in the same model means they cancel each other out.

In summary, regular churchgoers and church members who get involved in church activities and church groups are more likely to volunteer and they volunteer for wider range of activities, although they do not volunteer more hours. The influence of church attendance varies by denominational affiliation and by domain of volunteering. The reason why church attendance encourages volunteering has less to do with changing the way people think than it has with increasing the level of social interaction with others and the chances of being asked to volunteer.

The influence of church attendance on volunteering helps explain why other social characteristics are linked to volunteering. It helps explain why women are more likely to volunteer than men, home owners are more likely to volunteer than renters, married people are more likely to volunteer than singles, and parents more than the childless. It also throws more light on the racial gap in volunteering because it partially suppresses the positive effect of being White. Whites would volunteer at an even higher rate relative to other racial groups if they attended church as frequently. [20]

Conclusion

Informal social relations do increase the chances of volunteering, as long as they extend outside the family and the immediate neighborhood. Voluntary association memberships have a more powerful and extensive influence on volunteering. The more memberships a person has and the more intensely involved that person is in the voluntary association, the more likely he or she is to volunteer and the more activities for which he or she will volunteer. One important reason why joiners are also volunteers is that they are more likely to have been asked to volunteer. Memberships also help explain, at least in part, the influence of many individual attributes on volunteering, such as gender, race, and education. Middle class people enjoy the benefits of memberships more than working class people. Finally, church attendance, and particularly participation in church groups, has a positive effect on volunteering. In this concluding section we will outline some of the problems that remain to be solved in this area.

First, asking people about who they meet informally is an inadequate way of measuring social networks. Even quite serious attempts to measure social networks focus too much on the form of those networks (e.g., how many of your friends know other friends of yours) and rarely ask about their content or quality. It would be valuable to know, for instance, how many of those friends are currently volunteering. It would also be helpful to know something about the values and opinions of those friends and acquaintances. For example, a study of volunteers for a Swiss solidarity movement specializing in development-aid issues called the Bern Declaration tried to find out why some members were more active than others. Individual characteristics (e.g., education, age, gender, labor force participation) were unrelated to level of participation, but those who also belonged to organizations ideologically close to the cause were more active, as were those who belonged to informal networks made up of people (e.g., family, friends, acquaintances) sympathetic to or already involved in the cause (Passy and Giugni 2001:132). Sometimes, the content of a social network can be more important than its form.

Second, the distinction between social ties that connect us to new people and social ties that reinforce our ties to people we already know is rarely made in volunteer studies, but this distinction between "bridging" and "bonding" social ties is crucially important in the study of volunteering.

> Bonding networks involve dense linkages among relatively small numbers of people. Each member of a bonding network typically knows every other member, and these relationships often overlap into multiple dimensions of the members' lives—like the members of a small town who attend church together, work in the same factory, know one another's families, and shop at the same stores . . . bridging networks are composed of single-stranded ties that loosely connect large numbers of individuals. The relationships within these networks are generally less intimate or intense than those of the bonding networks . . . members of bridging networks are typically linked to one another through indirect ties—such as the ties connecting one neighbor to the CEO of a local company who plays squash with husband of the neighbor he chats with every morning at the bus stop. (Smock 2004:66)

Hall (1999:438) believes that bridging ties help explain the higher volunteer rates of the middle class. Working class social relations revolve around close contacts with kin and small sets of friends, while their memberships tend to be confined to trade unions. Members of the middle class have a wider range of social contacts, drawing their friends from a diverse range of sources, who are less likely to know each other, and who extend beyond the workplace.

Third, more attention needs to be paid to the *types* of volunteer work in which people are engaged. In the context of a highly stigmatized activity, such as AIDS-related volunteer work, social ties appear to be either relatively unimportant in drawing people into the work (Omoto and Snyder 1993:167) or a barrier to volunteering (Chambre 1995:128; Snyder et al. 1999). Family ties might discourage taking part in dangerous civil rights campaigning (McAdam and Paulsen 1993). If the type of volunteer work called for is quick response, collective action, as is the case in many disasters, then voluntary associations might well impede mobilization. After the bombing of the Murrah Federal Building in Oklahoma City in 1995, formal relief organizations quickly sprang into action to mobilize and help coordinate the volunteer work of the multitude of people who offered their services. However, voluntary associations played a minor role in mobilizing volunteers, at least compared to the role they play in more routine forms of volunteer work (St. John and Fuchs 2002:411). Voluntary associations might do a good job of mobilizing volunteers for more routine, everyday activities, but if the volunteer work is unconventional or controversial they might be less effective. For example, a conventional volunteer activity, such as Meals on Wheels, might be supported by social resources (such as membership in service clubs or religious congregations) but less conventional volunteer work, such as picketing an abortion clinic, might be discouraged by them (Anderson 1996; Lazerwitz et al. 1998:69). Similarly, when volunteer work is group-based (e.g., volunteers work as members of a group) memberships will be important but they will play a minor role where volunteer work is not group-based, as when a person signs on to help with a charity "fun-run." Parry et al. (1992:87) show that, in the case of group-based volunteering only 20 percent said they had become involved on their own initiative, compared to 43 percent who were volunteering on a more individual basis. Clearly, the social nature of the volunteer work will influence the role that social resources play.

Fourth, more attention needs to be paid not only to the type of volunteer work but to the type of voluntary association. Members of democratically run associations are more likely to volunteer because those organizations provide more opportunities to learn civic skills, but not all associations are governed democratically, and they do not all provide the chance to develop the skills that translate into volunteer work in the wider community (Verba et al. 1995). Voluntary associations vary widely in the beliefs and opinions they encourage in their membership. It is naïve to treat an environmental group and a fraternal organization as if they were equally likely to sponsor volunteer work in the community. For example, volunteers for Bread for the World (an anti-hunger campaign) were more likely to belong to political and religious organizations but *less* likely to belong to occupational, professional, farm, service, or school organizations (Cohn 1993:113–131). In this case, volunteers were undoubtedly mobilized by their other social involvements, but the content of those involvements is crucially important.

In conclusion, we acknowledge that social resources and volunteering are reciprocally related. Indeed, for many people

> organizing means both mobilizing volunteers and strengthening social ties in the community. In this situation, volunteering is both a desired outcome—a healthy neighborhood in which people are involved—and a means to that outcome—getting people involved. (Gittell and Vidal 1998)

And, just as friends recruit us to volunteer, volunteering can be a way of making friends. Qualitative studies abound with testimonials to the power of volunteering for making friends.

> About four of us became very good friends [working to raise money for public television]. If we had not worked . . . quite so seriously, it might have been that the station would not be able to continue. There is a good feeling in . . . helping establish something like that. In addition, we made strong friendships. (Daniels 1988:145)

Another woman remarked to Daniels (1988:179), "I would not have had the number of friends in a new community as a professional person that you make as a volunteer." Volunteering thus becomes a way of accumulating social resources that, in turn, can be reinvested in more volunteer work.

13

Volunteer Recruitment

Up to this point, we have demonstrated that people who have more resources at their disposal and who have the right personality traits and subjective dispositions are the most likely to volunteer. In other words, we have focused on the supply of volunteer labor, assuming that the problem is to explain why people, of their own volition, choose to help others. In so doing, we have postponed consideration of the fact that non-profit organizations are not passive recipients of volunteer labor. "Instead, they identify the set of individuals with the particular skills, experience and social capital they can most easily and productively use" and target those individuals for recruitment (Bryant et al. 2003:47). In some cases, the role of recruitment is obvious. Many boards of trustees are self-perpetuating entities: current members select new members (Ostrower 2002:1). Some voluntary associations that expect volunteer work from their members, such as the Junior League and Kiwanis, admit new members by invitation only. Many agencies screen would-be volunteers for their suitability. Many require training programs that "weed out" unsuitable applicants. Only those who pass the test are invited to volunteer.

There are two reasons why the recruitment process is important in the study of volunteers. The first is simply that many people will not volunteer *unless* they are asked. About a third of Canadians say they became a volunteer because someone asked them to do so (Hall et al. 2001). In the following quotation, the interviewee points out that having a friend volunteer was not enough to persuade him to volunteer also: he was waiting for his friend to ask him.

My friend C—— is very active in the resident's association. If he ever needed help to do something I would do it. I would be interested in that way, but I wouldn't go out of my way to get involved. He's a good leader. Some people are leaders and others just do what they are told. I'm like that. That's the trouble— there are too many of us that just sit back and do nothing. I must admit I am guilty of that. (Campbell and Wood 1999:149)

This person was prepared to volunteer but did not take the final step because his friend did not ask him for help. Janet Russo, a volunteer interviewed by Wuthnow (1991:36), agrees that simply being disposed to volunteer is not enough:

I think everybody is willing to volunteer. When we tried to set up a new PTA committee, we had a list of names, and everyone said how are we going to get them to do it, and I said try calling them on the phone and asking, and they all looked at me like it was a new and different idea, and I said just give me the list and a phone and I'll call, and they gave me the 'phone, and there were very few people who said no to me. I think that's what it takes, and don't expect more of them than they are willing to give.

A woman who joined a White supremacist group describes how others "volunteered" her for work she would not have done on her own volition: "I just kind of got volunteered into a lot of things I didn't really expect to, but when I got up and spoke at rallies and stuff, people really listened to what I had to say" (Blee 2002:6).

Being recruited covers many things other than an invitation to help. No doubt the invitation is part of a general discussion of the need for, and benefits of doing, the volunteer work. This information makes it easier for the person targeted to respond positively. When asked why they were not volunteering, 32 percent of Illinois residents said they had not been asked, but 26 percent said they did not know enough about the issues, 23 percent said they did not know how to get involved, and 9 percent said they did not feel welcome (Profile of Illinois 2001). Many of these obstacles would be removed by a personal invitation to help because the "personal touch" assures the prospective volunteer that his or her anxieties about being unable to perform the role are unwarranted. Being asked to help by another person can also be flattering. One focus group member explained that she agreed to volunteer because her boss had asked her. "She's an extremely hardworking person and is really dedicated and if she asked you to do something, it's because she knows that you're capable of doing a good job, and I would take that as a compliment" (Profile of Illinois 2001).

In the United States, nearly half the adult population is likely to be asked to volunteer in any given year. Those who are asked are four times as likely to volunteer as those who are not (Bryant et al. 2003). Recruitment evidently works, as we found when we analyzed the pooled Independent Sector data.

Regardless of socio-demographic differences and differences in church attendance, people were more likely to volunteer if they were asked. [64] Only 15 percent of those who had not been recruited last year had done any volunteer work during that time, compared to three-quarters of those who had been. [89] People who have been recruited also contribute more hours than "walkins." In the Independent Sector data we analyzed, recruits made up 44 percent of the sample but contributed 81 percent of the hours, a ratio five times higher than walk-ins. [1] This could result either from a "socialization effect" (people who have been asked feel more pressure to work longer hours) or a "selection effect" (only those who are likely to work hard are recruited).

The second reason why it is important to look closely at the recruitment process is that some people are more likely to be asked than others. Neither individuals nor organizations like to waste their time recruiting people who refuse. They prefer to target people with high "participation potential" (Brady et al. 1999:153). Although little is yet known about how this process works in volunteering, in the case of political participation it is quite apparent that recruiters follow rational strategies to mobilize people for political activities because the statistical models predicting political activity and recruitment are quite similar. It is as if recruiters knowingly use as selection criteria the factors that actually predict participation (Brady et al. 1999:156). This is not to claim, of course, that recruiters know all the biographical details of the prospects they target, but many behavior patterns linked with volunteering (e.g., frequent church attendance) are observable, some of the known personal characteristics of volunteers (age, gender, and race) can be determined quite easily, and desirable "qualifications" for doing volunteer work, such as education or income, can be inferred from occupation, neighborhood, or organizational memberships. Nor do we claim, of course, that recruitment is always rational or that rational prospecting always works: many college-educated people who are asked to volunteer refuse. Nevertheless, judging by the evidence of a number of surveys, recruiters act quite rationally when deciding whom to target for their recruitment drives.

If solicitation is not random but influenced by who is most likely to accept, and if those thought to be most likely to accept are middle class, then there is a built-in bias in the market for volunteer labor. Although our own study of this topic is the first major analysis of this important issue, the structural determination of volunteer recruitment is clearly foreshadowed in earlier research. Payne and Bull (1985:255) conclude that older people are less likely to be asked to volunteer than middle aged people because they are considered less reliable and less productive. Higher status people are more likely to be asked to volunteer partly because their position in society and their social connections are resources voluntary organizations can use. In the case of elite women, the social standing of their spouses is often the reason for extending an invitation (Daniels 1988:22). Brady et al. (1999:154) found that more educated and affluent people were more likely to be asked to volunteer.

Bryant et al. (2003:53) found that being female, White or Hispanic (rather than African American), a frequent churchgoer, and a home owner all increased the likelihood of being asked, as did having completed more than three years of college and having children. People living in rural areas and those who had been living in the community for a longer period of time were also more likely to be recruited. These are all attributes that suggest social integration (another middle class attribute) increases the chances of being recruited, whereas those who are more socially isolated, such as single people and the unemployed, are less likely to be asked (Lasby 2004:10).

Using the pooled Independent Sector data we were able to see if there was any pattern to volunteer recruitment in the United States. We found that women were more likely to be asked than men; White Americans (41%) more than Non-Hispanic Blacks (33%), Hispanics (34%), and members of other racial or ethnic groups (36%). Twenty-four percent of high school dropouts had been asked in the previous year, compared with 68 percent of those with advanced degrees. Thirty-two percent of those living in households with incomes less than $25,000 had been asked to volunteer, compared to 60 percent of those living in households with incomes more than $75,000. Part-time workers, especially if they were self-employed (56%), were more likely to be asked than full-time employees (46%), and much more than retirees (37%) and those not working for pay (38%). Nearly half (49%) of the parents had been asked, compared to 41 percent of the childless. Those who attended church every, or nearly every, week were asked at a rate of 58 percent, compared to 31 percent of those who never attended church. [31] All these differences were statistically significant and held up after controls in multivariate models, as shown in Table 3.[1]

Who Accepts?

How efficient is the recruitment process? If it is highly efficient, then every person targeted agrees to volunteer. The profile of the person most likely to be asked to volunteer, etched in the previous paragraph, is indeed very similar to the profile of the volunteer: female, White, better educated, wealthy, working part-time, and a parent who attends church frequently. This suggests that if we can predict who is likely to be recruited, we have gone a long way toward explaining who volunteers. Bryant et al. (2003) estimated the probability of volunteering among those who had been asked (in their data, eight out of ten people who had been asked actually volunteered). They found that only marital status influenced the chances of accepting the invitation. (Being divorced, separated or widowed lowered the probability of accepting an invitation to volunteer.) In other words, after the demand side of being asked was factored out, only marital status influenced volunteering. Among those who had not been asked, the picture was quite different. The probability of volunteering among those not asked was affected by marital status, age, gender, race, edu-

Table 3. Estimated Net Effects of Demographics and
Religious Activity on Being Asked to Volunteer.[1,2]

	Model 1
Demographics	
Female	.25***
Race: Black (a)	−.52***
Hispanic	−.34***
Other race	−.57***
Age: 25–34 years (b)	.05
35–49 years	.14+
50–64 years	−.07
65+ years	−.27*
Socioeconomic Status	
Education: High school (c)	.33***
Some college	.81***
College graduate	1.16***
Post-college	1.43***
Income: $25,000–$49,999 (d)	.27***
$50,000–$74,999	.27***
$75,000+	.42***
Owns home	.32***
Employment Status (e)	
Self-employed full-time	.30***
Self-employed part-time	.53***
Other-employed full-time	.01
Other-employed part-time	.30***
Retired	.06
Family Status	
Marital Status: Single (f)	.03
Divorced/separated	.07
Widowed	.05
Have kids	.24***
Other Factors	
Religious Service attendance	.37***
Intercept	−2.47***
R^2	.14

Notes:

[1] Unstandardized logistic regression coefficients are shown.

[2] Reference categories: (a) Non-Hispanic White; (b) <25 years;
(c) <High School; (d) <$25,000; (e) Unemployed; (f) Married.

  $p < .05$; ** $p < .01$; *** $p < .001$

cation, church attendance, residence, and whether or not one's parents volunteered.

The implication of the above findings is clear: one reason, perhaps the only reason, why some factors are associated with volunteering is that they increase the chances of being asked. Recruitment thus becomes the mechanism linking volunteering to several of the factors we have thus far described in the book. We explored this idea by first regressing having volunteered in the past year on all the usual socio-demographic and religious variables and then estimating a second model with being asked as an additional variable to see what happens to the coefficients for all the other variables. The results are shown in Table 4.[2] Adding recruitment to the model almost doubles its explanatory power. Comparing the coefficients in the two models, the mediating role of being asked is quite evident. It helps explain why women volunteer more than men, why Whites volunteer more than other racial and ethnic groups, why the elderly are less likely to volunteer, why better-educated and more affluent Americans are more likely to volunteer, why self-employed people are more likely to volunteer, why parents are more likely to volunteer, and why home owners volunteer more than renters. Note that it does not completely explain the influence of these variables because, as we have seen, they influence volunteering even among those who were not asked.

Bekkers (2005) conducted a similar analysis of data from the Netherlands. Interestingly, he found that being asked explained virtually none of the effect of socio-demographic or religious variables on volunteering in the Netherlands. One major reason is that, unlike the United States, neither income nor education increases the chances of being asked in the Netherlands. Of the remaining variables in his model, only home ownership is partially mediated by being asked.[3]

Another way of thinking about the connection between being asked and volunteering is to imagine there are four categories of people in the population. Some have been asked to volunteer and agreed to do so: we can think of these people as "conformists." A second group of people have been recruited but declined: we can think of these people as "rejecters." A third group volunteered without being asked: these are pure "altruists." A fourth group was not asked and had not volunteered: these people are "disengaged." What can the survey data tell us about who is most likely to be found in each of these groups? Conformists were more likely to be female, middle aged, White, better educated, more affluent, married, parents, self-employed, home owners, and frequent church attenders. Altruists tended to be White, better educated, lower income, self-employed, and frequent church attenders. Rejecters tended to be single or widowed, childless, and home owners who attend church infrequently. The disengaged tended to be male, older, non-Hispanic Blacks, poorly educated, lower income, retired or not employed, single, renters who rarely attend church. [32] This is in many ways a picture of "two nations," one consisting largely of those who enjoy a lot of the privileges of life and are

Table 4. Estimated Net Effects of Being Asked on Volunteering in the Past Year.[1,2]

	Model 1	Model 2
Demographics		
Female	.19***	.08
Race: Black (a)	−.63***	−.49***
Hispanic	−.46***	−.37***
Other race	−1.00***	−.89***
Age: 25–34 years (b)	.06	.05
35–49 years	.16*	.13
50–64 years	−.05	−.02
65+ years	−.26*	−.15
Socioeconomic Status		
Education: High school (c)	.54***	.51***
Some college	1.06***	.87***
College graduate	1.55***	1.26***
Post-college	1.89***	1.53***
Income: $25,000–$49,999 (d)	.26***	.16*
$50,000–$74,999	.21**	.09
$75,000+	.27***	.06
Owns home	.19***	.02
Employment Status (e)		
Self-employed full-time	.33***	.24*
Self-employed part-time	.60***	.41*
Other-employed full-time	.00	−.02
Other-employed part-time	.43***	.36***
Retired	−.17*	−.28**
Family Status		
Marital Status: Single (f)	−.02	−.05
Divorced/separated	−.03	−.10
Widowed	−.07	−.12
Have kids	.32***	.26***
Other Factors		
Service attendance	.56***	.50***
Asked to volunteer	—	2.57***
Intercept	−2.85***	−3.37***
R^2	.21	.39

Notes:

[1] Unstandardized logistic regression coefficients are shown.

[2] Reference categories: (a) Non-Hispanic White; (b) <25 years; (c) <High School; (d) <$25,000; (e) Unemployed; (f) Married.

$p < .05$; ** $p < .01$; *** $p < .001$

well integrated into their community and who enjoy some flexibility and autonomy in their jobs. They are recruited heavily and they have the time, resources, and motivation to respond positively. At the other end of the social scale is a population of people on the margins of society: they are not in the labor force, not married, their socio-economic status is lower, they are a member of a racial or ethnic minority group, and they are older. These marginal people are rarely asked to volunteer and, as if to justify this exclusion, are likely to refuse if they are asked.

Bearing in mind our discussion in chapter 3 of the influence of personality traits such as empathy and self-efficacy on volunteering, we also considered the possibility that these traits might help explain who accepts an invitation to volunteer. We hypothesized that more empathic people and people who think they have the power to make a difference would be more likely to agree to volunteer if asked. [90] We found people are more likely to decline an invitation to volunteer if they score low on efficacy. The score on empathy was only marginally significant, indicating a slight trend toward more empathic people being more likely to agree to volunteer if asked.[4]

Finally, we need to think more about the problem of whether recruitment is more important in getting some people to volunteer than others. One source of variation might be age. Young people have little experience of the volunteer role; they are less involved in the organizational life of their communities; and they are more self-conscious about taking on an adult role. This means they are less likely to be walk-ins. One survey of 12- to 17-year-olds suggests that being asked is especially important for people in this age group. Just over half (51.3%) had been asked to volunteer and, of this group, 93.4 percent had accepted (Brown 1999b:29). Such a high acceptance rate indicates either that they were just waiting for an invitation and eagerly accepted or that they perceive the invitation as having strong normative pressure: they found it hard to refuse because of their age and life course status.

Strong Ties, Weak Ties, Being Recruited, and Volunteering

Besides individual attributes such as education, race, and gender, sociological theory suggests that the quantity and quality of social relationships affect the chances of being recruited and whether the recruit will accept or decline. As far as quantity is concerned, it is likely that "the more people you know, the more likely you are to know a volunteer eager to recruit a co-worker" (Pearce 1993:67). But this says nothing about whether the invitation will be accepted, which probably has more to do with the quality of the relationship between the recruiter and the target. In this section we ask whether people are more likely to be asked by people close to them and if they are more likely to accept if they know the recruiter personally (Brady et al. 1999:154).

In a study of volunteers working for the National Foundation for Infantile Paralysis, Sills (1957:102) found that half the volunteers had signed up because a family member or close friend had asked them to serve. This would suggest that recruiters stay close to home when choosing their targets and slightly contradicts the argument outlined above that recruiters act rationally, selecting people for recruitment who bring the most resources to the work. In another study, about a third of Illinois volunteers said it was a friend who had persuaded them to volunteer. But relatives were no more likely to have asked them than co-workers or organization leaders (Profile of Illinois 2001). Who asks us to volunteer depends on our social position in life. For example, when we compare teenagers with adults we find that slightly more adults (46.2%) than teens (40.0%) said they had first learned about their volunteer experience through being asked. Of those who had been asked: slightly more adults (51.3%) than teens (43.5%) had been asked by a friend; many more teens (31.0%) than adults (18.1%) said they had been asked by a family member; more adults (30.7%) than teens (23.0%) had been asked by a member of their congregation. About a quarter (25.4%) of the teens named a teacher as a recruiter, an option not available to the adults. Because they were still in school, fewer teens (3.6%) than adults (15.7%) had been asked to volunteer by a fellow worker or employer (Hodgkinson and Weitzman 1996:111; Sundeen and Raskoff 2000). Compared to youth, adults were more likely to mention having an informal relationship with their recruiter, less likely to mention a school or college and more likely to mention their workplace, an informal social group, service clubs, or professional associations as places where the recruitment took place (Hodgkinson 1995:42). In other words, the pattern of recruitment tends to change over the life course as the social institutions in which people are embedded change.

Earlier, we suggested that the likelihood of us agreeing to volunteer depends on who asks. Being recruited by someone we know makes the work seem less risky and thus diminishes the anticipated costs. Being asked by someone we know who is already volunteering or with whom we have volunteered in the past is even more persuasive. As we have already noted, people prefer not to solicit volunteers at random but target those friends and acquaintances "with whom they have worked in other community volunteer activities" (Sills 1957:111). Recruiters know full well the power of close ties. In Japan volunteer firefighters are selected very carefully:

> When there is an opening and replacement candidate has been identified, the unit chief will ask someone close to the prospective volunteer, such as a parent, sibling, senior classmate, or neighborhood association president to recruit that person for the volunteer position. The community resident is then advised that it is a duty to accept the volunteer position and serve the community, and he or she capitulates. (Haddad 2004:20S)

In an analysis of Dutch data, Bekkers (2005) found that recruitment using strong ties was more successful. People were more likely to ignore or reject recruitment efforts by colleagues or strangers. We cannot replicate this analysis with the Independent Sector data because only volunteers were asked who had recruited them for volunteer work. Nevertheless, we can see if being asked by someone influences the intensity with which people volunteer—the number of hours they contribute and the number of different volunteer activities in which they are engaged. Looking first at all (volunteer) respondents, 22 percent had been asked to volunteer by a friend, 13 percent by a fellow church member, 8 percent by a family member, 4 percent by a co-worker, 3 percent by an employer, and the rest had been walk-ins. We sorted the volunteers into those who had been asked by a family member or friend (strong ties) and those who had been asked by people more distant from them such as fellow church members, co-workers and employers (weak ties). We focused first on volunteers who had been recruited, to see if the effect of being asked by someone close to them made a difference to the number of domains in which they volunteered. Compared to volunteers who had been asked by a church member, co-worker or employer, volunteers who had been asked by a family member or friend were active in more areas. We then looked at all volunteers, whether or not they had been asked. We used as a reference category those who were not recruited: compared to this reference category, both groups of recruits volunteered in more areas, but those who had been invited by people close to them volunteered for more. We then repeated this analysis, substituting volunteer hours as the dependent variable. Once again, we found that volunteers who had been asked by people close to them volunteered more hours than people invited by others socially distant from them. In the analysis of all volunteers, where the contrast category is those who had not been recruited, those who had been asked by either family members or friends volunteered more hours, but people who had been recruited by people distant from them volunteered *fewer* hours than people who had not been asked at all. This implies that people who respond to an invitation from a co-worker, an employer, or a fellow church member are "going through the motions" in their volunteer work and their level of commitment is actually lower than walk-ins. [91]

Conclusion

Many people who are currently volunteering did not start volunteering on their own initiative, but were recruited to do the work. Organizations with needs for volunteer workers try to cut the costs of recruitment by targeting people they believe are most likely to agree to help. This is one reason why current or former volunteers make attractive targets. Because people are not approached at random there is a bias in the mobilization of volunteers similar to that found by political scientists in the case of political mobilization. Part of the explanation why lower class people and members of minority groups volunteer at lower rates is that they have not been asked.

The analysis of being asked is deceptively simple, but many issues remain unresolved. First, the image of one person inviting another person to volunteer is somewhat deceiving because a certain amount of solicitation takes the form of organized reciprocity wherein people who belong to a voluntary association are asked to volunteer not as individuals but as members of groups. Eckstein (2001) describes this phenomenon in the Boston community where she studied the organization of volunteer work. Groups in the community would exchange volunteer labor on a regular basis. When extra volunteer help was needed to organize and fund a parade or other social event, the sponsoring organization would solicit help directly from leaders of other organizations in the community, knowing that it would in turn be solicited for help at some future time. In this case, people are being asked to volunteer because they belong to a group and, as often as not, they volunteered as a group. Other scholars have noted this tendency: "Often a community organization [e.g., the Lions Club] is asked by the chairman [of the local chapter of the March of Dimes] to assume responsibility for one phase of the March of Dimes, and individual members of the organization are subsequently asked by one of their members to carry out specific assignments" (Sills 1957:113). In this case, networks of organizations, not of individuals, influence the likelihood of being asked.

> Community organizations need time and money, and members call upon one another to pitch in, not only for that organization, but also for others. If I join the PTA, I'm very likely to be asked to volunteer for the fund-raising picnic, and someone I meet there may well invite me to help with the Cancer Society walk-a-thon. Once on the list of usual suspects, I am likely to stay there. (Putnam 2000:121)

A second issue has to do with who asks us to volunteer. We demonstrated that people are more likely to accept an invitation from people they know, but we did not consider the possibility that this varies by social class. We are more likely to be asked to volunteer by a stranger if we have a college degree, a prestigious job or belong to several voluntary associations, whereas the likelihood of being asked by someone known personally is not affected by these factors at all. When "prospecting" for volunteers, friends rely more heavily on indicators that can only be gained by acquaintance. They use criteria such as experience with the volunteer role, "cooperativeness," civic skills, and level of political engagement (Brady et al. 1999:154). It might well be that middle class people are more likely to accept a solicitation from a stranger than working class people.

A third issue has to do with domains of volunteer work. Where the volunteer is being asked to assume a burdensome work load, operate in stressful conditions or incur risk, being personally recruited might be more important than in the case of more casual or sporadic volunteering, which can rely more on walk-ins. For example, working in a hospice is one of the more demanding forms of volunteer work. In this setting, some kind of personal relationship between the prospective volunteer and the voluntary organization is probably most effective (Black and Kovacs 1999:482). Volunteering to help with a fund-raising "walk-a-thon" is more casual and informal and background checks or training are unnecessary.

Finally, in chapter 12 we explored the role of voluntary association memberships in volunteering, showing that "joiners" volunteer at a higher rate because they are more likely to be asked. We did not consider the possibility that recruitment could act as a substitute for memberships. In a preliminary analysis of this problem, using an interaction term for membership and being asked, we found that recruitment does indeed function as a substitute for memberships. The influence of memberships on volunteering was weaker for people who had been asked. Conversely, the influence of being recruited was weaker for people with many memberships. Although memberships and being asked are positively related and being asked is undoubtedly one reason why memberships encourage volunteering, they are also, to some degree, substitute pathways to volunteering. [33] People who belong to voluntary associations do not "need" to be asked as much as people who do not belong, probably because the social norms of the association make this redundant. People who do not belong to a voluntary association "need" recruitment because they are not embedded into a social network of fellow members who enforce the norm of volunteer work. This is issue deserves more investigation.

14

Schools and Congregations

In this chapter we focus on the most important social institutions in American community life, schools and religious congregations. We treat each as an important social context within which the volunteer role is organized, taught, encouraged, and rewarded. For various reasons, these institutions are probably much more important in maintaining the social fabric of community life in the United States than they are in other countries where volunteerism is found, but unfortunately we lack data on the role of schools and churches in the mobilization of volunteer labor in those other countries and we therefore focus mostly on the United States in this chapter.

Schools

In chapter 6 we described the influence of education on volunteering, but we did not consider the role of the school as an institution. We did not consider the possibility that schools might vary in the extent to which they encourage or discourage pupils from doing volunteer work when they are still enrolled in school and after graduation. Schools play a prominent role in organizing young people's time. Most educators encourage students to get involved in volunteer work because they believe it increases their sense of responsibility to the school and the community as a whole (Elder and Conger 2000:177). In this respect, the school, along with the church, functions as the first step in the generalization of ideas of social responsibility and compassion beyond the family to the community as a whole, from people the child knows personally to strangers. Of course, these are only potentialities. For schools to have these effects classrooms should be arenas for open discussion and disagreement; they should provide extra-curricular opportunities for students; and they should foster solidarity with the school and identification with its goals.

In this section, we consider how school characteristics alter the likelihood of volunteering, regardless of the student's own characteristics. As we shall, see, different schools take different approaches to the idea of encouraging or requiring community service from their students.

Public or Private

An Australian survey of high school students found that pupils in government (public) schools did less volunteering than students in either Catholic or independent (private) schools (Brown 2003:11). This study does not control for the individual characteristics of the student, and we cannot be sure whether there is something about the school or the characteristics of the pupils that accounts for this public-private gap. A survey of sixth through twelfth graders in the United States did control for parents' education, parents' volunteering, and whether or not the school required community service for graduation and still found that pupils in private, church-affiliated schools volunteered at a higher rate than students in public schools or secular private schools. Forty percent of the students enrolled in church-affiliated private schools were regularly volunteering at the time of the survey, compared to 29 percent in secular private schools and 24 percent in public schools (Nolin et al. 1997:15).

Size

Private schools tend to be smaller than public schools and this could be one reason for the differences described in the previous paragraph. Smaller groups are believed to be able to control the "free rider" problem better than large groups because they are able to monitor "shirking." Children who attend small schools therefore should face more pressure to become involved and contribute in meaningful ways to the life of the school. In large schools, on the other hand, a handful of students can dominate leadership roles, in which case the ratio of volunteers to non-volunteers is likely to fall (Elder and Conger 2000:172). Using data from National Household Education Survey, Kleiner and Chapman (1999) found no support for this hypothesis. Fifty-six percent of the students attending schools with less than three hundred pupils were currently volunteering, compared to 54 percent of students attending schools with one thousand or more pupils, an insignificant difference.

Service Requirements

Another possible reason why private schools have higher volunteer rates than public schools is that they encourage their students to do volunteer work, provide information on the means to do so, or even require it as a condition of graduation. "Community service" is the term used to describe a program of service that generally lacks explicit learning objectives or any attachment to regular curriculum courses. "Service learning" is the term used to describe volunteer work organized in relation to a course or curriculum with clear learning objectives that is intended to meet specific community needs. Community service becomes service learning when participants are given the opportunity, or are required, to talk and write about their experiences in an academic setting.[1]

Lately, more and more U.S. school districts have taken to mandating community service as a requirement for graduation.[2] In one recent U.S. survey, three-quarters of the high school students said their schools arranged or offered volunteer work and 21 percent said it was a requirement for graduation (Keeter et al. 2002a:33). It is safe to conclude that one reason why more teenagers are volunteering than their parents did when they were teenagers is that today more and more schools are encouraging it (Child Trends Data-Bank 2003). The support schools provide for doing volunteer work also explains why young adults volunteer at a lower rate than adolescents.[3] Recently, other countries have also begun requiring community service.[4]

If schools act as a social context for volunteering, then students attending schools that emphasize, and provide structures that facilitate, community service will be more likely to have students who are doing volunteer work. Two recent studies support this hypothesis. The first found 45 percent of the students attending high schools that arranged volunteer opportunities were volunteering compared to only a third of the pupils attending schools where no arrangements were made (Andolina et al. 2003). The second study found that 29 percent of the students attending a school that neither required nor arranged community serve were participating in community service, compared to 54 percent attending a school that arranged (but did not require) community service (Kleiner and Chapman 1999). Although these school effects are quite pronounced and certainly indicate that schools function to mobilize volunteer work among teenagers, we cannot conclude from these data that schools are the most important pathway to volunteering for Americans in this age range. Only 5 percent of American teenagers said they became involved with the organization for which they did most of their volunteer work as the result of a school requirement (Grimm et al. 2005:4). The reference to "requirement" here means mandated volunteer work in high school, and it is still possible that schools that merely encourage volunteer work will be a positive influence. But it is a reminder there are other pathways to volunteerism for teenagers, most prominently the church.[5]

School Effects on Future Volunteering

One reason school officials give for encouraging students to perform community service is that it sows the seeds for civic engagement in adulthood. People who volunteer in their youth become better citizens. In chapter 20 we will discuss the influence of youthful volunteering on adult citizenship, but here we are chiefly interested in the influence of the school as social context. It is one thing to argue that individuals who volunteered in adolescence are more likely to be civically engaged as adults and another thing to argue that individuals who attended schools that emphasized community service are more likely to be civically engaged as adults, *regardless of whether they did community service when in school.*

We cannot take it for granted that students who attended schools that encouraged community service are more likely to volunteer later in life. Where the school exerts pressure on students to do community service, a backlash against volunteering might occur. Many of the young people interviewed by Wuthnow (1995:72) were firmly against service-learning programs that were compulsory or rewarded them with academic credit because the service would not be appropriately motivated. Nevertheless, in chapter 10 we demonstrated that people who volunteered as teenagers are more likely to volunteer as adults and the pathway from service learning to adult volunteering might lie through volunteering in adolescence: students learn about volunteer work through the curriculum and as a result begin volunteering in their community and remain volunteers when they reach adulthood. A 1991 study of teenagers in the United States found that students who attended schools where community service was either encouraged or required were more likely to be volunteering outside of school than students who attended schools with no such encouragement (Sundeen and Raskoff 1994:395). A more recent study confirmed that teenagers attending schools that arranged or offered community service were more likely to volunteer outside of school. Whether or not the community service was required for graduation or merely arranged did not seem to make much difference. The authors of this study note,

> At least two hypotheses are available to explain how school policies affect students' participation in community service: schools policies might compensate for lower motivation to participate among some students (either by forcing students to participate regardless of their motivation, or by making participation easier so that less work or initiative is required to participate), or schools might help students to overcome other barriers to participation (e.g., the student may not know how to get involved, what opportunities are available, and whom to contact). It is possible for both these hypotheses to be true, but each might support a different kind of school policy: requiring students to participate might seem most directed at compensating for lower motivation, and arranging community service might seem most directed at removing barriers to participation. Based on this logic, the fact that arranging community service appears more im-

portant than requiring it provides some evidence that students are willing to participate but that many students need help in order to participate. (Nolin et al. 1997:18)

Metz and Youniss (2003) took advantage of the introduction of a mandatory community service requirement in a public high school in Boston to compare students who attended the school before and after the requirement was instituted. They were able to find out if students went on to do volunteer work in the community after completing the assignment. More importantly, they were able to use two successive cohorts to see if participation in the mandatory program changed students' intention to volunteer when they graduated. Far from discouraging volunteerism, the requirement improved the likelihood of volunteering. In addition, those who had participated in the mandated service work were more likely to have plans to volunteer after graduation. The positive effect of mandatory service was especially strong for those students who had shown no previous inclination to volunteer *outside* of the mandated work. These results are interesting because they demonstrate that, by changing the curriculum, rather than the individual attributes of the students, the rate of volunteering can be improved.

McLellan and Youniss (2003) compared two Catholic schools in the Washington, D.C., area because they adopted very different approaches to the question of community service even though it was required in both cases. One required service learning as part of the religion curriculum, hired a service coordinator, and asked faculty to encourage students to discuss their service learning experiences in class. The second school, which mandated the same number of hours of service, made no attempt to integrate it into the curriculum and allowed students to choose their own kind of service activity. In the study, students were asked about their participation in the service-learning component of the curriculum and about their volunteer activities outside of school. The researchers sorted the service-learning work into five categories: social service, working for a cause, teaching or coaching the needy, teaching or coaching the non-needy, and "functionary work," such as telephone fund raising. The voluntary work outside of school was classified into the same categories (with the exception of no distinction within the teaching or coaching category). Students attending the more "laissez-faire" school were just as likely to be volunteering outside of school as students attending the school where service learning was highly structured, but they preferred more "functionary" kinds of volunteer work. Pupils attending the school where service learning had been integrated into the curriculum were more likely to have chosen social service as their required activity in school. This, in turn, made it more likely they would choose to do social service work outside of school. Service learning might therefore do more to influence volunteer preferences than the overall amount of volunteering outside of school.

Panel studies provide a better picture of the consequences of school policies on later volunteering because it is possible to follow the same students as they graduate from school and enter adult life. The National Education Longitudinal Study (NELS) has been following a cohort of American high school students since 1988, when they were in eighth grade. In 1994, when the cohort was two years out of high school, 43 percent were currently volunteering. Sixty-one percent of those who had volunteered in high school were currently volunteering, compared to only 30 percent of those who had not volunteered in high school. Cohort members most likely to be volunteering in 1994 had attended a Catholic high school, where they had volunteered, and had gone on to college. However, the most interesting findings have to do with the school's approach to community service. Cohort members were more likely to be volunteering if they attended a school that organized community service in some way, *especially if the community service was strictly voluntary rather than required* (Smith 1997:124).

In chapter 10 we demonstrated that students are more likely to volunteer in college if they volunteered in high school, but we do not know what effect the policies of the school have on the likelihood of volunteering in college. According to the NELS data, 36 percent of students who volunteered in high school were not volunteering as sophomores in college. Socio-demographic characteristics do not explain who was more likely to quit volunteering, which had much more to do with school policies regarding volunteer work. Attending a school where community service was encouraged increased the likelihood the student would continue volunteering in college. Attending a school where community service was required, on the other hand, increased the likelihood of quitting volunteer work.

> Rather than performing service because they saw its importance, these students may have been conforming to group norms, responding to school expectations, or complying with graduate requirements for service—all extrinsic motivations. When volunteering is primarily a product of secondary socialization, it may be short-lived. (Marks and Jones 2004:331)

A later analysis of the NELS data updates these finding by using the 2000 panel. As with the previous analyses, high school students who volunteered were more likely to volunteer after high school than those who did not volunteer in high school. As in the earlier studies, students who attended a school that required community service were less likely to be volunteering than those who had attended a school where community service was merely encouraged—although they were more likely to be volunteering than students who attended schools where community service was neither encouraged nor required. Eight years after high school graduation (2000) the effect of high school volunteering was still apparent: 42 percent of those who volunteered in high school were volunteering compared to 26 percent of those who had not. However, by this time, the negative effect of attending a school that had mandated community service had disappeared (Planty and Regnier 2003:6). Obliging students to do volunteer work thus has only a short-term negative effect.

The Quality of Service Learning Programs

In the 2004 survey of school principals referred to earlier, the vast majority (80%) admitted that the service learning experience their school provided was a one-time event (Scales and Roehlkepartain 2004:16). Understandably, there is widespread skepticism about the effectiveness of programs that ask so little of the students. Critics of the service learning movement have questioned whether participation in a few school courses has the capacity to turn adolescents into active and engaged citizens who are capable of assessing and solving public problems. The skepticism is fostered by the lack of consistency in how service learning is defined and managed, and in the quality of the programs. Some activities are as fleeting and ephemeral as a Saturday afternoon car wash for charity; others require regular stints at a soup kitchen. Equally important, schools integrated service learning into the curriculum in many different ways. "In some schools, service is integrated into the academic curriculum so that it has a clear rationale, follows from the subject matter, and is the focus of reflective discussion. In other schools, however, students are left to their own devices for finding service placements and in making sense of their experience in the field" (Metz et al. 2003:48). Schools also vary in the kinds of activities they encourage or make available: in some cases the service work clearly targets the needy and the student is brought face to face with the people being served; in other cases, service work consists largely of performing manual labor for a non-profit or government agency, such as filing records or cleaning offices.

A number of conditions have to be met before a service-learning curriculum is a positive force for volunteering. The first is that mandated service work should involve direct interaction with people in need rather than dealing with social problems in the abstract or from a distance. The second is that service learning needs to be tightly managed. Schools need to "treat service with the same seriousness as they approach academics or athletics" (McLellan and Youniss 2003:56). When left to their own devices, students opt for the less challenging functionary work. Third, wherever possible, service learning should take advantage of student memberships in social networks outside of school consisting, in part, of membership in neighborhoods, clubs, and religious congregations. These social networks make it easier for high school students to find appropriate social service activities for their mandated service work and provide social support to maintain their commitment to it. Fourth, service learning should be integrated into classroom work. When students are given a chance to talk about their volunteer experience in the classroom they volunteer in the community at twice the rate of students not given a chance (Keeter et al. 2002a:33).

Morgan and Streb (2001:158) contrast two different approaches to service learning:

A project with a low level of student voice would be one where the teacher selects the specific service project, plans the logistics, and then has the students involved only in the actual performance of the service. For example, a project where the teacher decided that there was a need to clean up a park, made arrangements with the park staff, and then had the students involved only to do the cleanup would be considered a low-voice project. An example of a project with high levels of student involvement would be a project where middle school students in a home economics class began by doing some simple community needs assessment and picking their service project (a homeless shelter) based on their appraisal. Next the students would work with the staff and clients to develop the project and then plan the project (with appropriate support) and arranged funding. Then they would begin an ongoing tutoring program (literacy or life skills).

The question of whether or not mandating "volunteer" work creates a backlash against volunteerism remains an open one. When the Australian government introduced service learning into public schools under the title "active citizenship programmes" many skeptics argued that they would not help students internalize altruistic values or acquire positive attitudes toward citizenship because they were being forced to provide help to others. Focus groups of teenagers organized to discuss the programs revealed highly negative attitudes toward them. One student said: "Why would I want to volunteer for anything else when I've been forced to do something?" (Warburton and Smith 2003:779). A study of American high school students adds further support to the skeptics. Stukas et al. (1999) took advantage of the introduction of a service-learning requirement at the University of St. Thomas in St. Paul, Minnesota, to study its effect on intentions to volunteer in the future. They assumed that intention to volunteer might depend on whether the student had volunteered in the past and whether the student saw the service requirement as controlling his or her behavior. Students who answered that they were participating in the program only because it was required of them were scored high on feeling controlled. Students who felt more external control were indeed less likely to have plans to volunteer. In addition, when students perceived the experience as a controlling one, the positive effect of prior volunteer experience was blunted. The study suggests that service learning can dampen interest in volunteering among those who resent having to perform it. This outcome can be avoided by offering greater autonomy and choice for the individuals involved. However, the survey data we reviewed above indicates that, although there might be short-term negative consequences of attending a school where service is required, they disappear over time, and it is still better to have attended a school that required service than a school that did not have a community service program at all.

In conclusion, the school is one of the primary institutions for teaching young people how to do volunteer work. Although the institutional affiliation of the school (public versus private) makes some difference as to whether pupils volunteer, the most significant difference is whether or not the school has a policy of specifically encouraging volunteer work and, if so, what form that encouragement takes. If a school offers information on and supports volunteer work without specifically mandating it, the influence seems to be more durable. Schools *can* use service learning to promote long-term civic engagement, as long as the program is structured in such a way as to give students choice and time to deliberate on their experiences. Service learning that lacks reflection "can result in undesirable, rather than positive, effects" (Kenny and Gallagher 2003:6). For example, it can reinforce stereotypes of disadvantaged groups or distract attention from the root causes of the needs the volunteer is helping meet.

Much research remains to be done on the influence schools have on civic engagement in adult life. Although longitudinal data are being used with increasing frequency, little attention has been paid to the process of self-selection of more civic-minded students into community service programs or service learning courses where this is not a requirement, thus biasing the estimates of the success of the programs. Many studies rely on small samples or evaluations conducted at a single site. Too often, neither the quality of service programs nor intensity of commitment expected of students is measured. Nor is enough attention paid to the variety of service opportunities available or the variety of volunteer roles students play. Finally, appropriate multi-level methods are rarely used to isolate school effects. We cannot be sure we are witnessing the influence of the school on volunteerism rather than the characteristics of the individuals attending the school. For example, if schools that do a good job of promoting volunteer work are also schools more likely to be attended by students from families who encourage their children to do volunteer work, then the apparent effect of the school might be spurious.

Religious Congregations

Sociologically speaking, a religious congregation is a voluntary association, although this somewhat less true of Catholic parishes. In a time when traditional voluntary associations, fraternal orders, and mutual benefit associations are losing members, religious congregations remain strong and have become the most visible and active voluntary association in many American communities, especially in small towns and rural areas (Elder and Conger 2000:151). Compared to most other voluntary associations, a religious congregation is multifunctional, striving to meet a variety of individual, family, and community needs. It is both a bureaucratic entity and a social community. People are drawn to a particular congregation by social ties to others and they create new social ties once they become members. Being a member of a congregation is thus in many respects like being a member of an extended family. Social relationships seem to "count" for more if they are embedded in a religious congregation. Because a religious congregation strives to be a community and not just an organization, it is able to extract more voluntary labor from its members than most other voluntary associations. The volunteer role is defined less bureaucratically, framed instead as part of a set of personal responsibilities to other members. In this context "free riding" is a lot more difficult and shirking one's responsibility to the group is more noticeable. It is not surprising that people with lots of friends are more likely to volunteer, but especially if those friends also belong to the same church (Becker and Dhingra 2001:325; Park and Smith 2000:273).

The volunteer labor supply in the United States depends heavily on people recruited through religious congregations. The largest single concentration of volunteer work in the United States is organized by, or takes place in connection with, religious congregations: "well over 40 percent of all volunteer time is dedicated to religious organizations" (Salamon 1997:314). Forty percent of the total volunteers hours contributed by Illinois residents in 2000 related specifically to their religious faith (Profile of Illinois 2000). In turn, religious organizations rely heavily on volunteer labor to meet their survival needs. It is estimated that the average Mormon ward (congregation) has between 150 and 250 "callings" (volunteer activities) and receives between 400 and 600 hours of voluntary labor per week (Stark and Finke 2000:150).

We would be less interested in religious congregations if they mobilized only volunteer work on behalf of the church itself, but religious congregations are feeder systems for many other non-profit and voluntary organizations. People do not necessarily choose between volunteering for their church or a secular organization; many people who volunteer for religious causes also volunteer for secular causes (Clain and Zech 1999). Far from hoarding volunteer labor for their own use congregations provide volunteer labor to other organizations. A Canadian study coded non-profit agencies into religious and secular categories. Survey respondents were asked to indicate the number of hours they volunteered for up to three different organizations. Nearly eight in ten (79%) of the religious volunteers were also contributing time to a secular organization. Indeed, they contributed more of the total hours donated by all Canadians to volunteer work in that year than those who were volunteering only for secular organizations (Bowen 1999:17). In short, while religious congregations are effective mobilizers of volunteer labor intended for their own purposes, this is not at the expense of volunteer labor for organizations outside the church.

How Do Congregations Mobilize Volunteer Labor?

Like most voluntary associations, congregations play a crucial role in mobilizing volunteer workers by making it more difficult to say no. Members cannot say they are unaware of volunteer opportunities or that they are unfamiliar with the demands of the volunteer role. Congregations also make possible the recruitment of volunteers as groups of people. This, too, makes "shirking" more difficult.

> For example, in Council Grove, Kansas, the popular thrift shop, run entirely by volunteers from local congregations, has been in operation for more than twenty years. That the operation has been smooth and efficient over such a long period is a result of the fact that each congregation sends volunteers as a group. Working as a unit keeps members committed and accountable to one another, and this ongoing commitment is a key to the program's success. (Cnaan 2002:216)

From the standpoint of organizations such as the thrift shop, it is more efficient to recruit a group of congregants than to recruit individuals one at a time.[6]

Another reason why congregations mobilize volunteer work is the competition between churches for members. Congregations compete by offering a wide array of activities and programs intended to get members involved in the social life of the church and to appeal to different family members. Many of these activities take the form of volunteer work, which takes its place alongside basketball teams and reading groups as a way to keep members involved.[7] A final reason why religious congregations contribute so much to the supply of volunteer labor is that they are among the most "embedded" of voluntary associations. Some voluntary associations are relatively isolated, in that few of their members belong to other voluntary associations, and few members of other voluntary associations belong to them. Trade unions and veterans' organizations are isolated in this sense. Although this type of organization might mobilize volunteers on its own behalf, it is less likely to mobilize volunteer work on behalf of other organizations or sponsor joint volunteer campaigns. Religious congregations, on the other hand, are more embedded in the organizational life of their communities, sharing many members with other voluntary associations: their members belong to lots of other organizations and members of lots of other organizations belong to them. A recent study found that 68 percent of members of secular voluntary associations also belonged to a church. Overlapping church and secular memberships mean that churches are more likely than most secular organizations to act as feeder systems for volunteer work outside the congregation. Churches are a focal point of the network of memberships in any given community (Cornwell and Harrison 2004).

Which Congregations Recruit the Most Volunteer Workers?

As we learn more about the mobilizing role of religious congregations we become more aware of limitations of social surveys that gather information simply on church attendance. The religious congregation is actually a community with properties of its own that influences the rate of volunteering among members of the congregation quite apart from attendance at worship services. The congregation should be a unit of analysis in its own right, independent of the members who belong to it. For example, the members of a religious congregation might be affluent, which boosts the rate of volunteering among members of the congregation because rich people volunteer more, but their affluence also permits the congregation to have a larger operating budget and, as we shall see, big budget congregations develop more service programs and mobilize more volunteer labor.

As the result of a recent survey of over a thousand religious congregations in the United States (National Congregations Study) we know much more about what kind of congregation sponsors the most volunteer activities. Fifty-seven percent of the congregations were engaged in some kind of social service, community development or neighborhood organizing project. The average congregation supplied ten volunteers to these projects. The most common types of programs were food projects, housing projects, and services to the homeless. However, the median congregation participated in, or supported, only one social service program. The tendency was to focus on programs that promised to address immediate needs on a face-to-face basis. Although a small minority of congregations had instituted their own, stand-alone, programs manned by volunteers, sometimes with full-time paid staff, most provided volunteers to non-profit organizations or public agencies—sending teams of volunteers to cook and serve food at a homeless shelter one night a week, or organizing teams of people to help renovate housing at the weekends. Congregations most likely to sponsor social service activities were larger, middle class, and located in poorer neighborhoods (Chaves 2004:53).[8]

In another major study of religious congregations conducted in 1997 and 1998, a team of researchers interviewed representatives (usually pastors) from 549 religious congregations in the United States. In addition, questionnaires were distributed to over four thousand churchgoers. Nearly three-quarters of the congregations supplied volunteers to at least one secular service organization. The mainline Protestant congregations were the most likely to provide this kind of support (86%), followed by Catholic (77%), conservative Protestants (73%), and African American Protestants (65%). The number of service projects to which volunteers were supplied ranged from 3.71 for the mainline Protestants to 2.21 for the African American Protestants. On average, each congregation supplied five volunteers. The larger the budget of the congregation, the more connections to secular agencies it had, regardless of the individual incomes of members and denominational affiliation. Surprisingly, rural congregations sponsored fewer activities, probably because of the more pressing need for social services in the city. Regardless of denomination, human services, health, education, culture, and youth organizations were the most likely to receive congregational support. Outreach activities thus focused on providing relief for people in need, for educational missions, and for self-improvement: little support was given to economic development or advocacy activities (Ammerman 2002:154).

Most of these congregational studies indicate that size matters: the larger the congregation (measured by membership and budget) the more programs the congregation is likely to sponsor. One study found that three-quarters of those who belonged to congregations with less than three hundred members said their congregation helped sponsor a food pantry or soup kitchen, compared to 89 percent of those belonging to a congregation with a thousand or more members. Forty-two percent of the small congregation members said their church helped sponsor a shelter for the homeless, compared to 66 percent of those who belong to large congregations. Fifty-nine percent of those who belonged to small congregations said their church sponsored two or more programs, compared to 86 percent of those who belonged to large congregations (Wuthnow 2004:45). We cannot conclude from these associations that size is causing members to volunteer because volunteer activities might be attracting more members and is the cause rather than the effect of size, but these differences clearly indicate the importance of social context: two people, equally well disposed to doing volunteer work and with equal amounts of individual resources, have different chances of volunteering, depending on the size of the congregation they join.

Besides the size of congregation, the amount of volunteer work it mobilizes is also influenced by the way the congregation is organized, although we have only one study to support this contention. Becker and Dhingra (2001:322) distinguished four types of congregation. "Family" congregations concentrate on providing members with close and supportive personal relationships. "Houses of worship" focus on providing a satisfying main worship service. "Community" congregations foster lay participation and create a space for debate about political and social issues. "Leader" congregations play an active role in local civic life and social activism. Church members who saw their congregation as a place of debate (they belonged to "community"-type congregations) were the most likely to volunteer. Interestingly, belonging to the "house of worship" or the "leader" type of congregation lowered the odds of volunteering. "Both types denote congregational cultures that do not emphasize interpersonal connections of intimacy among members" (Becker and Dhingra 2001:326). In short, volunteering is encouraged by democratic structures and frequent interaction among congregation members.

In summary, more Americans belong to a religious congregation than any other voluntary association, and religious congregations are effective mobilizers of volunteer labor. Social surveys largely overlook this source of variation in volunteering because they gather information from individuals, not the social context in which those individual's lives take place. Congregational characteristics should therefore be treated as an independent—and important—social structure governing the supply of volunteer labor. It is unfortunate that, unlike schools, we have no nationally representative data on how congregational characteristics influence volunteering, after controls for the individual characteristics of the volunteer. On the other hand, it is important not to exaggerate the contribution of religious congregations. Few sponsor more than one social service program and the average number of volunteers supplied to programs outside the church is quite low considering the size of the congregations. Furthermore, the volunteer efforts religious congregations mobilize are quite limited in their scope. They are "much more likely to engage in activities that address the immediate, short-term needs of recipients for food, clothing, and shelter than in programs requiring more sustained and personal involvement to meet long-term needs, such as programs in the areas of health, education (excluding religious education), domestic violence, substance abuse, tutoring or mentoring work, or work or employment" (Chaves 2004:59). Religious congregations do supply volunteer workers, but on their own terms.

15

Community, Neighborhood, City, and Region

In this chapter and the one following we will describe how volunteering is influenced by where we live. We begin by looking at the way neighborhood characteristics affect the volunteer rate, paying particular attention to home ownership and residential stability. We then test the hypothesis that volunteerism is more common in rural areas and small towns by comparing the volunteer rates of city dwellers with the rate among suburbanites and people living in rural areas. At the end of this chapter we describe regional differences in volunteering and try to explain them. The following chapter will review, and add to, the research on volunteer differences between countries.

In chapters 15 and 16 we are discussing the role of ecological factors in volunteering. The ecological perspective is in many ways at the heart of sociology because it focuses on the way in which larger social structures mold individual behavior. Those individuals are, as often as not, unaware of the way their behavior is influenced by these larger social structures. From this perspective, community is objectively defined—as when we count how many people in a neighborhood own their own homes. We begin our review of the research in this area, however, by looking at community from a subjective point of view, where *our subjects define communities for us*. Psychologists refer to this as "psychological community" and sociologists refer to it as "social" or "collective identity." We will then look at how volunteering is affected by how people feel about their neighborhoods. People who think their neighborhood is worth preserving, feel safe going out at night, and trust their neighbors to share the burden of community housekeeping, might well be more likely to volunteer.

Strictly speaking, psychological communities and people's attitudes toward their neighborhoods are not ecological variables at all, but attributes of individuals. We include them in this chapter because they point to the influence of the *idea* of community on our disposition to volunteer. The objective meaning of community refers to a geographical space and its social and economic characteristics, ranging from neighborhoods to cities, regions, and countries. Wherever possible, we intend to distinguish the influence of the ecological unit from the influence of the individual. Assume, for example, that home owners are no more likely to volunteer than renters. This does not mean that home ownership has no effect on volunteering. People living in communities with high rates of home ownership might well have higher volunteer rates. This might be a function of lower population turnover, higher property tax revenues, better schools, and so on.

Imagined Communities

Many of the communities most important to us do not occupy physical space so much as mental space. Whether or not we even notice these communities or take them seriously helps determine whether we volunteer for them. These imagined communities can be considered under two headings. The first is social identity, or the sense of belonging to a social group from which one draws one's personal identity. The second is attachment to place. Here the community is "bricks and mortar" and spatially located, but residents vary in the degree to which they feel attached to it. Community attachment describes the extent to which individuals are committed to their place of residence and have a sense that they belong there, they can exert some control over it, that their personal needs can be satisfied there (Liu et al. 1998:433).

Social Identity

Social identity derives from membership in a social category, such as a religious, ethnic, racial, or sexual identity group. "In contrast to individual identity (I or me), collective identity (we or us) is a place that is shared with a group of other people" (Simon and Klandermans 2001:321). Social identity is subjective because people vary in the extent to which they identify with groups to which they "objectively" belong. It plays a crucial role in mobilizing volunteers because a person is more likely to volunteer for a group if he or she recognizes and identifies with it. Social identification alters the whole calculus of volunteering, lowering the costs and increasing the rewards of donating one's time freely. Volunteering can be rewarding not only because of its outcome (helping a client) but also because it forges an attachment between the volunteer and a social group: volunteering expresses our solidarity with the group (Rochon 1998:97). Because of our bond with the group we "feel bad" if we do not contribute to its welfare (Prentice and Ferguson 2000:131). Social identity is especially important wherever volunteer work calls for a collective effort (e.g., a demonstration), as it does in many forms of advocacy volunteering.

Social identity helps explain why groups high in social solidarity have higher rates of volunteerism. They overcome the free rider problem, not by offering incentives selectively only to those who volunteer, but by increasing solidarity between group members in the knowledge that people's primary motivation is to be accepted as a member of the group in order to affirm their social identity. Thus, rather than offering volunteers special recognition, acknowledging that only a few are willing to do the work of many, they concentrate on increasing social solidarity by, for example, imposing a "dress code." Such measures make it more difficult to stand back and let others do the work. This is one reason why those religious congregations that emphasize conformity and discipline are such fertile ground for recruiting volunteers. It explains why people who give high priority to their membership in racial and ethnic minority groups are more likely to volunteer (Burns et al. 2001:270). And it explains why the unions with the highest volunteer rate are located in industries where the workers are largely segregated from the rest of the community but closely integrated with each other, as in mining and dock work. In all these cases an ideology teaching that the group and its members are special further enhances solidarity and increases the chances that individual members of the group will step up and help the group meet its collective needs.

The more strongly people identify with the psychological community to which they belong (or aspire to belong) the more likely they are to adopt the reciprocity norms of the group. The more psychic benefits they derive from the community, such as status, self-esteem, and protection from stigma and castigation—the more they share histories and experiences—the more likely they are to volunteer to provide the material and psychological resources group members need. Omoto and Snyder (2003) found that AIDS volunteers ranked identification with the gay community as a very important reason for volunteering. Understandably, gay volunteers rated this reason even higher than straight volunteers. The majority of AIDS volunteers (57%) signed up because they had been asked by someone they knew, because they knew others who were volunteers or by participation in AIDS-related events, and because being recognized as part of the gay community was an important motivation for them.

In summary, people with strong social identities are more likely to volunteer. However, we cannot tell from the studies cited above whether social identity is the cause or the effect of volunteering. Although volunteering is one consequence of having a strong group identity, people volunteer *in order to* establish a sense of community or to legitimate or defend a social identity. The primary purpose of some kinds of volunteer work is gain recognition or rehabilitation for an identity or a group of people. In the words of one Japanese third generation immigrant to the United States:

> I think in the '60s I realized that there were needs that the government wasn't addressing and that communities must work for themselves. As ethnic minorities we must work for ourselves. . . . A place [agency] that has gone to the community to find out what their needs are does not just set up and say we are here to help. I think that in big organizations we lose control. I prefer community agencies where control isn't taken from the people. I feel it is important, because if we are talking about the Japanese community in general, it is important to maintain contact and identity within the community. . . . Through giving time and money we can maintain the identity of the community through programs and events. (Smith et al. 1999:125)

In cases where people volunteer in order to demonstrate their affinity with others, what they do might be less important than who they do it with. Black women who volunteer to mentor young and poor Black mothers as part of the "Birthing Project" see themselves as not only helping lower the infant mortality rate but also helping "preserve the race" in a time of family disintegration (McDonald 1997:783). White women who volunteer for racist groups speak of "taking responsibility" for the White race. They are not so much giving to others as volunteering on behalf of a racial community they are helping to define (Blee 2002:66). Even if strengthening group identity is not the motivation for volunteering it can be the unintended consequence. For example, the longer people volunteer to help people with AIDS the more likely are they to have social ties with others also volunteering for the same cause and the more likely are they to have tried to recruit others to join them in their work (Omoto and Snyder 2003:862). By volunteering they become more deeply immersed in the gay community. Similarly, women involved in rape crisis work "created, reinforced, or redirected a feminist identity as they simultaneously struggled to combat sexual assault within the community" (Abrahams 1996:773). Their volunteer work raised their consciousness of women as an oppressed group. Abrahams (1996:775) cites the case of a woman who developed her identity as a Chicana as a result of agreeing to volunteer for the Latino Student Organization at her college. There will also be cases where people volunteer in order to gain entry into a community. In this situation social identity is the intended outcome of the volunteer work, not the cause of it. For some of the search and rescue volunteers interviewed by Lois (2003:44), joining the group was a way to become part of the "real" people in a mountain community whose population was swelled each year by tourists. Getting to know and become accepted by the "regulars" was one way to become part of the community, to demonstrate that they shared the residents' commitment to preserving the community and its way of life. The decision to volunteer for that particular organization could not have been separated from the decision to volunteer at all. Search and rescue was one of the best ways to become identified as a "real" member of the community. Other kinds of volunteer activity would not have performed this job as well.

Attachment to Place

Attachment to place is the feeling that you belong in and are comfortable with a specific location, usually the neighborhood or community in which you live. Numerous studies show that people who are attached to their communities are more likely to volunteer. Volunteers are more likely than non-volunteers to: rate their community or neighborhood as an excellent place to live (Smith 1998:37); trust their neighbors (Profile of Illinois 2001); perceive a sense of community in their neighborhood; and think their neighborhood is important to them (Wandersman et al. 1987). Volunteers are more likely than non-volunteers to express pride in community institutions, such as parks, schools, libraries, and hospitals. For example, some of the volunteers in nursing facilities for the elderly were motivated by a desire to preserve and improve what they regard as an asset to their community: "This care facility is an important part of our community, and I, like others, feel it is one of the best and I want to keep it that way" (Keith 2003:25). Another study looked at volunteering among residents in low-income neighborhoods in Washington, D.C. Respondents were asked about their sense of community via questions assessing the degree of emotional connection with the neighborhood ("I feel connected to this neighborhood") and others focusing on shared action and spirit among residents ("If there is a problem in this neighborhood, residents will work together to get it solved"). Volunteers expressed stronger attachment to their community than non-volunteers (Zeldin and Topitzes 2002).[1]

It is popularly believed that people who live in rural areas, and particularly those who make their living off the land, are more attached to the communities in which they live and feel they have more of a "stake" in maintaining its social institutions, especially if they own farms and intend to pass those farms to the next generation. An Iowa study found that rural residents who were either currently operating farms or were from farm families (even though they were no longer farming) were more involved in the civic life of their community than were those with no direct ties to the land (Elder and Conger 2000:333). In another study, of elderly Iowa residents, respondents were asked to describe their level of involvement in local improvement activities and events and their attitudes toward their community (e.g., "Some people care a lot about feeling part of the community in which they live. For others, the community is not important. How important is it to you to feel part of the community?") (Liu and Besser 2003:355). Attachment to place explained 23 percent of the variation in volunteering, compared to 6 percent of the variation explained by education, family income, gender, and age combined.

In summary, volunteers are more attached to place than non-volunteers. Based on the studies we have reviewed, we cannot be sure that volunteering is the result of attachment because it might be the case that volunteer work makes people change their attitude toward where they live. In addition, it is quite plausible that volunteers—who are likely to be people who have a history of being active in their community—seek out places they think they will care about when they move. One study found that volunteers were more likely to say they looked for places to live that would be "good places to raise children" and where people seemed to know one another (Profile of Illinois 2001).

The Neighborhood

Ecological factors, which typically describe populations, are measured objectively and do not refer to the actor's perception of community. In this section we will review research where some objective measure of neighborhood characteristics has been linked to volunteering. Although the main goal of this part of the chapter is to ascertain the influence of ecological factors on volunteering we include a discussion of measures of home ownership and residential duration at the individual level because it is necessary to control for this variation when estimating the effects of ecological factors.

After some years of neglect, researching the influence of neighborhood characteristics on individual behaviors "has become something of a cottage industry in the social sciences" (Sampson et al. 2002:444). Much of this research focuses on the influence of poor neighborhood conditions, such as high unemployment and high residential turnover, on a variety of "problem behaviors" such as adolescent delinquency, teenage childbearing, school truancy, crime, and poor health. In their pre-occupation with the negative behavioral consequences of neighborhood social conditions, social scientists have largely overlooked the influence of neighborhood conditions on prosocial behavior such as volunteering. And yet there is every reason to believe that good as well as bad behavior is shaped by locality. Volunteer work is mainly a local phenomenon: most people travel only short distances to do their volunteer work and they contribute their services to local organizations, even if those organizations have a national presence; most volunteer work targets local problems, even if those problems are also found elsewhere; and most people decide to volunteer in response to a personal invitation from someone they know or in response to a call from an organization to which they belong or whose members they know. Unlike charitable donations of money, unpaid work is likely to be carried out close to home.

In this section we examine the proposition that people are less likely to volunteer if they live in a neighborhood that is run down, in the sense of having poor facilities, few safe public spaces, and high incidence of "problem behaviors." Without physical inspection of neighborhoods it is not possible to measure the extent to which neighborhoods are "run down" but Sampson et al. (2002:446) have concluded that among the more "durable correlates" of problem behaviors are low rates of home ownership and residential instability. We therefore treat these as proxy measures of neighborhood condition. Volunteer rates should be lower where few people own their own home and there is high residential turnover among the residents of the neighborhood. In what follows, we will first review the evidence connecting home ownership and duration of residence to volunteering at the individual level and we will then look at the ecological effects of these two variables, whether the rate of home ownership or the level of residential stability of the neighborhood have any influence on volunteering regardless of the individual characteristics of the people living in those neighborhoods.

Tenure Status

In a recent poll, nearly nine out of ten Americans agreed that people who own their own homes are more likely to be involved in community organizations and local government than people who rent (Homeownership Alliance 2004). Politicians frequently tout higher rates of civic engagement as one of the benefits of policies favoring private over public housing (DiPasquale and Glaeser 1999:355; Haurin et al. 2003:119). Although a noted researcher in this area (Saunders 1990) has argued that home ownership encourages volunteering because of its psychic benefits—home owners feel more secure—it is far more likely that home owners volunteer for financial reasons. Most people buy their homes because they want to save rent money. They also think a house is a good economic investment, albeit one that has the unique characteristic of being highly dependent on its surroundings for its value. For people to protect their investment in their homes, they must care about the quality of their neighborhood and its social institutions, and particularly its schools. Volunteering by home owners is thus a form of "enlightened self-interest" because they have a greater financial stake in the welfare of their community than renters (Wolpert 1999:240). A home owner might volunteer in connection with the neighborhood school even though she has no children of school age because a good school means good property values. In addition, home owners face higher transaction costs associated with moving than renters and thus have a stronger incentive to join neighborhood and community associations working to maintain the physical and social condition of the neighborhood (Rohe et al. 2000:24). Flight is more costly than fight.

The link between tenure status and civic engagement has been confirmed in numerous studies. Home owners are more likely than renters to be aware of local affairs, members of church and community organizations, involved in community political activities, attend a city council or board meeting, communicate with public officials, work with others to remedy local problems, work on a petition drive, and join neighborhood watch organizations (Blum and Kingston 1984; Cox 1982; Gilderbloom and Markham 1995: 1589; Greenberg 2001; Kingston et al. 1984:142; Profile of Illinois 2001; Ramakrishnan and Baldassare 2004:39; Rossi and Weber 1996:24). The impressive consensus shown in these studies conceals some unresolved problems. None of the studies distinguishes between different types of civic engagement, despite the probability that home owners are more likely than renters to volunteer for neighborhood and block associations, and school, civic, and public safety organizations, where their property interests are served, than for other organizations (e.g., international) that are unconcerned with local issues. None of the studies considers whether social conditions, such as the rate of poverty in the neighborhood, moderate the influence of home ownership on volunteering (Rohe and Basolo 1997). And only a few studies control for length of residence in the community, a crucial flaw considering that length of residence and home ownership are likely to be highly correlated.

We analyzed the Independent Sector data to test the hypothesis that volunteers are more likely to be home owners than non-volunteers. At the zero-order level, 53 percent of home owners had volunteered in the past year, compared to 39 percent of the renters. [76] In the past month, 40 percent of home owners had volunteered, compared to 27 percent of the renters. [34] The difference in monthly rates was found across all types of volunteering, but was most pronounced in the case of religious and educational volunteering. Home owners also volunteered for more activities than renters. [34] Regardless of race, age, gender, education, income, marital status, parental status, and church attendance, home owners were more likely to volunteer than renters, although with these controls tenure status made no difference in the case of volunteering for human services, environmentalism, political organizations, youth development, foundations, and international, nor did it make any difference to the number of hours volunteered. [20, 40]

We were not able to test the hypothesis that the gap in volunteering between home owners and renters is due to the greater financial stake of home owners in the community because we have no data on the economic value of the homes that are owned, but we are able to test a sociological theory, which is that home owners are more integrated into the social life of their community and this, in turn, increases the chances they will volunteer. Regardless of socio-economic differences, home owners attend church more frequently and belong to more voluntary associations than renters. [33] Undoubtedly, this helps explain why they volunteer more. Home owners are also more likely than renters to be recruited to do volunteer work: half of the home owners had been asked to volunteer, compared to a third of the renters. [67] Regardless of race, gender, age, education, income, marital and parental status, employment status, and church attendance, home owners were more likely to be asked to volunteer. Indeed, once being asked was entered into the model the effect of home ownership disappeared. [64] One reason they were more likely to have been asked is that they belonged to more voluntary associations.[2]

Duration of Residence

The longer people have lived in a community, the more people they know there and the more time they have had to develop bonds of affiliation, obligation, and reciprocity within the community. Newcomers are less likely to know their neighbors "and this lack of acquaintance with others also prevents mobilizers knowing the newcomers, excluding them from mobilization efforts" (Bowers 2004:527). People who have lived in their community for a long while tend to have more favorable attitudes toward it, in part because those with less positive attitudes have moved away (Sampson 1991:45). This is why we would expect long-term residents to volunteer at a higher rate than newcomers, because they are more attached to their community. One study found that people who expected to move in the next five years were 20–25 percent less likely to volunteer (Putnam 2000:204). But we have already demonstrated that home owners are more likely to volunteer than renters and home owners are less mobile than renters and it is therefore important to take the relationship between these two factors into consideration. In all likelihood, home owners are less mobile than renters because of the higher transaction costs of moving (Dietz 2003:12). We should therefore regard home ownership as one cause of duration of residence. In multivariate models including both variables, the effect of length of residence might well cancel out the effect of home ownership because of their high correlation. However, because "home ownership causes stability" it should be "credited" with its subsequent impact on volunteering (Dietz and Haurin 2003:403).

Numerous studies have demonstrated that long-time residents are more likely to volunteer than newcomers (Haezewindt 2002:24; Krishnamurthy et al. 2001:5; Perkins et al. 1996:103; Ravanera et al. 2002; Smith 1998:26; Thompson 1993a, 1993b; Wuthnow 2004:134). Most studies ignore the possibility that the influence of residence might vary by type of activity. Segal and Weisbrod (2002:436) found that being new to the community (less than two years) was associated with volunteering 1.3–1.6 fewer hours per month to health and religious organizations, but it had no effect on volunteering in connection with educational organizations.[3] Newcomers do not wait to get involved in schools. This interpretation is supported by a recent study of the social transformation of rural areas as suburban and city dwellers move out into agrarian communities, in which length of residence was positively correlated with involvement in community activities. Newcomers to the area were less involved in volunteer work, the one exception being volunteering in connection with schools. Many of them had moved out of the city precisely to find better educational opportunities for their children (Salamon 2003:123).

For the purposes of singling out the influence of length of residence on volunteering, each of these studies is flawed in one way or another: some are based on small samples; some report only zero-order effects; some do not measure volunteer work precisely; and none control for home ownership. There are three exceptions to these criticisms because they control for possible spuriousness in their analyses. The first study pooled GSS data from 1972–1994. Home owners were more likely to volunteer than renters, thus replicating the results of the earlier studies.[4] But when the authors controlled for how long respondents had lived in their community, the effect of home ownership on volunteering fell by 63 percent. In other words, home owners volunteer more mainly because they have lived in the community longer (DiPasquale and Glaeser 1999:355). DiPasquale and Glaeser (1999:379) used German data to replicate this analysis in a different country. In this case, the measure of length of residence was living at the same address. Respondents were asked, "How often do you volunteer in civic associations, civic groups, or other social services?" Nine percent of the renters and 16.5 percent of the home owners were volunteers. With controls for number of children, age, immigrant status, gender, marital status, education, income, region, and neighborhood, home owners were more likely to volunteer than renters. Once again, introducing a control for length of residence weakened the tenure status effect but did not eliminate it.

In our analysis of the Independent Sector data, the longer respondents had lived in their community, the more likely they were to volunteer: 30 percent of those who had lived in the community for less than two years had volunteered in the past month, compared to 40 percent of those who had lived in the community between five and nine years. [34] The correlation between home ownership and length of residence was quite high ($r = .33$). In our multivariate analysis we confirmed the positive effect of home ownership by first estimating a model with only that variable (plus controls) in the model. We then entered length of residence into the model. This coefficient was not significant and the coefficient for home ownership was unchanged. We conclude from this that the effect of length of residence is entirely due to the fact that long-term residents are more likely to own their homes than rent. [92] This provides more support to the investment theory than the social integration theory, but we also found that the longer a person had lived in the community, the stronger was the positive effect of home ownership, suggesting that home ownership becomes more important to us the longer we stay in the community. [77]

Ecological Effects

Tenure status and duration of residence are individual attributes. An ecological theory predicts that the *rate* of home ownership in a neighborhood has a positive effect on individual volunteering, regardless of the individual's own tenure status, and that the residential stability of a neighborhood has a positive effect on individual volunteering, regardless of how long the individual has lived there. There are two reasons for expecting ecological effects on volunteering. The first is that people who live in neighborhoods with high home ownership rates are surrounded by people who care a lot about the condition of their home because they own it. If our neighbors care about the upkeep of their homes we are encouraged to do likewise. Conversely, neighbors who let their property deteriorate discourage us from caring about our own (Rohe et al. 2000:20). The second is that a neighborhood populated by home owners is more stable than a neighborhood populated by renters, because home owners are less mobile than renters. Stable neighborhoods have higher rates of civic engagement (Haurin et al. 2003:123; Putnam 2000; Rohe et al. 2000:20). Communities with low residential turnover have an easier time reinforcing community networks and norms of reciprocity, which, in turn, encourage volunteerism (Eckstein 2001:845).[5]

Unfortunately, research on the influence of rates of home ownership and neighborhood stability is scarce because social surveys do not provide information on the neighborhood in which respondents live. An Iowa study found that residents living in stable communities were more likely to have engaged in a community involvement project last year (Rice and Steele 2001:398). Another study found that people living in more stable neighborhoods were more likely to have gotten together with other people to talk about the community's needs and to work with others to bring about change in their community, regardless of how long they had lived in the community themselves, but it did not consider the role of home ownership (Kang and Kwak 2003:92). Given the probable influence of neighborhood stability on volunteering, this is an issue deserving of more attention from researchers.

Economic Deprivation

Because much volunteer work is directed at providing services to those in need, it could be argued that deprived neighborhoods should have *higher* rates of volunteerism because the demand is higher. However, the weight of the evidence seems to support the counterargument, that poor neighborhoods spawn little volunteer activity. Communities in which many people are poor are unlikely to be able to sustain the infrastructure that makes associational life possible, such as buildings in which to meet and safe and lighted streets, and lack the "critical mass" of able willing people. The National Statistics Office in the United Kingdom has developed an "Index of Multiple Deprivation" that measures the level of deprivation in a ward (an election district) along a number of dimensions, including income, employment, health, education, and housing. The more deprived the community, the lower the rate of volunteering in that community, where volunteering is measured by active involvement in local organizations (Coulthard et al. 2002:9). Another study, using the same index, found that people living in deprived neighborhoods volunteered at half the rate of people living in less deprived neighborhoods (Prime et al. 2002:7).

Atkins and Hart (2003) found that the type of neighborhood in which they lived was one of the best predictors of whether or not school children in sixth through twelfth grade had done volunteer work not connected with their school in the past year. Controlling for race, sex, age, parent's educational attainment, and urbanicity, youth living in high poverty neighborhoods were less likely to have volunteered. Unfortunately, the mechanism linking community poverty with fewer memberships, independent of the individual's own level of poverty, is unclear. It could be lack of social resources, in the form of institutions serving the neighborhood, such as congregations and voluntary associations, or it could be a higher degree of social disorganization normally associated with poorer neighborhoods, such as broken families, a higher proportion of renters, more crime, and disorder in general. Two other studies have found that rates of volunteering are lower among residents of low-income neighborhoods but the samples in each case were restricted to special populations (adolescents and church members) and no controls were imposed for either home ownership rate or residential stability (Nolin et al. 1997:13; Wuthnow 2004:135). It is not clear at this time whether economic deprivation influences volunteering beyond its association with tenure status and stability and, if it does, what is the mechanism linking neighborhood poverty and volunteering.[6]

Problem Neighborhoods

Poor neighborhoods tend to be "problem" neighborhoods in that they have higher rates of social disorder and higher crime rates. When the social environment is risky, threatening or treacherous to navigate, one's sense of social responsibility is unlikely to extend beyond one's own family or circle of friends. Some people say they do not volunteer because they do not feel they belong in their community, or the community is not welcoming (Profile of Illinois 2001). People who have negative feelings about their community are less likely to feel responsible for taking care of it. In a comparison of a number of neighborhoods in the United Kingdom, Campbell and Wood (1999:127) noted that a fight outside a public house in the community

had . . . received widespread media attention. Negative reporting had a dampening effect on community morale, and people repeatedly said how dispiriting they found living in a place with a negative reputation. This undermined a sense of positive local identity, and made people less likely to be enthusiastic about community action.

A survey conducted in the United Kingdom found that people who live in neighborhoods with which they were comfortable were more likely to volunteer. In this survey, respondents were asked about the benefits and costs of living in their neighborhood. A "facilities" score measured respondent's satisfaction with community services, such as local health care and garbage collection. A "problems" score counted the number of problems the respondent saw in the neighborhood (e.g., crime, traffic congestion). The survey used a composite measure of social engagement in the community that included volunteer work to see how active residents were in community affairs. More of the socially engaged said they enjoyed living in their community (Coulthard et al. 2002:112). The unengaged were much more likely to say they lived in a community with few facilities. Another survey in the United Kingdom found a strong link between respondents' attitudes toward their local areas as a place to live and their involvement in volunteering. For example, half of those who said their neighborhood was a "very good place to live" were currently volunteering, compared to 31 percent of those who said it was "not at all a good place to live" (Smith 1998:37). In the United States, parents who rated their neighborhood as more safe than most were more likely to have done volunteer work for neighborhood schools (Wuthnow 1998:114).

Another study, focusing on people volunteering in connection with neighborhood organizations in three U.S. cities, yielded more mixed results. In Salt Lake City the organizations were community councils; in Baltimore they were neighborhood associations; in New York they were block associations. Their common goals were dealing with shared community problems, such as crime, youth gangs, graffiti, traffic, parking, and the condition of parks. Surveys administered to community residents included various questions about block and neighborhood physical and social problems. They were also asked if they had attended a meeting of a local community improvement voluntary association or done any work for such an organization. Quite independently, trained observers were sent into the communities to rate blocks by their "defensible space" (i.e., outdoor lighting, fencing in good repair, narrowness of streets) and their "incivilities" (i.e., litter, graffiti, run-down property). At the individual level (i.e., the respondent's own rating of the neighborhood) defensible space was unrelated to community activism. Surprisingly, in New York incivilities had a positive effect: the more incivilities in the neighborhood the more likely were people to be active in that neighborhood. What about the effect of neighborhood as rated by the objective observer? In this case there was no incivilities effect in any of the three cities. However, defensible space was positively related to activism in Baltimore and negatively related in New York. That is, in Baltimore, defensible spaces mobilized people to protect them; in New York, it seems, the absence of defensible space mobilized people to protest. This rather confusing set of results prevents us from drawing firm conclusions about the effect of neighborhood problems on volunteering. However, there is sufficient evidence here to suggest the utility of more research in this area. We should not always assume that neighborhood problems suppress volunteer activity: in the New York case, it seems as if they spurred people to action (Perkins et al. 1996).

In the Americans' Changing Lives survey, interviewers are asked to assign a score to the "neighborhood condition" of the respondent, as measured by level of maintenance of structures, yards and sidewalks in the neighborhood. This measure is very similar to the "defensible space" and "incivilities" measures referred to above. At the zero-order level, people living in problem-free neighborhoods were more likely to volunteer, but after controls for a number of socio-demographic factors were imposed, people living in problem-free neighborhoods were *less* likely to do so. The zero-order level correlation was simply expressing the socio-economic level of the respondent (Musick et al. 2000). In short, the worse the condition of the neighborhood in which people lived, the more likely they were to volunteer. This finding was replicated in a study of residents of Philadelphia and its surrounding suburbs without, however, the socio-economic controls. They were asked how much they volunteered and they were also invited to express their opinion about the severity of problems in their neighborhood, such as drug dealing and run-down or abandoned buildings. The more problems the resident reported, the more likely was he or she to volunteer (Kohut 1997:54). Once again, neighborhood problems can stimulate volunteer activity as well as stifle it. Another study found that women were less likely to volunteer if they felt unsafe in their community, but men were *more* likely to volunteer, suggesting not only that insecurity was a deterrent for women but that men were mobilized to do volunteer work by perceived public safety needs in the community (Caiazza and Hartmann 2001).

Social Homogeneity

According to the principle of homophily, "individuals prefer to interact with others who are similar to themselves in terms of income, race, or ethnicity" (Alesina and Ferrara 2000:850). According to this theory, the propensity to form clubs and be active in them is a function of the degree of social similarity in the population. This theory adds another dimension to the study of neighborhood effects. In addition to tenure status, residential stability, crime rate, and economic deprivation, neighborhoods vary in their degree of heterogeneity. Of course, these dimensions are likely to be correlated: communities with very high rates of home ownership are likely to be socially homogeneous. The effect of social heterogeneity has not received a lot of attention from social scientists seeking to understand why rates of volunteering vary from one community to another. One study looked at the consequences of racial heterogeneity. Regardless of their socio-economic position, people living in predominantly Black neighborhoods were more likely to volunteer for neighborhood associations and crime-watch organizations than people living in mixed or predominantly White neighborhoods. However, people living in predominantly White neighborhoods were more likely to volunteer for issue-based organizations and social and service organizations than people living in mixed or predominantly Black neighborhoods. In this case, social homogeneity did have a positive effect on volunteering, but the type of homogeneity made a difference to the kind of volunteer work people chose to do. Each race seemed to be able to set its own agenda (Portney and Berry 1997).

Neighborliness

Up to this point we have focused mainly on demographic measurements of neighborhood characteristics, but the word "neighborhood" suggests that people living in adjacent dwellings actually know each other: they are neighbors. In reality, neighborhoods vary a lot in the extent to which people living close to each other: have frequent and rewarding relations with each other; are expected to look out for or take care of unattended children; and feel responsible for the upkeep of public spaces such as streets and parks. We have no way of measuring actual neighborhoods for their level of neighborliness, but some surveys have asked individuals about their contact with their neighbors, and this information can be used to see if more neighborly people, or people who perceive others around them as being neighborly, are more likely to volunteer. Perkins et al. (1996:97) developed a measure of "neighboring" (e.g., watching a neighbor's home while they were away, lending a neighbor food or a tool, visiting with the neighbors, and discussing a neighborhood problem with a neighbor). Neighboring was a positively related to volunteering for block associations. In addition, residents who said they knew who their neighbors were, or felt a sense of attachment to their community or block, were more likely to volunteer.

In conclusion, the influence of neighborhood characteristics on volunteering has received insufficient attention from social scientists. Nevertheless, there is enough evidence to indicate that this would be a fruitful line of research in the future. Neighborhoods are important not only because they represent supra-individual influences on volunteering but also because they promise to help explain some of the socio-demographic differences in volunteering frequently observed. A good example of this is the influence of race on volunteering because residential segregation between Blacks and Whites in the United States remains high. The communities in which most Blacks live have fewer resources than those in which Whites live. Even outside the inner city, there are differences in the neighborhoods in which Blacks live that might lead us to expect them to volunteer less. Whites live in census tracts with higher average incomes and rates of home ownership. Even suburban Blacks live in poorer suburbs than Whites. More importantly, these differences are not simply a reflection of racial differences in human capital. "Even when many other individual characteristics are controlled, blacks live in suburbs with lower incomes than do non-Hispanic Whites" (Logan and Alba 1993:264). The socio-economic status of the community, in turn, affects the rate of organizational participation by people living in the community (Sampson and Groves 1989:788). In short, Blacks, of whatever social class, are less likely than Whites to live in the kinds of communities where there are abundant opportunities for social participation. This ecological theory does not ask us to assume that Blacks and Whites are competing for the same volunteer jobs but simply that Blacks have more limited access to volunteer job opportunities. Only one study thus far has looked at a neighborhood characteristic for an explanation of racial differences in volunteering. Portney and Berry (1997) surveyed a thousand residents in each of five cities in the United States. They asked respondents about their participation in volunteer work for neighborhood associations, independent issue-based citizen organizations (e.g., housing), neighborhood watch crime organizations, and social, civic, self-help, and service organizations. Racial differences in volunteerism varied by both the type of volunteer organization and the racial composition of the neighborhood. As far as neighborhood associations were concerned, Blacks were more active than Whites only if the racial composition of the neighborhood was 51 percent or more Black. In the case of crime watch organizations, Blacks were more active than Whites only if the neighborhood was racially mixed. In the case of social, service or self-help organizations, Blacks were *less* active only if the racial composition of the neighborhood was 51 percent or more Black. In summary, being in the majority helped Blacks become more active in comparison to their White neighbors but only on behalf of neighborhood associations. This kind of study needs to be replicated, not only for race but also for other major socio-demographic variables, such as education and income.

Population Density

In the public imagination cities are hostile to social interaction while rural areas foster it. In rural communities, social solidarity is strong and norms of reciprocity well known and enforced. It is more difficult to be a "free rider" in small communities. Cities, on the other hand, are places where it is possible to hide from social pressures: social contacts are fleeting and fragile. Social responsibilities become diffused to the point that few people take them seriously. This image of urban-rural differences encourages the belief that volunteerism is more common in rural areas and small towns and is therefore associated with population density (Smith 1994:245). "Agrarian communities are horizontally connected by members' participation in a vast array of civic activities" (Salamon 2003:18). It is no coincidence that the most rapid rate of growth of voluntary associations between 1850 and 1910 was not in major urban areas but in small cities with low growth rates and relatively homogeneous populations (Gamm and Putnam 2001:200). It is easy to see why people think that city dwellers are less likely to volunteer. Cities are more socially heterogeneous and, as we have seen, heterogeneity means less volunteering. Young, single people gravitate toward cities, as do newly arrived immigrants, and native members of minority groups, all populations with relatively low volunteer rates. In addition, sparse populations provide less support for public goods, such as parks and schools, and the private market provide fewer goods and services to them—hence the greater need for volunteer labor in rural areas (Mueller 1975:332).

The growth of suburbs after World War II created an even more hostile environment for civic engagement. The urban sociologist, Lewis Mumford, believed that suburbia was nothing but "a collective effort to lead a private life" (Putnam 2000:210). Suburbanization created longer commutes to work, reducing the time people had for doing volunteer work. Even non-commuters, including homemakers and the retired, face a scarcity of volunteer opportunities in the suburbs because a critical mass of people with the necessary time is missing (Putnam 2000:213). The more recent development of exurban populations, where rural areas have been invaded by subdivisions consisting largely of highly mobile, upper middle class people who commute to nearby urban areas to work and shop and whose commitment to the area is based largely on the prospect of good schools for their children and a taste of rural life, has created an even more sterile environment for volunteerism. "Subdivision people are 'too busy' to participate in volunteer efforts that make a small town work as a connected whole" (Salamon 2003:79).

Although many sociologists dispute the contention that urbanization means loss of community; that small town or rural life is rich in neighborliness and civic activities; and that suburban sprawl has undermined the volunteer spirit, the weight of the evidence supports the argument that densely populated areas are more hostile to volunteering (Barr et al. 2004:20; Carlin 2001:812; Day and Devlin 1996:44; Gaskin and Smith 1997:30; Putnam 2000:206; Reed and Selbee 2000a:25; Soo and Gong-Soog 1998; Vaillancourt 1994:823). Our own analysis of the Independent Sector data provided partial support for this argument. The volunteer rate was only slightly lower (44%) in the central city, compared to the suburbs (49%) and rural areas (49%). [34] Indeed, the mean hours volunteered in the past month (among volunteers) was slightly higher in the central city (twenty-two) than in the suburbs (twenty) or rural areas (eighteen). [24] After controlling for socio-demographic differences among respondents and using the city as the reference category, we found no difference in the rate of volunteering between city and suburban dwellers, but people living in rural areas were more likely to volunteer. [77]

Population Density as a Moderator

One topic that has been almost totally ignored by researchers is whether population moderates the influence of other variables on volunteering. Earlier in the book we argued that individual attributes, such as education, income, occupation, free time, and health, can all be treated as resources for doing volunteer work; but we cannot assume that resources always "count" the same. We have already explored the way in which socio-economic resources contribute more to White volunteering than Black volunteering, that school age children influence mother's volunteering more than father's. The value of a resource also depends to some degree on how scarce that resource is. Barr et al. (2004) found that professionals living in rural areas were more likely to volunteer than their counterparts in urban areas, the middle age peak in volunteering was more pronounced in rural areas, and part-time work was more closely associated with volunteering in rural areas. We suspect this is due to the fact that such resources are scarcer in rural areas and people who have them are more likely to be singled out by recruiters. We investigated the idea that population density moderates the influence of other variables in the Independent Sector data. We looked at age, gender, education, income, home ownership, church attendance, and race. The positive effect of owning one's own home was stronger in the suburbs indicating, perhaps, the significance attached to property values and keeping up the neighborhood in the suburbs. Second, the positive effect of income was stronger in rural areas, suggesting that rural volunteering might be more costly to perform. [93]

Another way of thinking how location might influence volunteering is to measure not population density but population *composition*. For example, cities are relatively young: they have a higher proportion of young people living in them compared to rural areas, which are relatively old. To the extent that these compositional differences involve factors associated with volunteering, they are likely to have an effect on how many people volunteer in any given area. For example, if educational achievement is primarily a "credential" or status marker by which people are selected for volunteer jobs, then its value depends on how many other people have achieved the same level. If lawyers are pressured to do *pro bono* work on behalf of poorer people in the community, the only lawyer in town is likely to do more volunteering than a lawyer living in an area where they are many other lawyers. One study found that educational gap in volunteering was wider in rural than urban areas because highly educated people were harder to find in rural areas (Barr et al. 2004:20). We used the Independent Sector data to test this hypothesis, dividing respondents into rural, suburban, and urban residents. We found no difference in the effect of education between suburbanites and city dwellers, but the education gap in volunteering was wider in rural than urban areas. [94]

Types of Volunteering

Up to this point all volunteer work has been treated as if it were the same, but the needs, interests and resources of rural, suburban, and urban residents are likely to be different enough to shape their volunteer needs and preferences. For example, if poverty rates are higher in the city, social service volunteering should be more common there. If environmental and wildlife protection are issues of more interest to rural dwellers, volunteer work in those areas might be more popular outside the cities. If tax support for public safety and fire and rescue services is limited in rural areas, volunteering for those activities might be more common there. In short, population density might influence the type of volunteer work as well as the amount. One study found that rural volunteers were more likely to volunteer for organizations devoted to culture, arts, and recreation, whereas volunteers in urban areas were more likely to volunteer for social services organizations. Local government support for culture, arts, and recreation might well be more limited in rural areas, increasing the demand for volunteers, while in the cities the demand for services might be playing some role in shaping what kind of volunteer work is performed (Barr et al. 2004). However, we found no difference by type of volunteering in the effect of place of residence in our analysis of the Independent Sector data set: regardless of type of volunteer work, rural dwellers were more likely to volunteer. [25]

Reasons for Volunteering

Life in the country is associated in the public mind with a different style of life. Rural life is depicted as more communal, more informal, and more stable than the dynamic, impersonal, and individualistic life of the city. Whatever the accuracy of these somewhat stereotypical images, they do raise the question of whether rural people think about volunteering in a different way from city people. Wuthnow (1998:136) is one sociologist who believes that place makes a difference to why we volunteer. In his study, people living in small towns were more likely to emphasize solidary benefits and norms of reciprocity—the kinds of reasons we would associated with life in cohesive communities—whereas suburbanites were more likely to emphasize self-development—the kind of reason we would associate with a more individualistic approach to life. Another study found that Canadian volunteers living in rural areas were more likely than city dwellers to say they agreed to volunteer because their friends were volunteering; and they were more likely to say they were volunteering because a family belonged to the organization. Although much of this difference is attributable to the fact that rural Canadians tend to be older, Canadian born, and long-term residents in their community it also suggests that the motivation to express solidarity with friends and family plays a more important role in rural than urban places (Barr et al. 2004).

We tested the hypothesis that rural and urban residents have different motives for volunteering by using the questions on reasons for volunteering in the Independent Sector data, but we found only two differences. City dwellers were more likely than suburban dwellers to say they volunteered to gain a new perspective on things and cope with a personal problem. [11] This might reflect the more "modern" outlook of city dwellers, but the most significant finding from this analysis is that where people live does not make much difference to why they volunteer.

City Heterogeneity

One reason often given for why rural areas have higher rates of volunteerism than cities is they are more socially homogeneous. By extension, this means that more homogeneous cities should have higher volunteer rates. In this section we will review the evidence in support of this hypothesis. We begin with a study that does not use a measure of volunteering but of political participation, meaning voting in local elections, contacting locally elected officials, attending community board meetings, and attending meetings of voluntary associations. Participation was lowest in the most affluent cities, slightly higher in the poorest cities, and higher still in the middle-income cities: that is volunteering was more common in economically heterogeneous cities. The city-level rate appeared to be a function of the combination of demand for services and supply of people most likely to volunteer (Oliver 1999). A similar study, of attending local board meetings and meetings of voluntary associations, also found that participation was highest in middle-income cities and lowest in affluent cities. This result was interpreted as showing that cities with economically diverse population (i.e., middle-income cities) have greater competition for public resources, which stimulates political conflict and sparks interest in civic affairs (Jacobs 1999). These two studies provide quite impressive support for the theory that diversity encourages volunteering, which contradicts the argument that homogeneity is good for volunteering. But note these are not really studies of volunteering and they both focus on political activities, which tend to be more contentious. Furthermore, there are studies that suggest homogeneity *is* good for volunteering.

Rotolo (2000) found that persons living in towns with more homogeneous populations were more likely to be members of voluntary associations. The effect of racial homogeneity was stronger than the effects of educational, economic, and industrial homogeneity, but each had a positive effect on memberships. Although this study did deal with volunteer work as such, given the correlation between volunteering and voluntary association memberships, it would be surprising if the same results were not found for volunteer work. Further support is given to the homogeneity thesis by a study of racial heterogeneity, income inequality, and club memberships by metropolitan area. Racial heterogeneity indicated the probability that two randomly drawn individuals in any given metropolitan area belonged to different races: the higher the score, the more heterogeneity. People living in more economically unequal communities were less likely to join groups, as were people living in racially mixed communities. The negative effect of racial heterogeneity was confined to church groups, service groups, hobby clubs, and sports clubs, all activities in which frequent interaction with other members is likely: the homophily principle was most likely to apply to these cases. Associations with a low degree of social interaction, such as professional associations, and those appealing to more homogeneous populations in rural areas, such as farmers' groups, were not affected by the degree of racial heterogeneity in the city. Income inequality had a much more pervasive effect. It was negatively related to membership in church groups, fraternities, service groups, hobby clubs, sports clubs, youth groups, school service groups, and political groups

(Alesina and Ferrara 2000). Reviewing "at least 15 different empirical economic papers" on the consequences of community heterogeneity, Costa and Kahn (2003b:104) found "the same punch line: heterogeneity reduces civic engagement." They studied the effect of racial heterogeneity across metropolitan areas in the United States on volunteer rates, using data from the DDB Lifestyle Surveys (1975–1998). They found that, regardless of age, the greater the racial fragmentation of the metropolitan area in which people lived, the less likely they were to volunteer. In another study, using census data on metropolitan areas, they found an inverse relation between volunteering and "birthplace fragmentation," where this meant the fraction of respondents born in different regions of the world. In other words, the greater the ethnic heterogeneity of the community in which one lives, the lower the odds of volunteering. However, they found no effect for racial fragmentation with this birthplace variable in the model (Costa and Kahn 2003a).

In conclusion, the belief that volunteerism thrives in rural communities but is declining in cities might be attributed to nostalgia for a rural way of life that perhaps never existed and a fear of the anonymity of city life that is perhaps exaggerated. But the survey evidence suggests that rural dwellers *are* more likely to volunteer, although the differences are not large and rural dwellers do not volunteer more hours. Despite the existence of areas of urban blight where residents feel unsafe and where inhabitants are transient, we now know that cities contain many communities where volunteer work can thrive. Conversely, rural areas can be so thinly populated or poor they find it hard to sustain the associations that provide the infrastructure for volunteer work. Finally, the composition of the population of an area is as important as its density. The homogeneity thesis suggests a very fruitful avenue for future research using geographical units small enough to capture meaningful differences in the racial and income differences in a population.

All of the studies we have described in this section are based on cross-sectional data. If urbanization causes a decline in volunteering, it would be helpful to have some longitudinal data on this issue. Urban sprawl has aroused increasing concern in recent years, not least because of its impact on the civic life of communities. As people grow more distant from their neighbors trust within the community declines. Suburbanization and ex-urbanization have added to these concerns because they create dispersed settlements, long commute times, and encourage the development of "big box" stores. Large retail establishments such as Wal-Mart and Home Depot drive out the small businesses that often sponsor local community activities. Residence, workplace, and consumption spaces no longer overlap or are even contiguous. People work in one place, live in another, and shop in yet another. Humphries (2001) examined the impact of economic scale on various political activities, including efforts to help the community, an example of volunteering. He found that rates of political participation were no higher in communities with higher levels of independent business ownership. Nor did the average size of the retail stores in the community (measured as number of employees per establishment) have any effect. However, the percentage of community residents who commuted to work outside the locality did have a negative effect on the likelihood of working in a political campaign—although there was no effect on working on community problems. Interestingly, time spent commuting to work had no effect on participation. Individuals living in communities with many commuters were less politically engaged because those were also communities in which rates of participation in voluntary organizations were lower and interaction with neighbors was uncommon.

It is fitting to end this section on ecological effects as measured by population density on this note: as far as volunteering is concerned, it does not matter whether you spend a lot of time commuting, but does matter if most of the people in your neighborhood spend a lot of time commuting. The "new urbanism" movement of recent years calls for "smart growth" to encourage the development of "sustainable" and "livable" communities built to a human scale where people once again live, work, and shop in the same community. One of the many purported virtues of this kind of community is that civic life would be healthy and vibrant. Salamon (2003:178) believes the most conducive environment for volunteering is a mixed-use community: "Coherent, organic small communities are those that sustain some productive work, shopping, different classes of residents, well-used public spaces, and houses clustered on streets with sidewalks." Stable communities of this kind share lifestyles and community norms, spawning a wide array of civic activities and higher rates of volunteerism. It remains to be seen whether the new urbanism movement will gain enough ground to provide a foundation for volunteer work.

Provinces and States

In this section we review the research on regional differences in volunteering. We focus on Canada and the United States because those countries have gathered the data necessary for analysis.

Canada is administratively divided into provinces, amongst which there are wide variations in volunteerism. The rates for 2000 were as follows (Hall et al. 2001):

Saskatchewan	42%
Alberta	39%
Prince Edward Island	37%
Manitoba	36%
Nova Scotia	34%
Newfoundland	31%
New Brunswick	29%

British Columbia	26%
Ontario	25%
Quebec	19%

Interestingly, two opposing theories have been put forward to explain the low rate of volunteering in Quebec. Vaillancourt (1994:823) argues that fewer people volunteer in Quebec because it is a relatively homogeneous region, as measured by language, ethnicity, and religion. Social and political homogeneity means more agreement over goods and services the public sector should provide and therefore less volunteer work. Arguing that homogeneity is not the same as social cohesion, Woolley (2003:169) believes quite the opposite. The Quebecois have a strong but divided sense of identity: some identify as French, others as Canadians. This polarization means trust is low, which discourages volunteering. There are fewer volunteers in Quebec, not because it is a very cohesive society but because it is a deeply polarized society. Woolley (2003:170) also points out that the high-voluntarism provinces, such as Saskatchewan and Alberta, have large Protestant majorities, whereas Quebec is strongly Catholic. Day and Devlin (1996:50) believe that regional variations in volunteering can be partly explained by the performance of provincial governments. Their analysis of 1987 Canadian survey data found a positive correlation between government expenditures in a province and the rate of volunteering. The implication is that if the government lowers expenditures there will be a reduction in volunteer work. Disaggregating government expenditure by type revealed that some spending programs increased volunteering (e.g., on recreation and culture) while others decreased it (e.g., social services). This study points to a flaw in Vaillancourt's argument, which assumes that public spending reduces the demand for volunteer workers.

In the United States, the equivalent of a province is a state. We analyzed the 2003 Current Population Survey (CPS) data on volunteering to measure the degree of inter-state variation in rates of volunteering. We found wide variations in the rate of any volunteering between the states, ranging from almost half (49.8%) of the residents of Utah to 21.3 percent of the residents of Nevada. The complete list of states showing the percentage of the population who volunteered in the past twelve months, who had volunteered only for religious organizations, only for secular organizations, or for both types of organization is to be found in Table 5. We should note, however, that the intensity of volunteering (the median number of hours contributed by each volunteer) does not correspond closely with these rankings. Utah has the most volunteers per capita and those volunteers contribute the most hours (ninety-six), but Nevadan volunteers, although they make up a smaller proportion of the population of their state, rank sixth in the number of hours each of them contributes (fifty-six). Conversely, Nebraskans rank second in the number of volunteers per capita but forty-seventh in the number of hours each of them contributes (forty-four). Indeed, North and South Dakota,

Table 5. Percentages of Respondents Volunteering for Religious and Secular Groups by State.

State	Religious or Secular	Religious Only	Secular Only	Religious and Secular
Utah	49.88%	23.02%	12.92%	13.23%
Nebraska	43.24%	11.43%	19.27%	10.75%
Iowa	40.33%	10.91%	19.52%	9.32%
Minnesota	40.24%	10.82%	20.00%	8.15%
North Dakota	40.01%	11.98%	17.40%	9.77%
South Dakota	39.72%	11.99%	18.18%	8.37%
Wyoming	39.46%	6.56%	25.60%	6.42%
Alaska	39.39%	7.79%	25.65%	4.35%
Vermont	38.48%	4.12%	28.42%	4.40%
Montana	38.33%	5.99%	25.98%	5.09%
Washington	37.67%	8.92%	22.45%	4.84%
Kansas	37.66%	9.63%	20.48%	6.89%
Wisconsin	37.19%	9.40%	20.44%	6.71%
Idaho	36.29%	12.10%	16.85%	6.13%
Maine	34.42%	5.48%	23.91%	3.76%
Colorado	33.97%	7.79%	20.83%	4.42%
Oregon	33.14%	7.39%	21.16%	3.31%
Connecticut	32.09%	6.19%	21.94%	3.25%
Indiana	31.70%	9.63%	16.78%	4.56%
Michigan	31.66%	8.63%	17.67%	4.65%
New Hampshire	31.65%	3.68%	22.37%	3.57%
Pennsylvania	31.54%	8.95%	17.00%	4.82%
Maryland	31.12%	6.57%	18.58%	4.31%
Ohio	31.06%	8.19%	17.10%	4.55%
Virginia	30.45%	8.51%	17.10%	4.16%
Missouri	30.32%	7.90%	16.40%	5.22%
Illinois	29.66%	7.89%	15.78%	4.85%
Kentucky	29.13%	9.11%	15.31%	4.18%
Dist of Columbia	28.53%	5.15%	19.05%	3.09%
Texas	28.45%	8.76%	15.10%	3.86%
Arkansas	28.07%	9.71%	14.12%	3.18%
Mississippi	28.04%	9.49%	13.75%	4.16%
New Jersey	27.81%	7.13%	16.10%	3.42%
Oklahoma	27.69%	8.67%	13.84%	4.09%
Alabama	27.69%	8.81%	13.46%	5.00%
South Carolina	27.28%	10.61%	12.94%	3.40%
Georgia	26.80%	9.09%	12.54%	3.92%
New Mexico	26.79%	7.54%	15.86%	2.13%
North Carolina	26.25%	9.56%	11.51%	4.33%
Massachusetts	25.92%	5.64%	16.10%	2.87%
Tennessee	25.66%	9.51%	11.31%	3.93%

(continued)

Table 5. *(Continued)*

State	Religious or Secular	Religious Only	Secular Only	Religious and Secular
Delaware	25.53%	6.30%	16.47%	2.21%
Florida	25.43%	7.49%	14.22%	2.57%
California	25.04%	6.21%	15.56%	2.24%
Hawaii	24.85%	5.34%	16.85%	2.09%
Arizona	24.61%	7.41%	14.81%	1.77%
West Virginia	23.77%	6.31%	12.96%	3.36%
New York	23.30%	5.29%	14.66%	2.34%
Rhode Island	23.17%	5.03%	15.27%	1.83%
Louisiana	23.06%	8.76%	11.44%	2.21%
Nevada	21.30%	5.54%	12.49%	2.85%

Iowa, and Minnesota would all be considered high volunteer states by the per capita measure but the intensity of volunteering in those states is relatively low as measured by median hours contributed (Corporation for National and Community Service 2006).

The reasons for these state variations are not clear at this time. Undoubtedly they have something to do with the composition of the population in the state. For example, Knack (2002:781) found that high volunteer states tend to have higher proportion of the population with high school diplomas or above. He found no association between level of income inequality and volunteering, but others think this is part of the explanation. Alesina and Ferrara (2000:850) argue that, because "individuals prefer to interact with others who are similar to themselves in terms of income, race, or ethnicity," states high in social homogeneity will have higher volunteer rates. Although Knack (2002) found no effect for income inequality, he did find that states with high volunteer rates were more racially homogeneous.[7]

Another possible explanation for state and regional differences in volunteering is variations in the levels of trust people have in one another. As we saw in chapter 3, trusting people are more likely to volunteer. According to the General Social Survey, trust levels tend to be higher in the West North Central Region of the country, where there are many Nordic and German immigrants, followed by New England (where many share a British ancestry), and the Mountain states, and tend to be lower in the Southern states, which have larger shares of African Americans, who are typically less trusting than Whites (Uslaner 2006:14).[8] Uslaner and Brown (2005) believe that the link between economic inequality and volunteering at the state level is the level of trust in the state.[9] They find that aggregate trust is a strong predictor of the share of people in a state who give their time in volunteering. They find no direct effect of income inequality on volunteering but an indirect effect "through" trust. In short, high levels of inequality undermine people's trust in each other and this in turn discourages volunteering. Note that these are aggregate level analyses: as the authors acknowledge, we can say nothing about the effect *on individuals* of state-level characteristics. For that, we need to turn to multi-level models.

Using the CPS data, we tested for the effects of two kinds of homogeneity—income and race—on volunteer rates, using logistic mixed models to estimate the effects of state-level variables on rates of volunteering, holding individual-level demographic variables constant. Because racial and income heterogeneity are highly correlated we estimated separate models.[10] In the model predicting any volunteering, income inequality was negatively related to the rate of volunteering: the greater the income inequality in a state, the lower the rate of volunteering. We arrived at the same result when racial heterogeneity was substituted for income inequality: the more racially heterogeneous a state, the lower its rate of volunteering. [95] The influence of income and race heterogeneity on volunteering did not vary by domain of volunteering, with one exception: racial heterogeneity did not affect religious volunteering. Thus we find fairly solid support for the homogeneity argument.[11]

Urban Density

We have already noted that large urban places are less congenial to communal life in general, including volunteering. This raises the possibility that more rural states have higher volunteer rates, regardless of the individual characteristics of the residents of those states. It is quite noticeable that, in the state rankings we reported earlier, the more sparsely settled states of the upper Mid-West have high volunteer rates. We used census data on state populations to examine the relation between a state's level of urbanization and its rate of volunteering.[12] Controlling for individual level socio-demographic variables, states ranking high in urban density had lower volunteer rates. [96] Population density therefore has both individual and ecological effects. Even people who do not themselves live in the city will volunteer less if they live in a state where most people live in the city.

Religious Composition

Up to this point we have focused on structural reasons for inter-state differences in volunteering but culture cannot be ignored. In a previous chapter we demonstrated that mainline Protestants volunteer at a higher rate than other denominational groups. Earlier in this section we noted that some of the variation in volunteering from one Canadian province is due to religious differences. If members of a particular religious affiliation have settled in states in disproportionate numbers, this might help account for variations in volunteering. Using data on religious memberships in the United States, we created three variables: the number of adherents of mainline Protestant denominations per thousand in the state; the number of adherents of evangelical Protestant denominations per thousand in the state; and the number of Catholics per thousand in the state. Because these data do not include counts of predominantly Black denominations, we controlled for racial heterogeneity in the mixed models we estimated. We found that states with majority mainline Protestant populations had higher volunteer rates and conversely states with high proportions of evangelical Protestants and Catholics had lower volunteer rates. However, with census data, we are unable to control for individual-level denominational affiliation, and we cannot be sure that the religious composition of state would make a difference to the individual's chances of volunteering, regardless of his or her own religious affiliation. Finally, we tested for the effects of religious composition on religious-only volunteering. Once more we found a positive effect for number of mainline Protestants per one thousand in the population and a negative effect for Catholics, but effect of the proportion of evangelical Protestants was the same as that of mainline Protestants—a reminder that conservative Protestants do volunteer in high numbers for work in connection with their church. [97]

Domains of Volunteering

For both structural and cultural reasons, states are likely to foster different kinds of volunteer work. To explore this issue, we disaggregated volunteer work into five broad domains (advocacy, human development, education, social services, and religion) to see if volunteer preferences vary by state. We found that state rankings varied somewhat depending on the domain. Thus, Utah was the top-ranked state overall and the top-ranked for religion, but ranked seventeenth for social services and twelfth for education and human development volunteering. A group of states was conspicuous for ranking high overall but lower on religious volunteering: Wyoming, Alaska, Vermont, and Montana. Many of the "Bible Belt" states ranked low overall but relatively high in religious volunteering: Kentucky, Tennessee, Mississippi, Alabama, South Carolina, and North Carolina. [98] However, we should note that, of the top ten states in religious volunteering, six were also in the top ten overall, evidence of the popularity of religious volunteering in the nation as a whole.

We then sorted respondents into those who volunteered in connection with a religious organization only, those who volunteered in connection with a secular organization only, and those who volunteered in connection with both. [99] For example, in Utah (the top-ranked state overall) 23.2 percent volunteered only in connection with a religious organization, 12.9 percent volunteered only in connection with a secular organization, and 13.2 percent volunteered in connection with both. This contrasts with Maine, where 5.4 percent were religious volunteers, 23.9 percent were secular volunteers, and 3.8 percent were both. In other words, the distribution of volunteer effort across sacred and secular activities varies from one state to the other.[13]

Conclusion

In a shrinking world, where even national differences are believed to be disappearing under the influence of globalization, the idea that there are regional differences within countries in everyday practices such as doing volunteer work is somewhat surprising. But in both Canada and the United States there are very large differences from one region to another in the proportion of residents who do volunteer work. Only fairly recently, with the advent of large-sample social surveys of volunteering, has the magnitude of these differences become apparent. Little is known about why these differences exist. Some theories point to demand factors: in some regions volunteer workers are busier because government spending, supporting non-profit agencies and providing social services for which people can volunteer their help, is more generous. Some theories point to supply factors: in some regions the population is comprised of more of the kind of people who typically volunteer. However, the influence of truly ecological factors on volunteering remains unclear. For example, it is true that people who live in cities are less likely to volunteer, but why should even people who live in rural areas be less likely to volunteer if the region in which they live is highly urbanized? And, although social heterogeneity seems to suppress the rate of volunteering in a region, we know little about how this works. Why would an individual living in a heterogeneous region be less likely to volunteer? How much of this is due to the scarcity of voluntary associations? How much of it is due to variations in the social networks of the residents of heterogeneous states?

16

Cross-National Differences

According to Boris (1999:1), the United States "has become the model for a robust civil society, a realm of independent citizen activity outside both government and business." Americans take such pride in their spirit of volunteerism that they regard it as a national trait setting them apart from other industrialized societies. In this chapter we will find out whether Americans are indeed more likely to volunteer than people living in other countries and whether they prefer different kinds of volunteer activities. However, our purpose is to go beyond simply describing these differences to find an explanation for them. We will think about these explanations at two levels. The first is compositional. Countries might exhibit different volunteer rates simply because their population is composed of different people. For example, we know that education predicts volunteering on a fairly consistent basis, regardless of the country in which the survey is conducted. One reason why country A has a higher volunteer rate than country B might therefore be that the proportion of highly educated people in the population is higher in country A. The second level is contextual. Context refers to a country-level measure: it describes a characteristic of a country, rather than an aggregate of individuals. For example, the level of economic development in a country might influence the rate of volunteering in that country by promoting certain values. All people living in an economically rich country will receive a "boost" from living in that country, even if they are not rich themselves. Ideally, analyses should take both of these levels into account.

Most of the studies we discuss below rely on the World Values Survey (WVS), conducted in 1981, 1991–1993, 1995–1998, and 1999–2001.[1] We base our analyses on data from fifty-eight countries providing information on volunteering in the 1999–2001 survey. The number of countries included in each analysis depends on the availability of data to measure other variables in the model. In this survey the respondents were first asked if they belonged to any of fourteen types of voluntary association and were then asked for which, if any, they were currently doing unpaid voluntary work.[2]

The WVS survey reveals wide differences in the rate of volunteering from one country to another.

0–10%: Russia, Serbia, Turkey

11–20%: Japan, Latvia, Lithuania, Ukraine, Montenegro, Northern Ireland, Poland, Portugal, Spain

21–30%: Austria, Argentina, Bosnia, Croatia, France, Italy, Luxembourg, Slovenia

31–40%: Belgium, Czech Republic, Denmark, Finland, Iceland, India, Ireland, Mexico, Moldova, Macedonia, Singapore

41–50%: Algeria, Canada, Chile, Korea, Netherlands, Peru, Puerto Rico, United Kingdom

51–60%: Albania, Philippines, South Africa, Sweden

+60%: Bangladesh, China, Tanzania, Vietnam, Zimbabwe, Uganda, United States

Considering that the survey asks respondents whether they are *currently* volunteering many of these estimates are inflated because, as we explained in chapter 2, the longer the period of time people are given to report volunteering the more will say they have done so. The WVS estimates that 43 percent of people living in the United Kingdom are currently volunteering, eleven percentage points higher than the rate for volunteering *in the past twelve months* reported by the Office of National Statistics Omnibus Survey conducted in 2001 (Haezewindt 2002:24). Another survey conducted in the same year estimated that only 26 percent of people living in England and Wales had volunteered in the past month, just over half the number the WVS reports as currently volunteering (Prime et al. 2002). In the United States, the WVS estimates that more than 64.7 percent of adult Americans are currently volunteering, whereas the Current Population Survey (CPS) special supplement on volunteering in 2003 estimated that less than half that figure (28.8%) had volunteered sometime in the past year. In Canada, the WVS reports a figure of 46.8 percent as currently volunteering compared to 27.0 percent of the population in the Canadian survey of volunteering and giving (conducted in 2000) who had volunteered at some point in the last year. The proportion currently volunteering would have been much lower than this. The estimates are also much higher than those given by the Johns Hopkins Comparative Nonprofit Sector Project (http://www.jhu.edu/~cnp/pdf/table201.pdf). For example, the WVS reports a rate of 28.1 percent for Ireland but the project reports a rate of 11 percent. The WVS reports a rate of 22.3 percent for Argentina, compared to the project's estimate of 8 percent. Although the directors of the project do not always make it clear how the volunteer rates for the countries it compares are estimated, the rates are consistently far below those reported by the WVS. These inconsistencies are rather troubling, but for our purposes the question is whether or not the figures for one country are inflated more than those of another and we have no reason to think this is the case. Our comparisons will therefore be unbiased by these measurement problems.

Explaining Cross-Country Variations in Volunteering

The comparative study of volunteer work has only just begun, in part because the necessary data have only recently become available. But this is not the only reason why scholarly work in this area is limited. Sociologists have not devoted much thought to *why* there should be any differences between countries in the proportion of people who do volunteer work. The theoretical work on national differences in volunteerism is "underdeveloped" (Curtis et al. 2001:785). In what follows, we review some of the theories proposed to explain why there are more volunteers in one country than another and assess the evidence to support these theories.

Structural Theories

The first set of theories explain variations in volunteering on the basis of structural features, such as the method of government, the size of the welfare state, the level of income or income disparity, the class structure, and the size or "carrying capacity" of the non-profit sector.

Experience with Democracy

Comparative sociologists generally assume that volunteerism cannot flourish in societies where there is no civil society, where the opportunity for free association and free discussion is limited. This is said to be the reason why few people volunteer in former communist countries, which have yet to develop a civil society (Flanagan et al. 1998:467). The same can be said for countries emerging from the grip of autocratic governments. Third sector organizations in South Korea began to flourish only with the advent of democratization in the early 1990s and when the government discovered the valuable role voluntary organizations could play in the provision of public services. Under the current more democratic regime "government support and acceptance of volunteerism is very high in Korea" (Ziemek 2003:78). Norris (2002:164) uses data on active voluntary association memberships from the 1995 WVS together with the score each country gets on a Freedom House measurement of political rights and civil liberties (an indicator of democratization) to measure the association between the two. Although the rate of volunteerism in a country was unrelated to the level of democratization in 1995, it was positively associated with the mean level of democratization between 1972 and 2000, suggesting that *stable* democracies are most conducive to volunteerism. This idea is supported by two other studies showing that years of democracy are positively related to the volunteer rate in a country (Curtis et al. 2001:80; Halman 2003:192).

Experience with democracy fosters volunteerism because it takes time to develop a vibrant and resilient "third sector" independent of the state and the market. Some scholars believe, however, that the important issue is how long a country has been deprived of democracy. If several generations have lived under non-democratic regimes they forget how to participate in civil society, how to organize themselves for the purposes of advocating a cause or meeting a need. The reason why former Soviet regimes have low volunteer rates is not simply because they are new democracies but because the people living under those regimes have never known what it is like to volunteer and organize voluntary organizations. In the Soviet system, volunteer work was organized by the state, and was compulsory. Recognizing the economic and ideological importance of having citizens do unpaid work for the state, Lenin institutionalized *subbotnicks* (later called "red Saturdays") when all Soviet citizens were expected to perform unpaid work at their workplace for no pay or did some other socially beneficial work. Volunteering was used to socialize young people into pro-communist values. During *perestroika* volunteerism declined precipitously because it was no longer mandated. In the embryonic civil society that began to emerge, truly voluntary associations were organized to express opposition to the vestiges of the totalitarian system (e.g., religious associations, environmentalist organizations) while some quasi-voluntary associations continued in association with the socialist state (e.g., professional associations). With further democratization, both of these forces have weakened. There has been a sharp decline, for instance, in the number of people working for trade unions or professional associations. The result is extremely low levels of volunteering in Eastern European societies. Despite the collapse of many of the safety-net provisions of the communist social system, few service-oriented non-profits have emerged to mobilize volunteer effort to help those in need. Significantly, the steepest rise in recent levels of volunteerism in Eastern Europe has occurred in countries most advanced on the road to democracy, such as the Czech Republic and Hungary (Juknevicius and Savicka 2003).

Many years of experience of totalitarian regimes undermines generalized trust, which in turn discourages volunteering. Not knowing whom to trust, people retreat into the private sphere, into the realm of their family and closest friends or into innocuous groups promoting government-tolerated cultural and recreational activities. The effect of these experiences lingers long after the totalitarian regime has collapsed. For example, in 1995, only 22.7 percent of Hungarians agreed that people could be trusted, compared to an average of 43.0 percent for other European countries. Lack of trust might help explain the negative association between years under "central planning" and the volunteer rate found in one study of OECD countries (Raiser et al. 2001:4). Inglehart (2003:67), however, found no association between years spent under communist rule and the rate of volunteering. His sample of countries was larger (forty-nine) and he included many current and former communist countries. Thus, although the introduction of a historical perspective into these cross-country comparisons is welcome, the results are far from consistent. It is by no means clear whether either years of democracy or years of communism have much influence on current volunteering.

Political Regime

Some social scientists believe that the nature of the political regime explains much of the variation in volunteering from one country to another. In "liberal" regimes such as Britain, Canada, Ireland, Northern Ireland, and the United States, volunteerism will flourish because it is a substitute for a strong welfare state. In "social democratic" regimes such as Denmark, Finland, Iceland, the Netherlands, Sweden, and Norway volunteerism will also flourish because political and work-related groups are expected to take an active part in policy formation, and the government provides funding to many nonprofit organizations and voluntary associations. In "corporatist" regimes such as Austria, France, and Italy, the centralization of decision making narrows the scope of civil society and provides few opportunities for volunteer work. In "Eastern Bloc" countries formerly under communist rule, such as Bulgaria, East Germany, Estonia, Hungary, Latvia, Lithuania, Romania, and Russia, an undeveloped civil society leaves little room for independent volunteer work. One analysis of the WVS data found no association between rate of volunteering and regime type. The authors speculate that a control for gross domestic product (GDP) in the model has eliminated the effect of regime type because liberal and social democratic countries are wealthier and wealthier countries have higher volunteer rates (Curtis et al. 2001). However, in another analysis of the WVS data, controlling for the wealth of the country did *not* eliminate the effect of political regime. This study used "degree of liberal democracy" to measure the political regime, where liberal democracy was defined as freedom of group opposition, political rights, and the effectiveness of the legislative body. Country wealth was measured by the purchasing power estimation of the gross national product. Despite the inclusion of this wealth measure, together with country-level controls for education and religiosity as well as individual-level attributes, the political regime measure was statistically significant: the more liberal the regime the higher the rate of volunteering (Parboteeah et al. 2004:438).

Schofer and Fourcade-Gourinchas (2001) also theorize that political regime makes a difference to volunteer rates, but their approach draws more heavily on institutionalist theory in which the *relation* between state and society is the focus. This relation can be conceptualized in a number of ways. One is to contrast corporatist with associational societies. In the corporatist model, society is envisioned as a communal order with subsidiary elements (e.g., occupational groups, churches, the military) carrying out differentiated public roles or functions: "Because they legitimize centralized incorporation, universalism, and collective organization, corporate social institutions should increase the level of associational activity" (Schofer and Fourcade-Gourinchas 2001:815). In the associational model, society is conceived as a fellowship of members (guilds, classes, occupational groups) who come together to form society. In these societies "individuals rather than groups, are supposed to be the best judges of their own interests" and the level of associational activity will be relatively low (Schofer and Fourcade-Gourinchas 2001:814).

There are some fairly obvious problems with this argument; at least as far as volunteer work is concerned. Countries such as the United States are anti-corporatist but they have high rates of volunteerism. Catholic countries tend toward more corporatist models but they have relatively low rates of volunteerism. Rothstein (2001:207) questions the "standard assumption" in the research on corporatism that it leads to high levels of associational activity. It is just as likely, he contends, that the government's support for and collaboration with interest organizations would make an organization's elite become more professional and less responsible toward their members and that the members' activity would then drop.[3] It is no surprise that Schofer and Fourcade-Gourinchas (2001:822) found no relation between corporatism and volunteering across thirty-two countries in the WVS of 1991.

For our own analysis of the WVS data, we tested for the effects of regime using a classification system developed by Huber et al. (2004). The first category is "liberal" and consists of Canada, the United Kingdom, Ireland, and the United States. The second category is "socialist" and consists of Austria, Belgium, Denmark, Luxembourg, and Sweden. The third category is "conservative" and consists of Finland, France, Germany, Italy, Japan, Portugal, and Spain. The fourth category is "transitional democracies" and consists of Albania, Bulgaria, Croatia, Czech Republic, Estonia, Hungary, Latvia, Lithuania, Moldova, Montenegro, Poland, Romania, Russia, Serbia, Slovakia, Slovenia, and Ukraine. The rest of the countries we put into an "other" category because they received no classification by Huber et al. (2004). In our analyses we used transitional democracies as the contrast category on the assumption they would have the lowest volunteer rates. Besides looking at volunteering in the aggregate, we constructed three types of volunteer work: "service' includes social welfare, youth work, sports, health, and the arts; "advocacy" includes labor unions, professional associations, political, local community activism, third world, environment, women's groups, peace movements; and religious volunteering is treated as a separate category.

There was considerable variation within each of the regime types: among the transitional democracies, volunteer rates varied from a high of 55.8 percent in Albania to a low of 7.5 percent in Russia; among the liberal regimes, the rates varied from a high of 64.7 percent in the United States to a low of 28.4 percent in Ireland; among the socialist regimes, the volunteer rate varied from a high of 53.9 percent in Sweden to a low of 28.3 percent in Austria; and in the conservative regimes, the highest rate was 36.5 percent in Finland and the lowest was 15.6 percent in Japan. [101] In our multi-level models, we controlled for individual differences in the population in socio-demographic status and frequency of church attendance. Compared to countries undergoing the transition to democracy, countries with both liberal and socialist regimes had higher volunteer rates. The conservative countries were, however, no different from the former communist countries. We found that same pattern regardless of type of volunteer work, although the regime effect was slightly stronger in the case of advocacy. [102] In short, despite considerable volunteering heterogeneity within the regime types, there are volunteer differences between countries that correspond to regime. The lowest rates are to be found in countries that are, in many ways, at the opposite end of the spectrum. In conservative countries, volunteer work is not encouraged by the state, which has few structures for engaging volunteers. Countries undergoing the transition to democracy have few independent voluntary associations and a poorly developed civil society, with resulting low volunteer rates. Both liberal and socialist regimes have higher volunteer rates that those two types, but probably for different reasons. In the more liberal regimes, volunteer work is a substitute for government programs; in the more socialist regimes, volunteer work is an adjunct to it.

Another explanation for why liberal and socialist regimes have higher volunteer rates is that they do a better job of protecting their citizens' rights and freedoms, which in turn makes it easier to volunteer. The Freedom House is a non-profit organization that ranks countries on their political rights and civil liberties using a seven-point scale where 1 represents the most free and 7 the least free.[4] Halman (2003:192) used these rankings to examine the proposition that volunteer rates are higher in countries with more political rights and civil liberties. He found no association between a country's ranking on civil liberties and its volunteer rate, but more extensive political rights did encourage volunteerism. We used both Freedom House measures to analyze the 1999–2001 WVS data, reverse coding such that a high score indicated more rights and freedoms. Controlling for individual-level socio-demographic and religious variables, we found that the fewer political rights a country enjoyed, the *higher* its volunteer rate. There was no association between civil liberties and the volunteer rate. This rather surprising finding could be attributable to two features of countries with few political rights (e.g., China). They are countries in which "volunteer" work is mandatory (e.g., on behalf of the party). Less likely, it could be due to the fact that countries with few political rights provoke more volunteer work to gain those rights. [103]

Welfare States

During the nineteenth century, charities were organized to meet social needs largely neglected by the state and the market. Between the 1880s and 1914, many European nations, together with Australia and New Zealand, launched social spending policies now considered the core of modern welfare states, aimed mainly at providing financial security in old age and temporary benefits for unemployed workers. The Great Depression accelerated the expansion of these programs. Given that charitable organizations and welfare programs were often seeking to perform the same role, it is reasonable to suppose that, as welfare programs expanded and their coverage became more universal, the demand for volunteers would fall. Some scholars believe that countries with strong welfare states not only have less need for volunteer services but also nurture a culture that stigmatizes volunteer work as charity (Ascoli and Cnaan 1997:321; Gaskin and Smith 1997:65).

Hofer (1999:115) believes that the welfare state in Germany has crowded out volunteerism: "Community service in Germany is not a natural part of the social system, although since the economic crisis of the 1980s there has been a reduction in public assistance programs and a call for increased self-help and volunteerism." Similarly, where the welfare state shrinks, the volunteer population should grow, as appears to be happening in Australia:

> The current Australian federal government is increasingly dominated by a neo-liberal ideology, which has resulted in a fundamental shift in the approach to welfare provision. Australian welfare is being transformed from a social right to a system based on the notion that welfare recipients have a responsibility to give something in return for support . . . Unemployed young people are expected to undertake their 'mutual obligation' requiring them to perform community service in exchange for unemployment benefit. (Warburton and Smith 2003:774)

In Italy, the term "volunteer" gained wide currency only during the 1980s, coincidental with a pan-European political turn toward neo-liberal political regimes advocating a larger role for the non-profit sector in supplying social services and a smaller role for government. The percentage of the Italian population volunteering rose from 10.7 in 1983 to 15.4 in 1989—although it fell back to 13.3 by 1994 (Ascoli and Cnaan 1997:305; Marta et al. 1999:73).

The idea that the welfare state and volunteer work are substitutes for each other suggests an explanation for cross-country variations in volunteering: the larger the welfare state, the lower the volunteer rate. The problem with this theory is that there is quite a lot of evidence to suggest that welfare states encourage volunteerism. For example, the Netherlands has one of the most generous welfare states in the world and also has a relatively high rate of volunteerism (De Hart and Dekker 1999:77). Sweden not only has an extensive welfare state but also a very high rate of associational memberships, a fact that can partly be explained by the very high rate of unionism in that country. The rate of volunteering is equally high: one in three Swedes is currently serving on the board or a committee of a voluntary organization (Rothstein 2001:214). Only 11 percent of Swedes agreed that, "If the government fulfilled all of its responsibilities, there should be no need for people to do unpaid work," compared to 37 percent of Europeans as a whole (Rothstein 2001:227). Swedes see no contradiction between an extensive welfare state and volunteerism. In fact, it is highly unlikely there is any relationship between opinions on the responsibility of government and the rate of volunteering in a country. Support for the welfare state does not mean antagonism to volunteerism (Gaskin and Smith 1997:59).

Nevertheless, we should not be too hasty in drawing the conclusion that welfare states actually encourage volunteering. Ruiter and De Graaf (2006: 206) found no relation between welfare state expenditures and the rate of volunteering in the country. Lundstrom and Svedberg (2003) are skeptical that variations in the size of the voluntary sector or the number of volunteers across countries can be explained by the size of the welfare state in that country. They focus on Sweden, a country with a large welfare state and higher volunteer rates. According to a 1999 national poll, 52 percent of Swedes had volunteered for a voluntary organization some time in the past year. They note that this high level of volunteerism has a long history in Sweden. There is one difference however, and that is the domain in which volunteer work is done. In countries like the United States, the United Kingdom, and Germany, much of the volunteer work focuses on social welfare, health, and education, but in Sweden the voluntary sector is dominated by cultural and recreational pursuits as well as trade union activities. In short, the expansion of the welfare state in Sweden has not led to any cutbacks in the voluntary sector as far as overall size is concerned. However, the welfare state "did force aside and tend to swallow up voluntary involvement in its core areas: health, education and social service" (Lundstrom and Svedberg 2003:222). The fact that there never was a voluntary sector in social services independent of the state made this easier and more acceptable. In other words, cross-sectional analyses of the relation between welfare state expenditures and the volunteer rate can be misleading. Sweden would appear to support the argument that the two go together, but closer examination reveals that the high volunteer rate in Sweden is largely attributable to activities that are unconnected to the welfare state and that the volunteer rate for social services *has* been reduced by government expenditures in those areas.

Another problem with the theory that welfare states encourage volunteerism is that they assume there are only two sectors in society, the market and the state. They ignore the presence of a third sector comprised of non-profit organizations and voluntary associations. This third sector, which relies heavily on volunteer labor, is not as well institutionalized in some countries as it is in others. For example, the laws pertaining to the establishment and operation of non-profit organizations are much more elaborate in a country such as the United States. This might help explain why the volunteer rate is relatively high there. Compared to the United States few societies "have anything approaching a coherent notion of a distinct private nonprofit sector, and those that do often include entities that would be unrecognizable to American students of the subject" (Salamon and Anheier 1996:2). The United Kingdom comes closest to the American model, but the organizations of which the British third sector consists are much more heterogeneous than is the case in the United States and the boundaries around the non-profit sector are much more vaguely drawn. In countries such as Germany and France the distinction between non-profit and private sectors is even fuzzier, while in a country such as Japan "the nonprofit sector hardly functions as a distinguishable sector" (Salamon and Anheier 1999:7). The situation is even more confused in developing countries where institutions to legitimate and recognize non-governmental organizations are almost entirely lacking. And, as we have already noted, a clear concept of the non-profit sector has yet to emerge in countries formerly part of the Soviet bloc.

Because the size and composition of the non-profit sector varies so much from one country to another, there will be no straightforward relation between welfare state expenditures and volunteering. Much will depend on how the welfare state and the non-profit sector relate to each other. In "liberal" countries, low government social welfare spending is combined with a large non-profit sector. This arrangement is most prevalent where "middle class elements are clearly in the ascendance, and where opposition either from traditional landed elites or strong working class movements has either never existed or been effectively held at bay" (Salamon et al. 2000:16). In "social democratic" countries, the state spends heavily on social welfare, leaving little room for non-profit agencies to operate. In "corporatist" countries, the state has made "common cause" with non-profit institutions, which thrive under this partnership while not leaving much room for volunteer contributions. In "statist" countries, the state is strong but does not provide much in the way of social welfare and non-profit activity remains "highly constrained" by "long traditions of deference." Anglo-Saxon countries (United States, United Kingdom, Australia) come closest to the liberal model: they are reluctant welfare states that rely heavily on private philanthropy to provide social services and therefore have a sizeable volunteer presence. Nordic countries (Finland, Norway, Sweden) come closest to the social democratic model because they do not rely much on private philanthropy, although a strong historical tradition of political and economic advocacy and the recent popularity of sports and recreation associations has resulted in a sizable volunteer component. European-style welfare "partnerships" (Austria, Belgium, France, Germany, Ireland, Israel, Netherlands) come closest to the corporatist model because they channel much of their social welfare protections through private voluntary organizations. But most of the people who work in these private voluntary groups are paid employees and the volunteer labor force is small. Asian industrialized countries such as Japan and South Korea come closest to the "statist" type because they have small and passive civil societies and low volunteer rates (Salamon et al. 2003).

Salamon and Sokolowski (2003:75) used this theory to predict differences in volunteering across twenty-four countries included in the Johns Hopkins Comparative Nonprofit Sector Project. They classified volunteer activities into "expressive," aimed "mainly at the actualization of participants' aesthetic, cultural or political preferences, or social bonding," and "service," denoting "activities that have a use-value to society and its members, such as fulfilling people's needs, solving social problems, or emergency relief." Social democratic countries, such as Finland and Sweden, had relatively high levels of volunteering but mostly of the "expressive" rather than "service" volunteering. Liberal regimes (such as Australia, the United Kingdom, and the United States) and corporatist regimes (such as Spain, Belgium, France, and Germany) tended to develop more service-oriented volunteering. In short, the welfare state does influence volunteering rates but this influence is apparent only after the role of the non-profit sector is factored in and volunteer work is sorted into different categories. This analysis is promising because it does not treat all volunteer work as if it were the same, but the authors are careful to note several anomalies in their results, such as the high rate of expressive volunteering in the Netherlands (classified as a "corporatist" political regime), an exception they attribute to the "growth of progressive political activism" and the "growing popularity of sports and leisure activities" (Salamon and Sokolowski 2003:87).

Economic Development

Many of the institutional differences described in the previous sections correspond with differences in the wealth of nations. Established democracies with generous welfare states and complex legal systems tend to be more economically developed. This raises the possibility that the institutional differences are simply a reflection of differences in national incomes. Besides, we know that, at the individual level, the likelihood of volunteering rises with income. Does this mean that affluent societies have higher volunteer rates than poor societies? Some scholars believe that economic development (or industrialization) is the key to explaining national differences in volunteer because it leads to structural differentiation that in turn leads to more associational activity and volunteer work (Curtis et al. 2001:785; Salamon and Anheier 1999). Inglehart (2003:56), on the other hand, argues that "economic development is not necessarily conducive to rising rates of civic participation" because economic modernization means a shift from traditional to secular values that discourages volunteering *and* a shift from survival to self-expression values that encourages it, the net effect of which is to render economic development ineffectual.

Studies on this topic have thus far failed to establish a clear consensus on the relation between economic development and volunteering. A widely used measure of country income (GDP) is unrelated to the volunteer rate (Curtis et al. 2001; Halman 2003:192; Inglehart 2003:67; Ruiter and De Graaf 2006). Another measure—the purchasing power parity estimation of gross national product, believed to more accurately reflect relative degrees of wealth across countries—is positively related to volunteering, although the regression coefficient is only $b = 0.02$ $p < 0.01$ (Parboteeah et al. 2004:438). Norris (2002:157) confirmed that the GDP measured by purchasing power was positively correlated with volunteering across forty-six countries in the WVS—and volunteering was unrelated to a simple measure of GDP. Raiser et al. (2001:11) found that cumulative economic growth between 1989 and 1998 was positively related to volunteering only for sports and professional associations.[5]

We used a World Bank classification system that divides countries into low, lower middle, upper middle, and high gross national income categories. Using multi-level models with controls for individual-level differences, we looked at service volunteerism, advocacy volunteering, and religious volunteering separately. Only advocacy volunteering was related to gross national income and, interestingly, it was more common in low-income countries. This is surprising because we associate more developed countries with more vibrant civil societies and less developed countries with restricted political rights and opportunities (gross national income and scores on Freedom House measures of political rights are very highly correlated) and we would expect higher volunteer rates in the high-income countries for this reason. Hence our surprise that the lowest-income countries have the highest rate of advocacy volunteering. Recall, that earlier we found that the fewer political rights citizens of a country enjoy, the more of them volunteered. When we controlled for GDP the effect of political rights went away. The countries with few political rights are also poor countries. It would seem this negative effect is attributable to low income more than it is having few political rights. Since we are focusing here on advocacy volunteering, in which labor unions and professional associations are included, it would seem that poorer countries encourage more advocacy volunteering because people are trying to improve their economic conditions. Otherwise, country-level income has no effect on volunteering. [104]

Income Inequality

A large middle class is needed to support a thriving non-profit sector with donations of money and time (Curtis et al. 2001). Societies in which money is concentrated in the hands of a few, where there is no intermediary group of middle-income earners between the rich and the poor would, according to this theory, have relatively low rates of volunteerism because it is unlikely people share values and interests or can find much common ground. This is a version of the homogeneity argument we encountered before: the more similar the incomes of the members of the population the higher the rate of volunteering in that population. For example, Woolley (2003:155) combined data on income inequality from the Luxembourg Income Study with data on volunteering from the WVS and found that fewer people volunteer when the gap between rich and poor is wide. We analyzed the WVS data using as a measure of income inequality the GINI coefficient for the country as reported by Hofstede (2001). The GINI coefficient is a widely used measure of income inequality. (A high score on the index indicates extreme inequality.) We included this measure in a multi-level model with controls for a range of individual attributes, including personal income (which had a positive effect on volunteering) and, at the country level, controls for mean level of education and gross national product. We found no relationship between income inequality and volunteering. [105] This does not mean the theory about the size of the middle class is invalid. Income from wages and salaries is not a particularly good indicator of disparities in economic well-being in a country because there can be other sources of income (e.g., tax credits, welfare payments) that level the playing field. Nor is it necessarily true that disparities in income undermine the cohesiveness of a society and the willingness of its population to work together as volunteers. The United States has a very high level of income inequality but one of the highest volunteer rates in the world. In addition, income alone is probably not enough to measure the strength and size of the middle class, which is as much a social as it is an economic entity. Dayton-Johnson (2001:78) also believes that volunteerism is higher in more socially homogeneous societies, but he uses level of education to test this theory. To explain why volunteer rates are higher in the United States than Italy he cites the fact that the standard deviation of years of schooling in the United States is 2.3 years, whereas in Italy it is 3.6 years. Using WVS data from 1999–2001 on seven advanced industrialized societies, he found a cross-country correlation of $r = 0.59$ between disparity in educational achievement and voluntary activity: the more similar the educational qualifications of population, the higher the volunteer rate in that population. In other words, the shared experience of a common education was as important in encouraging volunteer work as individual educational qualifications.

Age Structure

Up to this point we have ignored the influence of demand on volunteering, but it makes sense to expect the rate of volunteering to be higher where there is a greater need for volunteer services. Countries with large numbers of dependent people (e.g., children) would, according to this demand theory, have more volunteers. A young country is one in which a small proportion of the population is elderly and the fertility rate is high. To test the hypothesis that young countries have higher volunteer rates we created a mean score for each country in the WVS combining an inverse of the fertility rate with the percentage of the society over the age of 60. Higher scores on this measure indicate a combination of lower fertility rates and higher proportion over 60, thus an "older" society. Regardless of the gross national income of the society, this variable was a strong predictor of all types of volunteering: the younger the society, the higher the volunteer rate. [106]

Ethnic Heterogeneity

In the previous chapter we demonstrated that, at the level of the metropolitan area, state, and province, homogeneity is positively related to the volunteer rate. This might also be true at the country level. One study of a number of European countries found that the volunteer rate was higher in ethnically homogeneous countries (Costa and Kahn 2003b:107). As we noted in an earlier chapter, there is a strong possibility that trust explains why homogeneity is so conducive to volunteering. The WVS asks questions on trust and "civic cooperation," measured by respondents' answers to questions asking them if a number of behaviors are "always justified, never or something in between" (e.g., cheating on taxes if you have the chance; "keeping money you have found," avoiding a fare on public transport). According to one study, ethnically heterogeneous populations tend to be less trusting and less cooperative (Knack and Keefer 1997).

Cultural Theories

Cultural theories stress the influence of dominant values, beliefs, and attitudes on rates of volunteering. Most sociologists agree there are cultural differences between countries and (with somewhat less consensus) that these cultural differences help account for differences in behavior between countries. We have already noted that volunteer work is not regarded in the same way in all parts of the world. Anglo-Saxon countries seem to take the most favorable attitude, at least compared to countries such as Germany, France, Italy, and Spain (Dalton 2002:46), but even within the Anglo-Saxon world there are cultural differences: Americans regard volunteerism as an alternative to government action on social welfare, while Canadians are more inclined to rely on the state and think of volunteer work as second best (Lipset 1985:141; Uslaner 2002b:244).

Post-Materialism

While some scholars believe that the forces of modernization (e.g., rationalization, secularization, materialism, individualism) are eroding people's commitment to the public good, others take the opposite view: "While modern men and women may be less motivated by traditional feelings of duty and obligation, their individualist ideas of self-realization may stimulate prosocial behavior instead" (Dekker and Van den Broek 1998:16). If the latter argument were true, there would be more volunteers in countries high in self-expression and individualism than in more traditional countries.

The most vigorous proponent of the argument that modernization promotes volunteerism is Inglehart (2003). He acknowledges that structural changes, such as industrialization, with its attendant urban sprawl, long commuting times, two-career families, pervasive mass media, and widespread use of the Internet, account for some of the variation in volunteering, but regards these changes as chiefly the result of cultural differences between countries. Using data from the 1999–2001 WVS, he classifies volunteer work into three types: the first consists of environmental, peace, welfare, health-related, and international aid organizations; the second consists of political parties, local organizations concerned with poverty and unemployment, women's groups, and labor unions; the third consists of religious, youth, sports, educational, cultural, and professional associations. He classifies values along two dimensions. The first stretches from "traditional" to "secular-rational." Societies near the traditional end of this dimension attach importance to religion, parent-child ties, traditional family values, deference to authority, and absolute moral and sexual standards. The second value dimension stretches from "survival" to "self-expression." Societies ranking high on survival values are materialistic, relatively intolerant of minority groups, do not trust others, reject gender inequality, and emphasize hard work. Inglehart finds a strong positive correlation between a country's score on survival/self-expressive values and its volunteer rate: the more a society values self-expression, the higher the volunteer rate in that country. This is true for all three types of volunteer work. A country's score on the traditional/secular-rational dimension is related only to the third type of volunteering (church, youth, sports, professional, and cultural). The more secular a society, the fewer people volunteer for these kinds of organizations.

Political Values

We have already noted that established democracies have higher volunteer rates. As far as culture is concerned, this implies that volunteerism is more common in countries where commitment to democratic principles is widespread. Democracy is not only a way of behaving—holding elections, organizing campaigns—but is also a way of thinking. Halman (2003) used data on thirty-three countries to test the proposition that political values influence volunteer rates. To measure support for democratic principles, he used a battery of questions asking respondents their opinions about the effectiveness and fairness of democratic governments. At the individual level, he found no relation between support for democratic principles and the number of activities for which respondents volunteered. At the aggregate level, however, the broader the support for democratic principles in the population the higher the volunteer rate. Even people who themselves are not particularly strong supporters of democracy are more likely to volunteer if they live in a country where support for democracy is strong.[6]

Attitudes toward Philanthropy

The United Nations declared 2001 the Year of the Volunteer, thus signaling the gradual globalization of the idea of volunteerism (Anheier and Salamon 1999:44). Nevertheless, we are a long way from having a uniform global culture of volunteerism because the definition of and attitude toward philanthropy in general and volunteer work in particular varies so widely. Nothing could attest to this fact better than the absence of a word for the volunteer in many languages and the considerable problems social survey administrators face when conducting multi-national surveys. Attitudes are basically judgments about objects, and even if the volunteer role is clearly identified, this does not mean all cultures evaluate the role in the same way. Americans look favorably on the volunteer role because they are quick to believe governments are incapable of providing necessary services. In many European countries, volunteers are regarded as "amateurish 'do-gooders,'" as relics of the past to be replaced by paid professional staff capable of performing tasks more efficiently and effectively" (Anheier and Salamon 1999:43). In the transitional democracies, volunteerism bears the stigma of the obligatory "service" communist regimes tried to extort from their citizens and has only recently begun to acquire the favorable connotations associated with an emerging "free space" for political activity and discourse (Flanagan et al. 1999:151).

Japan provides an illustrative case history of how culture at first repelled volunteerism but as it began to modernize, found cultural space for the idea. Traditionally, charity toward strangers has been stigmatized in Japan, where people have been expected to be totally committed to their social group: primarily one's family and extended kin but also neighbors. Helping out within the group was not voluntary insofar as it was highly normative and harsh sanctions were imposed on those who failed to meet the obligation. Because the Japanese so rarely found themselves in any kind of role relationship involving giving help to strangers, it is hardly surprising the language did not contain a direct equivalent of the word "volunteer" (Stevens 1997:266). The few people who did volunteer were drawn into the work through the membership in organizations, often of Western origin, and "tainted with images of suspicious motives, meddling, 'high and mightiness' and backwardness" (Stevens 1997:230). Furthermore, few people had "care time" left over for formal volunteering. Powerful norms mandating help to extended kin left little time for the kind of impersonal, formal helping volunteer work demands. Volunteering was also stifled by the very close working relationship between local government and "volunteers" who were, in many respects, civil servants. In certain cases, local authorities and volunteers continue to work closely together to provide public safety benefits and social services. For example, volunteer fire departments receive most of their funding from municipal governments and volunteer firefighters are provided with a government pension when they retire. "Constant interaction between the volunteers and the city officials enables both sides to meet the needs of city residents and adjust services to adapt to changing conditions" (Haddad 2004:18S).

Despite these cultural forces militating against the institutionalization of volunteer work, modernization in Japan has helped change attitudes toward volunteerism. Virtually unheard of before the 1980s, the Japanese translation for volunteer (*borantia*) has become a "socially recognized identity and an accepted part of national policy, popular consciousness, and everyday vocabulary" (Nakano 2000:93). Japanese lifestyles have become more diversified with the growing wealth of the country and the rise of a more individualistic culture. "Japanese have turned to volunteering because it accommodates personal preference (to choose where, how and with whom one volunteers), wins public praise, and provides an accessible way of establishing oneself as a productive member of society" (Nakano 2000:94). This development thus pits the traditional Japanese view that individuals must devote themselves to the welfare of the larger group (e.g., family, company), on the one hand, and the newer view that individuals must develop themselves through self-expression. As a result, the Japanese today are volunteering at a rate quite comparable to other modern, industrialized societies. A recent survey of Japanese 10 years of age or more found that 27 percent of the men and 30.6 percent of the women had volunteered in the past year. This meant that over thirty-two million Japanese volunteered in 2001.[7] Among those who volunteered, working on behalf of "local improvement activities" was the most popular, but Japanese men and women could be found volunteering in a wide range of other activities, including helping children, the elderly, the sick and handicapped, sports, culture and the arts, public safety, environmental conservation, and disaster relief. In short, while it is difficult to measure cross-cultural differences in the cultural space available for the idea of volunteer work, we find the argument that it will influence the rate of volunteering in a country quite persuasive. Of course, the more volunteer activity there is, the more cultural space will be created to interpret and legitimate it.

Trust

In chapter 3 we discussed the theory that volunteering is encouraged by trust, treating trust as a personality trait. But according to some scholars, trust is more properly conceptualized as a property of a group or population. It describes an aggregate of people not a person. Thinking of trust in this way, we would hypothesize that volunteer work would be more common in high-trust societies even on the part of members who are not themselves particularly trusting. Levels of trust do seem to vary from one country to another and in some cases the rate of volunteering does seem to be linked to the level of trust. As a result of their recent experience of life under authoritarian regimes, the citizens of both Spain and Portugal tend to be distrustful (Torcal and Montero 1999:177). They also report some of the lowest rates of volunteering in Western Europe. More careful scrutiny, however, casts doubt on the validity of the trust hypothesis. Patulny et al. (2003) used information on trust drawn from the WVS and information on volunteering drawn from the Multinational Time Use Surveys (MTUS) to test the hypothesis that trusting societies volunteer more. There were wide variations in the level of trust from one country to another and also variations in the level of volunteering, but the two were not associated with each other. Delhey and Newton (2005) found no association between social trust and active voluntary association memberships in sixty countries participating in the WVS.[8] The hypothesis predicting high volunteer rates in more trusting societies appears to be invalid. This does not mean that the theory about high trust groups and volunteering is false because it might well apply to social collectivities of a smaller scale, such as neighborhoods, communities, and even cities.

Religion

In virtually all countries for which there are reliable data, frequency of church attendance is positively related to volunteering. The comparatively high rate of volunteering in the United States can be attributed to the religiosity of the American people. Greeley (1997a, 1997b) and Ladd (1999:139) conclude that virtually all the inter-country variation in volunteering is due to differences in religiosity. A comparison of two otherwise quite similar countries illustrates this argument. The volunteer rate in the United States is higher than the rate in Canada. Once country-level differences in frequency of church attendance are controlled, however, the Canadian rate exceeds that of the United States. The same could be said for Sweden and Norway because they, too, have higher rates of volunteering than the United States once frequency of church attendance is controlled. This is because much of the volunteer work in the United States is performed on behalf of churches. A higher proportion of Americans than residents of any other country say their volunteer work takes place in religious settings and that they found out about, and were encouraged to undertake, their volunteer work through their church (Davis 1990; Gaskin and Smith 1997:41; Hodgkinson and Weitzman 1996:8; Knapp et al. 1995; Marta et al. 1999). Americans rate religious reasons for volunteering more highly than Canadians, regardless of their own level of religiosity (Hwang et al. 2005). In Canada, by contrast, arts, culture, and recreation organizations are the largest beneficiaries of volunteer work, followed by social service organizations, with churches ranking third (McKeown et al. 2004:12).

Whereas religion helps account for the difference between the United States and other countries, it does not throw much light on differences *between* European countries. Halman (2003) used data from the 1999–2001 European Values Survey to construct two measures of religiosity. The first was an index of public religiosity, consisting of frequency of church attendance, confidence in the church, and the degree to which the respondent felt that the churches gave adequate answers to spiritual needs and moral, family, and social problems. The second was a measure of personal religiosity, consisting of: belief in a personal God; regarding God as important; considering yourself a religious person; getting strength from religion; and praying regularly. These two religious factors were highly correlated ($r = .71$; $p < .001$). There was no association between mean level of either score of religiosity and the rate of volunteering in that country. European countries are simply more secular than the United States and religion plays a minor role in mobilizing volunteer work. Another study of religiosity, using a larger sample of WVS countries, including many outside Europe, found that degree of religiosity (attending religious services weekly) was positively associated with volunteering. In this study there was more variation in religiosity from one country to another. It had a stronger effect than country wealth, level of education, and political regime (Parboteeah et al. 2004:438). Neither of the aforementioned studies controls for individual religiosity using multi-level models, which is the method used by Ruiter and De Graaf (2006:202) in their analysis of fifty-three countries included in the WVS survey. They found that people living in the most devout countries (as measured by church attendance) were almost four times more likely to volunteer than people living in the most secular countries. People living in more devout countries were more likely to associate with active church members who are, in turn, more likely to be volunteers, a social network explanation for societal variations in volunteering.

Americans are not only more religious than many other people but their religious tradition is somewhat different in a way that has consequences for volunteerism. The relatively high rate of volunteering among Americans probably has something to do with the kind of religious traditions they have adopted—and adapted. In some respects, the high priority Americans place on individual involvement in community affairs originated in America's revolutionary past, and in the separation of church and state. The dominant religion, Protestantism, promoted an ethic of voluntary provision for the needs of the community rather than relying on the state or the established church. It also encouraged the formation and self-governance of local churches and congregations in which democratic participation was encouraged and which were largely sustained by an ethic of voluntarism. Although the hegemony of the Protestant faith is declining, it has left its mark on the way Americans think about their relation between themselves and their community. Americans might well volunteer more than Europeans not because they are more frequent churchgoers but because more of them belong to, or are influenced by, religious denominations that are incubators of volunteer workers. Cross-country variations in volunteerism should therefore correspond to the proportion of the population belonging to Protestant denominations. One study, using WVS data from 1991 to compare a number of countries in Western Europe and North America, found a very strong positive correlation ($r = 0.76$) between the volunteer rate and the percentage of the population Protestant (Woolley 2003:156).

It is unwise to push this argument about religious faith too far because, as we noted above, national cultures both adopt and adapt religious traditions. Neither Protestantism nor Catholicism is the same in every country. Americans have developed a markedly democratic and individualistic version of Protestantism, particularly suited to fostering volunteer activities. Volunteering is higher in the United States because the individualistic and moralistic teachings of its mainstream Protestant churches give it special encouragement: "For Americans, religious people have a moral obligation to do good, for no one else will do so" (Uslaner 2002b:240). Most Canadians are also Protestant, but they have not been so quick to link volunteerism and the church. They are more inclined to believe that it is the responsibility of the state (working together with the church hierarchy) to solve social problems. The mainly Protestant English-speaking Canadians volunteer less than Protestant Americans because they give less time to religious organizations: volunteer rates for secular activities are about the same (Uslaner 2002b:242).

One problem with this "dominant religious tradition" hypothesis is that there are a number of countries that should have higher rates of volunteerism than the United States if being dominated by Protestantism were so important. The United Kingdom is an obvious example. This leads some scholars to argue that religious competition, rather than domination by one religious tradition, accounts for higher rates of volunteering. The sheer number and variety of churches in pluralistic religious systems sparks competition among them for members, which in turn leads to a proliferation of activities designed to keep members involved and committed (Woolley 2003:158). This truth is hidden by the fact that countries where a high proportion of the population is Protestant also tend to be pluralistic. Curtis et al. (2001:785–787) tested this theory of religious competition using 1991–1993 WVS data. They sorted countries into four categories: mainly Protestant (Britain, Denmark, Finland, Iceland, Norway, Sweden); mainly Roman Catholic (Argentina, Austria, Belgium, Brazil, Chile, France, Hungary, Ireland, Italy, Lithuania, Mexico, Portugal, Spain); mixed Protestant and Catholic (Canada, East Germany, Netherlands, Northern Ireland, the United States, and West Germany); and others (Bulgaria, Estonia, Japan, Latvia, Romania, Russia, and South Korea). The degree of religious competition had no effect on volunteering until trade union volunteering was excluded, whereupon the difference between the mixed Christian category and all the others became significant. In short, the countries with more pluralistic religious systems tended to have the higher volunteer rates. We sought to replicate this finding in an analysis of the 1999–2001 WVS data. We controlled for gross national income and individual-level socio-demographic attributes. We coded countries into the following categories, using information from the *World Christian Encyclopedia*: Protestant, Catholic, Orthodox, and Muslim-Hindu if at least 70 percent of the church affiliates belonged to that particular tradition. We created a mixed religion category for countries where no religious tradition had more than 70 percent of the affiliates. As shown in Table 6, the hypothesis that the mixed religion countries have the highest volunteer rates was partially validated. All the other types had lower volunteer rates, with the exception of the Protestant group. When we divided the volunteer work in service, advocacy, and religious volunteering, the connection between religious pluralism and volunteerism became clearer. It had no effect on advocacy volunteering (a category that would include trade unions). Orthodox countries had lower service volunteer rates than mixed religion countries, but otherwise there were no differences. As far as religious volunteering was concerned, the Orthodox, Catholic, and Muslim-Hindu countries all had much lower rates of volunteering than Protestant or mixed. These results provide support for both the dominant religion and the religious competition theories, but they suggest that the effect of religious competition is largely confined to religious volunteering. Mixed religion countries volunteer at no higher rates than Protestant countries but residents in both countries volunteer at higher rates than those living in countries dominated by the Orthodox or Catholic churches or where either Muslim or Hindu religions dominate. [107, 108, 109]

Individual Correlates

Up to this point, we have focused entirely on aggregate measures of difference between countries, estimating the influence of a number of country-level variables on the rate of volunteering. Throughout our own analysis, we have controlled for individual-level differences in socio-demographic variables and church attendance to try to ensure that the variation is caused by

Table 6. Estimated Net Effects of Country-Level Religion, World Bank GNI, Individual Religion and other Controls on Any Volunteering.[1]

	Any Volunteering	Service	Advocacy	Religious
Fixed Effects-Individual				
Intercept	.08	−.88**	−.96***	−2.97***
Demographics				
Female	−.23***	−.31***	−.08**	−.01
Age 25–34 (a)	−.07*	−.23***	.08+	.06
Age 35–44	.03	−.23***	.26***	.23***
Age 45–54	.09*	−.22***	.39***	.32***
Age 55–64	.08+	−.18***	.35***	.36***
Age 65+	−.07	−.31***	.24***	.32***
Socioeconomic Status				
Education	.39***	.43***	.41***	.18***
Income	.17***	.19***	.13***	.06**
Employment Status (b)				
Full-time work	.07**	−.03	.39***	−.07+
Part-time work	.30***	.35***	.41***	.10+
Self-employed	.12**	.07+	.34***	.06
Retired	.00	−.01	.01	.06
Marital Status (c)				
Married	.08*	.04	.08+	.08+
Single	.18***	.30***	−.07	.06
Religious Factors				
Service attendance	.30***	.15***	.14***	.72***
Orthodox Christian (d)	−.02	−.11	−.20*	1.02***
Protestant/Other Christian	.27***	.01	−.22***	1.51***
Catholic	.03	.03	−.16**	1.11***
Muslim-Hindu	−.09	−.15*	−.20**	1.10***
Other Religions	.29***	.02	−.05	1.45***
Fixed Effects-Country				
Protestant (e)	.12	.28	.40	−.61
Catholic	−.54+	−.45	−.34	−.80*
Orthodox	−.93*	−.82*	−.34	−1.18**
Muslim-Hindu	−.89*	−.58	−.41	−1.12*
GNI–Lower Middle (f)	−1.03**	−.96**	−1.02**	−.75*
GNI–Upper Middle	−.65+	−.37	−.84*	−.28
GNI–High	−.72+	−.21	−.87*	−.38
Mean Service Attendance	.08	.03	.14	.26+
Random Effects (variances)				
Intercept	.034***	.017***	.010***	.009***

Notes:
[1] Reference categories: (a) Age < 25; (b) Unemployed; (c) Divorced/separated/widowed; (d) No religion; (e) No single dominant religion; (f) GNI–low.

$+p < .10$; $^{*}p < .05$; $^{**}p < .01$; $^{***}p < .001$

country-level variables and not by differences between the individuals living in that country. For example, democratic societies might have many more educated people living in them than undemocratic societies and, since we know that educated people are more likely to volunteer, it is their over-representation that is causing the high volunteer rate, not the type of regime. Multi-level models tell us whether people feel the effects of country-level variations even though they do not themselves possess many of the resources needed for volunteering. For example, if education is positively related to volunteering, poorly educated people are less likely to volunteer, but the likelihood of even poorly educated people volunteering goes up if they live in a country where many people are well educated simply because the infrastructure supporting volunteer work (e.g., service learning curricula, voluntary associations) is more developed. Multi-level models also make it possible to see if the individual correlates of volunteering we have discussed earlier apply across all countries by enabling us to control for country-level variations in volunteering. A third benefit of multi-level models is that they make it possible to see if the influence of a particular individual attribute varies across countries. For example, religiosity might be more influential in one country than another. We have already dealt with the first issue: whether there are country-level differences in volunteering, net of individual differences. In this remaining section we will take up the last two issues: whether there is a "profile" of the volunteer that transcends national boundaries; and whether national boundaries moderate (change) the influence of individual attributes.

To begin building a pan-national profile of the volunteer we sorted the 1999–2001 WVS data on volunteering into three types: service volunteering includes social welfare, youth work, sports, health, and the arts; advocacy volunteering includes labor unions, professional associations, political, local community activism, third world, environment, women's groups, peace movements; and religious volunteering is a separate category. Using multi-level modeling we control for variations in the volunteer rate from one country to another. The resulting profile of the volunteer varied somewhat by type of volunteer work. Service volunteers were more likely to be male, single, working part-time, highly educated, affluent, and frequent churchgoers. This typical volunteer is different from that of the American volunteer on whom we have focused much of our previous analyses in being male and single, but this is probably due to the presence of youth and sports volunteering in this category. Advocacy volunteers were more likely to be male, middle aged, employed, well educated, affluent, and frequent churchgoers. This profile is quite similar to the American volunteer with the exception of being male rather than female, probably a result of work-related associations in the advocacy category. Religious volunteers tended to be older, married, better educated, earning higher salaries, part-time workers, and frequent churchgoers. This profile is also quite similar to that of the American volunteer, with the exception that the WVS religious volunteer is no more likely to be male than female. [59] In short, we agree with Gaskin and Smith (1997:3) that the socio-economic profile of the volunteer in different countries is quite similar (the main exception being the gender difference), but we would add that the mix of volunteer activities from one country to another does make some difference to who volunteers.

It is one thing to say that volunteers in all countries attend church more frequently than non-volunteers and quite another thing to say that church attendance has the *same* effect in all countries. This ignores country-level differences in the significance of particular domains of volunteer work (e.g., religious versus sports) and country-level differences in the social significance of individual attributes, such as religiosity or education. We cannot assume that these mean the same thing in all countries. As we have already demonstrated, gender does not always have the same effect on volunteering. In the United States, the gender gap in volunteering favors women, but in Italy men are more likely to volunteer. Family status varies in the same way: in the United States, married people are more likely to volunteer, whereas in Italy single people volunteer at a higher rate than married people (Ascoli and Cnaan 1997:310).

We used the WVS data to see if the influence of individual attributes varies by country, focusing on the attributes we have already discussed in the book and using multi-level models.

Gender

The WVS includes countries as different as Sweden, Italy, Mexico, South Africa, and Russia. The roles of men and women in these societies, and ideas about gender, vary widely across these societies. In traditional societies, women's freedom to participate in civil society is severely curtailed, whereas in more modern societies women have greater freedom to be active in civil society. Theoretically, this would predict some variation in the influence of gender on volunteering. In traditional societies we would expect men to more active in civil society, whereas modern societies might see more gender equality. "Women in most less developed countries generally occupy lower social positions and have fewer freedoms in joining clubs, associations and organizations" (Ziemek 2003:96). We tested this hypothesis with the WVS data, using gross national income as a proxy measure of modernization. We found significant interaction effects only in the case of service volunteering. In this area, although men were still more likely to volunteer than women the gap was narrower in higher-income countries, partially validating the hypothesis that women enjoy more freedom to participate in civil society in more affluent societies. [110]

Education

The more education people have, the more likely they are to volunteer, but the effect of education is relative (Nie and Hillygus 2001). Where education is scarce it increases in salience as a resource for civic action. In chapter 15 we reported that education has a stronger influence on volunteering in rural areas—where highly educated people are scarcer—than in urban areas. The same thing could be said of countries. In more highly developed countries, a higher proportion of the population is well educated. By the logic of this argument, the effect of education on volunteering should be stronger in less-developed countries (Ziemek 2003:98). A competing theory is that when individuals live in an environment where they interact with other highly educated individuals "they are more likely to be exposed to benevolent values and be more concerned about helping others" (Parboteeah et al. 2004:433). In their comparison of fifty-three countries, the level of education in the country had a positive effect on the volunteer rate in the country, regardless of the wealth or religiosity of the country or its political regime. However, they only control for individual-level education and do not explore the possibility that the positive influence of individual-level education is moderated by country-level education. We used the WVS data to test this by constructing a model containing an interaction term for respondent's education and the mean level of education for that country (as determined by the sample population). However, we found no interaction effect because the level of education of the country made no difference to volunteering. Neither theory was supported. More independent measures of the educational level in a country, not derived from the WVS itself, might provide more support.[9]

Employment

In chapter 7 we described how employed people are more likely to volunteer than those not in the labor force. Ziemek (2003:99) has suggested, however, that in less developed countries volunteer work might be more attractive to people without jobs because unemployed people in such countries are more likely "to consider volunteer work as a job market (re-entry) tool." If this is true, then the gap in volunteering between employed and unemployed should be narrower in less well-developed societies. The WVS does not contain information on unemployment, but we used labor force status to test this hypothesis. We found that the volunteer gap between people in the labor force and people not in the labor force was actually larger in low-income countries. [111] The more affluent the country, the more alike were the rates of volunteering among those with jobs and those without jobs. This could be due to the fact that being out of the labor force is not the same as being unemployed—it could mean being a student, a homemaker, or retired—and therefore we are not testing the same hypothesis. Nevertheless, this finding could also mean that unemployed people in rich countries find it easier to do, or see greater benefit in, volunteer work while they search for another job.

Church Service Attendance

Studies have repeatedly shown that frequent churchgoers are more likely to volunteer than those who never go to church. But this ignores the fact that the norm of frequent churchgoing varies considerably from one country to another and the fact that churchgoing is connected to volunteer work more closely in some countries than others. Ruiter and De Graaf (2006:203) argue that, in countries where most people go to church this "resource" loses its value and will not make much difference to the likelihood of volunteering. Analyzing the WVS data they found that church attendance had a stronger influence on volunteering in more secular societies (as measured by the average level of church attendance in the society). This is similar to the argument that education counts for less in countries where most people are well educated. The influence of church attendance on volunteering might also vary by whichever religious tradition is dominant in the country. We noted in chapter 5 that Americans, who are mostly Protestant, look upon volunteer work as an important way to "witness" their faith. This implies that religious zeal—as measured by church attendance—should have a more powerful influence on volunteering in that country than in others where the dominant religion does not place so much emphasis on volunteering. In our analysis of the WVS we created interaction terms for main religion in the country and level of church attendance in that country. We found that the positive effect of church attendance was stronger in Protestant countries than in any other type, thus validating the hypothesis. [112]

Age

In the United States and several other advanced industrial societies, the rate of volunteering peaks in middle age. This pattern is not found in all societies. In Germany and Romania, for example, older people are less likely to volunteer than younger people because of the negative experiences of the older generation under totalitarian regimes (Dalton 2002:54; Voicu and Voicu 2003). A comparative study of older Europeans (aged 50 years or more) found that the rate of volunteering drops off once people reach the age of 75. However, respondents aged 75 years or more were *more* likely to volunteer than younger people in Sweden, Denmark, and the Netherlands (all high volunteer societies) and *less* likely to volunteer than younger people in Mediterranean countries (Greece, Spain, and Italy). The overall rate of volunteering was influencing how long older people remained in the volunteer labor force (Erlinghagen and Hank 2006:577). Inglehart (2003:61) looked at the association between age and volunteering in seventeen rich countries and thirty-one "developing and former-communist countries." Age was unrelated to volunteering in the rich countries but negatively related to volunteering in the poor countries: that is, in the poorer countries, the young were more likely to volunteer than the old. It could be that the older generation in the former communist countries was socialized under the communist regimes where volunteer work was either mandated or forbidden. Once democracy arrived, they were simply uninterested in volunteering or not equipped to take advantage of the new civil society. In our own analysis of WVS data, we first sorted the countries by regime type, using the regime classifications we described earlier in the chapter. We used our classification of volunteer work into service, advocacy, and religion for the dependent variables. We then estimated mixed models with cross-level interactions between regime and age, using 16–24 as our reference category. As we discovered earlier, the volunteer rate in transitional democracies is comparatively low, but in these countries the youngest age group has the highest volunteer rate. Volunteering was more common in liberal countries but in those countries the middle aged did the most volunteer work. There were no regime-age interactions in the case of either religious volunteering or advocacy volunteering. Regime does therefore moderate the influence of age on volunteering but only in the case of service provision. [113] This could have something to do with the popularity of sports and recreation volunteering (included in the service category) in former communist countries, a type of volunteering that has special appeal to younger people, or simply the result of older people in former communist countries not having been socialized into performing service volunteer roles.

Conclusion

As we noted in the introduction to this chapter, the comparative study of volunteerism, now flourishing, is a relatively undeveloped area of scholarly investigation in the field of philanthropy. Progress in this area has been slowed by: the difficult of gathering comparable data; wide cultural variations in the understanding of the volunteer role; and lack of theoretical development. Recent work has altered this picture quite dramatically. A number of cross-national surveys using standardized definitions of volunteer work and other socio-demographic variables make comparisons easier. Much effort has been devoted to developing a conceptual framework for the measurement and analysis of the voluntary sector. A global civil society seems to be emerging, part of which is a common set of understandings as to the roles of non-profit and voluntary organizations. In countries with traditionally low volunteer rates more and more people are taking an interest in volunteer work. For example, the English-language South Korean newspaper *JongAng Daily* ran an article in June 2005 describing the results of a recent national survey reporting that one in five South Koreans had done volunteer work in the past twelve months. This is a remarkably high rate in a country where, as the newspaper reminded its readers, "volunteer work was not considered something the average person did" (http://www.worldvolunteerweb.org/dynammic/cfapps/news/news2).

Much work remains to be done in this area. First, more needs to be learned about how volunteer preferences and opportunities vary from one country to another. For example, Salamon et al. (1999) found that, after grouping the world into various regions, each seemed to have its own characteristic non-profit sector. In Western Europe, the non-profit sector was largely given over to social welfare services (often in association with religious institutions), sports, and recreation. In Central Europe, recreational and cultural volunteering dominated, reflecting the influence of previous communist regimes, although some of the newer voluntary organizations were targeting the environmental problems caused by those regimes. Extensive social welfare programs put in place under communism obviated the need for much social service volunteer work. In Latin American countries, the Catholic Church had sponsored many social service non-profits, while non-governmental organizations (many focusing on economic development issues) provided opportunities for advocacy volunteering. Other countries, such as Japan, Australia, Israel, and the United States, stood out as a result of their extensive health care non-profit sector, attractive many citizens to volunteer to work in that area. From this institutional perspective, the size and composition of the non-profit sector will have an effect not only on how much volunteer work people do but where they do that work.

17

Trends in Volunteering

This chapter describes recent trends in volunteering in countries for which there are trend data and reviews some of the theories that have been put forward to explain these trends. The number of people willing to do volunteer work has become something of a barometer of a society's civic health, which has heightened interest in changes in the size of the volunteer labor force. Throughout this chapter our discussion and analysis will be limited by the fact that surveying volunteerism in the general population is a relatively recent innovation, making it impossible to track changes in the rate of volunteering over more than a quarter of a century.

We are not interested in short-term fluctuations in volunteering. People frequently respond to emergencies by volunteering. Many of them have never volunteered before and will probably never volunteer again. At moments of crisis, people feel an urgent need to "do something." The terrorist attacks on the United States in September 2001 were such a moment for most Americans. The news media described how people from all over the country rushed to offer their services to aid in recovery from the disaster. The upsurge in volunteerism was recorded in the files of an organization called "Volunteermatch," which uses the Internet to link organizations in need of volunteer labor to people looking for volunteer opportunities. In the week following the attack, 13,227 people contacted Volunteermatch, compared to 3,802 in the corresponding week in 2000. Inquiries were not limited to crisis intervention organizations, although they experienced an eightfold increase, compared to a doubling of interest in other organizations (Penner 2004). These numbers are some indication of how many Americans *could* be mobilized for volunteer work if the circumstances were right. But within twelve weeks contacts with Volunteermatch had returned to their pre-attack levels.

Only by studying volunteer rates over several decades is it possible to get a clear picture of significant changes in people's interest in doing volunteer work and only by looking at social changes over a long period is it possible to explain why these trends have occurred. In what follows we will focus mainly on the United States, where the trend data on volunteering are most plentiful, but we will also examine trends in volunteering in other countries to see if there is anything exceptional about the United States.

United States

Many Americans judge the health of their community by the quality of its civic life. They become concerned if this quality begins to deteriorate because civic activities are treated as augurs of more fundamental and troubling changes in the fabric of community life. They wax nostalgic for a time when neighborhoods and other places showed more community spirit.

Volunteerism does indeed have a settled and honored place in American culture. Its roots can be traced to the eighteenth century when citizens were called upon to fight fires, act as night watchmen, staff libraries, visit patients in hospitals, help run benevolent societies and trade groups, teach in schools, and serve as missionaries, but America gained its reputation as "a nation of joiners" only after the explosion of voluntary association activity at the end of the nineteenth century. This growth only began to slow down after 1910.

> Economic and demographic changes disrupted patterns of work, leisure, churchgoing, and family roles. Women and men began to seek gender-defined associational attachments outside the home, adults began consciously to structure the social and educational worlds of children, native-born Americans sought to reform their own lives and the lives of immigrants, and African Americans and immigrants created organizations to respond to the erosion of traditional community interactions. (Gamm and Putnam 2001:192)

The slowdown in the rate of formation of new associations that began in 1910 prompted concern about the state of community in the United States. Voter turnout in presidential elections also fell, trust in government ebbed to a new low, club memberships declined, and habits of sociality such as entertaining at home and general neighborliness began to fall out of favor. Many feared that the habit of volunteering would go the same way. In their "solitary quest for private goods" Americans would simply not have the time, or the will, to work on behalf of others (Putnam 2000:403).

Without reliable survey data on volunteering prior to World War II it is not possible to say whether these fears of decline were justified, nor is it possible to say much about the extent of volunteerism in the American population prior to the 1970s, but since that time survey data have been gathered on a more regular basis. One motivation for gathering these data is that scholars and pundits have once again begun voicing concerns that "the unconstrained pursuit of profitability in a capitalist society" is resulting in "downsizing, insecurity, and a social psychology inimical to long-term commitments to family, neighborhood, and occupation" (Isaacs 2003:7). The sprawl of suburban and ex-urban ecologies, increasing geographical mobility, insecurity of employment and the diffusion of contingent work, and the need for households to send both spouses out to work to support a consumerist lifestyle are also believed to have sapped the volunteer spirit.

The evidence on recent trends in volunteering sends a mixed signal. Citing nearly thirty years of data from several different social surveys, Ladd (1999:64) reported that more and more Americans were engaging in "charity or social service activities, such as helping the poor, the sick or the elderly." The rate rose steadily from 26 percent in 1977, to 39 percent in 1987, and to 54 percent in 1995.[1] Using data from multiple years of the Multinational Time Use Study, Anderson et al. (2006:384) found that the amount of time spent daily on "civic association activity" had declined from about eight minutes or higher in 1965 and 1975 to under six minutes in 1992 and 1998.[2] Putnam (2000:12) also believes that volunteerism is declining in America. In his view, the volunteer rates reported by Ladd are deceiving because they disguise the fact that younger people are turning away from volunteer work. The increases are the result of older people volunteering in greater numbers. As these older people die or become incapable of doing volunteer work, the true decline of volunteerism will become apparent. Putnam bases his argument on the theory that younger generations of Americans are not as civic-minded as older generations, especially the older generation reared during the Great Depression. Dividing the American population into four cohorts—born before 1930, born between 1930 and 1945, born between 1946 and 1960 ("baby boomers"), and born after 1960—the data show an increase in the mean number of times volunteered per year between 1975 and 1997, but it is almost entirely confined to members of the 1930–1945 cohort, who grew up during the Depression and the Second World War. There was no equivalent increase in the rate of volunteering in succeeding generations (Goss 1999).

Putnam's generational theory resonates with popular feelings that Americans are becoming more materialistic, more selfish, withdrawing into their own private worlds, unconcerned about the future of the common good, in contrast to a generation of Americans who were taught the values of mutual trust, cooperation, and caring for one's fellow citizens by the hardships and privations of the Great Depression and the Second World War. Generation theory is an alternative way of accounting for age differences in behavior and attitudes when using cross-sectional data. Rather than attributing age differences to maturation and life course events, and assuming that the young will one day behave and think like the old, they are assumed to be permanent. It is further assumed that period effects, which influence all age groups in the population alike, will leave these generational differences intact. A generation is cultural phenomenon, distinguishing itself by a particular way of looking at itself.[3]

Many social scientists are skeptical of explanations for social change that rely on generation theory (Schuman and Scott 1989:360). They point to improvements in education and health among older people, more positive attitudes toward aging, and more opportunities for older volunteers as better explanations for the upward trend among older people (Chambre 1993). Putnam (2000:54) counters by arguing that the older generation is more civic-minded "*despite* the fact that it received substantially less formal education than its children and grandchildren" (Putnam 2000:254, our emphasis). But this begs the question of whether Putnam's thesis is based on reliable empirical data. Is it actually the case that the older generations are volunteering more and, if they are, is not simply due to the changing life circumstances of the old (e.g., better health) that younger people will also enjoy when they reach that age?

It is notoriously difficult to tease out the independent effects of generations because age, cohort (generation), and period effects can look very much alike.[4] One strategy for solving this analytical problem is to compare how much volunteer work two succeeding generations of Americans performed at the same stage of their life. This controls for age while testing for generation.[5] The National Longitudinal Survey of Labor Market Experience (NLS) provides an unusual opportunity to test the merits of this strategy because it has followed four population cohorts: men 45–59 years of age; "mature" women 30–44 years of age; young men 14–24 years of age; and "young" women 14–24 years of age. Only the women were asked about their volunteer work.[6] As it happens, members the mature cohort of women belong to the "civic generation" identified by Putnam, because they were born between 1923 and 1937, and the young women belong to the baby boom generation because they were born between 1944 and 1954. A comparison between these two cohorts at the same age thus affords an excellent opportunity to test the generation thesis.[7] The "young" women were more educated, more likely to be in the labor force, and they worked more weeks a year than the mature women. The mature women were more likely to be married and had more school age children in the household than the young women. They were slightly more likely to have professional and managerial jobs. Of primary interest was the fact that, unadjusted for any of the differences just described, there was no cohort difference in the number of weeks volunteered, although the younger women did contribute more of their time than the mature women.

Controls for these demographic differences between the two cohorts of women showed that more highly educated women volunteered more hours.

The effect of imposing this control was to give the advantage to the mature women: at any given level of education, mature women volunteered more than young women. Women who worked full-time volunteered less than women who worked part-time or did not work at all. The effect of controlling for work hours was to narrow the gap between the mature and young women. The mature women were volunteering more because they worked fewer hours. Controlling for marital status further diminished the gap in volunteering between mature and young women: mature women were volunteering more because, at the same age, they were more likely to be married. Controlling for parental status eliminated the volunteer gap entirely: mature women were volunteering more because they were more likely to have children in the household. In summary, there was a difference in the rate of volunteering between the two generations of women but the difference disappeared once the socio-demographic differences between them were held constant. The downward trend in volunteering is due not to changing consciousness but to changing demographics (Rotolo and Wilson 2004).[8]

Greeley (1997b) tested the generation theory in his analysis of World Values Survey (WVS) data from 1981 to 1991. His goal was to see which age groups in the American population changed their volunteer rate over the course of this decade. Looking only at the types of activity that were measured in both years, he found an overall increase in volunteer rate of ten percentage points. Grouping respondents by year of birth into ten-year categories and using both 1981 and 1991 panels, he found that the volunteer rate rose in both cohorts and, what is equally important, each cohort volunteered at a higher than its predecessor cohort did when it was the same age. The trend is, if anything, upward: "even those born during the 1970s and hence at the most only 20 at the time of the 1991 survey were already twice as likely to volunteer as those born in the 1960s were 10 years ago when they were in their twenties" (Greeley 1997b:70).

Putnam believes that his generation theory is supported because younger people are volunteering less in his data. Older people are taking on more and more of the burden of doing volunteer work. Trend data on volunteering among young people contradict this argument. Monitoring the Future is a survey of eighth, tenth, and twelfth graders in the United States that has been conducted annually since 1976. It covers over fifty thousand high school students. On each occasion they have been asked if they had participated in "community affairs or voluntary activities" in the previous year.

Since 1976, volunteering rates among high school seniors remained steady through 1990 at approximately 67 percent, but have risen to over 76 percent in 2001. Similarly, for eighth graders and tenth graders, volunteer rates have risen since 1991, with a volunteer rate of approximately 72 percent in 2001 for tenth graders and 66 percent in 2001 for eighth graders. (Lopez 2004:2)

Admittedly, there has been no increase in the proportion of high school students who say they volunteer on a *weekly* basis, but this proportion has remained fairly constant for all grades, at around 12 percent, and has not declined. In short, there has been an increase in volunteering among school age Americans in the last twenty-five years, but it has taken the form of episodic rather than regular activity.

Additional trend data on younger people are available from annual surveys administered to incoming college freshmen in the United States. Starting in 1984 they were asked if they had done volunteer work in the previous year (i.e., when they were seniors in high school). From about three-quarters in 1984 (males 70.5%, females 74.5%), the rate declined gradually until 1989 (males 62.9%, females 69.1%), but has trended upward since, to a rate of 78.1 percent for males and 86.3 percent for females in 2001. Another survey asked college freshmen how many hours during their senior year in high school they had spent doing volunteer work. The proportion that had not done any volunteer work at all fell from 56.6 percent for males and 56.1 percent for females in 1987 to 36.4 percent for males and 24.1 percent for females in 2001. The freshmen were also asked if they planned to volunteer now they were in college. In 1990, 10.9 percent of the males and 22.1 percent of the females were planning to do volunteer work. By 2001, this proportion had risen to 14.9 percent for males and 31.3 percent for females (Astin et al. 2002).

Surveys of the behavior, rather than the intentions, of college students show no evidence of a decline in volunteering. In 1997, a record-high 38.4 percent of college freshmen spent one or more hours per week volunteering, compared to 37.2 percent in 1995 and a low of 26.6 percent when this question first was asked in 1987 (http://www.gseis.ucla.edu/heri/norms_pr_96.html). Service learning courses are becoming more popular in college, but not so popular they could account for more than a tiny fraction of this increase. Once again, young adults show no signs of turning away from volunteer work. Indeed, some have argued that volunteer work is becoming *more* popular among young people as they lose their confidence in political institutions and processes. Today, young Americans seem more disposed to focus their civic activities on volunteering for local causes than getting involved with national organizations or in politics and government. Voting rates among young people are relatively low, as are other forms of direct political involvement. In a 2002 survey, twice as many 15- to 26-year-olds identified volunteer work as the most important kind of civic activity a citizen could engage in as did those who identified getting involved in politics and government (Center for Democracy and Citizenship 2002:42).

Although, as reported earlier, Anderson et al. (2006) also believe that volunteering in the United States has declined since 1965 they do not ascribe this to generational effects because the time contributed by all age groups is declining equally and, in any case, the decline is largely confined to American women who, they believe, are donating less time because they are working longer hours.

In summary, sociological investigation of trends in volunteering in the United States has yet to arrive at any definitive conclusions. This is mainly due to data inadequacies: time-series data using accurate and reliable measures of volunteering in the general population are simply not available. Surveys, such as those summarized by Ladd (1999) focus mainly on volunteerism defined mainly as charitable or service work, leaving a wide variety of other forms of volunteering unmeasured. These surveys suggest that volunteerism has not declined. Other surveys, such as the time-diary data used by Anderson et al. (2006) indicate a decline but the survey measures "civic association activity" which is not necessarily the same as the volunteerism denoted in the other studies. Putnam (2000) agrees with Ladd that volunteerism is one of the few civic activities that has not been declining but, it seems, wrongly assumes age or cohort differences in volunteering, assumptions that are nor borne out by studies of special populations, such as high school students and undergraduates. There seems to be little danger that the supply of volunteer workers will dry up as the "civic generation" moves on. As we shall see below, social changes do influence the supply of volunteer labor, but they do not all run in the same direction. Some discourage volunteer work while others encourage it.

Generations and Domains

Although there are no generational differences in the *rate* of volunteering, they can still influence what people volunteer for. There is no reason to believe that the range of volunteer opportunities remains the same: one has only to think of the enormous proliferation of environmental volunteer jobs in the past quarter century. In addition, formative experiences in youth and young adulthood influence people's volunteer preferences. For example, members of the baby boom generation were raised in the prosperous 1950s and they reached early adulthood in the late 1960s, at the height of the civil rights and peace movements of that era. According to some scholars, this generation acquired "an abiding confidence about the future" and its members were "prime candidates for collective political action" (Goldstone and McAdam 2001:211). They have retained this taste for political activism even though they are no longer young. This generation continues to volunteer its services to advocacy and community action groups, while the previous generation favors the more traditional voluntary associations (religious congregations, civic clubs, fraternal organizations) they were taught to see as centers of volunteer work in the community, and the subsequent generation turns to service-oriented volunteering. Of course, these changing priorities might not be due to differences in people's tastes for volunteer work but to changing social circumstances. The younger generation turns away from cooking meals for service clubs to assist in organizing a neighborhood environmental watch group because they are better educated, have better paying jobs, and are paying off a house mortgage.

The biennial surveys conducted by the Independent Sector are unusual in having surveyed Americans on their volunteer preferences over a number of years using the same classification scheme for different domains of volunteer work. Using data from 1990–1999, we computed the percentages volunteering for each of thirteen categories identified in the surveys. The changes were quite trivial: the greatest decline was experienced by religious organizations, down by five percentage points, and the largest gain occurred in youth-development organizations, up by six percentage points. Overall, the "winners" were environmental, arts, work, youth, international, and foundation-related volunteering. The "losers" were health, education, religion, human services, public benefit, recreation, and advocacy-related volunteering. One decade is too brief a spell for drawing conclusions about trends in volunteer preferences, but these changes are a reminder that the map of volunteering is constantly changing.

In an earlier study, we analyzed the NLS data to see if the young and mature cohorts of women described earlier volunteered for different kinds of activity (Wilson and Musick 2000). Women who indicated they had volunteered in the past twelve months were asked what type of organization they volunteered for. The options were (1) hospital or clinic, (2) school, (3) church, (4) political organization, (5) groups such as community chest, United Fund, Heart Fund, (6) Boy Scouts, Girl Scouts, Little League, (7) civic or community action, (8) social and welfare, or (9) other. This is a short list, but it does provide an opportunity to see if the two cohorts of women had different volunteer preferences. We noticed a number of differences between the two cohorts, regardless of the socio-economic differences and family status differences between them. First, young women were more likely to do school-related volunteer work than mature women. Ladd (1999:36) reported a similar finding: "all the surveys show the proportions of parents saying they have recently attended meetings dealing with local school needs and programs up over the last two or three decades." Unfortunately, Ladd does not indicate whether this trend is net of rising educational status, but the NLS data suggest that the rising popularity of school-related volunteering is not simply the result of women being better educated. This leaves the door open for a generational interpretation. Possibly the young women, schooled in the late 1960s, had acquired a stronger interest in educational issues from the many social movements aimed at educational reform active at that time. However, it is not possible to rule out a period effect either. Perhaps the 1990s saw more demand for school volunteers because of cutbacks in educational budgets or increasing concern about the quality of schooling in an increasingly competitive economic environment. Second, young women were more likely than mature women to spend time volunteering in connection with a civic group or an organization engaged in community action. This is not due to occupational differences between the two cohorts because this variable is controlled in the model and we can turn to a generational explanation for this trend. The young women were aged between 14 and 24 in 1968 and thus came of age during a time of considerable social and political turmoil. As we noted above, studies of Americans who were politically socialized in the 1960s indicate that they retain some of their interests in social activism. This could be causing the difference between the young and the mature women we observe. As usual, we cannot entirely rule out the possibility that the difference might be due to period rather than generation effects but it is worth noting that the mature women were first asked about their volunteer work in 1974, which is too early to have benefited from the explosion of advocacy groups and grassroots associations that occurred between the 1980s and the 1990s (Skocpol 2003). Third, the mature women were more likely than the young women to be doing "service" volunteering. This is probably a consequence of the decline in membership in service (e.g., Lions, Kiwanis) and fraternal associations (many of them sex segregated). Women have moved away from traditional clubs and federations toward other kinds of activity. Some might think the decline of service volunteering, which often demands a steady commitment of time, is a result of women entering the labor force, and this undoubtedly had something to do with it, but we control for labor force participation in our models. It is more plausible that, in an era that saw the expansion of women's rights and greater gender equality, voluntary associations that segregate the sexes lost popularity. The young women were no longer joining them or their women's auxiliaries. Fourth, although church-related activities remained the most popular choice across the generations, young women were less likely to choose them than the mature women. It is tempting to attribute this to secularization, the young women being less religious than the women born a generation before especially because Putnam (2000:70) believes there was a "slump" in church attendance during the mid-1980s. But there was no overall decline in church attendance between 1974 and 1991 (Wuthnow 1999:335) and, although participation in church-related groups did fall between 1974 and 1984, it had risen to its former level by 1994 (Rotolo 1999).

Social Trends and Their Influence on Volunteering

It might come as a surprise to learn that volunteer rates have not fallen in light of the well-documented decline in so many other forms of civic participation. This does not mean, however, that volunteer work has been unaffected by social changes. Rather, some of these changes have had an adverse effect on volunteering while others have had a positive effect, resulting in an overall rate of volunteering that has been quite stable. In this section we will document some of these influences and point out their countervailing effects.

Labor Force Participation

Putnam (2000:201) is one of many scholars who believe that the more hours people work for pay, the less volunteer work they will do. Any social trend toward people working longer hours would, according to this belief, lead to a downward trend in volunteering. The trend toward more women working full-time would be especially damaging to the volunteer labor supply, especially if middle class women start taking full-time jobs, because they are the most likely to volunteer (Schlozman et al. 1999:36). In chapter 7 we demonstrated that the relation between employment status and volunteering is quite complicated. We can therefore anticipate that tracing the relationship (if any) between employment trends and volunteer trends is not going to be a simple matter.

Tiehen (2000:510) used time diary data gathered at different times across four decades to describe trends in volunteering and assess the influence of changing employment patterns. Respondents were asked to record in time diaries each activity they engaged in during a twenty-four-hour period. The rate of volunteering was 13.5 percent in 1965, 13.0 percent in 1975, 9.5 percent in 1985, and 9.4 percent in 1993. Males and females, both married and single, exhibited the same downward trend. However, when it came to volunteer hours, single men and women, and married men volunteered more hours in 1993 than in 1965 while married women volunteered slightly fewer. Married women were, therefore, the only group to both volunteer at a lower rate and donate fewer hours. Married women's share of aggregate hours volunteered fell from 43.7 percent in 1965 to 29.8 percent in 1993. This was only partly due to the fact that their share in the population decreased, from 36.9 percent to 30.8 percent.

Tiehen (2000:520) believes that conflicting social forces explain the decline in married women's volunteering. Married women were being pushed *out* of volunteer work by full-time employment: "if married women's employment rate had maintained its 1965 level, their volunteer rate would have been almost 30% higher in 1993." Some of the decline was also due to the fact that women were having fewer children. On the other hand, married women were being pulled into the volunteer labor force by gains in educational attainment and by having fewer preschool children to look after. Because the push factors slightly outweighed the pull factors, the trend line for this group was downward. In the time diary study cited earlier Anderson et al. (2006) also found that a decline in the number of minutes Americans devoted to civic association activity was mainly attributable to an increase in the labor force participation of women.

Club Memberships

There is little doubt that membership in traditional, member-based, voluntary associations has been declining. Fewer and fewer Americans seem interested in joining and being active in the conventional, chapter-based organization. Depending on the extent of this trend, the consequences for volunteerism would be serious, because in the past so much of the volunteer labor in a community has been mobilized by these organizations. Looking at membership figures for thirty-two national chapter-based associations from 1900 to 1997, Putnam (2000:54) observes an initial upward trend (interrupted briefly by the Depression) but a downward trend beginning in the 1960s. Data from the General Social Survey (GSS) from 1975 until 1993 show a slight decrease in the overall percentage of the population claiming membership in at least one voluntary association. Acknowledging that nominal membership is not the same as volunteering, Putnam (2000:60) also looked at the percentage of men and women who took any leadership role in any organization during this time: the percentage declined from 17 percent in 1974 to 8 percent in 1993. This decline is even more remarkable considering the rise in educational attainment that occurred during this period, because educated people are more likely to perform leadership roles.

If voluntary association memberships are declining, if fewer and fewer people have the time to take on leadership roles in these organizations, and if volunteerism is closely tied to voluntary associations, why is the rate of volunteering not also falling? One answer is that there are many avenues for volunteering outside voluntary associations. We have already demonstrated that voluntary associations are an important gateway to volunteer work, and therefore it is important to consider Putnam's thesis about declining voluntary association memberships carefully. Several scholars have expressed skepticism about this thesis. Paxton (1999:114), analyzing the same GSS data as Putnam, concluded "there is *no* significant change in the general level of association" between 1975 and 1994.[9] More helpful in this context is Rotolo (1999), also using GSS data, because he focused exclusively on voluntary association memberships. The GSS has collected information on Americans' voluntary associations fifteen times between 1974 and 1994. The survey asks about membership in sixteen types of organizations.[10] The average number of memberships declined steadily between 1974 and 1984, but subsequently the number increased and by 1994 all the earlier losses had been regained. Only three organizational categories experienced a membership decline over the entire period: labor union membership fell from 17 percent in 1977 to 10 percent in 1991, a decline easily accounted for by the shipment of manufacturing jobs overseas; church-related memberships showed an initial decline and then a recovery in the 1980s, but did not regain all the ground they had lost; fraternal orders also suffered a net loss during the period. In other cases, it would be difficult to say whether there has been much of a trend at all. Sports group memberships did not begin to decline until the late 1980s. School service groups (e.g., the PTA) suffered losses in the 1970s but recovered most of that loss by the end of the period (18% of the population reporting membership in 1975 and 16% in 1994).

Other associations enjoyed growth during this period. Professional, literary, hobby clubs, and veterans associations all increased their memberships. Many remained stable: farm associations, service groups, political organizations, nationality groups, and youth groups all ended the period much as they began it.

In short, because the voluntary sector is comprised of such a wide variety of activities, it is impossible to make a summary statement that voluntary association activities are in decline and therefore it is unlikely trends in membership can account for trends in volunteering. In some areas membership rates are declining but in others they are not. Perhaps people are more ready to believe there has been an overall decline because membership in many "traditional" (and more familiar) voluntary associations, such as fraternal orders and service clubs, *has* been falling, since at least the 1930s. But other voluntary associations have sprung up to take their place. During the 1970s, many new grassroots social movement organizations (with permanent staffs) emerged, replacing or rivaling national organizations and, incidentally, opening the way for women to fill more leadership positions (Brudney 1990:14). The more traditional organizations declined because they demanded too much from people whose lives were becoming busier, more mobile and less predictable. Americans began to choose volunteer activities based on current interests, opportunities, and convenience. Their contributions became more episodic, restructured to reflect a more intermittent set of connections to new types of organizations. Although this allowed people to continue to volunteer despite increasing work commitments it altered the way volunteer work fitted into their lives. Voluntary organizations, including religious congregations, either adapted to this new mode of volunteering or became moribund. One of the reasons why the PTA staunched the decline in memberships was that it adapted to this environment, making it easier for working couples to participate, assigning volunteers tasks that could be accomplished in short bursts, placing new PTA branches in the workplace and allowing volunteer work during lunch hours. Organizations like the Junior League, once heavily reliant on non-working women available during the day, have re-scheduled their volunteer activities and lowered their expectations of how much each volunteer can contribute (Markham and Bonjean 1995).

The new forms of voluntary association are typically local, loosely structured, and energized by sporadic events (e.g., plant closings, music festivals, waste disposal, Special Olympics). Volunteer participation is intermittent and devoted mainly to the event, rather than to some long-term cause or even the organization itself. In consequence, the modern association focuses less on maintaining the loyalty of its members than on delivering a service to its clients that can be performed with relatively little demand on the time, and training, of volunteers. This helps explain why the proportion of the population who volunteer at least occasionally has risen while the number of organizational memberships has fallen.

> Volunteering has developed in ways that make it more amenable to people who are geographically mobile or who lead their lives in porous institutions. Volunteers' stories about how they became involved in community activities reveal the influence of living in a changing society. Some sign up as volunteers because they have just moved to a new community and are hoping to meet people. Some have been laid off when their company downsized and start volunteering to fill their time. Some have been forced into partial retirement, giving them the opportunity to volunteer. Some are hedging their bets by volunteering at organizations that might be potential employers. (Wuthnow 1998:51)

Describing changes in religious volunteering, Roof (1999:50) points out that in the past women contributed the bulk of volunteer labor to religious organizations. Mostly homemakers, they comprised "a cadre of workers ready to do whatever was needed in a gender-defined religious work, such as preparing and serving meals, teaching Sunday School, and fund-raising." As these women moved into the labor force they were no longer available to fulfill this role, but they did not abandon volunteer work. Rather than being "on call," they sought ways to get involved that would "extend their own spiritual fulfillment and allow them to use their own particular talents or professional skills." Rather than wait to be told where and when their services would be needed, they adopted a more "individualist" approach to service work, choosing what they wanted to do, and when, and how. Religious congregations had to adapt to this new definition of the role. Rossi's (2001a:46) personal reflection describes the same kind of change.

> In my panel study of the delegates to the first ever national women's conference in Houston in 1977, it was already clear that a marked contrast in the nature of political involvement differentiated younger from older delegates: the older delegates had an extensive array of organizational memberships (an astonishing average of twelve!). The younger delegates, by contrast, were not "joiners" and belonged to relatively few formal clubs and organizations. Instead, they reported a great number of political actions on issues of concern to them and a preference for informal peer groups.

In summary, there are two reasons why trends in memberships have not resulted in a decline in volunteering. The first is that it is not clear that there has been any decline in memberships at all, rather than a re-distribution of those memberships. The second is that volunteer work has become more detached from membership. There well might be emerging two types of volunteer, one volunteering on a regular basis, while the other volunteers sporadically. A 2002 survey of Americans found that, while 33 percent of Americans had volunteered for a group over the past twelve months, only 24 percent had done so on a regular basis. Significantly, sporadic volunteers were less likely to be members of a voluntary association than the regular volunteers, and they were also younger (Keeter et al. 2002:17).

Comparative Trends

In chapter 16 we described some of the differences in volunteering between countries. In this section we will examine the data on trends in volunteering in those countries outside the United States for which there are time series data. We will refer to data from the WVS and also data gathered from surveys conducted in individual countries.

One study of trends in volunteering in Europe and United States looked at data from the WVS from 1981 to 1983 and 1991 to 1993 (Baer et al. 2001). In both surveys respondents in thirteen European countries, Canada, and the United States were asked if they had done any "unpaid work" for a list of types of voluntary association. Focusing on these "working memberships" the authors found no sign of an overall decline in volunteering across the decade. However, the appearance of stability in the aggregate level of volunteering masked differences between the countries. Volunteering had increased in the Netherlands, the United States, and Belgium but had declined in Japan and Spain.[11] To assess whether changes within countries might be due to temporal differences in the demographic profiles of countries, the authors controlled for education, occupation, age, community size, marital status, and gender. Once again, no overall trend in the pooled data was visible, nor did the specific country trends change.

It is unlikely that major changes in any kind of social behavior will occur in one decade. Subsequent research has extended the study of WVS data to 1999, covering nearly two decades (Halman 2003). Between 1981 and 1999, the rate of volunteering fell in West Germany, Spain, France, Iceland, and Ireland but rose slightly in Belgium, Denmark, Italy, the Netherlands, Sweden, and Great Britain, although only Belgium and the Netherlands showed a consistent rise during this period and West Germany, Iceland, and Ireland showed a consistent decline. In the other countries, the rate of volunteering fluctuated over this twenty-year period.[12]

Baer et al. (2001:266) also looked at changes in volunteer levels for each of six individual association types. For the pooled sample (i.e., all fifteen countries aggregated), they found significant decreases between 1981 and 1990 in union and youth-related work, a significant increase in volunteering for education, arts, and cultural organizations, and no change in volunteering for religious, professional, or political organizations. Looking at individual countries, they found an increase in union activism in Sweden and volunteering for cultural and arts organizations in Norway, Denmark, the Netherlands, and West Germany. Religious volunteering declined in Spain, Northern Ireland, Ireland, Sweden, and Canada. The authors do not make much effort to explain these differences, and this seems to be a major research project waiting to be undertaken. It is little wonder that Halman (2003:193) writes, with seeming exasperation, that "there is no uniform pattern of change in Europe, and the trends are not consistent over time." However, one thing does seem to be clear: there was no noticeable or widespread decline in the rate of volunteering in European countries between 1981 and 1999. This explains why Halman (2003:193) found little evidence of generational differences in volunteer behavior in Europe. In the United Kingdom, the Netherlands, and Sweden, volunteering rose between 1981 and 1999 in all age groups, while it fell in all age groups in West Germany and Spain. In the countries experiencing an increase in volunteerism, young people were just as likely to be contributing to the increase as older people. There is no sign a "long civic generation" in Europe, the population of which also experienced the Great Depression and the Second World War.

Several of the countries included in the WVS as well as some that are not included have gathered their own data on volunteering. These data can be used to plot trends, albeit over a rather brief time period.

Canada

Three national surveys, carried out in 1987, 1997 and 2000, make it possible to plot changes in the rate and intensity of volunteering among Canadians 15 years of age or older for thirteen years. Between 1987 and 1997, the rate rose from 26.7 percent to 31.4 percent. Young Canadians, between the ages of 15 and 24, were almost entirely responsible for this increase. They almost doubled their rate of volunteering in one decade. One reason is that full-time enrollment in school went up during this decade, and volunteering is encouraged by school attendance. In addition, an economic downturn made it more difficult for young people to get full-time jobs (Jones 2000). Although the overall volunteer *rate* rose between 1987 and 1997, the average hours volunteered per person fell, from 191 hours a year to 149. More Canadians were volunteering, but they were each contributing fewer hours. This is more clearly seen in the decline of the median, from 95 hours a year to 66 hours a year. In Quebec, the decline in time spent volunteering was quite dramatic: volunteer hours per volunteer fell by 41 percent (Reed and Selbee 2000a:26). Between 1997 and 2000 the volunteer rate dropped, by just over four percentage points, to 27 percent. The decline was most noticeable among middle aged Canadians. But while the rate was falling the average hours volunteered per volunteer increased from 149 to 162.[13] In other words, fewer volunteers were contributing more hours each.

As with the United States, there is some evidence that Canadians today are volunteering in a different way from that of previous generations. Between 1987 and 1997, young Canadians entered the volunteer labor force in larger numbers than any other age group, but they brought with them a more casual commitment to volunteer work. The volunteer rate among teenagers and young adults (15–24) rose from 18 percent in 1987 to 33 percent in 1997 but the average number of hours per volunteer in this group fell from

174 to 125. McClintock (2000:26) used these trend data to argue that non-profit administrators and volunteer supervisors should restructure how they use volunteers' time: "If you have or can design volunteer activities that can be done in small chunks—such as meal delivery at lunch hour—or, in short, but fairly intensive spurts—such as handling games at a weekend fun fair—you have a better chance of getting people involved."

United Kingdom

The United Kingdom is included in the WVS, but there are additional data on trends in volunteering in the United Kingdom from surveys conducted solely in that country. Once again, the volunteer data do not extend far back in the country's history but we do know more about trends in voluntary association memberships. Hall (1999:423) found that the average number of associational memberships rose from 0.73 in 1959 to 1.12 in 1990. The increase was most pronounced in the more educated classes and among managerial and professional workers. In no social class did memberships decline.[14] Warde et al. (2003:518), updating this analysis to 1997 with data from The British Household Panel Study, found that levels of membership in the 1990s "were not that much different from those of previous decades."

As far as volunteer work is concerned, the U.K. General Household Survey provides comparable data by which trends can be plotted, although the time span is very short because after 1992 volunteer questions were no longer asked. In 1981, 23 percent of the respondents reported doing some voluntary work and by 1992 the proportion had risen slightly to 25 percent (Hall 1999:425). Another set of surveys found that the proportion of Britons who had volunteered in the last week was 18 percent in 1981, rising to 22 percent in 1991 but falling slightly to 21 percent in 1997. Smith (1998:158) believes this relatively flat rate is the result of two opposing trends. Younger Britons have more negative attitudes toward volunteering than older people and their rate of volunteering is declining. Older people in the United Kingdom are now volunteering at a higher rate than ever before. Although this argument does not rest on particularly sophisticated methods, it is compatible with Putnam's generational thesis: the volunteer labor pool has remained at the same level because older people are contributing at a higher rate than formerly.

Sweden

As in other countries, the rate of volunteering in Sweden has remained more or less constant over the last forty years. And, as in other countries, Swedes have changed how they volunteer and what they volunteer for. Many of the voluntary associations that formerly attracted the allegiance of Swedes spoke to the collectivization of identity (particularly social class). As a result of growing access to education, the notion of individual autonomy has gained popularity among Swedish citizens. This has not led to a decline in volunteerism because "an individualistically minded citizen is not necessarily an egoistic citizen" (Rothstein 2001:219). Today, Swedes are no less disposed to work on behalf of others than they were formerly, but they are more interested in being able to exercise individual autonomy in their choice of volunteer work, to ensure that their volunteer work fits into their lifestyle. As in other countries, the more traditional, established voluntary organizations face difficulties mobilizing this new kind of volunteer.

Norway

The story with Norway seems to be quite similar to that of Sweden: the rates of volunteering have not declined but the Norwegians are beginning to interpret the volunteer role differently. A Norwegian survey found that older people perform volunteer work in connection with long established voluntary associations of which they are members. They can be relied on for a certain level of loyalty and commitment to the organization. Younger people are less likely to belong to these traditional organizations or any voluntary association at all. As a result, their volunteer work is more specialized, more independent of national organizations, and seldom linked to larger, ideological projects. "The new model of participation is therefore characterized by a strong activity orientation, short-term commitment, extensive turnover and a weak or contained value basis" (Wollebaek and Selle 2003b:174). The survey, conducted in 1998, revealed quite distinct age differences in attitudes toward volunteering. Just over half (57%) of the 16- to 24-year-olds surveyed said it was important to volunteer for a particular organization, compared to 69 percent of those aged between 55 and 69. Twice as many of the 55- to 69-year-olds said it was important to volunteer for an organization of some kind other than on your own. Thirty-three percent of the young Norwegians agreed that volunteers could receive partial payment, compared to 18 percent among those aged between 55 and 69. Overall, the younger people were less attached or committed to organizations and took a slightly more calculating attitude toward volunteerism:

> The new volunteer, epitomized by today's young adult, is an individualist, but not necessarily an egoist. To drift from interest to interest, and actively choose what one wants to be a part of, is not only compatible with, but also the essence of the mantra of our times—to lead 'reflexive' and modern lives. (Wollebaek and Selle 2003b:176)

Unable to determine whether this is the result of generational or life cycle phenomena, the researchers argue the case for generation on the grounds of the decline of the "traditional, value based" organizations: "it is improbable that today's youth will develop the attitudes today's elderly attach importance to, even if they should become just as active" (Wollebaek and Selle 2003b:175). This is an interesting attempt to explain trends in the interpretation of the volunteer role by invoking changes in the nature of the organizations that mobilize volunteer work, resulting in a prediction, not that absolute levels will rise or fall as a result, but that people will change the way they volunteer.

Netherlands

The WVS data show a recent increase in volunteering in the Netherlands. Data from the Dutch Survey of Living Conditions spanning the years 1977–1995 confirm this by showing an increase in the percentage of the population volunteering. Most of this increase has taken place in the areas of "culture, sports and hobbies" and "childcare, schools and youth work" (De Hart and Dekker 1999:81). This is all the more remarkable in light of the fact that, although the average number of hours worked for pay has fallen over recent decades, the "free time" of the Dutch has not increased (De Hart and Dekker 1999:84).

Time diary data from 1980 and 1995 showed that the proportion of Dutch people mentioning having volunteered that day was unchanged. Men were less likely to have volunteered in 1995 than 1980 but women more. Volunteering declined among younger adults (18–34) but increased among those in the 55- to 74-year-old bracket. The rate of volunteering fell among the employed but rose among housewives. The college-educated were less likely to volunteer in 1995 than they were in 1980 but regular churchgoers were more likely (De Hart and Dekker 1999:87). These same data also reveal how people's lives have become fragmented and their leisure time more diversified. Despite the fact that Dutch people are feeling busier than they have ever done before they continue to volunteer at the same rate in part because the social forces making it more difficult to volunteer balance those making it easier (De Hart and Dekker 1999:89).

Australia

Australians have been studying volunteer work since the 1970s, but changes in the definition of volunteering and the way it is measured in social surveys make it very difficult to track changes. Ironmonger (2000) used data from surveys conducted in 1992 and 1997. He included informal volunteering (help given informally to kin and friends outside the household) but excluded "church or religious activity." Both surveys were based on nationally representative samples and both used a method of having respondents (aged 15 or more) keep diaries over a forty-nine-hour period. In this short span of five years, the average number of hours per week volunteered by men rose from 2.18 to 2.41 and by women from 2.85 to 3.50. There appears to be little room for the generation theory in Australia. One study used information collected in time diary studies to compare the volunteer rates of four birth cohorts of Australians: those born circa 1932, 1942, 1952, and 1962. Each successive cohort had a higher rate of volunteering than the earlier cohorts: "Most crucially the rate of volunteering among the allegedly disengaged post-war generation was higher than among their allegedly more civic predecessors" (Wilkinson and Bittman 2002:15).

In summary, the short-term trends in volunteering in a number of countries show just as many people volunteering as there were ten or twenty years ago, although there are trends in what people volunteer for and how they schedule their volunteer work to accommodate increasing demands on their time. Although there are trends and countertrends across countries, some gaining volunteers while others lose them, we need to know more about why these differences occur and whether or not they signal the beginning of divergent patterns of volunteer work.

The Non-Profit Sector and the Demand for Volunteer Labor

Up this point, we have focused entirely on factors that might affect changes in the supply of volunteer labor, but we cannot ignore the possibility that social changes influence the demand for volunteer labor also. As already noted in chapter 6, modern societies are comprised of private, public, and non-profit sectors. Most volunteer work is performed in the context of organizations located in the non-profit sector: in 1989, 68.3 percent of volunteer hours donated by Americans went to non-profit organizations, 5.6 percent to for-profit firms, and 26.1 percent to public sector organizations, mostly local public schools (Rose-Ackerman 1996:703). The size of the non-profit sector is bound to have some effect on the number of people who volunteer.

The expanding role of the state in modern economies has led some scholars to speculate that the non-profit sector will be squeezed by this expansion and the demand for volunteer labor will accordingly decline. Those on the political left wing see this as a good thing because it lessens reliance on demeaning private charity, but those on the political right wing see it as a bad thing because it is another example of an expansionary state stifling private initiative. In a 1981 speech Ronald Reagan said, "The truth is we've let Government take away many things we once considered were really ours to do voluntarily out of the goodness of our hearts and a sense of community pride and neighborliness" (Poppendieck 1998:92). As we shall see, although Reagan voiced his support for the volunteer role, the political reality was that "support for the volunteer effort was systematically eroded" during his administration because the social programs that formerly supported volunteers were cut with no provision for alternative funding to support them (Ellis and Noyes 1990:286).

In this section we look at how the development of the modern welfare state has affected the demand for volunteer work. During the nineteenth century, charities were organized to meet social needs largely neglected by the state or considered unprofitable by businesses. Between the 1880s and 1914, many European nations, together with Australia and New Zealand, launched social spending programs that constitute the core of modern welfare states, aimed mainly at providing financial security in old age and temporary benefits for unemployed workers. The Great Depression expanded these programs and in the countries affected the relative contribution of the voluntary sector declined fairly steadily (Wolch 1990:37). Ideological support for the welfare state, mainly from social democratic and left wing organizations, proved antithetical to the whole notion of providing social services on the basis of charity and "good works." Not only was volunteer work considered inefficient and unreliable but it also demeaned citizens who should regard any benefits they received as a right rather than an act of noblesse oblige.

The expansion of the welfare state also increased the number of people employed in the public sector and they soon became unionized. They felt they had a stake in the public provision of social services, which would be threatened by a parallel set of services provided by amateurs. They suspected that volunteer work would be used by public agencies to displace paid employees or drive down their wages, and they actively opposed it (Kieffer 1986:57).[15] The gradual professionalization of social work, psychological counseling, and nursing, together with the spread of licensing and certification for these and other helping professions, also helped breed an attitude of hostility toward the amateurish volunteer, depicted as woefully lacking in expertise, training, and accountability.

And yet, despite the continued expansion of the welfare state after the Second World War, the demand for volunteers has not declined. The crowding out hypothesis has not been validated. Countries with higher public social spending also have higher national levels of trust in public institutions, trust in other people, and active and passive participation (Oorschot 2005). There is little correlation between the size of the welfare state and the size of the non-profit sector. Among eleven countries with above-average expenditures on social welfare, five have relatively small non-profit sectors but six have relatively large ones (Salamon et al. 1999:14). In Canada, the more money a province spends on welfare, the higher the rate of volunteerism in that province (Day and Devlin 1996). In short, far from pushing volunteerism to the sidelines, government welfare programs seem to have encouraged it. In what follows we will consider some of the reasons why the expansion of the welfare state has not brought about the end of volunteerism.

First, although the goals and concerns of charitable organizations and of the welfare state overlap to some degree (e.g., taking care of the elderly), there are many areas in which their roles do not overlap at all. In the nineteenth century, people who volunteered for the temperance movement or for their local trade union branch were not doing work the government would otherwise have done. Many other areas of volunteer work (e.g., in connection with religious organizations) are unaffected in any discernable negative way by the expansion of the welfare state. Although the state has taken over some of the work formerly done by volunteers, it has also created more demand for volunteer work. For example, volunteers are needed to make sure that people are getting the public benefits to which they are entitled.

Second, the very feature of the welfare state that some find most appealing—its rationality—others find objectionable, believing that volunteer work is a better way to provide social services. Some even turn this logic on its head: the rationality of the state is itself inefficient. For example, volunteer Susan Robbins believes that government mandated programs to provide more educational opportunities for the deprived are inadequate because they treat everyone the same way, and are therefore wasteful (Wuthnow 1991:256). She believes volunteers are more efficient because they can tailor their efforts to individual needs. The provision of social services by volunteers is also preferred because civil servants often place clients in a subordinate and demeaning position, whereas volunteers treat them as people with a moral claim to the assistance they provide. Three out of four Britons agree that volunteers offer "something different that could never be provided by the state system" (Smith 1997:107). In a study of Home Start, an organization set up to help mothers having difficulties coping with their children, the mothers preferred to interact with the volunteers rather than social workers because they saw the volunteers as more generous with their time, more caring, less threatening, more practical, and more supportive emotionally (Bagilhole 1996:202). People think "compassion should have a human face" (Wuthnow 1991:270).

Third, support for the welfare state has weakened in recent years as a result of perceived inadequacies in the system and the promotion of market-driven solutions to social problems. Welfare state programs are no longer seen as panaceas but as having many limitations in scope and effectiveness. This leaves more room for volunteer work to exist alongside the welfare state. By more than three to one, Americans surveyed in 1998 rejected the idea that "most charities only do work the government should really be doing." Conversely, virtually all (96%) agreed, "no matter how much the government does, there is important work for private charities to do" (Ferree et al. 1998:6). It is hardly surprising that Americans want volunteer work to be practiced alongside government programs because their support for the welfare state has never been strong. Habitat for Humanity volunteers, whether from the political left or the right, contribute their time, in part, *because* they are skeptical of government attempts to alleviate the housing problem (Baggett 2001:107). In the 1990s, Americans were asked their opinions on various "strategies for helping the needy": only a quarter thought spending more money on government services would be useful, compared to half who thought that more people volunteering would help "a lot" (Wuthnow 1994:209). In 2001, Americans were asked who they thought would do the best job of providing social service to those in need: 37 percent chose religious organizations, 28 percent chose federal and state governments, and 27 percent opted for secular, community-based groups (Pew Research Center 2001:3). Religious organizations were respected for their role in feeding the hungry and counseling and educating prisoners, whereas government agencies were seen as doing the best job in the areas of literacy, health care, and job training. The relation between government and volunteer work is thus much more nuanced than one simply being a substitute for the other. Volunteers are regarded as being better at doing some things and public servants as being better at doing others. Americans do not reject government solutions because they lack faith in them. Rather, they support a vibrant and healthy non-profit sector because they want to people looking for help to have freedom of choice. Americans who oppose relying too much on faith-based voluntary work do not do so because they are more in favor of government solutions but because they are concerned that help-seekers will be forced to take part in religious services—again, a matter of freedom of choice (Pew Research Center 2001:11).

Another reason why Americans take the position that both volunteers and public servants are needed is that they are less inclined to trust the public servants than citizens of other countries. In a 2002 survey, Americans were asked if they felt they could trust each of a list of number of service-providing agencies. Forty-five percent said they trusted "people who run the public welfare in your community" a lot, or some, compared to 65 percent who said they trusted "people who run the Salvation Army in your community" and 72 percent who said they trusted people who run community organizations that help the needy (Wuthnow 2004:233). Not all Americans take such a cynical view of their government. Blacks have more confidence in government agencies than Whites, whereas college graduates and people earning higher incomes choose secular non-profits over both government and religious organizations. White evangelical Protestants are the most enthusiastic about religious strategies, and most supportive of faith-based social service (Pew Research Center 2001:5). Nevertheless, a culture of suspicion surrounding publicly provided services creates a fertile environment for private, volunteer work to flourish.

Fourth, proponents of the crowding out hypothesis assume that volunteers always oppose the welfare state and that advocates of the welfare state always oppose volunteerism. The evidence on this is rather mixed, although it is true that one can be a supporter of welfare state policies and volunteerism simultaneously. The leading architect of the welfare state in Britain, William Beveridge, was a firm believer in the voluntary sector, which he saw as "a counterweight to both the 'business motive' and a necessarily rule-based state bureaucracy" (Lewis 1999:260). Even in the United Kingdom, where support for the welfare state is quite strong, less than half of the population

(43%) believes the day will eventually arrive when public service has rendered volunteer labor unnecessary (Smith 1997:107). For their part, volunteers do not necessarily think they can replace government. They recognize the limits on what they can do for their clients. The Home Start program in the United Kingdom recruits volunteers to provide support and counseling to mothers referred by health visitors as having acute problems coping with their children. The responsibilities of the volunteer are extensive and often demanding. The volunteers do not pretend to substitute for trained caseworkers. One volunteer said,

> Some families, like last . . . it's a very disturbed family, and it really needs a lot of professional expertise . . . I've felt inadequate at times. I believe statutory bodies have failed this family. (Bagilhole 1996:197)

Volunteers are not necessarily more hostile to the idea of the public provision of social and individual needs. In a survey of middle class Australians, Pusey (2000:23) found that volunteers were half as likely as non-volunteers to agree that "most people on the dole are fiddling the system in one way or another" and twice as likely to reject the suggestion that "if welfare benefits weren't so generous, people would learn to stand on their own two feet." In the United States, a 1988 survey found that volunteers were no less likely than other people to think that the government has a responsibility to care for its citizens (Sundeen 1992).

Volunteers thus recognize the limitations of their role and acknowledge the contribution governments can make, but they are more inclined than non-volunteers to believe they have a comparative advantage over civil servants. In the United Kingdom, 34 percent of regular volunteers but 52 percent non-volunteers agreed that there would be no need for volunteer workers if the government fulfilled all its responsibilities; 9 percent of regular volunteers but 17 percent of non-volunteers agreed that volunteers are less efficient than paid workers; 83 percent of regular volunteers but 75 percent of non-volunteers agreed that volunteers offer something different that could never be provided by the state system (Smith 1998:113). In summary, volunteers are very similar to non-volunteers in their attitude toward the welfare state.

Even if there were any opposition between the welfare state and volunteerism, the growth of the welfare state has recently slowed in many advanced capitalist societies and significant restructuring has occurred in the relation between the state and the non-profit sector. In the interest of limiting "big government" and a "dependency culture" fostered by political entitlements and to encourage private initiatives, politicians have begun mapping out a new kind of partnership between voluntary agencies and the state whereby non-profit organizations could be contracted to provide some of the services the state formerly provided directly (Bales 1996:207). One consequence is that more and more volunteers end up working for the state.[16] When she came to power, Prime Minister Thatcher voiced her opinion that "the volunteer movement is at the heart of all our social welfare provision" (Bagilhole 1996:190) but she did not pursue ways of using the voluntary sector to cut public spending. It was left to "New Labour" to push this policy more aggressively in the 1990s (Kendall 2003:55). In the United States, public–non-profit partnerships date back to the 1950s, when the Eisenhower administration gave support to religiously affiliated social service agencies (Cnaan et al. 1999:11). Groups such as Catholic Charities, Lutheran Social Services, and the Federation of Jewish Philanthropies began receiving federal support to run hospitals, employment counseling, sheltered accommodation for the elderly, and the like. However, the conservative policies of the Reagan era "catapulted mainline religious organizations and charities into increasing provision of social services, both on their premises and in support of community agencies, by providing volunteers, money, and use of facilities" (Cnaan et al. 1999:8). Under the Clinton administration a new partnership between the state and the voluntary sector increased the proportion of the revenues of non-profit agencies provided by the government. Of all the money contributed to the U.S. non-profit sector in 1992, half came from membership dues, usage fees, and investment income, and close to a fifth from private donations, but the balance came from the government (Rose-Ackerman 1996:703). Government support for the non-profit sector tripled between 1977 and 1997 (mainly to health, social services, and the arts), while individual charitable giving only doubled (Salamon 2002:33, 36).

The large presence of religious organizations in the provision of social services in the United States was, for a long time, a serious barrier to the government giving more assistance to volunteer agencies because so many of them were closely tied to churches. In 2001, President Bush signed two executive orders, one establishing a White House Office of Faith-Based and Community Initiatives and another establishing Centers for Faith-Based and Community Initiatives in five federal agencies. Although problems with church-state separation issues meant that no legislation on these policy changes was possible, the intention of the Bush administration was to use the executive power to direct funds in support of faith-based voluntary efforts to deliver social assistance and attack community problems. Religious/public partnerships were not new. But the Bush initiative marked a change because it broke down the wall separating the social service function from the religious functions discharged by these groups. In 1996, the United States congress signed into law the Personal Responsibility and Work Opportunities Reconciliation Act of 1996. A key provision of the act allowed congregations and other religious bodies not incorporated as regular non-profit organizations to apply for public funds to provide social services while maintaining their religious character. Popularly known as "charitable choice" this new policy created organizations such as Be-

yond Welfare, founded in 1997. Funded by private foundations, individual donations, and local and state grants, the goal of the organization is to encourage
people on welfare or in poverty to work toward economic self-sufficiency. Besides providing job coaching, mental health counseling, help locating affordable housing and child care, and support during emergencies, the organization
sets up "partnerships" between middle class volunteers and "clients" trying to
make it off welfare.

State-church boundary issues have not figured so prominently in the new
partnership between the state and the non-profit sector in other countries, but
most have experienced changes in the way governments relate to agencies organizing voluntary workers. Increasingly, governments are negotiating partnerships with non-profit agencies to deliver social services and those agencies
are becoming increasingly reliant on public funds to operate. In the 1990s,
just over half the revenues of registered charities in Canada came from Canadian governments (Day and Devlin 1996:38). In Australia, the government
provides twice as much funding to the non-profit sector as private foundations (Warburton and Mutch 2000:38). In Germany, the state provides 68
percent all non-profit revenues (mainly hospitals), with France, at 59 percent,
quite close behind (Rose-Ackerman 1996:707).

Part of the emerging alliance between the state and the non-profit sector
is a new role for the state as a direct recruiter, organizer, and mobilizing
agent for volunteer workers. The state no longer leaves it to private initiatives
to create a supply of volunteer labor but takes on some of this responsibility
itself. As we shall see, getting more service delivery workers is not the only
reason for taking on this role: many politicians think that volunteer work
provides other social benefits. This is made plain in a white paper issued in
1989 by the Tory government entitled *Caring for People: Community Care in
the Next Decade and Beyond,* which argued that volunteer work is a valuable way of getting people "to take responsibility for their own needs whenever possible." In other words, volunteer work is not only good for the client
but good for the volunteer as well (Hudson 1998:456). "New Labour" has
taken a much more public and aggressive attitude toward encouraging volunteer work than preceding governments, inspired by a communitarian philosophy designed to steer a middle course between the individualism of free
market thinking and the old-style collectivism of the Socialist Party. One of
the principal tenets of communitarianism is that a healthy voluntary sector is
vital to the survival of democracy. During the Blair administration, the Home
Office adopted a goal of increasing the number of volunteers in the United
Kingdom as part of official government policy. The "Millennium Volunteers"
scheme was designed to get more young people volunteering in their local
community. The Experience Corps, launched in 2001, targeted people 50 and
over. In 2001, the Home Office drew up an Active Communities Agenda with
a target of making substantial progress by 2004 toward involving one million people in their communities. That same year, it carried out a citizenship

survey of people aged 16 and over living in England and Wales to provide an evidence base by which to gauge progress. In 2005, the home secretary, Charles Clark, launched the Year of the Volunteer, designed to increase opportunities for volunteering and raise public awareness of them, in the interest of strengthening communities, helping people learn and care about democracy, and building their own confidence and skills.

Contemporaneously, and guided by the same political philosophy, federal and provincial governments in Canada have instituted programs to encourage volunteerism. In 2000, the federal government committed nearly a hundred million Canadian dollars to a five-year plan called the Voluntary Sector Initiative, the purpose of which was to improve the delivery of government social services through more extensive use of volunteers (Brock 2001:55). In 2002, then Prime Minister Jean Chretien appointed the minister of Canadian heritage as the person responsible for strengthening the relationship between the state and the voluntary sector. In December, the minister, Sheila Copps, announced the establishment of three new national centers to support volunteerism across Canada. In addition, local networks were to be set up in each province and territory to ensure that the centers' programs met the needs and priorities of voluntary organizations and volunteers. As part of the Canada Volunteerism Initiative, funding of $35 million was to be provided to the centers over the next five years.

In the United States, the National and Community Service Act of 1990 created a private, non-profit organization (Points of Light Foundation) and a new federal agency (Commission on National and Community Service) to promote volunteerism. Three years later, the National and Community Service Trust Act created the Corporation for National Service (CNS) to house all domestic service programs. Several existing national service programs were brought under the CNS umbrella (e.g., Volunteers for Service in America, the Retired and Senior Volunteers Program). A new program, AmeriCorps, was also started. In return for a ten-month commitment, members of AmeriCorps receive a small stipend for their services, averaging about $7,500 a year, and they accrue credits of $4,725 in an educational trust that can be allocated either to tuition expenses or accumulated loans. According to Perry et al. (1999:229) "Americorps was envisioned as a way to enhance civic commitments by providing a way for participants to contribute to the solution of public problems and to build communities." President Clinton hoped it would also bring together people of different races and social backgrounds. Data from the first year of service indicate this hope was, to some degree, realized. Forty-seven percent of AmeriCorps volunteers were White, 31 percent were African American, and 14 percent were Hispanic (Perry et al. 1999:243).

In some cases, and quite controversially, governments have turned to volunteer work as a condition for receiving "entitlements" such as unemployment benefits and subsidized housing. Conservative politicians want clients to work in return for the government benefits they receive, and they believe that community service will help instill values and attitudes that will prevent the client from needing government "handouts" in the future. In 1998 the United States Congress passed into law the Quality Housing and Work Responsibility Act. It requires public housing residents not working full time, studying, disabled, or over the age of 62 to perform community service every year. Supporters of the legislation argued that volunteer work would instill a greater sense of discipline and responsibility among public housing residents. Chen (2004:1) estimated that the legislation could affect 350,000 people nationwide in 2004. New York City gives its public housing residents who are not exempt twelve months to complete ninety-six hours of volunteer work. If one household member does not comply the whole household runs the risk of eviction. Welfare was thus made conditional on "giving something back." Australia has a similar scheme, tied to employment: "so-called mutual obligation requirements mean that many welfare recipients are obliged to work in unpaid positions to maintain their [unemployment] payments" (Brown et al. 2003:2).

In summary, the growth of the welfare state has not squashed the volunteer spirit or reduced the size of the non-profit sector. This is partly due to the fact that the voluntary sector addresses needs the state cannot meet. It is partly due to the fact that volunteers seek goals (e.g., moral education) that are outside the purview of state action. To the extent they do not perform the same functions in a society they can co-exist. Recent trends have seen a closer relation between the state and the non-profit sector as governments funnel more social service funds through non-profits and provide assistance to non-profits in finding and keeping volunteer workers. The state is thus having a positive effect on the supply of volunteers, directly through quasi-public agencies such as the Corporation for National Service, mandated to mobilize volunteers, and indirectly, in the form of volunteers recruited to replace staff who have been fired because of budget cuts, and in the form of charitable organizations that have been placed under contract to provide social services, whose labor force is comprised partly of volunteer workers. The state's wish to be a partner to the non-profit sector is motivated not only by the need to deliver services more efficiently. There is also a political agenda. By encouraging volunteerism, governments believe they will promote individual and civic responsibility. They will also promote what Isaacs (2003:6) calls "the principle of subsidiarity" whereby social problems are tackled at "the lowest and most proximate level of engagement consistent with their solution." In this vein, skeptics of AmeriCorps argue that paying people to volunteer does little to inspire long-term civic commitment and that much of the work volunteers perform does little to develop job-related or civic skills. Furthermore, encouraging people to think of "service to their community" as meaning primarily one-on-one service or "clean up" activities does little to educate people about the structural causes of social problems or encourage a more activist, social justice, stance toward solving them. The state's encouragement of volunteer work does not, therefore, come without a price. The principle of subsidiarity means that groups wishing to address more deep-seated, macro-level social problems, such as high rates of unemployment or wage stagnation, are unlikely to get support from governments. Feeding a hungry person is not the same as ending hunger. Justice issues are pushed to the background in favor of "compassionate conservatism." Indeed, government agencies are usually prohibited from funding or offering material support to groups that advocate political positions. As Isaacs (2003:7) notes, it may be true that problems such as the recidivism of youthful offenders can be tackled by granting money to local community or faith-based organizations but rates of juvenile delinquency are more likely to come down if the minimum wage is raised or more affordable public housing is made available. This would not be such a serious concern were it not for the fact that volunteer work is touted as a substitute for rather than a complement to government efforts, as if tutoring programs for the illiterate were an effective substitute for good public schools.

Conclusion

Despite widespread alarm that people today are less interested in doing volunteer work, survey data indicate that there is no cause for concern, that the volunteer spirit is not diminished. Major structural changes, such as the movement of many women into the full-time labor force, the decline of traditional voluntary associations and small town life, and the expansion of the welfare state, have not dampened the volunteer spirit. There have certainly been some changes. First, the composition of the volunteer labor force is changing: fewer married women, more young adults and older people. Second, the types of activities that draw the most volunteer labor are constantly changing. Fifty years ago protecting the environment was hardly on the map as a volunteer activity. Predominantly rural and small town populations supported a host of religious, civic, service, and public safety groups, many of which have declined as that way of life disappears. Third, the way people volunteer is changing from long-term commitments in affiliation with an organization to more sporadic, contingent volunteer activities. Fourth, more volunteers are working for organizations with some kind of relationship to government agencies, subject, in part, to the regulations imposed by these agencies—a subject we will return to in a later chapter. But the net effect of these changes has been stable or even slightly rising rates of volunteering. This is because the social changes have conflicting consequences for volunteering: higher education levels boost the rate of volunteering, but higher urbanization rates depress it; the movement of women into the labor force depresses the volunteer rate, the decline of the extended family boosts it;

secularization weakens support for religious volunteering but increases support for advocacy groups and new social movements interested in issues of recognition and identity. Thus, despite the widespread concern that social and economic changes are eroding the basis for community concerns and action, there is little evidence that a consistent, secular trend downward has occurred—so far.

Part 5.

The Organization of Volunteer Work

In part 5, we look in detail at the actual tasks volunteers perform and the way the work of the volunteer is organized. For the first topic we will rely on social survey data and for the second we will rely on ethnographic data. In the book thus far we have used the generic term "volunteer work" to refer to unpaid labor people perform on behalf of an organization. We have distinguished between different types or domains of volunteering, based largely on the product or service the volunteer provides. But these concepts are very blunt instruments for identifying and measuring the actual work that volunteers perform on the job. When volunteers go to work they might be asked to knock on doors, paint doors, lock doors after a meeting, write checks for the purchase of doors, help infirm people negotiate doors, design doors for a Web page, teach young children to spell "doors," or open metaphorical doors into a business corporation or city council. Some of these jobs demand physical skills, manual dexterity, and strength; other jobs call for a high level of literacy, mathematical ability, organizational skills, and the ability to get along with people. Some jobs require, or permit, making decisions, being creative, supervising others, and being a spokesperson for the organization; other jobs are routine, menial, and demand obedience to the commands of others. Some jobs bring the volunteer face-to-face with the client; others jobs are backstage, in the office, or the kitchen. In short, the world of unpaid work is very similar to the world of paid work: it embraces a wide array of different "jobs" or tasks.

Ethnographic studies, with their microscopic focus on volunteer activities, provide a rich and detailed picture of the tasks that volunteers perform, but this picture is inevitably limited in scope. Survey research offers another strategy for studying volunteer tasks. Volunteers can be asked to identify the specific tasks they perform as volunteers, thus making it possible to count the number of tasks volunteers perform, to identify those tasks most commonly performed, and to construct a demographic profile of who does what kind of task. The limitation of survey research, as we shall see, is that it is a very blunt instrument for measuring tasks. Surveys are limited in the amount of detail they can provide on the nature of tasks performed. The task categories we find in social surveys tend to be rather inclusive and include quite heterogeneous activities or they sometimes fail to identify any actual task at all. For example, the Independent Sector identifies nine different religious tasks and thirty-nine different secular tasks. Some are quite specific (poll taker) but others are rather general (fire/rescue squad volunteer). The 2002 Current Population Survey (CPS) supplement on volunteering identifies ten different "activities," but most of them are too general (engage in activities to protect the environment or animals) or lump together activities (provide care or transportation) that are too heterogeneous to be useful for analytical purposes. That being said, we certainly have much more data on the kinds of things people do as volunteers than we had thirty years ago, and it is now possible to see much more clearly which activities volunteers are most likely to be asked to perform and who is most likely to perform them. The purpose of chapter 18 is to document how many tasks the average volunteer performs, which of the tasks are more commonly performed, and who is most likely to be assigned to a given task. The data provide a valuable source of information on the division of volunteer labor.

In chapter 19 we look inside the organizations that hire volunteers to see how their work is managed. The emphasis is less on what the individual volunteer brings to the experience and more on how the organization of volunteering makes certain kinds of experiences more likely. Organizations do not completely determine how people think about volunteering and how they act as volunteers any more than business firms completely the determine the thoughts and behaviors of their employees, but we are interested in the ways organizations channel and use volunteers' needs and motivations to mobilize their energies and strengthen their commitment to the organization. The volunteer role is defined principally in organizational terms: the rights and responsibilities of the volunteer are defined in relation to those of the other volunteers with whom they work, the paid staff who oversee their work, and the clients they serve. The role is not a given: its terms and meanings are defined in relation to these other roles and, of course, roles performed in the workplace and at home. The organization must manage the inevitable tensions that arise as their various roles relate to each other and as volunteers seek to balance their often-conflicting demands.

Throughout most of the book we have ignored the fact that, for many people, their volunteer work is something like a career. It can last many years. In chapter 19 we focus on attachment to volunteer work and commitment to volunteer organizations. By attachment we simply mean the number of years a person has been volunteering. By commitment we mean the length of time a person has been volunteering for the same organization. Recruiting volunteers is a tedious and time-consuming business, giving volunteer organizations a strong incentive to reduce turnover among their volunteers. And yet paid staff have few of the incentives—or sanctions—that are available to managers and supervisors of paid employees. Much of the sociological research in this area has been devoted to trying to explain variations in the levels of attachment and commitment, looking both at the characteristics of the individual volunteers (who is most likely to quit?) and at the characteristics of organizations (which organizational practices do the best job of reducing turnover?). We end this chapter with a discussion of the changing organizational environment of volunteer work as the "partnership" with government bureaucracies develops and the probable consequences of these changes for the volunteer and for volunteer work.

18

Volunteer Tasks

People say they volunteer because they "want to make a difference," to "help people," to "get involved," or to "do God's work" but the chances are that, for most of them, volunteer work provides an opportunity to do something specific: edit a newsletter, mentor a child, cook a meal, build a house, comfort a cancer patient, work with animals, drive a truck, teach young children, or share a love of music. In other words, they did not first decide to volunteer and then choose what to do as a volunteer. They sought out, or were offered, the chance to perform a particular task, in much the same way they would seek out, or be offered, a particular paid job.

Formal volunteering is defined as help provided to or on behalf of an organization. This is another reason to pay close attention to the tasks volunteers perform because organizations typically recruit people to perform specific tasks rather than recruit volunteers and then decide what to do with them. They need someone to help raise funds, keep the books, maintain the building, distribute leaflets from door to door, and organize meetings. These organizational needs create a demand not for volunteer work in general so much as specific types of volunteer work. The volunteer's "choice" of task to perform is therefore partly a function of his or her own preferences and aptitudes, but also a function of organizational needs. Few people take up volunteering because they actually like begging strangers for money, but this is one of the most common volunteer tasks, simply because the organizations with which volunteers are associated are in constant need of money. Conversely, the supply of certain "jobs" such as serving on a governing board is structurally limited, which is why few volunteers have these jobs.

In this chapter we look in detail at the actual tasks volunteers perform and who is most likely to do a particular task. Because we are primarily interested in analyzing how social characteristics determine who does what, we sort volunteer tasks along two dimensions. The first is vertical: it describes the social stratification of tasks according to a dimension running from simple, repetitive, and low-skill jobs offering little room for autonomy or initiative to complex, varied, and high-skill tasks offering much room for autonomy and decision making. The tasks at the bottom of this hierarchy resemble the work of blue-collar and service workers, while those at the top resemble the work of professionals and managers. Implicit in this dimension is a hierarchy of status whereby more esteem is bestowed upon the more complex tasks that require strategic decision making. The second dimension is horizontal, pointing to differences within strata. The chief criterion used in horizontal differentiation is gender. The same level job (according to the first dimension) can be either predominantly male or predominantly female in its connotation. We assume that cultural understandings as to the suitability of men and women for particular jobs found in the household and the workplace also inform the division of labor in volunteer work. The purpose of this chapter is to see if social characteristics influence what kind of task volunteers do, using these two dimensions to distinguish between types of task. To what degree does social class help determine the quality of the task volunteers are assigned to? To what extent does gender determine what type of task volunteers perform? Is the pattern of occupational segregation found in paid employment also found in the world of volunteer work?

Our ability to analyze volunteer tasks is necessarily limited by how many tasks are identified in social surveys. The number of tasks and how precisely they are defined and distinguished are largely a function of the time limits imposed by the cost of administering social surveys. We have no way of knowing if all the tasks have been identified and measured. The Independent Sector survey asks only respondents who had volunteered in the past month to identify up to two activities for each of the organizations for which they volunteer. By gathering data on tasks only from volunteers who were active in the past month the survey probably inflates the number of tasks volunteers perform because respondents who have volunteered in the past month are more committed to their work. The CPS allows respondents to name up to ten tasks, but only for the organization for which they volunteered the most hours. This measure probably under-counts the number of tasks volunteers perform because many volunteer for more than one organization.[1] The 2000 National Survey of Giving, Volunteering and Participating asked Canadians whether they had performed any of fifteen tasks (e.g., office work), allowing multiple mentions. The 1997 National Survey of Volunteering in the United Kingdom showed respondents a list of ten "types of activity" and asked them if they performed that activity in each of the areas ("fields") in which they volunteered (Davis 1998:40).

We will analyze the Independent Sector data on tasks below but before we get to that we will describe the raw percentages found in other surveys. In the 1997 United Kingdom survey, the percentage mentioning each listed task among those volunteering was as follows:

Fund-raising (66%)
Organizing or helping run events (55%)
Committee member (36%)
Driving (26%)
Representing (21%)
Visiting people (20%)
Other (20%)
Counseling (17%)
Clerical (19%)
Social service (18%)

About half the volunteers named at least one task and 22 percent named five. The 1992 United Kingdom General Household Survey asked volunteers which tasks they had performed in the past year from a list provided (Goddard 1994:10):

Fund-raising, other than collections (45%)
Committee member (31%)
Collecting money directly (30%)
Helped at a club (26%)
Administration (19%)
Organized or helped with entertainment (18%)
Tutor (15%)
Canvass (12%)
Visiting people (10%)
Practical help (10%)
Counsel (8%)

The ten most frequently reported tasks among Canadian volunteers were (Hall et al. 2001:41)

Organize or help out at events (57%)
Committee member (41%)
Canvass or fund-raise (40%)
Office work (30%)
Provide information, lobby (29%)
Teach or coach (28%)
Provide care or support (27%)
Collect or serve food (25%)

Drive (20%)
Maintenance (16%)

The fact that activities are classified differently in these surveys makes it almost impossible to draw general conclusions or compare the results, but some patterns are fairly clear. "Helping out" is mentioned often not only because it is a rather generic category but also because it describes accurately a lot of what volunteers do. Even if a volunteer is "hired" to perform one task (e.g., drive) he or she is likely to list helping out as another task (when needed). The frequency with which fund-raising is mentioned illustrates the heavy reliance of non-profit organizations on revenues generated by volunteers. Committee memberships are by definition in short supply, but a surprisingly large proportion of volunteers mention serving on a committee. This attests to the democratic structure of many voluntary associations and also to the tendency for these organizations to create offices as rewards to give to volunteers.

Number of Tasks

In 1992, 1994, and 1996 the Independent Sector survey asked those respondents who volunteered in the previous month about specific tasks they might have performed. Respondents were shown a list of tasks and asked to check off no more than two tasks for each area in which they volunteered. For example, a respondent who volunteered only in the areas of health and education could have a minimum of zero tasks and a maximum of four. Respondents were free to say they had performed the same task (e.g., fund-raising) in more than one area. The list of forty tasks was subdivided into ten tasks in connection with religious organizations and thirty tasks in connection with secular organizations. To make multivariate analysis possible, we aggregated the tasks into thirteen categories in order to get sufficiently large cell sizes. The categories are listed below together with the percentage of respondents who had performed the task indicated. Because the respondent could mention more than one task, the percentages do not add up to one hundred. Just over a third (35.8%) of the volunteers had performed at least one religious task and 58 percent had performed at least one secular task.[2]

Religious Organizations

Assist paid staff (aide to clergy, choir member/director, or church usher) 18.8%.
Administration (deacon/deaconess) 2.9%
Counseling (parish visitor) 2.87%
Teaching (Sunday school/Bible teacher) 11.6%
Clerical (office work) 6.2%

Secular Organizations

Assist paid staff (assistant to paid employee) 8.1%
Clerical (library work, office work, campaign worker, poll taker) 9.6%
Teaching (tutor, guide, arts volunteer, coach) 21.3%
Nursing (nurse, assistant at blood bank, hospital or nursing home aide, assistant to the elderly or handicapped) 10.5%
Manual (baby-sitting, cleaning, driving, or fire/rescue squad) 9.7%
Administrative (community coordinator, spokesperson, or meeting planner) 7.7%
Counseling (social service counselor, counselor Big Brother/Big Sister, telephone hotline, youth group leader) 19.9%
Leadership (officer, board member, committee member) 13.2%

Recall that volunteers could list up to two tasks for each domain in which they volunteered, but some volunteered in only one domain while others volunteered in several. This means that the number of tasks a respondent lists is a function of the number of domains in which he or she volunteers. Indeed, the beta coefficient for the influence of number of domains on number of tasks is $b = .66$, $p < .001$ for secular tasks and $b = .07$, $p < .001$ for religious tasks. In our estimates of the influence of socio-demographic variables on the number of tasks performed, *we therefore control for the number of domains in which the respondent is active.*

The number of secular tasks performed declines gradually as people grow older, falling more steeply once they pass their 65th birthday. Middle class people are busier than working class people, as indicated by the fact that the number of tasks is positively related to education, income, and tenure status (home owners). There are no gender or race differences. Frequent churchgoers perform fewer secular tasks than volunteers who rarely attend church. [74] In a second analysis we focused on employed respondents to better measure the influence of occupational status on number of tasks performed. Professionals and managers do more tasks than workers lower down the occupational ladder. This is only partly explained by the fact they volunteer in more areas. [114]

Religious tasks are distributed differently. Whites do fewer religious tasks than either Non-Hispanic Blacks or Hispanics. As might be expected, frequent churchgoers do more religious tasks than infrequent churchgoers. Age has the same debilitating effect on religious as it does secular task performance. Neither education nor income has any effect on the number of religious tasks performed. Finally, married people performed more religious tasks than singles. Interestingly, then, frequency of church attendance increases the number of religious tasks performed but reduces the number of secular tasks performed. Racial minorities do more religious tasks but are no different from Whites when it comes to secular tasks. Middle class people do more secular tasks than working class people but the same number of religious tasks. Race influenced who did the most religious tasks but class influenced who did the most secular tasks. In short, social class, age, and race not only influence who will volunteer but also how busy volunteers are. [74]

Job Segregation in Volunteer Labor

The sheer variety of tasks volunteers perform clearly indicates that volunteer labor has been divided into a number of specific functions (e.g., bookkeeping). As we noted in the introduction to this chapter, tasks can be categorized both horizontally and vertically. The horizontal dimension refers to the specialization of tasks: the work of preparing food is separated from the work of delivering the food. In many instances, one person will prepare the food and another person will deliver it. If the route for delivering the food has to be reconfigured, the chances are that another person will do that job. And if the local government authority begins a debate about allocating public funds to help buy the ingredients to make the food, the chances are a different person will attend the meetings to make sure the voice of the hungry is heard. This kind of division of labor is found in all organizations. The vertical dimension means that tasks are distinguished according to their rank as measured by criteria such as power, prestige, autonomy, and agreeableness. For example, Harris (1996:58) is clearly referring to the vertical dimension when she classifies volunteer tasks into three groups: governance (e.g., sitting on boards and committees); operational (e.g., actual delivery of services); and support (e.g., facilities maintenance or fund-raising). The stratification of volunteer tasks replicates the way jobs are ranked in other sectors and, like those jobs, some volunteer tasks are more desirable than others. "At one end of the continuum are volunteer project managers, often retired from government or industry, running large programmes. At the other end the occasional volunteer shuffles papers and licks stamps" (Bales 1996:207).

When volunteer organizations screen applicants for volunteer positions they have both horizontal and vertical dimensions in mind, knowing that not all volunteer tasks are alike. They use the background, experience, and skills of applicants to determine where to place them. Likewise, volunteers have their own preferences as to the kind of work they would like to do, based on their experiences, their self-perceptions as to the skills they can offer, their motivations for doing volunteer work, and the demands (e.g., schedules) they are prepared to meet. The social determination of volunteer tasks is therefore somewhat like the social determination of domestic chores or paid work activities. To some degree, people are selected for a job, based on their apparent qualifications, and to some degree people select jobs, based on their interests and capabilities. Both selection processes are influenced by ideas about who is most fitted to do what kinds of work. For example, if most paid nurses are female there is every reason to believe that most unpaid nurses' assistants will be female also. If most accountants are male, there is every reason to believe that the person who volunteers to prepare a non-profit organization's tax returns will also be male.

This is not to say that there is always a perfect match between volunteer and job. Nor does it imply that people will volunteer only if they are assigned a task they find agreeable. It is quite common for volunteers to say uncomplainingly that their volunteer work makes no use of the skills they have acquired in the course of performing other roles. One recent survey showed that, while some volunteers want to use their skills in their volunteer work, others are less concerned. Forty-two percent said their paid jobs and their volunteer tasks called for "really quite different" skills. Only one in five said they called for the same skills (Ferree 1998:15). Nor should we overlook the fact that a lot of volunteer work is unskilled labor—a generalized "helping out"—the kind of work almost anyone could do, regardless of any job skills they might have acquired.

In what follows we set out to disprove a simple proposition: that people are assigned at random to particular volunteer tasks. To do this we will conduct a number of multivariate analyses estimating the influence of various social characteristics on the odds of being assigned a particular task.

Gender

As we noted in chapter 8, the gender gap in volunteering is not as wide as many people believe, but this does not mean that men and women do the same kind of volunteer work. In the paid labor force occupational segregation along gender lines is very common (Reskin 1993). For example, physically demanding jobs, such as truck driving, are considered men's work while caring jobs, such as nursing (often just as physically arduous) are seen as more appropriate for women. Sex typing of tasks is also evident in the domestic sphere: preparing meals, washing dishes, cleaning house, and washing, ironing, and mending clothes are identified as women's work, while outdoor and other household maintenance tasks and equipment maintenance and repair are considered men's work (Presser 1994:352). Many of the tasks performed in the course of the working day or around the house are also performed by volunteers in the course of their work: buildings must be maintained, food prepared, equipment maintained, clothing sorted, counseling provided, pupils taught, financial records kept, meetings organized, newsletters written, and personal care provided. The intriguing question is whether the pattern of occupational segregation by gender found in the workplace and at home diffuses into the volunteer world.

For two reasons, it could be argued that volunteers are sheltered from the kind of discrimination and gender ideology found in other spheres. The first has to do with the voluntary nature of volunteer work, as opposed to paid work and even domestic chores, which are serious obligations for most adults. If women object to be asked to cook food in the course of their volunteer work they are free not to volunteer at all. In short, it is more difficult to enforce gender ideologies within the context of voluntary work. The second reason for expecting less job segregation in volunteer work is that many voluntary organizations are predominantly male or female. Sex-linked organizations are compelled to break down gender barriers between tasks because there are no members of the other gender around to do those tasks. In exclusively female organizations, for example, women lead, administer, and make the kind of decisions denied to them in other roles. Indeed, this might be the reason they are volunteering in the first place (Daniels 1988; Moore and Whitt 2000:310; Steinberg and Jacobs 1994:95). For their part, predominantly male organizations, such as emergency squads and fraternities, cannot assign "women's work" to women because there are no female members.[3]

Although non-profit organizations and voluntary associations do create a different work environment from that found in the workplace and at home, this not really sufficient to disturb the traditional pattern of occupational segregation. Women are assigned to routine and often undervalued work while men are preferred for board and committee memberships (Odendahl and Youmans 1994:207). McAdam (1992:1226) describes how, during the civil rights campaigns of the 1960s, men performed the riskier (and hence more prestigious) task of going into the field to register voters while women were assigned to the support roles of clerical workers, Freedom School teachers, and community center staff. This was not because women were afraid of the more challenging volunteer work: when they applied to join the campaign, they were just as likely as men to ask to do voter registration work.

Gender is used to allocate volunteers across the horizontal dimension as well. There is "women's work" in the volunteer world as well as in other spheres. In general, men are considered more appropriate for the more public, political, and instrumental tasks, whereas women's volunteer activity "tends to mirror traditional 'feminine' caring work" (Prentice and Ferguson 2000:122). This pattern replicates the division of labor between "instrumental" tasks and "expressive" tasks found in the typical American family. In the environmentalist grassroots organization Cable (1992:38) studied, women

> did the "shitwork" . . . in line with gender specialization. Bake sales, yard sales, and raffles raised funds. They kept the meeting minutes and attendance records, speaking out less often than men.

On one occasion,

> The group erected a billboard urging residents to express their concerns about [the chemical pollution of] Yellow Creek. Men assembled the materials and built the billboard, and a man offered to place it on his property. Women, on the other hand, arranged a contest in the public schools to design a billboard message. Thus, the men undertook the physical labor and more public and dra-

matic aspects, while women used their interpersonal skills, organizing through social networks related to their children. (Cable 1992:43)

Although all volunteer work shows a concern for the welfare of others, there are different ways to display this concern, some of them more prestigious and attractive than others. Providing care *for* other people is "dirty work." It means spending time in the cancer ward, being a buddy to an AIDS patient, mentoring fatherless boys, visiting shut-ins, and coaching handicapped athletes. These tasks resemble the care work that goes on in families, which is considered women's work. Other tasks are more congenial and seem to carry more weight because they ask us to *care about* others and the wider community. The task is more formal and rational, less personal and emotional. It is men's work.

Evidence of a gendered allocation of tasks can be found in a number of social surveys. Fischer et al. (1991:270) looked at task assignments in the Retired and Senior Volunteer Program, using the program's own job descriptions to sort tasks into leadership and non-leadership positions. Tasks were also coded according to contact with client, contact with supervisory staff, and use of clerical, technical or communication skills. Although gender made no difference to the last three measures, men were more likely to be assigned to leadership tasks. Significantly, the volunteer's job prior to retirement had no influence on the assignment: only gender mattered. Moore and Whitt (2000) analyzed the gender composition of non-profit boards of trustees in Louisville, Kentucky. Regardless of social class, men occupied the large majority of trustee seats overall, they were far more likely than women to hold seats on more than one board, and they were less likely than women to specialize in one field within the non-profit sector. Blee (2002:132) observed that the few women who joined the White supremacist movement were largely excluded from leadership positions and worked primarily as "social facilitators." In Britain, women are more likely than men to be involved in fundraising and giving practical help, while men are more likely than women to serve on committees and to give non-professional advice (Haezewindt 2002:24). Also from the United Kingdom, Smith (1998:47) found that women were more likely than men to be engaged in fund-raising and social services; men were more likely than women to be engaged in committee work, counseling, providing transportation, and being a spokesperson for the organization. Two other British surveys also found gender differences in volunteer task assignments. One, conducted in 1992, found that women were more likely than men to raise funds, while men were more likely than women to tutor or train, give advice, and serve on a committee (Goddard 1994:9). The other, conducted in 2001, largely replicated these findings: women were more likely than men to raise money and give practical help, while men were more likely than women to give advice and serve on committees (Haezewindt 2002:24). Hooghe (2001:164) found that, in Belgium, men were more likely than women to be serving on the board of voluntary associations. A Canadian survey showed that women were more likely than men to canvass, campaign, and fund-raise, provide care and support, and collect, serve, or deliver food, whereas men were more likely to teach or coach, maintain or repair facilities, or provide transportation (Mailloux et al. 2002:9). The top six jobs for women were making items; preparing or serving food; selling items; collecting or distributing food or goods; providing care and companionship; and office administration, bookkeeping, or library work. The top six jobs for men were repairing or maintaining buildings and facilities; professional consulting; fire-fighting, first aid, search and rescue; coaching, judging and umpiring; serving on a board; and researching, writing, and speaking. Canadian male volunteers were more likely think of themselves as leaders. When asked if they helped "run this organization," 42 percent of the men replied affirmatively compared to 31 percent of the women. In the United States, men are more likely than women to coach or teach, provide counseling or emergency care, serve on a board or engage in general labor; women are more likely than men to prepare and serve food, fund-raise, and provide general office services (U.S. Bureau of Labor Statistics 2003). Finally, a 1994 survey of eleven European countries asked volunteers if they had performed a number of different tasks: men were more likely than women to have served on a committee; women were more likely than men to have volunteered to visit shut-ins (Gaskin and Smith 1997:37). In short, there does seem to be a patriarchal structure to volunteer work whereby the more desirable tasks tend to be assigned to men and the less desirable tasks (e.g., asking for money) are assigned to women. In the list of task assignments given above the horizontal division of labor is also evident. Typically, women are more likely than men to be assigned to (or select) personal service or clerical positions; men are more likely to do more physical tasks, such as maintenance, providing transportation, and coaching a sport.

Most of the studies we cite describe only zero-order differences. They do not control for socio-economic differences between men and women. For example, the fact that men are more likely to be asked to serve on a board might simply reflect their socio-economic advantages. In a multivariate analysis of 2002 data gathered by the Census Bureau in which these and other variables were controlled, Rotolo and Wilson (2007) found that women were less likely than men to build, maintain, or repair physical structures, serve on boards or committees, to teach or coach, and to provide care or transportation. They were more likely than men to solicit money, prepare and deliver food or goods, and help out generally during events. They were no more likely than men to provide consultations or do administrative work. Some tasks were associated with a specific gender, regardless of the volunteer domain: building and maintenance was men's work whether volunteers were working on behalf of a religious organization or a civic group; preparing and serving food was women's work whether volunteers were working in a hospital or for a youth recreation group.

Analyzing the Independent Sector data, we found no gender difference in the absolute number of tasks performed in either religious or secular organizations. [115] We then looked at the net effect of gender on the likelihood of performing specific tasks. In the religious domain, men were more likely than women to assist clergy and serve as a deacon—two leadership positions. Women were more likely than men to teach (e.g., Sunday school) and do clerical work. [116] In the secular domain, men were more likely than women to teach or coach and serve as leader (i.e., as an organization officer, committee member, or board member); women were more likely than men to do office work, provide nursing care, and assist paid staff. [117] These results provide some support to the theory that leadership in voluntary organizations is gendered and that tasks at the same level are allocated differentially to men and women.

Race

In the conventional labor market, race is often used to allocate people to particular jobs. Minority groups are forced to take on the "dirtier" and more menial tasks. As we noted earlier, the volunteer world is somewhat different because no one is forced to volunteer. We can refuse to do volunteer jobs we dislike. This means that racial discrimination in volunteer work should be less than racial discrimination in paid work. In the Independent Sector data, Black and Hispanic volunteers reported doing more religious tasks than Whites, but the same number of secular tasks. [74] We found virtually no evidence that race is used to assign volunteers to particular jobs. In religious organizations, Blacks were more likely to than Whites serve as a deacon, and Hispanics were more likely than Whites to be doing office work—but we should note that the vast majority of religious congregations are racially homogeneous. [116] In secular organizations, Non-Hispanic Blacks were the most likely to do administrative work, and members of "other" races were more likely to be doing manual work. [117] In short, the division of labor in the volunteer world does not seem to be influenced much by race. Blacks and Hispanics are not systematically consigned to lower-level tasks and Whites do not occupy positions of leadership at a higher rate than Blacks or Hispanics. Of course, these data say nothing about the use of race and ethnicity to allocate tasks *within particular organizations* where there are members of all racial and ethnic groups.

Employment Status

In chapter 6 we demonstrated that paid work hours influence the number of hours that people volunteer. Since it takes time to perform tasks employment status should make some difference to the number of tasks performed as well as, perhaps, the types of task to which people are assigned.[4] According to the 2003 CPS supplement on volunteering, having a job results in less time spent collecting, preparing, or distributing food and clothing, providing general office services, and more time spent coaching or teaching, fund-raising, counseling, providing transportation, and serving on a board or committee. Since these raw percentage differences are rarely more than three or four points it is unlikely that work hours have much influence on the kinds of task volunteers do (U.S. Bureau of Labor Statistics 2003).

In our analysis of the Independent Sector data, the influence of employment status on volunteer tasks was trivial. We compared all respondents with part-time workers. In one area only (teaching or coaching) were part-time workers most likely to be performing a religious task. In the only other religious task influenced by employment status—counseling—part-time workers were the least likely to be performing it and retirees and full-time self-employed workers the most, suggesting that much of this counseling is coming in the form of services provided by lawyers, ministers, accountants, psychologists, and other professionals. [116] In the secular domain employment status was influential in only three areas. Full-time self-employed workers and retirees were most likely to be assisting paid staff. Part-time workers were more likely than full-time workers to do office work but no more likely than retirees or those not in the labor force. Retirees were the most likely to be nursing, which might be associated with their propensity to do volunteer work on behalf of the elderly. [117] In short, there is little support in these findings for the idea that the time demands of paid work make much difference to the kinds of work volunteers do.

Occupation

In some cases, the connection between occupational status and type of volunteer work is quite specific, as when a lawyer uses legal skills to do pro bono work, a nurse provides comfort to hospice residents, or a teacher tutors illiterates. A contributor to *The Practicing CPA* described one instance of her volunteer work:

> Several attorneys had filed a class-action suit against the Social Security Administration and the state of Tennessee, charging that Social Security benefits belonging to children in state custody had been improperly used. The attorneys wanted to understand the discrepancies they had discovered in state and federal documents. They needed help in preparing to take depositions from state financial officers. I advised them about the questions they should ask and gave them a primer on financial jargon. (Steinberg 1999:5)

She goes on to describe a group of volunteers in Philadelphia, known as Community Accountants, who provide free accounting-related services to non-profit organizations. In Moore and Whitt's (2000) study of non-profit boards of trustees, board members were drawn mostly from the White upper middle class: all the men and 89 percent of the women were either professionals or managers.

These are, of course, isolated cases and sample surveys are needed to establish any association between occupational status and task assignment. Survey data on the relation between occupational status and volunteer tasks are scarce. A United Kingdom survey found that professional and managerial workers were more likely to help organize events, counsel, visit the sick and elderly, and do clerical work. Rather surprisingly, they were no more likely than unskilled manual workers to fund-raise or serve on committees (Smith 1998:53). Goddard's (1994:11) findings from another British survey are more in line with expectations. Professionals and managers were less likely to engage in fund-raising, more likely to give presentations, give advice, serve on a committee, and do administrative work. Conversely, unskilled manual workers were the least likely to tutor or train, give presentations, give advice, serve on a committee, or do administrative work.

In their analysis of the CPS data from the United States, Rotolo and Wilson (2007) found that, compared to those not in the labor force, craft workers and, more consistently, operatives, were more likely to do the manual, routine, and relatively unskilled work of maintenance, helping out during events, providing care or transportation, and teaching or coaching. Managers were no more likely to do this kind of work than volunteers with no job at all. Somewhat surprisingly, they found that, compared to people without jobs, all workers were less likely to serve on committees or boards. Although number of hours worked for pay is controlled in this analysis, it is likely that homemakers and retirees simply have more *disposable* time to give to working on boards and committees. It is also possible that some homemakers have decided not to work for pay in order to be able to devote time to committee work or to serving on a board.

Education

Employers routinely use educational credentials when hiring workers for paid jobs, but it is an open question as to whether the same process occurs in the case of volunteer work. A number of studies have found that the managerial and white-collar volunteer tasks are more likely to be done by more highly educated people (Johnson et al. 2004:60; McClintock 2000:9). The CPS survey on volunteering found that, compared to high school dropouts, college graduates were more likely to coach or teach, provide information or serve as usher, fund-raise, provide counsel, work in the office, serve on a committee, and engage in music or performance, whereas they were less likely to collect, prepare, or distribute food or engage in manual labor (U.S. Bureau of Labor Statistics 2003). In their analysis of the 2002 CPS data, Rotolo and Wilson (2007) found that well-educated volunteers were more likely to serve on a board or committee and to provide consultations or do administrative work. Conversely, poorly educated people chose (or were assigned to) more menial tasks, such as building maintenance, fund-raising, preparing food and goods, helping out during events, providing care and transportation, and teaching or coaching. In our analysis of the Independent Sector data we found that, in the religious domain education had a positive effect only on the likelihood of doing office work. Twice as many volunteers with postgraduate degrees as volunteers with high school diplomas had done office work. [116] In the secular domain the influence of education was more extensive. Education was positively related to doing office work, teaching or coaching, and occupying a leadership position. It was negatively related to doing manual work. [117] In short, there is fairly solid evidence that education not only influences who volunteers but also who does specific volunteer jobs. These findings are of considerable interest because they raise the possibility that some of the difference in volunteering by education we noted in chapter 6 is actually a result of the kinds of jobs people are asked to do. Would college educated people be as ready to volunteer if they know they would be assigned to more menial tasks, such as washing dishes in a soup kitchen? On the other hand, would people whose education is limited to a high school diploma be more willing to volunteer if they thought they would have an equal chance of doing "white-collar" jobs?

Age

In chapter 11 we pointed out that one reason older people are attracted to volunteering is that gives them a chance to meet people. This implies that they are more likely to choose tasks that bring them into contact with clients. On the other hand, physical limitations might prevent them from doing physically demanding work and they might not be too ready to take on serious responsibilities such as serving on a board or committee. Chappell and Prince (1997) found that older volunteers were more likely to engage in direct service provision to clients (e.g., food, clothing, befriending) and less likely to be performing governance tasks such as administration, supervision or sitting on committees. The peak of volunteering that occurs in middle age is largely a function of parents' involvement in their children's activities. We might expect people in this age range to choose teaching or coaching jobs disproportionately. An affinity with clients might also play a role in task assignments. Goddard (1994:10) found that older people were more likely than younger people to visit people in institutions, perform administrative tasks, serve on a committee or provide practical help, and less likely to offer tutoring or training. The rate of offering tutoring or training was highest in the 35–59 age range, a pattern no doubt explained by another, which is that the rate of performing this task was highest among adults whose youngest children were between 5 and 15 (Goddard 1994:11). However, survey findings are not consistent on the influence of age on task assignment. Other surveys report that, compared to people aged between 25 and 34, elderly people were more likely to be fund-raising, more likely to be serving on a committee, more likely to be visiting people, more likely to be counseling, and more likely to be doing clerical work. No differences between these two groups were found in organizing events, driving, and representing a volunteer organization (Smith 1998:49). The 2003 CPS survey found that, compared to Americans aged between 16 and 24, those aged 65 or more were less likely to coach or teach, fund-raise, or engage in manual labor. They were more likely to provide information or serve as an usher, and collect and prepare food. Otherwise, there were no age differences (U.S. Bureau of Labor Statistics 2003). We do not know how much of this is self-selection and how much of it is discrimination against older volunteers. However, it should be noted that they are just as likely to be serving on a board or committee as any volunteers younger than themselves.

We used the Independent Sector data to test the hypothesis that task preferences change as people age, regardless of their socio-economic, family, and religious status. We found that, in the religious domain, age influenced only the distribution of teaching or coaching activities: older volunteers were indeed less likely to be performing this task. [116] In the secular domain the influence of age was confined to three tasks. Age was positively related to leadership and negatively related to teaching or coaching. In the case of personal care volunteering both the youngest and the oldest reported the high activity rates compared to the middle aged. [117]

In summary, although the pattern is not always clear and there are variations from one survey to another, age does seem to make a difference to task selection or assignments. Either people's preferences change as they age or volunteer supervisors use age when they are screening people for particular volunteer jobs.

Church Attendance

Like education, church attendance is a reliable predictor of volunteering, but little is known about whether it makes any difference to what volunteers do. A Canadian survey found that frequent churchgoers were more likely to provide care or support, to collect, deliver or serve food. This was not simply the result of religious congregations focusing more of their volunteer efforts on providing care or food service. The differences remained even when the analysis was confined to non-religious organizations. For example, among those who had volunteered for a secular organization, 30 percent of the weekly churchgoers had collected, prepared or served food, compared to 18 percent of the non-attenders (McKeown et al. 2004:12). However, for most of the tasks, there were no differences by church attendance.

In our analysis of the Independent Sector data frequent churchgoers were more likely to perform all five of the religious tasks, the influence being strongest in the case of assisting clergy and teaching. [116] Church attendance influenced only two tasks in the secular domain: those who never attended church were the most likely to have done office work; those who attended church occasionally were the most likely to have done manual labor. [117] On the basis of these results, there is little evidence here that frequent churchgoers select, or are selected for, any particular secular task. In the case of religious tasks, it makes some sense that the task most closely associated with frequent church attendance is assisting clergy because attendance at church is probably required for this task

Conclusion

In summary, the data from social surveys indicate that the division of volunteer labor is influenced by social characteristics. Generally speaking, the allocation of volunteers to tasks replicates the way people are assigned to jobs in the workplace and in the household. As far as gender is concerned, women do the more typical "female" jobs and men occupy leadership positions. As far as social class is concerned, the more highly educated volunteers are more likely to be serving on committees or boards and the volunteers with limited education are more likely to be doing the unskilled, manual labor. Volunteers who have manual jobs are also more likely to be doing manual work as volunteers. Finally, there are life course differences in the kinds of jobs volunteers do.

Still in its infancy, the study of volunteer tasks stands at the frontier of research on volunteering. Survey research can tell us whether a person is a volunteer, but that term is so vague as to tell us very little about what that person does as a volunteer. It is the equivalent of knowing that someone is employed or "in the labor force" without knowing much about how they spend their working day. Until we penetrate to the level of the volunteer task, we are no better off than we would be knowing that a person has a job in a hospital or a school: we do not know whether that person is sweeping floors or performing brain surgery, teaching math or maintaining security. Only at the level of task is it possible to glimpse the real work millions of volunteers are doing.

Although recent surveys have begun to throw much more light on the division of volunteer labor, two problems remain to be solved. The first is that there is little consistency from one survey to another in how tasks are defined and measured. As we noted earlier, some categories are so broad they do not identify a task at all. One reason why the task definitions vary so widely is that there is no consensus among researchers as to what these tasks might be. For example, the 2002 CPS special supplement included "organize, supervise, or help with events or activities" in the list of activities presented to respondents. Forty-three percent of the respondents indicated having performed this task. The 2003 survey redesigned the list of tasks to eliminate this amorphous category and added two new tasks: "engage in music, performance, or other artistic activities" and "engage in general labor." But in the process, an important category (maintenance) included in the 2002 survey disappeared, to be absorbed (presumably) in the "general labor" category (U.S. Bureau of Labor Statistics 2003). A further change tackled the problem created in 2002 by grouping the provision of care and transportation in the same category by identifying providing transportation independently. However, the provision of care (a very common volunteer task) disappeared in this redesign. One of the practical problems created by these *ad hoc* conceptual adjustments is that it becomes almost impossible to discern associations between specific tasks and demographic groups. For example, women are likely to do a higher proportion of the care work but a smaller proportion of the emergency medical service work and yet these activities are in the same category. Coaching is likely to be a predominantly male activity but teaching is likely to be a predominantly female activity and yet they are defined as the same task.

The second major problem that remains unresolved is that the conceptualization and measurement of tasks is not guided by sociological theory but is largely substantive and intuitive. It is as if a sociologist of work walked onto a college campus and noted that some workers were mowing the lawns, some were cooking food, some were filing documents, some were teaching, some were counseling troubled students, some were writing reports, and some were chairing a committee to select a new provost. These are undoubtedly different activities, but it is difficult to know what to make of this list without some conceptualization of the important differences between them. Generally speaking it is difficult to build a theory to explain differences when the differences are conceptualized and measured poorly. If volunteer work is simply labor that is unpaid, then it should vary along much the same lines as does paid work. Sociologists who study paid work classify activities according to more abstract categories, such as whether the worker is dealing with data, things or people; whether the work is repetitive, complex, and allows room for creativity; whether the work is closely supervised or the job affords autonomy to the worker (Karasek 1990). In the study of paid work, it is assumed that these differences in job characteristics will help explain why some demographic groups are more likely to be found doing one job rather than another. It is assumed some jobs are more attractive and intrinsically rewarding than others; that competition for attractive jobs will be keen; and that certain groups will have an advantage in getting these jobs. When it comes to volunteer work, too much emphasis has been placed on the substance of the work (e.g., office work) and not enough attention to these kinds of characteristics. After all, some office jobs can be dull and boring while others are exciting and fulfilling. Volunteers are attracted to the job not because it takes place in an office but because it offers them the chance to be creative.

19

The Volunteer Role

Volunteer work is distinguished from informal helping (e.g., mowing a neighbor's lawn) and caring (e.g., helping an elderly parent shop for groceries) by the fact that it takes place in or on behalf of an organization, such as a government agency, a non-profit organization, an advocacy group, a fund-raising campaign, a club, or a recreational association. Volunteer work is, above all, an organized experience. The principal difference between informal helping and volunteering is that the individual exchanges personal control over his or her resources (e.g., deciding how to help an elderly neighbor) for the financial, physical, and social resources provided by the organization.

The organization of volunteer work has helped institutionalize the volunteer role in modern societies in much the same way that schools have institutionalized the role of the mentor and hospitals have institutionalized the role of the healer. A sure sign of the institutionalization of the volunteer role is the emergence of a field called "volunteer administration," complete with college training courses, professional associations, and specialized journals. Volunteer administration concerns itself with, among other things, job descriptions for volunteers, setting standards of performance, devising incentive systems, monitoring compliance with organization rules, establishing selection procedures, combating turnover and attrition, and dealing with liability issues. It is highly significant that the *Dictionary of Occupational Titles* issued by the U.S. Department of Labor now lists jobs such as "supervisor of volunteers," "coordinator of volunteers," and "director of volunteers" (Ellis and Noyes 1990:345).

Roles are behavioral expectations of what a person should do. Performing a role means conforming to expectations others have about the proper
conduct associated with a position, or status, in society. As roles become
more institutionalized, the expectations become clearer and the sanctions for
failure to meet those expectations become more severe. According to one
noted scholar, the most important function of the volunteer role is to limit
compassion. Wuthnow (1991:195) describes a busy volunteer who

> had learned to draw a sharp distinction between her role as a care giver and her
> self. The one was manageable because it was restricted . . . the role defined how
> she should behave. When she visited people in hospital, there was a script for
> her to follow. She might feel their pain, or feel rewarded by having visited them,
> but she could fall back on a specified set of norms and expectations.

Working through an organization, rather than independently, she is brought
into contact with the needy but only for brief periods of time and the help for
which she is responsible is limited, quite unlike the care role she might perform in relation to her children or elderly parents. Organizational rules also
help her coordinate the volunteer role with the other roles she plays in her
life. She is expected to narrow her compassion to "a small circle of concern"
to ensure that the care work does not overwhelm her (Eliasoph 2003). Likewise, volunteers for Habitat for Humanity "are provided with identifiable
volunteer roles that facilitate their service to others while limiting it to manageable levels appropriate for their busy lives and multiple responsibilities"
(Baggett 2001:218). Harris (1996:59) describes how religious congregations
try to overcome the reluctance of members to undertake volunteer work by
limiting the demands made on them, by asking them to take only a small part
of the role, or asking them to take their turn in performing the role. Sometimes these limits chafe against the volunteer's altruistic impulses. Holden
(1997:118) observed that volunteers came to the homeless shelter where she
was conducting her research with good intentions, "desires to help others, to
give something back to the community, and to live out their religious values,"
but the organization had its own limited expectations of what volunteers
should do and often undermined many of these good intentions.

The Institutionalization of the Volunteer Role

There are two principal ways in which the volunteer role is institutionalized. First, the expectations attached to the role are standardized and incum-
bents are socialized into accepting them. Perhaps an extreme example is that
of emergency squad volunteers, who are typically expected to commit to a
minimum number of hours per week (between sixteen and thirty), undergo
rigorous training, and regularly update their skills (Gora and Nemerowicz
1985:27). Another example is people whose volunteer work is very stressful.

For example, helping arthritis sufferers deal with their pain is closely circum-scribed work. Initiates undergo an arduous period of training, during which they are taught a number of specialized skills, following a training manual carefully. All volunteers must meet the same high standards of competence (Barlow and Hainsworth 2001:214). Not all volunteer roles are so exacting by any means, nor is rigid bureaucratization the only way to standardize ex-pectations, but nevertheless institutionalization includes defining and enforc-ing expectations concerning the tasks to be performed in the role. In some cases a "career ladder" is instituted: more experienced volunteers become trainers of novice volunteers. The Oregon Long Term Care Program pro-motes advanced veteran ombudsmen to the rank of Certified Ombudsman In-vestigator (Nelson et al. 2004:117).

The second way to institutionalize the volunteer role is to ensure that people perform it for the right reasons. As we noted in chapter 2, the volun-teer role is defined partly in cultural terms: people who are not "sincere" are not performing the role correctly. For the volunteer role to function properly, the people who perform it must be properly motivated. Just as the role of the priest is partly defined by a sense of calling so the role of the volunteer is de-fined by altruism. For example, volunteers at a homeless shelter were careful to define the proper behavior and motivation of the "real" volunteer, thereby helping to institutionalize the role (Holden 1997). They distanced themselves from the "resume-padder" motivated largely by self-interest with no desire to "connect" with clients or think much about homelessness as an issue. Resume-padders defined the volunteer role in very narrow terms and were re-luctant to take on additional responsibilities. On the other hand, "do-good-ers" were morally suspect because they were condescending, motivated mainly by pity for their clients. Do-gooders were judgmental and not partic-ularly empathic.

Other Roles Define the Volunteer Role

As is the case with all social roles, the volunteer role is defined and cir-cumscribed by the other roles to which it is routinely connected. In the popu-lar mind, the volunteer role is defined partly by the fact that it is unpaid work. In turn, of course, the role of the paid employee is defined by the fact that he or she charges for labor performed. Occupants of both roles work hard to define the boundary separating them: one is professional and com-modified; the other is amateur and a gift. This is clearly shown in a fascinat-ing study of paid and unpaid emergency medical technicians (EMTs) by Nelsen and Barley (1997). For each group to fully understand its role, it con-trasted itself with the role of the other. Paid EMTs were quick to note their superior training and expertise, their ability to make crucial decisions and act decisively in emergencies, their cool detachment under pressure and self-control under trying circumstances, and their professional obligation to respond to

calls whatever the inconvenience. Professionals depicted volunteers as amateurish, unreliable, emotional, and "trauma junkies." In contrast, volunteers
emphasized their personal involvement in the role, their commitment to community, their humanitarian concern for patients' welfare, their ability to provide warm and nurturant support to accident victims and their relatives, and
their refusal to be motivated by monetary gain. The volunteers regarded their
service as a gift to a community largely populated by kin, friends, and neighbors. For them, treating patients was a moral obligation owed to others with
whom they had primary ties. "They considered the rational, efficient, coolly
detached approach of the paid provider alienating because it reduced patients
to cases and EMTs to functionaries who lacked compassion and a proper
sense of social responsibility" (Nelsen and Barley 1997:637). They were volunteers *because* they were not professionals. The same pattern was observed
in a study of women helping in day care centers for children. Paid staff positioned themselves as experts and treated both children *and* their parents as
clients. The women working as volunteers in the center (most of them mothers) saw their volunteer role as a way of avoiding the perceived drawbacks associated with professionalism. One volunteer complained about staff "with a
paper educational background," intimating that no special training other
than mothering skills was required to operate day care centers (Prentice and
Ferguson 2000:129).

If, on the one hand the volunteer role is defined in contrast to the paid
work role, on the other it is defined in contrast to the client role. In order to
perform their role as helpers, volunteers must have needy people with whom
to connect. Some volunteers get frustrated because clients perform their role
as grateful recipients of needed help inadequately. Hillary, a volunteer at a
homeless shelter, expresses her frustration at the recalcitrant behavior of her
clients:

> And they didn't have this and they didn't have that, and I am, like, just frus-
> trated sometimes with the entitlement mentality like, "I'm here so everything
> ought to be here for me." And food should be great. I guess as a volunteer,
> when you are donating your time and people are donating supplies and cooking
> the food and donating the food . . . It would be nice if people were grateful for
> the fact that, yes, there is a shelter here. (Holden 1997:137)

Volunteers find expressions of gratitude from clients psychically rewarding
but they are also welcomed because they help legitimate their role as help
provider.

Attachment and Commitment

Although the volunteer role is organized and therefore subject to the constraints and demands of an organization, for most people it is an ephemeral
role. "An ephemeral role is a temporary or ancillary position-related behav-

ior pattern chosen by individuals to satisfy social psychological needs incompetently satisfied by the more dominant and lasting roles they regularly must enact in everyday life positions" (Zurcher 1983:135). Ephemeral roles can be taken up and put down in subordination to primary roles such as those associated with work and family. It is rare for a person to occupy the volunteer role for a prolonged period of time without interruption because more important life events impede their work. In this section we will discuss not the incidence but the duration of volunteering—not how many people in a population volunteer—but for how long people volunteer. We are interested in why some people occupy the role longer than others.

We use two concepts to describe duration of volunteering. *Attachment,* a term borrowed from labor economists, describes the volunteer work history of the individual: what proportion of that person's life has been spent in the volunteer role and whether the role has been performed intermittently or continuously. Note that attachment is defined as a pattern of behavior: it is not a state of mind. Vela-McConnell (1999:154) describes one of the volunteers he interviewed as being more passionate about being a volunteer than about any particular cause. Strong attachment *can* be a sign of devotion to a cause (e.g., animal welfare) or a decision to dedicate one's life to helping others but it could also be a consequence of objective factors, such as being a homemaker. Thus, while some people are strongly attached to volunteering because they are fond of it, other are strongly attached because they trapped in the role. Some people speak of being tied to volunteer work in the same way they are tied to family obligations. During focus group conversations one participant who was no longer volunteering was heard to say,

> It depends at what stage your life is at. There are different demands. I've got kids and everywhere you go they want you on a committee for this, a committee for that. I've just decided to pull the plug for a little while and have a break because once you're on there, no one wants to take over. . . . It's like "can you do another 12 months?" "Can you do this?" because no one else will do it. You sort of feel trapped in there. (Flick et al. 2002:58)

Commitment means the strength of a person's ties to a particular organization or a particular volunteer role. Commitment is also measured behaviorally. A highly committed volunteer is loyal to the organization, willing to work long hours, to put the volunteer role and its demands first. Commitment is influenced strongly by the concrete relations volunteers have with other volunteers, the paid staff, and the clients of the organization. A highly committed volunteer is the last to leave.

Attachment

People who make a "career" out of volunteering display the strongest attachment to the role. One focus group member told Australian researchers,

In a way it [volunteering] becomes an addiction. You think well I can't walk away from volunteering because there is so much to do. (Flick et al. 2002:56)

A study of Japanese volunteers found three distinct levels of attachment to the work. "Professional" volunteers devoted much of their life to volunteer work, regarded their volunteer role as primary and the roles of worker and family member as secondary. Men sacrificed middle class status and a secure income whereas the women gained social status and power. "Second-career" volunteers attached more importance to their work and family roles but were able to find time for volunteer work without too much conflict. "Regular volunteers" did not attribute much importance to the volunteer role, which was clearly subordinated to their primary roles. Their involvement in volunteer work was intermittent. They were quickest to forgive themselves for being unable to devote their lives to volunteering by citing the demands of their mainstream roles (Nakano 2000:104).

Labor economists believe that one important indicator of labor force attachment is the pursuit of a career rather than holding a sequence of unrelated jobs. A career is marked by a series of stages of upward mobility: prior experience and learning are considered important for later work performance. Compared to conventional careers, the volunteer role does not have a very distinct progression. Nevertheless, one study showed that upper class women thought about volunteer work as having a ladder of upward mobility. Hard work and success at a lower level was expected to lead to promotion to the next. Volunteers emphasized the importance of "moving on" from one office, organization, or cause to another for the sake of both the organization and their own personal growth as volunteers (Daniels 1988:208). Even where the volunteer role does not take on these career characteristics, there is certainly a tendency for people to continue volunteering once they begin. A person who has volunteered previously is more likely to agree to volunteer again if asked and will continue to volunteer longer (Moen 1997).

Social surveys are not very helpful when it comes to describing attachment to volunteering because they typically only ask respondents if they volunteered during the year prior to the survey. Repeated measures of the rate of volunteering in a population are not very helpful either. A constant rate of volunteering across consecutive surveys could be the net result of some people leaving and other people entering the volunteer labor force and therefore tell us nothing about whether the *same people* were volunteering in all surveys. To find out how much of their lives people have devoted to volunteering we either have to ask them to recall their history of volunteer work or we have to follow them as they age. Both methods have been used to obtain a clearer picture of attachment to volunteering.

The National Education Longitudinal Study of 1988 has been following the same cohort of young Americans since they were in eighth grade. When they were in twelfth grade (1992) they were asked if they had participated in any unpaid volunteer or community service activity. They were asked the same question in 1994 and 2000. Although 68 percent of the young American students had volunteered at least once during the three survey periods, only 12 percent had volunteered on all three occasions (Planty and Regnier 2003:3). This is a rather volatile stage in the life course as far as commitments such as volunteer work are concerned, and it is no surprise that the attachment is weak in this period. Oesterle et al. (2004:1141) looked at volunteering activities during adolescence and young adulthood covering the nine-year period from age 18–19 to age 26–27. They found that respondents were almost *eight times* more likely to volunteer in a given year if they had volunteered the year before. This is a clear indication that volunteering can become a habit, even among younger people.

Longitudinal data covering more of the adult years are perhaps a more accurate measurement of attachment to volunteering. In 2000, a random sample of participants in the 1997 Canadian National Survey of Giving was re-interviewed. Nearly three-quarters (70.5%) of those who had volunteered in 1997 were still volunteering in 2000 and at the same level. Eight percent were volunteering fewer hours and 2.3 percent were volunteering more. As might be expected, people who were volunteering below the median hours in 1997 were more likely to have taken on more volunteer work. The vast majority of those not volunteering in 1997 were still not volunteering in 2000: only 11.8 percent of those not volunteering in 1997 had become volunteers by 2000 (Reed and Selbee 2000a:6). A longer time span is covered in a previous analysis we conducted of the Americans' Changing Lives (ACL) data using information from 1986, 1989, and 1994. We found that 27 percent of respondents had volunteered in all three waves, 21 percent had volunteered in two waves, and 23 percent in one wave (Musick and Wilson 2003:265). An even longer time span is covered in a study using data from the NLS, which tracked mid-life women over a fifteen-year span. Only 9 percent had volunteered on all five occasions they were asked (Segal 1993:79). Another study asked women how long they had volunteered over the past thirty years. The average duration was twelve years (Robison et al. 1995). Johnson et al. (2004) looked at volunteering among an elite cohort of highly intelligent females first surveyed between 1921 and 1928. In 1940, 1950 and 1960 these women were asked whether they were doing volunteer work. In 1940, when their average age was 29, 32.8 percent were volunteering. In 1950, when their average age was 39, 61.7 percent were volunteering. In 1960, when their average age was 49, 45 percent were volunteering. For those who answered the question on community service in all years, 26 percent volunteered in all three survey years, 24 percent had volunteered in none of the survey years and the rest volunteered on one or two occasions. The correlation between consecutive measurements was $r = 0.3$ and $r = 0.4$ (Johnson et al. 2004:55). In summary, the volunteer population consists of three broad groups of people: some have developed a habit of volunteering, some move in and out of the volunteer labor force in response to changing resources and opportunities, and some volunteer only once.

Explaining Attachment

Despite the fact that the studies described above reveal wide variations in volunteer work histories, the task of explaining these variations has only just begun. It is likely that some of the same factors that explain why someone becomes a volunteer in the first place also explain attachment to volunteering (Barkan et al. 1995:131). Individual resources, such as education, time, and money, not only make it easier to be a volunteer but also ensure better volunteer assignments (Penner 2002). As far as time is concerned, it is easier for people who never entered the labor force (or withdrew from it permanently) to devote more of their life to volunteering. A volunteer at a well woman's clinic told Merrell (2000a:35),

> I've always, since I first got married been involved, because I didn't actually work, physically work for money. I've always loved this sort of work and I should have done probably social work training, but because I didn't, this is my way of sort of fulfilling my ambition.

As far as other individual resources are concerned, in an earlier study we found that highly educated White people were not only more likely to volunteer in the first place but were also more attached to volunteering (Wilson and Musick 1999).[1] Penner (2002) identifies pressure from significant others, either negative—in the form of demands for time and attention—or positive—in the form of support and encouragement—as influences on attachment. Young Americans who volunteered for the Mississippi Freedom Summer Campaign of 1964 were most likely to still be volunteering in the 1980s if they had stayed in touch with other volunteers from that campaign (McAdam 1988:190). Peace activists had been involved in volunteer work longer if they had formed close friendships with other activists (Downton and Wehr 1997:65). Volunteers working for the Plowshares organization (an anti-war movement) described how opposition from others to their work made the support of fellow members especially important:

> My family doesn't support me at all. I've also gone through hard times with church leaders. But I have a community that says, 'You're not crazy. What you're doing is right.' I have friend who are behind me one hundred percent. . . . You have to meet with like-minded activists. All of the long-haul activists have learned that. It simply isn't possible to continue working for peace without community. (Nepstad 2004:51)

People with few social ties in general have less attachment to volunteering: they escape the social monitoring to which the socially embedded are exposed and find it easier to backslide.

Penner (2002) also mentions having the appropriate motivation and sharing the values of the organization for which the individual volunteers as sources of attachment These factors are somewhat difficult to measure in social surveys, but in an earlier study we examined data from three waves of the ACL gathered in 1986, 1989, and 1994 to see if the type of volunteering made any difference to attachment. We found that people volunteering in connection with a church in the first wave were much more likely than volunteers for secular causes in the first wave to volunteer across all three waves (Musick and Wilson 2003:265). This is not to say that religious people are more "appropriately" motivated than people volunteering for secular causes or that their values are somehow "better" but it does suggest that religious organizations provide a more supportive environment for consistent volunteering.

We partially replicated this finding in an analysis of the Independent Sector data. In the 1992 survey respondents who said they had volunteered in the past twelve months were asked how long they had been a volunteer. We compared respondents who said they had volunteered for five years or more with those who had never volunteered, those who had volunteered for less than three years and those who had volunteered for between three and five years. Just over a quarter of the sample had volunteered for five years or more. Twenty-nine percent had never volunteered. As might be expected, older people were more likely to say they had volunteered for five years or more, but the only other variable that consistently predicted length of volunteering was frequency of church attendance. The more frequently the respondent attended church, the longer he or she had volunteered. [118]

Commitment

Up to this point we have described and tried to explain variations in attachment to volunteering, by which we mean the length and structure of an individual's volunteer work history. Much work remains to be done on this topic, but there is another level at which the topic of the duration of volunteering can be analyzed, which is the length of time an individual stays in a particular volunteer job—or at least the length of time the individual volunteers for a particular organization. A long volunteer work history can consist of many different volunteer jobs. Commitment means staying with the same job. Lack of commitment to a particular job or organization is a serious problem for volunteer organizations because it is costly and time consuming to recruit and train new volunteers. Volunteer administrators look for ways of managing volunteers in such a way as to strengthen their commitment to their task, but it is in the nature of volunteer work that the "exit" option is always available because the individual does not rely on volunteer work to make a living. The task thus becomes that of trying to control an already high turnover rate. For example, Bread for the World, an anti-hunger lobbying organization, experienced a 60 percent turnover in volunteer personnel in six years (Cohn et al. 1993:128). A study of hospice volunteers found that 43 percent had left the program between four and eleven months after completing training (Black and Kovacs 1999:483).

The high turnover rate among the hospice volunteers could be attributed to the stressful nature of the volunteer work, but there are other stressful volunteer tasks that do not have such high turnover rates. Volunteer firefighters, for example, average ten and a half years of service. Fighting fires can be stressful, but the firefighting squads also have very high social solidarity: most firefighters draw the majority of their friends from the squad, and this solidarity probably accounts for the low turnover rate (Perkins 1988). Accounting for variations in commitment is thus an important sociological task. How do organizations manage volunteers in such a way as to limit attrition? Because of the nature of volunteer work, organizations do not have available to them many of the mechanisms used when dealing with paid employees and they must seek other ways of ensuring the loyalty of their volunteers. In this section we will discuss some of the problems of promoting organizational commitment faced by volunteer administrators and some of the ways in which they have tried to tackle this problem. As we shall see, volunteer administrators face a dilemma: they must foster the volunteer spirit of those who have offered their services for free, but they must also control that spirit to meet organizational needs. They want to energize their volunteers but also to discipline them, and they are denied many of the methods of energizing and controlling available to people who manage paid employees.

The task ahead of us is to explain commitment to volunteer jobs. We will look at two sets of factors. The first has to do with the relation between the organization and the volunteer. What does the organization do to influence the commitment of the volunteer? The second set of factors has to do with the individual volunteer. What attitudes are most conducive to long-term commitment to the volunteer task? What is the role, for example, of satisfaction with the work?

Organizational Practices

As noted earlier, one difference between "informal" and "formal" volunteering is that, by joining or affiliating in some way with an organization, the individual trades personal control over his or her resources in exchange for the benefits of being a member of an organization. In other words, a volunteer organization, like any other organization, has to provide incentives in exchange for the discipline it imposes on its members.

INCENTIVES

Organizations can use a variety of incentives to ensure the compliance and loyalty of their staff but the type of reward most suited to volunteer work is "normative," so called because it consists of the manipulation of esteem, prestige, and other ritualistic symbols and the allocation of social acceptance. This type of reward is sometimes referred to as "purposive" because it assumes people can be motivated to work for an organization by emphasizing the worthiness of the values for which it stands. "The intrinsic worth or dignity of the ends themselves are regarded by members as justifying the effort" (Clark and Wilson 1961:146). Unlike the other types of reward, purposive incentives are inseparable from the ends being sought. Purposive incentives mean "motivating a person, by exhortation or example, to share the goals of the organization and instilling in him a sense of duty or a feeling of guilt that impels him to work toward those goals" (Wilson 1973:31). Normative rewards include solidary incentives, the type that derives from the act of associating itself. The volunteer is attracted by the congeniality of social interaction and the social status provided by doing volunteer work. For example, by agreeing to serve "on a women's auxiliary to the hospital board, raising funds with a ball or fashion show for unobjectionable cause, and promoting a symphony orchestra or an art institute" (Clark and Wilson 1961:142), women no doubt raise money for worthy causes, but they also affirm their social standing in the community. Solidary incentives are one reason why voluntary associations develop a wide array of titles, offices, and committees, because they are ways of signaling acceptance into the group. Solidary incentives also include the promise of new friends and new social relationships. These relationships make the volunteer work more satisfying (Barkan et al. 1995:128).

Because they rely heavily on normative incentives volunteer organizations must often tolerate sub-optimal performance by volunteers, simply because it is better than none at all "and sometimes because the organization made an explicit commitment to include all who were interested in its goals even if they could not contribute much to the organization" (Pearce 1993:51). For example, Habitat for Humanity relies heavily on volunteer labor to construct and renovate houses for the poor. Often the labor is unskilled and the work less than top quality. This raises the question of whether people should be allowed to simply buy their sweat equity, contributing money to the organization so that it could hire a professional to do the job, such as wiring or plumbing. An affiliate board chairperson responded to this question in the following manner:

> No, if you did that then Habitat's basic precept of people helping people would be ruined. There is no sense of community if people just write checks and let someone else do the work for them. You also can't forget that there's more going on than just hammering nails. Working in a hands on way allows people to meet other people, to learn about other cultures, and to basically get out of their comfort zone. (Baggett 2001:125)

On the other hand, while employers of paid workers must remain vigilant against "shirking" because they think their employees will perform as little labor as possible for the most pay, volunteers can become dissatisfied if they are not kept busy, precisely because they are giving their time for nothing. This is one reason employing a mix of paid and unpaid staff creates problems, because the compliance of the paid staff is secured by material incentives, whereas the volunteers must be offered incentives of another kind. Volunteers are likely to balk at doing tasks that contradict their values, whereas the paid staff will do what they are paid to do. In addition, whereas paid workers want money or promotion, volunteers want honor or recognition. They become disillusioned not because of low pay or being denied promotion but because their work is unappreciated (Gora and Nemerowicz 1985:31).

Normative incentives work best on people who have thoroughly internalized the values of the organization. The "more closely a member's interests match an organization's inducements, the more he or she will contribute time, money, psychological commitment, participation and other valued personal resources to the group" (Knoke 1988:316). For this reason, volunteer organizations need to pay careful attention to their members' reasons for volunteering and match their incentives to those reasons. "Volunteers are likely to make greater contributions of time and energy when the volunteer roles they play are consistent with other salient aspects of self-identity" (Farmer and Fedor 2001:193).[2]

In real life organizations use a range of incentives. For example, on their Web page, the Kiwanis announce that volunteering for the organization means that "communities are improved, friendships are built, leadership skills are developed, and business contacts are made," examples of purposive, solidary, and utilitarian rewards, respectively, but the most important incentive for joining the Kiwanis is a purposive one: the promise that "the lives of children around the world are changed for the better." Offered a range of incentives, volunteers can choose which to respond to, depending on their own motivations. For example, "members who desire interpersonal social benefits engage in internal activities that allow them frequent interaction with other persons" (Knoke 1988:326). Problems will arise if volunteers are not able to choose which compliance incentive to respond to or if they consider the incentive used inappropriate. For example, if volunteers are motivated primarily by normative reasons they might consider the promotion of solidary incentives (e.g., recognition ceremonies) a waste of time. They might also find it difficult to work alongside staff members who are getting paid for their work. Volunteers motivated by solidary needs—a desire to meet others or be with other like-minded people—balk at devoting too many resources to serving clients or to organizing demonstrations and marches.

Volunteer coordinators need to be aware of the fact that the reasons why people take up volunteering might not be the same as the reasons why they *continue* volunteering. In one study of abortion rights activists (both for and against), Gross (1995) measured the level of engagement in a number of activities. He also asked activists to evaluate various reasons for volunteering on a five-point scale ranging from not very important to very important. Activists ranked moral and values reasons as being most important for becoming a volunteer and material and solidary incentives lowest. When it came to their current level of activism, however, they ranked material and solidary reasons highest and the moral or value reasons lowest. Idealism drew them into the work but more mundane rewards determined how committed they were to the organization.

VOLUNTEER MANAGEMENT

Organizations that hire volunteers need to ensure compliance, but they must also deal with the fact that most volunteers give priority to their work and family roles. People can take "time out" from the volunteer role, but few can take time out from being a parent or earning a living. This creates particular management problems for organizations that depend on volunteer labor. Volunteers become disgruntled if they think their voluntary services are being mismanaged and if their relations with paid staff and other volunteers are unsatisfying.[3]

First, volunteers are more likely to quit if they feel put upon and "used." In many situations, volunteers experience the free rider problem at first hand. They are working to provide some collective benefit (e.g., raising funds for a membership organization) from which all members will benefit even if they do not volunteer themselves. In the absence of rewards and punishments to control "shirking" it is difficult to sanction those who do not pull their weight, but even among volunteers there are bound to be different levels of commitment. Volunteers need to feel they can trust their fellow volunteers to do their assigned tasks. Disaffection results not so much from lack of rewards but from inequities in rewards. Volunteers will also become disaffected if they are supplied with fewer resources (e.g., training, support from paid staff) than other volunteers, despite being expected to do the same amount of work. This kind of mismanagement seems to be quite common. One study found that 61 percent of volunteers said other volunteers had let them down and 42 percent had experienced conflict with other volunteers (Wuthnow 1998:170). In short, volunteers want to be treated fairly: they will quit if they think the organization's policies and procedures are at fault.

Second, volunteers are more likely to quit if they get inadequate support from paid staff in the form of training, answers to questions, and coordination of activities. One study divided volunteers enrolled in a program to help people on probation into three groups: the "committed" had six months of service or more, the "partially committed" had under six months of service and the "uncommitted" were screened into the program but did not volunteer. "Volunteers in the committed group were significantly more satisfied with the orientation and with staff support, and felt they received more help from the probation officer" (Pierucci and Noel 1980:248). They also spent less time attending meetings and completing reports than the partially committed. Significantly, commitment was unrelated to the quality of the volunteer's relation to the client.

Third, organizations need to have in place methods of distributing normative incentives on an equitable basis. Volunteers want to be provided with a clear structure of opportunities so that merit can be earned and acknowledged. They are no different from other workers in wanting their good work to be encouraged and rewarded (and to see poor or shoddy work corrected and sanctioned).

> A hospital recognizes its volunteers by promoting them. Senior and excellent volunteers are given the responsibility for training newer volunteers. The manager of volunteer resources at the hospital says that "this act of faith is more valuable than pins and certificates." In fact, she says, "Our volunteers love training and are hungry for it. We have better attendance at training sessions than at teas, dinners, etc." (McClintock 2000:36)

An organization that treats all volunteers alike, no matter their contribution of time, the costs they pay, the number of tasks they perform, the risks they run or the dangers they face, will likely have a high turnover. In short, volunteers are more likely to quit if they feel that the organization does not appreciate or recognize the work they do as individuals. Such recognition should be supplied on an ongoing basis rather than in elaborate ceremonies.

Fourth, volunteers are more likely to quit if they feel there is too much bureaucracy. The increasing use of contracts into the voluntary sector, whereby the state contracts with non-profits for the provision of specific services, has formalized the volunteer role. Government regulations require stricter accountability with respect to quality control and performance. These trends might be attractive to volunteers who would like to see a clearer definition of the volunteer role and more explicit training and career enhancement opportunities, but they are unappealing to those who resent close supervision and task specialization because it turns volunteer work into an ordinary job (Horne and Maddrell 2002:87). When volunteers are required to provide services according to someone else's specification they tend to lose their intrinsic motivation. Many kinds of volunteer work are no more amenable to rationalization than childcare: "a role of personal caring and attentiveness—is not one for which specialized training exists" (Deegan and Nutt 1975:345). Volunteers complain about the proliferation of rules, protocols, and paperwork (which gets in the way of the "real" volunteer work) and about having too little autonomy on the job (Phillips et al. 2002). A study of church volunteers found that many had signed up because they looked forward to working autonomously and in ways that would be self-fulfilling. They did not want to be "managed" or "controlled" or "monitored" (Harris 1996:61). Barbara, a volunteer at a soup kitchen, complained to Bender (2003:55) that her job had been bureaucratized as the agency for which she volunteered expanded and more paid staff were hired:

Many, many things were different. Mostly, it was a lot more fun. We *never* spent three hours doing just one thing. This is kind of boring; two weeks in a row we do onions for three hours. Now, it's hard to feel that you're really helping someone. You don't see much of the process. You see just one thing.

Wharton's (1991) study of a program matching adult women volunteers ("family friends") with pregnant or newly delivered teenage mothers found that volunteers resented being asked to record their interactions with teenage mothers on "contact sheets" broken down into ten-minute units. Perkins (1988) found that efforts to rationalize firefighting by requiring skills training and adding administrative layers to the squads created tension between the newer members, who welcomed the change, and the older members, who believed the changes sullied the voluntary spirit and who looked upon the squad not merely as a means to fight fires but as a means to preserve community solidarity. In human services volunteering, too much rationalization widens the gaps between paid staff, volunteers, and clients and the increased social distance makes it more difficult to have a satisfying caring relationship with the clients (Holden 1997:132).

Fifth, too much bureaucracy can alienate volunteers but too little can also be alienating. Roles are behavioral expectations of what a person should do. If the rights and responsibilities of the volunteer in the organization are unclear or contradictory the result is role ambiguity, which can be stressful. Volunteers for social service organizations, when asked how they thought people could be encouraged to volunteer more, suggested more careful explanation of the expectations placed on volunteers and the limits to their work (Phillips et al. 2002). A volunteer told Australian researchers,

I think people are afraid. . . . I've learned about rights and responsibilities of volunteers but I don't think that is out there in the community. . . . people are frightened that they are going to be taken over and that they don't have a right to say what their limits are. (Flick et al. 2002:73)

All too often, there *is* ambiguity in the definition of the volunteer role, in part because the work is unpaid. Jobs that are paid are defined more precisely because performance has to be measured and rewarded. Ironically, there may be more need for precision in the case of the volunteer role than there is in the case of paid workers. Careful volunteer job descriptions place limits on the responsibilities of the volunteer, thus minimizing the chances that "free" labor will become slave labor. Failure to define the volunteer role precisely places the volunteer at a disadvantage to the paid staff.

I think women have known for many years that to work without pay means that you are in many ways not given the same recognition as someone who is a paid employee. The same thing applies to volunteers in an organization where the paid staff can tend to assume things about their role and that has an effect in seeing volunteers as in some way there to supplement their role, rather than volunteers being there in their own right, contributing their own time. (Flick et al. 2002:66)

Clear role definition includes setting realistic goals. Unrealistic expectations are a major source of dissatisfaction and quitting. Ironically, burnout is more common among more idealistic volunteers, who start their job with unrealistically high expectations of what they can achieve (Klandermans 1997:104). When volunteers are asked to say what they find most satisfying about their work they are more likely to mention the feeling they are making a difference in the lives of those they serve than any other aspect of the job. The satisfaction is even greater where the work involves face-to-face interaction with clients (Pancer and Pratt 1999:53). But this satisfaction is dependent on having expectations clearly identified. As one volunteer put it: "What keeps me volunteering is the continuance of a challenge that is fulfilling *and within my ability to do so*" (Phillips et al. 2002:3, emphasis added).

Non-profit organizations are well aware of the importance of clearly defining the volunteer role to prevent high turnover. That is why many of them offer orientation sessions and training to make sure volunteers understand the role they will be expected to perform in the organization. Hospice volunteers undergo extensive training, much of it devoted to helping them deal with death and dying (Chambre 1995:130). Training is considered a necessity, not a luxury, when volunteer work involves intimate contact with children, if only out of concern for legal liability (Phillips et al. 2002:3). The importance of the volunteers understanding how their work fits into the larger scheme of things is illustrated in an anecdote told by Eisner (1997:41) about Benjamin Barber, director of the Walt Whitman Center for the Culture and Politics of Democracy at Rutgers University:

> His Rutgers students were divided into groups to work on specific service projects. Some were sent to work at a homeless shelter, others to paint the plugs of fire hydrants in a nearby community. After a couple of weeks, the painting crew complained. This is community service? We should be helping the needy, not painting fire hydrants. Barber then had the students meet with an official from the community, and his explanation made all the difference. It turns out that the community's firefighters had wanted the plugs painted because it would help them locate the plugs more quickly when the hydrants were knee-deep in snow and ice. It was a particularly urgent job because the previous year, a year of heavy winter weather, two residents may have died in fires because the hydrant plugs were so difficult to find. And the community itself didn't have the money to pay municipal workers to do the job. Once given the context, the students returned to work with zeal, convinced that they were contributing to a healthier community.

Designing a training scheme to avoid role ambiguity will define the rights and responsibilities of the volunteer, even to the point of a written job description; ensure volunteers understand and accept their role in the organization; boost volunteers' sense of efficacy in their roles by training, careful supervision, positive feedback, and role modeling; tie the work of the volunteer to the overall goals of the organization; and demonstrate how the work of the organization is making a difference to people's lives and to the community.

RELATIONS WITH PAID STAFF

Most people volunteer through agencies staffed by paid professionals such as social workers, teachers, nurses, and the clergy, or their work is supervised by paid managers and other administrators. The paid staff are necessary to plan campaigns, coordinate activities, mobilize volunteers, lobby politicians, raise funds and obtain sponsorship, forge alliances, provide continuity from one campaign to another, keep books, and so on. With the exception of very rare cases, where volunteers supervise paid staff (e.g., governing boards of museums), volunteers occupy a position of subordination to paid employees. Most people recognize that paid staff are necessary to manage and coordinate the work of volunteers.

> It's not like people are just walking in and are in the project. There's some active, intentional, hard work going on to bring people in, to get them oriented and supported, to remove the barriers, to support them . . . If you took that away and said, okay volunteers, do it all on your own, I suspect what you would have would be a dwindling number of people who without that support would become more discouraged, they'd feel more stress, they'd get more mad at each other. It would grind to a halt, I think. (Reitsma-Street et al. 2000:666)

Despite the fact that paid staff and volunteers recognize their need for each other, there are inherent problems built into their relationship. Many of the paid workers are "career activists" who have chosen to work in the nonprofit sector for ideological reasons. They are very committed to their work and have often accepted lower wages in order to get the chance to do nonprofit work. Volunteers' reluctance to make a similar commitment creates strain between paid staff and volunteers. Paid employees complain, "volunteers come in and leave whenever they want, lay down conditions on their availability that conflict with the needs of their supervisors, and yet demand high status jobs and recognition" (Kieffer 1986:59). They resent volunteers because they can pick and choose when to show up for work and how long to work, and they can avoid most of the dirty work. In some cases, such as long-term care facilities, the tenure of volunteers might exceed those of the paid staff, especially those doing the more menial kinds of tasks to which volunteers will also be assigned (Keith 2003:112). An awkward reversal of roles occurs, whereby volunteers have to teach paid staff how to do their job. But generally, the tenure of the volunteer is much shorter than that of the paid employee and this transience makes it difficult for the paid staff to sanction volunteers, especially if the organization is understaffed or the supply of fresh volunteers is uncertain.

In some instances, paid workers view volunteers as competitors for their jobs, or at least people who, by working for nothing, depress their wages: hence union opposition to the use of volunteers. Parents who help out in school as teacher's aids can threaten not only teachers but ancillary staff as well if volunteers are asked to work alongside them doing a similar job but for no pay. Social workers can feel threatened by volunteers, especially where the volunteers are assuming the role of advocates on behalf of the clients, implicitly setting themselves against the paid staff. Payne (2001:108) found that paid staff in hospices felt threatened by volunteers with skills earned in their work roles, such as nursing. Chambre (1987:121) cites a study showing that paid staff were more at ease with two types of volunteer, teenagers and older people, because they felt more in control and less threatened by them. Far from feeling they pose a threat to paid staff, volunteers often feel denigrated by them because they think that, because volunteers work for nothing, their work has no value (Daniels 1988:15). The paid staff disrespect them because they are unpaid. While volunteer firefighters decorate their cars with bumper stickers that read "Paid or volunteer, we're all professionals," paid firefighters dismiss volunteers as mostly inept and unreliable (Simpson 1996:32).

Ironically, the very informality of the relationship between volunteers and staff can make it difficult to determine whether in fact problems exist and quit rates can be high without their cause being identified (Deegan and Nutt 1975:347). Non-profits try to solve this problem by clearly stating the adjunct role of the volunteer in relation to paid staff so that there is no confusion over who is in control. The downside to this management strategy is that skilled volunteers, or people with prior management skills who have taken up volunteering, resent being shunted to marginal roles. Non-profits must steer a fine line between closely regulating the role of the volunteer in relation to paid staff to prevent volunteers from infringing on paid staff roles and prerogatives and marginalizing or downgrading the volunteer role.

Paid employees are often responsible for the rationalization of the volunteer role in an attempt to clarify the relation between them. The organization faces the problem of defining the volunteer role clearly enough so that its rights and responsibilities are obvious to all but leaving it diffuse enough to avoid over-regulation and dampening volunteers' enthusiasm. Too little structure and volunteers are likely to overstep their role; too much structure and the work begins to resemble paid employment and volunteers leave. Volunteers resent being too closely supervised by paid staff and "get quite defensive" (Payne 2001:111). They balk at attempts by paid staff to rationalize their work because it gets in the way of their motivation for volunteering.

Making egg salad in the mixer was both more efficient and more sanitary than doing it by hand. Sean assumed that these were the most important aspects of making food in large quantities for people with AIDS, especially when he was running behind schedule. Roger and Barbara thought otherwise: moments after laughing with Sean about Bill's crazy, time consuming tasks, they argued against the shortcut. Like Sean, they based their argument on the expectation that the client's needs came first; but they started with the idea that aesthetics was first among those needs. 'Food is love' overcame practical kitchen issues, including efficiency and food safety. It was not enough just to get the meals out . . . preserving the texture of the egg salad was just as important, if not more so, since it also preserved volunteers' practices and by extension their authority, meaning and imaginative work. (Bender 2003:60)

This kind of conflict has its roots in different goals. The paid staff gives priority to efficiency; volunteers give priority to the expression of values.

RELATIONS WITH CLIENTS

As we noted earlier, social roles are defined by the other roles to which they are related. The volunteer role is defined in contrast to the paid staff role. It is also defined in contrast to the client role. Volunteering is primarily about helping people in need with no expectation of a return for that help. In other words, the help is not provided on a contingent basis such that it would be halted if no returns were received. Ironically, this means that, for the volunteer experience to be satisfying, there have to be people in need who deserve the volunteer's help. Although the volunteer does not look for reciprocity, he or she does feel the need for some positive outcome, even if it is simply an acknowledgement of the help or expression of gratitude from the client. However, this places the recipient of the help in a subordinate position and this, in turn, makes some volunteers feel uncomfortable and awkward. Organizational failure to deal with these problems can result in high turnover-rates. In this section we will draw on ethnographic research to discuss these issues in more detail.

First, volunteers do not necessarily expect anything in return for their services, but they want to believe their clients need their help, and one of the ways those clients can express their need is to acknowledge and show gratitude for the help received. Baggett (2001:119) notes how Habitat for Humanity volunteers pressured prospective home owners to work at the construction site where the volunteers could meet them and thus have a more fulfilling experience: "as one affiliate board member explained, many think the home owners should be made to work alongside the volunteers, who, without a chance to interact with the home owners, would be 'robbed of the feeling of helping the needy.' " If clients do not seem to need their help (e.g., they could get a job and feed themselves) or do not show gratitude for the help they receive, volunteer work becomes unsatisfying. Stein's (1989) ethnographic study of volunteers and clients at food pantries and soup kitchens shows that clients do not always behave in the "appropriate" way and therefore make it difficult for volunteers to help them. Food servers in the soup kitchen were occasionally asked for extra helpings in a demanding way or complaints were made about the speed and manner of the table service. Food pantry clients sometimes complained about how little food they were given. In order to perform their role properly, volunteers needed their clients to be "deserving" and appropriately grateful for the help they were receiving without, however, submitting to being stigmatized as feckless and untrustworthy—hence the importance of being deserving. Some volunteers avoided this problem by denying the need for reciprocity altogether. Clients need not express their gratitude as an emotional payoff because the volunteer was intrinsically motivated. "I'm doing this more for me than for them" (Stein 1989:245). Volunteers inspired by spiritual motives were more likely to think that the clients had a right to their services and thus were not as upset when the clients failed to reciprocate with proper expressions of gratitude. Indeed, the need for sacrifice might well be enhanced under these conditions. So anxious were volunteers to receive the appropriate response from clients they were highly sensitive to departures from role expectations:

> I noted earlier that a volunteer at a food pantry said he was angered by recipients who asked, "Is that all?" on receiving their groceries . . . but I believe that the intonation could convey at least two meanings. One, of course, is that of a complaint: "Don't I get any more?" In addition . . . this question could mean, "Is there anything else I need to do before leaving with the groceries? (Stein 1989:247)

White volunteers in the civil rights movement in the south during the 1960s often encountered the same type of problem: the African Americans did not always seem to be grateful for the contributions they were making. Indeed, they were often confronted with suspicion, distrust, and outright hostility from the people they were trying to help. Black distrust of Whites in general led them to suspect the motives of the volunteers. They were incredulous that White people would give something to Blacks without expecting a return. They refused to believe that Whites were paying the same price for their volunteer work as their Black companions. In response, White volunteers took pains to demonstrate they were indeed "paying the price." One White volunteer "cleaned the toilet of a civil rights organization because he was afraid the Negroes working there might think it degrading" (Levy 1968:110).

Second, while many people are drawn to volunteer work that involves face-to-face contact with clients with whom they seek a close and mutually satisfactory relationship, the volunteer role limits compassion. Volunteers are not allowed to get too close to their clients or to care too much about them. Stepping over this line causes distress for the volunteer. Professional staff often limit contact with clients in order to protect volunteers from emotionally draining experiences. Hospice volunteers are mainly assigned to tasks such as driving, reception, and staffing the snack bar, where contact with dying people is kept to a minimum (Field and Johnson 1993:1627). In the absence of formal guidelines, volunteers must find what works for them and their clients. A study of AIDS volunteers found that the "buddies" were less satisfied with their work than they had expected to be after three months. The more frequently they visited their client and the longer the visit lasted the more satisfied they were, but this was true only up a point. If they got too close, satisfaction declined. By the time six months had passed the relation between closeness of contact and satisfaction was positive and linear. Seemingly, after six months volunteers and clients had fully negotiated their relationship with each other (Omoto et al. 1998:120).

Getting too close is one thing, not getting close enough is another. For people who want to express compassion in their volunteer work, bureaucratic rules can be stifling. Holden (1997) shows how bureaucratic regulations imposed by a homeless center conflicted with the motivation to affirm a moral identity as a helper. Volunteers came to the shelter infused with a desire to help others and, in this case, a desire to treat others with respect, as equals, not to demean them or treat them as inferiors. This was a problem, not only because of the class difference between volunteers (college students) and clients, but also because shelter rules made it difficult for volunteers to treat the "guests" as equals. Volunteers wanted to live up to the demands of the idealized volunteer role, which required them to help in a compassionate and uncondescending way, and encouraged their clients to see them as friends. In practice, however, volunteers discovered that "their role in the shelter was limited to enforcing seemingly petty rules, prying into resident's lives, and doling out supplies" (Holden 1997:123). They were encouraged to believe that the guests were untrustworthy. In turn, the guests reacted to the volunteers' supervision with hostility or evasion. Thus, organizational imperatives forced the volunteers into a hierarchical relationship instead of the egalitarian one they desired. One volunteer explained:

> Sometimes somebody is going off and any time you are forced to give a warning, you know, you just feel like shit . . . It's hard for me because I want to be on, like, equal ground—like feel equal to them and not feel a superior or something because it's not my situation. But every time I have to give a warning . . . you have to put yourself on the, you know, the different level . . . you're not equal anymore. (Holden 1997:124)

So strong was the desire to affirm a moral identity in the context of bureaucratic rules that volunteers took special pride in acts that signaled their desire for equality or signs of friendship from guests. "I like nights when, I like to talk to people, I really, I think sometimes I really feel like I am connecting" (Holden 1997:127). In the ethnography of the soup kitchen cited above, the volunteers often found themselves placed in an unwelcome disciplinary position over the clients.

> At all of the soup kitchens I observed, people gathered outside until the doors were opened to admit them. At one of the soup kitchens, recipients were di-

rected where to sit; plates of food were brought to them, as were second help-ings. The task of the condiment dispenser consisted of adding catsup and mus-tard to the sandwiches of those who wanted them. The condiments were not set on the table or passed from person to person; instead a volunteer was in charge of distributing them to adults and children alike. Such policies, although more practical than venal, are indicators of control. (Stein 1989:247)

Third, providing a "service" frequently places the client in a subordinate position to the volunteer whether the volunteer wants this or not. In the case of Habitat for Humanity, the need for volunteers and the comparative needi-ness of the home owners "creates a power differential between them based on social class" (Baggett 2001:115). Volunteers had a tendency to presume that the families they were working with were inferior to and less respectable than themselves, otherwise they would not be asking for help. Middle class Black women who volunteered to mentor young and poor Black mothers as part of the "Birthing Project" found it difficult to overcome the class divide between helper and helped. Some found they had to convince their "sister" that they did not feel superior to them. They had to account for why they would give their time to others without expecting a return. Others felt exploited by their clients. "The young lady I got was a real opportunist. She came in thinking that she'd get in this project and I would be her taxi and I would be her bene-factor and I would take her out and do all this stuff for her" (McDonald 1997:788).

In the homeless shelter study described above, the mainly middle class volunteers, imbued with the notion that compassion must be combined with egalitarianism, wanted to treat their clients as equals. This was made difficult not only by the class difference but also by bureaucratic roles governing volunteer-client relations. Some clients reacted with hostility to the hierarchy but others ignored this aspect of the relationship and treated volunteers as in-dividual people with personal lives of their own. Volunteers wanted clients to "accept" them as more than rule enforcers or service providers. The clients therefore had to do their part to overcome the social differences between giver and receiver. One way in which volunteers avoided being placed in a su-perior position to their guests was to get the paid staff to enforce the rules for them. "Although the volunteers were invested with the power to enforce the rules by giving warnings [of expulsion], they usually and almost uniformly relinquished this power to the managers" (Holden 1997:133). Another strat-egy was to pretend ignorance of the rules and thus not enforce them. "I don't really . . . have a handle on the rules, so I don't feel comfortable enforcing them" (Holden 1997:134). Some volunteers dealt with this problem by "oth-ering" the clients. "Volunteers could thus construe rule-enforcement as nec-essary to compensate for guests' moral weakness, rather than as a reflection of their own non-egalitarian impulses" (Holden 1997:135). In order to do this, volunteers had to classify guests into "good" and "bad" as defined by how they accepted help. Good guests were compliant and friendly and bad ones were ungrateful and cranky.

Individual Attributes

Up to this point, we have focused on organizational and relational issues and their bearing on volunteer commitment. But volunteers come to organizations with different resources, different self-perceptions, and different expectations with respect to volunteer work, and these differences are bound to have some influence on their commitment to their jobs.

ROLE IDENTITY

If a role is important to our sense of who we are we are more likely to be committed to that role. A good sign that a role is salient to a person is if it is invoked in many different social situations. For example, if a person discusses her children frequently with her work colleagues, her fellow book club members, her friends and neighbors, even the mail carrier, her mothering role identity is highly salient to her. In short, people do not simply perform a role but identify with the role to varying degrees, and this helps determine how committed they are to the role (Piliavin 2002:473).

People have strongly identified with the volunteer role when they refer to their work as an expression of "who they really are." They have difficulty separating themselves from the role, as in: "I am being true to my own self and to my own commitments and following through on something that is really important to me" (Teske 1997:121). Such people *must* volunteer, regardless of whether their actions are condemned or praised (Schervish and Havens 1997:240). One peace activist told Downton and Wehr (1997:66),

> Being personally responsible gives meaning to my life. I feel very identified with the women and children who suffer the most from way, violence, and sexism. It's a personal issue. I feel I would personally benefit from the changes. And the injustices make me furious, so my activism is an outlet for that. It's a constructive outlet for my anger, and I feel bad if I don't do it, and I feel good if I do, generally. I feel crummy if I'm not doing something, crummy about myself. It is part of my ideal self to be involved, definitely a part of my value system—a good person is involved. And if I'm not involved, then I'm not living up to my ideals.

A pro-life activist told Teske (1997:128): "It is not something you choose to do. It is something you have to do or you can't live." Another sign of identification with the volunteer role is when people speak of being impelled to "practice what they preach." They do not wish to appear hypocritical, pretending to be something other than they are, saying one thing and doing another (Blee 2002:70).

It is tautological to say, as Farmer and Fedor (2001:193) do, that contributing a lot of time and energy to volunteer work is a sign that the volunteer role is salient to that person. The expenditure of time and energy is a *consequence* of identification with the role. A person who spends long hours volunteering has not necessarily identified with the role. People can distance themselves from a role they are obliged to perform if they do not identify with it. They might protest they are unsuited to, or unqualified for, the volunteer work to which they have been assigned, or complain they are volunteering in spite of themselves. One of the volunteers interviewed by Vela-McConnell's (1999:188) admitted he was "not really a big activist, which is kind of sad." Being an activist was not part of who he was.

One way of finding out how much volunteers identify with their role is to ask them to express their agreement or disagreement with two statements: "Time donation is something I rarely think about"; "Time donation is an important part of who I am." People who think often about time donations and who feel time donations are an important part of who they are have identified strongly with the role. They tend to think that more people should be volunteering more of their time (Lee et al. 1999). In a study of volunteer emergency medical technicians, Reich (2000) found that the volunteers who saw more of their "real me" in the emergency medical technician role were more committed to it. They took on a range of activities in the organization above and beyond those narrowly prescribed by the role. Furthermore, older and more experienced volunteers viewed their volunteer role-identity as more similar to their "ideal me," suggesting either a socialization effect, as volunteers gradually brought their actual and ideal roles into line or a selection effect, as those who failed to bring them into line dropped out.

The turnover rate among volunteers with a weak role identity is higher than it is for people who identify strongly with the volunteer role (Miller et al. 1990). A person who develops a specific role identity linked to a particular organization is likely to be more committed to that organization. Volunteers for the American Cancer Society (ACS) were asked how many hours they worked for the organization, how many hours they volunteered for other organizations, and whether they had any intention of leaving the ACS. Role-identity merger was measured by: perceived prestige of the organization, having other ACS volunteers who are important and who might be lost if the volunteer quit, and personal importance ("I feel certain that the work I do contributes in important ways to the mission and aims of the American Cancer Society"). The stronger they identified as a volunteer for ACS, the more hours they volunteered for the organization, the fewer hours they volunteered for other organizations, and the less likely were they to express an intention to leave the organization (Grube and Piliavin 2000).

Role identity theory helps explain why people become more identified with their volunteer work as they do more of it. The longer they volunteer, the larger the "stake" they have in their volunteer role and, as their investment increases, they become more committed. The person then strives to make his or her behavior consistent with this role identity. On three occasions, four months apart, Penner et al. (1998) surveyed volunteers working for an organization set up to help people infected with the AIDS virus. On each occasion respondents were asked: their feelings about being a volunteer; their satisfaction with the organization; and their commitment to the organization (e.g., willingness to do more assignments). In the initial survey, volunteers who were more satisfied with the organization and had more positive feelings about being a volunteer contributed more hours. The longer the volunteers served, the more satisfied they became with the organization.

Role identity theory is important for the study of commitment because it challenges the view that volunteers decide to quit on the basis of a rational calculation of the costs and benefits of doing the work. We evaluate the costs and benefits of volunteer work in light of our identity, or the identity we would like to have. Our identity thus becomes an independent basis for evaluating our interests. An action that might seem to call for extreme sacrifice and dedication, and which people would be unlikely to perform without incentives or soon grow tired of, becomes routine and quite unheroic once the volunteer identity has been embraced. No rewards are necessary because no costs are entailed. We think to ourselves: "I am a person who habitually does these actions without need for praise or comment." Because we judge the worthiness, or the utility, of our actions in light of our identity, or the identity to which we lay claim, they become rewarding because they enable us to express our values, talents, and abilities. Our actions gratify us by allowing our self-concept to approach our self-ideal ("I *am* being the type of person I want to be"). A young woman volunteering at a rape crisis center told Abrahams (1996:773) that she found the work rewarding because it "made me into a person that I really want to be and am proud of being." Role identity theory therefore obliges us to re-think what people mean when they say they volunteer in order to "make a difference." They do not necessarily mean this instrumentally (e.g., helping build a house) and they do not necessarily get frustrated and quit if the house does not get built. They are referring to their own identity. Helping someone learn to read or building them a house to live in has an instrumental purpose but it also helps the volunteer "become a better person" or realize a desired identity. And once volunteer work has become a way for us to affirm a desired identity, the more we do, the more central that identity will be to us. The identity is reinforced by the personal investments and sacrifices volunteer work demands. The more the individual invests in the role the greater the incentive to continue to perform it.

PROPER MOTIVATION

In chapter 4 we pointed out that motivational theories assume people volunteer to meet certain needs. It is logical to extend this line of argument and predict that people will quit volunteering if these needs are not met. Because we associate volunteer work with charity it is natural to assume that people who volunteer for the "right" motives—altruism—will be more committed to the work. Nelson et al. (2004:118) found that volunteers acting as ombudsmen in long-term care facilities contributed more time to the job if they were altruistically motivated: self-development and affiliation motives made no difference to time contributed. Penner et al. (1998) surveyed AIDS volunteers to examine the effect of motivation on length of service. Using the VFI, they found that only the values motive predicted length of service (measured over three waves eight months apart). A study of turnover among hospital volunteers found that having an inconvenient schedule was the best predictor of leaving the hospital within six months. However, volunteers whose main motivation was to gain work-related experiences—those who saw the volunteer work as a means to end—were more likely to quit than those whose motivation was more altruistic (Miller et al. 1990). Serving as a Big Brother/Big Sister volunteer can be quite demanding. Volunteers are expected to contribute many hours and, because of their behavior problems, children often cannot give the volunteers the personal fulfillment the volunteers may seek. Volunteers often say they quit this program because of relationship problems with the child or parents' lack of involvement with the child, or their feeling of not being appreciated either by the child, the parents, or the agency. But if all volunteers in the program faced these difficulties why did only some people quit? One study found that volunteers who had mentioned being motivated by the "need for or expectation of egoistic benefits" were the most likely to quit the program (Rubin and Thorelli 1984:230). Snyder and Omoto (1992:213), also studying AIDS volunteers, found that volunteers who invoked esteem enhancement or personal development reasons for their work they were more likely to be active at a one-year follow-up. Surprisingly, perhaps, these more "selfish" reasons functioned to maintain commitment whereas value motivations had no effect.

Volunteers have a tendency to select activities that match their motivations. Snyder and Omoto (1992:229) found that AIDS "buddies" scored higher on motivations revolving around concerns for others whereas those working for AIDS organizations without direct contact with people with AIDS scored higher on motives of self-enhancement or sociality. But it is not always possible to assign volunteers to tasks to match their needs and this creates problems. Indeed, it likely to be the case that there is no particular motive that explains commitment: rather, commitment is explained by the extent to which the tasks volunteers are given match their motives. McClintock (2000:36) recommends that volunteer resource managers use motives to design incentives:

A museum's volunteers are highly motivated by the desire to learn. The museum's recognition program builds on that and thanks volunteers by giving them behind-the-scenes tours, special lectures, special awards of merit based on performance, a performance evaluation system where staff evaluate their performance and vice versa, end of project and exhibition programs where they have wine and cheese and do a "post-mortem" on the event or celebrate with champagne.

In other words, individuals whose motivational needs are met by their participation probably derive greater satisfaction from their work and are less likely to drop out. In a study of elderly volunteers at a community hospital Clary et al. (1998:1525) found that volunteer satisfaction was higher among those receiving benefits related to their reasons for volunteering. Another study found that college students were not only more satisfied with their volunteer tasks if they matched their motivations for volunteering they were also more likely to plan on volunteering in the future (Clary et al. 1998:1526). In her study of search and rescue volunteers, Lois (2003:44) found that the more senior members of the organization believed that "those who joined for the 'wrong reasons' subsequently quit." In this case, wrong reasons would include thrill seeking, glory seeking, joining just to acquire outdoor or survival skills, or discounted outdoor equipment.

A mismatch between motivations and activities need not be a problem as long as volunteers change their motivation as they gain more experience with the volunteer work. A motivation that leads people to become volunteers is not the same as the motivation that leads them to stay involved. "It seems that once volunteers are attracted to the work [emergency squads] by a service-to-the-community ethic, they begin to receive the unanticipated rewards of personal development, personal growth, good feelings about themselves, new friendships, and intrinsically interesting work" (Gora and Nemerowicz 1985:35). For some search and rescue volunteers, the initial appeal of the work was the element of thrill and excitement of the rescue or the prestige of being on the team in the community or simply getting to know others and make friends. Eventually, however, performing altruistic acts led them to reinterpret their actions and their motives became more altruistic in nature (Lois 2003:53). Perhaps initial motivations would not have been enough to sustain long-term commitment, or those who did not develop motivations conducive to long-term commitment would have dropped out. If excitement is the reason we join search and rescue squads and we develop no other reason to belong, we will leave when we get bored and go in search of other thrilling opportunities.

Another reason why a mismatch need not weaken commitment is that people have multiple motivations for volunteering and organizations offer a variety of incentives to encourage volunteer workers. It then becomes a matter of finding the incentive to match the motivation. If an organization offers a variety of incentives, volunteers can choose which to respond to depending on their own motivations. For example, "members who desire interpersonal social benefits engage in internal activities that allow them frequent interaction with other persons" (Knoke 1988:326). If volunteers are motivated primarily by normative reasons they might consider the promotion of solidarity incentives (e.g., recognition ceremonies) a waste of time. They might also find it difficult to work alongside staff members who are getting paid for their work. Volunteers motivated by solidary needs—a desire to meet others or be with other like-minded people—balk at devoting too many resources to serving clients or to social activism.[4]

In light of the above argument about the functionality of having multiple motives, it would seem logical to argue that multiple motives strengthen commitment to a voluntary organization. Surprisingly, the little research that has been done on this topic suggests otherwise. In a longitudinal study of AIDS volunteers, 62.9 percent gave more one motivation for volunteering. In a companion longitudinal study of hospice volunteers, almost the same proportion (61%) gave more than one motivation. In both populations, volunteers with multiple motivations reported *more* stress, rated their volunteer work as *more* costly to them, saw it as *less* fulfilling, and were *less* satisfied with what they were doing. It is difficult to interpret this pattern. Perhaps volunteers who have multiple motives fail to focus on any one in particular and thus experience an overall lack of satisfaction (Kiviniemi et al. 2002). It could also be that highly focused volunteers are for some other reason having to do with personality or social background also more likely to derive satisfaction from their volunteer activities.

JOB SATISFACTION

People say they volunteer because they want to "make a difference." While they do not expect to get paid for their labor, they do expect their gift of time to be "recognized" and they expect to see some results for their labors. In the words of one volunteer,

> The major reason [for continuing to volunteer] is my opportunity to be able to come back to meetings and see that some of the things that we've discussed have been acted upon and that, therefore, we've made a difference, whether it's a small difference or a large difference. And that really is payment enough as a volunteer to be able to say, 'I've given some input. I've made a difference here in this organization.' And as long as that continues on then my interest is still there with that organization. I know that I'm a valuable part of the organization. (Basok et al. 2002:2)

Another woman explained why she volunteered for an agency devoted to finding after-school activities for children:

> You see the kids when they come in from school. They are happy to be here. I see less kids [*sic*] on the street than I used to in my younger day because they didn't have a place like that. It is good. It has helped the community to survive. It has helped against breaking and entering. Kids are off the street. They have a place to go. Without no [*sic*] volunteers there would be no place. It we can't help, they can't survive. (Reitsma-Street 2000:661)

If their work seems to be futile, volunteers will become disillusioned and frustrated. A peace activist told Hunt and Benford (1994:509),

> I've lost energy. I'm not energized like I was. The meetings, the sacrifices I've made, no evidence of progress, all that—it adds up. It wears you out until you're burned out. I just need a break . . . I'll probably get involved later on, I don't know, but for now I need a change.

While volunteer work can be very pleasurable and rewarding, it can also make people feel angry, embittered, disillusioned, cynical, despairing, and useless. Eventually, it can lead to "burnout." Coles (1993:136) heard so many references to burnout in his many years of working with volunteers that he "almost came to expect to hear the phrase in every conversation with someone who is doing community service." Burnout is often produced by a combination of high levels of commitment and high levels of tension with society and is more likely in the case of advocacy volunteering because the measures of success are so intangible, at least compared to direct face-to-face volunteering, where a smile on a face can provide an immediate reward, but it is a staff problem that faces all volunteer administrators. Nelson et al. (2004:116) describe the role of the long-term care ombudsman (an advocacy role) as stressful because volunteers "need to have the wherewithal to challenge administrators and sometimes elders' family members."

In this section we will examine the simple proposition that people who are dissatisfied with the volunteer role are most likely to quit. Dissatisfaction could, of course, stem from the factors we have discussed in the chapter so far. Volunteers become dissatisfied because the paid staff do not respect them or because the client is ungrateful. We expect paid employees who are dissatisfied with some aspect of their job—its pay, the working conditions, or prospects of advancement—to quit if they have an option. We expect them to be less committed to those jobs, more likely to slack off and take sick days because, as often as not, they would rather be doing something else. At first glance, volunteer work seems to be very similar. The disillusionment of the young Canadian volunteer in the following quotation is evident: "There's times . . . especially working with the developmentally challenged . . . when you're putting a lot out and not getting a lot back and not seeing anything happen and you know, it's things like that that can . . . make it more difficult to keep doing it" (Pancer and Pratt 1999:51). Indeed, while we might tolerate a dissatisfying paid job because of the money or the belief we have little choice, we have much higher expectations of our volunteer job. After all, we have chosen it, perhaps because it promises to give us something our other job lacks, or because we want to use our special gifts, or because we want to have some control over our work, but the freedom with which we chose it means we attach so much more importance to being satisfied with it. And, because we are not getting paid for the work, we want it to be intrinsically gratifying, perhaps more than we would demand of a job for which we were getting paid.

On the other hand, there are reasons to wonder whether job satisfaction plays such a pivotal role in volunteering commitment. First, many of the frustrations involved in volunteer work are exactly the kind of "cost" volunteers imagined they would incur when they signed up. They *expect* their altruism to be costly to them. They regard it as a measure of their worth and significance. Indeed, they might become dissatisfied if the costs of doing the work were less than they anticipated. People volunteer in order to give something. Like any gift, if it were costless it would lose its value to the donor. "Paying the price" therefore makes the activity worthwhile and meaningful. One of the AIDS volunteers interviewed by Bender (2003:66) contrasted her gift of time to provide food for people with AIDS to people who gave money, where

> you just write the check and put it in the envelope and that's it. In a sense, it doesn't cost you anything. There's nothing of yourself there.

Second, volunteers tend to judge success differently from paid employees. Paid workers whose salaries do not reflect their performance are expected to be dissatisfied. Paid workers who see no tangible outcome of their labors— sales staff who sell nothing—are expected to become frustrated and disillusioned. But volunteers see things differently. Many acknowledge that the goals for which they strive (e.g., eradicating hunger) will never be achieved. For example, although many Americans have been involved in peace movements and organizations whose goal is to end the arms race between nations it is difficult for them to see measurable results from their efforts. Under these circumstances it would be easy to lose faith in the mission. But peace activists are not necessarily motivated only by the prospect of winning. As one member of Plowshares put it: "Our goal, our purpose, our approach is not primarily to have an effect. It is first of all to be faithful. When you follow the gospel, it's not in order to be a success. It's an attempt to be faithful to God, to God's will for today, to be the voice of conscience" (Nepstad 2004:54). Volunteers do not fool themselves that they will solve the world's problems on their own. Why would anybody waste time trying to eradicate hunger when the problem is so intractable? The answer is that people do not volunteer to eradicate hunger but to provide food to hungry people:

> You come in, prepare the food, they box it up, it goes out. . . . This seemed like a very simple thing I could do. I can't fix the whole world, but one morning a week I could go make some food for people who need it. (Bender 2003:65)

Habitat for Humanity volunteers see themselves as helping "chisel the corner off the problem" (Baggett 2001:112). By reducing social problems, such as inadequate housing, to individual acts of kindness they make the task manageable, even conceivable, and as a result have difficulty understanding why more people are not volunteering when so little is required of them. Far from having fixed goals they must achieve else frustration will set in, volunteers are capable of adjusting their goals to fit their real expectations (Eliasoph 1998:82).

Third, for many volunteers, the means are as important as the end. So long as they are "doing the right thing" the attainment of long-term goals is less important. This is why volunteers do not get frustrated if others fail to volunteer. The "free rider" problem is not necessarily a reason to quit.

> If people are involved in homelessness or hunger, or any social service, and they're doing it to be successful, it's going to be very frustrating. Because even Jesus said, "the poor are with you always." But I think if people do it, not to be successful, but to be faithful, then I think you find the energy and the strength and the hope to continue. I'd love to think that we could eradicate homelessness, but I don't know if that's going to happen in my lifetime. My motivation is to do it because I feel I've been called, as a religious person, to feed the hungry and clothe the naked and provide shelter for those with no shelter. (Poppendieck 1998:193)

There is important therapeutic dimension to helping behavior, a dimension of self-knowing. When people volunteer they demonstrate that "being good and caring is possible" (Eliasoph 1998:83). This is a more performative way of thinking about volunteering. Rather than a cost to be borne in pursuit of a gain, volunteer work is a way of expressing and dramatizing a particular view of the world. People volunteer not to preserve or advance their interests but to preserve the feeling that the world makes a certain kind of sense. Volunteers "wanted to reassure themselves through their own activity that the world makes sense because good citizens really can make a difference on issues that matter. Volunteers are, above all, " 'moral'—in the sense of *meaning making*—rather than 'rational' actors" (Eliasoph 1998:64). Their volunteer work reflects their need to "witness," to "create a self in keeping with particular moral ideals" (Allahyari 2000:111). In short, while there is certainly "a large dose" of self-interest in volunteering, it is misguided to think that the search for some "rewarding outcome" explains it and the failure to achieve that outcome explains why people quit (Wuthnow 1991:42). Intrinsically motivated, volunteers are relatively indifferent to external rewards. Indeed, offering these rewards can blunt the altruistic impulse. Emergency squad volunteers are no less satisfied for not getting paid for what they do. Indeed, "there was some suggestion that monetary rewards would diminish the emotional boost they got from volunteering" (Gora and Nemerowicz 1985:14).

Given these arguments, it is far from obvious that volunteers will quit their job if they become dissatisfied with it. In the rest of this section we will review the research on the role of satisfaction in volunteer turnover. One study interviewed AIDS volunteers first during the original orientation and training sessions, again after three months, six months, twelve months, and finally after two and half years. Because volunteering to help people with AIDS carries with it a social stigma, the researchers assumed the volunteer work would be stressful. In subsequent interviews, the most stigmatized volunteers were the least satisfied with their work. Indeed, the individuals most apprehensive about this stigmatization left the program before the two-week training session was over. A year after the program began, half the initial volunteers had dropped out because the stigma associated with the work was more than they could bear (Snyder et al. 1999). A follow-up study two and half years later found that volunteers who had earlier expressed satisfaction with the work were more likely to be volunteering for the same organization (Omoto and Snyder 1995).

This kind of detailed study of volunteers in a particular organization supports an argument that is intuitively plausible: if volunteers do not like the work for some reason they will quit. Other studies, however, have failed to find a link between level of satisfaction with volunteering and subsequent exit from the volunteer role (Penner and Finkelstein 1998:534; Wilson and Musick 1999). Davis et al. (2003) analyzed data from 238 individuals who began volunteering for one of nine organizations in the Tampa Bay region of Florida in 1996–1997. Subjects were interviewed during the orientation session for new volunteers and were contacted four times during the next twelve months. Attrition was fairly steady: nearly a third (32%) had dropped out after only three months; by six months this figure had reached 56 percent; and by the end of the year only 27 percent were still volunteering. Volunteers' level of satisfaction at time of first follow-up did not predict whether the subject would still be volunteering twelve months later. Only twelve of the 101 volunteers who had quitted expressed dissatisfaction with their work assignments. Quitters were much more likely to mention time conflicts, emergencies, vacations, or changes of residence. They were also younger and more poorly educated. Miller et al. (1990) surveyed 165 hospital volunteers. They were asked a number of questions about their level of satisfaction with their volunteer job and with the specific tasks to which they were assigned. They were also asked whether they were volunteering to gain work experience and whether they intended to quit in the next six months. Six months later, the researchers contacted the directors of volunteer services at the hospitals where the research was conducted to get the names of those who had quit. Neither the level of satisfaction nor the specific task assigned had any effect on quitting.

Based on this review of the limited research on this topic, it is unclear what role job satisfaction plays in the level of commitment people have to the volunteer role. We cannot rule out the possibility that people will quit if they are dissatisfied even if dissatisfaction at one time does not predict quitting at a later time very well. This raises the question of what makes people dissatisfied with their volunteer work. In this chapter we have described some of the structural reasons, such as role ambiguity, that might create dissatisfaction, but social psychological factors also play some part. Our satisfaction with any role is influenced by our expectations regarding that role. One study of AIDS volunteers found that psychological burnout occurred most rapidly among those who had not anticipated the social stigma associated with the work (Snyder et al. 1999).

The influence of expectations on volunteer satisfaction opens up a whole new field of sociological exploration. People from different social backgrounds, with different resources, with different reasons for volunteering will react to the same tasks in different ways because they have different expectations about the volunteer role they are assigned. On study showed that men tended to be more critical than women of the way their volunteer work was organized, were more pessimistic about the organization achieving its objectives, less likely to feel their efforts were appreciated by the organization, and less likely to have been asked to do the things they would really like to do. It is probable, on the basis of this evidence, that men would have higher quit rates than women. Women volunteers also expressed some dissatisfaction with their work, but they were more likely to feel that too much was expected of them and they were not always able to cope with the things they had been asked to do (Smith 1998:97). Older volunteers tend to be more satisfied than younger volunteers (Smith 1998:97). This might reflect an adjustment from the idealism of youth or simply the fact that the unsatisfied volunteers had dropped out.

Much more work needs to be done on the causes of dissatisfaction with the volunteer role and the influence of dissatisfaction on the quit rate. But we should not exaggerate the role of this social psychological element in the commitment of volunteers. If people are asked why they quit volunteering, they rarely mention dissatisfaction with the work. In other words, dissatisfaction might indeed cause some people to stop volunteering but it is not the main reason why people abandon the role. In a 2000 survey of Illinois residents, a quarter of those volunteering said they were contributing fewer hours this year than last. When asked why, 20 percent mentioned increased family obligations, 17 percent increased work obligations, 16 percent deteriorating health, 11 percent residential relocation, and 8 percent increased demands from multiple sources. Only 4 percent said they had become bored or burned out (Profile of Illinois 2001). Keith (2003:135) asked a sample of volunteers serving as hospital ombudsmen to speculate why fellow volunteers had left their work. Some (15%) mentioned burnout as the cause, but the more frequently mentioned reasons were quite practical: 30 percent mentioned lack of time, 23 percent mentioned health problems, and 12 percent were "too old." Downton and Wehr (1997:83) found that only a minority of peace activists who quit did so because they were dissatisfied with the impact their work was having. Most of the activists had multiple definitions of success. In asking if their volunteer work had made a difference, most of them said it had made a difference—to them.

RESOURCES

Up this point we have focused on the subjective factors that might affect commitment to the volunteer role, but we mentioned at the beginning of this chapter that some people are more "available" for volunteer work because of their resources. Here we will apply this idea to commitment to the volunteer role. The socio-demographic profile of the more committed volunteer is indistinct at this time, but surveys of specific organizations and ethnographic studies suggest that commitment is, to some degree, socially determined by factors that volunteers bring to the organization. When the director of volunteer services in a North Carolina hospital was asked to rate the "dependability" of ninety-nine volunteers working in the hospital, the older, female volunteers were rated as more dependable (Zweigenhaft et al. 1996). A study of young urban adolescents (mean age 12) who applied to the Big Brother/Big Sisters program also gathered data on the adult Big Brothers and Big Sisters who had volunteered to help them. Although the study was mainly interested in the outcomes for the adolescents, it also gathered information on the volunteers. Because attrition from the program on the part of the youth was important to the study, it is possible to see if there is any variation in the length of the relationship by the characteristics of the volunteer, holding the characteristics of the youth constant. Volunteers with larger household incomes tended to be in matches that lasted longer than lower income volunteers, probably because they had greater flexibility in the use of their time and could more easily afford child care and transportation expenses. Married volunteers aged 26–30 faced a greater risk of termination, probably because of competing demands of small children (Grossman and Rhodes 2002:215).

Conclusion

In this chapter we have described the institutionalization of the volunteer role and the social factors that influence people's attachment to volunteer work in general and their commitment to specific volunteer roles in particular. The volunteer role has gradually become more formalized, as new screening, training, and supervisory methods are introduced and rewards and sanctions systematized. Many welcome these innovations because they help clarify the often vague expectations associated with the volunteer role while others resent rationalization because it undermines the genuine spirit of volunteerism. The new "partnership" between the state and the non-profit sector has served to accelerate this process of rationalization as governments impose their requirements for record keeping, accountability, and efficient management. Governments, in turn, have adopted more "business-like" approaches in an attempt to achieve greater efficiencies and counter opposition from conservatives opposed to "tax and spend" policies. They are increasingly subcontracting work to private non-profits in the same way that major corporations subcontract work out to peripheral manufacturers of parts and providers of services. The result is a new definition of managing volunteers. Zappala et al. (2001:3) call this new way of organizing volunteer services the "social enterprise" model. According to this model, greater efficiency in the provision of services can be achieved if non-profits organize themselves more along business lines and solicit social partnerships primarily with the state but also with private enterprise. This marks a shift from the traditional "charity" model where financial and logistic support comes from below, where the volunteer work is largely client driven in response to perceived need, and where rationalization is kept to a minimum. In the social enterprise model, non-profits are expected to adopt a more "business-like and professional approach" (Zappala et al. 2001:4). They are expected to look for innovative ways to provide services to meet changing social and client needs, to be more accountable for performance, and to provide incentives to motivate volunteers. In the charity model, volunteers are expected to "walk in" and are recruited from the community in general. In the new model, volunteers might be recruited, for a limited time, on the basis of their special contributions or availability, like contingent workers in the paid labor force. In the charity model, the job is adapted to suit the volunteer; in the enterprise model, the volunteer must adapt to suit the job. In the charity model, long-term commitment is valued and rewarded; in the enterprise model, volunteering is need-base, fixed-term, and not necessarily based on membership or commitment to the organization. In the charity model the principal motivation is altruism; in the enterprise model this motivation is combined with motivations having to do with self-improvement and the acquisition of job skills.

Finally, we should note that the "problem" with which the second half of this chapter deals—getting volunteers to make a commitment—is less serious now than it has been in the past because people are not looking to make long-term commitments and organizations are no longer expecting it of them. In chapter 17 we noted that more and more volunteers contribute their volunteer hours in a more sporadic, infrequent pattern. The style of volunteering might be undergoing a change. People no longer join a voluntary association and expect to make a long-term commitment to volunteering for that association alone. More and more people seem to be choosing to contribute their hours on a sporadic basis to events or causes without joining an organization or making a commitment or choosing to contribute the same number of hours as before but distributing those hours across more organizations without necessarily being tied to one or the other. When Zappala et al. (2001:12) surveyed volunteers for the Smith Family (a large non-profit organization in Australia) they found that quite a large proportion of the volunteers contributed time only once or twice a year. These infrequent volunteers were more, not less, likely to also be volunteering for another organization. They tended to be younger and more mobile. From the Smith Family standpoint they were less committed, even though they volunteered just as much.

Part 6.

The Consequences of Volunteering

We usually think of volunteers as people who give their time to help others without benefit to themselves. Perhaps this is why so little attention has been paid to what volunteers get out of the volunteer experience. Volunteer service is intended to be a gift and the giving should not be conditional on receiving anything in return except, perhaps, an expression of gratitude. The psychic reward of gift giving, the positive feeling about ourselves as we do our duty, fulfill an obligation, or receive the thanks of others, is perhaps the most often cited of the benefits of volunteering, in large part because people have little hesitation in allowing volunteers to receive this kind of benefit. Volunteering can also provide material benefits, although this is less often acknowledged, because volunteers are not expected to be interested in material gain. But, while acting altruistically might rule out acting selfishly, it does not mean we must act *selflessly,* as if we must abnegate ourselves when helping others. Volunteering can include fulfilling some vision of ourselves. Self-fulfillment and volunteering can therefore go together. It is not necessary to think of actions being either self-interested or not. Many actions provide joint rewards: the volunteer derives enjoyment from the experience and therefore satisfies his or her interests, but the action is also of benefit to others. This is different from engaging in an action only because it gratifies self-interests or engaging in an action that is not rewarding although it might benefit others.

In one sense, it is obvious that volunteers gain from their work in quite material ways: helping maintain a sports club cuts the annual membership fees; helping to run a cooperative keeps the cost of groceries down; volunteering in a child's private school lowers tuition fees; serving on the committee of the local trade union branch helps win wage increases. But these are all material benefits that accrue not only to the volunteer but to those who did not volunteer at all: they are all "public" or "collective" goods. In part 6 we are interested in "private goods": those that accrue only to the person doing the volunteer work. We use the term "private goods" to describe any tangible outcome of volunteer work enjoyed exclusively by the volunteer. Despite seeming to paint volunteerism in a more selfish light, the prospect of earning private goods is a powerful incentive. It helps explain why people do not succumb to the temptation to "ride free." Wood (2001:268) believes that private incentives help explain why some people risked their lives to fight for the redistribution of land in El Salvador. This behavior is hard to explain in rational terms because all peasants would have benefited from the land redistribution, not just those who incurred risks. She argues, "the assertion of agency itself constituted part of the meaning of those acts." Unlike the other benefits of the insurgency, these emotional benefits were available only to participants. Likewise, Stein (2001:116) sees the motivation of Christian activists (e.g., against abortion clinics) as being primarily to construct a positive sense of themselves and their families as strong and independent: their activism is "a reparative act."

Both of the topics we cover in chapter 20 have to do with ways of thinking and behaving believed to be good for society, habits that parents and mediating institutions, such as schools and churches, are expected to endorse and encourage. The reference to "good for society" betrays the normative assumptions informing the discussion of the topics in this chapter. Democracies must ensure that each new generation of citizens identifies with the common good and becomes engaged in the civic life of their communities. Successful political socialization means the development of civic literacy, civic skills, and civic behaviors. These are the "goods" discussed in the first part of the chapter. We are interested in whether volunteers make better citizens than people who do not volunteer. Are they more likely to vote? Are they more engaged in political activities at the local level? It could be argued that volunteers are better citizens by definition because their volunteer work might well consist of helping raise funds for political campaigns, leafleting the neighborhood before a school board election, or writing letters to the mayor on behalf of a neighborhood improvement association. But volunteer work is not *necessarily* political and is sometimes explicitly motivated by a concern to avoid "politics." Indeed, insofar as volunteer work distracts people from conventional politics, it might be detrimental to good citizenship. It is therefore an empirical question whether volunteers make good citizens.

The second topic covered in chapter 20 is the influence of volunteering on antisocial behavior. "Antisocial behavior" is a rather loose term but it is normally used to refer to delinquent or criminal behaviors such as illicit drug use, stealing, school truancy, or vandalism. Again, the normative assumptions informing this discussion are that it is better to be prosocial in one's attitudes and behaviors than antisocial and that antisocial behavior should be sanctioned and potentially very costly. Avoiding antisocial attitudes and behaviors is therefore a possible benefit of volunteer work. According to the theory we endorse, when it comes to explaining antisocial behavior, the issue is not why certain individuals commit crimes but what keeps the rest of society's members from engaging in criminal activity. Many people believe that getting involved in "constructive activities" such as volunteer work limits the propensity to "get into trouble."

Chapter 21 discusses the influence of volunteering on two kinds of personal benefits, namely labor market rewards and health. It is quite common for people to cite a desire to acquire job-related skills as one reason for volunteering. In chapter 6 we speculated that self-employed workers volunteer more than other workers because their jobs will benefit: they can "advertise" their services and make new business contacts. Some unemployed people volunteer to maintain their skills and work habits or to get a foot in the door of an organization that might eventually hire them. These are, however, only intentions: we do not know whether volunteering actually has the intended effect. In any case, the vast majority of volunteers do not give instrumental motivations for the work they do. It could be that too much time spent on volunteering detracts from one's career. In the Japanese case we cited in chapter 19, the "professional" volunteers devoted much of their life to volunteer work, treating their volunteer role as primary and the roles of worker and family member as secondary. Chapter 21 will review the empirical evidence on the relation between volunteering, occupational prestige, and income. As we have already discovered in earlier chapters, volunteers are drawn disproportionately from the middle class. Chapter 21 will ask whether volunteering has anything to do with them being there.

The idea that volunteering provides health benefits might seem surprising, given that it is an additional and unpaid work role, but the second half of chapter 21 will provide a number of reasons for expecting that volunteers are healthier than non-volunteers. Sociological research has already shown that "social ties have a salutary effect on mental health" (Kawachi and Berkman 2001:459) and that socially isolated people face substantial risk of negative health outcomes, such as depression (Mirowsky and Ross 1989:141; Pillemer and Glasgow 2000:3). Since people develop more social ties as a result of their volunteer work, they should be healthier than non-volunteers. According to the role enhancement perspective, people occupying more roles are healthier "because of the augmentation of the individual's power, prestige, resources, and emotional gratification" (Rozario et al. 2004:414). Since the volunteer role is an addition to primary roles, such as the family and the work role, it should, for this reason also, provide health benefits. In chapter 21 we will look first at mental health. As we noted earlier, volunteer work is unquestionably capable of providing psychic benefits: volunteers frequently describe themselves as feeling better as a result of their volunteer work. When volunteers in the Retired and Senior Volunteer Program, Foster Grandparent Program, and the Senior Companion Program were asked if they had changed in any way since they began participating in the program, almost all had positive things to say. They had a new sense of accomplishment and a new purpose in life. They looked forward to each new day because now they were making a positive difference in the life of another. In short, their sense of well-being had improved (Gartland 2001). In some cases, volunteering can transform one's whole outlook on life (Omoto et al. 1993:334). One of the remarkable results in the survey of elderly volunteers just cited is that not only had the volunteers improved mentally, two-thirds of them said they felt *physically* healthier as a result of their volunteer work (Gartland 2001). In the second half of chapter 21 we will discuss the effect of volunteer work on physical health and mortality. We will rely heavily on longitudinal studies to disentangle the relation between health and volunteering. We hypothesize that volunteers lead healthier lives and live longer, but we acknowledge that healthy people are more likely to volunteer.

20

Citizenship and Prosocial Behavior

In the first section of this chapter we consider the argument that volunteering creates good citizens. "Citizenship" is a broad umbrella term covering a range of behaviors, attitudes, skills, beliefs, and values. According to the most expansive definition it includes participation in various forms of democratic politics: voting, working in political campaigns, contacting public officials, serving on local government boards, attending demonstrations, and the like; preferences for political involvement and feelings of attachment to community; skills and cognitive capacities, such as the ability to understand complex social issues; and other-regarding ethics (Perry and Katula 2001:331–333).

It might seem strange to suggest that citizenship is a consequence of volunteering because many forms of citizenship *are* volunteer work. This is certainly true, but it also true that many forms of citizenship (e.g., voting, running for office) are not volunteer work and many forms of volunteer work (e.g., teaching Bible study class) are not forms of citizenship. Conover et al. (1993) used the focus group method to explore Americans' conception of what it means to be a good citizen and whether or not volunteering is included in this conception. All focus group members agreed that the responsibilities of a good citizen were to vote, pay taxes, and contribute to the defense of their country. All agreed that a bad citizen was someone who broke the law, violated the rights of others, or did something to hurt his or her country or injure its citizens. Beyond that, there was no consensus. A majority of members took the view that citizens have obligations that go beyond legal requirements such as paying taxes and obeying laws and include giving something back to one's community, simply because one benefits from belonging to it. They seemed to regard this kind of community service as a natural extension of family ties, although they looked on people who actually do volunteer as especially virtuous citizens. Aside from this majority, there were several other factions: one group interpreted the duties of citizenship quite narrowly and regarded volunteer work as strictly an individual choice, neither obligatory nor particularly meritorious, although something worth encouraging; another believed active engagement in community affairs was an essential part of being a citizen and accepting the benefits that went with it; and another went even further to argue that good citizens have no choice but to volunteer. Clearly, only the last group would argue that volunteering and being a good citizen are the same thing. For most others, there is either no, or only some, overlap between them.

Why Volunteering Encourages Good Citizenship

There are a number of reasons why volunteer work encourages good citizenship. First, volunteering builds trust in other people and public institutions, and trusting people are more likely to get involved in politics (Flanagan et al. 1998:460). Second, volunteering encourages the belief that a social contract underlies orderly social life. By volunteering, people develop an understanding of the bargain between the ordinary person and the polity. They come to realize that for political systems to work everyone must "do their part." In the case of younger people, working with others on a volunteer project helps combat their customary self-centeredness. They learn "that actions are interdependent, that group discipline serves a common purpose, that differences among participants can be negotiated, and that multiple perspectives can be coordinated" (Youniss et al. 1997:625). Third, doing volunteer work gets people more intensely involved in the organizational life of voluntary associations and other non-profit organizations, where they meet a wider range of people and learn more about local issues and local politics: participation breeds participation. Fourth, volunteer work teaches civic skills, such as the ability to write letters and memoranda, plan and organize meetings, and give presentations or speeches, which can then be used in the political arena. The kind of civic training volunteer work can provide is illustrated in the following quotation:

> Arlene spoke about developing more confidence as a communicator. She had found speaking in public a traumatic experience when she was younger. Her activism required her to speak about peace issues in elementary schools, book clubs, service groups like Kiwanis and Rotary, retirement homes, and city council meetings. Called upon to speak often, she eventually overcame her fear of public speaking. (Downton and Wehr 1997:119)

Nothing demonstrates the importance of learning civic skills more than the contrast between students who get involved in extra-curricular activities, such as school clubs or school government, and those who get involved in school sports. Members of the first group are more likely than the average student to become civically engaged as adults but members of the second group are less likely. The problem with sports is they teach no civic skills: activities are planned, decisions are made at the top, and the athlete is permitted little autonomy (Verba et al. 1995).

Fifth, volunteer work makes people more aware of the structural nature of social problems and the need for political solutions. In the case of many young people, volunteer work is their first opportunity to understand the social experiences of other groups of people. It deepens their understanding of how larger social structures impinge on their lives and those they are trying to help (Flanagan et al. 1999:150). Volunteer work can also be a consciousness-raising experience for adults, For example, by volunteering to help AIDS patients, people become aware of the seriousness of the problem and its underlying causes. They become truly aware of the existence of a "gay community" for the first time. They come to see AIDS and its treatment as a civil rights issue rather than a personal problem. Volunteering to help the poor can have the same effect. For example, the goal of the non-profit organization called Beyond Welfare is to help poor people gain economic self-sufficiency. Partnerships are set up between middle class volunteers and clients trying to make it off welfare. While helping the client is the main goal of the program, it is also intended to teach political lessons to the volunteers, who "are expected to examine their biases toward people with low incomes and take steps to move past these biases, to listen with an open mind and heart to participants and allow participants to 'call the shots' about what help they need" (Bloom and Kilgore 2003:434).

These arguments why volunteerism encourages good citizenship are intuitively plausible, but what is the empirical evidence that such a relationship exists? We will begin by looking at the association between volunteering and citizenship among young people. Development psychologists believe the roots of good citizenship are planted early in life. For those who are concerned about political ignorance and apathy among the young, encouraging them to volunteer might help them get involved.

Volunteering and Civic Values among Youth

Sociological theories of socialization emphasize that practical learning is as important as internalizing norms or learning values. This is why doing volunteer work, as opposed to taking civics lessons, is believed to be more effective when teaching young people citizenship because it allows civic virtues to be demonstrated and practiced. Niemi and Chapman (1998) used data from the 1996 National Household Education Survey (NHES) to examine the civic development of ninth through twelfth graders in the United States.[1] In addition to questions measuring civic development, students were asked whether they participated in school government, other school activities (e.g., sports), out-of-school activities (e.g., church), or community service.[2] The more hours the students spent on community service the more they knew about politics. However, students who participated in student government or other in-school or out-of-school activities *also* knew more about politics than students who did not participate in any of these activities (Niemi and Chapman 1998:30). Volunteer work did not appear to make a distinctive contribution. To rule out the possibility these differences might be spurious, the researchers controlled for the social class background and academic performance of students. After controlling for these factors, irregular or infrequent volunteering had no influence on political knowledge. Students who volunteered more than thirty-five hours a year knew more about politics than both the irregular volunteers and those students who did not volunteer at all ($b = 0.23$ $p < 0.05$). After these controls, participation in school government and in other extra-curricular activities continued to have a positive effect on political knowledge, albeit not quite as strong as the effect of doing volunteer work. The lesson is clear: causal or intermittent volunteer work is unlikely to have much effect on political awareness among youth.

As far as attention to politics was concerned, students who volunteered more than thirty-five hours a year were more likely to read a national newspaper weekly than students who did not volunteer; they were more likely to watch the news daily; almost twice as likely to talk about the news with their parents at least once a week; and more likely to watch the news with their parents (Niemi and Chapman 1998:31). Even students who volunteered infrequently were more interested in politics than students who did not volunteer at all, regardless of their academic performance and parents' education. Political efficacy was also linked to volunteering. Less than half (48.5%) of the non-volunteers said they understood politics or government, compared to 67.2 percent of those volunteering more than thirty-five hours a week, regardless of their or their parent's education.[3]

The results of this study certainly suggest that volunteers have developed attitudes toward the political system conducive to good citizenship. Because these are cross-sectional data we cannot be sure whether volunteering is causing civic development or civic development is causing volunteering. Niemi and Chapman (1998:58) attempt to deal with this problem by looking at NHES data on service learning. Students were asked if their school arranged or offered any service activities and whether these activities were required. Students were selected who attended schools that either arranged or required service learning. Even among those students whose "volunteering" was not voluntary but mandated, or those attending schools where service learning was arranged or offered, volunteering was associated with more political knowledge, more frequent discussion of the news with parents, greater perceived participation skills, and a stronger sense of political efficacy. These findings are consistent with the argument that participation leads to changes in civic development rather than vice versa (i.e., it is not a case of the more politically knowledgeable students electing to volunteer).

A study conducted in Britain suggests that the same relation between young people's volunteering and political knowledge is to be found there. A survey of 14- to 16-year-old school children found that a surprisingly large proportion had been politically active: 70 percent had signed a petition to campaign about something; 59 percent had participated in a boycott; 48 percent had joined a campaign about something happening in their local area; 16 percent had written to a local politician; and 7 percent had gone on a march or rally. In addition, 12.6 percent were involved in regular volunteer work. The study does not say whether volunteers were more likely to have been politically active than non-volunteers, but the volunteers were more politically sophisticated than the non-volunteers. They had a better understanding of the needs of different groups in society; stronger feelings of political efficacy; they were more interested in politics and more determined to vote when they reached legal age; they were more aware of the structural forces underlying individual actions; and they were more likely to believe they had acquired the skills necessary for political campaigning, such as how to contact people and how to work in a group: "you just get the knack, what to do, when, who to speak to, that sort of thing" (Roker et al. 1999:195).

Flanagan et al. (1999:147) studied "civic commitments" among youth in the United States, Australia, and five European countries. Adolescents were asked how important it was for them to achieve various goals, including contributing to their community, contributing to their society, helping the less fortunate, preserving the earth and protecting the environment, combating pollution, and being active in politics. In all seven countries volunteers rated contributing to their community, contributing to their society, and helping the less fortunate more highly than non-volunteers. However, with a few exceptions, volunteerism was not associated with political goals further removed from service-oriented activities. Only in the former Soviet bloc countries did volunteers rate environmental concerns more highly; and only in Sweden and the United States did volunteers rate being active in politics more highly than non-volunteers. In none of the countries did young people rank the goals of getting involved in politics very highly, and volunteering did little alter this.

These comparative data on volunteering make it possible to see if the connection between volunteer work and civic commitments varies from one country to another. This is important because, as we have already noted, the meaning of volunteer work varies considerably from one country to another, as does the nature of politics. There is no standard "curriculum" for civic education. In some countries with a strong tradition of voluntary associations being active in political life, the association between volunteerism and civic commitment might be strong. Where the voluntary sector is less well developed, or where its role in society is different, the association might be weaker. A 1995 study of 12- to 18-year-olds in three "stable" and four "transitional" democracies found that the influence of volunteering on citizenship among young people varied from one country to another. Respondents were asked the following question: "When you think about your life and your future, how important is it to you personally to: (a) contribute to your country; and (b) do something to improve your society?" (Flanagan et al. 1998:465). The relation between the respondent's opinion on these items and volunteerism was highly inconsistent: volunteers were more likely than non-volunteers to rank these goals highly—but only the male volunteers in the United States, Sweden, and the Czech Republic, and only the female volunteers in the Czech Republic, Bulgaria, and Russia (Flanagan et al. 1998:467). There is no obvious explanation for these differences. Another study used data from a 1999 survey of adolescents in Chile, the Czech Republic, Norway, Poland, Portugal, Sweden, and the United States. The adolescents were asked whether they expected to be politically active later in life (e.g., join a political party, vote in a national election). On average, 37 percent expected to vote and 19 percent expected to join a political party. Those who were currently volunteering had greater expectations of being politically active in the future than those who were not volunteering, the one exception being the United States. The American adolescents seem to draw a sharper line between volunteer work and political activity (Torney-Purta and Amadeo 2003).

Adolescent Volunteering and Adult Citizenship

Adolescents are too young to engage in most types of "good citizenship" behavior. It is therefore important to know whether encouraging a young person to volunteer has any long-term influence on citizenship. In the United States, the debate over whether schools should encourage and arrange volunteer work in order to promote adult democratic values and practice has been going on for over a hundred years (Nolin et al. 1997:1). Amidst growing concerns that younger generations of Americans are turning away from conventional politics, some school districts have made community service a requirement of graduation, one purpose being to promote civic virtues in adulthood. As we noted in chapter 14, these programs have been quite controversial. Claims about their effectiveness often exceed what the empirical data show. Specifically, there is a "significant gap between scholars who assert that service, by its very nature, promotes citizenship and those who argue that only particular types of service activities nurture citizen development" (Perry and Katula 2001:338). Most community service work performed by adolescents does little to encourage them to think broadly about the social issues surrounding the problems they are dealing with. It is not certain that service learning does much to encourage toleration for others or a greater sense of social responsibility. On the other hand, service learning can develop "citizenship skills," such as negotiation and public speaking, and enhance the learner's sense of agency, so that individuals can make a difference if the service learning program is properly managed.

Astin et al. (1998) analyzed data from a cohort of young Americans from whom information was first collected when they were in their freshman year in college (1985), again when they were college seniors (1989), and again five years after graduation (1994). On each occasion, respondents were asked if they had participated in any volunteer work in the previous year. They were also asked to express their degree of commitment to participate in community action programs, their willingness to help others in difficulty, their willingness to participate in programs to clean up the environment, promote racial understanding, and develop a meaningful philosophy of life. Respondents who had volunteered in college were more likely to be volunteering in 1994. In 1994 they were also more likely to express support for each of the values. Controlling for current volunteering, the influence of college volunteering on values persisted, with the exception of cleaning up the environment and developing a meaningful philosophy of life. In short, early volunteering had a long-term effect on three of the civic and social values, an effect that was not attributable to current level of volunteering or educational achievement.

In another longitudinal study, Fendrich (1993) contacted a random sample of alumni of Florida A and M and Florida State Universities after they had graduated. The first contact was made ten years after they had left college and the second contact was made twenty-five years after graduation. In the first wave of interviews, he found that students who had been activists while in college belonged to more civic organizations than non-activists. By the time he re-surveyed the alumni fifteen years later these differences had disappeared among the Florida A and M alumni, who were predominantly African American. Students who had been activists were no longer more civically engaged than those who had not been active in college. Among the alumni of Florida State, who were predominantly White, the differences between activists and non-activists remained. The adults who had been activists in college were more likely to have recently participated in a protest march, and to have attended a protest meeting. In a rather similar study, McAdam (1988) studied young people who participated in the "Freedom Summer" voter registration campaign in the South during the civil rights movement, comparing them to those who had applied to join the campaign but never participated. In a follow-up survey conducted twenty years later, he found that those who had taken part in the campaign were more politically active in their adult life than those who applied to join but did not participate.

As with the cross-sectional surveys we described earlier, it is not altogether clear from these longitudinal studies that volunteer work has anything distinctive to contribute to citizenship that other extra-curricular activities could not also contribute. Verba et al. (1995) found that adults were more likely to participate in an effort to achieve better racial understanding if they had volunteered while in high school, but the same effect was found for almost any kind of high school organizational participation.

Adult Volunteering and Adult Citizenship

In this section we will review the evidence that adult volunteer work concurrently influences citizenship behavior. Few of the cross-sectional studies described in this section control for the influence of earlier volunteering as described in the previous section and we cannot know, therefore, whether this influence has disappeared or continues to manifest itself through adult volunteering.

Survey data largely support the notion that adult volunteers tend to be more active in politics than non-volunteers. For example, data from the GSS show that being an *active* member of a voluntary association (serving on a committee, serving as an officer, attending conferences and workshops) goes along with being active in local politics, such as voting frequently in local elections, lobbying local political officials, and working with others to solve some community problems (Knoke 1990:1058). Jenkins et al. (2003) analyzed data from a nationally representative sample of Americans aged 15 and older to see if volunteers were more likely than non-volunteers to be involved in politics. They created nineteen survey questions to measure the level of civic engagement in the population.[4] People who were civically engaged were also likely to be active in election campaigns and to express their opinions to public officials. The researchers went on to identify types of people based on the frequency with which they engaged in specific behaviors. "Civic specialists" were those who engaged in two or more civic activities. "Electoral" activists were those who engaged in two or more election related activities. Some were "dual activists" because they scored high in both areas. About 6 percent were civic specialists, 20 percent were electoral specialists, 16 percent were dual specialists, and the remainder (48%) was disengaged. The disengaged tended to be less educated, poorer, Latinos, and young adults (15–25). Dual activists were more highly educated and more affluent than either the electoral or the civic specialists. Finally, the authors found that despite the fact that civic engagement (volunteering) seemed to be a separate dimension from conventional politics, civic specialists were just as likely as electoral specialists to voice their opinions through channels such as petitions, boycotts, letters to the editor, and direct contacts with public officials. The voice of the volunteer was heard clearly. Focus group research by the authors revealed that civic specialists tended to reject conventional political activities. They felt politicians were corrupt or unresponsive and they believed their own volunteer efforts were more likely to succeed than pursuing the path of electoral victory and legislative representation.[5]

The link between volunteering and political activity is of special significance for minority groups, who might lack the socio-economic resources needed to participate fully in the political system. Volunteer work might provide them with the skills and self-confidence to get involved politically. In the African American community, the church's role in mobilizing political behavior among members of that community has often been noted. This raises the question of whether or not volunteering for one's church encourages African Americans to vote, campaign, support political parties, and otherwise become civically engaged. Brown and Brown (2003) use data from the 1993–1994 National Black Politics Survey to answer this question. The survey asked respondents if they volunteered for their church—serving on a committee, given time to a special church project, or helped organize a meeting. They were also asked if they had been politically active in the past year—contacting public officials, engaging in political campaigns, and the like. Interestingly, frequency of church attendance had no influence on political activism, but respondents who volunteered for their church were more likely to have voted and to have been politically active. The study also helped explain why middle class Blacks were more politically active than lower class Blacks: they were more likely to volunteer in their church.

Case studies of non-profit organizations provide further evidence of the link between volunteering and politics. AmeriCorps is a form of quasi-volunteering insofar as members are paid a small stipend and get credit toward college tuition for doing volunteer work. It is relevant to this discussion because one of the aims of the program is to encourage more active citizenry and stronger democracy. There is some evidence that the organization is having its intended effect:

> Survey responses indicate that Americorps made a positive difference in corps members' lives by increasing their personal, professional, and social skills (such as self-confidence). Many corps members also indicated an increased awareness of the needs of their communities and the efficacy of their direct service activities. (Perry et al. 1999:234)

However, we should also note that people who volunteer for AmeriCorps already have high levels of public service motivation. They do not sign up simply because they cannot find a job (Simon 2002:528). Skeptics would point out how unlikely it is that the ten-month experience will increase commitment to active citizenship among people who are already strongly committed. They would be more confident that the AmeriCorps experience is positive if the studies included a control group of non-volunteers with whom to compare those who join AmeriCorps.

Mechanisms Linking Volunteer Work and Citizenship Behavior

Earlier, we described some of the reasons why volunteer work might foster good citizenship. Only a few of these ideas have been subjected to empirical testing.

Trust

In order to develop the "other-regarding ethic" believed to be an essential component of good citizenship, people must be willing to trust strangers not to wish them harm.[6] High trust tends to be associated with citizenship behaviors: "people who trust others are all-round good citizens" (Putnam 2000:137). Trust is a vital part of the social fabric out of which democratic politics are woven. If more people can be persuaded to trust others, democracy will flourish. We discussed the influence of trust on volunteering chapter 3. Trust is a positive personal attribute—some of us are trusting persons, others are not—that encourages us to volunteer. But personality traits are not immutable, and the relation between volunteering and trust could well be reciprocal: trusting people are more likely to volunteer, but volunteer work makes them more trusting.

The standard trust question on social surveys is actually a measure of trust in a "generalized other." It asks us if we trust people *in general,* not particular people, such as members of a particular religious or racial group. The latter would be a form of "particularized" trust because it is limited to specific groups of people. It makes sense to believe that volunteering—a formal way of giving help to others, who are often strangers, in the company of other volunteers who we might not know that well—influences generalized trust more than particularized trust. Generalized trust is "thin" trust and it rests on "weak" ties; particularized trust is "thick" trust and rests on "strong" ties (Uslaner 2000:28). This is similar to the distinction drawn by Putnam (2000) between "thin" trust, based on everyday contacts between co-workers, neighbors, team-members, and "thick" trust, embedded in family and friendship ties. Only thin or generalized trust makes it possible to build bridges to others. Thick trust tends to sediment social ties with our in-group but weaken ties to out-groups.

This distinction is important because volunteering might foster one kind of trust and not the other. Volunteering might make us more trusting of other members of the group for which we volunteer but *less* trusting of people outside it. For example, volunteering to teach Bible class might foster reciprocity and mutual trust *within* religious congregations. When a member of our congregation volunteers to tutor our children in a Bible study class, we become indebted to them:

> [w]hen someone voluntarily teaches my child what I consider to be important, I am happy to reciprocate by helping that individual, as well as other members of the group, using the skills and abilities that I uniquely possess, whether by baking a cake or recommending a good mechanic. Now, multiply this network of reciprocation to include choir members, ushers, committee members, and other congregational volunteers, and the level of social embeddedness, exchanges, and trust becomes quite tangible. (Cnaan 2002:261)

This network of reciprocation, however, does not extent beyond the group itself, in which case volunteer work has little effect on more generalized trust or it may weaken it. Thus, if volunteer work creates interactions with dissimilar people it may encourage generalized trust, but if it creates interaction with similar people it will develop only in-group trust. The social diversity of the interaction is thus crucially important. To the extent that volunteer work encourages people's natural tendency to associate mostly with people like themselves, it will not have much positive effect on the kind of trust believed to be important for a healthy civil society. Although volunteer work is often painted as an opportunity to help, and thereby meet, people from different social backgrounds, the volunteer-client relationship does not necessarily create this kind of interaction or build more generalized trust. Baggett (2000:133) describes how volunteers for Habitat for Humanity believe in an ideal of integrating people from different social backgrounds into the same community for the purpose of building trust and toleration. Too often, however, this means screening clients so that they resemble the volunteers (who are mainly middle class) and socializing and disciplining clients so that they internalize and adhere to the same social norms as the volunteers. The "common ground" Habitat for Humanity finds is already occupied by the volunteers, not the clients. The volunteer-client relationship in this case does not create a great deal of empathy between the two and does not create much of a foundation for mutual trust. In short, volunteering for Habitat for Humanity will not necessarily make you more knowledgeable about, tolerant of or trusting in people very different from you. People might well be more likely to *say* they have become more trusting as a result of their volunteer work, but we cannot be sure they are any more trusting than non-volunteers.

In summary, while it is probably true that trusting people are more likely to volunteer, it is not certain at all that volunteering makes us more trusting of people in general. If, in their volunteer work, people associate mainly with those of a similar social background—as might be the case in a religious congregation—it is more likely that volunteering will build particularized trust and indeed foster distrust of people who are not members of the group. Indeed, one skeptic has concluded, after a review of the research on this topic, that volunteering does not have much effect on trust even of one's fellow group members (Hooghe 2003:91).[7] The link between volunteering and citizenship is unlikely to be generalized trust.

Self-Efficacy

In chapter 3 we discussed the influence of self-efficacy on volunteering. People are more likely to volunteer if they believe their efforts will bear fruit: they have a "can do" outlook on life. Although we characterized self-efficacy as a personality trait in that chapter, this does not mean it is incapable of change. Ethnographic data suggest that the relation is reciprocal: self-confident people are more likely to volunteer, but volunteer work builds self-confidence that in turn spills over into the political arena. In one study of volunteers at community centers in Canada organized to provide activities for people in poorer neighborhoods to find safe places for children and "a variety of nutrition, play, family home visiting, drop-in, educational, cultural, and social action programs," the empowering effect of doing volunteer work was clearly evident (Reitsma-Street et al. 2000:655). Mostly unemployed women, the volunteers spoke enthusiastically about the way in which helping out at the center provided them with an opportunity to make important decisions and take responsibility for organizational matters, including hiring paid staff, setting program goals, and distributing funds. After six years "[r]elationships in the centers had to include significant space for conflict and resolution procedures as power to decide had become highly valued by volunteers especially over decisions that affected the whole community" (Reitsma-Street et al. 2000:663).

Another study showed how women who might otherwise have been hesitant to be visible and audible in public settings gained the confidence to do so through their volunteer work, in this case an organization set up to advocate for better public safety in poorer neighborhoods.

> Before getting involved in our organization, you know . . . [she] never really thought that her voice—nobody gave a shit what she had to say. But now, this woman, after being involved for a year with our organization ran negotiations with [the] Deputy [Police] Chief, one of the top police officials in the city. And we're sitting in these negotiations, the guy's half an hour late, and Carrie is chairing and she starts off by scolding him, saying "you know we all took a half day off work to be with you, and you can't even be on time. Do you not respect us?" This is someone who when she first started working with the organization, wouldn't do anything but sit at a sign-in table and sign people in as they walked in the door [to a meeting]. (Smock 2004:37–38)

In chapter 11 we discussed the way in which memberships in voluntary associations foster "civic skills." There is also a social psychological component to this process, whereby mastering these skills in the context of volunteer work instills confidence in people that they can use them in the more public world of politics.

Social Networks

Volunteering does not have to change subjective dispositions to have an influence on citizenship behavior. The pathway from volunteer work to a life in politics is fairly well trodden, at least in the United States. "Volunteer work is a traditional avenue into the world of politics in this country" (Daniels 1988:189). An interview with an upper class American woman illustrates how this works:

I was president of the PTA in another school seven or eight years later when my oldest child was in junior high. It was an active PTA with twenty on the board. Then when I was President of the PTA, I became a delegate to the citywide advisory council on school integration. During this time I also was a volunteer in the schools. I did individual tutoring in math for ghetto kids. When my kids went on I was president of the PTA and then secretary of the citywide PTA. At that point I left the PTA . . . [But] the PTA had gotten me into the political scene. Through the labor friends I had developed I was appointed to various commissions by the mayor. I'm just going on some state and national boards [concerned with integration, civil rights, and equal opportunity]. (Daniels 1988:71)

For this woman the mechanism linking volunteer work to politics was social networks. Her volunteer work not only built a reputation for getting things done but also connected her to members of local, and eventually national, political networks.

Comparative Data on the Link between Adult Volunteering and Citizenship

The World Values Survey makes it possible to compare the association between volunteering and political behavior in several different countries. The latest data (1999) show that volunteers are more likely to be politically engaged than non-volunteers (where this means discussing politics and being willing to sign a petition) in thirty-five of forty-seven countries (Hodgkinson 2003:50). In the 1991 survey, volunteering was measured as being an active rather than passive member of a voluntary organization. Membership alone was sufficient to increase political knowledge, political interest, and engagement in protests and demonstrations over non-membership, but active members were even more civically engaged. Comparing five of the WVS countries, Dekker and Van den Broek (1996:139) found that in the United States active members were more likely than passive members to be interested in politics, to be members of a political party, to have contributed time to a political organization, and to have engaged in a protest or demonstration; in Great Britain they knew more about politics, were more likely to have contributed time to a political organization and to have engaged in a protest or demonstration; in West Germany they knew more about politics, were more likely to belong to a political party, to have contributed time to a political organization, and to have engaged in a protest or demonstration; in Italy they were more likely to have contributed time to a political organization. Only in Mexico were active members no different from passive members on any measure of political engagement. In summary, data from the United States and comparative data largely support the hypothesis that volunteers tend to be more civically engaged than non-volunteers although, as we see from then WVS data, the range of civic behavior with which volunteering is associated varies from one country to another.

Judging by the evidence reviewed above, adult volunteers do make better citizens. However, a number of issues remain to be explored in this field. First, the conventional definition of good citizenship is highly normative: that is, it is based upon a certain set of value-based assumptions as to which kinds of political behavior are desirable. Not all people would necessarily agree with this definition. Where good citizenship means getting involved in fairly conventional activities, such as voting, doing jury duty, paying taxes, and attending town hall meetings, the link between volunteerism and being a good citizen is fairly straightforward. But what if good citizenship includes being "political" in the sense of challenging the status quo? Volunteer work would appear to steer people away from this kind of confrontational politics toward more accommodative political strategies. The influence of volunteering on democratic politics is therefore not necessarily benign.

A second issue is that, despite the evidence linking adult volunteering and civic engagement cited above, there are signs that volunteer work among younger people is becoming an alternative to politics, rather than a stepping-stone toward more civic engagement. Young people today have low voting rates but high volunteer rates. One concern it that volunteer work will actually depoliticize them by encouraging them to think that social problems can be solved by individual, direct acts of charity rather than structural reform. This is one criticism that is made of service learning. It fosters an individualized notion of citizenship, encouraging us to assume responsibility for the provision of a social service that formerly belonged to the government. In this respect, service learning does not encourage civic engagement at all but a particular way of thinking about the relation between the government and its people, a particular way of defining democracy. Volunteer work can similarly send political messages unconsciously by fostering a special kind of relationship between volunteer and client. A good example is Habitat for Humanity, in which volunteers undertake to help build or renovate houses for eligible families. Part of the volunteers' job is to help define eligibility and screen families for eligibility. Whereas most of the volunteers are middle class, most of the clients are drawn from the working class, many of them members of racial minorities. Clients are expected to help with the building and renovating work—"sweat equity." The program probably does cultivate a political awareness but it is suffused with middle class values of self-sufficiency and individualism.

A third issue has to do with the volunteer experience itself. Volunteer work does not always train people for democracy. More and more volunteer work is taking place in the context of bureaucracies, such as government agencies, or consists of helping professionals do their work (e.g., in schools or hospitals) where there is little opportunity to learn civic skills. Volunteer work performed in isolation, such as delivering meals to shut-ins or mentoring youth, also has limited political significance. "If I were a citizen searching for a public forum in which to learn how to participate in and clarify my thoughts about the wider world, volunteer groups would not usually have been good places to search" (Eliasoph 2003:202).

A fourth issue has to do with the assumption that lessons learned in volunteer work generalize to politics at the local or national level. Even where volunteer work focuses on quite politicized issues at the local level—such as the location of a waste dump or a homeless shelter in the area—it is not clear that getting involved in a "single issue" prepares people for more conventional politics. Campbell and Wood (1999:135) found little evidence that volunteering in connection with local issues (e.g., traffic control, noise pollution) encouraged involvement, or even interest, in national politics. Volunteering in this case had to do with local issues, where actions could have a direct and immediate effect, and where the actions had a direct bearing on the activist's safety and well-being. They found little evidence that sporadic and targeted involvement generalized to other issues, to other kinds of involvement or interest and engagement in politics beyond the local level.

A fifth issue is methodological and takes us back to the beginning of the section. Is it logical to think of volunteering as cause and politics as effect? Would it not make more sense to think of them both as part of the same syndrome of civic activities? These activities tend to form clusters. For example, Andolina et al. (2003) found that volunteers are typically more active politically. But they are also more likely to have worked with others to solve a community problem, more active in voluntary associations, more likely to have raised money for charity, more likely to have contacted public officials and the media, and more likely to have signed a petition. They found that when children who were reared in households where political discussions were common grew up they not only volunteered more regularly but also voted, followed politics closely, signed petitions, and so on.

The truth is that volunteering and citizenship go together in people's minds. Not surprisingly, those most engaged already are the most likely to link them. As part of a research project on the civic engagement of the residents of Illinois, seven focus group discussions were conducted in seven locations. In three of the groups, members were selected to be highly engaged in civic activities; in four of the groups the participants were screened to make sure that they had not been involved in group activities and did not consider themselves active in their community. All members had jobs. Members of the civically engaged groups tended to be older, married, parents, college graduates, and frequent churchgoers. Members of all groups agreed that living in a community involves a sense of belonging, meaning that you know your neighbors, people watch out for each other, and residents are actively involved in what is going on in the neighborhood. Members of the civically engaged groups were more likely to say they had sought out communities that were "good places to raise children." They expressed strong interest in maintaining and improving the positive aspects of their community and they accepted some responsibility for the welfare of the community. They also saw their volunteer work as a way to "connect" with other people in the community. Members of all groups agreed that citizenship required active involvement in one's community. But civically engaged respondents were more likely to express the view that citizenship involved "giving something back"—otherwise a person had no right to complain (Profile of Illinois 2001). Similar results were found in a British survey conducted in 2000. Asked if they felt "civically engaged," 18 percent replied in the affirmative. By this they meant they were well informed about local issues, they believed they could influence political decisions, and they agreed that local people could influence decisions relating to their neighborhood. People who felt civically engaged were more likely to have taken an action to solve a local problem (e.g., writing a letter to an elected official) and to be actively involved in a local organization (Coulthard et al. 2002:6). For example, 27 percent of those who felt civically engaged had been actively involved, with responsibilities, in a local organization some time in the past three years, compared with only 10 percent of those who did not feel civically engaged. In summary, the populations represented by both of these samples, one from the United States and the other from Britain, are probably comprised of several different clusters of people. Members of these clusters share certain socio-economic characteristics and they also share patterns of behavior. It makes little sense to think of the individual components of those clusters of behavior as existing independently of one another. Volunteering and civic engagement do "go together" but it is misleading to think of one causing the other.

Volunteering and Adolescent Development

In the second half of this chapter we consider the argument, usually applied to adolescents, that doing volunteer work contributes to a "healthy" human development. Adolescence is a period in the life span when a person changes from being a child to being an adult. During this phase of human development positive outcomes are measured by the young person acquiring a firmer sense of identity, a sense of initiative, emotional competence (e.g., ability to control anger), teamwork and social skills, toleration of diversity, internalization of prosocial norms, and an ability to interact with adults (Hansen et al. 2003). Negative outcomes are measured by "problem" or "risky" behaviors such as substance abuse, unsafe sex, delinquency, crime, and violence.

As with citizenship, there are those who would argue that volunteering is not the cause of healthy human development but an indication of it. Others believe that volunteering should not be viewed as a sign of good moral character but as an "exceptionally powerful means" of facilitating it (Hart et al. 2006:634). The developmental benefits of volunteering motivate the many programs that aim to get young people involved in helping others (Flanagan et al. 1999:144).[8] In many American school systems, community service is encouraged, and in some cases required, because parents and educational administrators believe it will promote positive self-identity and a sense of caring and compassion.[9] Although a 2002 survey found that only four in ten adults were familiar with the term "service learning," nine out of ten "support the presence of service-learning programs in their schools once the programs are explained" (Kenny and Gallagher 2003:151). This does not mean that parents believe volunteer work is an effective antidote to juvenile delinquency. Mostly, they seemed to want academic courses that deal with "real world" situations so as to better prepare their children for a job after school, and they think more service learning will help achieve this goal. Indeed, a minority of parents resist the idea that ethics of responsibility and compassion could be taught in schools, claiming they are the responsibility of parents and others.

Nevertheless, volunteer programs for youth typically include the rationale that young people given an opportunity to participate in constructive, supervised activity outside of school are less likely to engage in behaviors harmful to themselves and others. One prominent sociological theory of juvenile delinquency suggests why this should be true. Control theory does not ask why certain individuals commit crimes but what keeps the rest of society's members from engaging in criminal activity. The theory states that people's criminal activity is controlled by their attachment and commitment to conventional institutions, individuals, and processes. Some of this control is direct, as in the form of parental guidance. Some of it is indirect, in the form of the adolescent's desire to avoid causing pain and displeasure to those with whom he or she has a close relationship. Some of the control is internal, in the form of shame or guilt that prevents a person from committing deviant acts. A prominent exponent of this theory argues that four types of bonding serve to encourage conformity (Hirschi 1969). Attachment is the emotional bond between the juvenile and others, such as parents, teachers, and peers. Commitment is measured by motivation to succeed at conventional goals. Involvement means engaging in law-abiding activities, such as after-school programs. Belief is measured by strength of conviction in the rightness of conventional values. Each of these types of bonding could be fostered by volunteer work. Control theory is not the only reason to think that volunteering will curb delinquency. Volunteer work has the potential to boost self-esteem, self-efficacy, positive relations with peers and adults and a sense of belonging to the community, all of which promise to encourage social conformity.

In this part of the chapter we will review the evidence concerning the influence of volunteering on "healthy" human development. The term "human development" is very broad, and most of the studies we cite have focused on the development of attitudes and behaviors considered healthy from the standpoint of abstaining from anything that is antisocial. We begin by looking at studies asking volunteers how they think they have benefited from their volunteer experiences. These studies are necessarily limited in that people who do not volunteer are not included and we have no way of knowing if volunteer work is making any distinct contribution. They are also limited in that we have no way of knowing if the perceived benefits of volunteer work spill over into other areas of life and actually influence the way adolescents behave.

Volunteers Evaluate Their Experience

A number of studies of volunteers who were asked to evaluate their participation in volunteer programs suggest that it is normally a positive experience, resulting in a change in attitudes in a positive direction, toward greater feelings of social responsibility and self-confidence. In one study, American school children in the ninth, eleventh, and twelfth grades were asked to say whether they had positive or negative experiences in organized youth activities and to evaluate whether these experiences occurred more often in these activities than in other parts of their lives, such as participating in a school class or socializing with friends. Compared to academic classes and hanging out with friends, organized youth activities were consistently rated higher. The more active students reported higher rates of goal setting, problem solving, more experiences of identity exploration, more opportunities to learn how to express and control emotions, and more frequent opportunities to learn teamwork and social skills. Organized activities did not, however, forge new ties to adults or develop relations with children from different social backgrounds. As far as specific organized activities were concerned, involvement in faith-based, service, and community and vocational activities was especially likely to yield experiences relating to the development of identity, prosocial norms, and ties to adults. Youth participating in faith-based and service activities were especially likely to report that their volunteer work was a "positive turning point" in their life. Arts activities (e.g., band), academic activities, and leadership activities (e.g., student government), on the other hand, brought few additional learning experiences beyond those encountered in class or even hanging out with friends (Hansen et al. 2003). In summary, activities that more closely resembled volunteer work were more likely to be associated with the development of prosocial norms and ties to the community, helping students involved in them become more integrated into the wider world.

A 1992 survey of American teenagers asked those who had volunteered in the last year whether any of a list of outcomes had been a "very important benefit" of their volunteer work. The teenagers responded most positively to "I learned to respect others." Nearly half mentioned this benefit. Most of the benefits rated as very important had to do with improved social relations: "I gained satisfaction from helping others"; "I learned to be helpful and kind"; "I learned how to get along with and relate to others." More practical or material benefits were less likely to be cited. Only 16.6 percent said improved school grades were an important benefit; and only 20.3 percent saw new career goals as a benefit of volunteering (Hodgkinson 1995:38). These responses are subject to bias, of course, as volunteers might feel disposed to rate as important to them the more acceptable reasons for volunteering and downplay the more utilitarian benefits. Nor do we know if the same results (e.g., learning to respect others) could not have been achieved in some other way, such as attending church frequently. But these findings support the view that adolescents who volunteer have attitudes and beliefs that are more conducive to social conformity. Young Canadian volunteers described their benefits in much the same way: they had learned to appreciate what they already have ("I realize that I have a lot compared to what some people have you know . . . some people don't have anything"); they had gained more self-confidence ("I gained a lot of confidence in myself and just what I can tackle and the challenges I can take on in my life"); and they had clarified their life goals ("I've learned so much . . . and working with them [disabled children] is actually what has helped me decide on what I want to do for the rest of my life") (Pancer and Pratt 1999:51).

One study looked at young people involved in Teen Outreach Program, an organization sponsored by the Junior League designed to get young people involved in volunteer service in their communities. One of the goals of the program is to enhance young people's sense of autonomy while improving their ability to have mature and self-confident relationships with adults. The study used data from sixty-six different programs. Upon entry into and exit from the program students were asked to report on the incidence of a number of "problem behaviors" such as pregnancy or causing a pregnancy, having failed a school course, and school suspension. These measures were also applied to a comparison group of teenagers who had not volunteered. The volunteers significantly decreased their levels of each of the problem behaviors from program entry to program exit, compared to the teenagers who were not involved in the program. Although the number of hours volunteered made no difference to change in problem behaviors, the decrease in problem behaviors was greatest for those who rated the experience positively. Those who saw the volunteer experience as promoting their own autonomy and their relatedness to adults in the program reported the steepest decline in problem behaviors (Allen et al. 1994).

These studies, where volunteers are questioned about the benefits they believe they have derived from their volunteer work are valuable, but a rigorous test of the theory that volunteering inhibits delinquency and promotes positive human development requires that both volunteers and non-volunteers be included in the study. We will first note the studies using representative samples but cross-sectional data, where causal imputation is difficult. We will then describe some studies that used a more suitable longitudinal design.

Volunteer Work and Antisocial Behavior

Regardless of what volunteers think about their experience, what is the evidence that volunteers are less likely to get into trouble than non-volunteers? One source of data on this subject is Monitoring the Future, a survey of American high school students conducted every year. Among the many questions asked of the students is whether or not they did community service in the previous year. The more frequently students participated in community service the less likely they were to have used marijuana in the past twelve months (Youniss et al. 1999:249).[10] Another nationally representative survey (NELS) asks twelfth graders if they had performed any unpaid volunteer or community service work during the past two years. They are also asked how many times in the past year they had got involved in a fight in or out of school, been put on suspension by their school, been suspended from school, transferred for disciplinary reasons, or spent time in a juvenile detention center. Hoffman and Xu (2002) summed the responses to form an index of delinquency. Students who had volunteered in the past two years scored lower on the index.[11] Hart et al. (1998) also looked at the association between having volunteered in the past two years and "problem behaviors" among a cohort of adolescents and young adults from the NLSY (1994). Volunteers were less likely than non-volunteers to have stolen something worth more than $50, used force to get something, attacked someone to inflict serious injury, broken into a building, or been required by authorities to bring their parents to school. The magnitude of these associations was, however, quite small.

"Binge drinking" on college campuses is a chronic source of concern to parents and administrators. Youth alcohol abuse is not only deviant and, for many students, illegal, but also has many harmful consequences: "binge drinking is arguably the No. 1 public health hazard and primary source of preventable morbidity and mortality for the more than six million full-time college students in America" (Weschler et al. 1995:921). The sociological research on binge drinking has thus far detected only very weak correlations with demographic variables such as age, gender, and parents' education. Low religious salience, membership in fraternities or sororities, spending a lot of time socializing with friends, and spending little time studying are better predictors. A 1993 survey of students in 140 colleges in the United States asked students if they had consumed five or more drinks in a row over the past two weeks (four for women). They were also asked how many hours a day they had spent volunteering over the past month. Volunteering was associated with a 5 percent reduction in risk of binge drinking (Weitzman and Kawachi 2000:1937).[12]

Intervention Studies

The theory that participation in community service restrains adolescent deviance implies that planned intervention might make a difference. This intervention could take the form of asking one group of adolescents to volunteer and comparing the consequences with a control group of adolescents who did not volunteer. The Teen Outreach Program we described earlier is an example of such an intervention study. Working in conjunction with volunteers from the Junior League, students were assigned to volunteer activities such as an aide in a hospital or peer tutoring. The primary purpose of the classroom activities was to promote discussion among students about such issues as dealing with family stress, improving communication skills, dealing with lack of self-confidence, making the transition to adulthood. The program was thus not entirely about volunteering. Evaluations of the program were generally positive. A study reported by Allen and Philiber (2001) used data collected over a four-year period from over sixty sites in the United States where the program was active. Participants in the program averaged 37.4 hours of community service work over the course of the academic year.[13] Students participating in the program had half the risk of pregnancy (or, for males, having caused pregnancy) shown by the comparison group. They faced only 60 percent the risk of course failure as demonstrated by members of the comparison group and 50 percent the risk of academic suspension. The buffering effect of participation in the program was stronger (in the case of pregnancy) for those who had already given birth to a child; that is, for those most at risk of having another. In the case of academic suspension, the volunteer work was more efficacious for those who had been suspended before. The implication is that the program works better for high-risk youths. Moore and Allen (1996:236) describe a similar study—the Valued Youth Program—in which "efforts were made to form school-home-community partnerships" with the goal of improving academic skills, decreasing truancy, and lowering dropout rates. A two-year evaluation of the program, comparing participants with a control group, showed that the program reduced the school dropout rate as well as improving self-concept and reading grades.

O'Donnell et al. (1999) assessed the influence of participation in community service on violence among adolescents. They used students in the seventh and eighth grade at two urban schools in their study, one serving as an intervention school and the other as a control school. All students at the intervention school participated in a classroom curriculum that included a ten-lesson unit focusing on violence prevention. In addition, half the students in the intervention school were randomly assigned to participate in a community service program, in which they spent several hours each week providing service in local health care agencies under the guidance of teachers and community nurses. Measures of violent behavior were taken before the program began, and at a six-month follow-up, after the program had been in operation for some time. Among the eighth-graders, participation in community service reduced violent behavior. The eighth-graders who volunteered reported lower levels of violence than both the eighth-graders who participated only in the violence prevention curriculum, and students from the control school, who had neither the curriculum nor community service participation. The curriculum-only students did not differ from the control students in level of violence, suggesting that participation in community service was the key factor in producing reduced violence levels. In summary, there is "good evidence that volunteering, along with school-based support, relates to a reduction in teen pregnancy, course failure, suspension from school, school drop out, and an improvement in reading grades and self-concept" (Moore and Allen 1996:242). Furthermore, "dosage" seems to be important: the more hours volunteered, the longer the program lasted, and the more chances students had to reflect on and discuss their volunteer experiences, the more protective were the effects of volunteer work. The programs also seemed to work better if students felt they had a choice in the volunteer work and that it fulfilled their motives for volunteering.

After reviewing a number of intervention studies using volunteer work to cultivate prosocial values and discourage antisocial behavior, Moore and Allen (1996:251) identify a number of shortcomings in the research in this field. Several studies did not use a control group matched on age and socio-economic status. Sample sizes were often very small. Most studies relied heavily on the adolescents' own reports rather than the reports of third parties about their behavior. Even when adults were used as informants they were subject to bias because they knew of the adolescents' participation in the program. Few studies ascertained whether the benefits of volunteering are permanent or long lasting. Studies rarely considered whether volunteer work might be more effective for older than younger students. Nevertheless, the results reported above suggest this would be a fruitful area for future research.

Longitudinal Studies

Longitudinal studies are especially valuable when studying the association between volunteering and delinquency because causal ordering can be seen more easily. Without such data we cannot rule out the possibility that delinquents avoid volunteer work. But there is another reason why being able to trace individuals over time is so important. In the case of young people, there is a "natural" increase in problem behaviors during the teenage years: "deviant activities and emotional problems increase over the adolescent years, on average" (Elder and Conger 2000:199). The real question is not whether volunteering reduces the likelihood of deviance but whether it does anything to limit the increase we would otherwise expect.

Uggen and Janikula (1999:336) used the first eight waves of the Youth Development Study, which began in 1988 with a cohort of 1,139 14-year-olds, to look at the influence of volunteer work on the likelihood of having been arrested by 1995. Because the retrospective arrest data were gathered only when the respondents reached age 17, the study covers the ages 17–21. The researchers use as their dependent variable the timing of the first arrest. Most of the arrests reported were for violation of liquor laws. In 1991, when the students were 17, 27 percent reported having been arrested for this reason. This percentage rose to 33 in the next year, 30 percent at age 19, 31 percent at age 20, and 3 percent at age 21. Arrest rates for other offences (e.g., narcotics, larceny, and assault) followed a similar downward trend. *Current* volunteer work was measured when students were in the eleventh and twelfth grades. About a quarter of the students reported doing volunteer work in either their junior or senior years of high school. Volunteers were more likely to be White, come from higher family income homes, and have higher GPAs and higher educational aspirations. They were also less likely to have been arrested: 3 percent of the volunteers had been arrested, compared to 11 percent of the non-volunteers. Event history analysis revealed the impact of volunteering on the timing of first arrest: by the end of 1993, when the respondents were 19 or 20 years old, 99 percent of the volunteers had not been arrested compared to 96 percent of the non-volunteers. This 3 percent gap widened to 8 percent by 1995. The risk of arrest for volunteers over the study period was about 28 percent the risk for the non-volunteers.[14]

As we have already noted, one problem with studying the influence of volunteering on deviance is self-selection. That is, the negative association between volunteering and delinquency might be due to the fact that delinquent youth choose not to volunteer. Social control theorists would argue that adolescents with greater self-control select into volunteer work and those lacking self-control select out of it. Uggen and Janikula (1999:348) tackle this problem by introducing into their analysis measures of "prosocial attitudes" gathered in 1988 (the first wave of the study) when the students were 14 and measures of volunteering before eleventh and twelfth grades. These variables help control for the possibility that prosocial students (i.e., those with prosocial attitudes and a prior record of volunteering) were more likely to be volunteering in eleventh and twelfth grade in the first place. Even with these controls in place, the rate of arrest for volunteers was less than the rate of arrest for non-volunteers.

Community Volunteering and Deviance

A promising line of research on the etiology of deviance and criminal behavior focuses on neighborhood characteristics. The theory guiding this research is that neighborhoods lacking in community cohesion and organizational participation are more likely to experience problems with crime and juvenile delinquency (Hoffman and Xu 2002:569). Insofar as volunteer work could be considered one measure of organizational participation this would suggest that communities with high rates of volunteering have lower deviancy rates. Weitzman and Kawachi (2000) used a nationally representative survey of 17,592 young people enrolled in 140 four-year colleges in the United States to examine the influence of volunteering on "binge drinking." Binge drinking was defined as consuming five or more alcoholic drinks per drinking occasion (four for women) at least once in the two weeks before the survey.

Forty-four percent of respondents reported binge drinking. The students were asked how many hours they had spent volunteering per day over the past month. Responses were used to calculate a campus aggregate level of volunteering, ranging from 0.11 hour to 1.16 hours, with a mean of about twenty-two minutes. Students at campuses with high rates of volunteering were 26 percent less likely to binge drink than were their peers at campuses with low levels of volunteering. The findings were unchanged by controlling for fraternity or sorority membership. The mechanisms whereby this effect is produced are unclear at this time. Perhaps campuses where many students volunteer are places where students bond closely with one another and enforce social norms and offer social support. This cross-sectional study is unable to completely rule out the theory that campuses where binge drinking is widespread and condoned provide an unfavorable climate for volunteerism or that students inclined to binge drinking avoid campuses where volunteer rates are high.

There are few studies of the influence of actual neighborhood or community-level volunteering and the incidence of problem behaviors among the residents of that community. A "citizens audit" carried out in Britain in 2000 asked respondents, "Not counting anything you do for your family, in your work, or with voluntary organizations, how often, if at all, do you actively provide help for other people?" Using responses to this question it is possible to measure the percentage of individuals in each community (county and district local authorities) who spent at least some time on voluntary activity in the average month. The average varied from 15 percent in some communities to 1 percent in others. A comparison of the level of volunteering in a community with the number of burglaries per thousand people in that community showed they were negatively correlated (Whiteley 2004).[15] In other words, local authority areas with many volunteers have fewer burglaries than local authority areas with low levels of such activity. This is a highly suggestive study, but more work needs to be done on this problem. The analysis does not control for the population composition of the local authority area using multi-level models and does not control for important neighborhood characteristics such as home ownership and residential stability.

Parent's Volunteering and Children's Delinquency

We cannot leave the subject of the influence of volunteering on delinquency without touching on the issue of whether the volunteer work of other members of the family has any effect on an adolescent's delinquent behavior. Why should there be any connection between the volunteer work of one family member and the delinquent behavior of another? Parents who volunteer are more likely to be involved in their community, more likely to know where their children are and who they are associating with, more likely to have a relationship with their children that involves them in adult-type roles, and less likely to leave their children alone without supervision (Elder and Conger 2000:123). The influence of volunteering is therefore somewhat indirect.

Focusing on rural and small town populations in one state highly dependent on agriculture, Elder and Conger (2000:213) categorized youth into five groups, depending on their level of "competence" in academic work and social activities. A student whose mother was a PTA leader and whose father was a church trustee represented the most competent group. In her senior year this student was co-captain of the cheerleading squad and the girl's basketball team, simultaneously serving in the student senate, singing in the church choir, and playing an active role in the local chapter of the National Honor Society. The "socially recognized" type of youth, on the other hand, did not excel academically but enjoyed positive relations with peers and was very involved in school extra-curricular activities. A third group, "self-critical achievers," were successful academically, had quite good relations with their peers but lacked self-confidence, and were less involved in social activities. A fourth group felt socially ignored by teachers, parents, and even their peers, performed poorly in academic work, and lacked the self-confidence to get involved in social activities. Finally, there were students who lacked support from parents, had poor grades, disliked school intensely, and were completely uninvolved in organized social activities connected to the school. Boys were over-represented in this last group, as girls were over-represented in the most competent group. The parents of the most competent children tend to be much more highly educated than the parents of the least competent group. Children in the most competent group have lived in the same community all their life. Children in the least competent group have moved frequently. It need hardly be added that children in the "socially ignored" and "least competent" groups were much more at risk of engaging in problem behaviors than children in the other three groups (Elder and Conger 2000:196).[16]

It is likely that rural areas are somewhat distinctive in the role parents play in controlling the deviant behavior of their children. In rural areas, within-generation ties, such as those between peer group members, are less effective in shaping the social attitudes and activities of youth than they are in urban settings. While it is true that parents with strong community ties are better able to monitor their teenagers' social activities outside the home because they are part of a larger network of community adults (Elder and Conger 2000:112), this is likely to be more true in rural than urban areas. In other words, the size and population density of the community moderates the positive influence of parental volunteering.

Conclusion

The study by Elder and Conger (2000) described in the previous paragraph reaffirms that it is unwise to think of volunteer work as being the *cause* of social conformity, as if these behaviors existed independently. More accurately, they are behaviors that tend to go together: they are both the result of some common factor, probably having to do with family background. Volunteering is not the cause of moral behavior so much as it is an indicator of it. Community service is typically included in the "assets" child psychologists believe are necessary to raise caring and responsible children (Moore et al. 2001:64). "Social capacity" is a measure of "good child outcomes." Good children are empathic and behave in such a way as to display concern for family members, friends, members of the community, and the larger society.

Most of the studies reviewed in this section confirm a positive association between volunteering and keeping out of trouble. Does this mean that we can cut back on juvenile delinquency by *requiring* community service? The answer is almost certainly no. For example, the Quantum Opportunities Program has a requirement that all youth involved in the program complete 250 hours of service in the community. The purpose of the program is to help disadvantaged youth in the areas of education (e.g., tutoring), developmental activities (e.g., career choices) and community service (e.g., neighborhood cleanups). Although participants in the program are less likely to be delinquent as a result, members of the staff in the program are not ready to attribute this to community service, mainly because participants in the program resented the community service—they regarded it as "punishment" (Penn 2000:24).

An important issue that remains unresolved is whether there is anything distinctive about volunteer work when it comes to encouraging prosocial behavior. A recent review of the research on activity participation among young people and its consequences concluded that the results "demonstrate a strong connection between participation in constructive, prosocial activities and psychosocial, behavioral and academic adjustment" (Bartko and Eccles 2003:234). Volunteer work is one form of prosocial activity but it is not at all clear that volunteering has a unique effect on child development and adjustment to adult roles. Typically, of course, volunteering is one of a number of activities in which adolescents are engaged. The reality is that individual adolescents are different not because some volunteer and others do not but because they combine activities in different ways. A "person-centered" approach constructs profiles of activities for each adolescent and looks at the consequences for outcome variables for each profile. In a recent study, adolescents were asked their rate of participation in eleven different activities over the past year, ranging from less than once a month to nearly every day, on a six point scale (Bartko and Eccles 2003). Using cluster analysis the activities were sorted into six profiles. One of these was a volunteer profile. The mean for volunteering for adolescents in this group was 4.71 compared to 1.76 for the sample as a whole. The volunteer mean for students in the "uninvolved" group was 0.26. This last group scored much higher on the measure of "hanging out with friends" (3.87) but it should be noted that the adolescents with the volunteer profile reported a mean of 3.6 for hanging out with friends. In other words, most students engaged in a variety of activities, but these activities clustered together in different ways. Knowing which cluster students were in predicted a number of psychosocial and behavioral outcomes: for example, students who were highly involved in many activities showed the lowest mean problem behaviors. As it happens, volunteers scored very close to the mean for the sample as a whole as far as other activities were concerned. This study, which by its method represents the experience of youth in multiple activity settings better than single variable measures that focus on one activity at a time, suggests caution in concluding that volunteer work offers anything distinctive to the adolescent as far as human development is concerned.

21

Occupation, Income, and Health

In chapter 2 we described how volunteers are expected to be altruistically motivated: they should not provide a service for gain, especially material benefits. But this does not rule out the possibility of material benefits as the unintended consequence of volunteer work. In chapter 4 we described how some people volunteer specifically in order to improve their job skills or to establish contacts with prospective clients or employers: among the volunteers in a recent survey who were unemployed at the time, nearly half were convinced they would stand a better chance of getting a job as a result of their volunteer work; and among volunteers who were employed, a quarter believed their volunteer work had helped them get their job (Hall et al. 1998:30). The majority of people do not volunteer for these reasons, however, and in any case, volunteering with the intention of getting a better-paying job does not mean to say that one will succeed. We must turn to the empirical evidence to see if volunteers do better in the job market than non-volunteers. In the first part of this chapter we review, and add to, the research on the occupational and income benefits of volunteering, and in the second part we do the same for health benefits.

Why Volunteering Leads to Better Jobs

There are three major reasons why volunteering might improve a person's chances of getting a better job. The first is that volunteers do better in school, get better educational credentials, and, as a result, get better jobs. The second is that volunteer work is a form of occupational training in which important job skills are learned, which in turn makes it easier to compete for good jobs. The third reason is that volunteer work forges social ties with a wider network of socially heterogeneous people, which, in turn, enhances job prospects by increasing the chances of learning about, or having personal contact with someone who is offering, a desirable job.

Education

In chapter 6 we discussed the influence of education on volunteering: more educated people volunteer at higher rates. Education is thus a resource for volunteering. But volunteers tend to do better in school, and people who do well in school tend to get better jobs. The recent emphasis on service learning in schools in the United States is partly motivated by the belief that getting students involved in community service work will improve their academic performance. In 1993, the National and Community Service Trust Act (P.L. 103-82) established the Learn and Serve America School and Community-Based Programs to support school and community-based efforts to involve school aged youth in community service. The Learn and Serve program is administered by the Corporation for National Service and funded through grants to states and national organizations, and through them to individual school districts, schools, and community organizations. In 1994–1995, the first year of the program, the corporation awarded approximately $30 million in grants supporting over 2,000 local efforts involving over 750,000 school aged youth. An example of the kind of program sponsored by Learn and Serve is that organized by a high school in Florida in which service learning was integrated into the alternative education program for at-risk students. Every other week students in the at-risk program, along with high achieving students, worked for half a day with staff from the parks and recreation department to revitalize a neighborhood park. Students worked in small groups on tasks that reinforced social, behavioral, and academic skills. An organized group discussion followed each service session. Teachers in the alternative education program then used the park experience over the year to illustrate lessons in the classroom. An evaluation of the program looked at the consequences of participation six months and one year after completion of the program, comparing the volunteers with a group of non-volunteers. At the first follow-up the high school volunteers had improved their math grades at a higher rate than the non-volunteers and the middle school students had improved their social studies grades more than the comparison group. There was no impact on English and social studies grades or on measures of course failure, absenteeism, homework hours, or educational aspirations. When the students were re-surveyed one year later the science grades of the high school volunteers were higher than the comparison group but other differences had disappeared. At the last follow-up "repeaters" (those who had continued in the service learning program for another year) were identified. No educational differences were found (Center for Human Resources 1999). Although the service learning students scored higher on a measure of "school engagement," this evaluation casts doubt on the idea that volunteerism (at least in the form of service learning) has any short-term positive influence on academic achievement.

Looking at longer term outcomes, Astin et al. (1998) analyzed data from a national sample of former college students from whom data were collected when they were in the freshman year (1985), four years later (1989), and again nine years after college entry (1994–1995). They found that students who volunteered in college were more likely to attend graduate school and to earn higher degrees. This was true even after controlling for volunteering in 1994–1995. Why volunteering has this positive effect is not known at present. It is unlikely that volunteering has much effect on young people's cognitive abilities. It is much more likely that volunteering builds self-confidence, maturity, and poise, which are useful for successful performance in the classroom and in academic assignments. Doing community service is also a form of "ability signaling" (Devlin 2001:64). It marks an adolescent as a "well-rounded" person, the type of student eagerly sought by selective colleges and universities (Aschaffenburg and Maas 1997:585). Economists refer to this as the "investment model" of volunteering (Duncan 1999).

Job Skills

The notion that volunteer work is a form of "ability signaling" assumes that people do indeed obtain job-related skills when they volunteer. In this respect, volunteering contributes to a person's stock of human capital. This term conventionally refers to formal education but it also includes job skills. These skills are usually acquired on the job, but volunteer work provides an alternative training ground. For example, when people sign up as an unpaid member of an emergency rescue squad they are required to undergo training in a number of skills that could qualify them for a job in the health services industry. Civic skills, such as the ability to plan and run a meeting, coordinate a fund drive, edit a newsletter, or give a presentation, acquired through many forms of volunteer work, are also marketable, especially for more desirable white-collar jobs (Verba et al. 1995). One-third of Canadians surveyed in 1997 believed their volunteer work provided them with managerial, communication, and interpersonal skills they could use directly in their paid jobs or businesses (Hall et al. 1998:30, 35, 39). A later Canadian study, in 2000, found that most volunteers believed their communication and interpersonal skills had improved as a result of their volunteer work. Younger volunteers were most likely to see these benefits: just under half (49%) of the employed volunteers aged 15 to 24 said their volunteer activities gave them new skills they could apply directly to their job. But even among those aged between 55 and 64, 29 percent said their volunteer activities had given them new skills to apply to their job ("The Benefits of Volunteering," www.givingandvolunteer ing.ca). We cannot tell how accurate these estimations are, but judging by the volunteers' own reports, volunteer work can improve one's chances in the labor market by increasing one's stock of human capital.

Social Networks

Volunteering builds social networks, which makes it easier to get a good job. Volunteering forges connections to people who might contribute advice, information, and further connections, all of which improve the chances of getting a good job, especially if those persons possess a lot of economic and cultural capital (Lin 1999). Previous research has shown that volunteers have more social contacts than non-volunteers (Wuthnow 1998:235).[1] Volunteers go to church more frequently, attend more association meetings, have more friends, and have more people with whom they would feel comfortable discussing "important matters" (Wilson and Musick 1998). A survey of teenage volunteers found that 28 percent thought their volunteering would help them "get my foot in the door at a place where I would like to work"; 29 percent expected to "make new contacts that might help my future career"; two-thirds had learned about new career options as a result of their volunteering; and just over half had developed new career goals (Wuthnow 1995:216, 266). Nearly a quarter of adult Americans say that one of their reasons for volunteering is to "make new contacts that might help my business or career" (Hodgkinson and Weitzman 1996:112).

Labor Market Rewards

To estimate the possible beneficial effects of doing volunteer work we will use two measures of labor market rewards, occupational status and income. In chapter 6 we observed that both occupational status and income have a positive effect on volunteering. Here we trace the influence running in the other direction: the effect of volunteering on occupational status and income. In order to do this, longitudinal data are preferable because they make it possible to discern the influence of volunteering on subsequent *changes* in occupation and income.

Occupation

Two studies of cohorts of women in the National Longitudinal Surveys have examined the influence of volunteering on occupational achievement. The first looked at the cohort of "mature women," who were first asked about their volunteer work in 1974 and again in 1976, 1979, and 1981. The researchers limited their study to the women who had been out of the labor force for most of the years prior to 1974 with the aim of seeing if volunteer work increased the chances returning to work. The more often the women had volunteered in the year prior to the survey, the more likely they were to have re-entered the labor force by 1981. The authors of the study surmised that these women had spent their time out of the labor force doing volunteering work, thus accumulating the human capital to smooth their transition back into employment. However, the more hours a woman volunteered during that period the *less* likely was she to re-enter the labor force. Clearly, some women were using volunteer work to prepare themselves for entering the labor force while others had adopted volunteer work as a vocation to which they were intensely committed: for this reason they were less likely to have taken a job. This implies that the relation between volunteer work and occupational achievement is not linear: intense involvement in volunteer work might well be a sign that the woman has detached herself from a "regular career" and substituted a career in volunteering. Volunteering also affected the status of the job the women took if they did enter the labor force. Compared to women who did volunteer work for one year or less, women who volunteered for more than one year were more likely to be professionals and less likely to be blue-collar or service workers. Their volunteer work seems to have qualified them for better jobs. Strikingly, volunteering *only* in 1974 had no influence on occupational prestige in 1981. Only women who had accumulated a lot of volunteer experience did better in the job market (Statham and Rhoton 1985).

In a similar analysis of the same NLS data we looked at the "young women" cohort (Wilson and Musick 2003).[2] On average women were not very mobile during this period: mean occupational status rose only slightly between 1973 and 1991. The women followed a conventional life course trajectory as they moved from early adulthood to middle age: by 1991 they had completed their education, spent most of their time since leaving school at work, had married and borne children, most of whom were still living with them. We estimated the effect of 1973, 1978, and 1988 volunteering on 1991 occupational status, net of level of occupational status in 1973. All three measures of volunteering—whether they were volunteering at all, the number of different activities, and the number of hours—were positively related to occupational status. Most significantly, the earliest measure of volunteering (1973) had a positive effect, *even with later measures of volunteering in the model.* In other words, the positive effects of volunteering were additive: the longer the women volunteered the better the job they had when they reached middle age. We then restricted our study to women who had jobs in both 1978 and 1991. Because women could have moved in and out of the labor force between 1978 and 1991 we controlled for the number of times a respondent reported working in the intervening period. Among this group of continuously employed women, volunteers were more upwardly mobile than the non-volunteers.

In short, although the evidence is based on very few studies confined largely to women, volunteer work does seem to have a positive effect on occupational status. More studies of this topic are needed before we can conclude these findings are robust. It would be particularly useful to know if these same patterns are found among men.

Income

A significant component of labor market rewards consists of wages and salaries. As we shall see, it is not altogether clear that volunteering increases earnings. Two Canadian studies found that volunteer and income were positively related (Day and Devlin 1997, 1998). Because the 1987 Canadian survey of volunteering gathered data only on family income, the first analysis was restricted to employed individuals who were the sole wage earners in their household. A binary variable was used to measure volunteering: whether the respondent had volunteered at all in the last year. On average, volunteers earned about 7 percent more than non-volunteers. Interestingly, when volunteer work was differentiated by domain (e.g., education and youth development, health, religion) volunteering in connection with a religious organization had a negative influence on earnings whereas volunteering for an "other category" (e.g., environmental and international) had a positive influence. Men experienced more income benefits from volunteering than women: male volunteers earned 21.5 percent higher incomes than male non-volunteers while female volunteers earned only 11.2 percent more than female non-volunteers. Once various socio-demographic variables (e.g., education, children, and marital status) were controlled, female volunteers earned less than female non-volunteers. One possible explanation for this is that religious organizations are the most important type of volunteer organization for women, and "participation in such groups yields strong negative returns to women on the labor market" (Day and Devlin 1997:711).[3] To partially replicate this analysis, Devlin (2003) used data from a later Canadian survey, the 1997 National Survey of Giving, Volunteering and Participation. Excluding those who earned no income at all, she replicated the positive income effect of volunteering and the gender difference: the earnings differential between male volunteers and non-volunteers was 14 percent, compared to a differential for women of only 2.5 percent. She also found that the income of more highly educated people benefited more from volunteering than the income of poorly educated people.

One major problem with these analyses is that they are based on cross sectional data. As we argued in chapter 6, it is just as likely that highly paid people are more likely to volunteer. Longitudinal data have the potential to disentangle cause and effect in this relation but unfortunately studies using panel data have yielded conflicting results. An investigation of the long-term effects of volunteering among 12,376 college students who were surveyed when they were freshmen in 1985, again as seniors, and once again nine years later, found that those who volunteered while in college earned higher wages, in part because they were more likely to stay in college and get an advanced degree (Astin et al. 1998). Statham and Rhoton's (1985) study of the NLS mature women cohort found that women who had volunteered in 1974 were earning *lower* incomes in 1981, apparently paying the cost of devoting some of their time to unpaid work. In an earlier analysis of the effect of volunteering in 1973 on wages and salaries in 1991 among the young women in the NLS, we found that volunteers were no better off than non-volunteers as far as income was concerned although we did, as noted above, find they had better occupations (Wilson and Musick 2003).[4] This study suggests a reason why volunteers do not make more money than non-volunteers. Perhaps volunteers are drawn to occupations that are respected and highly esteemed (and thus score relatively high on the occupational prestige scale) but do not pay so well. Another possible explanation lies in the role of social networks. As we noted above, innumerable studies have shown that social networks have a positive effect on occupational achievement but they rarely show that social networks have much effect on incomes, net of occupation. This might explain why volunteering helps people get better jobs without helping them earn more money. Social networks are certainly useful in helping us get a "foot in the door" but they have little influence over how much we earn once we have got the job.

In conclusion, although many people express ambivalence about the idea that volunteers can benefit from their sacrifices the evidence seems to suggest they do, whether or not they are motivated by this goal. Admittedly, the evidence to support this contention is limited because so few longitudinal studies have been carried out and the case for occupational status seems stronger than the case for income. This might be due to the fact that long-term volunteers select into occupations that score relatively high on the prestige scale but do not pay particularly well.

Apart from the need to replicate the studies described above, a number of issues remained unresolved. First, more research is needed on the mechanisms whereby volunteering leads to better jobs. As we noted earlier, one possible mechanism is social networks. But social networks come in different sizes and forms. It is important to distinguish between networks that largely function as support structures, helping individuals "get by" or cope with demands of everyday living, where the social ties are strong (overlapping and close, as in family, friends, and neighbors), as opposed to networks that are comprised of weak ties that offer social leverage helping individuals 'get ahead' or change their opportunity structure. Ties that offer leverage can promote upward mobility by providing access to further education, training, and employment. Such ties typically extend across class, race and even gender lines (Dominguez and Watkins 2003). Until measures of social networks are improved and used in research little progress in testing the social networks hypothesis is likely.

Second, not every kind of volunteer work brings economic benefits. No doubt volunteering for the local branch of the realtor's association could help one's career as a real estate agent but there are many instances where volunteer work could equally well put a brake on career advancement. Many advocacy volunteers allow their beliefs and values to dictate their choice of job, to protect their self-identity as an idealist or an activist. Klatch (2000:508) found that former members of Students for a Democratic Society had gravitated toward jobs in non-profit organizations, social service agencies, and educational institutions because those environments enabled them to preserve their identities as activists even though the actual level of volunteer work had declined. These kinds of jobs do not pay very well and the jobholder might well be over-qualified. Another example is "Plowshares," a high-risk peace organization where imprisonment for protest actions was a realistic threat. Volunteers for this organization were disproportionately well educated (44% of them had graduate degrees) but they had given up professional careers for which they were qualified in order to devote more time to the movement. Others had chosen self-employment or contract work to ensure they were available for volunteer work when needed (Nepstad 2004:56).

Third, it is unclear how many people actually use the "investment model" when choosing whether to volunteer or what to volunteer for. This model assumes that people rationally decide that the "payoff" from volunteer work is worth the investment of (unpaid) time. In chapter 4 we discussed the various motivations for volunteering. "Career" motivations are included in the Volunteer Functions Inventory. But this kind of motivation is given priority by only a small minority of volunteers, the exact proportion varying from under 10 percent in the Independent Sector surveys to nearly a quarter in the 2000 Canadian survey data. Prouteau and Wolff (2003:19) found no evidence that unemployed people who were actively seeking work were any more likely to volunteer than the unemployed who are not seeking work. Nor were employed people who were actively seeking another job any more likely to be volunteering. On the other hand, the fact that the importance of this motivation varies by age gives support to the investment model. As we noted in chapter 4, Canadian students enrolled full-time in college were much more likely to say they volunteered to improve their job opportunities than volunteers already in the labor force. In the same survey, Canadian volunteers who were unemployed were much more likely to say they were volunteering to improve their job prospects than Canadian volunteers who had jobs. In other words, the investment model is by no means generally valid, but for certain segments of the population it might well apply.

Volunteering and Health

In this section we examine the influence of volunteering on mental and physical health. Many volunteers speak about the positive feelings they experience as a result of their volunteer work, but these accounts are not a reliable basis for concluding that volunteering is beneficial: those who have not benefited might have become disillusioned with volunteer work and dropped out. We will pay most attention to surveys that make it possible to compare the mental and physical health of volunteers and non-volunteers.

Volunteering and Mental Health

The term "mental health" refers to a wide range of measures of psychological well-being, including indexes overall life satisfaction, indicators of positive self-concept, such as self-esteem, and to symptoms of mental disorders or illnesses, such as depression. Mental illness is not the absence of mental health and mental health is not the absence of mental illness. Mental health includes a number of dimensions, such as self-esteem, realization of one's potential, the ability to maintain fulfilling and meaningful relationships, self-acceptance, autonomy and a sense of competence, and ability to manage the world. Mental illness, defined psychiatrically, includes disorders such as anxiety, mood (e.g., depression), eating disorders, and obsessive-compulsive behaviors. Sociologists also include behaviors that deviate from expectations in ways that are difficult to explain or interpret. Whereas the psychological approach treats mental illness as a disorder of the mind, the sociological perspective views it as a failure to adapt to or manage stressful life-events. Variations in mental health in the population can be attributed to the fact that some people experience more stressful events than others *and* that some people are more vulnerable to their negative effects than others. People can protect themselves (or are protected) from stress by marshalling coping resources. Chief among these coping resources are social networks—ties to other individuals from whom support, or simply contact, in times of stress is forthcoming. Social activities can also help cope with stress by affirming a sense of purpose and mastery over life events. For example, we have already learned in chapter 4 that dealing with one's own problems is one motivation for volunteering. Gay men might cope with the stress imposed by the threat of AIDS by volunteering to be a "buddy" for a man who already has the disease.

Much of the sociological research on the etiology of mental illness has focused on the role of social integration in reducing people's vulnerability to stress. Social integration helps mainly because it increases perceived social *support*. The more ties people have to others the more support they expect to receive. Although volunteer work means *giving* social support rather than taking it, plausible arguments can be made that doing volunteer work improves mental health. These arguments can be grouped into two main categories: volunteer work re-shapes our social relationships; and volunteer work changes the way we think about ourselves.

Social Integration

The first reason to think that volunteer work is good for our mental health is that it links us to a wider social world, drawing us into more intense person-to-person interactions with a wider range of people (including other volunteers). Many volunteer jobs require us to work with others. They occur in organizational settings and engage us in social interactions that are usually positive and emotionally warm. Displays of solidarity, as when other volunteers show up on a regular basis, can be rewarding, especially if the volunteer work is costly or risky, as in doing civil rights work or helping with search and rescue. In short, volunteering is beneficial not so much because it is a form of helping but because it changes the way we are connected to other people.

Social integration can take many forms, ranging from interpersonal social networks to active memberships in numerous organizations. Research has shown that, whereas social isolation causes psychological distress, social integration has many positive psychological consequences (Greenfield and Marks 2004:S259; Thoits 1986). The question is whether there is anything beneficial about volunteering as a social activity as opposed to simply knowing a lot of people or joining many organizations. To answer this question, it is necessary to determine if there are indeed psychological benefits to *providing a service* to others in an organizational setting. It is quite conceivable that social ties can provide benefits regardless of whether they involve helping: any form of social integration "augments an individual's power, prestige, resources, and emotional gratification, including social recognition and a heightened sense of identity" (Moen et al. 1995:260).

Self-Concept

The second group of arguments as to why volunteering improves mental health focuses on how helping others changes the way we think about ourselves. Generally speaking, people say that helping others makes them feel good (Wuthnow 1991:87). Volunteers are typically rewarded with gratitude and, not infrequently, social recognition and approbation. Helping others therefore places us in a pleasingly superior position morally; we have the advantage over our clients and over others who declined to help (Clark 1987:298). Even if we are not rewarded by the gratitude of our clients, or even meet clients in the course of our work, volunteer work is typically morally informed and guided. People say they volunteer because they want to "make the world a better place" or "do the right thing" and any time we do the right thing we feel better about ourselves. Doing our duty, living up to our responsibilities, meeting our obligations, are intrinsically rewarding behaviors.[5] Furthermore helping others, or working on behalf of a cause, provides a sense of mission, giving purpose and significance to our lives. Doing volunteer work is also one way to be productive: it allows us to use personal skills and strengths in which we take pride, or allow us to develop these aptitudes and thus an enhanced sense of self. Being an active and productive member of society (where being productive and active is highly valued) is intrinsically rewarding and has positive psychological benefits, such as higher self-esteem, higher self-confidence, and sense of control over one's environment (Midlarsky 1991).[6] By looking at the results of their work, volunteers learn they can influence the lives of others, and such feelings of self-efficacy are positively associated with better mental health (Piliavin 2002:5). An interview with a search and rescue volunteer serves as an illustration of this point: "It was neat to be part of that [rescue operation] where I honestly felt like my decision made a difference" (Lois 2003:159). Volunteer work can also build social competence and assuage anxiety about social relationships, bringing us into contact with a wide range of people and giving us the chance (or obliging us) to develop and refine social skills. Eight in ten of Canadian volunteers said their volunteer work helped them with their interpersonal skills, such as understanding people better, motivating others, and dealing with difficult situations. Just over two-thirds (68%) said that volunteering helped them develop better communication skills. The more hours they volunteered the more likely were they to report skill improvement ("The Benefits of Volunteering," www.givingandvolunteering.ca). Finally, although in chapter 20 we learned that volunteering does not seem to foster a sense of trust in other people in general, it can develop a sense of trust in specific groups of people—the people belonging to the same church, the same neighborhood or the same voluntary association. Distrusting people tend to be anxious and insecure.

These are quite plausible arguments for expecting volunteer work to be good for us, but is there any evidence to support these arguments? Most volunteers speak highly of the psychological benefits of their work. For example, Omoto et al. (1993) found that after twelve months of working with people with AIDS, volunteers felt less lonely and more self-confident as a result of their experience. The problem with this kind of study is that the volunteers who did not think they were getting any benefits, or who were stressed by the work, are likely to have quit. And those who have volunteered a lot of their time might be tempted to justify the cost by exaggerating the benefits enjoyed. A more scientific way of judging the mental health benefits of volunteer work is to use a nationally representative sample that includes both volunteers and non-volunteers so that the "before and after" effects of volunteer work can be compared to a "control" group of people who have not volunteered. In addition, the study should use longitudinal data to help determine the causal order because people with better mental health might be more disposed to volunteer.

The Americans' Changing Lives (ACL) longitudinal data set has been used on two occasions to estimate the influence of volunteering on mental health. Using the 1986 and 1989 data, Thoits and Hewitt (2001) looked at the influence of volunteering in 1986 on change in mental health between

1986 and 1989. Life satisfaction, happiness, self-esteem, and sense of mastery were all positively related to volunteer hours. Volunteering even helped alleviate symptoms of depression. Volunteer hours in 1986 had a minimal *direct* effect on well-being in 1989. Rather, people who volunteered in 1986 had better mental health in 1989 because they were more likely to be volunteering in 1989. In other words, volunteering had no long-term (three-year) health benefits: if the individual stopped volunteering between 1986 and 1989, the mental health benefits disappeared. This suggests that health benefits derive more from the way volunteer work changes social interactions than from the way it changes the way we think about ourselves because if the latter were true, 1986 volunteering would have a more enduring effect.

The possible influence of social interactions is one of the issues we explored in our own analysis of the ACL data. We used measures of how often respondents attended meetings of groups or clubs and how often respondents talked on the telephone and got together with friends and relatives, testing the hypothesis that volunteers enjoyed better mental health because they were more socially integrated. We found that volunteers did indeed have fewer depressive symptoms and that people who attended meetings frequently had fewer depressive symptoms (informal social interaction had no effect), but meeting attendance was not the mechanism linking volunteering and depression (Musick and Wilson 2003). This does not rule out the possibility that the volunteer work itself increases the rate of social interaction with others and thus mental health, but it does rule out the possibility that mental health is improved by volunteering because it draws people into more social groups.

Finally, panel data gathered during the reunification of Germany suggests these patterns are not unique to the United States. Unification was a trying time for all East Germans especially, and their level of life satisfaction declined rapidly during this period. Furthermore, the collapse of the communist regime caused a steep decline in volunteering because many of the nationally owned firms that had sponsored volunteer organizations were privatized. The rate of volunteering at least once a month fell from 18 percent in 1990 to 8 percent in 1992. Those who chose to continue volunteering during this period did not experience the same decline in life-satisfaction as the rest of the population, suggesting that volunteer work was to some extent buffering them from the stresses of the transition to a new form of society (Meier and Stutzer 2004).

Volunteering and Well-Being among the Elderly

Much of the research on volunteering and mental health has focused on elderly populations because "successful aging"—an idea that includes good mental health—is believed to depend on getting engaged in exactly the type of productive activity volunteering represents so well. The mental health benefits of volunteering for elderly people have been demonstrated in a large number of studies. Wheeler et al. (1998:74) concluded from a meta-analysis of sixteen studies of volunteering among older people (where appropriate controls had been used) that volunteers enjoy "a greater quality of life" according to various life satisfaction measures. A study of Americans aged between 50 and 75 found that 60 percent of the volunteers but only 50 percent of the non-volunteers felt optimistic about their future; 63 percent of the volunteers but only 50 percent of the non-volunteers felt productive "often"; 59 percent of the volunteers but only 44 percent of the non-volunteers felt they were part of a team (Peter D. Hart 2002:5). Midlarsky and Kahana (1994:211) found that elderly volunteers scored higher than non-volunteers on an index of well-being consisting of morale, happiness, subjective social integration, and self-esteem. Harlow and Cantor (1996) studied participants in a longitudinal survey following a cohort of Californians from childhood into old age. In 1972 and 1977, respondents were asked to rate their satisfaction with life in nine different domains. An overall life satisfaction index was constructed by calculating the mean score across these domains. Controlling for level of life satisfaction in 1972, community service activity in 1972 had a positive effect on life satisfaction in 1977 (when the median age of the respondents was 65). Although there is always some likelihood that satisfied people are more likely to volunteer in the first place, the control for 1972 level of satisfaction in this study suggests that volunteer work causes satisfaction. Perry (2001) describes an evaluation study of the Senior Companions Program conducted between 1979 and 1985 in which seniors engaged in the program were compared with those on the waiting list. Volunteers showed significant improvements in mental health, while the health of those on the waiting list declined. Even more tellingly, seniors who remained active in volunteer work throughout the five-year period maintained the same level of health while those who dropped out experienced a decline. In Szinovacz's (1992) study of "adaptation" to retirement, those who were volunteering (especially women) adapted more successfully to retirement: they were less likely to miss having work responsibilities and work colleagues or feel bored, lonely, or useless.

In another study, data from MIDUS were used to examine the influence of volunteering on the mental health of adults between the ages of 59 and 74. They were asked how many hours a month they spent on average doing volunteer work for four types of voluntary organization. (36% of respondents were coded as volunteers by this measure.)[7] In general, volunteers had more positive affect but no less negative affect than non-volunteers. In other words, volunteering made the elderly respondents more cheerful but did not protect them from feeling sad. Elderly people who had suffered role loss (e.g., losing a spouse) were more likely to have lost their sense of purpose in life, but not so much if they were volunteers (Greenfield and Marks 2004). Another major survey—of Americans 55 and older—found that retirees who were volunteering were more likely to say they were "very satisfied" or "somewhat satisfied" with their retirement than those who were not volunteering (Butrica and Schaner 2005).

An analysis of the ACL data set looked at the influence of volunteering on depression in respondents aged 60 years or older at baseline (1986) and in two subsequent panels (1989 and 1994). Li and Ferraro (2005) found that volunteering in 1986 reduced depression in 1989, which in turn reduced depression in 1994. There was no effect of 1989 volunteering on 1994 volunteering: that is, volunteering in 1989 did not add to the already beneficial effect derived from the 1986 volunteering. Interestingly, depression in 1989 had a *positive* effect on volunteering in 1994, suggesting a compensatory mechanism—people taking up volunteering in order to deal with depression.[8]

Although they are limited to cross-sectional comparisons, studies of European populations confirm the positive association between volunteering and mental health in elderly populations. In almost all ten countries in the Survey of Health, Ageing and Retirement in Europe (aged 50 or more years) "the share of respondents who showed symptoms of depression in the last month was four to five percentage points lower than those who were not bothered by such problems" (Borsch-Supan et al. 2005:249). The English Longitudinal Study of Aging uses a slightly unusual measure of well-being. It asks participants (all aged 65 or older) to respond to a number of items measuring sense of control (e.g., "I feel free to plan for the future"), autonomy (e.g., "I feel that I can please myself with what I can do."), pleasure (e.g., "I feel full of energy these days"), and self-realization (e.g., "I feel that life is full of opportunities"). Respondents were also asked if they were doing volunteer work. Volunteers scored higher on the measure of well-being than nonvolunteers. Although the health of the respondent and relationships with children and family were the strongest influence on well-being, volunteer work had just as much influence as education, retirement status, and whether or not the respondent was living at home. Among those aged 75 or more, volunteer work was even more important than types of interaction such as frequency of contacts with children, family or friends (Netuveli et al. 2006).

A few studies have found no psychic benefits from volunteering among the elderly. Krause et al. (1992:P300) found that volunteering was associated with lower rates of "somatic symptoms," such as loss of appetite, trouble sleeping, and feelings of listlessness among a sample of Americans age 60 or more, but there was no effect on sense of personal control or depressed affect. Chambre (1987:92) found that elderly volunteers were no more satisfied with life than elderly people who did not volunteer. Much the same findings were reported in an intervention study where a group of retirees, some of whom were currently volunteering, some of whom had volunteered in the past but not in the past six months, and some of whom had never volunteered, were invited to participate in a program designed to get more seniors to volunteer. Being placed in the program had no influence on the seniors' sense of well-being over a six-month period.

> Those currently volunteering at the start of the study who had a lengthy history of volunteering had significantly higher well-being and extraversion scores through the three stages than other groups. However, the fact that the volunteer group status became insignificant at all stages when health and personality traits were entered in regressions on well-being suggests that these individual characteristics are responsible for both becoming long-term volunteers and greater well-being. (Pushkar et al. 2002:157)

While this rather limited study suggests caution in thinking that doing volunteer work can act like a "pick-me-up" for seniors, at least in the short run, the overall trend in these studies is that volunteering can help older people feel better about themselves.

How Much Volunteering Does It Take?

In epidemiological terms, it would be interesting to know the "dose-response" relation between volunteering and mental health. What level of volunteering is necessary to bring about the desired result? When participants in the Retired and Senior Volunteer Program, Foster Grandparent Program, and the Senior Companion Program were asked if they had changed in any way since they began participating in the program, almost all had positive things to say. They mentioned a sense of accomplishment, having a purpose in life, making a positive difference in the life of another, looking forward to each new day, pleasure gained from daily activities, sense of self-esteem, sense of well-being, the feeling that someone was looking out for them, and ability to make ends meet. The more hours they contributed, the more enthusiastic they were about the benefits, suggesting a linear positive relation between the amount of volunteering and mental health (Gartland 2001). If some volunteer work is good, more will be even better.

The results of research on this topic, however, suggest that the picture is not quite so simple. For example, our motivation for volunteering might shift from extrinsic to intrinsic as we contribute more hours (Fischer and Schaffer 1993). Intrinsically motivated volunteering is believed to be more beneficial to our health. This would mean that we must work a certain number of hours before the health benefits "kick in." The occasional or sporadic volunteer would reap no benefits. At the other end of the scale, people who contribute many volunteer hours begin to suffer from role overload, which is stressful and likely to have negative health consequences. To help answer this question, Morrow-Howell et al. (2003) examined the effect of volunteering on depressive symptoms using three waves of data from the ACL, focusing on respondents who were 60 years of age or older in the first wave. The more hours respondents volunteered in the first wave, the fewer depressive symptoms they reported in the last wave, *but if the hours volunteered exceeded one hundred hours a year the positive effect tapered off.*

While the results of this study suggest that more is better—up to a point —volunteer work is often treated as if it existed in a vacuum. But the same number of volunteer hours can have very different consequences, depending on other role demands. An aspect of Emile Durkheim's theory of suicide that is often overlooked is his contention that, while some integration protects us from having suicidal thoughts, too much social integration can be a cause of stress. Taking on too many roles becomes stressful as people struggle to meet the expectations of all the other actors to whom they are connected by these roles. For some people, an extra hour of volunteer work has to be squeezed into many other demands on their time, while for others it might be the only work obligation they have. Volunteers who are squeezed for time might not enjoy so many of the health benefits because their stress level has risen. In short, the protective effect of volunteer work is contingent on other demands on people's time. This topic has rarely been studied. A 1986 survey of American women examined the effect of caring for relatives on well-being. Contrary to expectations neither currently caring nor having cared for a relative in the past had any effect on any of the measures of well-being used (mastery, self-esteem, depression, general life satisfaction, and role conflict). However, women who were volunteering as well as providing care to relatives reported more symptoms of depression. Volunteering and caring thus combined to make women depressed. This might have something to do with the kind of volunteering work women who are providing care to relatives choose to do. They might be more inclined to choose volunteer work that resembles the caregiving work they are already doing (such as helping out at an adult day care center). They might be better off if they chose to do volunteer work that provided alternative activities and relationships (Moen et al. 1995). A study of retired Americans aged 50 years or more presents a different picture. Volunteers were more satisfied with their retirement than those who were entirely inactive, but those who were volunteering *and* providing informal help were even more satisfied with their retirement. And, although retirees whose activity was confined to caring for relatives were less likely to be satisfied than retirees who were entirely inactive, those who combined caregiving with volunteering were more satisfied than the inactive—volunteering effectively countered the negative influence of caregiving (Butrica and Schaner 2005). Although this study does not measure activities in number of hours it contradicts the notion that too many roles create dissatisfaction with life.

Besides the number of hours volunteered, another measure of "dosage" is how long people have been volunteering. If mental health is improved by volunteer work, people who have made a "career" out of it should be healthier. Two recent studies suggest that long-term experience is indeed beneficial. Moen (1997:146) looked at the influence of volunteering on the health of women who were first interviewed in 1956 and again in 1986. On the second occasion, the women were asked about their volunteer work since the first interview. The women who were currently volunteering were in better mental health than the women not volunteering, but women who had volunteered off and on since they were last interviewed, thirty years before, were the healthiest. Women who had volunteered for most of their life were more socially integrated—measured by number of friends, frequency of church attendance, and club memberships—which in turn enhanced their sense of well-being. In a similar study, but over a shorter time-span, we examined the association between volunteering and depression across three panels of the ACL survey, in 1986, 1989, and 1992 (Musick and Wilson 2003). Both men and women who volunteered in all three waves were enjoying better mental health in 1992. People who did not volunteer at all were the most depressed. This was not due to the fact that long-term volunteers had, by definition, volunteered more recently. If this were the case, respondents who volunteered in only one wave but did so in 1992 would have the same levels of depression as those who volunteered in all waves, but this was not what we found. Indeed, those who volunteered in 1992 and in at least one other wave were more depressed than the three-wave volunteers. In short, both studies suggest that, the longer people volunteer, the better their mental health.

The Stress-Buffering Model

The studies we have described above assume that volunteering has a beneficial effect on mental health, regardless of whether the individual is under stress. The stress-buffering model assumes that volunteering is related to well-being only, or mainly, for persons under stress and has little or no effect on people who are stress free. In this "stress-buffering" model, volunteering prevents or at least modulates the responses to stressful events that would otherwise damage health. The issue is not whether volunteering improves health but whether volunteering prevents health from getting worse, given the stress being experienced. The model predicts that people experiencing stress will show more positive effects of volunteering than people not under stress.

A number of studies have tested this hypothesis, with varying results. When volunteers in the Retired and Senior Volunteer Program, Foster Grandparent Program, and the Senior Companion Program were asked if they had changed in any way since they began participating in the program, almost all had positive things to say. They mentioned a sense of accomplishment, having a purpose in life, making a positive difference in the life of another, looking forward to each new day, pleasure gained from daily activities, sense of self-esteem, sense of well-being, the feeling that someone was looking out for them, and ability to make ends meet. However, the low-income volunteers mentioned more benefits than the high-income volunteers (Gartland 2001). This might have something to do with the fact that participants in the programs receive a small stipend, which would be more significant for poorer people, but it might also have something to do with the fact that low-income people were subject to more stress than higher income people, and derived more benefits from their volunteer work.

More reliable conclusions can be drawn from survey data based on larger random samples of the population. Rogers (1996) used data from a 1985 community study to see if scores on a Depression Scale were related to frequency of attendance at voluntary association meetings. Although this is not exactly a measure of volunteering, meeting attendance is quite highly correlated with volunteering, as we have seen. The study included a measure of the stresses to which subjects in the study might have been exposed: a thirty-one-item checklist covering a range of incidents affecting relationships, health, finances, work, and other types of events measured exposure to stress. The respondents in the data set ranged in age from 22 to 89, with a mean age of 59. Participation in voluntary associations was associated with a small but significant reduction in psychological distress. Participation especially benefited those experiencing more stress. In other words, the benefits of group membership increased as stress levels increased. Even though respondents with higher self-esteem coped with their stresses better, participation provided additional buffering effects. These results suggest that the buffering effects of group membership are not due to higher levels of psychological resources. The author suggests some other possibilities. Perhaps social integration itself is having beneficial effects, for example, in providing social support. Perhaps social participation changes the meaning and significance of stressors (e.g., worries about one's job), ameliorating their effect.

Moderating Effects

In earlier chapters we described the way in which people from different social backgrounds volunteer for different reasons. For example, women are more likely than men to cite the rewards of social interaction and support, as are older people. If volunteering acts as a resource, protecting people from the negative effects of stress, and if volunteering does this because it provides social support then it would follow that volunteer work is "worth" more to some groups than others as far as mental health benefits are concerned. In short, we would expect socio-demographic attributes to moderate the positive effect of volunteering. In this section we consider some of the possibilities.

AGE

As we age, the role context within which volunteer work takes places also changes. Many gerontologists believe that the protective effects of volunteering are especially valuable to older people because of the role loss they are likely to be experiencing. To the extent that volunteer work is a way of being "useful" or "productive" it will enhance mental health by offering substitute roles to make up for the loss. There are a number of ways in which volunteer work could be implicated in this process. First, younger people's self-esteem is based more on their paid work, whereas most elderly people are retired and volunteering can give them better protection against the feelings of powerlessness and insignificance caused by this loss of role (Fischer et al. 1991:262; Midlarsky 1991:24; Okun 1994). Second, the elderly experience social withdrawal as the result of retirement and other life changes, such as declining health or financial resources (Moen et al. 1995:242; Pillemer and Glasgow 2000:34). As their social networks shrink, their mental health declines. Volunteer work is a way of keeping connected to others and replacing lost social relationships. Third, growing old makes many people anxious because it robs them of their independence and self-sufficiency. By volunteering, they enter into chains of reciprocity that hold the promise of receiving assistance from others when the need arises (Krause et al. 1992:P300). Fourth, when older people volunteer they are doing it entirely by choice and not as the result of some social obligation, such as those imposed on parents or employees (Chambre 1987:82). This element of choice is important because activity theory argues that only if the activity is an expression of individual choice do psychological benefits accrue (Midlarsky and Kahana 1994:54).[9] Finally, younger people adopt a more instrumental attitude toward volunteer work, being more inclined to treat it as a way to improve other social roles. Older people are less likely than younger people to be motivated to volunteer by material rewards for themselves or their families or by some prospect of gaining work experience or job skills (Fischer and Schaffer 1993:49). Since intrinsic rewards are ultimately more satisfying than extrinsic rewards, the volunteer work of older people is more gratifying.

A number of studies have compared the influence of volunteering on the mental health of older and younger people. One study followed up hospice volunteers after six months of service to see if their work had changed the way they thought about themselves. The self-esteem of the older volunteers had improved, but the self-esteem of the younger and middle aged volunteers declined. It is likely that the younger and middle aged volunteers found the hospice environment more difficult to cope with than the older volunteers (Omoto et al. 2000:189). Van Willigen (2000) used panel data from the ACL to examine the influence of volunteering in 1986 on life satisfaction in 1989 (controlling for level of life satisfaction in 1986). She divided the sample into two groups, one aged between 25 and 59, the other consisting of adults 60 years of age and older. She used two measures of volunteer work: the "range" of volunteer work, or how many different volunteer activities the respondent was involved in; and the number of hours volunteered. The more hours the older people volunteered the more satisfied they were with life in general. Among younger people, however, the positive effects of volunteer work began to decline above one hundred hours a year. The effect of range of volunteering was different. For older people, the more activities they were involved in the more satisfied they were with their lives. For younger people, the more activities they were involved in the *less* satisfied they were with their lives. These results support the argument that volunteering is of special benefit to older people, who are less likely to have other social roles to keep them feeling productive and useful. Younger adults who volunteer a lot reach a point where they experience role overload. The consequent stress creates dissatisfaction with life in general. Another study, drawing on the same data set, found that volunteering reduced depressive symptoms, but *only* among those aged 65 or older (Musick and Wilson 2003). Young people's mood was much more closely tied to their jobs. Older people substituted volunteer work for paid employment as a source of good feelings about themselves. This conclusion is supported by the results of another study, of a random sample of residents of New York State aged between 50 and 72 (1994), which found that volunteering improved the mental health only of the retirees in the study, particularly the men. Among the "retired" people who had subsequently returned to the paid labor force, volunteering did not provide any health benefits. Indeed, retirees who had returned to the labor force were *more* likely to report depressive symptoms if they volunteered. They were overloaded by taking on volunteer work as well as paid work in their retirement (Moen and Fields 2002:40).

RACE

The world of voluntary associations, including the church, provides an alternative source of self-esteem to minority groups excluded from mainstream economic, political, and social rewards. This raises the question of whether African Americans get more mental health benefits from their volunteer work than White Americans. One study of Americans 60 years old and over used two measures of subjective health from the ACL data set. A "positive affect scale" consisted of three items asking respondents how often during the past week they enjoyed life, were happy, and felt there were people who really understood them. A "negative affect scale" asked how often the respondent had felt depressed, sad, or lonely, whether everything they did was an effort, and whether they could not get going. Respondents could choose between "hardly ever," "some of the time," and "most of the time." Respondents were also asked about their volunteer work for (a) religious organizations and (b) all other kinds of organization. Religious volunteering enhanced positive affect, but only for the Whites in the sample. Secular volunteering enhanced positive affect, but only for White males. Religious volunteering reduced negative affect, only for Black females. Secular volunteering reduced negative affect, but only for Black males. These results, while difficult to summarize, are very interesting because they dispute the notion that the church is an especially valuable community institution for African Americans. Blacks who volunteer for their church do not feel any better for doing so while Whites who volunteer for their church do feel an improvement. *Indeed, neither religious nor secular volunteering improves the mood of African Americans.* The effects of volunteering on Blacks are confined to protecting them from feeling bad about themselves. On the other hand, while Whites felt better about themselves as a result of their volunteering, it did little to prevent them from having negative feelings (McIntosh and Danigelis 1995).

EMPLOYMENT STATUS

Self-concept is influenced by all of the salient roles we play, including work roles and family roles, as well as the volunteer role. Work and family roles are primary roles, the most important to us, while volunteering is a secondary role. Earlier, discussing the moderating effect of age, we noted that volunteering has a stronger effect on well-being among the elderly than among the middle aged or the young. The reason is that the volunteer role becomes more salient after we retire. This, in turn, suggests that employment status moderates the effect of volunteering on mental health. Volunteer work functions as a substitute for paid employment as a source of self-esteem. Nakano (2000:99) shows how, in Japan, volunteer work is an important source of status for women whose opportunities in the paid labor market are limited to low-level white-collar work or blue-collar low-paying and low status jobs. Roy and Danileviciute (1999) examined the relation between two measures of mental health (overall life satisfaction and degree of control over everyday life) and volunteering among Canadians aged between 50 and 64. Volunteers were more satisfied with, and felt more in control of, their lives than non-volunteers. The more hours they volunteered, the more satisfied with life they were, but this was true only for those who were employed. This is contrary to the substitution hypothesis. People with jobs were getting more out of their volunteer work than people not in the labor force. This could result from employed volunteers having more rewarding volunteer assignments or it could be that unemployed people feel they have, in some way, been forced to volunteer by their circumstances and this lack of choice makes the work less rewarding for them. The question of whether or not volunteer work can substitute for paid work as a source of self-esteem or self-confidence in the pre-retirement population deserves further study.

DOMAINS

We have had many occasions to note the wide variety of activities included under the heading of volunteer work. Very little is known about whether different volunteer activities yield different health benefits. One possibility is that volunteer work framed by a larger sense of purpose and meaning is more fulfilling. On the other hand, volunteer work that is an adjunct to other social roles might provide less psychic nourishment. A mother who volunteers for the PTA because her child is in school, the lawyer who does pro bono work because his firm expects it, the farmer who serves as membership secretary of the growers' association, are doing chores that closely resemble work obligations. These are quite *instrumental* forms of volunteering. At the other end of the spectrum, volunteer work guided by ultimate values, by a sense of duty endorsed and recognized by the local community, or by some aesthetic interest (e.g., museum docent), might be altogether more beneficial. It is a more *expressive* mode of volunteering.[10] The important point to remember is that intrinsically rewarding activities yield more positive mental health consequences. Another possible reason why type of volunteering might make a difference is the social setting in which the work takes place. If the connection between volunteering and well-being is partly explainable in terms of social interactions, activities that involve the volunteer in more social interactions should have a more positive effect. Also, settings where the volunteer role is well institutionalized and where the volunteer's contribution is recognized and supported should yield more health benefits.

To find out if type of volunteering moderates the effect of volunteer work on depression, in an earlier study we divided respondents in the ACL data set into four groups: those who volunteered for both the secular and religious activities (e.g., a church group and a school); those who volunteered exclusively for religious activities; those who volunteered for no religious activities; and those who did not volunteer at all. As reported earlier, only the older volunteers derived any benefit from their volunteer work. However, the type of volunteer work did have something to do with how much they benefited. Church-related volunteering had a more beneficial effect than secular or mixed volunteering or no volunteering at all. Why should church-related volunteering be more beneficial? Compared to most other voluntary associations, religious congregations emphasize the value of caring more forcefully and therefore promote the intrinsic rewards of volunteering; they institutionalize the role of the caregiving more clearly; and they offer group support and encouragement for performing the role. It is probably no accident that people who volunteer in connection with their church are more likely to do so year after year than people who volunteer in connection with a secular organization (Wilson and Musick 1998:268).

Tasks and Benefits

With the exception of the occasional attempt to link health benefits to the particular types of volunteer work, the studies cited in this chapter largely ignore the wide range of jobs volunteers actually do. In chapter 18 we described how some volunteers spend their time teaching or coaching, some serve on committees or governing boards, some do clerical work, and so on. Some of these activities could well be more rewarding than others and consequently have different health benefits. A 1994 survey of eleven European countries asked respondents whether they had performed a number of specified tasks and also asked respondents what benefits they felt they had received from doing volunteer work. Just over half (51%) said one benefit of volunteering is that "I really enjoy it." The proportion was highest among those teaching (66%) and lowest among those providing transportation (41%). Thirty-four percent said they got satisfaction from seeing results; the proportion was highest among those engaged in advocacy (48%) and lowest among those providing therapy (19%). Just under a quarter (24%) said their volunteering had broadened their experience of life: the rate was highest among those providing counseling (46%) and information or advice (44%) and lowest among those providing therapy (17%) or transportation (18%). Just over a third (36%) said they enjoyed meeting people and making new friends: this benefit was most often mentioned by counselors (52%), committee members (51%), and advocates (49%) and least often mentioned by therapists (15%) and drivers (33%). Eighteen percent said volunteering had provided a chance to learn new skills: the rate was highest among those providing information and advice (38%) and lowest among those providing therapy (12%) or transportation (16%). Sixteen percent appreciated their volunteer work because it gave them a change to do things they were good at: this was especially true of those providing information and advice (33%) and counseling (29%) and least likely to be true among those providing therapy (10%) or transportation (18%). Eighteen percent of the volunteers as a whole but 60 percent of those providing therapy and only 13 percent of fund-raisers mentioned social recognition in the community. Twenty-nine percent thought their volunteer work help them stay active and healthy: this was especially true of those providing therapy (64%), transportation (50%) and not so common among fund-raisers (21%) and office workers (27%). Volunteering was an opportunity to uphold religious or moral principles for 18 percent of all volunteers, but 37 percent of the advocates and 32 percent of the counselors. Only 15 percent of the drivers and 18 percent of the committee members saw this benefit (Gaskin and Smith 1997:50). Clearly, volunteer tasks vary in the kinds of rewards they provide. If these rewards are, in turn, linked to health benefits, then some tasks will be more conducive to good health than others. For example, if meeting people and making new friends have positive health consequences, then volunteering to provide transportation is probably not going to provide this benefit. Tracing this link between the actual work that volunteers do and mental benefits they might enjoy is one of the more important tasks awaiting researchers in this area.

Community-Level Volunteering and Mental Health

To this point, we have discussed volunteering from an egocentric perspective. We have treated volunteer work as an individual attribute, an activity that connects us to a wider social world. Guided by Durkheim's theory of social integration, we have argued that volunteering, as a form of social integration, has a salutary effect on mental health, but the original theory focused on communities rather than individuals: the concept of social integration described a property of a collectivity. Social integration measured at the individual level might well miss the influence of social integration measured at the collective level. Specifically, this means that volunteering can influence an individual's well-being in two ways. At the first level, we predict that volunteers enjoy better health than non-volunteers. At the second level, we predict that people who live in communities where the volunteer rate is high enjoy better health, on the average, than people who live in communities where the volunteer rate is low. Even people who do not volunteer benefit if they live in a community where many others volunteer. Indeed, they might benefit more than volunteers living in communities where few others are volunteering.[11]

Volunteering and Physical Health

Sociologists have long argued that social ties have a beneficial effect not only on mental but also physical health (House et al. 1988; Lin et al. 1999:345; Okun et al 1984; Rietschlin 1998; Umberson et al. 1996; Weatherington et al. 2000:56). Because volunteer work increases the number, variety, and quality of our social ties it promises to protect us against illness and even prolong life. Social ties have a positive effect on our physical health not because they prevent illnesses but because they help us deal with them better and recover more quickly.[12]

Social Participation and Physical Health

We will first review a number of studies that include a question on volunteer work in their measure of social participation or a measure of something resembling volunteer work, without specifically identifying the unique effect of volunteering itself. Many of these studies have focused on the elderly, for obvious reasons.

Young and Glasgow (1998) include volunteer work in an index of "instrumental social participation" they created out of data gathered from Americans aged 60 years or older living in the Middle Atlantic region in 1993.[13] High instrumental social participation was positively associated with higher levels of self-reported health, net of socio-economic level, years of retirement, level of medical care use, and religious participation. Men and women benefited equally. Data from a panel study of a representative sample of the New Haven population aged 65 and older were used to examine the relation between "social engagement" and various physical health outcomes (De Leon et al. 2003:633). Baseline data were gathered in face-to-face interviews in 1982. Volunteer data were also gathered at baseline. Disability data were gathered in eight subsequent years, the last being in 1991.[14] The physical health of all subjects declined with age, as might be expected. Subjects who were highly engaged were in better health at the beginning of the study than those who were disengaged, but the positive effect of engagement diminished over time. By providing a greater sense of purpose and a sense of control over one's life, social engagement enhanced resilience in the face of disease processes that become more severe over time, up the point where a "dose" of engagement was having little effect.

Another analysis of the same data used an index of "productive activities" to predict variations in mortality (Glass et al. 1999).[15] Mortality from all causes thirteen years after baseline (1982) was measured using newspaper and hospital records, annual contact with study participants or their next of kin, and the national death index. By 1994, 62 percent of the original respondents had died. Eighty-five percent those in the lowest activity quartile had died compared to 60 percent of those in the highest activity quartile. These differences in survival rates were about the same magnitude as those brought about by fitness activities (74.0% and 55.2%, respectively). The protective effect of productive activities was strongest among those leading the least physically active lives. Unpacking the productive activities measure into its separate components, the authors found that all components except paid community work increased survival rates. In short, when singled out for special attention, volunteering had unique beneficial effects, but no more than those provided by a wide variety of "productive activities" including gardening. This study suggests a number of conclusions: health benefits should be attributed to the performance of meaningful social roles, which in turn lead to a stronger sense of self-efficacy; productive activities increase involvement in chains of reciprocity and mutual help and support; productive activities increase the likelihood of engagement in wider networks of social support, information, resources, and the like. It would be difficult to conclude on this basis that there was anything special about volunteerism in prolonging life.

In our review of the effect of volunteering on mental health we raised the question whether long-term volunteering yields more benefits than sporadic or short-term volunteering. The same question can be posed with respect to physical health. Moen et al. (1992) used data from a two-wave panel study involving mothers first interviewed in 1956 and again in 1986. The survey measured how much time elapsed between 1956 and the first onset of serious illness and functional disability (e.g., inability to do heavy work around the house). The researchers looked at the influence of both an index of multiple roles measured in 1956 (e.g., worker, club member) and individual roles (e.g., volunteer) on these health outcomes. Although the number of roles in 1956 had no effect on the timing of the onset of first serious illness, it did delay the onset of functional disability. In addition, compared to not having volunteered at all, volunteering intermittently between 1956 and 1986 was positively related to functional ability in 1986. This study is valuable for the long span of time during which volunteer work was measured (retrospectively). It shows that commitment to volunteer work over the long haul can have positive physical health benefits.

Volunteer Work and Physical Health

In the studies reviewed thus far, volunteer work has been included in general measures of social integration and it has not been possible to say whether there is anything distinctive about it as a health-promoting activity. A number of studies have focused on volunteer work more precisely. Two studies of the ACL data from 1986 and 1989 found that people who volunteered in 1986 were physically healthier in 1989 than people who did not volunteer, regardless of their health status in 1986. The older respondents benefited especially from volunteer work. However, the physical benefits of volunteering began to wane above one hundred hours of volunteer work a year, indicating that role overload was beginning to take a physical toll (Thoits and Hewitt 2001; Van Willigen 2000). Oman et al. (1999) analyzed data from a 1990 study of Marin County, California, residents 55 years of age or older.[16] Just under a third had been volunteers in 1990, with the highest rate (41%) occurring among those aged between 65 and 74. Between 1990 and 1995, 23.8 percent of those interviewed in 1990 died. The highest mortality rate (30.1) occurred among those who were not volunteers in 1990. The lowest mortality rate (12.8) occurred among those who had been volunteering for two or more organizations. Those who had been volunteering for one organization had an intermediate mortality rate (24.2). The mortality rate was unaffected by how many hours the volunteer worked. Volunteers tended to exercise more, smoke less, and (for women) consume more alcohol. They were also better educated, had higher income, were more religious and (for men) more likely to be married and have good self-rated health. After adjustments for these controls, intense volunteerism (more than two organizations) was associated with a 44 percent reduction in mortality compared to not volunteering. Volunteering delayed death better than physical exercise and frequent church attendance and almost as well as not smoking.

A very similar study is reported in Musick et al. (1999), but this time a nationally representative sample is used. Selecting respondents aged 65 or older from the 1986 ACL survey, the researchers ascertained who among the respondents interviewed in 1986 had died by 1994, when another round of interviews was conducted among the survivors.[17] Volunteers were less likely to have died than non-volunteers, but only if they limited their volunteer work to one organization: those who volunteered for more than one had a *greater* chance of dying, although not as great as those who did not volunteer at all. Once again, we see that some integration is good for you but too much might not be a good idea. The protective effect of volunteering was not equally effective for all the seniors in the study. It was strongest for those who did not socialize with friends and family much, another sign that too many roles can be hazardous to your health. Taking on the volunteer role while you are also busy with informal social interactions does not necessarily increase your chance of survival.

Another study used a different method to track the association between volunteering and mortality, but the results are much the same. Rogers (1996) used data from the 1984 National Health Interview Survey, a national probability sample of the civilian population age 55 and over.[18] In 1986 respondents were asked whether they had performed volunteer work for an organized group in the previous twelve months. In his analysis, Rogers compared those who survived the period 1986–1991 with those who died. Volunteers were less likely to have died than non-volunteers.

A study of subjects in the Asset and Health Dynamics among the Oldest Old deals with a much older population: in 1998 their average age was 76. Volunteers were healthier than non-volunteers, but more important, those who volunteered one hundred hours or more in 1998 were more likely to have survived until 2000. They were also in better physical health than non-volunteers, having fewer limitations on daily living, such as being unable to bathe themselves (Luoh and Herzog 2002). As several of the studies previously cited have found, the positive effects of volunteering faded once the number of hours contributed exceeded a certain point.[19] Another analysis of the same data focused on all respondents who were aged 70 or older in 1993, using the 2000 panel to construct the outcome measures, thus covering a longer time span. Volunteers were 28 percent less likely to have died before 2000 than non-volunteers.[20] Volunteering also slowed the decline in self-reported health and the decline in functional status (e.g., bathing, shopping). Among volunteers only, the more hours contributed, the better the self-reported health. However, volunteering had no effect on the number of physician-diagnosed medical conditions, such as heart conditions, strokes, and arthritis. The authors of the study conclude that the connection between volunteering and health among the elderly "may have nothing to do with the likelihood that one would obtain a medical condition, but rather that volunteering would increase an older person's social and psychological resources necessary to cope with the onset of a medical condition" (Lum and Lightfoot 2005:51).

Community-Level Volunteering and Physical Health

As we noted earlier, social integration has two meanings in sociological writings. It refers to the extent to which an individual is connected to others through multiple roles but, in Durkheim's original formulation, it also refers to a characteristic of a group. Some groups are more integrated than others and being a member of an integrated group is good for one's health. It is one thing to say that individuals who volunteer are healthier but it is another to say that some neighborhoods create such a positive atmosphere by the number of people volunteering in them that all neighbors benefit. Studies investigating the link between community-level measures of social integration and physical health are rare, but it is quite plausible that the volunteer rate in the community would have an affect on the health of that community. More volunteering could encourage better promotion of norms of behavior promoting good health (e.g., control of excessive drinking) and provide more mutual aid and social support. Lochner et al. (2003:1798) looked at 1995 neighborhood-level data from the city of Chicago to identify 343 "neighborhood clusters," using geographic boundaries and "knowledge of traditional Chicago neighborhoods." Each cluster contained about eight thousand residents. Survey respondents were asked about memberships in a variety of voluntary associations, including religious organizations, neighborhood associations, business and civic groups, and neighborhood ethnic or nationality clubs as well as political organizations. This information was used to construct a measure of the average per capita associational membership in each cluster. For each cluster data were gathered on mortality rates for residents aged between 44 and 66. As might be expected, poor neighborhoods had lower per capita associational memberships and higher levels of mortality. More intriguingly, the higher the rate of civic participation in the cluster, the lower the mortality rate, regardless of material deprivation. Unfortunately, because the authors are unable to control for socio-economic status at the individual level, they cannot rule out the possibility that these contextual effects are actually the result of the composition of the population. And, although voluntary association memberships and volunteering are quite highly correlated, we cannot be sure the same results would be found if the dependent variable was hours of volunteer work. Another community-level study of volunteering and physical health comes from the United Kingdom. A "citizens audit" carried out in Britain in 2000 asked respondents, "Not counting anything you do for your family, in your work, or with voluntary organizations, how often, if at all, do you actively provide help for other people?" This response was used to measure the percentage of individuals in each community (county and district local authorities) who spent at least some time on voluntary activity in an average month. This variation was then compared to the percentage of people who reported being in good health in that community in the 2001 census. The correlation coefficient was $r = 0.37$, $p < 001$. Communities with low levels of voluntary activity had poorer health (Whiteley 2004).

Conclusion

Although much research remains to be done on the relation between volunteering and health, there is no question that people are healthier as a result of their volunteer work. In this concluding section we will discuss some of the issues that deserve more attention.

First, social integration theory assumes that adding the volunteer role to other roles will improve health, without questioning how significant the role is. But social roles vary in how salient they are. Adding insignificant roles might benefit people less than adding roles that are considered important. Without more information on where people rank their volunteer work alongside all their other activities, it is difficult to predict its health consequences accurately. For example, one study found that Black women were more depressed than White women. It also found that volunteers reported fewer depressive symptoms than non-volunteers, regardless of race. This would suggest that Blacks could improve their mental health and catch up with Whites by volunteering more. But the study also found that Black women were less likely to be married or employed (both sources of self-esteem) and more likely to be providing care to a relative (a source of stress). The positive effect of volunteering was trivial for this group compared to the effect of being married or employed. If a Black woman wanted to be as healthy as a White woman it would behoove her to get married, not start volunteering (Cochran et al. 1999). In short, the health consequences of performing the volunteer role can only be understood in the context of the other roles being performed.

Second, the mental health benefits of volunteering seem to depend somewhat on whether the work provides intrinsic rewards. Volunteering that is (or feels) mandatory (e.g., PTA, scouting, or coaching soccer for a parent; required community service for a delinquent teenager; volunteer work "expected" by an employer) may not provide the benefits that flow from more freely chosen helping activities (Stukas et al. 1999). Some critics argue that the current emphasis on volunteering as a vital component of "productive aging" comes dangerously close to creating a social norm that older people *should* do volunteer work, just as they should eat healthy foods or exercise regularly, not only stigmatizing older people who choose not to volunteer but removing some of the intrinsic rewards of volunteer work that is freely chosen (Martinson and Minkler 2006).

Third, it is not yet possible to identify anything unique about the contribution of volunteer work to health. "In roughly descending order of importance, people who are married, have close friends, go to church or are members of clubs have significantly better health than those who do not" but the key issue here seems to be that the relationship be supportive and positive. Just knowing someone is not enough (Halpern 2005:111). It is easy to imagine all kinds of volunteer activities that neither involve us in much social interaction with others nor are particularly supportive or, indeed, positive. We should not be too quick to link volunteer work to the kind of social integration that has been proven to benefit our health.

Finally, social selection presents a conundrum to researchers who argue that social integration and health are related. Volunteering has positive health benefits, but healthy people are more likely to be engaged in multiple roles and broader social networks. We discussed the role of health as an individual resource for volunteering in chapter 7. Ill health is a reason people often give for not volunteering or not volunteering more: people who are not limited by physical ailments, people who are self-confident and happy, are more likely to volunteer. With cross-sectional data we are unable to assign causal effects. In the case of mortality studies, of course, this is less of a problem, but where the outcome measure is physical or mental health, only the studies described above that use panel data and suitable methods of analysis are able to draw any conclusions at all as to whether volunteering leads to better health.

22

Conclusion

In this concluding chapter we take up a number of issues left unresolved in the book thus far and point ahead to a number of theoretical and empirical problems that remain for scholars in this area to solve. We begin by returning to the discussion in chapter 2 of how volunteering should be conceptualized and discuss briefly the political implications of how we define volunteering.

The Discourse of Volunteering

In this book we have used a definition of volunteer work that suits our heavy reliance on survey data. Ours is, in many respects, an operational definition: volunteering is what the surveys measure. This approach is similar to the majority of social scientists working in this field, most of whom believe that useful distinctions can be drawn between volunteering, activism, and caring and who write as if they are categorically different species of action. In part, this is a reflection of a scientific approach to the study of volunteering that *requires* that the concept refer to some objective reality, the goal being to delineate this reality accurately, but it also reflects the institutionalization of the voluntary sector. If the U.S. Bureau of Labor's *Dictionary of Occupational Titles* contains a reference to "supervisor of volunteers" there must be some consensus as to who is a volunteer.

In chapter 2 we described the difference between essentialist (realist) and constructionist approaches to concept formation in sociology. The essentialist approach assumes there is some essence in nature that the conceptual definition can pin down; the social constructionist approach assumes that words like "volunteering" are "tools" people use to think about and define their actions and the actions of others. Rather than trying to explain why someone becomes a volunteer, social constructionists investigate why and how an activity (e.g., cooking) is labeled volunteer work. They see data (such as labels) as a discursive strategy, a second order reality; a text that must be continually questioned and subverted. They believe it is a mistake to assume there is a "real" set of acts that is unequivocally volunteering and another set of acts that is unequivocally activism, and so on. Words like "volunteer" and "activist" refer not to objects in the social world but are vernacular terms, used by "lay" actors in everyday settings to make sense of their activities. The different meanings attributed to these terms represent nothing more than social convention as to where to draw the line between them. Rather than describing categories of action that are essentially different (in nature), they describe ideas in people's heads.

Although the social constructionist perspective can be quite disconcerting for the social realist, who wants to "pin down" an activity in order to measure it, it has the advantage of drawing attention to the strategic use of social labels like "volunteering" and "activist." It is a reminder that the same activity can be labeled as one or the other depending on political and economic interests. Some people, for example, would prefer to avoid being labeled an activist because they do not want their actions to be seen as about power. A group of volunteers studied by Eliasoph (1998) proclaimed themselves volunteers rather than activists because, by so doing, they could articulate their conviction that their relative powerlessness in the political system was a result of their own shortcomings rather than with the system itself. Another group of volunteers were more willing to attach to themselves the label "activist" because they had less faith in personal generosity than they did in "solutions that would be built into official institutions" (Eliasoph 1998:75). In actual fact, both groups were engaged in very similar activities, the only difference being the language in which they chose to speak about them.

The strategic use of volunteer discourse is also demonstrated in Abrahams's (1996:790) study of mainly middle class, White, female activists who "tended to view power as something negative." To avoid seeming interested in power, they preferred to think of themselves as volunteers rather than political actors. Similarly, Teske (1997:82) noted how pro-life "activists" tried hard to shed the activist label because they regarded their work as personal rather than political: "more about affecting the specific people they encountered than about trying to change the laws or even the attitudes of society more generally." Although the women "activists" interviewed by Gittell et al. (2000) were trying to change people's lives by improving the quality of life in their neighborhood and their access to social resources and institutions, they chose not to identify themselves as activists or as political. They regarded politicians as opportunistic and self-serving, the very opposite of altruists. Believing that communities could be improved by changing people's lives one at a time, they were not so much denying politics as refusing to accept a discourse that divided the personal and the political, the private and the public, the individual and the collective.

Social actors are not entirely free to select which discourse to use to describe their activities. Their interpretive choice is influenced by the behavior of others around them and by the threats they receive and the promises made to them. For example, in the early stages of the AIDS epidemic, many in the gay community were ambivalent about going public with their gay identity. The dominant emotions of shame and fear discouraged activism, "pointing instead toward volunteerism, community-based service provision and lobbying" (Gould 2001:143). In the face of government inaction the emotional tone shifted toward that of anger and resentment. A new discourse of gay pride included and legitimated activism. Gender also determines framing choices. In the opinion of one author, women are encouraged to care enough to help others, but not to "care in a way that might disrupt existing social institutions and social organization" (Blackstone 2004:352). For example, breast cancer volunteers take pains to emphasize the sociable aspect of their work and play down the political aspect, even though a major part of their work is lobbying for increases in the funding for cancer research. They couch their demand for more research funding for women's illnesses in terms of "fairness" rather than more overtly political arguments about the misallocation of resources. Averse to causing conflict, they prefer to see their work as an expression of morality rather than the exercise of power, despite (or perhaps because of) the fact that the cancer foundation to which they are donating their time has taken on the mission of empowering women, to help see themselves as having rights in the medical arena. The focus on individual morality undermines the attempt to construct breast cancer as a political problem (Blackstone 2004:360). Empowerment is defined in individual rather than collective terms.

In all these cases, actors are making use of a discourse that effectively depoliticizes volunteer work, a very common practice in American history, during which volunteer work has traditionally been framed as service work (Ellis and Noyes 1990:10). Defining an activity as "charity" removes it from the troublesome and contentious world of activism into the much less challenging and socially approved world of caring. "Do-gooders" are politically harmless. What is politically threatening about being virtuous, compassionate, and caring for other individuals? How could volunteers be inspired by anything other than "good thoughts"? Whereas social activists are often treated with suspicion, volunteers are welcomed. They are on our side, while activists are all too inclined to "take issue" with us. But by making this distinction we reproduce a version of volunteerism that is stripped of all political meaning when, in fact, the definition of problems as individual in nature and solution is itself a political statement.

By adopting the service discourse to describe volunteering, we emphasize the positive, or virtuous, side of volunteerism, forgetting that helping others or working for a cause can be inspired by negative emotions, such as fear, anxiety, guilt, and anger, and forgetting that people can volunteer to help others, or to change laws, because they hate others and wish to exclude them. "Not all nonprofits are of the conventional, mainstream, and law-abiding sort that most people, including scholars, think of as non-profits" (Smith 2000:5). Neighbors who band together to form an organization to prevent a homeless shelter from being built in their neighborhood, an action some might condemn as selfish and mean-spirited, are nevertheless volunteers because they are a minority doing unpaid work from which all others in the community will, in their view at least, benefit. Writers such as Ellis and Noyes (1990:3) and Rossi (2001), who define volunteer work as socially responsible behavior and who leave it up to the actor to decide what this means, *seem* to be giving an ethically neutral definition of volunteering, but in so doing they downplay the fact that volunteer work is institutionalized, supported by an infrastructure of non-profit and voluntary organizations, government agencies, and advocated by business corporations, all of whom conceive of volunteering exclusively in terms of service work that supports the status quo.

By insisting that volunteer work is individually focused and not about structural change or collective action, a particular way of thinking about volunteer work is built into the definition. For example, volunteering to work in a soup kitchen or construct temporary shelters for the homeless is not innocent of political messages. It promotes an ideology of charity, reinforcing (or at least tolerating) the continued dominance of a culture of individual responsibility, hard work, home ownership, and the like, and forestalls challenges to the ideological justification for real estate development, rental policies, and private home construction. In the opinion of some of their critics, this is precisely what is wrong with high school and college service learning programs. Bickford and Reynolds (2002:229) tell the following story about students enrolled in a service learning course they were teaching:

> One student was particularly pleased with her experience: her group had gone to a local beach and picked up litter. The instructor asked her: "Don't you think it would have been more effective if your group had targeted the source of the pollution on the beach, perhaps picketing at the local businesses that contribute most to the need for beach cleanup?" This student balked at the idea. She was keen on volunteering but almost offended at the idea of activism.

The authors also describe how a service learning program aimed at bringing literacy tutors from a nearby college campus into the local public schools completely overlooked the political dimension to the literacy problem:

What does it mean that the schools must rely on volunteer labor to achieve their educational mission? What does it mean that they are designed in such a way that teachers cannot give sufficient individual attention to students? What does it mean that some students do not belong to families that encourage them to read? (Bickford and Reynolds 2002:250)

In short, service learning provided instruction in volunteering, not activism. The students should have been encouraged to ask not "why are these people poor?" but "why is there poverty?" Not "why can't Johnny read?" but "what causes illiteracy?" (Bickford and Reynolds 2002:238).

It might be too cynical to describe volunteers as well meaning but often ineffectual and sometimes harmful helpers, reproducing social inequalities by masking the real power differences on which the charitable work on behalf of the "deserving" poor rests, but the political damage inflicted by promoting volunteer work as a solution to social problems can be quite severe if it results in the neglect of political solutions. Upper class volunteer work clearly betrays its class bias. The elite women volunteers interviewed by Daniels (1988:xxi) saw their work as benefiting the entire community rather than a special segment of it, but they were oblivious of the fact that the privileges that made it possible for them to give time freely were part of the problem they were trying to solve. Also, they included in community service volunteer work they did on behalf of expensive private schools and other social institutions and social spaces from which they benefited disproportionately. The elite women interviewed by Kendall (2002:172) focused their volunteer work either on efforts from which they, as a class, would disproportionately benefit (e.g., the arts) or on human welfare services identified with very particular populations (e.g., abused children), where the larger structural forces that might underlie the issue (e.g., low wages) were all but invisible. They took pains to frame their work as "philanthropy" aimed at encouraging individuals to use private initiative to overcome their problems. They also distanced themselves from the needy by thinking of themselves working with an organization rather than for the clients of that organization. Despite these denials, their philanthropic work was intensely political. They were acting as gatekeepers of the boundaries of social class in the community but chose not to recognize or emphasize this characterization of their work.

The positive bias toward volunteerism and against activism has been perpetuated by the way historians treat voluntary associations. In the United States especially, voluntary associations are depicted as spontaneous collective responses to perceived social problems and are assigned a democratic role. From this perspective, they are clearly functional for society, so much so that Americans in particular are inclined to judge the health of their communities by how many clubs and associations there are and how many people join them. Voluntary associations are believed to be good not only because they improve social welfare without government intrusion but also because they help meet integrative goals, linking people of different social class, race, and region together, and because they help build community by encouraging a sense of sharing, social responsibility, and community. They are a kind of social glue. In this analysis, little consideration is given to what some scholars have taken to calling "the dark side of social capital" (Putnam 2000:350). Voluntary associations, and the people who work on behalf of them, can divide as well as unite; preach intolerance as well as fraternity; exclude as well as include; foster distrust as well as trust.

All of this would be less important were it not for the fact that the state is playing an increasing role in defining what counts as volunteer work, and the probabilities are that this definition will be closer to care than to activism. As we have documented in this book, Western governments have, with varying degrees of emphasis, adopted the position that volunteer work, properly defined and regulated, should be supported and encouraged. Governments are assuming an active role in the funding, mobilization, and organization of volunteer work. The consequences of this new "partnership" are not yet fully apparent, but it will likely encourage safe, non-controversial, and "non-political" volunteering at the expense of advocacy volunteering and social activism. In the United States, non-profit or philanthropic organizations—religious, educational, health, scientific, cultural, social service, membership groups, and trade unions—are treated as tax exempt under federal law and contributions to them are tax deductible. Other organizations, while they do not have the benefit of tax exemption on contributions, are exempt from federal tax on surplus revenues because they are believed to be acting in the public good. In return, they are prohibited from engaging in partisan politics. People who work for these organizations unpaid are considered volunteers. Current rulings exclude groups such as the Ku Klux Klan because they are considered antisocial, despite the fact that their members believe they also have the public good in mind. In short, these official policies and programs foster the notion that volunteering is good for society or, more accurately, *only activities that are good for society could possibly be volunteering*—and governments get to decide what is good for society.

Recent policy initiatives on volunteering in the United States, the United Kingdom, Canada, and Australia reflect the influence of communitarian thinking. In the United Kingdom, this philosophy is enshrined in a "discussion document" issued in 2002 entitled "Next Steps on Volunteering and Giving in the UK" over the signature of the then Home Secretary David Blunkett and Chancellor of the Exchequer Gordon Brown.[1] The document spelled out the Labour government's vision of the role of the state as an "enabler," helping communities develop by providing a framework within which volunteerism could thrive, disputing the right-wing notion that government action crowds out volunteerism on the one hand *and* the left-wing notion that the need for universal public services is too important to leave to "charity" on the other. The document thus expressed the government's commitment to a "third way" for social services to be delivered, in which governments formed partnerships with voluntary agencies. Being a "good partner" meant recognizing there are limits to what governments can achieve; that building a "compassionate society" is not within the government's mandate or capabilities; that centralized government is less effective than decentralized, local government working in conjunction with grassroots organizations; that these organizations have more flexibility and often show more creativity than government agencies; and that volunteers frequently have stronger motivation and personal commitment than paid employees.[2]

In 2004, the Labour government appointed the Russell Commission to develop a new national framework for youth action and engagement. The aim of the commission was to find ways to increase the level of volunteering by younger people in the United Kingdom. In setting up the commission it was guided by the belief that, by doing volunteer work, young people would develop their civic skills and contribute in an active way to their local communities; the capacity of communities and of non-profit organizations would be enhanced; society at large would be more cohesive; and, through job skills development, the United Kingdom's competitive advantage in the world economy would be improved. The commission issued its report in 2005. It called for a "new national framework for youth action and engagement" by broadening access to volunteer opportunities, enhancing the benefits that young people get from volunteering, and raising the value other people place on their contribution.[3]

In Canada, a task force set up by the Privy Council Office concluded that "Volunteerism is an important act of citizenship where individuals give their time and energy to their community by choice and without pay" (Dreesen 2000:23). The task force credited volunteerism with improving the "well-being and quality of life of Canadians"; providing "a vehicle for involving citizens in civic participation and public decision-making"; sustaining "social cohesion"; and making a "substantive economic contribution" to society. All kinds of other benefits were listed: reinforcing social trust, public education, support for individuals, families and communities "in transition," reinforcing common values and a "sense of purpose."[4]

In the United States, the federal government has become much more assertive in promoting volunteer work, principally through the Corporation for National Service (CNS), a joint agency including representatives from both the public sector and voluntary sectors. In a report issued in 2000, the corporation's board of governors recommended increasing the use of volunteers to achieve the goals of federal and state agencies, more corporate support for employees who want to perform volunteer service, expanding partnerships with faith-based organizations, more service learning in high schools and colleges, and more service opportunities for older Americans. In addition to the CNS the federal government channels financial aid to non-profit agencies, including "faith-based organizations." The long-term consequences of these new initiatives are yet to be seen, but already concerns are being expressed about the political costs of a closer relationship between non-profit and voluntary agencies and governments. Some worry that governments, especially of the right, are eager to promote the idea that individual and community needs are the result of individual failings and meeting these needs requires individual change. Furthermore, where governments and philanthropic efforts are joined, it is all too possible to allow moral considerations to enter into the helper-helped relationship in which only the "deserving poor" are given aid. The Reagan administration of the 1980s did much to promote this understanding of volunteering as it sought to justify budget cuts by encouraging private sector initiatives. "Efforts to promote social justice, equality, and quality of life have suffered a loss of legitimacy as direct charity for the poor is promoted as the only useful form of philanthropy . . . Even the sector's name has been changed to refer generically to nonprofits as 'service providers' rather than as community organizations, voluntary associations, or social action groups" (Boris 1999:5). By distancing volunteer work from activism or even advocacy, the idea that volunteerism is about "damage control rather than prevention" is perpetuated and talk of justice or rights excluded (Poppendieck 1998:5). We turn the needy into "clients" who need our help rather than people with rights we need to acknowledge and respect. "Poor people might be, and often are, very well treated in charitable emergency food programs, but they have no rights, at least no legally enforceable rights, to the benefits that such programs provide" (Poppendieck 1998:12).

These trends are cause for concern, but it is important not to exaggerate the influence of this ideology of accommodation on volunteers, many of whom are quite capable of providing services to individuals or local groups while at the same time understanding the broader, structural basis of the problems they are helping deal with:

> volunteers are for the most part concerned about the wider society and committed to the view that it can be improved. Their volunteer work is in this sense not exclusively directed toward individuals in need but is symptomatic of their concern for the good of society. (Wuthnow 1991:261)

They are perfectly aware of the difference between individually focused "band-aid" solutions to social problems and social change solutions focused on structural issues. They know that their work offers only temporary solutions to chronic problems. But temporary solutions are, in their opinion, better than no solutions at all: "To participate in voluntary organizations means we are making a choice for the better, siding with the good, doing something, rather than sitting idly by while the specter of chaos and corruption advances" (Wuthnow 1991:233). In Beyond Welfare, an organization founded in 1997 to support people on welfare or in poverty to work toward economic self-sufficiency, "partnerships" are set up between middle class volunteers and "clients" trying to make it off welfare. Who would be drawn to engage in this often-fruitless work? Are they volunteers naively interested in band-aid solutions to difficult social problems? On the contrary: they are highly politically motivated, incensed by the 1996 changes in the welfare laws that made it more difficult for the poor and unemployed to stay on welfare. One respondent explained her motivation to help as being triggered by the recent legislation: "what a horrible law; what a horrible thing to do to people" (Bloom and Kilgore 2003:438).

Volunteering and Caring

As shown in chapter 2, the discourse of volunteering also draws a line between caring and volunteering. There is considerable room for interpreting the same act (such as helping a neighbor or visiting a shut-in) in many different ways. Pinning the label of care work on an activity consigns it, by definition, to the domestic sphere. This has two consequences: it privatizes the activity and it identifies the activity as women's work. Historically speaking, men's "volunteer work" has been political or civic in nature; women's "volunteer work" has been service-oriented and private (Ellis and Noyes 1990:10). The use of the care label pushes the activity deeper into the private sphere and further separates the volunteer work of men and women. In the process, much of the volunteer work women do becomes invisible, because it is misnamed as care. "When women specialize in giving care in communities and men specialize in taking care of others by coordinating voluntary effort or focusing on advocacy, women's care easily remains a less influential activity, inferior to more visible civic activity" (Cancian and Oliker 2000:145).

Women who volunteer for political causes must therefore struggle with the tendency to dismiss their work as merely the expression of their instinctive compassion for others. They must take steps to avoid being categorized as caregivers if they want to be taken seriously in the public arena. For example, one of the biggest obstacles faced by animal rights activists is that empathy for animals, even as the victims of human cruelty, is considered emotionally deviant in many social settings. To deal with this problem, people within the movement draw a distinction between volunteers who work at animal shelters, sponsor dog washes, and the like (who are described as "animal lovers" and characterized as "welfarists" and "emotional") from activists who engage in "rights talk" and seek "justice" (Groves 2001:219). By accusing animal rights activists of sentimentality opponents devalue their work, classifying it as care work and thereby blunting its political impact. Ironically, the animal rights activists cannot afford to be seen as "caring" and must develop a "frame" for their actions that emphasizes rights and justice over compassion and care.

Animal rights activists seek to move their actions along the continuum toward activism and away from caring for strategic reasons, particularly if they are women. Sometimes, however, strategic considerations require moving actions from activism to caring. For example, women are more often leaders of grassroots environmental groups than men. While this seems to invalidate the theory that men are more likely to be seen as political actors than women, it does not if we bear in mind that these terms are labels available for use in political struggle. Grassroots environmental groups do not fare well against polluting corporations when they fight them on the grounds of science and expertise because they lack resources and credibility. They do, however, have privileged access to "mom discourse." This is a more legitimate-sounding language for citizen involvement in such movements than "expert discourse." If they frame their volunteer work as "caring" they are more effective than if they frame their work as "activism." Reciprocally, the language of caring makes it possible for women to assume leadership positions, albeit at the cost of reinforcing gender stereotypes (Eliasoph 1998).

This is where the social constructionist standpoint described above becomes particularly insightful. We are reminded that terms like "volunteer" and "activist" are simply part of a "cultural toolkit" for use in defining activities in particular ways. The same activity could be defined as volunteering, activism, or caring depending on a wide variety of social circumstances and political interests. Naples's (1992) concept of "activist mothering" illustrates this point well. For working class African American women, volunteering to help one's community is an extension of mothering, or caring. African American women think about the wider Black community as a family in which caring for children takes place. Conversely, mothering in African American neighborhoods necessarily takes on some of the aspects of community maintenance, or activism. Proper care for one's children *is* involvement in the community and is a way of combating the political neglect of the needs of the community's residents. Community maintenance (what some might call volunteering) thus doubles as caring, with some tinge of activism thrown in. A similar pattern would probably be found among Hispanics. Diaz et al. (2001:3) note that Hispanic volunteering is more "personal." The identity of the person who asks you to volunteer and of the person who receives the help you provide is very important in the Hispanic community. The distinction between volunteering (for strangers) and caring (for family and friends) has not emerged with the same degree of clarity as is found in the Anglo community. "Showing care" means defining the problems over which you think you can have control, limiting the circle of concern to that which seems to be manageable. In the process, caring becomes domesticated: it is "close to home." The discourse here is reciprocal because help provided close to home is called care. "Care" does not describe a fixed set of social practices but the kind of help provided if one wants to limit one's concerns, to de-politicize them. Care work helps define the domestic sphere; in turn, the domestic sphere is used to identify caring work and to distinguish it from volunteering and activism.[5]

Who Volunteers?

In this book we have sketched a psychosocial profile of the volunteer. Thanks to the recent explosion of interest in volunteerism, data are available to provide a much more detailed picture of the volunteer, complete with information on personality traits, reasons for volunteering, socio-economic status, gender and race, religious beliefs and practices, marital and parental status, social ties and memberships, and the role of recruitment. We also have a much better idea of the kinds of social communities from which volunteers are most likely to be drawn—the kinds of schools and religious congregations they attend, the characteristics of the neighborhood in which they live, whether they are more likely to live in rural areas, suburbs, or in cities, and in which region of the country they are most likely to live. We have even been able to compare volunteer rates across many different countries and explore the idea that the chances of volunteering depend on the country in which people live.

Our profile of the volunteer is, however, far from complete. Many details are missing. Some of this is attributable to missing data and some of this is due to analyses of existing data that have yet to be completed. In this section we will discuss some of these outstanding issues.

Resources

In chapters 6 and 7 we presented the argument that volunteer labor, like any other kind of labor, consumes resources, such as time and money. Volunteer work is less costly if one is endowed with plentiful supplies of resources such as education, occupation-based skills, and good health. While in some cases (e.g., health) the reason why it functions as a resource for volunteering is fairly obvious, in others it is not. For example, education is a consistent and strong predictor of volunteering, but how can we account for this association? There are many possible answers to this question. Education helps shape attitudes and dispositions that encourage volunteering. Better-educated people have more self-esteem, self-efficacy, and ability to empathize, and they are more trusting. Education provides the skills needed to perform volunteer work and improves knowledge of social problems and an analytical understanding of their possible solutions. Education is also a form of "ability signaling": it makes sense to recruit more highly educated people because if they are good at one thing they will be good at another. Educated people are more mobile, have weaker primary ties with kin and neighbors, and are more likely to use voluntary associations, churches, and volunteer work as substitutes for these ties. Pursuing an education also means spending more time in schools and colleges, which are similar to religious congregations in being places where volunteering is encouraged and the resources to perform it are provided. Much of this remains, however, speculation either because the data on these mechanisms linking education to volunteering do not exist or because the analyses have yet to be done.

Social Relationships

One drawback of using survey data is that information is typically gathered from individuals whose relationships with others are unmeasured. This encourages us to focus on individual attributes, such as free time, to the neglect of social relationships and social contexts. Human beings are first and foremost social actors whose thinking and behavior are shaped by those around them. We explored some of these issues in part 4 of the book but many remain to be tackled.

The Household

Although the people who complete social survey questionnaires are typically members of a household, this is rarely acknowledged in studies of volunteer behavior. It is very different in studies of philanthropy, where it is simply assumed that decisions about how much money to give to charity are made as part of the household budget management. As we demonstrated in chapter 11, in many marriages, both husbands and wives volunteer.[6] Married couples will volunteer jointly; parents will take their children with them to share the experience of volunteering. In order to fully understand the practice of volunteering, we must take into account the inner dynamics of the household to explore the ways family members encourage, or discourage, volunteer work by other family members. Two examples can be provided of potential analyses of household effects on volunteering.

Most social scientists acknowledge that doing volunteer work can cost money, which makes the weak influence of personal income on volunteering rather puzzling. The solution to this riddle is that, in most cases, income is a household phenomenon: it is jointly produced and jointly consumed. How it is spent depends on whether one or two people produce it and who contributes the larger share. For example, one study showed that family income had a positive effect on volunteering, but only for women. This is easily explained once we recall that women typically earn less than men, which means they enjoy the benefits of higher family income without paying the high opportunity costs (of volunteering rather than working for pay) that men face. They can switch from paid work to volunteering at less cost to themselves than can the men to whom they are married (Wilson and Musick 1997a). It is therefore important in future studies of the influence of income on volunteering to consider this relationship in light of the needs of the household as a whole.

Role Sets

To many sociologists, the fundamental unit of analysis is "persons-in-roles." As occupants of roles, actors are necessarily involved in role sets: an employed woman might be a mother, wife, teacher, and hockey coach. She must manage the often-conflicting demands made by the other role players in this set of roles. Regrettably, the idea that volunteering is a role embedded in a larger set of roles is almost entirely lost in the social survey research on volunteering. Instead, being a volunteer is reduced to a "state" of the individual, similar to being in the labor force. Attributes are treated as proxies for interaction and role incumbencies. Thus liberated from the network of roles in which it is embedded, volunteering is free to be causally connected to other individual "states," such as work hours or number of children. In reality, work, family, and volunteering constitute a *set of roles*. Although survey researchers frequently gather information on these roles, they rarely consider the way they combine to affect choices. For example, it is typically assumed that people allocate their time in a sequence of decisions. First they choose how many hours to work for pay and only then do they decide how many hours to volunteer. But it is highly likely that a significant number of people, especially women, choose how many hours to work for pay and how many hours to volunteer simultaneously. They decide how to allocate their time across paid and unpaid work at the same time, trading them off against each other (Tiehen 2000). In other words, they choose to volunteer under those conditions where their work and family roles can be combined in a satisfactory way. For example, some surveys show that married people are more likely to volunteer than single people. They also show that part-time workers volunteer more often than full-time workers. Must we assume that the effect of work is "added to" the effect of marriage? It is more likely that a certain social relationship (i.e., being married) has made possible a particular combination of work and volunteer roles. Married women find it easier to choose a combination of paid and unpaid work than single women.

Social Networks

The social network concept is more abstract than either household or role sets. Social networks are comprised of friends, extended kin, workmates, fellow church or club members, and so on. These networks connect us to volunteer opportunities and increase the chance of being recruited. Unfortunately, social surveys typically use inadequate network measures, if they use them at all. Typically, information is drawn from the respondent. The social networks are therefore ego-centered. Because little is known about the linkages between other members of the respondent's circle of acquaintances, it is a misnomer to call them social networks at all. We know how often the respondent has contact with friends but not how often those friends contact each other. We know if the respondent draws friends from all walks of life but we know nothing of the heterogeneity of the social networks of which he or she is a member. We know how many friends the respondent has but we do not know how many of them volunteer. We can therefore examine the impact of the number of friends on volunteering but we cannot examine the impact of different kinds of friends, or friendship networks, on volunteering.

Neighborhood

We devoted part of chapter 15 to the influence of neighborhood characteristics on volunteering, but research on this topic has only just begun. Residential stability and higher rates of home ownership clearly have an influence on volunteering, but exactly why this is so remains obscure. Is it mostly a matter of social networks and social trust or is it more a matter of financial stake in neighborhood welfare? What are the other neighborhood characteristics that might influence the level of volunteering? It is here that Eckstein's (2001) study of the Boston neighborhood, reported in chapter 15, is so valuable. Neighborhoods rich in voluntary associations are capable of fostering "collective volunteering," in which people volunteer as members of a team. The "team" might be a religious congregation, a youth organization, or the local branch of the American Legion. A team agrees to supply volunteers to the community for a specific purpose, such as mounting a Christmas-gift-to-the needy drive. The leverage achieved by local voluntary associations is readily apparent: many more individual members of such groups are drawn into volunteer work in this way than would otherwise be the case. This kind of volunteering is not merely the aggregation of individual decisions to volunteer, because community characteristics have made the collective mobilization possible. It makes sense that more people will volunteer if they live in a neighborhood with strong norms of community building or one that is institutionally well endowed with voluntary organizations. And, since we know that the quality of schools, the availability of parks and clubs, and the outreach programs of religious congregations vary across neighborhoods, we can expect the volunteer rate to vary also. The intriguing point is that an increase in volunteering could be brought about by improving neighborhoods as well as "improving" individuals. Conversely, failure to maintain a given rate of volunteering or community involvement might be attributable to the disintegration of a neighborhood rather than to a decline in altruism.

The Local Market for Volunteers

Volunteerism is predominantly a local phenomenon: it is the coming together of the demand for and supply of volunteer labor on a local level. National surveys tell us a lot about the demographics of volunteering but very little about how the relation between volunteers and the groups or organizations for which they work is structured by the organization of social life, the local population mix, and the shared norms guiding the types of helping relationships that are sanctioned and supported in the community. In national surveys, the respondents are spread too widely among locales with different norms, opportunities, and supports for various kinds of volunteer work for it to be possible to see how the market for volunteer labor works. Organizations are looking for volunteers; people are looking for volunteer opportunities. How do these two meet? Exploring the mediating role of institutions such as schools, churches, workplaces, and voluntary associations would be a good place to begin because they cut the cost of searching for volunteers. Too much emphasis on individual resources and motivations leaves these structural constraints on volunteering largely unspecified. The central problem facing participants in the volunteer labor market is not comparing alternative volunteer opportunities, weighing their various costs and benefits against not doing any volunteer work at all, but finding out what the alternatives are in the first place.

Attachment and Commitment

In chapter 19 we sought answers to the question why some people make a career out of volunteering or show great loyalty to a particular volunteer organization while others volunteer only once or very sporadically. We discovered that, to some degree, the very factors that predict who will become a volunteer also predict who will be most attached to the work. For example, more highly educated people are not only more likely to volunteer in the first place but tend to volunteer for longer spells. They are less likely to get disillusioned with, or tired of, volunteer work. Perhaps it has something to do with the nature of the volunteer work they do. We found that matching motivation to specific tasks, providing psychic rewards and adequate support, were also important. However, we were surprised to find that satisfaction with volunteer work was unrelated to length of service or, in the case of one study, was negatively related—the most satisfied volunteers were the most likely to quit. We discussed some of the reasons why satisfaction seemed to have so little to do with attachment or commitment to a particular organization, but there are much larger issues involved here. We normally expect workers to quit if they are unsatisfied with their job and there are other jobs available. For people doing care work (such as looking after children) quitting is not really an option, but volunteer work is rather different. Quitting is certainly an option and is frequently exercised, and yet quitting volunteer jobs does not seem to be motivated by the same reason as quitting paid jobs. Intriguingly, the cost-benefit approach to explaining career volunteers is not all that helpful. Some of this might have to do with the fact that survey researchers tend to think in terms of *absolute* satisfaction when predicting commitment to volunteering. But we need to know whether volunteer work is more or less satisfying than other roles being performed.[7] We also need to know whether volunteer work is more or less satisfying in relation to expectations. The volunteer might be thinking, "Does the activity satisfactorily express who I am?" The soup kitchen volunteer is there because she wants to learn more about herself or to affirm an identity as a caring person. Ridding the world of hunger is not necessary to reach these goals. By the same logic, the opposite set of circumstances can be imagined. A woman might sign up to prevent rezoning of nearby land in order to protect the quality of the neighborhood in which she lives, but she learns nothing more about herself as a result of her participation and her expressive rewards are few, although the rezoning is prevented. In both cases, value is endogenous to participation because the volunteer herself instills it through her participation. Finally, we need to know whether volunteer work is satisfying in comparison with the level of satisfaction obtained by other volunteers. In chapter 19 we learned that volunteers could get upset at inequities in their job assignments and rewards compared to other volunteers. This is an old sociological truth: that our level of satisfaction with rewards is determined, in part, by the rewards being earned by those around us who are putting in the same number of hours and doing the same kind of work.

Benefits of Volunteering

Public officials frequently mention the benefits of volunteering when campaigning to get more people to volunteer. Being political actors, they are most interested in the way in which volunteer work develops political skills and promotes broader civic engagement, a lesson they are particularly keen to teach to young people, who seem uninterested in civic affairs. And yet, as we have seen, the evidence to support this idea is rather uneven and based on only a few longitudinal studies using inconsistent definitions of volunteer work and civic engagement. Only some kinds of volunteer work teach the lessons of democracy or promote interest in or commitment to democratic politics. And, while getting young people involved in volunteer work might well encourage them to be "better citizens" as adults, it is uncertain whether volunteering is the only or even the best method of producing this outcome.

Politicians also allude to "personal development" as a benefit of volunteering, as in the UK Home Office discussion paper described above. This is a policy objective—using volunteer work to promote the healthy moral, cognitive, and expressive development of the individual—which many social scientists have endorsed in their research on the antecedents of antisocial behavior. Volunteering thus becomes a method of deviance control. Unfortunately, research on this topic is very limited and entirely restricted to younger populations. A few longitudinal research projects have yielded promising findings—children who volunteer are less likely to get into trouble—but we do not know how much of this is due to selection effects (juvenile delinquents do not become volunteers); how much of the benefit is due to volunteer work as such rather than any structured activity that gives the young person some responsibility, brings him or her into contact with adults, and limits his or her time hanging out with friends; and how much of the "effect" is actually due to some third factor—such as family background—that both keeps the young person out of trouble and encourages the young person to volunteer.

Also implicit in the government calls for more volunteers is the assumption that volunteerism is good for one's mental and physical health. Increasing life spans have created "third age" problems as more and more people spend a large proportion of their lives in retirement, many of them looking for "productive" roles to play. Governments regard this older population as a pool of skilled and motivated volunteers to help provide public services (e.g., park guides). Gerontologists tout the advantages of keeping active in old age. Social scientists have been able to contribute to this debate by drawing on fairly recent developments in the research on health, showing the benefits of social support, social integration, and—perhaps—volunteering. And yet the evidence on the health benefits of volunteer work is again rather weak and inconsistent. It is unclear whether young and middle aged people gain significant mental health benefits from doing volunteer work. Some positive influences on morbidity and mortality have been documented, but we are unsure of the reasons for these influences, the mechanisms that connect volunteering with physical health. And again it is unclear whether volunteer work is necessary to produce these outcomes rather than simply having an active social life.

The Future of Volunteerism

In this book we have largely avoided using the term "social capital" because of its nebulous quality. However, we cannot ignore the debate about the alleged decline in social capital in our assessment of the current state of social science research on volunteering and where it might be going. Advocates of the Third Way have been highly receptive to the thesis that democratic government must rely heavily on an active and engaged citizenry, and that social problems are best dealt with at the local level with projects inspired and managed by local or grassroots organizations. Many people were quite ready to believe, as Putnam (2000) maintained, that civic life was under threat from big government, longer work hours, the growth of suburbs and "exurbs" where community life was harder to sustain, and the growth of mass media, with their tendency to privatize and individualize social life. Putnam's writings set off a prolonged debate about the empirical evidence for a decline in "social capital," the reasons for it, and the possible remedies for this decline in civic life. This, in turn, sparked academic debate about the reasons for volunteer work, the obstacles preventing people from doing it, and the uneven distribution of volunteer work across class, gender, race, and age groups, much of it in the interest of finding ways to sustain the supply of volunteer labor in the face of threats posed by socio-economic changes.

As we have discovered, reliable data on volunteering do not reach back far enough for trends to be accurately measured. Observed changes might simply be temporary adjustments to events, such as the economic decline of the 1980s. The rates of volunteering in most of the countries for which we have reliable data have been more or less stable over the past quarter century. This is not to deny changes in what people volunteer for, in how people contribute their volunteer hours, and in which segments of the population show the most interest in volunteering, but there is no master trend. If volunteering is a component of social capital it is a component that is not declining. On the other hand, it shows little signs of becoming more inclusive. Most of the government documents alluded to above state broader participation in volunteer work as one of their goals. In some countries, such as Canada and the United Kingdom, the social capital debate has been framed within a larger context of social inclusion: a healthy democratic society means the involvement of all groups in society regardless of their financial or other resources. But although some studies show increasing proportions of young people volunteering and other studies show increasing proportions of older people volunteering (depending on the country), there is no evidence to suggest any change in the class bias of volunteering or in the relative exclusion of racial and ethnic minority groups from volunteer work.[8]

The Globalization of Volunteerism

Another important development at the end of the twentieth century was the globalization of volunteering, "a massive upsurge of organized, private, voluntary activity in virtually every region of the world—in the developed countries of North America, Western Europe, and Asia; throughout Central and Eastern Europe; and in much the developing world" (Salamon et al. 2003:2). A number of factors have encouraged this trend. The spread of information technologies and literacy not only makes it easier to share information on volunteerism and the volunteer role, but it also helps spread the demand for volunteer work by informing more people of civil and human rights issues, global problems such as environmental degradation, and economic injustice. The citizens of many of the more advanced industrial societies share disillusionment with welfare state policies but distrust the market as a solution to social problems. In addition, volunteering is officially sanctioned as a vital component of "social capital," and governments are interested in promoting social capital because "it can potentially encourage economic growth, educational achievement, reduced crime and better health" (Ruston 2003:2).

The globalization of volunteering was acknowledged in November 1997, when the United Nations Assembly passed a resolution declaring 2001 the International Year of Volunteers.[9] Among the initiatives attributed to the year were research in individual countries into the extent and distribution of volunteering; the preparation of a "toolkit" for measuring volunteering; the introduction of volunteer awards and other methods of recognizing exemplary volunteer contributions; the establishment of volunteer centers and institutes in individual countries to provide information, training, education, and matching services; the acceptance by many governments of the responsibility to promote an environment favorable to volunteerism; revising existing laws to provide a legal framework to protect volunteers; increased funding from governments, corporations, and foundations for non-profit agencies; improved networking of voluntary agencies across national borders (China hosted its first national conference on volunteerism); and promotional campaigns and events.

These globalization trends do not necessarily mean uniformity in the size and structure of the voluntary sector in the countries of the world. At the current state of development of the "global civil society" the Anglo-Saxon countries (the UK, Canada, the United States, and Australia) have developed strong service-oriented voluntary sectors that rely quite heavily on volunteers; the Nordic countries have strong advocacy-oriented voluntary sectors that rely very little on volunteer labor; European welfare-state countries (e.g., Germany, Austria) have quite strong service-oriented voluntary sectors that depend very little on volunteer labor, in part because they received government funding to hire people; the Asian industrialized societies have small service-oriented voluntary sectors that rely minimally on volunteer labor; Latin American countries have large service-oriented voluntary sectors that do not rely heavily on volunteers; African countries have relatively large service-oriented voluntary sectors that are heavily reliant on volunteers for labor; the countries of Central and Eastern Europe have very small advocacy-oriented voluntary sectors with a volunteer component below the average for all the thirty-five countries compared in this study (Salamon et al. 2003). In other words, while it is undoubtedly true that volunteerism is undergoing a process of globalization, there are few signs that the role of the voluntary sector in society, or the role of the volunteer, is becoming more uniform. Much depends on the political, economic, and social history of the country involved.

Appendix: Data Description

Independent Sector

The Independent Sector data contain information from respondents surveyed over five waves in 1990, 1992, 1994, 1996, and 1999. The goal of these surveys was to collect information from American adults about their levels of volunteering and giving and motivations for doing so. Although the data collection for each wave was similar, there are some discrepancies. For this reason, each of the years of data collection is described separately. In each survey a new sample of adults was drawn, leaving no overlap in respondents between the waves.

1990 The data were collected by the Gallup Organization using a multi-stage area probability sample of non-institutionalized civilians aged eighteen and older and living in the United States. Blacks, Hispanics, and those with household incomes over $60,000 per year were over-sampled to facilitate sub-group analyses. Weights were employed in analyses to ensure that the sample was representative of the population from which it was drawn. Interviews were conducted from March 23 to May 20, 1990, on an in-person basis. The final sample size was 2,727.

1992 Data for this wave were collected in a manner similar to that for the 1990 wave. The interviews were conducted between April 3 and May 17, 1992, and yielded 2,671 completed surveys.

1994 Data for this wave were collected in a manner similar to that for the 1990 wave; however, this wave did not include the over-sample of Blacks, Hispanics, and affluent Americans. Nevertheless, weights were still employed to ensure the representativeness of the sample. In-person interviews were conducted between April 22 and May 15, 1994, and yielded 1,509 completed surveys.

1996 Data for this wave were collected in a manner similar to that for the 1990 wave, including over-samples for Blacks, Hispanics, and affluent Americans. Interviews were conducted between May 4 and June 16, 1996, and yielded 2,719 completed surveys.

1999 Data for this wave were collected in a manner similar to that for the 1990 wave, including over-samples for Blacks, Hispanics, and affluent Americans. Interviews were conducted in May–July 1999 and yielded 2,553 completed interviews.

The Independent Sector data contain a bounty of valuable information on volunteering and its motivators. However, some analyses of these data would be difficult if not impossible without combining the data across waves.

Consequently, the data used in this volume are a combination of these five waves of data, yielding an overall sample size of 12,179. Many of the variables used in our analyses, such as volunteering during the previous year, were asked during all waves of data collection. Some (e.g., motivations) were asked only in some or one of the waves.

Of those variables asked in multiple waves, most used question wordings and response categories that were similar across waves. However, in some cases, questions were slightly re-worded or response categories were changed. In our efforts to combine the variables from different survey years, we took these changes into consideration and created new combined variables that retained the measurement goals of the concepts under study.

The most important variables used from these data were the questions that assessed volunteering. To collect data on this behavior, respondents were asked a series of questions in the area.

Any volunteering in the past twelve months First, respondents were read a list of areas in which people sometimes do volunteer work. For each area, respondents were asked to indicate whether they had volunteered in that area during the past twelve months. The areas were (a) health organizations, (b) education, (c) religious organizations, (d) human services, (e) environment, (f) public/society benefit, (g) recreation—adults, (h) arts, culture, humanities, (i) work-related organizations, (j) political organizations, (k) youth development, (l) private and community foundations, (m) international/foreign, (n) informal/alone, and (o) other. Because of the ambiguity of the informal/alone and other categories, we did not count these areas when determining levels of volunteering over the past year. Instead, we coded respondents as having volunteered during the past year if they said they had volunteered in any of the (a) through (m) areas. Occasionally, we use a measure of volunteering range, which is a sum of all of the areas mentioned.

Volunteering in the past month For each area respondents said they had volunteered in, they were asked whether they had done any volunteer work in that area in the past month. If they had done so, they were then asked to provide the number of hours. In certain parts of the volume we use a measure of volunteering hours garnered from these questions. We identified the respondents who had volunteered in the past month and then summed the number of hours they reported for each area.

Volunteering types We classified the original thirteen areas of volunteering into larger thematic groups. As noted in the volume, the purpose of this grouping was to determine whether the predictors of volunteering behaved differently depending on the type of volunteering under study. Respondents were coded as having volunteered in a group if they had volunteered in any of the areas making up the group. The groups were composed as follows:

Advocacy: (a) environment, (b) political organizations, (c) public/society benefit, (d) private and community foundations, (e) work-related organizations, and (f) international foreign;

Education: (a) education and (b) arts, culture, humanities;
Human services: (a) health organizations and (b) human services;
Development: (a) recreation—adults and (b) youth development;
Religious: (a) religious organizations.

Americans' Changing Lives

The Americans' Changing Lives data were collected by the Survey Research Center at the University of Michigan on a stratified, multi-stage area probability sample of non-institutionalized persons aged 25 and over and living in the coterminous United States (House 1994). African Americans and persons aged 60 and over were sampled at twice the rate of non-African Americans and persons under age 60. Initial face-to-face interviews lasting eighty-six minutes on average were completed in the homes of 3,617 respondents between May and October of 1986. A second wave of in-person data was collected from the same respondents in 1989. Due to sample attrition, the number of respondents interviewed during this wave was 2,867. Weights were employed in analyses to ensure that the sample was representative of the population from which it was drawn.

Because the data from the same respondents were collected in both waves, we are able to examine changes in volunteering over time using this data set. The fact that the measures of volunteering were consistent across waves makes it possible to examine changes in the volunteer behavior of individuals over time. Respondents were asked if they had done any volunteer work in the past twelve months in each of the following areas: (a) church, synagogue, or other religious organization, (b) school or educational organization, (c) political group or labor union, (d) senior citizen group or related organization, and (e) other national or local organization. If respondents indicated that they had volunteered in one or more of these areas, they were asked how many hours they spent doing that volunteer work during the past twelve months. Response categories for this question included (1) less than 20 hours, (2) 20–39 hours, (3) 40–79 hours, (4) 80–159 hours, and (5) 160 hours or more. In the analyses we report in the book we use three measures of volunteer work drawn from this data set: any volunteering at all during the past twelve months; hours volunteered in the past twelve months; and number of different areas in which volunteer work took place.

Current Population Survey

The Current Population Survey is a monthly survey of approximately fifty-seven thousand American households conducted by the Bureau of the Census (U.S. Bureau of Labor Statistics 2003). The goal of the survey is to provide a source for government statistics on employment and other social and economic indicators. The CPS sometimes includes supplemental survey data collected for a single month during the year. The data on which our analyses of CPS are based come from one of these supplements: the September 2003 Volunteer Supplement. During this month, the Bureau of the Census conducted their normal monthly CPS but added a series of questions on volunteering. Respondents were asked numerous questions about their volunteering activities since September 1, 2002, until the date of the interview (interviews were conducted between September 14 and 20, 2003).

The CPS is designed to ensure that the sample is representative of households in all fifty states and the District of Columbia. The sample size of interviewed persons varies from month to month; in the September 2003 data we examined, the useable sample size was 95,337. This final sample consists of interviewed civilians in identified households aged 15 and older. Weights were employed in the analyses to adjust for household non-response and other forms of sampling errors. The CPS begins by asking respondents if they had done any volunteer activities through or for an organization since September 1st of the last year. If respondents said they had not, they are then asked the following, "Sometimes people don't think of activities they do infrequently or activities they do for children's schools or youth organizations as volunteer activities. Since September 1st of last year, have you done any of those types of volunteer activities?" Respondents who said they had volunteered were then asked how many different organizations they had volunteered for. Once that number was elicited, respondents were asked to identify the type of organization. The number of organizations could range between one and seven or more. The types of organizations were (a) religious organization, (b) children's educational, sports, or recreational group, (c) other educational group, (d) social and community service group, (e) civic organization, (f) cultural or arts organization, (g) environmental or animal care organization, (h) health research or health education organization, (i) hospital, clinic, or healthcare organization, (j) international organization, (k) labor union, business, or professional organization, (l) political party or advocacy group, (m) public safety organization, (n) sports or hobby group, (o) youth services group, and (p) some other type of organization. Based on this series of questions, we created the following variables:

Any volunteering Respondents were coded as having volunteered if they mentioned having volunteered in this series of questions.

Volunteering types As was the case with the Independent Sector data, we created a series of variables to indicate whether respondents had volunteered in various areas. Although the organizations listed in the CPS data do not completely overlap with those listed in the Independent Sector data, we attempted to make these volunteering types as similar as possible across surveys. Respondents were coded as having volunteered for a specific type if they mentioned having volunteered for one or more of the following organizations in each type:

Advocacy: (a) environmental or animal care organization, (b) political party or advocacy group, (c) labor union, business, or professional organization, (d) international organization, and (e) civic organization;

Development: (a) children's educational, sports, or recreational group, (b) youth services group, and (c) sports or hobby group;

Education: (a) other educational group and (b) cultural or arts organization;

Human services: (a) health research or health education organization, (b) hospital, clinic, or healthcare organization, (c) social and community service group, and (d) public safety organization;

Religious: (a) religious organization.

After respondents mentioned volunteering for a particular organization, they were then asked the number of weeks and number of hours per week they volunteered for each organization over the past year. Although this information could be useful for a variety of research purposes, it was not used in this volume.

World Values Survey

The World Values Surveys (Inglehart et al. 2004) were designed to facilitate research on social values, beliefs, and behaviors of adults from countries around the world. The surveys contain data from representative samples of adults 18 and older living in approximately sixty countries spread across all six of the non-Antarctica continents. Sampling varied from society to society, but in most some form of stratified multi-stage area probability sampling was used. All interviews were conducted in person with the exception of a few telephone interviews used to reach respondents in the most remote areas of Iceland. Although the World Values Surveys were collected over four waves, we only use data from the fourth wave (conducted in 1999–2001) in this volume. Weights were employed in the analyses to adjust for non-response and other forms of sampling error.

Sample sizes within each country varied a great deal, but most obtained data from at least one thousand respondents. Because the volunteering questions were not asked in all countries, we used a subset of the full data in our analyses. Limiting the data to respondents who were asked the volunteering questions, we obtained an overall sample size of approximately seventy-nine thousand respondents. This number of respondents was not always used, however, due to missing data on predictor variables for various countries. In addition, because we included data from outside sources (e.g., World Bank) that sometimes had missing or incomplete data for particular countries, we were not always able to use all of the countries where the volunteer question had been asked.

Volunteer work was measured by first showing respondents a list of fifteen groups and activities and asking which ones respondents belonged to. The list of groups included (a) social welfare services for elderly, handicapped, or deprived people, (b) religious or church organizations, (c) education, arts, music, or cultural activities, (d) labor unions, (e) political parties or groups, (f) local community action on issues like poverty, employment, housing, and racial equality, (g) third world development or human rights, (h) conservation, environment, and animal rights groups, (i) professional associations, (j) youth work (e.g., scouts, guides, youth clubs, etc.), (k) sports or recreation, (l) women's groups, (m) peace movement, (n) voluntary organizations concerned with health, and (o) other groups. For each group or activity named by respondents, they were asked for which they were doing unpaid voluntary work. This questioning sequence assumed that all volunteers are members of groups, and as such, probably does not capture volunteering done by people who do not belong to groups. Based on these measures, we created several indicators of volunteering.

Any volunteering Respondents who mentioned doing unpaid voluntary work for any activity or group, other than "other groups," were coded as having volunteered.

Volunteering types We created three variables to capture the different areas in which respondents volunteered. Because volunteering rates are very low in some countries, we could not use the categorization scheme we were able to use in the Independent Sector and Current Population Survey data sets. Respondents who mentioned doing unpaid voluntary work for any of the groups in each type were coded as having volunteered for that type.

Activism: (a) labor unions, (b) political parties or groups, (c) local community action on issues like poverty, employment, housing, and racial equality, (d) third world development or human rights, (e) conservation, environment, and animal rights groups, (f) professional associations, (g) women's groups, and (h) peace movement;

Service: (a) social welfare services for elderly, handicapped, or deprived people, (b) education, arts, music, or cultural activities, (c) youth work (e.g., scouts, guides, youth clubs, etc.), (d) sports or recreation, and (e) voluntary organizations concerned with health;

Religious: (a) religious or church organizations.

Number of groups This measure is a sum of the number of groups or activities for which respondents had done unpaid voluntary work.

Notes

2. What Is Volunteering?

1. As if these definitional problems were not enough, the advent of multi-country surveys of volunteerism has created even more severe difficulties because the meaning of volunteerism varies so widely from one country to another. "The British and American concept of volunteering, the French *voluntariat,* the Italian *voluntariato,* the Swedish *frivillig verkshamhet,* or the German *Ehrenamt* have different histories and carry different cultural and political connotations" (Anheier and Salamon 1999:48). For example, in Germany volunteering is associated with "honorary work," which is given a special interpretation as an activity necessary for upkeep of the political community. This is quite different, in meaning and scope, from the understanding of volunteerism in Anglo-Saxon countries, where politics and advocacy are pushed to the margins of volunteer work (Dekker and Halman 2003:2). These cultural differences make it very difficult to compare volunteer activities across countries. In light of these problems, some experts advise that the use of the word "volunteer" be avoided in multi-country surveys because of the ambiguity of the term. "Instead, the questionnaire should list various clearly defined types of behavior that are relevant to the survey, and then ask the respondents whether they have engaged in those forms and, if so, for how long" (Dingle 2001:23). But this only pushes the problem back to deciding that types of behavior are "relevant."

2. A follow-up study found international agreement on this net-cost definition. The more a person benefited from an activity, the less likely was that person to be thought of as a volunteer. The more costly the activity was to the person (e.g., it consumed more time), the more likely was that person to be defined as a volunteer. Opportunity costs, such as income and social pleasures foregone by doing volunteer work, were not, however, factored into this equation, probably because people simply do not see these costs when they think about volunteer work (Handy et al. 2000:63).

3. Kleidman (1994:264) argues against treating paid and unpaid labor as a dichotomy and proposes instead that we consider a "range of voluntariness" that varies by amount of compensation and sacrifice. This echoes an idea voiced earlier by Smith (1982), who suggested that all altruism is relative, the degree of altruism depending on the reward received. Employees working in non-profit organizations who work long hours, are poorly compensated, and have little or no job security should, perhaps, be considered "quasi-volunteers." Baldock and Ungerson (1991) describe people in Britain who agree to provide services under the supervision of a state agency or a non-profit organization working under contract to the state in return for a small stipend as "quasi-volunteers."

4. AmeriCorps was created in 1993 when President Clinton signed into law the National and Community Service Trust Act. The act provided for the establishment of the Corporation for National and Community Service and, under its auspices, the AmeriCorps program. The intention was to recruit volunteers aged 18–24 for one year of service to help in a number of areas: schools, community restoration projects,

working with the sick and the elderly, job training, environmental conservation, and public safety.

5. Frey and Goette (1999) demonstrated this in a study using the Swiss Labor Force Survey, conducted in 1997. Respondents were asked whether they performed "volunteer activities" and whether or not they had received financial compensation for it. One in five of the volunteers had been paid for their work. Volunteers who were paid worked four hours less a month. It would be premature to argue that this shows that offering financial incentives causes people to reduce the amount of volunteer work they do, but this one study does suggest that stipends can backfire.

6. Ellis and Noyes (1990:3) argue that social responsibility is the essence of volunteering. They ground this argument in motivation theory by conceding that what is important is that the volunteer believes his or her actions are socially responsible, whether or not outside observers might think so.

7. The imputation of improper motives helps explain why trade union activists are rarely treated as volunteer workers, even by social scientists. Theirs is seen as self-interested behavior. They are working to boost their pay, benefits, job security, working conditions, and the like. Trade union activists are also marginalized because they have not freely chosen to do the work—another motivational reason. Admittedly, membership in a trade union is frequently involuntary, as in a closed shop, and the same could be said of people who are active in professional associations, such as the American Medical Association, another activity likely to be excluded from the category of volunteerism. However, these reasons for exclusion are not persuasive because they apply to *membership*, not activism. On the first count, trade unions face a serious free rider problem: although only some are active, all members will benefit from gains achieved at the bargaining table. And even if membership is involuntary, activism is not. It is still necessary to explain why, of all those workers who are forced to join the union as a condition of their job, only a few volunteer. Self-interest is not absent from union activism. Studies indicate that active members tend to have a higher "stake" in their job—they have more seniority and they have more dependents—but this alone does not explain why a worker devotes free time to attending union meetings and running for elected office because not all those with a high stake volunteer. And in any case, the "greater stake" argument can be made about many other forms of volunteer work, such as mothers who volunteer for the PTA only while their children are in school, HIV-diagnosed people who become active in AIDS organizations, or home owners who become active in neighborhood clean up campaigns.

8. Teske (1997:84) draws a similar distinction between the "service-providing type" of activist, who engages in direct hands-on work with the disadvantaged, and the "social change activist," who sees social justice work as endeavoring to bring about fundamental change in the structure of society.

9. Volunteers occasionally express frustration at the "Band-Aid" approach of their work: "Sometimes I think I'm just kidding myself. I think I should just forget tutoring and mentoring, and field trips and summer camps and just go out and work as a political organizer—something like that—try to change the whole system" (Coles 1993:41).

10. Stewart and Weinstein (1997:810) maintain it is impossible to separate AIDS volunteerism from AIDS activism: "the personal and the political do not separate easily." Creating safe spaces for gay and lesbians to build their own communities of mutual support ("communion-oriented" work) is also a civil rights issue ("system-ori-

ented" work). Some AIDS volunteers are trying to build community awareness of AIDS. Some focus primarily on education to the gay community (e.g., distributing literature, manning hotlines). Some are there to provide emotional and practical support to AIDS patients. And yet, they acknowledge that these different tasks draw different kinds of people, suggesting that they are different in practice or in meaning. Those advocating political change tend to be young gay or bisexual males. Those offering individual support tend to be older and are more likely to be female and heterosexual. Those who focus more on education and outreach "were about one third female and heterosexual, and midway between the others in terms of age" (Stewart and Weinstein 1997:817).

11. Kayal's (1993:141) interviews with volunteers at the Gay Men's Health Crisis center in New York revealed that most volunteers wanted the organization to focus on taking care of people with AIDS, leaving the more political activities to other gay organizations. However, they also saw their volunteer work as "a political act or statement," and many agreed that the AIDS problem was one of public health as well as individual suffering. In the case of AIDS, the threat was not only to this or that individual but also to the gay community. AIDS volunteers wanted to alleviate the suffering of the ill and dying and to prevent others from contracting the disease, but they also wanted to save the "gay community" (Kayal 1993:131).

12. Another reason why the line between activism and volunteerism becomes blurred has to do with the idea that volunteering is about individuals and activism is about collectivities and collective action. This distinction does not withstand scrutiny in the light of empirical research on volunteerism and activism. In one important respect, all volunteer work targets collective goods. A person who helps out at a local food distribution center might do so because she feels compassion toward a hungry person, but her decision to contribute her time is influenced by how many others she believes are also likely to help. Working at the food distribution center involves no collective action in the conventional sense, but having insufficient numbers of people show up might well deter her from volunteering. Even volunteering to help the hungry feed themselves thus encounters the free rider problem. Volunteer organizers know this well, which is why recruitment often takes place through social networks. Religious congregations supply *teams* of volunteers for a given evening. This is a form of collective action.

13. A greater appreciation of the similarities between volunteerism and activism has also resulted from social movement scholars changing the way they think about activism. Formerly, they focused on highly contentious, non-routine events, tending to describe activists as rather unusual, even social misfits. More recently, they have begun to pay attention to the more mundane, local, and routine forms of advocacy and to acknowledge that activists might be more embedded in social institutions and social networks than those who remain on the sidelines. Social activism has thus been normalized and come to resemble in many ways participation in more conventional social organizations, such as trade unions, political parties, and voluntary associations. Today's social movement scholars freely admit, "most movement participants . . . are volunteers" and often use the words "activist" and "volunteer" interchangeably (Passy and Giugni 2001:124). Piliavin and Grube (2002:470) regret the exclusion of "attempts at structural change" from the studies of altruism, prosocial behavior, and volunteerism. Excluding social protest, acts of dissent, and other forms of community activism draws the boundaries around volunteerism too restrictively. We agree that

there is no point in treating the analysis of mechanisms of recruitment and participation of individuals in voluntary associations and in social movements as separate. How and why individuals decide to engage in the production of collective goods instead of acting as free riders reflects very similar logics in the two cases. (Diani 2001:7)

The very same cases are often treated as instances of social activism or volunteerism depending on the professional identities and affiliations of the researchers involved. To be sure, social movements are somewhat different from voluntary associations in focusing on conflict and being part of a broader collective entity (e.g., environmentalism), but the similarities are greater than the differences. This does not mean that all volunteer work takes place in the context of voluntary associations. Much of it is mobilized and organized by social institutions such as hospitals, schools, churches, and the like. Nevertheless, the argument is sound: it is wiser to treat volunteering and activism as part of the same *genus* than treat them separately. The distinction between care work and volunteering is somewhat more justifiable. The various tasks of the household such as taking care of kin, young and old, cooking, washing, cleaning, maintenance, and the like fall undeniably toward the obligatory end of the spectrum. Admittedly, time spent on these chores varies over time and varies across social groups, but they are primary roles, whereas volunteer work is a secondary role.

14. In the United Nations document referred to at the beginning of the chapter, informal helping is described as "unmanaged" volunteering:

Unmanaged volunteering is the spontaneous and sporadic helping that takes place between friends and neighbors—for example, child care, running errands, and loaning equipment—or in response to natural or man-made disasters. It is the dominant form of volunteering in many cultures. By contrast, managed volunteering takes place through organizations in the non-profit, public, and private sectors, and tends to be more organized and regular." (Dingle 2001:9)

15. The word "volunteer" derives from the Latin word *voluntas*, meaning choice.

16. This tendency to blur the line between care work and volunteer work seems to be especially common among women who, compared to men, "speak and act in ways that are more altruistic, more communal, more peaceful and more nurturing" (Schlozman et al. 1995:268).

17. For a number of years, social scientists have been asking people in a number of countries to keep diaries in which they record their activities on a designated day. One advantage time diary methods have over survey methods is that recall is not a problem. The Multinational Time Use Study (MITUS) aggregates data from twenty-three countries around the world, gathering information on time use in the previous forty-eight hours. The most recent surveys for which comparison data are available were conducted between 1989 and 1995. It is possible, by comparing the incidence of volunteering in the MITUS with the incidence of volunteering in the 1995 version of the World Values Survey, to see how the incidence rate varies. For example, in the World Values Survey 34% of Norwegians said they were "active" members of a voluntary association, compared to 4% who had volunteered within the past forty-eight

hours. In the United States, 42% of the World Values Survey respondents had volunteered during the past year, and 3% had volunteered in the past forty-eight hours. Only in the Netherlands were the figures close: 31% of the World Values Survey sample had volunteered in the past year and 28% of the MITUS sample had volunteered in the past forty-eight hours (Patulny et al. 2003). Respondents in the United Kingdom 2000 Time Use Survey were asked to keep time use diaries. On any given diary day, 3% of the respondents had spent time volunteering. But when they were asked if they had volunteered at any time in the past month the rate rose to 12% (Ruston 2003:5).

18. As far as age is concerned, the greatest disparity is found in the case of people aged between 34 and 50, who contribute 39% of the total hours although they comprise only 30% of the sample. Their ratio is two times higher than that for the under 25s. Whites over-contribute, with a ratio of 1.05, and "other" races under-contribute with a ratio of .60. The more highly educated the group, the higher its ratio: the ratio for people with advanced degrees is five times higher than that for high school dropouts. The same pattern is found with income, although the difference is not as pronounced: the ratio of the top earners is twice that of the poorest. Married people make up 63% of the sample but contribute 71% of the hours (ratio 1.13): their ratio is double that of widowed people. Parents make up 43% of the sample but contribute 51% of the hours. As far as employment goes, self-employed part-time workers contribute at a ratio of 2.01, twice that of retirees. Non-profit sector workers also have a high ratio of hours to sample size, two and a half times that of people working in the private sector. Professionals make up only 25% of the sample but contribute 40% of the hours. Their ratio is three times higher than blue-collar workers. Home owners assume a disproportionate share as do frequent church attenders (the ratio for the "every week" group is three times that of the "not at all" group). Interestingly, being asked affects the ratio. Those who were asked to volunteer make up 44% of the sample but contribute 81% of the hours. Their ratio is five times higher than those who were not asked.

19. A survey asked Illinois residents if they volunteered for any of six types of volunteer work at any time in the past year and, if so, whether they volunteered on a regular basis (Profile of Illinois 2001).

Type	Any	Regularly
Religious	36%	15%
Education	37%	14%
Social Service	35%	11%
Youth	22%	11%
Civic	14%	6%
Hospital	15%	5%
Arts	10%	4%

20. A 2003 study of Americans 45 and older found that, among those who had volunteered in the past month at all, only 38% said they had done so regularly, while 48% said they had no regular volunteer schedule (Kutner and Love 2003).

21. The Independent Sector survey, on which we rely most heavily, first asks respondents if they volunteered in the past month and if so, for which organizations. They are then asked how many hours they volunteered for each organization. They

are subsequently asked if they have done any volunteer work for organizations other than those mentioned in response to the first question. They are not asked how many hours they had volunteered for these additional organizations.

22. One thing is certain; the more prompts respondents are given the more volunteer activities they list (Steinberg et al. 2002:489). For example, a 1994 survey of several European countries first asked respondents if they had done any unpaid work in the previous year. Twenty-three percent said they had. The respondents were then prompted using a list of organizations for which they might have done unpaid work. The rate rose to 27% (Gaskin and Smith 1997:28).

23. The CPS changed its classification scheme between 2003 and 2004.

3. Personality

1. The association between personality traits and volunteering can be the result of certain kinds of personalities seeking out volunteer work or selective recruitment. For example, if volunteers assigned to desk work scored lower on empathy than volunteers assigned to deal with clients face-to-face, this might mean that less empathic people opt for the desk work, or it could mean that the volunteer agency has selected volunteers who seem more empathic people for work dealing directly with clients (Okun and Eisenberg 1992). Many volunteer agencies have training programs that "unsuitable" candidates fail to complete. If most people volunteering at a crisis counseling center score high on a personality trait such as empathy part of this reflects the fact that the agency will have rejected those who lack this characteristic.

2. We are aware that concepts such as self-efficacy and trust are considered by social psychologists to be components of the self-concept that are highly susceptible to influence by social situations. We will take up this issue in the conclusion.

3. Social psychologists do not necessarily subscribe to the view that these dispositions are personality traits.

4. The questions are, "Are you a talkative person?" "Do you usually take the initiative in making new friends?" "Do you tend to keep in the background on social occasions?" "Are you mostly quiet when you are with other people?"

5. Regardless of age, race, gender, education, income, occupation, marital status, level of participation in formal organizations, and informal social contacts.

6. The list consists of the following items, the numbers in parentheses being their loadings on the latent factor:

"We all have a right to concern ourselves with our own goals first and foremost, rather than with the problems of other people." (.69)

"I often become more irritated than sympathetic when I see someone crying." (.87)

"Individuals can do little to alleviate suffering in the world." (1.00)

"You cannot blame a person who is completely involved in important work for being insensitive to those around him." (.89)

"Most people with serious problems brought their problems on themselves." (.86)

7. Using the Youth-Parent Political Socialization Study to construct parent-child pairs, Jennings and Stoker (2001) found that parental scores on a standard trust measure in 1965 were only modestly correlated with the child's score. But the more important fact is that *the strength of this association did not waver in subsequent panels*

of the study (1973, 1982, and 1997). The children's trust scores hardly changed at all in twenty-four years. The correlation between the 1965 and 1973 score was $r = .32$; the correlation between the 1973 and 1982 score was $r = .43$; the correlation between the 1982 and 1997 score was $r = .46$ (Jennings and Stoker 2001:11). If the children were trusting in high school they were likely to be trusting in middle age.

8. Claibourn and Martin (2000) draw on data from the Youth-Parent Socialization Study to examine the influence of trust on changes in volunteering over time. In this panel study, information was gathered from high school students and their parents, beginning in 1965, with follow-ups in 1973 and 1982. Respondents were asked about whether they were "active" in nine types of voluntary association. This is not quite the same as volunteering. Respondents were also asked the standard question on personal trust: whether they believed other people, in general, could be relied on to be trustworthy, fair, and helpful. Level of trust in 1973 had no effect on change in activity level between 1973 and 1982.

9. Our findings thus contradict those of Herzog and Morgan (1993) and Thoits and Hewitt (2001), but this could result from using a different measure of efficacy. The Independent Sector question makes a direct reference to efficacy in the context of volunteer work.

10. The factor loadings are shown in parentheses.

11. Our conceptualization thus separates us from those who treat trust as a component of "social capital," stocks of which can become depleted. We agree with Veenstra (2000) that a distinction needs to be drawn between trust as a psychological attribute (with a rather continuous character), trust as a property of social relations (as in the trusting relations exhibited by close family members), and trust as a property of social systems (as in the trust people might have in currency exchanges). The last two kinds of trust are appropriate indicators of "social capital" because that term correctly refers to a group attribute, but surveys rarely measure them.

4. Motives

1. Among Canadians aged between 15 and 24, 59% of the full-time students gave "improve job opportunities" as one motive for volunteering, compared to 43% of those who were already in the labor force (Jones 2000:39). As one young volunteer put it, "I think at an early age I realized that . . . I would like to go into a medicine related field, and I figured the best way to see what was actually going on in a hospital was to become a volunteer" (Pancer and Pratt 1999:48).

2. Between 1997 and 2000 the level of participation of Canadians (15–24) in the labor force increased from 61.5% to 64.4% while their rate of volunteering declined from 33% to 29%. "By contrast, from 1987 to 1997, when job prospects for youth in Canada were not nearly as good, there was an increase in volunteerism among young people" (Canada Council on Social Development 2002:2).

3. Close to two-thirds (62%) of Canadian unemployed volunteers said they volunteered in order to improve their job prospects and an even higher proportion of people actively looking for work (78%) were volunteering for this reason. Some of the trade union volunteers surveyed by Fosh (1981:34) were motivated by a desire to become full-time, paid union officials. According to an accountant writing in a professional journal, "Pro bono activities can help you build confidence, increase your leadership and managerial skills, strengthen your organizational and planning skills

and increase your overall morale" (Steinberg 1999:5). A business executive told Moore and Whitt (2000:312), "You're damn right it's helpful to be on several boards. It extends the range of your network and acquaintances, and your experience. That's why you go on a board, to get something as well as give." Thirty percent of the EMS volunteers surveyed by Thompson (1993a) said their service on the squad had helped them obtain either their current or earlier employment. The coordinator of volunteering at a Woman's Health Clinic in Winnipeg noticed that many of her volunteers were university students in fields like social work who were looking for a chance to develop job-related skills (Adair 1997:25).

4. Including the protective function in the list of motivations reminds us that volunteer work can be one way of meeting emotional needs. Volunteering can be inspired by "hatred, desire for revenge, and a host of other motives that lead people to do something that then benefits their group" (Mansbridge 2001:245). Often, negative emotions created by the violation of moral principles, such as justice, will spur volunteer work. Some mothers who volunteer at day care centers clearly do so out of a feeling that, as mothers, it is their duty to get involved. They "regularly express feelings of guilt, regret, and longing when they are unable to meet expectations" (Prentice and Ferguson 2000:127).

5. All of these associations were net of controls for socio-economic status.

6. Non-volunteers were asked to rate the importance of a motive if they did choose to volunteer.

7. One study concluded, somewhat improbably, that there is only one motivation. Cnaan and Goldberg-Glenn (1991) surveyed 258 volunteers for human agencies and 104 non-volunteers. Their factor analysis of answers to twenty-eight motives questions reached a single factor solution. Twenty-two of the twenty-eight motives loaded on one factor comprising a scale with high reliability (alpha = .86). The authors conclude that there is an altruistic motivation indicating a general disposition to be helpful.

8. The analysis controlled for education and employment status.

9. Items are rated on a four-point scale ranging from the statement "never applies to you" (0) to the statement "applies to you very often" (3). Examples of items on the list are, "I believe that society cannot be responsible for providing food and shelter for all homeless people"; "I feel as though I have done nothing of worth to contribute to others"; "I have a responsibility to improve the neighborhood in which I live"; "I feel as though I have made a difference to many people."

10. It is somewhat surprising that the generativity concept does not figure more prominently in the psychological research on volunteerism because volunteer activities, in many cases, are generative activities, and generative concerns are often expressed through volunteerism. The parallels between this approach and the functionalist theory of motivation are quite striking. In particular, there is a great deal of similarity between the values motive and generativity. Snyder and Clary (2003) administered a survey to American undergraduates including both the Loyola Generativity Scale and the VFI. The correlation between the scale and the values motivation measure was $r = .26$ ($p = .002$). There were also modest associations between the generativity scale and all the other motivation measures except protective.

11. The questions on motivation in the Independent Sector surveys draw largely on the VFI. Because only some of the motivation questions were asked on more than one occasion, to conduct an analysis of pooled data we focused on the following items, with the VFI label noted in brackets:

"Volunteering makes me feel needed." [Enhancement]
"I feel compassion toward people in need." [Values]
"I can make new contacts that might help my business or career." [Career]
"Volunteering is an important activity to the people I respect." [Social]
"Volunteering allows me to gain a new perspective on things." [Understanding]
"Volunteering helps me deal with some of my own problems." [Protective]

Respondents were shown a list of reasons and asked if they thought each was very important, somewhat important, not too important, or not at all important. Every respondent answered the question for every reason, *even those who were not currently volunteering.* ("If you have not volunteered before, I'd like to know what reasons for volunteering would be important to you.").

12. Among Canadian volunteers, women were more likely to mention exploring personal strengths, while men were more likely to mention developing skills and gaining new experience and the fact that their friends volunteered (McClintock 2000:13). Okun et al. (1998:619) found that female volunteers had higher "protective motive scores" than male volunteers. For example, they were more likely than men to agree that "Volunteering helps me work through my own personal problems." In a small study comparing male and female medical students, Fletcher and Major (2004:111) found that women scored higher than men on four of the six motives in the VFI. However, we should note that a study of volunteers for homeless shelters and animal shelters found no difference in the motivation of the men and women involved (Ferrari et al. 1999:43).

13. In a modest but highly suggestive study Latting (1990) found that Whites were more likely to mention self-improvement motives for participating in a Big Brothers and Big Sisters of America program ("It seemed like an opportunity to learn new things"), while Blacks are more likely to mention community improvement motives ("I believed it was my duty to help contribute to the community").

14. The pattern of association between age and motivation in previous research is unclear because different studies use different measures of motivation. There are also occasional contradictions from one study to another even when measures are identical. Not surprisingly, younger people are more likely to say they volunteer in order to improve their job prospects or to gain work-related experience, explore their own strengths, and because their friends volunteer (i.e., peer pressure). For teenagers, volunteering is partly a way to fit in with the group and find one's identity. Older people are more likely to cite value motivations, including religious obligation and believing in the cause, and social motives such as a desire to meet new people (Black and Kovacs 1999:487; Bowen et al. 2000; Chappell and Prince 1997:346; Ferrari et al. 1999:44; Hall et al. 2001:46; McClintock 2000:13; Miller et al. 1990; Okun et al. 1998:619; Okun and Schultz 2003; Omoto et al. 2000:187; Schondel and Boehm 2000).

15. Among those already volunteering, however, education made no difference to the importance attached to this motivation, indicating its special significance for educated people who are not yet volunteering. [14]

16. Throughout this analysis we have controlled for socio-demographic and religious differences. The patterns of association we have uncovered are not, therefore, attributable to the fact that people from different social backgrounds both prefer different kinds of volunteer work and have different motivations for doing it. There is some tendency for people volunteering in different domains to give different reasons for doing volunteer work. This is a topic that deserves further investigation.

5. Values, Norms, and Attitudes

1. We will discuss the institutionalization of the volunteer role in chapter 19.

2. One survey asked respondents to agree or disagree with two statements designed to measure materialism. In each case, materialists were less likely to volunteer: "making a lot money is very important" (volunteers 35%, non-volunteers 51%); "materialism is an extremely serious problem" (volunteers 35%, non-volunteers 26%) (Wuthnow 1994a:253). In addition, respondents were asked to rate the importance of a number of topics to their "basic sense of worth as a person." Volunteers attributed more importance than non-volunteers to family, community, helping the needy, and one's relationship with God. Volunteers were more likely to say they wanted more out of life than just a good job and a comfortable lifestyle. They were less likely to say making money was very important to them (Wuthnow 1994a:243).

3. Steger et al. (1989) examined value differences between environmental activists and a random sample of the population of Ontario and Michigan. They distinguished materialist and post-materialist values. Materialist values were measured by giving priority to maintaining order in the nation and fighting rising prices. Post-materialist values were measured by giving people more say in important government decisions and protecting freedom of speech. Environmentalists in both countries were more likely to adhere to post-materialist values and slightly less likely to espouse materialism.

4. Almost all the difference between the affiliated and unaffiliated was due to the fact that the non-affiliated did not volunteer for church-related groups. Religious affiliation did not increase volunteer work at random; it simply gave the affiliated an additional opportunity to volunteer.

5. One study found no interfaith differences in volunteering (Smith 1998:39) and another study, of teenagers, found that, while Catholics were less likely to have volunteered in the previous month than Protestants and members of other religions, they were *more* likely than the other two groups to volunteer in connection with human services (Sundeen and Raskoff 1994:395).

6. One reason why Catholics volunteer less than Protestants might be that many Catholics attend parochial schools, which either do not encourage community service or fail to foster ideals conducive to volunteer work. But Dee (2003) found that adults who had attended Catholic schools were no less likely to have volunteered in the past month than people of the same cohort who had attended non-Catholic schools.

7. The mean number of social service programs reported by people attending mainline or liberal Protestant denominations was 3.9, compared to 3.9 for Jews, 3.5 for Catholics, and 2.2 for evangelical Protestants. Eighty-six percent of the mainline and liberal Protestant congregations participated in a social service, community development, or neighborhood project, compared to 68% of evangelical congregations.

8. We should note one study, based on a more limited sample, which found no difference in sponsorships by the denominational affiliation of the congregation (Cnaan 2002).

9. When people are asked specifically if they do community work *through* their churches almost twice as many evangelicals as mainline Protestants say they have done so. Evangelicals were much more involved in church activities overall. And level of overall church activity was strongly correlated with volunteer work in the areas of child and youth programs; helping the poor, sick, and homeless; civic and community

groups; and arts and culture organizations (Pew Research Center 2001:22). Liberal and mainline Protestants, on the other hand, are more likely to mobilize their congregants to volunteer directly for volunteer activities such as support programs for battered women, abused children, pregnant teenagers, migrants or refugees, and foster care (Hodgkinson et al. 1990). In short, mainline Protestants *are* more likely to volunteer in secular agencies than any other religious family, with evangelicals most likely to focus their volunteer efforts on religious organizations.

10. Warburton et al. (2001:597) showed elderly people a list of other people and asked them which of these people would expect them to volunteer. For each "other"—spouse, family member, friend, doctor, people in general, and charitable groups—volunteers were more likely to report expectations than non-volunteers.

11. It is hardly surprising that advocacy volunteering is frequently motivated by the conviction that people's rights are at stake. However, this conviction is rarely sufficient to mobilize volunteer energies. Norms themselves are not enough to instigate action, which has to be "triggered" by an event or experience, often emotional. Volunteers often speak of being "touched by" something that happened to them. In 1992, the NAMES Project AIDS Memorial Quilt was displayed on the mall in Washington, D.C. The quilt was displayed for three days. It required the participation of around four thousand volunteers to set up and break down the quilt each day, staff information booths, and the like. A sample of these volunteers was subsequently surveyed. The survey asked them about their participation in a variety of political activities, not all of them having to do with AIDS. They turned out to be "exceptionally well-educated, financially well to do, politically engaged, and ideologically intense" (Jennings and Andersen 2003:194). Most were either gay or lesbian. The most powerful predictor of involvement in political activities turned out to be having suffered pain or loss as a result of having a partner, friend, or family member become an AIDS victim. Surprisingly, this was a stronger predictor than the respondent's own HIV status. In this case, emotional arousal was necessary to spark the outrage informed by the justice principle.

12. Almost all (95%) of the American high school students surveyed in 1991 agreed that it is important for people to volunteer their time to community activities; 62% said it was *very* important. Seventy-one percent thought their communities would be better places to live if more adults volunteered (Wirthlin Group 1995b:8). Interestingly, Hispanics were the most likely (71%) to regard community service as an obligation, compared to African Americans (62%) or Whites (57%). Girls (67%) were more likely than boys (53%) to take the obligation seriously to the point of suggesting it be made a graduation requirement (Wirthlin Group 1995b:15).

13. Controlling for family status, religiosity, age, education, and gender.

14. The index consisted of the following items: "When something needs to be done, the whole community usually gets behind it"; "Community clubs and organizations are interested in what is best for all residents"; "Most everyone in (name of community) is allowed to contribute to local government affairs if they want to."

15. Controlling for education, family income, gender, age, formal and informal ties, and sense of community.

16. Not all those who are aware of or subscribe to a norm pay heed to it when time comes for action. Many more people express support for prosocial norms than actually behave prosocially and, as reported above, many people volunteer while simultaneously expressing only weak or no support for these norms. The National Sur-

vey on Philanthropy and Civic Renewal (1997–1998) asked respondents, "How important do you feel it is for community life for people to volunteer money and time to charitable organizations?" Six in ten of the respondents declared it to be "very important" (Ferree et al. 1998:5). The survey then asked respondents if they felt some obligation to volunteer time to community service. Only a fifth of those surveyed believed that volunteer work was an "absolutely essential" citizen obligation. To slightly more than half the respondents, volunteer work was "entirely a matter of personal preference" (Ferree et al. 1998:9).

17. It consists of two items:

"The need for charitable organizations is greater now than five years ago."
"Charitable organizations are more effective now in providing services than five years ago."

18. This factor consisted of the following items:

"Most charitable organizations are honest and ethical in their use of donated funds."
"Generally, charitable organizations play a major role in making our communities better places to live."
"Most charitable organizations are wasteful in their use of funds."
"Generally, charitable organizations make very little difference in dealing with major problems."

6. Socio-Economic Resources

1. Controlling for parents' occupational status, parents' volunteering, and their own frequency of church attendance.

2. This difference held up even after controls for parents' education, parents' volunteer activity, whether the school was public or private, and whether or not the school required or arranged community service activities.

3. Another study found that Britons who left school after age 21 volunteered at twice the rate of those who left school at age 18 (Smith 1998:31).

4. Controlling for gender, age, income, marital status, employment status, and frequency of church attendance.

5. This difference remained even after controls for other socio-demographic differences and church attendance. [50]

6. See Table 3 in chapter 13.

7. The exceptions are Herzog and Morgan (1993:133), who found no association between family income and the likelihood of volunteering, but their study was restricted to Americans aged 55 years or older; and Prouteau and Wolff (2003), who found that serving on the board or as an officer of a voluntary association was not associated with higher wages, but their sample is small and their measurement of volunteering limited.

8. One reason why income might make a difference to volunteering is that people on limited incomes have less favorable attitudes toward charitable organizations. Perhaps they regard them as mainly benefiting the middle class, whereas higher income people value charitable organizations because of their contribution to social order. To

test this hypothesis, we looked at the role played by the attitudes we discussed in chapter 5 in linking income with volunteering. As it turned out, income was not a very good predictor of these attitudes. In consequence, it is hardly surprising that the influence of income on volunteering cannot be explained by attitudinal differences. [51]

9. Segal (1993:47) found that volunteer hours were positively related to wages, but for men only. The implication is that single men will volunteer if they can afford it; single women will volunteer whether they can afford it or not. However, his sample included only single adults aged between 18 and 54. Carlin (2001:810) did not include a comparison group of men but found no effect of married women's wages on their volunteer participation. Significantly, however, family income from other sources (including the husband's wages) had a positive effect on the women's volunteer hours. This suggests that married women's volunteer time is less affected by the opportunity costs incurred because they are secondary earners. The loss of their income due to volunteering is less costly than would be the loss of income from the husband.

10. Nevertheless, as Jones (2006) discovered, social integration variables are more important when predicting volunteering and individual resource variables are more important when predicting giving.

11. In their analysis of charitable donations, Schervish and Havens (1997:254) found "Households in which the respondent expresses a social commitment by volunteering their [*sic*] time to one or more philanthropic organizations give an average of 0.1 per cent more of their household income to philanthropy for every five hours the respondent volunteers per month."

12. In Canada, the mean hours volunteered by managers in 1997 was 57.2, compared to 62.0 for professionals, 45.8 for white-collar workers, and 30.8 for blue-collar workers (Reed and Selbee 2000a:48). In Britain, professional and managerial workers volunteer at almost twice the rate of unskilled manual workers (Smith 1998:29). This pattern is confirmed in another British survey, the General Household Survey of 1992, which found that 40% of professionals, 33% of employers and managers, 35% of "intermediate non-manual" but only 12% of unskilled manual, and 17% of semi-skilled manual and personal service workers had volunteered in the past year. Forty-four percent of volunteers were either professionals or managerial workers, compared to 24% of non-volunteers (Goddard 1994:7). In Japan, the volunteer rate of professionals is 35.5%, for managers 39.3%, clerical 30.7%, sales 24.5%, service 27.1%, craft 26.4%, transport 21.3%, mining 21.9%, and laborers 27.1% (Statistics Bureau 2002).

13. This is precisely what Gomez and Gunderson (2003) found in their analysis of the 1994 Canadian General Social Survey data. After controlling for education, income, work schedule, hours worked, and various socio-demographic factors, people working in more prestigious jobs were slightly *less* likely to volunteer. However, another multivariate study of Canadians found that "production workers" were less likely to volunteer than office workers, sales people, or managers and professionals, regardless of income, hours of work, education, marital or parental status, or gender (Vaillancourt 1994:820).

14. A number of studies by industrial sociologists have demonstrated that workers with better quality jobs are more active in their leisure time overall and more likely to be active in community affairs, including volunteering. Conversely, blue-collar and service jobs tend to be highly stressful, tiring, and tightly structured, allowing workers little room for discretion over the pace and timing of work. Such jobs leave little

time or energy for very active leisure time pursuits and little taste for more "productive work" outside one's own job (Greenberg et al. 1996; Hagedorn and Labovitz 1968; Herzog and Morgan 1993; Meissner 1971; Parry et al. 1992; Roxburgh 2002; Sobel 1993; Torbert and Rogers 1973; Wilensky 1961).

15. Although these results are a striking confirmation of much previous research in this area, we should note that the workplace is not the only place to acquire and develop civic skills for volunteering, and perhaps not the most important. Ayala (2000) compared the contribution of civic skills learned on the job with that of the same civic skills learned in the context of a voluntary association. The effect of civic skills learned and used in the workplace was only half as strong as the effect of civic skills learned and used in voluntary associations. The impact of "job level" was insignificant with job skills in the model, which is partial confirmation of the idea that they mediate the effect of work on volunteering, but the fact that the effect was so weak in comparison with skills learned in non-profit organizations suggests that the *context* in which the skills are acquired and used makes a difference. Ayala (2000:109) believes this is because "As opposed to the workplace, where the decision to participate is much more a case of avoiding high penalties for inaction, the decision to perform most time-based political acts is similar in nature to the decision to take an active role in an NPO." In short, when people are coerced into performing "skill acts," such as organizing a meeting at work, they do not take away the same aptitudes for or inclination toward volunteer work in general. The idea that the workplace can be the training ground for civic participation should therefore be treated with caution: it may not be the best training ground.

16. Kelley et al. (2005:370) found that several of the volunteers working in needle exchange programs in San Francisco were paid as community health outreach workers "and would make contacts during their syringe-exchange volunteer shifts." There was little difference between the paid work for the public sector and their private work as volunteers. In some Canadian provinces social service workers are being coerced into "contributing" extra time to jobs, such as probation officer and child welfare worker. "One Alberta immigrant aid worker, who was paid for 20 hours a week reported that the part-time workers in her agency felt that 'it is an expectation that you will be there 40 hours per week'" (Baines 2004:281). Social service managers estimated that at least 60% of the volunteers working in connection with their agencies were public sector employees. More broadly, public sector employees were expected to volunteer to raise funds to help offset the cuts in public expenditures on their agencies. In Ontario, the provincial government has mandated that high school students do volunteer work as a requirement for graduation. Teachers are expected to "volunteer" their time to help supervise these activities (Brock 2001:56).

17. The 1996 Independent Sector Giving and Volunteering Survey found that the percentage of part-time self-employed respondents who volunteered (73.6%) far exceeded any other group surveyed (Hodgkinson and Weitzman 1996:D143). Self-employed workers also rank high in volunteering in the United Kingdom, Canada, and Japan (Jones 1999:10; Smith 1998:334; Statistics Bureau 2002).

18. Controlling for occupation, number of hours worked for pay, number of jobs, education, race, age, gender, and marital status.

7. Time and Health

1. A 2000 survey found that nearly half (47%) of employed Canadians were working for companies that provided some kind of support for volunteering. On average, volunteers who received employer support contributed more hours (151 a year) than those employees who did not receive support (131 hours a year). The most common type of support was approval to use equipment or facilities, followed by approval to take time off to volunteer and approval to modify work hours. The most effective kind of support (measured in hours volunteered) was being able to modify work hours. Interestingly, volunteers who received support from their employers were more likely to report job-related motivations for volunteering. Employers' support for volunteer work might not be entirely disinterested: they stand to gain if their employees enhance their job skills while volunteering ("Employer-Supported Volunteering," www.givingandvolunteering.ca).

2. This is true even for college students: those who have part-time jobs while in college have a higher volunteer rate (51.3%) than students not working (39.5%)—although students working thirty-five hours a week or more had the lowest rate of all (35.4%) (Horn and Berktold 1998).

3. One study, of Americans 45 years of age or older, found that those with zero work hours volunteered at a lower rate than the employed, but they contributed more hours a month if they *did* volunteer (Kutner and Love 2003). In a British study, volunteers not in the labor force contributed the most hours in the past month (17.2), followed by the unemployed (15.9), part-time workers (15.6), and full-time workers (14.1) (Goddard 1994:15). In the Canadian survey, the most hours (193) were contributed by those not in the labor force, followed by the unemployed (175), part-time workers (155), and full-time workers (145) (Lasby 2004:3).

4. This study, limited to young adults aged between 19 and 27, controlled for marital status, parental status, education, race and gender, and volunteering in the previous year.

5. Many European countries, faced with high levels of unemployment in the 1970s and 1980s, began discussing the role of volunteerism in providing skills training or useful work for those outside the labor market. In the United Kingdom, "a succession of special employment measures during the eighties and nineties stressed the part volunteering could play in training unemployed people for work" (Gaskin and Smith 1997:11). In 1982, for example, the Thatcher government provided eight million pounds sterling to the Manpower Services Commission to organize voluntary unpaid work for the unemployed. The Labor opposition attacked the scheme as "slave labor" to do work that should have been undertaken by local authorities. Proponents pointed to a safeguard in the program that prevented projects from involving work what would put existing jobs at risk. Critics also worried that unemployed people would be reluctant to take on volunteer work at the risk of losing unemployment benefits for which looking for work was a requirement. Although only 3% of respondents to a 1994 United Kingdom survey gave this as a reason for why they were not volunteering (i.e., concerns about losing unemployment benefits), we do not know how high this might be amongst the unemployed.

6. Taniguchi (2006) found the same gender difference in the MIDUS data.

7. We controlled for whether the respondent was retired and also for the usual socio-demographic and religious variables.

8. This is no trivial measurement issue. A recent Canadian study of volunteering found that 81% of all volunteer hours were contributed by just one-third of the volunteers. This implies the existence of a relatively small group of people who are intensely committed to volunteer work and possibly impervious to the time demands of their job.

9. This pattern is also found in Japan. A 2001 survey found that the more time Japanese workers spent commuting the less likely they were to volunteer. Thirty-six percent of Japanese who worked at home volunteered, compared to 28.6% of those whose one-way commute was between fifteen and thirty minutes and 20.4% of those who commuted two hours a day one way (Statistics Bureau 2002).

10. Her interviews revealed that women became volunteers because they were linked to other people while men became volunteers *in order to* link to other people.

11. Rossi (2001b:106) found no relation between time spent giving "unpaid assistance" to relatives, neighbors, and friends and time spent volunteering.

12. For example, among those who volunteered for just one area, 24% had helped informally during the past year, compared to 75% of those who had volunteered in six or more areas.

13. Because the author was interested in the division of labor between husbands and wives, only married people were included in this study.

14. This study does not distinguish between caring for family members and housework.

15. Psychological distress was a latent factor comprised of perceived stress and depression symptoms.

16. Gomez and Gunderson's (2003) analysis of the Canadian General Social Survey data from 1994 showed the same pattern. Respondents who rated their health as poor or fair were less likely to volunteer than those who rated their health as good, very good, or excellent, even after controlling for socio-demographic variables. Identical results were found in a study of the Canadian survey data on volunteering from 2000 (Ravanera et al. 2002).

17. Chambre (1987:110) suggests that good health increases life satisfaction: "People in poorer health are pitied by other older people. By extension, being in excellent health places an older person in an envied position relative to others which, in turn, either improves or reinforces higher levels of well being." Greater satisfaction with life, in turn, encourages elderly people to volunteer.

18. Other studies of older populations have arrived at very similar results (Gallagher 1994a:573; Kincade et al 1996:481; Okun 1993:67). Baum et al. (2000) suggest that the positive effect of physical health might well vary by the type of volunteer work. They found that participation in a "volunteer group" and engaging in a campaign to improve social or environmental conditions were both positively related to physical health—but only for those over 65—and several types of community engagement that would normally be included under the heading of volunteer work, such as participating in a political campaign, working on behalf of a trade union, working with a community action group or a school-related group, were not related to health at all.

19. In another analysis of the ACL data we factor analyzed the items to create a combined health score. After controls for socio-economic status we found that health had a *negative* effect on hours volunteered. There are a number of possible explanations for this somewhat surprising result. The first is that our analysis factored in

whether or not the respondent was providing help informally. We found that healthier people were more likely to provide health informally. The chances are that healthy people were volunteering less because they were providing more informal care (Wilson and Musick 1997a). Another possible explanation is suggested by Rossi (2001b:118) who, in an unpublished analysis of the MIDUS data, found that health self-rating was consistently negatively associated with volunteer service. She attributes this to the fact that people in "truly excellent health may prefer to spend their leisure hours in more active pursuits" than volunteer work.

8. Gender

1. We do not mean to imply that the distinction between private and public domains is so rigid that women cannot overcome it. Indeed, volunteer work can be one way in which women break down this barrier. Women who become active in their communities do so, in part, because they are mothers. Their mothering role leads them to be active. But this activism transforms how they think about the identity "mother" by questioning the barrier between private and public that, according to traditional conceptions of mothering, confines helping behavior to the domestic sphere (Abrahams 1996:770). Black women who volunteered to work for a local advisory council to organize youth programs and block watches and plan events in a public housing project in Chicago treated the project as an extended family network: they were often called "mothers" by unrelated activists (Feldman and Stall 2004:95). Nevertheless, we maintain that there are domains of volunteer work where the service ethos is more pronounced and these domains are more closely associated with women, whereas there are domains of volunteer work that are more political, more advocacy driven, more instrumental, and these are the domains in which men choose to be active.

2. Recent experiments on Israeli adolescents cast doubt on the argument that females volunteer more than males *because* they have a stronger ethic of care. The teenagers were asked a battery of questions intended to measure their gender role orientation. Another set of questions measured how strongly they were committed to an ethic of care. They were also asked if they would be willing to volunteer for one of two projects (e.g., tutoring children in socio-economically deprived areas). The researchers found that girls and individuals (of either sex) who scored highly feminine on the gender role orientation measure had higher caring scores than boys and individuals who scored high in masculinity: that is, both gender and gender role orientation made a difference to how strongly adolescents felt they should care about, and for, others. (Interestingly, gender accounted for more of the variation in the adoption of an ethic of care than gender role orientation.) Turning to the volunteer measure, the researchers found that girls were more likely to express a willingness to volunteer than boys, but caring scores made no difference to willingness to volunteer among the girls, although they did increase the willingness of boys to volunteer. Ironically, an ethic of care, argued by Gilligan to motivate more care work on the part of females, made a difference only among males (Karniol et al. 2003). This very limited study attempting to link gender, gender role orientation, an ethic of care and volunteering deserves replication.

3. Controlling for race, parents' education and income, number of parents in the household, academic performance, public or private school, and whether or not the school arranged community service.

4. We also analyzed the World Values Survey data to see if gender differences existed after controls for socio-economic and religious variables. We used as a measure having volunteered during the past year and we pooled the data from different countries. We found that women were *less* likely to volunteer than men. [59] In the United States, women volunteer at a higher rate than men; in Europe it is the reverse.

5. One study of a hospice day care center in the United States found that only one in ten volunteers was male (Field and Johnson 1993:1627) and another in New Zealand reported an almost identical distribution (Payne 2001:111).

6. Handy and Srinivasan (2004) conducted a survey of hospital volunteers in Ontario, Canada, whose work consisted mainly of accompanying patients on outings, offering companionship, providing support to patients and families in waiting rooms, shopping and doing errands, and taking patients from one facility to another. Three-quarters of the volunteers were female. Phillips et al. (2002b) studied forty-nine volunteers working in agencies providing home and community care services to the elderly and disabled. Once again, three-quarters of the volunteers were women.

7. A Canadian survey found that men were more likely than women to belong to trade unions, political parties, professional associations, and sports and recreation groups. Women were more likely than men to belong to social welfare, religious, education and cultural, women's groups, animal rights organizations, and health associations. Gender made little or no difference to membership in community action, third world development, and environmental groups (Woolley 1998:28).

8. Controlling for race, age, education, employment status, and marital and parental status.

9. The items were "I find it hard to be sympathetic toward starving people in foreign lands when there is so much trouble in our own country"; "Maybe some minority groups do get unfair treatment, but that's no business of mine"; "I get very upset when I see people treated unfairly"; "I would agree to a good plan to help the poor even it is cost me money"; "It's not really my problem if others are in trouble and need help."

10. For details on how these variables were measured see chapter 3.

11. For how these measures were constructed, see chapter 5.

12. Some feminists might regard the "power" women enjoy as volunteers as not very consequential, largely circumscribed by the superior power of men. For example, Little (1997) describes how, by serving on committees of local voluntary organizations, women in the rural parts of England gain entry into the politics of the local community. By helping to organize and operate local charitable organizations they identify themselves as someone who should be consulted about village activities. At the same time, of course, this work reflects their powerlessness in the public world of jobs and electoral politics and, often, in the domestic sphere as well: "Male approval for the amount and type of voluntary work of women appeared to be a very necessary basis for that involvement" (Little 1997:262). In many respects the women's volunteer work was expressive rather than instrumental, part of a package of activities intended to maintain and protect the rural way of life. Several women interviewed felt trapped in the volunteer role, having taken care of an individual, group of individuals, or organization in some way and feeling that the welfare of those they had helped would suffer were they to stop volunteering.

13. This is not to deny that, for some women, volunteering is a means of getting a job (Mueller 1975:334; Stephan 1991:228). Women in general are different from

men in how they regard their volunteer role, but not all women are alike. Some see their volunteer work as a career, a substitute for a job, but others see their volunteer work as only a temporary replacement for a job they would prefer to have (Jenner 1981).

14. There is another line of argument that points to a different hypothesis: that women are more affected by their work role than men. The volunteer role has traditionally been seen as women's work. If men get some free time, they are less likely than women to fill this free time with volunteer work. This should mean that the influence of work hours on volunteering is stronger for women than men. As women get more free time they feel more pressure to fill it up with "good works." A number of studies support this hypothesis. Wuthnow (1994a:239) found that men with part-time jobs were no more likely to volunteer for their church than men with full-time jobs. While women who worked full-time were slightly more likely to volunteer than all men, women who worked part-time were even more likely. In short, work hours made a difference to the religious volunteer work of women but not men. British data (from 1992) show that the positive effect of part-time work (over full-time work) was stronger for women than men (Goddard 1994:7). In Australia, the gender difference in rate of volunteering among full-time workers was only three percentage points but among part-time workers it was thirteen percentage points (Australian Bureau of Statistics 2002). Time diary data from Britain show that men enjoy about an hour more free time (i.e., free from all demands) at the weekends than women, but this has no effect on their relative rate of volunteering (Ruston 2003:5). Taniguchi (2006) uses MIDUS data to show that, relative to full-time employment, part-time employment encourages women's volunteer work but not men's. (This might be a function of the fact that few men work part-time—a larger sample might reveal an association.)

15. This was the conclusion of a study of the connection between occupation, gender, and political participation. (This is not a study of volunteering as such, although the index of political participation does include volunteering for a political campaign.) Men were more likely to participate in politics because they were more likely than women to have professional and managerial jobs, and their jobs were more likely to provide the kinds of experiences (e.g., supervising others) associated with the volunteer role (Schlozman et al. 1999).

16. The interaction measure was constructed from a list of seven items asking respondents how often they spent a social evening or spent time with a list of friends and acquaintances (e.g., friends at work, in the neighborhood.)

17. Gallagher (1994b) found no gender difference in the number of hours spent volunteering by the elderly, nor did she find that men and women volunteered for different types of work: men were just as likely to volunteer for "charity work" (helping the poor, sick, elderly, or other needy persons) as women. Nor did older men and women divide volunteer labor. Controlling for age, health, income, race, and employment, only fund-raising was gendered—and men did more of it than women. One explanation for this lack of gender difference in her sample is that the men and women belonged to pretty much the same type of voluntary association. Only in groups whose membership was almost entirely male (e.g., fraternal orders, veterans groups, or service groups such as the Kiwanis) were men more involved than women: "if an ethic of care is to be found in the types of groups to which older men and women belong, it is a gender neutral ethic of care reflecting a long history of helping others" (Gallagher 1994b:83). The small size of her sample (thirty-two men and fifty-five

women) means she might have missed significant effects that would have shown up in a larger sample.

18. It could be the case that men might under-report and women over-report some kinds of helping behavior because of the normative expectations attached to gender (Roker et al. 1999a:190).

9. Race

1. One study found that Black professionals were more likely to volunteer than White professionals (Chambre 1987:77).

2. A 2004 special study of Hispanics in the United States reported higher volunteer rates than the CPS survey cited earlier. Overall, 53% of respondents said they had volunteered in the previous twelve months: just over a third (35%) had volunteered for a church or religious group, 27% had volunteered for a school or tutoring program, 21% had volunteered for a neighborhood, business, or community groups, and 12% had volunteered for a nationality or ethnic or racial group (Pew Hispanic Center 2004).

3. Although Black volunteers might be more generous with their time, the fact that a smaller proportion of them volunteer means they contribute less than their "fair share" of the volunteer hours. [1] Blacks make up 11% of the sample and contributed almost 11% of the total volunteer hours, for a ratio of .98. Whites make up 78% of the sample but contributed 82% of the hours, for a ratio of 1.05. Hispanics make up 8% of the sample but contribute 6% of hours, for a ratio of .79.

4. A study of adult Canadians found that recently arrived immigrants were more likely than established residents to give as a reason for not volunteering that nobody had asked them ("The Giving and Volunteering of New Canadians," www.givingandvolunteering.ca).

5. An analysis of data from a nationally representative sample of Americans (1990 Citizen Participation Survey) and a 1994 Texas survey of minority groups also found that the rate of volunteering varies by immigration status. In the Texas survey 14% of the first generation Hispanics and 16% of the Asian Americans worked with others to solve local problems, compared to 34% of the third generation Hispanics and 40% of the third generation Asian Americans (Junn 1999:1425). (The author did not report regression results for this activity but instead used overall political participation as a dependent variable. Controlling for socio-economic status, the longer members of either ethnic group had been in the country, the more politically active they were.)

6. The first variable (frequency of telephone contact with friends, neighbors, and relatives) used a six-item response scale with ranges from (1) never to (6) more than once a day. The second variable (frequency of going out or visiting with friends, neighbors, and relatives) also employed a six-item response format where values ranged from (1) never to (6) more than once a week.

7. Controlling for education, income, functional health, age, gender, marital and parental status,

8. We used three different dependent variables: any volunteering in the past twelve months, number of volunteer activities, and number of hours donated in the past month by those who volunteered in the past month. We measured social networks by frequency of church attendance, number of voluntary associations member-

ships, and level of informal social interaction, constructed from a list of seven items asking respondents how often they spent a social evening or spent time with a list of friends and acquaintances (e.g., friends at work, in the neighborhood).

9. Blacks are more religious than Whites, by any measure used (Robinson and Godbey 1997:225; Taylor 1988; Taylor et al. 1996).

10. Controlling for education, income, religious salience, and functional health.

11. This pattern of results seems to confirm that Black churches play a more prominent role in the philanthropic life of the African American community, which is why church attendance is so influential a resource for Black volunteering. Interestingly, however, social surveys show little support for the argument that Black churches are more engaged in their communities. A 1998 survey of 1,236 religious congregations in the United States asked informants (typically the pastor), "Has your congregation participated in or supported social service, community development, or neighborhood organizing projects of any sort within the past 12 months?" Informants reported on the number of social service programs, the amount of money spent on social services in the past twelve months, and the number of volunteers from the congregation working on social services. Defining a congregation as Black if at least 80% of the membership was African American, Tsitsos (2003) found that African American congregations were more likely to support tutoring and substance abuse programs and less likely to support clothing programs but, overall, *there were no racial differences in the level of support congregations gave to social service programs.*

12. Not only are Whites more likely to be recruited, they are more likely to accept if asked. African Americans seem to be more skeptical of the utility of "charitable" solutions to their problems. They are more likely than Whites to say they have no interest in volunteering or that people should be paid for their time. [12]

13. The author of one report speculated that the lower rate of volunteering on the part of African Americans might be a consequence of being less trusting of "neighbors, coworkers and club members" (Kohut 1997:25).

14. Only three studies have found *higher* rates of volunteering among Blacks than Whites after controls for social class. Kohut (1997:37) found that Blacks were marginally more likely to volunteer than Whites; Freeman (1997) found that Blacks volunteer more *hours* than Whites; Fischer and Schaffer (1993) found that Blacks volunteer more than Whites, but their sample was restricted to the elderly.

15. If religiosity and class were highly correlated this argument would make little sense because it would make no difference whether we were measuring religion or class, but Black religion is less stratified along class lines than White religion (Beeghley et al. 1981:407). Not only are Blacks more uniformly religious than Whites, but also the Black church is less differentiated from community and secular life than is the White church (Lincoln and Mamiya 1990:187).

16. "Informal philanthropy remains the most prominent way that African-Americans display their giving and serving traditions" (Hall-Russell and Kasberg 1997:6).

17. "In poorer communities, taking care of one's children is almost as much an obligation to the peace, security, and well-being of neighbors and fellow community members as it is the success and comfort of the next generation of the family" (Newman 2001:161).

18. To some extent these ethnic differences are a function of the poverty of re-

cent immigrants to the United States. "Guatemalan people are very hospitable and kind; they want you to eat with them and so on. People are poor and can't really give money. There is not really an infrastructure for formal giving. People are very caring and giving" (Smith et al. 1999:56).

10. The Life Course: The Early Stages

1. Young adults are less familiar with the volunteer role: 29% of Canadians aged 15–24 but only 18% of those aged between 35 and 44 cited as a reason for not volunteering that they did not know how to do so (Lasby 2004:10).

2. Longitudinal data clearly show this decline in volunteering as people make the transition from adolescence to young adulthood. In the Youth Development Study, half the people who were volunteering in 1992, when they were aged 18 or 19, had quit volunteering by 2000, when they were aged 26 or 27 (Oesterle et al. 2004).

3. The same pattern of preferences is found in the United Kingdom, where young adults are drawn mostly to sports-related volunteering, while advocacy volunteering is more popular in the 45–54 age group (Smith 1998:48).

4. If this is the case, one explanation for why a person is currently volunteering is that he or she has volunteered before. In a longitudinal study of women who were first interviewed in the 1920s, the correlation between volunteering in 1940 and 1950 was $r = 0.3$ and the correlation between volunteering in 1950 and 1960 was $r = 0.4$. Although previous volunteer experience accounted for only 9–16% of the variation in current volunteering, this is nevertheless an impressive demonstration of the enduring influence of previous volunteering, considering the time that had elapsed between interviews (Johnson et al. 2004). If cohorts are tracked at shorter intervals the connection becomes even stronger.

5. Just over two-thirds (67%) of American high school students surveyed in 1995 were *currently* volunteering (Wirthlin Group 1995b:11). According to a special survey of U.S. teenagers conducted in 1992, 60% had performed volunteer work in the past twelve months, boys and girls equally, averaging 3.5 hours a week for each volunteer. The most popular type of volunteer work was in connection with a religious organization. Twelve- and 13-year-olds were just as likely to volunteer as 17-year-olds, although older teens were engaged in a wider range of volunteer activities and they contributed more hours. Just over half (56%) of the 12-year-olds said they had done volunteer work when they were even younger (Brown 1999b:29; Wuthnow 1995:261). The National Longitudinal Survey of Youth found that 58% of the teenage girls and 42% of the teenage boys had volunteered in the last year (Hart et al. 1999:380).

6. If the parents volunteer, the children are likely to volunteer also (Hall et al. 2001:39; Hofer 1999:119; Nolin et al. 1997:12; Roker et al. 1999a; Rosenthal et al. 1998:490; Sundeen and Raskoff 1994:392; Wuthnow 1995:260; Yates and Youniss 1998).

7. "Volunteering teaches us ways in which to be kind that are limited, that pertain to strangers, and that do not require an investment of our entire being" (Wuthnow 1995:105).

8. For Rossi (2001c:290), the pathway from parents to children is somewhat more complex. She believes that generative parents tend to have children who score high on personality traits such as communion and agency. (As we saw in chapter 3,

generativity is a measure of commitment to the next generation and to activities that contribute a positive legacy that will outlive the self. It is measured by agree/disagree items such as, "You feel that other people need you.") Communion is a personality trait measuring agreeableness, helpfulness, caring, and sympathy. Agency is a personality trait measuring self-confidence, forcefulness, and assertiveness. According to Rossi, more generative parents tend to have children who are more caring, helpful, self-confident, and assertive, and these children, in turn, are more likely to volunteer.

9. Eisenberg (1992) argues that children are more likely to engage in prosocial behaviors if they have been raised in warm and loving families by parents who were emotionally available and supportive and who taught the importance of helping others.

10. "Our interview data cast doubt on the assumption that children must see their parents volunteering . . . to begin volunteering themselves" (Wuthnow 1995:47).

11. The study was limited to two-parent families including a seventh-grade child and a sibling close to that child in age.

12. Jennings and Stoker (2001) looked at the influence of parents' voluntary association activity on their children's activity. The regression coefficient estimating the effect of parental *overall* activity in 1965 on children's overall activity in 1973 was $b = 0.10$. This is quite modest, but stronger effects were found where the parent was active in a religious congregation or an ethnic or racial group.

13. The study controlled for student's academic performance and whether the student was attending a public or private school. The positive influence of parental socio-economic status on children's volunteering lasts into adult life (Planty and Regnier 2003:5).

14. This particular panel is not representative of all Americans in that age range. The sample consists of young people born to women aged 14–21 in 1979 who were unmarried and poor. They are already "at-risk" children, likely to have relatively high rates of antisocial behavior and low rates of volunteering.

15. The survey did not measure volunteer work specifically but included a battery of questions on "political participation" (e.g., contacting public officials, engaging in protests and demonstrations, and working on a campaign), which we treat as a proxy measure.

16. The actual measure was "level of activity" in a voluntary association.

17. It should be noted, however, that, for other groups, the effect of youth volunteering is positive. Although this analysis confirms that youth volunteering is an important foundation for later volunteering and this relation is not simply the side effect of attitudinal differences, it is important to note that the attitudes in this study are measured when the respondent is an adult, not a teenager, and a further test of the hypothesis that the link between volunteering across the life course is indeed a matter of building on experience would require a measure of the attitudes people had when they were young.

11. The Life Course: The Later Stages

1. It is possible that the men were using volunteer work to find a new partner.

2. This analysis controlled for children, age, labor force participation, education, income, and church attendance.

3. This might be the result of cohabiting unions being newer than marriage unions but the CPS does not provide data on length of marriage.

4. Parents of preschool children have about four hours less free time per week than those with older children and about nine hours less than married couples without children (Robinson and Godbey 1997:130). When Illinois residents were asked why they had cut back on their volunteering hours, 20% gave the birth of a child or the illness of an aging parent (Profile of Illinois 2001).

5. A number of volunteers in the Girl Guide Association in the UK signed up to help because they had a child in the guides and were concerned to prevent their local unit from closing (Bussell and Forbes 2002:249).

6. The 1992 UK General Household Survey shows how children affect the likelihood of volunteering. Only 22% of the childless had volunteered in the past year compared to 35% of those with three or more children. The number of dependent children under 16 in the household increased the likelihood of volunteering for both men and women. The age of the youngest dependent child told an even more revealing story. Only 18% of those with a child younger than 2 had volunteered in the past year compared to 35% of those whose youngest child was between 5 and 9 years old (Goddard 1994:7). Among volunteers, 37% of the parents of children under 2 years of age volunteered only one to five days in the past year, compared to 25% of parents of children between 5 and 9. Conversely, 10% of parents of very young children volunteered for fifty to ninety-nine days, compared to 16% of parents of school age children (Goddard 1994:13).

7. A few studies have reported contradictory findings. For example, Moen (1997:139) found that preschoolers in the household had a *positive* effect on women's volunteering compared to having school age children. One explanation for this might be that the measure of having school age children is actually a measure of the total number of children the woman has, and having lots of children in the house might inhibit volunteering, but the Goddard study cited above shows a positive effect for the number of children. Time diary data from 1976 analyzed by Carlin (2001:815) showed that married women with children under 6 in the household were less likely to volunteer: however, they contributed more hours if they did so. Data from the Youth Development Study spanning a nine-year period in young people's lives (18–19 to 26–27) showed parents of preschoolers were about half as likely to volunteer as respondents without children, but school age children did not have the expected positive effect (Oesterle et al. 2004). Mustillo et al. (2004), on the other hand, found that, whereas school age children did have the expected positive effect on mother's volunteering, preschool children did not have a negative effect—they simply had no effect at all. Clearly, this is an issue that deserves further exploration. For example, studies need to pay more attention to the employment status of the parents because it might be easier for a homemaker mother to volunteer while caring for young children than it is for a woman working full-time outside the home, an issue we discuss in the following section.

8. One study found that mothers who worked thirty-five or more hours a week were less likely to be highly involved in their children's schools than mothers who worked part-time (Nord et al. 1997:51). In this case "involvement" meant attending a general school meeting, a regularly scheduled parent-teacher conference, or a school or class event or volunteering in the child's school.

9. Young mothers can be socially isolated by having to tend to their children (Munch et al. 1997). Research has shown that having preschool children in the house cuts into the free time of both mothers and fathers but the effect is three times as strong for women as men (Schlozman et al. 1999:42).

10. Adjusted for other demographic variables, such as gender, race, age, and education.

11. As one parent put it, "[Politics] is not what's important to me. My family's what's important to me. Especially now as a single parent . . . If I have time, I want to spend it around the home with my children. I'm very active in church stuff" (Klatch 2000:516).

12. A survey of Black Americans' voluntary association memberships found that the more children they had the more likely they were to belong to church-related organizations, block clubs, the PTA, sports clubs, and women's rights and veterans' groups, and the less likely they were to belong to political and civil rights organizations (Woodard 1987).

13. Holding constant gender, occupational prestige in 1986, race, education, age, and church attendance in 1986.

14. This is not specifically a measure of volunteering, but one of the groups of organizations they were shown was civic groups, such as voluntary service organizations, environmental groups, political parties, and scouts or guides associations, which we treat as a proxy measure of volunteering.

15. They do not single out volunteer work as a measure of social participation but include it in a composite index in which the other two items are attendance at the meetings of organizations, programs, or groups and attendance at religious services.

12. Social Resources

1. We constructed a mean score for each respondent by summing all the informal social interaction measures.

2. With controls for demographic and religious variables and number of memberships.

3. The positive association between number of extra-curricular activities and volunteering held up even after controls for academic performance, grade in school, parental education, and whether or not parents were volunteering.

4. Because membership in voluntary associations is not random but structured by race, gender, age, and socio-economic differences, we control for these factors in our analysis, together with informal interaction and church attendance.

5. The most popular type of organization was school-related: 13% were members. Membership rates in the other types of organization were fraternal order 3%; sorority, fraternity or alumni group 8%; civic organization 8%; professional association 11%; voluntary association 8%; religious organization 7%; political organization 7%; veterans' organization 6%; labor union 7%; and "other" 10%. [88]

6. Controlling for socio-demographic and religious variables.

7. Although respondents were allowed to name more than seven memberships, we truncated this graph at seven because so few respondents exceeded that number. The chart predicts the probability of volunteering. In the group made up of very trusting people who belong to seven or more groups the predicted probability is .95, meaning that 95% of the group volunteer. In contrast, the predicted probability of people in the low trust, zero-membership group is about .05, meaning that only 5% of the people in this group would be volunteers.

8. We created two dummy variables to measure intensity. The first is coded 1 if the respondent said he or she participated only a few times a year or not at all and 0 if

otherwise. The second is coded 1 if the respondent said he or she participated once or twice a month or every week or nearly every week and 0 if otherwise.

9. To test this hypothesis, we created a summary variable where 1 = non-member or member but not active, 2 = only a few times a year, and 3= participated once or twice a month or every week or nearly every week.

10. There are numerous examples of studies that use social resources to connect an exogenous variable with volunteering. For example, social resources have been shown to explain the link between education and volunteering (Liu and Besser 2003:361; Nie et al. 1996:75; Wilson and Musick 1997a); church attendance and volunteering (Wilson and Janoski 1995); and extroversion and volunteering (Herzog and Morgan 1993:136).

11. We partially replicated this study using data from the Independent Sector survey by constructing interaction terms for number of memberships and level of education and for number of memberships and income. [79] We looked at three measures of volunteering: any volunteer work at all; range of volunteering; and (for those who volunteered) number of volunteer hours. The influence of memberships on the odds of volunteering actually *declined* as education increased. The same was true of income: the more income the respondent earned, the weaker the effect of memberships on the odds of volunteering. We then looked at the range of volunteering. The result for income was exactly the same but education made no difference to the effect of memberships. Finally, we looked at hours volunteered. Memberships had the same effect regardless of education, and their influence on hours volunteered became weaker as income increased. These results contradict those found in our earlier study. This could be due to different measures of the variables or a different sample but this interesting question deserves more attention. It is highly unlikely that individual and social resources operate independently of each other, and their precise interaction needs to be better understood.

12. Wuthnow (1995:163) found that, among teenagers, females were more likely to volunteer in the company of friends, to see volunteering as a way to make friends and have a social life, and to indicate that peer approval and support was an important condition for their volunteering. Social relations seemed to play a more crucial mobilizing role for girls than boys. Boys were more likely than girls to seek out volunteer opportunities on their own. Among the elderly, women linked their involvement as volunteers to their existing friendships with other women. Men mentioned this pathway less often: they were more likely to volunteer *in order to* make friends (Gallagher 1994b:84). Another study suggesting that social resources are more important for women than men focused on farm couples. Spouses were asked if they volunteered in connection with a political organization at any time over the past five years. Sixteen percent of the husbands and 14% of the wives had volunteered, a statistically insignificant difference. However, wives were more likely to have been drawn into volunteering by memberships than were husbands. Wives were more likely to have volunteered if they belonged to traditional farm organizations, commodity organizations, or political action groups. Only belonging to a commodity organization made any difference to the husbands' volunteering (Meyer and Lobao 1996).

13. Wuthnow (2004:107) found that people who attend religious services weekly or almost weekly were more likely to have done volunteer work than those who attended once or twice a month or only a few times a year. The widest gap was found in

the case of activities related to the church, schools, youth development, and the distribution of food, and the narrowest gap was found in the case of building houses for the poor, community organizing, violence prevention efforts, and shelters for abused women or children.

14. One study found that Canadians who identified themselves as religious but never attended church volunteered *less* than those who were not religious at all (Ravanera et al. 2002).

15. There were no interaction effects for mainline Protestants: in other words, the positive effect of belonging to a mainline Protestant denomination (as opposed to having no religious affiliation at all) was no stronger for frequent churchgoers than for infrequent churchgoers.

16. American teenagers who attend church frequently have more prosocial values, where these values are measured by importance attached to (1) giving time through volunteer work to charitable, religious, or community organizations; (2) making financial contributions to charitable, religious, or community organizations; (3) making the world a better place; and (4) doing things for people, regardless of gender, race, age, and whether or not their parents were volunteering (Beutel and Johnson 2004).

17. McKeown et al. (2004:16) found that two-thirds of Canadians who attended religious services weekly were a member of at least one voluntary association, compared to 45% of those who did not go to church at all.

18. We do not wish to claim that they are more socially integrated because they attend church more often, although this is certainly possible. It could well be that they attend church frequently because they are more socially integrated or both could be the result of some unmeasured variable.

19. Liu et al. (1998) looked at the influence of participating in church groups and church attendance on participation (not volunteering) in non-church groups (e.g., recreational, political and civic groups, service and fraternal organizations, job-related organizations). Respondents were asked how often they attended church and how often they participated in church-related groups. Frequency of church attendance was positively associated with participation in church-related groups, and participation in church-related groups had a positive effect on participation in non-church groups. Church attendance thus had both a direct effect on participation in secular groups and an indirect effect "through" church groups.

13. Volunteer Recruitment

1. In this regression analysis the omitted categories are as follows: gender (male), race (White), age (16–24), education (less than high school), residential status (renter), labor force status (not in the labor force), marital status (married), parental status (no children).

2. The coefficients in this table are slightly different from those shown in Table 1 in chapter 6 because that table contains information only on respondents who were asked the membership question, whereas this table includes all respondents.

3. It is worth noting that he includes in his model a variable measuring "social pressure" ("In my social environment it is obvious to volunteer"), which might well be highly correlated with the probabilities of being asked, and it is positively correlated with volunteering.

4. We used multinomial logit modeling to see if these two personality traits predicted the difference between being recruited and accepting and being recruited and refusing.

14. Schools and Congregations

1. The term "service learning" originated in the late 1960s to describe an internship program in which college students gained credit for service endeavors linked to the curriculum. The idea of service learning is no longer limited to school settings but can be found in youth groups and religious organizations although, of course, educational credits cannot be earned.

2. In 1984, 27% of high schools offered opportunities to perform community service and 9% provided service learning opportunities (Kenny and Gallagher 2003:130). A survey of school principals conducted in 1999 found that 64% of all public schools (83% of all public high schools) in the United States had students participating in community service activities recognized by or arranged through the school. In 2004, an identical survey found that 66% of all public schools (81% of all public high schools) were providing community service opportunities. In 1999, 31% of all public schools (46% of all public high schools) included service learning components in their curriculum. By 2004 these percentages had dropped slightly, to 28% and 44%, respectively (Scales and Roehlkepartain 2004). While the diffusion of community service and service learning programs seems to have slowed recently, there can be no denying that social forces promoting volunteer work are present in the lives of today's teenagers that were absent from the lives of previous generations. Adolescents say their schools place more emphasis on doing community service than their parents (Wirthlin Group 1995b:11).

3. In 2003, the nationwide volunteer rate for Americans aged 16–18 was 32% compared to 24% among those aged 19–24. It is worth noting that the gap was widest (thirty-one percentage points) in Maryland, the only state with mandatory community service requirements for high school students (Helms 2004:1).

4. In 1999, the Ontario government in Canada mandated volunteer work in the secondary school system. It provided the authority to force teachers to supervise extra-curricular activities as part of their regular duties and it required students to complete forty hours of community involvement activities as part of the requirements for graduation (Brock 2001:56).

5. Some would dismiss community service and service learning as suitable topics for research on volunteering because frequently they are not voluntary, and service learning is rewarded with academic credits. But many kinds of volunteer work are not voluntary, as when members of the congregation take turns making the after-service coffee or mothers rotate supervisory duties at the child care center. Nor is service learning alone in bringing side benefits and, besides, the fact that a student who takes a service learning course gets credit does not explain why he or she chose that precise method of earning the credit. It is certainly more questionable when community service work is mandated as a requirement of graduation, but even then it is possible that attending a school where service work is required encourages a student to volunteer later in life because it creates the norm that such work is socially desirable. (In chapter 20 we will take up the question of whether service learning that is not freely undertaken and not designed and managed by the student has long-term benefits.)

6. Many community service programs would not survive without the organizational support of congregations or alliances of congregations. Many non-profit organizations were started by and continue to rely on congregations. For example, the largest membership-based lobbying organization in the anti-hunger movement of the 1980s was Bread for the World. The organization expected its members to communicate regularly with their congressmen about hunger legislation. It was organized and staffed with volunteers entirely by religious congregations. Not surprisingly, 89% of its members said religion was very important in their lives, 86% prayed everyday, and 90% attended church once a week or more, proportions far in excess of the averages for the American population (Cohn et al. 1993:122). Similarly, most Habitat for Humanity affiliates got their start and initial funding from local congregations and are supplied with volunteers by religious congregations on a regular basis (Baggett 2001:190).

7. A survey of 128 congregations in Greensboro, North Carolina, found that nine out of ten provided volunteers for one or more human services activities in the community (Cnaan et al. 1993:36). A 1991 study of 152 churches and synagogues in Chicago found that 77% housed at least one community program or organization and 59% funded their own social service program (Cnaan et al. 1999:179). A 1998 study of twenty-four Philadelphia congregations occupying "historic properties" found that 58.3% were operating food pantries, 58.3% organized summer camps for children, 50% offered recreational programs for children, 45.8% managed clothing closets, 45% had tutoring programs and programs to arrange visits to the sick and elderly. Forty-two percent were engaged in advocacy programs for civil rights and social justice. In all, eighty-nine programs were reported by the twenty-four congregations, with an average of 3.7 per congregation (Cnaan et al. 1999:232). A later expansion of this study covered 251 congregations in eight cities. Among them they were operating 175 service activities (e.g., hospital visitation, food pantries) with an average of 3.9 service activities per congregation. Nine out of ten congregations reported at least one activity, while about half reported five or more. In 78.4% of the service activities volunteers were used (Cnaan 2002:61).

8. The level of congregational support for volunteer work reported in this survey is much lower than that described in Cnaan's research reported above, which is based on much smaller samples of congregations. Wuthnow (2004:38–40) suggests the National Congregations Study under-estimates the number of congregations sponsoring service programs by about 10% because of the survey's low response rate and a tendency for smaller congregations to under-report the volunteer work they sponsor.

15. Community, Neighborhood, City, and Region

1. There was no relation between attachment to place and volunteering among the adolescents in the survey.

2. Further analysis showed that it is not a matter of renters refusing invitations to volunteer. Renters were more likely than owners to neither have been asked nor volunteered. Home owners were more likely than renters to be asked and to volunteer and to have been asked but not volunteered. [100] There was no difference among those who were asked but declined. The effect of being asked is thus mainly associated with renters not being approached at all. They seem to be less visible to recruiters and that is because they are less socially integrated.

3. Regardless of gender, race, age, education, income, and marital status.

4. Regardless of age, race, gender, marital status, income, and education.

5. Working class people, who normally would have quite low volunteerism rates, are more likely to volunteer if they live in stable communities, especially if the community is socially homogeneous (Eckstein 2001:847).

6. The Los Angeles Survey of Urban Inequality (1994) does not include a measure of volunteering but does ask respondents about their memberships in voluntary associations and the close association between voluntary memberships and volunteering warrants using data from the survey to examine the association between community poverty (the percent of households in a census tract living below the poverty line) and participation in voluntary organizations. Regardless of socio-economic status, residents in poorer neighborhoods participated in fewer organizations. "These findings indicate that neighborhood poverty is not a proxy for individual-level socio-economic characteristics, but that it is independently and negatively related to the number of organizations to which individuals belong" (Stoll 2001:542).

7. Putnam (2000) found a negative relation between income equality and social capital—where social capital was defined as trust in others, organizational memberships, volunteering, voting, and socializing with friends. Using the same measure of social capital Hero (2003) found a negative relation between a state's level of social capital and "minority diversity" (i.e., percent Black, Latino, and Asian): diverse states had less social capital. Like Knack, he found no income inequality effect but, by focusing on the income disparities between Blacks and Whites rather than income inequality in general, he found a *positive* relation between income inequality and social capital. In other words, if heterogeneity means income inequality between races, the greater the inequality, the more social capital; if heterogeneity means income inequality within races, the greater the inequality, the less social capital there is.

8. The concentration of religious fundamentalists in the Southern states might also help account for the somewhat lower level of volunteering in that region because they tend to be less trusting, especially if they attend church frequently.

9. Trust is measured by the standard question, "Generally speaking, do you believe that most people can be trusted, or can you not be too careful in dealing with people?"

10. We used the GINI index as a measure of state level of income inequality. We constructed a measure of racial heterogeneity by calculating the proportion of the state's total population represented by each of the five racial/ethnic groups identified (White, Black, Native American Indian, Asian, and other), squaring those proportions and summing them, and then subtracting the total from one. According to this measure, state racial heterogeneity ranges from 0 to 0.8. The larger the heterogeneity number, the more even the distribution of the races.

11. We were unable to test the trust hypothesis because the CPS does not contain a question on this topic.

12. We used as a measure of urban density the percentage of the state population living in metropolitan areas in 1994, where metropolitan is defined as an area containing a city of fifty thousand or more inhabitants. The percentages ranged from 100 in the District of Columbia to 27.2 in Vermont. (Table A-2. States, in the *State and Metropolitan Area Data Book*.)

13. Because the "secular-only" category includes such a large number of activities, the percentage reporting this concentration is higher in all states but Utah, where

there are two religious-only volunteers for every secular-only volunteer. But the ratio of secular to religious volunteers varies considerably. In Maine there are six secular-only volunteers for every religious-only volunteer; in South Carolina the ratio is almost one-to-one. States in which there are twice as many secular-only volunteers as religious-only volunteers are Wyoming, Alaska, Vermont, Montana, Washington, Kansas, Wisconsin, Maine, Colorado, Oregon, Connecticut, New Hampshire, Maryland, Ohio, Virginia, Missouri, Illinois, D.C., New Mexico, Massachusetts, Delaware, California, Hawaii, West Virginia, New York, Rhode Island, and Nevada.

16. Cross-National Differences

1. The World Values Survey is administered by a global network of social scientists whose goal is to obtain a sample of at least one thousand respondents 18 years of age or older in each country. In most countries, some form of stratified multi-stage random sampling is used to obtain nationally representative samples. Face-to-face interviews are used in most cases. The survey asks respondents if they belong to any voluntary organization from a list of types of organization (one organization for each category) and they are then asked if they are currently doing "unpaid work" for that organization. They are not asked how many hours of work they contributed. In the 1995–1998 survey the wording for this question was changed to ask if the respondent was a member, active member, or not a member of an organization. Because the word "active" is an imprecise measure of volunteer work, this survey is rarely used in studies of volunteerism.

2. The response rate for the 1999–2001 survey ranged from a low of 25% in Spain to a high of 95% in Slovakia.

3. Recall that Curtis et al. (2001) predict lower rates of volunteerism in corporatist countries.

4. The political rights measure focuses on the freedom and fairness of elections, the capacity for competition by political opposition, freedom from domination by the military, foreign powers, or other powerful groups, and minority rights and participation. The civil liberties measure uses a fourteen-item checklist focusing on freedom of expression and belief, freedom of association and organization, the rule of law and human rights, and social and economic rights (e.g., choice of marriage partner.)

5. In an intriguing and innovative analysis, Van Schaik (2002) looked at the association between economic development and volunteering across fifty-four regions *within* European countries. He used as a measure of economic growth the level of GDP per capita, the investment ratio, and the school enrolment ratio (the total number of pupils at first and second level in 1977, divided by total number of people in the corresponding age group). He found a positive association between the rate of regional economic growth and the rate of volunteering in the region.

6. The author is careful to note cases that do not fit this generalization: "The numbers of volunteers are highest in Sweden, the Netherlands and Slovakia, but these societies do not appear to be most in favor of the democratic attitude. Democracy is most favored in Germany, Austria, Iceland, and Denmark, countries where volunteering is less widespread" (Halman 2003:190). As other sociologists have noted (see the earlier discussion of structural theories), the analysis of variance over a relatively small number of cases is almost certain to result in these anomalies, each of which must be accounted for by arguments unique to the country.

7. Volunteer activity was defined as "the act of providing one's own efforts, time, knowledge or skill for society or community without receiving remuneration for the work" (Statistics Bureau 2002).

8. Knack (2003) did not distinguish passive from active memberships but he did distinguish between two types of voluntary associations: the first focuses on economic interests (professional associations, trade unions, political parties or groups); the second focuses on more civic activities (education, arts, culture, youth work, human services). He found that social trust was not associated with membership in the first group at all but was positively associated with membership in the second group. He surmises that the economic incentives for joining the first group make trust unnecessary. "For groups where the benefits of membership are primarily social, low-trust individuals may refrain from joining" (Knack 2003:352).

9. Comparative sociologists are frequently faced with the question of how to measure individual attributes consistently across different countries. In our analysis we follow the recommendations of the project directors on how to measure education and income. Education was measured using the following categories: 1—inadequately completed elementary education; 2—completed elementary education; 3—elementary education plus basic vocational qualification; 4—secondary, intermediate vocational education; 5—secondary, intermediate general qualification; 6—full secondary, maturity level certificate; 7—higher education, lower-level tertiary certificate; 8—higher education, upper-level tertiary certificate. To code income, respondents were shown a scale of incomes appropriate for the country in question and asked to place themselves in the appropriate decile for that country.

17. Trends in Volunteering

1. We should note that Wuthnow (2004:102) used the same wording in a survey he conducted in 1999, by which time the rate had fallen to 35%.

2. Civic association activity includes attendance at community, political, church, or trade union meetings; voluntary tutoring or coaching; paperwork and other organizational work associated with voluntary activities; and other voluntary community or political activities, such as demonstrations and providing meals or refreshments.

3. Not every birth cohort becomes a generation. For example, the birth cohort succeeding the baby boomers has been labeled "Generation X" precisely because it lacks a generational consciousness. "Few, if any galvanizing events or movements occurred around which a special identity could be formed" (Jennings and Stoker 2001:4).

4. This confusion is sometimes apparent in Putnam's argument. For example, he observes a more rapid decline in social participation among the younger than the older birth cohorts and concludes that "about half the overall decline in social capital and civic engagement can be traced to generational change" (Putnam 2000:266). But he knows this method of detecting generation effects compounds birth cohort and period effects because each successive birth cohort reaches a given age in a different year, often decades apart. He cannot rule out the possibility that any difference in social participation is due to changes in social context that occur in the time that elapses between the different birth cohorts reaching a given age. As far as separating generation and period effects is concerned, Putnam (2000:485) finds that "if both year of birth and year of survey are included in the same regression, year of survey becomes

virtually insignificant in these measures." In this case, he is unable to control for age because it overlaps with cohort (year of birth). Therefore, he cannot rule out the possibility that the generation effect is actually the result of a change in the composition of the sample due to age-related factors, such as retirement or lower morbidity.

5. Admittedly, it measures volunteering in two different periods because the members of the two cohorts will reach the same stage of their life roughly twenty-five years apart. However, it is possible to control for period effects on volunteering by conducting a pooled time series analysis to see if either of the two periods selected for comparison are unusual in their rate of volunteering.

6. The mature women were first surveyed in 1967, when they numbered 5,083; the young women were first surveyed in 1968, when the sample size was 5,159. Questions on volunteering were included in only some of the NLS panels: the mature women were asked about their volunteer work in 1974, 1976, 1979, 1981, and 1984; the young women were asked about their volunteer work in 1973, 1978, 1988, and 1991.

7. It is not possible to pool the data from *all* the women. The brief period during which the women were asked about their volunteer work means that only women between ages 37 and 48 can be compared. The reason for this is as follows: The earliest measure of volunteering for the mature women occurred in 1974, when the youngest of them was 37. The latest measure of volunteering for the young women was taken in 1991, when the oldest of them was 48. The women available for comparison are therefore the mature women who were between 37 and 48 in 1974 and the young women who were between 37 and 48 in 1991.

8. The generation theory of trends in volunteering is further undermined by the results of another study of longitudinal data. Although the measurement in this case is voluntary association memberships, we believe the results have a bearing on trends in volunteerism because so much volunteer work takes place in connection with voluntary associations. In the survey used, the first generation was born between 1910 and 1940—half of them between 1917 and 1924. This generation "easily falls within Putnam's high praised 'long civic generation' " (Jennings and Stoker 2001:3). Its members were parents of the survey respondents comprising the second cohort, who were high school seniors when they were first surveyed in 1965. The high school students were early members of the baby boomer generation. The age-standardized voluntary association memberships of the first generation in 1965 can be compared with those of the second generation in 1997. The data show that, in mid-life, members of the second generation belonged to more voluntary associations than their parents at the same age, regardless of current income, education, workforce participation, and home ownership. Much of this was due to an increase in membership in professional or business groups and neighborhood associations.

9. This is not a direct challenge to Putnam's argument because her measure of "association" is a latent variable comprised of group memberships, spending an evening with neighbors, and spending an evening with friends.

10. It should be noted that this is a question about membership in a *type* of organization (e.g., nationality group) and that the respondent could well be a member of more than one organization in this category without this information being gathered. However, this problem is consistent across the surveys and therefore looking at trends is only biased if many Americans increased their memberships in a given type over this period.

11. The decline in Japan was entirely due to less union volunteering.

12. Unfortunately, this later study reported only the change in the percentage of people volunteering in each country between 1981 and 1990, and 1990 and 1999, whereas the Baer et al. (2001) study used negative binomial regression analysis to estimate whether any change in number of people volunteering was statistically significant.

13. The largest increase occurred among Canadians 55 years of age and older, among those with less than high school education, and among the unemployed and those earning less than $20,000 a year.

14. As with the United States, there have been changes in the popularity of different types of voluntary organizations. Women's organizations have lost members while other organizations, such as those concerned with the environment, have gained members (Hall 1999:421). A change in the mix of voluntary association memberships reflects rising educational levels and the growth of the middle class occupations.

15. Trade union collective bargaining agreements in Canada still limit the activities of volunteers in hospitals and schools.

16. The number of public sector programs in the United Kingdom relying to some extent on volunteer labor increased rapidly in the 1960s and 1970s. Local governments were authorized to spend some portion of property taxes to fund voluntary organizations and, in 1972, the government established a Volunteer Center and a Voluntary Services Unit in the Home Office (Hall 1999:442).

18. Volunteer Tasks

1. In 2005 30% of American volunteers contributed time to more than one organization.

2. Nearly a quarter of the volunteers (22.4%) are excluded from the analysis to follow. Some of them listed "other" as a task, some did not know whether they did any tasks and others simply did not answer this question. (By definition, volunteers must perform some task or other, but social surveys frequently locate respondents who do not, or cannot, identify a task they have performed. For example, 57% of the volunteers in a survey of Indiana residents had done none of the ten tasks they were shown [Gronberg and Never 2004:268].) We also excluded being a blood donor because it is not a volunteer task and fund-raising because it was not included in the list of tasks in all years.

3. Many men's organizations have circumvented this problem by setting up "ladies auxiliaries."

4. Goddard (1994:11) found that the "economically inactive" were most likely to report visiting people in institutions and providing practical help; part-time workers were the most likely to mention fund-raising; and the unemployed were most likely to mention helping at a club. Full-time workers were most likely to mention giving presentations, serving on a committee, and organizing entertainment, a reflection of their superior education, income, and occupational status.

19. The Volunteer Role

1. We should note here the results of a study looking at women's volunteering over a thirty-year span (1956–1986). Women with a job were less likely to become a volunteer in the first place, whereas more highly educated women were more likely.

Neither factor, however, had any effect on exit from the volunteer role. Having a job did not increase the odds of dropping out of volunteer work and being highly educated did not increase the odds of continuing to be a volunteer (Moen 1997).

2. Simon et al. (2000) developed an "organizational identification" scale to help explain differences in willingness to volunteer among people who had signed up to help an AIDS volunteer service organization ("AH"). For example, one item in the scale read, "In general, belonging to AH is an important part of my self-image." Those with the strongest identification with the organization were the most willing to volunteer. A study of emergency medical volunteers found that those who saw more of their "real me" in the emergency medical technician role were more "committed" in the sense of taking on a range of activities in the organization "above and beyond" those required (Reich 2000).

3. A number of studies of volunteers and volunteer organizations indicate that management practices can influence volunteers' commitment to their jobs (Black and Kovacs 1999:482; Caro and Bass 1995; Chambre 1987; Deegan and Nutt 1975; Dorsch et al. 2002; Merrell 2000; Penner 2002; Phillips et al. 2002a).

4. Perhaps it is unrealistic to assume that people have needs that are clearly formulated ahead of the time they start volunteering and that the volunteer experience will either satisfy those needs or not: "there is evidence that volunteers may not engage in elaborate rational analysis of their options before joining, but 'try on' the work and decide later whether or not they want to stay" (Pearce 1993:11).

20. Citizenship and Prosocial Behavior

1. Civic development was measured by political knowledge (e.g., "What name is given to the first ten amendments to the U.S. Constitution?"); attention to politics (e.g., how often the respondent watched the national news on television); political participation skills (e.g., whether the respondent felt as if he or she could make a statement at a public meeting); political efficacy (e.g., respondents were asked if they felt they had a say in what the federal government does); and tolerance of diversity (e.g., respondents were asked if they believed that people should be allowed to make public statements against religion).

2. The hours of community service variable was developed by combining information about the number of weeks and the number of hours per week students reported spending in each of up to three service activities.

3. Volunteering was not associated with the student's feelings about whether his or her family had a say in what the government does. Nearly all students agreed they could write a letter to a government office and nearly 90% agreed people should be allowed to speak against religion publicly. As a result neither of these attitudes was related to volunteering.

4. They asked about conventional political behavior, such as voting, displaying campaign materials, working for candidates, and fund-raising. They then asked about activities outside the electoral arena: regular volunteering, active group memberships, fund-raising for charities, and informal group activity to work on community problems. A third dimension measured political voice: contacting public officials, protesting, boycotting, contacting newspaper editors, and canvassing, among others. Factor analysis of the entire nineteen items revealed that they tended to cluster into three groups. In the group called "civic" fell regular volunteering, community problem

solving, being an active member of a group, and raising money for charity. In the group called "electoral" fell the activities associated with elections such as voting and donating money to a campaign. A third group contained all of the "voice" measures, such as contacting the media. For example, the correlation between volunteering and being an active member of a voluntary association was stronger than the correlation between volunteering and donating money to an election campaign. However, the important point is that these dimensions or factors were related to each other.

5. In a separate analysis of a sub-set of the same sample, focusing on young people aged between 14 and 26, Jenkins (2005) found that the association between volunteering and electoral engagement (e.g., working for a candidate) was stronger for women than men.

6. Perry and Katula (2001:331–333) identify toleration as another component of "other-regarding ethics." Democratic polities require a certain level of toleration of diversity, respect for others' values and practices, and willingness to compromise for the sake of collective goals. It is widely believed that getting involved in secondary groups is one way in which other regarding ethics can be learned. Cigler and Joslyn (2002) used data from the 1974–1994 GSS surveys and from the Citizen Participation Survey (1995) to see if joining voluntary associations made people more tolerant of others. (While this is not a study of volunteering, voluntary association memberships are, as we have seen, an important precursor of volunteering.) Both the GSS and Citizen Participation Study have an extensive list of questions designed to elicit respondents' positions on civil liberties issues, including the right of various "non-conformists" such as communists and homosexuals to access to the public arena. The more memberships respondents had the more tolerant they were. There was some variation across types of membership. In the Citizen Participation Study survey, members of veterans' and ethnic groups were less tolerant than people who belonged to no organizations at all, while members of political and cultural groups were more tolerant. In the GSS survey members of unions, college fraternities, and farm and religious organizations were less tolerant than non-members, while members of literature and professional groups were more tolerant. All of these effects are net of gender, age, religiosity, education, race, income, and region of the country. Although this study is not about volunteering, its lesson is clear: some types of membership do encourage people to be more "other-regarding" but other types of membership have precisely the opposite effect.

7. Volunteering is a collective resource, as well as an individual resource. Communities in which there is a lot of volunteering going on might well produce more trusting citizens—regardless of whether those citizens are volunteering themselves. This topic has not received much attention from social scientists. One study used membership in at least one civic association or social group to see if neighborhoods high in memberships produced more trusting people. The results of this study provided only partial support for the theory that "social capital" creates generalized trust. Whereas the rate of memberships in the community had a positive effect on the level of trust of Blacks, it had no effect on the level of trust of Whites (Marschall and Stolle 2004). While this study did not measure volunteer work directly and its findings are inconsistent across racial groups, it does suggest a fruitful direction of future research on the link between volunteering, trust, and civic engagement. The link might not exist at the individual level at all, but at the level of community. This would certainly fit one way of thinking about trust, as a property of groups rather than individuals.

8. "Participation in community service provides a real-world context in which participants can explore moral questions, engage in moral discourse, perform moral actions, and reflect on complicated moral issues" (Hart et al. 2006:644).

9. "Through engagement in service activities with peers and caring adults, service can enhance healthy connections with others, offer constructive use of leisure time, and provide chances for youth to contribute in a meaningful way to their communities" (Kenny and Gallagher 2003:3).

10. Controlling for gender, religious denomination, attendance at Catholic school, socioeconomic status, race, and intact versus single parent family.

11. Regardless of gender, parental socio-economic status, race, academic grades, hours worked for pay, and type of school attended.

12. These negative associations between volunteering and antisocial behavior are weak. We should also note that not all studies show that volunteering suppresses antisocial behavior. A survey of Vermont public school students in grades eight through twelve asked them how many hours during an average week they had spent helping other people without getting paid. Forty-eight percent of the students had provided some help. Students were also asked if they had engaged in any health risk behaviors in the past month, such as binge drinking, fighting, and engaging in sexual intercourse. Volunteering was positively related only to frequency of aerobic exercise, no doubt a reflection of the fact that much of the volunteer work was in connection with sports or recreation organizations, a preferred volunteer activity for younger people (Murphy et al. 2004).

13. The evaluation study compared 1,673 students who participated in the program with 1,604 students matched on school grade, race, mother's educational level, single-parent households, and prior record of course failures, academic suspensions, and pregnancies.

14. Eccles and Barber (1999) use data from the Michigan Study of Adolescent Life Transitions to examine the connection between various kinds of extra-curricular activities and risky behaviors, such as getting drunk, skipping school, and using drugs. Subjects were surveyed for the first time when they were in sixth grade and were followed until they reached the age of 26. In tenth grade they were asked about their participation in a number of extra-curricular activities, including volunteering. Unfortunately for our purposes, the researchers grouped volunteering with church attendance to form one "prosocial activity" category. Nevertheless, they find differences that hint at the positive effect of volunteer work in secondary school. Looking at the rate of involvement in problem behaviors in twelfth grade, students who had engaged in prosocial activities were less likely to report delinquency. Specifically, students involved in prosocial activities showed less of an increase in risky behaviors during their high school years than their non-involved peers. They also had higher grade point averages. Other extra-curricular activities did not yield such positive results. Athletes actually showed an increase in drinking between tenth and twelfth grades. No effects on risky behavior were found for participation in the performing arts (e.g., band), school-related clubs (e.g., student council), or academic clubs (e.g., foreign language club).

15. The correlation coefficient was $r = 0.30$, $p < 001$.

16. Problem behavior was defined as above-average participation in such activities as theft, vandalism, petty larceny, selling drugs, and violence toward others as well as substance abuse.

21. Occupation, Income, and Health

1. Controlling for the hours spent volunteering, level of education, number of group memberships, employment status, neighborhood income, church membership, and number of children.

2. We used the Duncan Socio-Economic Index to measure the occupational status of women who were working in 1973 and in 1991.

3. The authors acknowledge that by restricting the data analysis to households where the respondent is the sole breadwinner, and where the income is measured at the household level, they might have under-estimated the effect of volunteering on women's income.

4. One possible reason why these studies of the NLS data do not replicate the findings reported in Astin et al. (1998) is that they pertain only to women.

5. "In general, if I act as I think I ought, I will probably feel good about it. But it is not that I think I ought to do it because it makes me feel good, but rather that it makes me feel good because I think I ought to have done it" (Miller 1982:47).

6. The "helper-therapy" principle in many self-help groups institutionalizes the idea of being helped through helping others (Banks 1997).

7. Respondents received a summative score of major role-identity absences by adding together the number of absent roles in major life domains: partner (not married), employment (not employed), and parental (no living children). Mental health was measured as: *negative affect* (e.g., "During the past 30 days how much of the time did you feel so sad nothing could cheer you up"); *positive affect* (e.g., "During the past 30 days, how much of the time did you feel cheerful"); and *sense of purpose in life* (e.g., "Some people wander aimlessly through life, but I am not one of them").

8. The attrition in this sample of elderly Americans, which was not random but tended to be more likely among the more depressed and the non-volunteers, means that the true relationship between depression and volunteering is probably underestimated in this analysis.

9. This is one reason why older people have more positive attitudes toward volunteering than younger people (Midlarsky and Kahana 1994:135).

10. For example, church-related volunteering is more likely to be undertaken for its own sake: young people who volunteer through their churches are less likely than young people who volunteer through secular organizations to offer instrumental reasons for their behavior, such as expecting others to help them in return, making career contacts, developing job opportunities, or using their volunteering to improve their resume (Wuthnow 1995:269).

11. Helliwell and Putnam (2004:1443) suggest that our sense of well-being is affected not only by our own volunteer efforts but also of those around us because we get more satisfaction from volunteering if others are also volunteering. Although they measure voluntary association memberships rather than volunteering they find that nations with greater membership densities have higher average levels of life satisfaction even after accounting for individual-level participation. The authors note that "until this result is replicated among communities within nations, there remains risk that it is capturing, in part, the effects of other important factors that differ among nations" (Helliwell and Putnam 2004:1443).

12. Gerontologists have been among the most vocal proponents of the idea that getting engaged in social activities helps slow the physical deterioration experienced

in old age. For example, a 1974 investigation of the mortality rate of a sample of California residents (first interviewed in 1965) found that survival rates were higher among those who had many friends and saw their relatives frequently (this effect was stronger for women than men), those who belonged to a church or temple, those who belonged to one or more formal or informal groups, and for married men (but not married women). The effect of social contacts was partially mediated by the use of preventive health services: in other words, belonging to social groups and having lots of friends increased the chances of hearing about and using services that prevent the onset of illnesses (Berkman and Syme 1979). Strawbridge et al. (1999) found lower mortality rates among frequent churchgoers in a sample of California residents who were followed from 1965 to 1994. One reason why frequent churchgoers survived longer was that they belonged to more voluntary organizations. In short, there is good reason to suspect that volunteer work has positive effects not only our self-concept but also on our physical condition.

13. Other components of the index were club memberships and involvement in local politics.

14. Although the study asked specifically about frequency of engagement in unpaid community work, the researchers constructed a summary "social engagement" index comprised of eight items: visits to theater or sporting events; shopping; gardening; meal preparation; game playing; day or overnight trips; paid community work; and unpaid community work. The study used multiple measures of disability status, including the ability to perform essential self-care tasks such as bathing, mobility (e.g., walk up and down stairs), and body functions such as kneeling or handling small objects.

15. Productive activities were gardening, preparing meals, shopping, paid community work, and unpaid community work.

16. Mortality experience was determined by screening local newspapers for obituary notices or by attempted contact for re-interview in 1995.

17. Just over four hundred of the 3,617 respondents interviewed in 1986 had died.

18. He matched data from the nearly sixteen thousand Americans interviewed with data from the National Death Index through the year 1991.

19. Paid work had the same health benefits for this elderly population. Paid and unpaid work were alternative means of maintaining good health in old age.

20. Controlling for demographic differences, marital status, socio-economic status, and baseline health and functioning.

22. Conclusion

1. The document pointedly rebutted the notorious remark of Margaret Thatcher that "there is no such thing as society" by declaring that, "This Government rejects the view that society is composed of selfish individuals each pursuing solely their own ends. There is such a thing as society, and everybody, young and old, can make a contribution to it."

2. Aside from new initiatives to encourage more charitable donations to volunteer organizations, the document outlined a number of ways in which volunteering could be promoted by government: providing an infrastructure of volunteer centers to coordinate volunteer work; using Web sites to create "virtual markets bringing potential volunteers and opportunities together"; developing volunteer projects aimed principally at younger people; introducing citizenship education into the national curricu-

lum; and encouraging business corporations to institute volunteering schemes for their employees. The Home Office established an "Active Communities Unit" in 2002 to coordinate these activities.

3. The commission recommended a "series of campaigns to promote awareness of volunteering"; a national volunteering "portal" to provide information and advice on volunteer opportunities for young people; the appointment of "Youth Volunteer Development Managers"; encouraging schools to develop "a volunteering ethos"; the institutionalization of awards and recognitions for youth volunteers; encouraging government agencies to use youth volunteers; clarifying the rights and responsibilities of volunteers; making it easier for unemployed youth to volunteer without losing benefits; and more public funding for voluntary agencies.

4. In an "accord" published in 2001, the federal government announced a new partnership with the voluntary sector. The accord recognized that the "voluntary sector is one of three pillars that constitute Canadian society, together with the public and private sectors." The voluntary sector was recognized for encouraging people to participate and work together for common causes, strengthening citizen engagement, allowing for multiple perspectives to be heard on a variety of issues, and providing opportunities for people to practice the skills of democratic life. The accord acknowledged the essential contribution of volunteers to "services critical to Canadians" and as "advocates for common causes." The minister for social development took responsibility for managing the government side of this partnership and the Voluntary Sector Forum comprised of leaders from a variety of voluntary sector organizations managed the partnership from the voluntary sector side.

5. There are other ethnic groups that simply make no distinction between volunteering and care work. Wilson et al. (2001:129), noting that the Maori people of New Zealand report less volunteer work than the White settlers, attribute this to the fact that the Maori do not have a word for volunteering and do not distinguish between caring for people in the household and caring for people in the community.

6. In just over one-third of all American households, two members of the family volunteer together, a fraction that rises to nearly one-half in middle class families (Points of Light Foundation, 1994).

7. A survey of teenagers found that 83% got a "great deal" or a "fair amount" of satisfaction from "doing things for others." Is this high or low? It is high in relation to satisfaction with schoolwork (70%) but low in relation to satisfaction with family (94%) (Wuthnow 1995)?

8. In recognition of this fact, the British government has funded the Black and Minority Ethnic Twinning Initiative to encourage mainstream organizations to twin with at least two Black and minority ethnic organizations in order to improve the level and quality of volunteer opportunities for formerly excluded groups.

9. One hundred and twenty-four countries endorsed the resolution. The resolution noted "the significant contribution that volunteers make in their own countries to improve welfare and realizing the aspirations of their fellow citizens for improved economic and social well-being" and "that much volunteer activity is performed by women and that such socially useful work should be appropriately recognized and supported." The proposal called for member countries to "enhance the recognition, facilitation, networking and promotion of volunteer service." A follow-up report issued by the secretary-general in September 2002 proclaimed the International Year of Volunteers "successful by any account."

References

Abrahams, Naomi. 1996. "Negotiating Power, Identity, Family, and Community: Women's Community Participation." *Gender and Society* 10: 768–796.

Adair, Andrea. 1997. "Volunteer Work: Do Feminists Do It Differently?" *Herizons* 11: 24–25.

Alesina, Alberto, and Eliana La Ferrara. 2000. "Participation in Heterogeneous Communities." *Quarterly Journal of Economics* 115: 847–904.

Allahyari, Rebecca. 2000. *Visions of Charity: Volunteer Workers and Moral Community.* Berkeley: University of California Press.

Allen, Joseph, and Susan Philiber. 2001. "Who Benefits Most from a Broadly Targeted Prevention Program?" *Journal of Community Psychology* 29: 637–655.

Allen, Joseph, Susan Philliber, Scott Herling, and Gabriel Kuperminc. 1997. "Preventing Teen Pregnancy and Academic Failure: Experimental Evaluation of a Developmentally Based Approach." *Child Development* 68: 729–742.

Allison, Lora, Morris Okun, and Kathy Dutridge. 2002. "Assessing Volunteer Motives: A Comparison of an Open-Ended Probe and Likert Rating Scales." *Journal of Community and Applied Social Psychology* 12: 243–255.

Almeida, David, Daniel McDonald, John Havens, and Paul Schervish. 2001. "Temporal Patterns of Social Responsibility." Pp. 135–157 in *Caring and Doing for Others*, ed. Alice Rossi. Chicago: University of Chicago Press.

Amato, Paul. 1990. "Personality and Social Network Involvement as Predictors of Helping Behavior in Everyday Life." *Social Psychology Quarterly* 53: 31–43.

Amato, Paul, and A. Booth. 1997. *A Generation at Risk: Growing up in an Era of Family Upheaval.* Cambridge: Harvard University Press.

Ammerman, Nancy. 1997. *Congregation & Community.* Piscataway, N.J.: Rutgers University Press.

———. 2002. "Connecting Mainline Protestant Churches with Public Life." Pp. 129–158 in *The Quiet Hand of God: Faith-Based Activism and the Public Role of Mainline Protestantism*, ed. Robert Wuthnow and John Evans. Berkeley: University of California Press.

Anderson, Christopher. 1996. "Political Action and Social Integration." *American Politics Quarterly* 24: 105–125.

Anderson, Ralph, and Kyra Osmus. 1988. "Cold Night and Long Day: A Comparison of Male and Female Volunteers in a Night Shelter." *Journal of Voluntary Action Research* 17: 54–59.

Anderson, Robert, James Curtis, and Edward Grabb. 2006. "Civic Association Activity in Four Democracies." *American Sociological Review* 71: 376–400.

Andolina, Molly, Krista Jenkins, Cliff Zukin, and Scott Keeter. 2003. "Habits from Home, Lessons from School: Influences on Youth Civic Engagement." *PS: Political Science and Politics* 36: 275–280.

Anheier, Helmut, and Jeremy Kendall. 2002. "Interpersonal Trust and Voluntary Associations." *British Journal of Sociology* 53: 343–362.

Anheier, Helmut, and Lester M. Salamon. 1999. "Volunteering in Cross-National Perspective: Initial Comparisons." *Law and Contemporary Society* 62: 43–65.

Ardelt, Monika. 2000. "Intellectual versus Wisdom-Related Knowledge: The Case for a Different Kind of Learning in the Later Years of Life. *Educational Gerontology* 26(8): 771–789.

Aschaffenburg, Karen, and Ineke Maas. 1997. "Cultural and Educational Careers: The Dynamics of Social Reproduction." *American Sociological Review* 62: 573–587.

Ascoli, Ugo, and Ram Cnaan. 1997. "Volunteers for Human Service Provisions: Lessons from Italy and the USA." *Social Indicators Research* 40: 299–327.

Astin, Alexander, Leticia Oseguera, Linda Sax, and William Korn. 2002. *The American Freshman: Thirty-Five Year Trends, 1966–2001*. Los Angeles: Higher Education Research Institute, University of California.

Astin, Alexander, Linda Sax, and Juan Avalos. 1998. "Long-Term Effects of Volunteerism during the Undergraduate Years." *Review of Higher Education* 22: 187–202.

Atkins, Robert and Daniel Hart. 2003. "Neighborhood, Adults, and the Development of Civic Identify in Urban Youth." *Applied Developmental Science* 7:156–164.

Australian Bureau of Statistics. 2002. *Australian Social Trends 2002: Voluntary Work*. Canberra, Australia: Australian Bureau of Statistics.

Ayala, Louis. 2000. "Trained for Democracy: The Differing Effects of Voluntary and Involuntary Organizations on Political Participation." *Political Research Quarterly* 53: 99–115.

Baer, Douglas, James Curtis, and Edward Grabb. 2001. "Has Voluntary Association Activity Declined? Cross-National Analyses for Fifteen Countries." *Canadian Review of Sociology and Anthropology* 38: 249–274.

Baggett, Jerome. 2001. *Habitat for Humanity*. Philadelphia: Temple University Press.

Bagilhole, Barbara. 1996. "Tea and Sympathy or Teetering on Social Work? An Investigation of the Blurring of the Boundaries between Voluntary and Professional Care." *Social Policy and Administration* 30: 189–205.

Baines, Donna. 2004. "Caring for Nothing: Work Organization and Unwaged Labour in Social Services." *Work, Employment and Society* 18: 267–295.

Baldock, John, and Clare Ungerson. 1991. " 'What D'ya Want if You Don't Want Money?'—a Feminist Critique of 'Paid Volunteering'." Pp. 136–160 in *Women's Issues in Social Policy*, ed. Mavis Maclean and Ducie Groves. London: Routledge.

Bales, Kevin. 1996. "Measuring the Propensity to Volunteer." *Social Policy and Administration* 30: 206–226.

Banks, Eric. 1997. "The Social Capital of Self-Help Mutual Aid Groups." *Social Policy* 28: 30–38.

Barkan, Steven. 2004. "Explaining Public Support for the Environmental Movement: A Civic Voluntarism Model." *Social Science Quarterly* 85: 913–937.

Barkan Steven, Steven Cohn, and William Whitaker. 1995. "Beyond Recruitment: Predictors of Differential Participation in a National Anti-hunger Organization." *Sociological Forum* 10: 113–134.

Barlow, Julie, and Jenny Hainsworth. 2001. "Volunteerism among Older People with Arthritis." *Ageing and Society* 21: 203–217.

Barr, Cathy, Larry McKeown, Katie Davidman, David McIver, and David Lasby. 2004. *The Rural Charitable Sector Research Initiative.* Toronto: Canadian Centre for Philanthropy.

Barrett, David, George Kurian, and Todd Johnson. 2001. *World Christian Encyclopedia.* New York: Oxford University Press.

Bartko, W. Todd, and Jacquelynne Eccles. 2003. "Adolescent Participation in Structured and Unstructured Activities: A Person-Oriented Analysis." *Journal of Youth and Adolescence* 32: 233–241.

Basok, Tanya, Suzan Ilcan, and Branka Malesevic. 2002. *Social Justice Volunteers: Motivation and Engagement.* Toronto: Canadian Centre for Philanthropy.

Bass, Scott, and Francis Caro. 2001. "Productive Aging: A Conceptual Framework." Pp. 37–80 in *Productive Aging,* ed. Nancy Morrow-Howell, James Hinterlong, and Michael Sherridan. Baltimore: Johns Hopkins Press.

Batson, C. Daniel, Nadia Ahmad, and Jon-Ann Tsang. 2002. "Four Motives for Community Involvement." *Journal of Social Issues* 58: 429–445.

Batson, C. Daniel, Patricia Schoenrade, and W. Larry Ventis. 1993. *Religion and the Individual.* New York: Oxford University Press.

Baum, Frances, Robert Bush, Carolyn Modra, Charlie Murray, Eva Cox, Kathy Alexander, and Robert Potter. 2000. "Epidemiology of Participation: An Australian Community Study." *Journal of Epidemiology and Community Health* 54: 414–423.

Beck, Paul, and M. Kent Jennings. 1982 "Pathways to Participation." *American Political Science Review* 76: 94–108.

Becker, Peggy, and Pawan Dhingra. 2001. "Religious Involvement and Volunteering: Implications for Civil Society." *Sociology of Religion* 62: 315–335.

Beeghley, Leonard, Ellen Van Velsor, and E. Wilbur Brock. 1981. "The Correlates of Religiosity among Black and White Americans." *Sociological Quarterly* 22: 403–412.

Begley, Thomas, and Henry Alker. 1982. "Anti-busing Protest: Attitudes and Actions." *Social Psychology Quarterly* 45: 187–197.

Bekkers, Rene. 2002. *Giving Time and/or Money: Trade-Off or Spill-Over?* http://www.fss.uu.nl/soc/homes/bekkers/arnova0202.pdf.

———. 2005. *The Intergenerational Transmission of Volunteering.* http://www
.fss.uu.nl/soc/homes/bekkers/transmission2.pdf.

Bender, Courtney. 2003. *Heaven's Kitchen: Living Religion at God's Love We Deliver.* Chicago: University of Chicago Press.

Bengtson, V. L., and Roberts, R. E. L. 1991. "Intergenerational Solidarity in Aging Families: An Example of Formal Theory Construction." *Journal of Marriage and the Family* 53: 856–870.

Berkman, Lisa, and S. L. Syme. 1979. "Social Networks, Host Resistance and Mortality: A 9 Year Follow-Up Study of Alameda County California Residents." *American Journal of Epidemiology* 109: 186–204.

Bettencourt, B. Ann 1996. "Grassroots Organizations: Recurrent Themes and Research Approaches." *Journal of Social Issues* 52: 207–221.

Beutel, Ann, and Monica Kirkpatrick Johnson. 2004. "Gender and Prosocial Values during Adolescence." *Sociological Quarterly* 45: 379–393.

Beutel, Ann, and Margaret Mooney Marini. 1995. "Gender and Values." *American Sociological Review* 60: 436–448.

Bickford, Donna, and Nedra Reynolds. 2002. "Activism and Service-Learning: Reframing Volunteerism as Acts of Dissent." *Pedagogy* 2: 229–252.

Billis, David, and Howard Glennerster. 1998. "Human Services and the Voluntary Sector: Toward a Theory of Comparative Advantage." *Journal of Social Policy* 27: 79–98.

Black, Beverly, and Pamela Kovacs. 1999. "Age-Related Variation in Roles Performed by Hospice Volunteers." *Journal of Applied Gerontology* 18: 479–497.

Blackstone, Amy. 2004. " 'It's Just About Being Fair': Activism and the Politics of Volunteering in the Breast Cancer Movement." *Gender and Society* 18: 350–368.

Blau, Peter. 1964. *Exchange and Power in Social Life.* New York: Wiley.

———. 1977. "A Macrosociological Theory of Social Structure." *American Journal of Sociology* 83: 26–54.

Blee, Kathleen M. 2002. *Inside Organized Racism: Women in the Hate Movement.* Berkeley: University of California Press.

Bloom, L. R., and Kilgore, D. 2003. "The Volunteer Citizen After Welfare Reform in the United States: An Ethnographic Study of Volunteerism in Action." *Voluntas: International Journal of Voluntary and Nonprofit Organizations* 14(4): 431–454.

Blum, A. F., and P. McHugh. 1971. "The Social Ascription of Motives." *American Sociological Review* 36: 98–109.

Blum, Terry, and Paul Kingston. 1984. "Homeownership and Social Attachment." *Sociological Perspectives* 27: 159–180.

Blumberg, Rhoda. 1990. "White Mothers as Civil Rights Activists." Pp. 166–179 in *Women and Social Protest,* ed. Guida West and Rhoda Blumberg. New York: Oxford University Press.

Bobo, Lawrence, and Franklin D. Gilliam. 1990. "Race, Sociopolitical Participation, and Black Empowerment." *American Political Science Review* 84: 377–393.

Boraas, Stephanie. 2003. "Volunteerism in the United States." *Monthly Labor Review* 126: 3–11.

Boris, Elizabeth T. 1999. "The Nonprofit Sector in the 1990s." Pp. 1–34 in *Philanthropy and the Nonprofit Sector in a Changing America,* ed. Charles Clotfelter and Thomas Ehrlich. Bloomington: Indiana University Press.

Borsch-Supan, Axel, Karsen Hank, and Hendrick Jurges. 2005. "A New Comprehensive and International View of Ageing: Introducing the 'Survey of Health, Ageing and Retirement'." *European Journal of Aging* 2: 245–253.

Bowen, Deborah, M. Robyn Anderson, and Nicole Urban. 2000. "Volunteerism in a Community-Based Sample of Women Aged 50 to 80 Years." *Journal of Applied Social Psychology* 30: 1829–1842.

Bowen, Kurt. 1999. *Religion, Participation, and Charitable Giving.* Ottawa: Canadian Centre for Philanthropy.

Bowers, Jake. 2004. "Does Moving Disrupt Campaign Activity?" *Political Psychology* 25: 525–543.

Bowlby, Jeffrey, and Kathryn McMullen. 2002. *At the Crossroads: First Results for the 18- to 20-Year-Old Cohort of the Youth in Transition Survey.* Hull, Quebec: Human Resources Development Canada.

Bowman, Woods. 2004. "Confidence in Charitable Institutions and Volunteering." *Nonprofit and Voluntary Sector Quarterly* 33: 247–270.

Brady, Henry, Kay Schlozman, and Sidney Verba. 1999. "Prospecting for Participants: Rational Expectations and the Recruitment of Political Activists." *American Political Science Review* 93: 153–168.

Brady, Henry, Sidney Verba, and Kay Schlozman. 1995. "Beyond SES: A Resource Model of Political Participation." *American Political Science Review* 89: 269–295.

Braungart, Richard, and Margaret Braungart. 1989. "Political Generations." *Research in Political Sociology* 4: 281–319.

Brewer, Gene. 2003. "Building Social Capital: Civic Attitudes and Behavior of Public Servants." *Journal of Public Administration Research and Theory* 13: 5–26.

Broadbridge, Adelina, and Suzanne Horne. 1996. "Volunteers in Charity Retailing: Recruitment and Training." *Nonprofit Management and Leadership* 6: 255–270.

Brock, Kathy. 2001. "Promoting Voluntary Action and Civil Society through the State." *ISUMA* 2: 53–61.

Brooks, Arthur, and Gregory Lewis. 2001 "Giving, Volunteering, and Mistrusting Government." *Journal of Policy Analysis and Management* 20: 765–769.

Brown, Eleanor. 1999a. "Patterns and Purposes of Philanthropic Giving." Pp. 212–231 in *Philanthropy and the Nonprofit Sector in a Changing America,* ed. Charles Clotfelter and Thomas Erlich. Bloomington: Indiana University Press.

———. 1999b. "Volunteering and Public Service." *Law and Contemporary Problems* 62: 17–42.

Brown, Kevin. 2003. *Active Citizenship and the Secondary School Experience:*

Community Participation Rates of Australian Youth. Camberwell: Australian Council for Educational Research.

Brown, Phil, and Faith Ferguson. 1995. " 'Making a Big Stink': Women's Work, Women's Relationships, and Toxic Waste Activism." *Gender and Society* 9: 145–172.

Brown, S. Kathi. 2003. *Staying Ahead of the Curve: The AARP Working in Retirement Study.* Washington, D.C.: AARP.

Brown, Stephanie, Randolph Nesse, Amiram Vinokur, and Dylan Smith. 2003. "Providing Social Support May Be More Beneficial Than Receiving It." *Psychological Science* 14: 320–324.

Brudney, J. L. 1990. *Fostering Volunteer Programs in the Public Sector.* San Francisco: Jossey-Bass.

Bryant, W. Keith, Haekyung Jeon-Slaughter, Hyojin Kang, Aaron Tax. 2003. "Participation in Philanthropic Activities: Donating Money and Time." *Journal of Consumer Policy* 26: 43–73.

Burns, Nancy, Kay Lehman Schlozman, and Sidney Verba. 1997. "The Public Consequences of Private Inequality: Family Life and Citizen Participation." *American Political Science Review* 91: 373–389.

———. 2001. *The Private Roots of Public Action: Gender, Equality, and Political Participation.* Cambridge: Harvard University Press.

Burr, Jeffrey, Francis Caro, and Jennifer Morehead. 2002. "Productive Aging and Civic Participation." *Journal of Aging Studies* 16: 87–105.

Burr, Jeffrey, Namkee G. Choi, Jan E. Mutchler, and Francis G. Caro. 2005. "Caregiving and Volunteering: Are Private and Public Helping Behaviors Linked?" *Journals of Gerontology Series B: Psychological Sciences and Social Sciences* 60: S247–S256.

Bussell, Helen, and Deborah Forbes. 2002. "Understanding the Volunteer Market: The What, Where, Who and Why of Volunteering." *International Journal of Nonprofit and Voluntary Sector Marketing* 7: 244–257.

Butrica, Barbara, and Simone Schaner. 2005. "Satisfaction and Engagement in Retirement." *The Retirement Project: Perspectives on Productive Aging.* (Number 2): Washington, D.C.: Urban Institute.

Cable, Sherry. 1992. "Women's Social Movement Involvement: The Role of Structural Availability in Recruitment and Participation Processes." *Sociological Quarterly* 33: 35–51.

Cacioppe, Ron, and Philip Mock. 1984. "A Comparison of the Quality of Work Experience in Government and Private Organizations." *Human Relations* 37(11): 923–940.

Caiazza, Amy, and Heidi Hartmann. 2001. *Gender and Civic Participation.* Paper prepared for the John S. and James L. Knight Foundation.

Campbell, Catherine, and Rachel Wood. 1999. *Social Capital and Health.* London: Health Education Authority.

Campbell, David. 2004. "Acts of Faith: Churches and Political Engagement." *Political Behavior* 26: 155–180.

Campbell, David, and Steven Yonish. 2003. "Religion and Volunteering in America." Pp. 87–106 in *Religion and Social Capital,* ed. Corwin Smidt. Waco, Tex.: Baylor University Press.

Canada Council on Social Development. 2002. *What Influences Youth to Volunteer?* Toronto: Canadian Centre for Philanthropy.

Cancian, Francesca M., and Stacey Oliker. 2000. *Caring and Gender.* Lanham, Md.: Rowman and Littlefeld.

Caputo, Richard. 1997. "Women as Volunteers." *Nonprofit and Voluntary Sector Quarterly* 26: 156–174.

Carlin, Paul. 2001. "Evidence on the Volunteer Labor Supply of Married Women." *Southern Economic Journal* 67: 801–824.

Carlo, Gustavo, Morris Okun, George P. Knight, and Maria Rosario de Guzman. 2005. "The Interplay of Traits and Motives on Volunteering: Agreeableness, Extraversion and Prosocial Value Motivation." *Personality and Individual Differences* 38: 1293–1305.

Caro, Francis, and Scott Bass. 1995. "Increasing Volunteering among Older People." Pp. 71–96 in *Older and Active: How Americans over 55 Are Contributing to Society,* ed. Scott Bass. New Haven, Conn.: Yale University Press.

———. 1997. "Receptivity to Volunteering in the Immediate Post-Retirement Period." *Journal of Applied Gerontology* 16: 427–442.

Caspi, Avshalom, Brent Roberts, and Rebecca Shirer. 2005. "Personality Development: Stability and Change." *Annual Review of Psychology* 56: 433–584.

Center for Democracy and Citizenship. 2002. *Short-Term Impacts, Long-Term Opportunities.* Washington, D.C.: Center for Information and Research in Civic Learning and Engagement.

Center for Human Resources. 1999. *National Evaluation of Learn and Serve America (Summary Report).* Waltham, Mass.: Brandeis University.

Chambre, Susan. 1987. *Good Deeds in Old Age.* Lexington, Mass.: D.C. Heath and Co.

———. 1993. "Volunteerism by Elders: Past Trends and Future Prospects." *Gerontologist* 33: 221–228.

———. 1995. "Being Needful: Family, Love, and Prayer among AIDS Volunteers." *Research in the Sociology of Health Care* 12: 113–139.

Chan, Christopher, and Glen Elder, Jr. 2001. "Family Influences on the Social Participation of Youth: The Effects of Parental Social Involvement and Farming." *Rural Sociology* 66: 22–42.

Chappell, Neena. 1999. *Volunteeering and Healthy Aging: What We Know.* Toronto: Volunteer Canada.

Chappell, Neena, and Michael Prince. 1997. "Reasons Why Canadian Seniors Volunteer." *Canadian Journal on Aging* 16: 336–353.

Chaves, Mark. 2001. "Religious Congregations and Welfare Reform." *Society* 38: 21–27.

———. 2004. *Congregations in America.* Cambridge: Harvard University Press.

Chaves, Mark, Helen Giesel, and William Tsitsos. 2002. "Religious Variations in

Public Presence: Evidence from the National Congregational Study." Pp. 108–128 in *The Quiet Hand of God: Faith-Based Activism and the Public Role of Mainline Protestantism,* ed. Robert Wuthnow and John Evans. Berkeley: University of California Press.

Chavis, David, and Abraham Wandersman. 1990. "Sense of Community in the Urban Environment." *American Journal of Community Psychology* 8: 55–82.

Chen, David. 2004. "In Public Housing, It's Work, Volunteer or Leave." *New York Times,* April 15th, section A, p. 1.

Child Trends DataBank. 2003. *Volunteering.* http://www.childtrendsdatabank .org. Accessed November 7, 2003.

Choi, Lona. 2003. "Factors Affecting Volunteerism among Older Adults." *Journal of Applied Gerontology* 22: 179–196.

Christenson, James, James Hougland, Thomas Ilvento, and Jon Shepard. 1988. "The 'Organization Man' and the Community: The Impact of Organizational Norms and Personal Values on Community Participation and Transfers." *Social Forces* 66: 808–826.

Cigler, Allan, and Mark Joslyn. 2002. "The Extensiveness of Group Membership and Social Capital: The Impact on Political Tolerance Attitudes." *Political Research Quarterly* 55: 7–25.

Claibourn, Michael, and Paul Martin. 2000. "Trusting and Joining? An Empirical Test of the Reciprocal Nature of Social Capital." *Political Behavior* 22: 267–291.

Clain, Suzanne, and Charles Zech. 1999. "A Household Production Analysis of Religious and Charitable Activity." *American Journal of Economics and Sociology* 58: 923–946.

Clark, Candace. 1987. "Sympathy Biography and Sympathy Margin." *American Journal of Sociology* 93: 290–321.

Clark, Peter, and James Q. Wilson. 1961. "Incentive Systems: A Theory of Organizations." *Administrative Science Quarterly* 6: 129–166.

Clary, E. G., and J. Miller. 1986. "Socialization and Situational Influences on Sustained Altruism." *Child Development* 57: 1358–1369.

Clary, E. Gil, and Mark Snyder. 1991. "A Functional Analysis of Altruism and Prosocial Behavior: The Case of Volunteerism." Pp. 119–148 in *Prosocial Behavior,* ed. Margaret Clark. Newbury Park, Calif.: Sage.

Clary, E. G., M. Snyder, R. D. Ridge, J. Copeland, A. A. Stukas, J. Haugen, et al. 1998. "Understanding and Assessing the Motivations of Volunteers—a Functional Approach." *Journal of Personality and Social Psychology* 74(6): 1516–1530.

Clary, E. Gil, M. Snyder, R. Ridge, P. Miene, and J. Haugen. 1994. "Matching Messages to Motives in Persuasion: A Functional Approach to Promoting Volunteerism." *Journal of Applied Social Psychology* 24: 1129–1150.

Clary, E. Gil, Mark Snyder, and Arthur Stukas. 1996. "Volunteers' Motivations: Findings from a National Survey." *Nonprofit and Voluntary Sector Quarterly* 25: 485–505.

Cnaan, Ram. 2002. *The Invisible Caring Hand: American Congregations and the Provision of Welfare*. New York: New York University Press.

Cnaan, Ram, and R. Goldberg-Glenn. 1991. "Measuring Motivation to Volunteer in Human Services." *Journal of Applied Behavioral Science* 27: 269–285.

Cnaan Ram, Femida Handy, and Margaret Wadsworth. 1996. "Defining Who Is a Volunteer: Conceptual and Empirical Considerations." *Nonprofit and Voluntary Sector Quarterly* 25: 364–383.

Cnaan, Ram, Amy Kasternakis, and Robert Wineburg. 1993. "Religious People, Religious Congregations, and Volunteerism in Human Services: Is There a Link?" *Nonprofit and Voluntary Sector Quarterly* 22: 33–52.

Cnaan, Ram, Robert Wineburg, and Stephanie Boddie. 1999. *The Newer Deal: Social Work and Religion in Partnership*. New York: Columbia University Press.

Cochran, Donna. 1999. "Racial Differences in the Multiple Social Roles of Older Women: Implications for Depressive Symptoms." *Gerontologist* 39: 465–472.

Cohn, Steven, Steven Barkan, and William Halteman. 2003. "Dimensions of Participation in a Professional Social-Movement Organization." *Sociological Inquiry* 73: 311–337.

Cohn, Steven, Steven Barkan, and William Whitaker. 1993. "Activists against Hunger: Membership Characteristics of a National Social Movement Organization." *Sociological Forum* 8: 113–131.

Coleman, John. 2003. "Religious Social Capital: Its Nature, Social Location, and Limits." Pp. 33–48 in *Religion and Social Capital*, ed. Corwin Smidt. Waco, Tex.: Baylor University Press.

Coles, Robert. 1993. *The Call of Service: A Witness to Idealism*. Boston: Houghton Mifflin Company.

Conover, Pamela Johnston, Stephen Leonard, and Donald Searing. 1993. "Duty Is a Four-Letter Word: Democratic Citizenship in the Liberal Polity." Pp. 147–171 in *Reconsidering the Democratic Republic*, ed. George Marcus and Russell Hanson. University Park: Pennsylvania State University Press.

Conway, Margaret, and Alfonso Damico. 2001. *Building Blocks: The Relationship between High School and Adult Associational Life*. Paper presented at the 2001 Annual Meeting of the American Political Science Association, San Francisco.

Conway, Margaret, Sandra Damico, and Alfonso Damico. 1996. "Democratic Socialization in the Schools." Pp. 421–442 in *Democracy, Socialization and Conflicting Loyalties in East and West*, ed. Russell Farnen, Henk Dekker, Rolf Meyenberg, and Deiter German. New York: St Martin's Press.

Cooper, Helen, Sara Arber, Lin Fee, and Jay Ginn. 1999. *The Influence of Social Support and Social Capital on Health*. London: Health Education Authority.

Corey, Elizabeth, and James Garand. 2002. "Are Government Employees More Likely to Vote?" *Public Choice* 111: 259–283.

Cornwell, Benjamin, and Jill Ann Harrison. 2004. "Labor Unions and Voluntary Association Membership." *American Sociological Review* 69: 751–767.

Corporation for National and Community Service. 2006. *Volunteering in America: State Trends and Rankings.* Washington, D.C.: Corporation for National and Community Service, Office of Research and Policy Development.

Costa, Dora, and Matthew Kahn. 2003a. "Understanding the American Decline in Social Capital, 1952–1998." *Kyklos* 56: 17–46.

———. 2003b. "Civic Engagement and Community Heterogeneity: An Economist's Perspective." *Perspectives on Politics* 1: 103–111.

Coulthard, Melissa, Alison Walker, and Anthony Morgan. 2002. *People's Perceptions of Their Neighborhood and Community Involvement.* London: Office of National Statistics.

Cox, Kevin. 1982. "Housing Tenure and Neighborhood Activism." *Urban Affairs Quarterly* 18: 107–129.

Curtis, James, Douglas Baer, and Edward Grabb. 2001. "Nations of Joiners: Voluntary Association Memberships in Democratic Societies." *American Sociological Review* 66: 783–805.

Cutler, Stephen, and Nicholas Danigelis. 1993. "Organizational Contexts of Activity." Pp. 146–163 in *Activity and Aging,* ed. John Kelly. Newbury Park, Calif.: Sage.

Cutler, Stephen, and Jon Hendricks. 2000. "Age Differences in Voluntary Association Memberships: Fact or Artifact." *Journal of Gerontology* 55B: S98–S107.

Damico, Alfonso, Sandra Bowman Damico, and Margaret Conway. 1998. "The Democratic Education of Women: High School and Beyond." *Women and Politics* 19: 1–31.

Daniels, Arlene. 1988. *Invisible Careers: Women Civic Leaders from the Volunteer World.* Chicago: University of Chicago Press.

Davis, Mark, Jennifer Hall, and Marnee Meyer. 2003. "The First Year: Influences on the Satisfaction, Involvement, and Persistence of New Community Volunteers." *Personality and Social Psychology Bulletin* 29: 248–260.

Day, Kathleen, and Rose Anne Devlin. 1996. "Volunteerism and Crowding Out: Canadian Econometric Evidence." *Canadian Journal of Economics* 29: 37–53.

———. 1997. "Can Volunteer Work Help Explain the Male-Female Earnings Gap?" *Applied Economics* 29: 707–721.

———. 1998 "The Payoff to Work without Pay: Volunteer Work as an Investment in Human Capital." *Canadian Journal of Economics* 31: 1179–1191.

Dayton-Johnson, Jeff. 2001. *Social Cohesion and Economic Prosperity.* Toronto: James Lorimer and Co.

De Hart, Joep. 2001. "Religion and Volunteering in the Netherlands." Pp. 89–103 in *Social Capital and Participation in Everyday Life,* ed. Paul Dekker and Eric Uslaner. London: Routledge.

De Hart, Joep, and Paul Dekker. 1999. "Civic Engagement and Volunteering in the Netherlands: A 'Putnamian' Analysis." Pp. 75–109 in *Social Capital and*

European Democracy, ed. Jan van Deth, Marco Maraffi, Kenneth Newton, and Paul Whiteley. London: Routledge.

Delhey, Jan and Kenneth Newton 2005 "Predicting Cross-National Levels of Social Trust: Global Pattern or Nordic Exceptionalism?" *European Sociological Review* 21:311–327.

De Leon, Carlos Mendes, Thomas Glass, and Lisa Berkman. 2003. "Social Engagement and Disability in a Community Population of Older Adults." *American Journal of Epidemiology* 157: 633–642.

Dee, Thomas. 2003. The Effects of Catholic Schooling on Civic Participation. Circle Working Paper 09, College Park, Md.: Center for Information and Research on Civic Learning and Engagement.

Deegan, Mary Jo, and Larry Nutt. 1975. "The Hospital Volunteer: Lay Person in a Bureaucratic Setting." *Sociology of Work and Occupations* 2: 338–353.

Dekker, Paul, and Andries Van den Broek. 1996. "Volunteering and Politics: Involvement in Voluntary Associations from a 'Civic Culture' Perspective." Pp. 125–152 in *Political Value Change in Western Democracies,* ed. Loek Halman and Neil Nevitte. Tilburg: Tilburg University Press.

———. 1998. "Civil Society in Comparative Perspective." *Voluntas* 9: 11–38.

Dekker, Paul, and Loek Halman. 2003. "Volunteering and Values: An Introduction." Pp. 1–18 in *The Values of Volunteering: A Cross-Cultural Perspective,* ed. Paul Dekker and Loek Halman. New York: Kluwer Academic.

Devlin, Rose Anne. 2001. "Volunteers and the Paid Labour Market." *ISUMA* 2: 62–68.

Diani, Mario. 2001. *Social Movement Analysis and Voluntary Action Analysis.* Paper presented at the conference "The Third Sector from a European Perspective," University of Trento, Italy, 15–16 December 2001.

Diaz, William, Nadine Jalandoni, Kristen Hammill, and Tamara Koob. 2001. *Hispanic Giving and Volunteering: Findings from the Independent Sector's National Survey of Giving and Volunteering.* Washington, D.C.: Independent Sector.

Dietz, Robert. 2003. *The Social Consequences of Homeownership.* Unpublished paper, written for the Homeownership Alliance.

Dietz, Robert, and Donald Haurin. 2003. "The Social and Private Micro-Level Consequences of Homeownership." *Journal of Urban Economics* 54: 401–450.

Dingle, Alan. 2001. *Measuring Volunteering: A Practical Toolkit.* Washington, D.C.: Independent Sector.

DiPasquale, Denise, and Edward Glaeser. 1999. "Incentives and Social Capital: Are Homeowners Better Citizens?" *Journal of Urban Economics* 45: 354–384.

Dominguez, Sylvia, and Celeste Watkins. 2003. "Creating Networks for Survival and Mobility: Social Capital among African-American and Latin American Low-Income Mothers." *Social Problems* 50: 111–135.

Donahue, Michael, and Peter Benson. 1995. "Religion and the Well-Being of Adolescents." *Journal of Social Issues* 51: 145–161.

Dorsch, Kim, Harold Reimer, Valerie Sluth, David Paskevich, and Packianathan

Chelladurai. 2002. *What Affects a Volunteer's Commitment?* Toronto: Canadian Centre for Philanthropy.

Downton, James, Jr., and Paul Wehr. 1997. *The Persistent Activist: How Peace Commitment Develops and Survives.* Boulder, Colo.: Westview Press.

Duncan, Brian. 1999. "Modeling Charitable Contributions of Time and Money." *Journal of Public Economics* 72: 213–242.

Duncan, Cynthia, Margaret Walsh, and Gemma Beckley. 1999. "Doing Good While Doing Well: Professional Black Women in the Mississippi Delta." Pp. 138–160 in *Neither Separate nor Equal: Women, Race and Class in the South,* ed. Barbara Ellen Smith. Philadelphia: Temple University Press.

Eagly, Alice, and Maureen Crowley. 1986. "Gender and Helping Behavior: A Meta-Analytic Review of the Social Psychological Literature." *Psychological Bulletin* 100(3): 283–308.

Eccles, Jacquelynne, and Bonnie Barber. 1999. "Student Council, Volunteering, Basketball and Marching Band: What Kind of Extracurricular Activity Matters?" *Journal of Adolescent Research* 14: 10–43.

Eckstein, Susan. 2001. "Community Gift-Giving: Collective Roots of Volunteerism." *American Sociological Review* 66: 829–851.

Edwards, Patricia Klobus, John Edwards, and Ann Dewitt Watts. 1984. "Women, Work, and Social Participation." *Journal of Voluntary Action Research* 13: 7–22.

Egerton, Muriel. 2002. "Higher Education and Civic Engagement." *British Journal of Sociology* 53: 603–620.

Eisenberg, Nancy. 1992. *The Caring Child.* Cambridge: Harvard University Press.

Eisner, Jane. 1997. "No Paintbrushes, No Paint." *Brookings Review* 15: 39–41.

Elder, Glen, and Rand Conger. 2000. *Children of the Land: Adversity and Success in Rural America.* Chicago: University of Chicago Press.

Eliasoph, Nina. 1998. *Avoiding Politics: How Americans Produce Apathy in Everyday Life.* Cambridge: Cambridge University Press.

———. 2003. "Cultivating Apathy in Voluntary Associations." Pp. 199–212 in *The Values of Volunteering: A Cross-Cultural Perspective,* ed. Paul Dekker and Loek Halman. New York: Kluwer Academic.

Ellis, Susan, and Katherine Noyes. 1990. *By the People: A History of Americans as Volunteers.* San Francisco: Jossey-Bass.

Ellison, Christopher G., and David A. Gay. 1989. "Black Political Participation Revisited: A Test of Compensatory, Ethnic Community, and Public Arena Models." *Social Science Quarterly* 70: 101–119.

Elshaug, Carol, and Jacques Metzer. 2001. "Personality Attributes of Volunteers and Paid Workers Engaged in Similar Occupational Tasks." *Journal of Social Psychology* 141: 752–763.

Emig, Arthur, Michael Hesse, and Samuel Fisher.1996. "Black-White Differences in Political Efficacy, Trust, and Sociopolitical Participation." *Urban Affairs Review* 32: 264–277.

Emler, Nicholas, and Elizabeth Frazer. 1999. "Politics: The Education Effect." *Oxford Review of Education* 25: 253–273.

Erlinghagen, Marcel, and Karsten Hank. 2006. "The Participation of Older Europeans in Volunteer Work." *Ageing and Society* 26: 567–584.

Eurostat. 2004. *How Europeans Spend Their Time: Everyday Lives of Women and Men.* Luxembourg: Office for Official Publications of the European Communities.

Farkas, Janice, and Christine Himes. 1997. "The Influence of Caregiving and Employment on the Voluntary Activities of Midlife and Older Women." *Journal of Gerontology* 52B: S180–S189.

Farmer, Steven, and Donald Fedor. 2001. "Changing the Focus on Volunteering: An Investigation of Volunteers' Multiple Contributions to a Charitable Organization." *Journal of Management* 27: 191–211.

Feldman, Roberta, and Susan Stall. 2004. *The Dignity of Resistance: Women Residents' Activism in Chicago Public Housing.* Cambridge: Cambridge University Press.

Fendrich, James. 1993. *Ideal Citizens: the Legacy of the Civil Rights Movement.* Albany, NY: State University of New York Press.

Ferrari, Joseph, Michael Loftus, and Julia Pesek. 1999. "Young and Older Caregivers at Homeless Animal and Human Animal Shelters: Selfish and Selfless Motives in Helping Others." *Journal of Social Distress and the Homeless* 8: 37–49.

Ferree, G. Donald, John Barry, and Bruno Manno. 1998. *The National Survey of Philanthropy and Civic Renewal.* Washington, D.C.: National Commission on Philanthropy and Civic Renewal.

Field, David, and Ian Johnson. 1993. "Satisfaction and Change: A Survey of Volunteers in a Hospice Organization." *Social Science and Medicine* 36: 1625–1634.

Fischer, Karla, Bruce Rapkin, and Julian Rappaport. 1991. "Gender and Work History in the Placement and Perception of Elder Community Volunteers." *Psychology of Women Quarterly* 15: 261–279.

Fischer, Lucy, and Kay Schaffer. 1993. *Older Volunteers.* Newbury Park, Calif.: Sage.

Fisher, Bradley, Michele Day, and Caroline Collier. 1998. "Successful Aging: Volunteerism and Generativity in Later Life." Pp. 43–66 in *Social Gerontology,* ed. David Redburn and Robert McNamara. Westport, Conn.: Auburn House.

Flanagan, Constance. 2003. "Developmental Roots of Political Engagement." *PS: Political Science and Politics* 36: 257–261.

Flanagan, Constance, Jennifer Bowes, Britta Johnson, Beno Csapo, and Elena Sheblanova. 1998. "Ties That Bind: Correlates of Adolescents' Civic Commitments in Seven Countries." *Journal of Social Issues* 54: 457–475.

Flanagan, Constance, and Nakesha Faison. 2001. "Youth Civic Development: Implications of Research for Social Policy and Programs." *Social Policy Report* 15: 3–15.

Flanagan, Constance, Britta Jonsson, Luba Botcheva, Beno Csapo, Jennifer

Bowes, Peter Macek, Irena Averina, and Elena Sheblanova. 1999. "Adolescents and the 'Social Contract': Developmental Roots of Citizenship in Seven Countries." Pp.135–155 in *Roots of Civic Identity: International Perspectives on Community Service and Activism in Youth,* ed. Miranda Yates and James Youniss. Cambridge: Cambridge University Press.

Fletcher, Anne, Glen Elder, and Debra Mekos. 2000. "Parental Influences on Adolescent Involvement in Community Activities." *Journal of Research on Adolescence* 10: 29–48.

Fletcher, Thomas, and Debra Major. 2004. "Medical Students' Motivations to Volunteer: An Examination of the Nature of Gender Differences." *Sex Roles* 51: 109–114.

Flick, Mardi, Michael Bittman, and Jenny Doyle. 2002. *The Community's Most Valuable Asset—Volunteering in Australia.* Sydney: University of New South Wales Social Policy Research Centre.

Folbre, Nancy. 2001. *The Invisible Heart: Economics and Family Values.* New York: New Press.

Forrest, Ray, and Ade Kearns. 2001. "Social Cohesion, Social Capital and the Neighborhood." *Urban Studies* 38: 2125–2143.

Fosh, Patricia. 1981. *The Active Trade Unionist.* Cambridge: Cambridge University Press.

Fox, Mary Ann, Brooke Connolly, and Thomas Snyder. 2005. *Youth Indicators 2005: Trends in the Well-Being of American Youth.* Washington, D.C.: National Center for Educational Statistics.

Freedman, Marc. 1999. *Prime Time: How Baby Boomers Will Revolutionize Retirement and Transform America.* New York: Public Affairs.

Freeman, Richard. 1997. "Working for Nothing: The Supply of Volunteer Labor." *Journal of Labor Economics* 15: 140–167.

Frey, Bruno, and Lorenz Goette. 1999. Does Pay Motivate Volunteers? Working Paper #7, Institute for Empirical Research in Economics, University of Zurich, Switzerland.

Friedland, Lewis, and Shauna Morimoto. 2005. The Changing Lifeworld of Young People: Risk, Resume-Padding, and Civic Engagement. Circle Working Paper 40, Washington, D.C.: Center for Information and Research on Civic Learning and Engagement.

Frisch, Michael, and Meg Gerrard. 1981. "Natural Helping Systems: A Survey of Red Cross Volunteers." *American Journal of Community Psychology* 9(5): 567–579.

Funder, David. 2001. "Personality." *Annual Review of Psychology* 52: 197–221.

Furstenburg, Frank, and Sarah Kaplan. 2004. "Social Capital and the Family." Pp. 218–232 in *The Blackwell Companion to the Sociology of Families,* ed. Jacqueline Scott, Judith Treas, and Martin Richards. Oxford: Blackwell.

Gallagher, Sally.1994a. "Doing Their Share: Comparing Patterns of Help Given by Older and Younger Adults." *Journal of Marriage and the Family* 56: 567–578.

————. 1994b. *Older People Giving Care: Helping People and Community.* Westport, Conn.: Auburn House.

Gamm, Gerald, and Robert Putnam. 2001. "The Growth of Voluntary Associations in America, 1840–1940." Pp. 173–220 in *Patterns of Social Capital,* ed. Robert Rotberg. New York: Cambridge University Press.

Garcia, Immaculada, and Carmen Marcuello. 2002. "Family Model of Contributions to Non-Profit Organizations and Labor Supply." *Applied Economics* 34: 259–268.

Gartland, Peter. 2001. *Senior Corps Volunteer Participation.* Washington, D.C.: Corporation for National Service.

Gaskin, Katharine, and Justin Davis Smith. 1997. *A New Civic Europe? A Study of the Extent and Role of Volunteering.* London: National Center for Volunteering.

General Social Survey: Housing, Family and Social Statistics Division. 1999. *Overview of the Time Use of Canadians in 1998.* Ottawa: Statistics Canada.

Gerstel, Naomi. 2000. "The Third Shift: Gender and Care Work Outside the Home." *Qualitative Sociology* 23: 467–483.

Gerstel, Naomi, and Sally Gallagher. 1994. "Caring for Kith and Kin: Gender, Employment, and the Privatization of Care." *Social Problems* 41: 519–539.

Gerstel, Naomi, and Sally K. Gallagher. 2001. "Men's Caregiving: Gender and the Contingent Character of Care." *Gender & Society* 15 (2): 197–217.

Gerth, Hans, and C. Wright Mills. 1953. *Character and Social Structure.* New York: Harcourt Brace and Co.

Giddens, Anthony. 1998. *The Third Way: The Renewal of Social Democracy.* Cambridge: Polity Press.

Gilderbloom, John, and John Markham. 1995. "The Impact of Home Ownership on Political Beliefs." *Social Forces* 73: 1589–1607.

Giles, Dwight, and Janet Eyler. 1994. "The Impact of a College Community Service Laboratory on Students' Personal, Social and Cognitive Outcomes." *Journal of Adolescence* 17: 327–339.

Gilligan, Carol. 1982. *In a Different Voice: Psychological Theory and Women's Development.* Cambridge: Harvard University Press.

Gittell, Marilyn, Isolda Ortega-Bustamente, and Tracy Steffy. 2000. "Social Capital and Social Change: Women's Community Activism." *Urban Affairs Review* 36: 123–147.

Gittell, Ross, and Avis Vidal. 1998. *Community Organizing: Building Social Capital as a Development Strategy.* Thousand Oaks, Calif.: Sage.

Glaeser, Edward. 2001. "The Formation of Social Capital." *ISUMA* 2: 34–40.

Glaeser, Edward, David Laibson, Jose Scheinkman, and Christine Soutter. 2000. "Measuring Trust." *Quarterly Journal of Economics* 115: 811–846.

Glass, Thomas, Carlos Mendes de Leon, Richard Marotti, and Lisa Berkman. 1999. "Population Based Study of Social and Productive Activities as Predictors of Survival among Elderly Americans." *British Medical Journal* 319: 478–483.

Glass, Thomas, Teresa Seeman, A. Regula Herzog, Robert Kahn, and Lisa Berkman. 1995. "Change in Productive Activities in Late Adulthood." *Journal of Gerontology* 50B: S565–S76.

Goddard, Eileen. 1994. *Voluntary Work: A Study Carried Out on Behalf of the Home Office as Part of the 1992 General Household Survey.* London: HMSO.

Gold, Doris. 1971. "Women and Volunteerism." Pp. 384–400 in *Woman in Sexist Society: Studies in Power and Powerlessness*, ed. Vivian Gornick and Barbara Moran. New York: Basic Books.

———. 1979. *Opposition to Volunteerism: An Annotated Bibliography.* Chicago: CPL Bibliographies.

Goldstone, Jack, and Doug McAdam. 2001. "Contention in Demographic and Life-Course Context." Pp. 195–221 in *Silence and Voice in the Study of Contentious Politics*, ed. Ron Aminzade. New York: Cambridge University Press.

Gomez, Rafael, and Morley Gunderson. 2003. "Volunteer Activity and the Demands of Work and Family Life." *Industrial Relations* 58: 573–591.

Gora, Joann, and Gloria Nemerowicz. 1985. *Emergency Squad Volunteers: Professionalism in Unpaid Work.* New York: Praeger.

Goss, Kristin. 1999. "Volunteering and the Long Civic Generation." *Nonprofit and Voluntary Sector Quarterly* 28: 378–415.

Grabb, Edward, and James Curtis. 2005. *Regions Apart: The Four Societies of Canada and the United States.* Don Mills, Ontario: Oxford University Press.

Gracia, Enrique, and Juan Herrero. 2003. "Determinants of Social Integration in the Community." *Journal of Community and Applied Psychology* 14: 1–15.

Greeley, Andrew. 1997a. "Coleman Revisited: Religious Structures as a Source of Social Capital." *American Behavioral Scientist* 40: 587–594.

———. 1997b. "The Other Civic America: Religion and Social Capital." *American Prospect* 32: 68–73.

Greenberg, Edward, Leon Grunberg, and Kelly Daniel. 1996. "Industrial Work and Political Participation: Beyond 'Simple Spillover'." *Political Research Quarterly* 49: 305–330.

Greenberg, Michael. 2001. "Elements and Test of a Theory of Neighborhood Civic Participation." *Research in Human Ecology* 8: 40–51.

Greenfield, Emily, and Nadine Marks. 2004. "Formal Volunteering as a Protective Factor for Older Adults' Psychological Well-Being." *Journal of Gerontology: Social Science* 59B: S258–S264.

Greeno, C., and Eleanor Maccoby. 1993. "How Different Is the 'Different Voice'?" Pp. 193–198 in *An Ethic of Care*, ed. M. J. Larrabee. New York: Routledge.

Greenslade, Jaimi, and Katherine White. 2005. "The Prediction of Above-Average Participation in Volunteerism." *Journal of Social Psychology* 145: 155–173.

Grimm, Robert, Jr., Nathan Dietz, Kimberly Spring, Kelly Arey, and John Foster-Bey. 2005. *Building Active Citizens: The Role of Social Institutions in Teen*

Volunteering. Washington, D.C.: Corporation for National and Community Service.

Gronberg, Kirsten, and Brent Never. 2004. "The Role of Religious Networks and Other Factors in Different Types of Volunteer Work." *Nonprofit Management and Leadership* 14: 263–290.

Gross, Michael. 1995. "Moral Judgement, Organizational Incentives and Collective Action: Participation in Abortion Politics." *Political Research Quarterly* 48: 507–534.

Grossman, Jean, and Jean Rhodes. 2002. "The Test of Time: Predictors and Effects of Duration in Youth Mentoring Relationships." *American Journal of Community Psychology* 30: 199–219.

Groves, Julian McAllister. 1995. "Learning to Feel: The Neglected Sociology of Social Movements." *Sociological Review* 43: 435–461.

Groves, Julian. 2001. "Animal Rights and the Politics of Emotion." Pp. 212–232 in *Passionate Politics: Emotions and Social Movements*, ed. Jeff Goodwin. Chicago: University of Chicago Press

Grube, Jean, and Jane Piliavin. 2000. "Role Identity, Organizational Experiences, and Volunteer Performance." *Personality and Social Psychology Bulletin* 26: 1108–1119.

Gunn, Christopher. 2004. *Third-Sector Development: Making Up for the Market*. Ithaca, N.Y.: IRL Press.

Guterbock, Thomas M., and Bruce London. 1983. "Race, Political Orientation, and Participation: An Empirical Test of Four Competing Theories." *American Sociological Review* 48(4): 439–453.

Haddad, Mary Alice. 2004. "Community Determinants of Volunteer Participation and the Promotion of Civic Health: The Case of Japan." *NonProfit and Voluntary Sector Quarterly (Supplement)* 33: 8S–31S.

Haezewindt, Paul. 2002. "Investing in Each Other and the Community: The Role of Social Capital." Pp. 19–26 in *Social Trends No 33: 2003 Edition*. London: Home Office.

Hagedorn, Robert, and Sanford Labovitz. 1968. "Occupational Characteristics and Participation in Voluntary Associations." *Social Forces* 47: 16–27.

Hakim, Catherine. 1996. *Key Issues in Women's Work*. London: Athlone.

Hall, Michael, Tamara Knighton, Paul Reed, Patrick Bussiere, Don Macrae, and Paddy Bowen. 1998. *Caring Canadians, Involved Canadians: Highlights from the 1997 National Survey of Giving, Volunteering and Participating*. Ottawa: Statistics Canada.

Hall, Michael, Larry McKeown, and Karen Roberts. 2001. *Caring Canadians, Involved Canadians: Highlights from the 2000 National Survey of Giving, Volunteering and Participating*. Ottawa: Statistics Canada.

Hall, Peter. 1999. "Social Capital in Britain." *British Journal of Political Science* 29: 417–461.

Hall-Russell, Cheryl, and Robert Kasberg. 1997. *African-American Traditions of Giving and Serving*. Indianapolis: Indiana University Centre on Philanthropy.

Halman, Loek. 2003. "Volunteering, Democracy, and Democratic Attitudes." Pp. 179–198 in *The Values of Volunteering: A Cross-Cultural Perspective,* ed. Paul Dekker and Loek Halman. New York: Kluwer Academic.

Hamilton, Stephen, and Mickey Fenzel. 1988. "The Impact of Volunteer Experience on Adolescent Social Development: Evidence of Program Effects." *Journal of Adolescent Research* 3: 65–80.

Handy, Femida, Ram Cnaan, Jeffrey Brudney, Ugo Ascoli, Lucas Meijs, and Shree Ranade. 2000. "Public Perception of 'Who Is a Volunteer': An Examination of the Net-Cost Approach from a Cross-Cultural Perspective." *Voluntas* 11: 45–65.

Handy, Femida, and Narasimhan Srinivasan. 2004. "Hospital Volunteers: An Important and Changing Resource." *Nonprofit and Voluntary Sector Quarterly* 33: 28–54.

Hansen, David, Reed Larson, and Jodi Dworkin. 2003. "What Adolescents Learn in Organized Youth Activities: A Survey of Self-Reported Developmental Experiences." *Journal of Research on Adolescence* 13: 25–55.

Harlow, Robert, and Nancy Cantor. 1996. "Still Participating After All These Years." *Journal of Personality and Social Psychology* 71: 1235–1249.

Harris, Margaret.1996. "An Inner Group of Willing People: Volunteers in a Religious Context." *Social Policy and Administration* 30: 54–68.

Harry, Joseph. 1970. "Family Localism and Social Participation." *American Journal of Sociology* 75: 821–827.

Hart, Daniel, Robert Atkins, and Thomas Donnelly. 2006. "Community Service and Moral Development." Pp. 633–656 in *Handbook of Moral Development*, ed. Melanie Killen and Judith Smetana. Mahwah, N.J.: Erlbaum.

Hart, Daniel, Robert Atkins, and Debra Ford. 1998. "Urban America as a Context for the Development of Moral Identity in Adolescence." *Journal of Social Issues* 54(3): 513–530.

———. 1999. "Family Influences on the Formation of Moral Identity in Adolescence: Longitudinal Analyses." *Journal of Moral Education* 28: 375–386.

Hart, Holly, Dan McAdam, Barton Hirsch, and Jack Bauer. 2001. "Generativity and Social Involvement among African Americans and White Adults." *Journal of Research in Personality* 35: 208–230.

Haurin, Donald, Robert Dietz, and Bruce Weinberg. 2003. "The Impact of Neighborhood Ownership Rates: A Review of the Theoretical and Empirical Literature." *Journal of Housing Research* 13: 119–151.

Hayghe, Howard. 1991. Volunteers in the U.S.: Who Donates the Time?" *Monthly Labor Review* 114: 17–23.

Healy, Kieran. 2004. "Altruism as an Organizational Problem: The Case of Organ Procurement." *American Sociological Review* 69: 387–404.

Heinz, John, and Paul Schnorr. 2001. "Lawyer's Roles in Voluntary Associations." *Law and Social Inquiry* 26: 597–620.

Helliwell, John, and Robert Putnam. 2004. "The Social Context of Well-Being." *Philosophical Transactions of the Royal Society of London* 359: 1435–1446.

Helms, Sara. 2004. *Youth Volunteering in the States: 2002 and 2003*. College Park, Md.: Center for Information and Research on Civic Learning and Engagement.

Hendricks, Jon, and Stephen Cutler. 2004. "Volunteerism and Socio-emotional Selectivity in Later Life." *Journal of Gerontology: Social Sciences* 59B: S251–S247.

Hero, Rodney. 2003. "Social Capital and Racial Inequality in America." *Perspectives on Politics* 1: 113–122.

Herzog, A. Regula, and James Morgan. 1993. "Formal Volunteer Work among Older Americans." Pp. 119–142 in *Achieving a Productive Aging Society*, ed. Scott Bass, Francis Caro, and Yung-Ping Chen. Westport, Conn.: Auburn House.

Hitlin, Steven, and Jane Allyn Piliavin. 2004. "Values: Reviving a Dormant Concept." *Annual Review of Sociology* 30: 359–393.

Hodgkinson, Virginia. 1995. "Key Factors Influencing Caring, Involvement, and Community." Pp. 21–50 in *Care and Community in Modern Society*, ed. Paul Schervish, Virginia Hodgkinson, and Margaret Gates. San Francisco: Jossey-Bass.

———. 2003. "Volunteering in Global Perspective." Pp. 35–54 in *The Values of Volunteering: A Cross-Cultural Perspective*, ed. Paul Dekker and Loek Halman. New York: Kluwer Academic.

Hodgkinson, Virginia, and Murray Weitzman. 1996. *Giving and Volunteering in the United States: Findings from a National Survey*. Washington, D.C.: Independent Sector.

Hodgkinson, Virginia, Murray Weitzman, and Arthur Kirsch. 1990. "From Commitment to Action: How Religious Involvement Affects Giving and Volunteering." Pp. 93–114 in *Faith and Philanthropy in America*, ed. Robert Wuthnow. San Francisco: Jossey-Bass.

Hofer, Manfred. 1999. "Community Service and Social Cognitive Development in German Adolescents." Pp. 114–134 in *Roots of Civic Identity: International Perspectives on Community Service and Activism in Youth*, ed. Miranda Yates and James Youniss. Cambridge: Cambridge University Press.

Hoffman, John, and Jiangmin Xu. 2002. "School Activities, Community Service, and Delinquency." *Crime and Delinquency* 48: 568–591.

Hofstede, Geert. 2001. *Culture's Consequences: Comparing Values, Behaviors, Institutions, and Organizations Across Nations*. Thousand Oaks, CA: Sage Publications.

Hoge, Dean, Charles Zech, Patrick McNamara, and Michael Donahue. 1998. "The Value of Volunteers as Resources for Congregations." *Journal for the Scientific Study of Religion* 37: 470–481.

Hogg, Michael, Deborah Terry, and Katherine White. 1995. "A Tale of Two Theories: A Critical Comparison of Identity Theory and Social Identity Theory." *Social Psychology Quarterly* 58: 255–269.

Holden, Daphne. 1997. "'On Equal Ground': Sustaining Virtue among Volunteers in a Homeless Shelter." *Journal of Contemporary Ethnography* 26: 117–145.

Holloway, Sue, Sandra Short, and Sarah Tamplin. 2002. *Household Satellite Account (Experimental): Chapter 8 Voluntary Activity.* London: Office of National Statistics.

Homeownership Alliance. 2004. *The Benefits of Homeownership.* Washington, D.C.: Homeownership Alliance.

Hooghe, Marc. 2001. " 'Not for Our Kind of People': The Sour Grapes Phenomenon as a Causal Mechanism for Political Passivity." Pp. 162–175 in *Social Capital and Participation in Everyday Life,* ed. Paul Dekker and Eric Uslaner. London: Routledge.

———. 2003a. "Voluntary Associations and Democratic Attitudes." Pp. 89–112 in *Generating Social Capital,* ed. Marc Hooghe and Dietlind Stolle. New York: Palgrave MacMillan.

———. 2003b. "Participation in Voluntary Associations and Value Indicators: The Effect of Current and Previous Participation Experiences." *Nonprofit and Voluntary Sector Quarterly* 32: 47–69.

Hook, Janet. 2004. "Reconsidering the Division of Household Labor: Incorporating Volunteer Work and Informal Support." *Journal of Marriage and Family* 66: 101–117.

Horn, Laura, and Jennifer Berktold. 1998. *Profile of Undergraduates in U.S. Post-Secondary Education Institutions: 1995–6.* Washington, D.C.: National Center for Education Statistics, U.S. Department of Education.

Horn, Laura, Katherine Peter, and Kathryn Rooney. 2002. *Profile of Undergraduates in U.S. Post-Secondary Education Institutions: 1999–2000.* Washington, D.C.: National Center of Educational Statistics, U.S. Department of Education.

Horne, Suzanne, and Avril Maddrell. 2002. *Charity Shops: Retailing, Consumption and Society.* London: Routledge.

Hougland, James, and Jon Shepard. 1985. "Voluntarism and the Manager: The Impact of Structural Pressure and Personal Interest on Community Participation." *Journal of Voluntary Action Research* 14: 65–78.

House, James. 1981. "Social Structure and Personality." Pp. 525–561 in *Social Psychology: Sociological Perspectives,* ed. Morris Rosenberg and Ralph Turner. New York: Basic Books.

———. 1997. *Americans' Changing Lives: Waves I and II, 1986 and 1989* [Computer file]. ICPSR version. Ann Arbor: University of Michigan, Survey Research Center [producer], 1994. Ann Arbor, Mich.: Inter-university Consortium for Political and Social Research [distributor].

House, James, Debra Umberson, and Kenneth Landis. 1988. "Structures and Processes of Social Support." *Annual Review of Sociology* 14: 293–318.

Hoyert, Donna, and Marsha Mailick Seltzer. 1992. "Factors Related to the Well-Being and Life Activities of Family Caregivers." *Family Relations* 41: 74–81.

Huber, Evelyn, Charles Ragin, John D. Stephens, David Brady, and Jason Beckfield. 2004. *Comparative Welfare States Data Set,* Northwestern University, University of North Carolina, Duke University, and Indiana University.

Hudson, Pete. 1998. "The Voluntary Sector, the State, and Citizenship in the United Kingdom." *Social Service Review* 72: 452–465.

Hughes, Diane. 2001. "Cultural and Contextual Correlates of Obligation to Family and Community among Urban Black and Latino Adults." Pp. 179–226 in *Caring and Doing for Others*, ed. Alice Rossi. Chicago: University of Chicago Press.

Humphries, Stan. 2001. "Who's Afraid of the Big, Bad Firm: The Impact of Economic Scale on Political Participation." *American Journal of Political Science* 45: 678–699.

Hunt, Scott, and Robert Benford. 1994. "Identity Talk in the Peace and Justice Movement." *Journal of Contemporary Ethnography* 22: 488–517.

Hunt, Scott, Robert Benford, and David Snow. 1994. "Identity Fields: Framing Processes and the Social Construction of Movement Identities." Pp. 185–208 in *New Social Movements*, ed. Enrique Larana, Hank Johnson, and Joseph Gusfield. Philadelphia: Temple University Press.

Hunter, Kathleen, and Margaret Linn. 1980. "Psychosocial Differences between Elderly Volunteers and Non-volunteers." *International Journal of Aging and Human Development* 12: 205–213.

Hwang, Monica, Edward Grabb, and James Curtis. 2005. "Why Get Involved? Reasons for Voluntary-Association Activity among Americans and Canadians." *Nonprofit and Voluntary Sector Quarterly* 34: 387–403.

Independent Sector Nonprofit Sector Almanac. 2004. http://www.independent sector.org/PDFs/npemployment.pdf.

Inglehart, Ronald. 2003. "Modernization and Volunteering." Pp.55–70 in *The Values of Volunteering: A Cross-Cultural Perspective*, ed. Paul Dekker and Loek Halman. New York: Kluwer Academic.

———. 2004. *World Values Surveys and European Values Surveys*, 1999–2001 [Computer file]. ICPSR version. Ann Arbor, Mich.: Institute for Social Research [producer], 2002. Ann Arbor, Mich.: Inter-university Consortium for Political and Social Research [distributor].

Inglehart, Ronald, Miguel Basanez, and Alejandro Moreno. 1998. *Human Values and Beliefs: A Cross-Cultural Sourcebook*. Ann Arbor: University of Michigan Press.

Ironmonger, Duncan. 2000. "Measuring Volunteering in Economic Terms." Pp. 56–72 in *Volunteers and Volunteering*, ed. Jeni Warburton and Melanie Oppenheimer. Annandale, Australia: Federation Press.

Isaacs, Jeffrey. 2003. "Faith-Based Initiatives: A Civil Society Approach." *Good Society* 12: 3–10.

Jackman, Mary. 1994. *The Velvet Glove: Paternalism and Conflict in Gender, Race, and Class Relations*. Berkeley: University of California Press.

Jackman, Robert, and Ross Miller. 1998. "Social Capital and Politics." *Annual Review of Political Science* 1: 47–73.

Jackson, Elton, Mark Bachmeier, James Wood, and Elizabeth Craft. 1995. "Volunteering and Charitable Giving: Do Religious and Associational Ties Promote Helping Behavior?" *Nonprofit and Voluntary Sector Quarterly* 24: 59–78.

Janoski, Thomas. 1998. *Citizenship and Civil Society.* New York: Cambridge University Press.

Janoski, Thomas, Marc Musick, and John Wilson. 1998. "Being Volunteered? The Impact of Social Participation and Pro-social Attitudes on Volunteering." *Sociological Forum* 13: 495–520.

Janoski, Thomas, and John Wilson. 1995. "Pathways to Voluntarism: Family Socialization and Status Transmission Models." *Social Forces* 74: 271–292.

Jenkins, Krista. 2005. Gender and Civic Engagement. Circle Working Paper 41, Washington, D.C.: Center for Information and Research on Civic Learning and Engagement.

Jenkins, Krista, Molly Andolina, Scott Keeter, and Cliff Zukin. 2003. *Is Civic Behavior Political? Exploring the Multidimensional Nature of Political Participation.* Paper presented at the Annual Conference of the Midwest Political Science Association, Chicago.

Jenner, J. 1981. "Volunteerism as an Aspect of Women's Work Lives." *Journal of Vocational Behavior* 19: 302–314.

Jennings, M. Kent, and Ellen Ann Andersen. 2003. "The Importance of Social and Political Context: The Case of AIDS Activism." *Political Behavior* 25: 177–199.

Jennings, M. Kent, and Richard Niemi. 1971. "The Division of Political Labor between Mothers and Fathers." *American Political Science Review* 65: 69–82.

Jennings, M. Kent, and Laura Stoker. 2001. *Generations and Civic Engagement: A Longitudinal Multiple-Generation Analysis.* Paper presented at the 2001 American Political Science Association Convention, San Francisco.

Johnson, Monica Kirkpatrick, Timothy Beebe, Jeylan Mortimer, and Mark Snyder. 1998. "Volunteerism in Adolescence: A Process Perspective." *Journal of Research on Adolescence* 8: 301–332.

Johnson, Monica Kirkpatrick, Kristie Foley, and Glenn Elder, Jr. 2004. "Women's Community Service, 1940–1960: Insights from a Cohort of Gifted American Women." *Sociological Quarterly* 45: 45–66.

Jones, Frank. 1999. "Seniors Who Volunteer." *Perspectives on Labor and Income* 11: 9–17.

———. 2000. "Youth Volunteering on the Rise." *Perspectives on Labor and Income* 12: 36–42.

———. 2001. "Volunteering Parents: Who Volunteers and How Their Lives Are Affected." *ISUMA* 2: 69–74.

Jones, Keely. 2006. "Giving and Volunteering as Distinct Forms of Civic Engagement: The Role of Community Integration and Personal Resources in Formal Helping." *Nonprofit and Voluntary Sector Quarterly* 35: 249–266.

Jones-Correa, Michael, and David Leal. 2001. "Political Participation: Does Religion Matter?" *Political Research Quarterly* 54: 751–770.

Juknevicius, Stanislovas, and Aida Savicka. 2003. "From Restitution to Innovation: Volunteering in Postcommunist Countries." Pp. 127–142 in *The Values of Volunteering: A Cross-Cultural Perspective,* ed. Paul Dekker and Loek Halman. New York: Kluwer Academic.

Junn, Jane. 1999. "Participation in Liberal Democracy: The Political Assimilation of Immigrants and Ethnic Minorities in the United States." *American Behavioral Scientist* 42: 1417–1438.

Kang, Naewon, and Nojin Kwak. 2003. "A Multilevel Approach to Civic Participation." *Communication Research* 30: 80–106.

Karasek, Robert. 1990. *Healthy Work: Stress, Productivity, and the Reconstruction of Working Life.* New York: Basic Books.

Karniol, Rachel, Efrat Grosz, and Irit Schorr. 2003. "Caring, Gender Role Orientation, and Volunteering." *Sex Roles* 49: 11–19.

Katz, Daniel, and Robert Kahn. 1966. *The Social Psychology of Organizations.* New York: John Wiley.

Kawachi, Ichiro, and Lisa Berkman. 2001. "Social Ties and Mental Health." *Journal of Urban Health* 78: 458–467.

Kayal, Philip. 1993. *Bearing Witness: The Gay Men's Health Crisis and the Politics of AIDS.* Boulder, Colo.: Westview Press.

Keeter, Scott, Molly Andolina, Krista Jenkins, and Cliff Zukin. 2002. *Schooling and Civic Engagement in the United States.* Paper presented at the 2002 Annual Meeting of the American Political Science Association, Boston.

Keeter, Scott, Krista Jenkins, Cliff Zukin, and Molly Andolina. 2003. *Three Core Measures of Community-Based Civic Engagement: Evidence from the Youth Civic Engagement Indicators Project.* Paper presented at the Child Trends Conference on Indicators of Positive Development, Washington, D.C.

Keeter, Scott, Cliff Zukin, Molly Andolina, and Krista Jenkins. 2002. *The Civic and Political Health of the Nation: A Generational Portrait.* Washington, D.C.: Center for Information and Research on Civic Learning and Engagement.

Keith, Pat. 2003. *Doing Good for the Aged: Volunteers in an Ombudsman Program.* Westport, Conn.: Praeger.

Kelley, Margaret, Howard Lune, and Sheigla Murphy. 2005. "Doing Syringe Exchange: Organizational Transformation and Volunteer Commitment." *Non-Profit and Voluntary Sector Quarterly* 34: 362–386.

Kendall, Diane. 2002. *The Power of Good Deeds.* Lanham, Md.: Rowman and Littlefield.

Kendall, Jeremy. 2003. *The Voluntary Sector: Comparative Perspectives in the UK.* London: Routledge.

Kenny, Maureen, and Laura Gallagher. 2003. *Teenagers and Community Service.* Westport, Conn.: Praeger.

Kerestes, Michael, James Youniss, and Edward Metz. 2004. "Longitudinal Patterns of Religious Perspective and Civic Integration." *Applied Developmental Science* 8: 39–46.

Kieffer, Jarold. 1986 "The Older Volunteer Resource." Pp. 51–72 in *America's Aging: Productive Roles in an Older Society,* ed. Committee on an Aging Society, Institute of Medicine and National Research Council. Washington, D.C.: National Academy Press.

Kincade Jean, Donna Rabiner, Shulamit Bernard, Alison Woomert, Thomas Konrad, Gordon DeFriese, and Maria Ory.1996. "Older Adults as a Community Resource: Results from the National Survey of Self-Care and Aging." *Gerontologist* 36: 474–482.

Kingston, Paul, John Thompson, and Douglas Eichar. 1984. "The Politics of Homeownership." *American Politics Quarterly* 12: 131–150.

Kiviniemi, Marc, Mark Snyder, and Allen Omoto. 2002. "Too Many of a Good Thing? The Effects of Multiple Motivations on Stress, Cost, Fulfillment, and Satisfaction." *Personality and Social Psychology Bulletin* 28: 732–743.

Klandermans, Bert. 1984. "Social-Psychological Expansions of Resource Mobilization Theory." *American Sociological Review* 49: 583–600.

Klandermans, Bert. 1997 *The Social Psychology of Protest.* Oxford: Blackwell.

———. 2002. "How Group Identification Helps to Overcome the Dilemma of Collective Action." *American Behavioral Scientist* 45: 887–900.

Klatch, Rebecca. 2000. "The Contradictory Effects of Work and Family on Political Activism." *Qualitative Sociology* 23: 505–519.

Kleidman, Robert. 1994. "Volunteer Activism and Professionalism in Social Movement Organizations." *Social Problems* 41: 257–276.

Kleiner, Brian, and Chris Chapman. 1999. *Service Learning and Community Service among 6th through 12th Grade Students in the United States: 1996 and 1999.* Washington, D.C.: U.S. Department of Education.

Kluegel, James R., and Eliot R. Smith. 1986. *Beliefs About Inequality: American's Views of What Is and What Ought to Be.* New York: Aldine de Gruyter.

Knack, Stephen. 2002 "Social Capital and the Quality of Government: Evidence from the States." *American Journal of Political Science* 46: 772–785.

———. 2003. "Groups, Growth and Trust: Cross-Country Evidence on the Olson and Putnam Hypotheses." *Public Choice* 17: 341–355.

Knack, Stephen, and Philip Keefer. 1997. "Does Social Capital Have an Economic Payoff? A Cross-Country Investigation." *Quarterly Journal of Economics* 112: 1251–1288.

Knoke, David. 1988. "Incentives in Collective Action Organizations." *American Sociological Review* 53: 311–329.

———. 1990. "Networks of Political Action: Toward Theory Construction." *Social Forces* 68: 1041–1064.

Knox, Trevor. 1999. "The Volunteer's Folly and Socio-economic Man: Some Thoughts on Altruism, Rationality and Community." *Journal of Socio-Economics* 28: 475–492.

Kohut, Andrew. 1997. *Trust and Citizen Engagement in Metropolitan Philadelphia: A Case Study.* Philadelphia: Pew Research Center for the People and the Press.

Krause, Neal, A. Regula Herzog, and Elizabeth Baker. 1992. "Providing Support for Others and Well-Being in Later Life." *Journal of Gerontology* 47: P300–P311.

Krishnamurthy, Anita, Duncan Prime, and Meta Zimmeck. 2001. *Voluntary and Community Activities: Findings from the 2000 British Crime Survey.* London: Home Office.

Kulik, Liat. 2002. "Perceived Effects of Voluntarism on Marital Life in Late Adulthood." *Journal of Sociology and Social Welfare* 29: 35–52.

Kutner, Gail, and Jeffrey Love. 2003. *Time and Money: An In-Depth Look at 45+ Volunteers and Donors.* Washington, D.C.: AARP Knowledge Management.

Ladd, Everett. 1999. *The Ladd Report.* New York: Free Press.

Lam, Pui-Yan. 2002. "As the Flocks Gather: How Religion Affects Voluntary Association Participation." *Journal for the Scientific Study of Religion* 41: 405–422.

Landry, Bart. 2000. *Black Working Wives: Pioneers of the American Family Revolution.* Berkeley: University of California Press.

Lasby, David. 2004. *The Volunteer Spirit in Canada: Motivations and Barriers.* Toronto: Canadian Center for Philanthropy.

Latting, J. 1990. "Motivational Differences between Black and White Volunteers." *Nonprofit and Voluntary Sector Quarterly* 19: 121–136.

Laumann, Edward. 1973. *Bonds of Pluralism.* New York: John Wiley.

Lawson, Ronald, and Stephen Barton. 1990. "Sex Roles in Social Movements: A Case Study of the Tenant Movement in New York City." Pp. 41–56 in *Women and Social Protest,* ed. Guida West and Rhoda Blumberg. New York: Oxford University Press.

Lazerwitz, Bernard, and Michael Harrison. 1979. "American Jewish Denominations: A Social and Religious Profile." *American Sociological Review* 44(4): 656–666.

Lazerwitz, Bernard, J. A. Winter, et al. 1998. *Jewish Choices: American Jewish Denominationalism.* Albany, N.Y.: SUNY Press.

Lee, Lichang, Jane Allyn Piliavin, and Vaughn Call. 1999. "Giving Time, Money, and Blood; Similarities and Differences." *Social Psychology Quarterly* 62: 276–290.

Levy, Charles. 1968. *Voluntary Servitude: Whites in the Negro Movement.* New York: Appleton-Century-Crofts.

Lewis, Jane. 1999. "Reviewing the Relationship between the Voluntary Sector and the State in Britain in the 1990s." *Voluntas* 10: 255–270.

Lichter, Daniel, Michael Shanahan, and Erica Gardner. 2002. "Helping Others? The Effects of Childhood Poverty and Family Instability on Prosocial Behavior." *Youth and Society* 34: 89–93.

Li, Yunqing and Kenneth Ferraro. 2005. "Volunteering and Depression in Later Life: Social Benefit or Selection Processes?" *Journal of Health and Social Behavior* 46:68–84.

Lin, Nan, Xialan Ye, and William Ensel. 1999. "Social Support and Depressed Mood: A Structural Analysis." *Journal of Health and Social Behavior* 40: 344–359.

Lincoln, Eric, and Lawrence Mamiya. 1990. *The Black Church in the African-American Experience*. Durham, N.C.: Duke University Press.

Lipset, Seymour Martin. 1985. "Canada and the United States: The Cultural Dimension." Pp. 109–116 in *Canada and the United States,* ed. Charles Doran and John Sigler. Englewood Cliffs, N.J.: Prentice-Hall.

Lisman, David. 1998. *Toward a Civil Society*. Westport, Conn.: Bergin & Garvey.

Little, Jo. 1997. "Constructions of Rural Women's Volunteer Work." *Gender, Place and Culture* 4: 197–209.

Liu, Amy, and Terry Besser. 2003. "Social Capital and Participation in Community Improvement Activities by Elderly Residents in Small Towns in Rural Communities." *Rural Sociology* 68: 343–365.

Liu, Amy, Vernon Ryan, Herbert Aurbach, and Terry Besser. 1998. "The Influence of Local Church Participation on Rural Community Attachment." *Rural Sociology* 63: 432–450.

Lochner, Kimberly, Ichiro Kawachi, Robert Brennan, and Stephen Buka. 2003. "Social Capital and Neighborhood Mortality Rates in Chicago." *Social Science and Medicine* 56: 1797–1805.

Logan, John R., and Richard D. Alba. 1993. "Locational Returns to Human Capital: Minority Access to Suburban Community Resources." *Demography* 30: 243–267.

Lois, Jennifer. 2003. *Heroic Efforts: The Emotional Culture of Search and Rescue Volunteers*. New York: New York University Press.

Lopez, Mark. 2004. *Volunteering among Young People*. College Park, Maryland: Center for Information and Research on Civic Learning and Engagement, University of Maryland.

Lum, Terry, and Elizabeth Lightfoot. 2005. "The Effects of Volunteering on the Physical and Mental Health of Older People." *Research on Aging* 27: 31–55.

Lundstrom, Tommy, and Lars Svedberg. 2003. "The Voluntary Sector in a Social Democratic Welfare State—the Case of Sweden." *Journal of Social Policy* 32: 217–238.

Luoh, Ming-Ching, and A. Regula Herzog. 2002. "Individual Consequences of Volunteering and Paid Work in Old Age: Health and Mortality." *Journal of Health and Social Behavior* 43: 490–509.

Lynd, Robert, and Helen Merrell Lynd. 1929. *Middletown: A Study in American Culture*. New York: Harcourt, Brace and Co.

Lyons, Mark, and Susan Hocking. 2000. "Australia's Highly Committed Volunteers." Pp. 44–55 in *Volunteers and Volunteering,* ed. Jeni Warburton and Melanie Oppenheimer. Annandale, Australia: Federation Press.

MacDonald, Robert. 1996. "Labours of Love: Voluntary Working in a Depressed Local Economy." *Journal of Social Policy* 25: 19–38.

Mackie, Gerry. 2001. "Patterns of Social Trust in Western Europe and Their Genesis." Pp. 245–282 in *Trust in Society,* ed. Karen Cook. New York: Russell Sage Foundation.

Macy, Michael. 1988. "New-Class Dissent among Socio-Cultural Specialists: The Effects of Occupational Self-Direction and Location in the Public Sector." *Sociological Forum* 3: 325–356.

Mailloux, Louise, Heather Horak, and Colette Godin. 2002. *Motivation at the Margins: Gender Issues in the Canadian Voluntary Sector.* Ottawa: Voluntary Sector Initiative, Government of Canada. http://www.vsi-isbc.ca/eng/whats_new.cfm.

Mansbridge, Jane. 2001. "Complicating Oppositional Consciousness." Pp. 238–264 in *Oppositional Consciousness: The Subjective Roots of Social Protest,* ed. Jane Mansbridge and Aldon Morris. Chicago: University of Chicago Press.

Marini, Margaret Mooney, Pi-Ling Fan, Eric Finley, and Ann Beutel. 1996. "Gender and Job Values." *Sociology of Education* 69: 49–65.

Markham, William, and Charles Bonjean. 1995. "Community Orientations of Higher-Status Women Volunteers." *Social Forces* 73: 1553–1572.

———. 1996. "Employment Status and the Attitudes and Behaviors of Higher Status Women Volunteers, 1975 and 1992." *Sex Roles* 34: 695–717.

Marks, Helen, and Susan Jones. 2004. "Community Service in Transition." *Journal of Higher Education* 75: 307–339.

Marschall, Melissa, and Dietlind Stolle. 2004. "Race and the City: Neighborhood Context and the Development of Generalized Trust." *Political Behavior* 26: 125–153.

Marshall, Victor. 1983 "Generations, Age Groups and Cohorts: Conceptual Distinctions." *Canadian Journal of Aging* 2: 51–61.

Marta, Elena, Giovanni Rossi, and Lucia Boccacin. 1999. "Youth, Solidarity, and Civic Commitment in Italy." Pp. 73–96 in *Roots of Civic Identity: International Perspectives on Community Service and Activism in Youth,* ed. Miranda Yates and James Youniss. Cambridge: Cambridge University Press.

Martin, Mike. 1994. *Virtuous Giving: Philanthropy, Voluntary Service, and Caring.* Bloomington: Indiana University Press.

Martinson, Marty, and Meredith Minkler. 2006. "Civic Engagement and Older Adults: A Critical Perspective." *Gerontologist* 46: 318–324.

McAdam, Doug. 1986. "Recruitment to High-Risk Activism: The Case of Freedom Summer." *American Journal of Sociology* 92(1): 64–90.

———. 1992. "Gender as a Mediator of the Activist Experience: The Case of the Freedom Summer." *American Journal of Sociology* 97: 1211–1240.

McAdam, Doug, and Ronelle Paulsen. 1993. "Specifying the Relationship between Social Ties and Activism." *American Journal of Sociology* 99: 640–667.

McAdams, Dan, and Ed. de St. Aubin. 1992. "A Theory of Generativity and Its Assessment through Self-Report, Behavioral Acts, and Narrative Themes in Autobiography." *Journal of Personality and Social Psychology* 62: 1003–1115.

McAdams, Dan, Holly Hart, and Shadd Maruna. 1998. "The Anatomy of Generativity." Pp. 7–43 in *Generativity and Adult Development: How and Why We Care for the Next Generation*. Washington, D.C.: American Psychological Association.

McClintock, Norah. 2000. *Volunteering Numbers: Using the National Survey of Giving, Volunteering and Participation for Fundraising*. Toronto: Canadian Centre for Philanthropy.

McDonald, Katrina Bell. 1997. "Black Activist Mothering: A Historical Intersection of Race, Gender, and Class." *Gender and Society* 11: 773–795.

McIntosh, Barbara, and Nicholas Danigelis. 1995. "Race, Gender and the Relevance of Productive Activities for Elders' Affect." *Journals of Gerontology* 50: 229–240.

McKeown, Larry, David McIver, Jason Moreton, and Anita Rotondo. 2004. *Giving and Volunteering: The Role of Religion*. Toronto: Canadian Center for Philanthropy.

McLellan, Jeffrey, and James Youniss. 2003. "Two Systems of Youth Service: Determinants of Voluntary and Required Youth Community Service." *Journal of Youth and Adolescence* 32: 47–58.

McPherson, J. Miller, and Lynn Smith-Lovin. 1972. "Women and Weak Ties: Differences by Sex in the Size of Voluntary Organizations." *American Journal of Sociology* 87: 883–904.

———. 1986. "Sex Segregation in Voluntary Associations." *American Sociological Review* 51: 61–79.

Meadows, Lynn. 1996. "Discovering Women's Work: A Study of Post-Retirement Aged Women." *Marriage and Family Review* 24: 165–191.

Meier, Stephan, and Alois Stutzer. 2004. Is Volunteering Rewarding in Itself? Working Paper No. 180, Institute for Empirical Research in Economics, University of Zurich.

Meijs, Lucas, Femida Handy, Ram Cnaan, Jeffrey Brudney, Ugo Ascoli, Shree Ranade, Lesley Hustinx, and Idit Weiss. 2003. "All in the Eyes of the Beholder? Perceptions of Volunteering Across Eight Countries." Pp. 19–34 in *The Values of Volunteering: A Cross-Cultural Perspective,* ed. Paul Dekker and Loek Halman. New York: Kluwer Academic.

Meissner, Martin. 1971. "The Long Arm of the Job: A Study of Work and Leisure." *Industrial Relations* 10: 239–260.

Menchik, Paul, and Burton Weisbrod. 1987. "Volunteer Labor Supply." *Journal of Public Economics* 32: 159–183.

Merrell, Joy. 2000. " 'You Don't Do It for Nothing': Women's Experiences of Volunteering in Two Community Well Woman Clinics." *Health and Social Care in the Community* 8: 31–39.

Metz, Edward, Jeffrey McLellan, and James Youniss. 2003. "Types of Voluntary Service and Adolescents' Civic Development." *Journal of Adolescent Research* 18: 188–203.

Metz, Edward, and James Youniss. 2003. "A Demonstration That School-Based

Required Service Does Not Deter—But Heightens—Volunteerism." *PS: Political Science and Politics.* 36: 382–286.

Meyer, Katherine, and Linda Lobao. 1996. "Farm Couples and Crisis Politics: The Importance of Household, Spouse, and Gender in Responding to Economic Decline." *Journal of Marriage and Family* 59: 204–218.

Michaud, Jacinthe. 2004. "Feminist Representations of Women Living on Welfare." *Canadian Review of Sociology and Anthropology* 41: 267–289.

Midlarsky, Elizabeth. 1991. "Helping as Coping." Pp. 238–264 in *Prosocial Behavior,* ed. Margart Clark. Newbury Park, Calif.: Sage.

Midlarsky, Elizabeth, and Eva Kahana. 1994. *Altruism in Later Life.* Thousand Oaks, Calif.: Sage.

Miller, Harlan. 1982. "Altruism, Volunteers and Sociology." Pp. 45–53 in *Volunteerism in the Eighties,* ed. John Harman. Washington, D.C.: University Press of America.

Miller, Lynn, Gary Powell, and Joseph Selter. 1990. "Determinants of Turnover among Volunteers." *Human Relations* 43: 901–917.

Milroy, Beth Moore, and Susan Wismer. 1994. "Communities, Work and Public/Private Sphere Models." *Gender, Place and Culture* 1: 71–91.

Mirowsky, John, and Catherine Ross. 1989. *Social Causes of Psychological Distress.* New York: Aldine de Gruyter.

Mixer, Joseph. 1994. "Women as Professional Fundraisers." Pp. 223–253 in *Women and Power in the Nonprofit Sector,* ed. Teresa Odendahl and Michael O'Neill. San Francisco: Jossey-Bass.

Moen, Phyllis. 1997 "Women's Roles and Resilience: Trajectories of Advantage or Turning Points?" Pp. 133–156 in *Stress and Adversity over the Life Course,* ed. Ian Gottlib and Blair Wheaton. Cambridge: Cambridge University Press.

Moen, Phyllis, Donna Dempster-McClain, and Robin Williams. 1992. "Successful Aging: A Life Course Perspective on Women's Multiple Roles and Health." *American Journal of Sociology* 97: 1612–38.

Moen, Phyllis, and Vivian Fields. 2002. "Midcourse in the United States: Does Unpaid Community Participation Replace Paid Work?" *Ageing International* 27: 21–48.

Moen, Phyllis, Vivian Fields, Rhoda Meador, and Helen Rosenblatt. 2000. "Fostering Integration: A Case Study of the Cornell Retirees Volunteering in Service Program." Pp. 247–264 in *Social Integration in the Second Half of Life,* ed. Karl Pillemer, Phyllis Moen, Elaine Weatherington and Nina Glasgow. Baltimore: Johns Hopkins University Press.

Moen, Phyllis, Vivian Fields, Heather Quick, and Heather Hofmeister. 2000. "A Life-Course Approach to Retirement and Social Integration." Pp. 75–107 in *Social Integration in the Second Half of Life,* ed. Karl Pillemer, Phyllis Moen, Elaine Weatherington and Nina Glasgow. Baltimore: Johns Hopkins University Press.

Moen, Phyllis, Julie Robinson, and Donna Dempster-McClain. 1995. "Caregiving and Women's Well-Being: A Life Course Approach." *Journal of Health and Social Behavior* 36: 259–273.

Moore, Cynthia, and Joseph P. Allen. 1996. "The Effects of Volunteering on the Young Volunteer." *Journal of Primary Prevention* 17: 231–258.

Moore, Gwen, and J. Allen Whitt. 2000. "Gender and Networks in a Local Voluntary-Sector Elite." *Voluntas* 11: 309–328.

Moore, Kristin, Jeffrey Evans, Jean Brooks-Gunn, and Jodie Roth. 2001. "What Are Good Child Outcomes?" Pp. 59–84 in *The Well-Being of Children and Families,* ed. Arland Thornton. Ann Arbor: University of Michigan Press.

Morgan, James N. 1986. "Unpaid Productive Activity over the Life Course." Pp. 73–109 in *America's Aging: Productive Roles in an Older Society,* ed. Committee on an Aging Society, Institute of Medicine and the National Research Council. Washington, D.C.: National Academy Press.

Morgan, William, and Matthew Streb. 2001. "Building Citizenship: How Student Voice in Service-Learning Develops Civic Values." *Social Science Quarterly* 82: 154–169.

Morrow-Howell, Nancy, Jim Hinterlong, Philip Rozario, and Fengyan Tan. 2003. "Effects of Volunteering on the Well-Being of Older Adults." *Journals of Gerontology* 58B: S137–S145.

Morrow-Howell, Nancy, James Hinterlong, Michael Sherraden, and Philip Rozario. 2001. "Advancing Research on Productivity in Later Life." Pp. 285–312 in *Productive Aging,* ed. Nancy Morrow-Howell, James Hinterlong and Michael Sherraden. Baltimore: Johns Hopkins University Press.

Morrow-Howell, Nancy, Susan Kinnevy, and Marylen Mann. 1999. "The Perceived Benefits of Participation in Volunteer and Educational Activities." *Journal of Gerontological Social Work* 32: 65–80.

Morrow-Howell, Nancy, and A. Mui 1989. "Elderly Volunteers: Reasons for Initiating and Terminating Service." *Journal of Gerontological Social Work* 13: 21–34

Mueller, Marnie. 1975. "Economic Determinants of Volunteer Work among Women." *Signs* 1: 325–333.

Munch, Allison, J. Miller McPherson, and Lynn Smith-Lovin. 1997. "The Effects of Childrearing for Men and Women." *American Sociological Review* 62: 509–520.

Murphy, David, Kelly Lamonda, Jan Carney, and Paula Duncan. 2004. "Relationships of a Brief Measure of Youth Assets to Health Promoting and Risk Behaviors." *Journal of Adolescent Health* 34: 184–191.

Murray, Sylvie. 2003. *The Progressive Housewife: Community Activism in Suburban Queens, 1945–1965.* Philadelphia: University of Pennsylvania Press.

Musick, Marc, A. Regula Herzog, and James House. 1999. "Volunteering and Mortality among Older Adults: Findings from a National Sample." *Journal of Gerontology* 54B:S173–S180.

Musick, Marc, and John Wilson. 2003. "Volunteering and Depression" *Social Science and Medicine* 56: 259–269.

Musick, Marc, John Wilson, and William Bynum, Jr. 2000. "Race and Formal Volunteering." *Social Forces* 78: 1539–1570.

Mustillo, Sarah, John Wilson, and Scott Lynch. 2004. "Legacy Volunteering: A Test of Two Theories of Intergenerational Transmission." *Journal of Marriage and Family* 66: 530–541.

Mutchler, Jan, Jeffrey Burr, and Francis Caro. 2003. "From Paid Work to Volunteer: Leaving the Paid Workforce and Volunteering in Later Life." *Social Forces* 81: 1267–1293.

Nakano, Lynne. 2000. "Volunteering as a Lifestyle Choice: Negotiating Self-Identities in Japan." *Ethnology* 39: 93–107.

Naples, Nancy. 1991. " 'Just What Needed to be Done': The Political Practice of Women Community Workers in Low Income Neighborhoods." *Gender and Society* 5: 478–494.

Naples, Nancy. 1992. "Activist Mothering: Cross-Generational Continuity in the Community Work of Women from Low-Income Urban Neighborhoods." *Gender and Society* 6: 441–463.

Negrey, Cynthia. 1993. *Gender, Time and Reduced Work*. Albany: State University of New York Press.

Nelsen, Bonalyn, and Stephen Barley. 1997. "For Love or Money? Commodification and the Construction of an Occupational Mandate." *Administrative Science Quarterly* 42: 619–653.

Nelson, H. Wayne, Karen Hooker, Kimberly De Hart, John Edwards, and Kevin Lanning. 2004. "Factors Important to Success in the Volunteer Long-Term Care Ombudsman Role." *Gerontologist* 44: 116–120.

Nepstad, Sharon. 2004. "Persistent Resistance: Commitment and Community in the Plowshares Movement." *Social Problems* 51: 43–60.

Netuveli, Gopalakrishnan, Richard Wiggins, Zoe Hildon, Scott Montgomery, and David Blane. 2006. "Quality of Life at Older Ages: Evidence from the English Longitudinal Study of Aging (Wave 1)." *Journal of Epidemiology and Community Health* 60: 357–363.

Newman, Katherine. 2001. "Local Caring: Social Capital and Social Responsibility in New York's Minority Neighborhoods." Pp. 157–178 in *Caring and Doing for Others*, ed. Alice Rossi. Chicago: University of Chicago Press.

Nie, Norman, and D. Sunshine Hillygus. 2001. "Education and Democratic Citizenship." Pp. 30–57 in *Making Good Citizens*, ed. Diane Ravitch and Joseph Viterriti. New Haven, Conn.: Yale University Press.

Nie, Norman, Jane Junn, and Kenneth Stehlik Barry. 1996. *Education and Democratic Citizenship in America*. Chicago: University of Chicago Press.

Niemi, Richard, and Chris Chapman. 1998. *The Civic Development of 9th-through-12th Grade Students in the United States: 1996*. Washington, D.C.: National Center for Educational Statistics, U.S. Department of Education.

Niemi, Richard, Mary Hepburn, and Chris Chapman. 2000. "Community Service by High School Students." *Political Behavior* 22: 45–69.

Nolin, Mary Jo, Bradford Chaney, Chris Chapman, and Kathryn Chandler. 1997. *Student Participation in Community Service Activity.* Washington, D.C.: US Department of Education, National Center for Educational Statistics.

Nord, Christine, Deeann Brimhall, and Jerry West. 1997. *Fathers' Involvement in Their Children's Schools.* Washington, D.C.: Department of Education, National Center for Education Statistics.

Norris, Pippa. 2002. *Democratic Phoenix: Reinventing Political Activism.* Cambridge: Cambridge University Press.

———. 2004. "Still a Public Service Ethos?" Unpublished paper, John F. Kennedy School of Government, Harvard University.

Odendahl, Terry, and Sabrina Youmans. 1994. "Women on Nonprofit Boards." Pp. 183–221 in *Women and Power in the Nonprofit Sector,* ed. Teresa Odendahl and Michael O'Neill. San Francisco: Jossey-Bass.

O'Donnell, Lydia, Ann Stueve, Alexi San Doval, Richard Duran, Rebecca Atnafou, Deborah Haber, Norma Johnson, Helen Murray, Uda Grant, and Gregory Juhn. 1999. "Violence Prevention and Young Adolescents' Participation in Community Youth Service." *Journal of Adolescent Health* 24: 28–37.

Oesterle, Sabrina, Monica Kirkpatrick Johnson, and Jeylan Mortimer. 2004. "Volunteerism during the Transition to Adulthood: A Life-Course Perspective." *Social Forces* 82: 1123–1151.

Okun, Morris. 1993. "Predictors of Volunteer Status in a Retirement Community." *International Journal of Aging and Human Development* 36: 57–74.

———. 1994. "Relation between Motives for Organizational Volunteering and Frequency of Volunteering by Elders." *Journal of Applied Gerontology* 13: 115–126.

Okun, Morris, Alicia Barr, and A. Regula Herzog. 1998. "Motivation to Volunteer by Older Adults: A Test of Competing Measurement Models." *Psychology and Aging* 13: 608–617.

Okun, Morris, and Nancy Eisenberg. 1992. "A Comparison of Office and Adult Day-Care Center Older Volunteers." *International Journal of Aging and Human Development* 35: 219–233.

Okun, Morris, and Amy Schultz. 2003. "Aging and Motives for Volunteering: Testing Hypotheses Derived from Socioemotional Selectivity Theory." *Psychology and Aging* 18: 231–239.

Okun, Morris, William Stock, Marilyn Haring, and Robert Witter. 1984. "The Social Activity/Subjective Well-being Relation." *Research on Aging* 6: 45–65.

Oliver, J. Eric. 1999. "The Effects of Metropolitan Economic Segregation on Local Civic Participation." *American Political Science Review* 43: 186–212.

Oliver, Pamela. 1984. "'If You Don't Do It, Nobody Else Will': Active and Token Contributors to Local Collective Action." *American Sociological Review* 49: 601–610.

Oman, Doug, Carl Thoresen, and Kay McMahon. 1999. "Volunteerism and Mortality among Community Dwelling Elderly." *Journal of Health Psychology* 4: 301–316.

Omi, Michael, and Howard Winant. 1986. *Racial Formation in the United States: From the 1960s to the 1980s.* New York: Routledge.

Omoto, Allen, Diane Odom Gunn, and A. Lauren Crain. 1998. "Helping in Hard Times: Relationship Closeness and the AIDS Volunteer Experience." Pp. 106–128 in *HIV and Social Interaction,* ed. Valerian Derlega and Anita Barbee. Thousand Oaks, Calif.: Sage.

———. 1993. "Volunteers and Their Motivations: Theoretical Issues and Practical Concerns." *Nonprofit Management and Leadership* 4: 157–176.

———. 1995. "Sustained Helping Without Obligation: Motivation, Longevity of Service and Perceived Attitude Change among AIDS Volunteers." *Journal of Personal and Social Psychology* 68: 671–686.

Omoto, Allen, and Mark Snyder. 2002 "Considerations of Community: The Context and Process of Volunteerism." *American Behavioral Scientist* 45: 846–867.

Omoto, Allen, Mark Snyder, and James Berghuis. 1993. "The Psychology of Volunteerism: A Conceptual Analysis and a Program of Action Research." Pp. 333–356 in *The Social Psychology of HIV Infection,* ed. John Pryor and Glenn Reeder. Hillsdale, N.J.: Lawrence Eerlbaum Associates.

Omoto, Allen, Mark Snyder, and Steven Martino. 2000. "Volunteerism and the Life Course: Investigating Age-Related Agendas for Action." *Basic and Applied Social Psychology* 22: 181–197.

O'Neill, Michael. 2001. "Research on Giving and Volunteering: Methodological Considerations." *Nonprofit and Voluntary Sector Quarterly* 30: 505–514.

Onyx, Jenny, and Rosemary Leonard. 2000. "Women, Volunteering and Social Capital." Pp. 113 in *Volunteers and Volunteering,* ed. Jeni Warburton and Melanie Oppenheimer. Annandale, Australia: Federation Press.

Oorschot, Wim van. 2005. "The Social Capital of European Welfare States: The Crowding Out Hypothesis Revisited." *Journal of European Social Policy* 15: 5–26.

Ostrower, Francie. 2002. *Trustees of Culture: Power, Wealth, and Status on Elite Art Boards.* Chicago: University of Chicago Press.

Pancer, S. Mark, and Michael Pratt. 1999. "Social and Family Determinants of Community Service Involvement in Canadian Youth." Pp. 32–55 in *Roots of Civic Identity: International Perspectives on Community Service and Activism in Youth,* ed. Miranda Yates and James Youniss. Cambridge: Cambridge University Press.

Parboteeah, K. Praveen, John Cullen, and Lrong Lim. 2004. "Formal Volunteering: A Cross-National Test." *Journal of World Business* 39: 431–441.

Park, J., and C. Smith. 2000. " 'To whom has much been given . . . ': Religious Capital and Community Voluntarism among Churchgoing Protestants." *Journal for the Scientific Study of Religion* 39: 272–286.

Parker, John. 2003. *Social Theory*. New York: Palgrave Macmillan.

Parry, Geraint, George Moyser, and Neil Day. 1992. *Political Participation and Democracy in Britain*. Cambridge: Cambridge University Press.

Parsons, Talcott. 1949. *Essays in Sociological Theory Pure and Applied:* Glencoe, Ill.: Free Press.

Pascarella, Ernest, Corinna Ethington, and John Smart. 1988. "The Influence of College on Humanitarian/Civic Involvement Values." *Journal of Higher Education* 59: 412–437.

Passy, Florence. 2001. "Political Altruism and the Solidarity Movement." Pp. 3–25 in *Political Altruism? Solidarity Movements in International Perspective*, ed. Marco Giugni and Florence Passy. Lanham, Md.: Rowman and Littlefield.

Passy, Florence, and Marco Giugni. 2001. "Social Networks and Individual Perceptions: Explaining Differential Participation in Social Movements." *Sociological Forum* 16: 123–153.

Pattie, Charles, Patrick Seyd, and Paul Whiteley. 2003. "Citizenship and Civic Engagement: Attitudes and Behavior in Britain." *Political Studies* 51: 443–468.

Patulny, Roger, Michael Bittman, and Kimberly Fisher. 2003. "Trust and Volunteering: Contrasting Time Diaries with Values Data." Paper presented at the 25th IATUR Conference on Time Use Research, Brussels, September, 2003.

Pavalko, R. M. 1988. *Sociology of Occupations and Professions,* 2nd ed. Itasca, Ill.: Peacock.

Paxton, Pamela. 1999. "Is Social Capital Declining in the United States?" *American Journal of Sociology* 105: 88–127

Payne, Barbara, and C. Neil Bull. 1985. "The Older Volunteer: The Case for Interdependence." Pp. 251–272 in *Social Bonds in Later Life*, ed. Warren Peterson and Jill Quadagno. Beverly Hills, Calif.: Sage.

Payne, Sheila. 2001. "The Role of Volunteers in Hospice Bereavement Support in New Zealand." *Palliative Medicine* 15: 107–115.

Pearce, Jone. 1993. *Volunteers: The Organizational Behavior of Unpaid Workers*. London: Routledge.

Penn, Everette. 2000. *Reducing Delinquency through Service*. Washington, D.C.: Corporation for National Service.

Penner, Louis. 2002. "Dispositional and Organizational Influences on Sustained Volunteerism: An Interactionist Perspective." *Journal of Social Issues* 58: 447–467.

———. 2004. "Volunteerism and Social Problems: Making Things Better or Worse?" *Journal of Social Issues* 60: 645–666.

Penner, Louis, John Dovidio, Jane Piliavin, and David Schroeder. 2005. "Prosocial Behavior: Multilevel Perspectives." *Annual Review of Psychology* 56: 365–392.

Penner, Louis, and Marcia Finkelstein. 1998. "Dispositional and Structural Determinants of Volunteerism." *Journal of Personality and Social Psychology* 74: 525–537.

Penney, Cynthia. 1998. "Single-Minded Volunteers." *Good Housekeeping* 227: 27.

Perkins, Douglas, Barbara Brown, and Ralph Taylor. 1996. "The Ecology of Empowerment: Predicting Participation in Community Organizations." *Journal of Social Issues* 52: 85–110.

Perkins, Kenneth. 1988. "Note on Commitment and Community among Volunteer Firefighters." *Sociological Inquiry* 58: 117–121.

———. 1990. "Volunteer Fire and Rescue Departments." *Nonprofit and Voluntary Sector Quarterly* 19: 359–370.

Perren, Kim, Sara Arber, and Kate Davidson. 2003. "Men's Organizational Affiliations in Later Life: The Influence of Social Class and Marital Status on Informal Group Membership." *Ageing and Society* 23: 69–82.

Perry, James. 2001. *The Outcomes of Senior Service*. Testimony before the U.S. Senate Special Committee on Aging, Field Hearing, Indianapolis, Indiana.

Perry, James, and Michael Katula. 2001. "Does Service Affect Citizenship?" *Administration and Society* 33: 330–365.

Perry, James, Ann Marie Thompson, Mary Tschirhart, Debra Mesch, and Geunjoo Lee. 1999. "Inside a Swiss Army Knife: An Assessment of AmeriCorps." *Journal of Public Administration Research and Theory* 9: 225–250.

Peter D. Hart Research Associates. 2002. *The New Face of Retirement: An Ongoing Survey of American Attitudes on Aging*. Washington, D.C.

Pew Hispanic Center. 2004. *The 2004 National Survey of Latinos: Politics and Civic Participation*. Washington, D.C.: Henry Kaiser Foundation.

Pew Research Center for People and the Press. 2001. *Faith-Based Funding Backed, But Church-State Doubts Abound*. http://people-press.org/reports /print.php3?ReportID=15.

Phillips, Susan, Brian Little, and Laura Goodine. 2002a. *Recruiting, Retaining, and Rewarding Volunteers: What Volunteers Have to Say*. Toronto: Canadian Centre for Philanthropy.

Phillips, Susan, Brian Little, and Laura Goodine. 2002b. *Caregiving Volunteers: A Coming Crisis?* Toronto: Canadian Centre for Philanthropy.

Phipps, Shelley. 2003. "Social Cohesion and the Well-Being of Canadian Children." Pp. 79–121 in *The Economic Implications of Social Cohesion*, ed. Lars Osberg. Toronto: University of Toronto Press.

Pierucci, J., and R. Noel. 1980. "Duration of Participation of Correctional Volunteers as a Function of Personal and Situational Variables." *Journal of Community Psychology* 8: 245–250.

Piliavin, Jane. 2002. "Doing Well by Doing Good: Benefits for the Benefactor." Unpublished paper.

Piliavin, Jane, and Jean Grube. 2002. "Role as Resource for Action in Public Service." *Journal of Social Issues* 58: 469–485.

Pillemer, Karl, and Nina Glasgow. 2000. "Social Integration and Aging: Backgrounds and Trends." Pp. 19–48 in *Social Integration in the Second Half of Life*, ed. Karl Pillemer, Phyllis Moen, Elaine Weatherington and Nina Glasgow. Baltimore: Johns Hopkins University Press.

Planty, Mike, and Michael Regnier. 2003. *Volunteer Service by Young People from High School through Early Adulthood.* Washington, D.C.: National Center for Education Statistics.

Poppendieck, Janet. 1998. *Sweet Charity? Emergency Food and the End of Entitlement.* New York: Viking.

Portney, Kent, and Jeffrey Berry. 1997. "Mobilizing Minority Communities: Social Capital and Participation in Urban Neighborhoods." *American Behavioral Scientist.* 40: 632–644.

Prentice, Susan, and Evelyn Ferguson. 2000. "Volunteerism, Gender, and the Changing Welfare State." Pp. 118–141 in *Restructuring Caring Labour,* ed. Sheila Neysmith. New York: Oxford University Press.

Presser, H. B. 1994. "Employment Schedules among Dual-Earner Spouses and the Division of Household Labor by Gender." *American Sociological Review* 59: 348–364.

Prime, Duncan, Meta Zimmick, and Andrew Zurawan. 2002. *Active Communities: Initial Findings from the 2001 Home Office Citizenship Survey.* London: Home Office.

Profile of Illinois: An Engaged State. Report of the Illinois Civic Engagement Project. 2001. http://civic.uis.edu/report/release.html.

Prouteau, Lionel, and Francoise-Charles Wolff. 2003. "Does Voluntary Work Pay Off in the Labor Market?" http://www.lameta.univ-montpl.fr/jma2003/Articles/JMA2003_Prouteau.pdf. Accessed December 1, 2003.

Puffer, Sheila, and James Meindl. 1992. "The Congruence of Motives and Incentives in a Voluntary Organization." *Journal of Organizational Behavior* 13: 425–434.

Pusey, Michael. 2000. "Middle Australians in the Grip of Economic 'Reform' . . . Will They Volunteer?" Pp. 19–31 in *Volunteers and Volunteering,* ed. Jeni Warburton and Melanie Oppenheimer. Annandale, Australia: Federation Press.

Pushkar, Dolores, Myrna Reis, and Melinda Morris. 2002. "Motivation, Personality and Well-Being in Older Volunteers." *International Journal of Aging and Human Development* 55: 141–162.

Putnam, Robert. 2000. *Bowling Alone: The Collapse and Revival of American Community.* New York: Simon and Schuster.

Raiser, Martin, Christian Haerpfer, Thomos Nowotny, and Claire Wallace. 2001. Social Capital In Transition. Working Paper No. 61, European Bank of Reconstruction and Development.

Ramakrishnan, S. Karthick, and Mark Baldassare. 2004. *The Ties That Bind: Changing Demographics and Civic Engagement in California.* San Francisco: Public Policy Institute of California.

Raskoff, Sally, and Richard Sundeen. 1995. "Teenage Volunteers and Their Values." *Nonprofit and Voluntary Sector Quarterly* 24(4): 337–357.

Ravanera, Zenaida, Roderick Beaujot, and Fernando Rajulton. 2002. "The Family and Political Dimensions of Social Cohesion: Analyzing the Link Using the 2000 National Survey on Giving, Volunteering and Participating." Paper presented at the Annual Meeting of the Canadian Population Society, Toronto, 2002. [http://www.ssc.uwo.ca/sociology/popstudies/dp/do02–07 .pdf].

Reed, Paul, and L. Kevin Selbee. 2000a. *Volunteering in Canada in the 1990s: Stasis and Change.* Ottawa: Statistics Canada

———. 2000b. "Distinguishing Characteristics of Active Volunteers in Canada." *Nonprofit and Voluntary Sector Quarterly* 29: 571–593.

———. 2001. "The Civic Core in Canada: Disproportionality in Charitable Giving, Volunteering, and Civic Participation." *Nonprofit and Voluntary Sector Quarterly* 30: 761–780.

———. 2003. "Do People Who Volunteer Have a Distinctive Ethos? A Canadian Study." Pp. 91–110 in *The Values of Volunteering: A Cross-Cultural Perspective,* ed. Paul Dekker and Loek Halman. New York: Kluwer Academic.

Reich, Warren. 2000. "Identity Structure, Narrative Accounts, and Commitment to a Volunteer Role." *Journal of Psychology* 134: 422–435.

Reinarman, Craig. 1987. *American States of Mind.* New Haven, Conn.: Yale University Press.

Reitsma-Street, Marge, Mechthild Maczewski, and Sheila Neysmith. 2000. "Promoting Engagement: An Organizational Study of Volunteers in Community Resource Centers for Children." *Children and Youth Services Review* 22: 651–678.

Reskin, B. 1993. "Sex Segregation in the Workplace." *Annual Review of Sociology* 19: 241–270.

Rhodes, Jean. 2002. *Stand by Me: The Risks and Rewards of Mentoring Today's Youth.* Cambridge: Harvard University Press.

Rietschlin, John. 1998. "Voluntary Association Membership and Psychological Distress." *Journal of Health and Social Behavior* 39: 348–355.

Rigney, Daniel, Jerome Matz, and Armando Abney. 2004. "Is There a Catholic Ethic of Sharing?" *Sociology of Religion* 65: 155–165.

Robinson, John, and Geoffrey Godbey. 1997. *Time for Life: The Surprising Ways Americans Use Their Time.* University Park: Pennsylvania State University Press.

Robinson, Robert, and Elton Jackson. 2001. "Is Trust in Others Declining in America? An Age-Period-Cohort Analysis." *Social Science Research* 30: 117–145.

Robison, Julie, Phyllis Moen, and Donna Dempster-McClain. 1995. "Women's Caregiving: Changing Profiles and Pathways." *Journal of Gerontology* 50B: S362–S373

Rochon, Thomas R. 1998. *Culture Moves: Ideas, Activism, and Changing Values.* Princeton: Princeton University Press.

Rogers, Richard. 1996. "The Effects of Family Composition, Health, and Social Support Linkages on Mortality." *Journal of Health and Social Behavior* 37: 326–338.

Rohe, William, and Victoria Basolo. 1997. "Long-Term Effects of Homeowner-ship on the Self-Perceptions and Social Interaction of Low-Income Persons." *Environment and Behavior* 29: 793–820.

Rohe, W., G. McCarthy, and S. Van Zandt. 2000. The Social Benefits and Costs of Homeownership: A Critical Assessment of the Research. Working Paper No. 00-01, Washington, D.C.: Research Institute for Housing America.

Rohe, William, and Michael Stegman. 1994. "The Impact of Homeownership on the Social and Political Involvement of Low-Income People." *Urban Affairs Quarterly* 30: 152–172.

Roker, Debi, Katie Player, and John Coleman. 1999a. "Young People's Voluntary and Campaigning Activities as Sources of Political Education." *Oxford Review of Education* 25: 185–198.

———. 1999b. "Exploring Adolescent Altruism: British Young People's Involve-ment in Voluntary Work and Campaigning." Pp. 56–72 in *Roots of Civic Identity: International Perspectives on Community Service and Activism in Youth,* ed. Miranda Yates and James Youniss. Cambridge: Cambridge Univer-sity Press.

Romero, Carol Jusenius. 1986. "The Economics of Volunteerism: A Review." Pp. 23–50 in *America's Aging: Productive Roles in an Older Society,* ed. Committee on an Aging Society, Institute of Medicine and National Research Council. Washington, D.C.: National Academy Press.

Roof, Wade Clark. 1999. *Spiritual Marketplace: Baby Boomers and the Remak-ing of American Religion.* Princeton: Princeton University Press.

Roper ASW. 2004. *Baby Boomers Envision Retirement II.* Washington, D.C.: AARP.

Rose-Ackerman, Susan. 1996. "Altruism, Nonprofits, and Economic Theory." *Journal of Economic Literature* 343: 701–728.

Rosenberg, Morris, Carmi Schooler, Carrie Schoenberg, and Florence Rosenberg. 1995. "Global Self-Esteem and Specific Self-Esteem." *American Sociological Review* 60: 141–156.

Rosenthal, Saul, Candice Feiring, and Michael Lewis. 1998. "Political Volunteer-ing from Late Adolescence to Young Adulthood: Patterns and Predictions." *Journal of Social Issues* 54: 471–493.

Rossi, Alice. 2001a. "Contemporary Dialogue on Civil Society and Social Re-sponsibility." Pp. 3–72 in *Caring and Doing for Others,* ed. Alice Rossi. Chi-cago: University of Chicago Press.

———. 2001b. "Domains and Dimensions of Social Responsibility." Pp. 97–134 in *Caring and Doing for Others,* ed. Alice Rossi. Chicago: University of Chi-cago Press.

———. 2001c. "Developmental Roots of Adult Social Responsibility." Pp. 227–320 in *Caring and Doing for Others,* ed. Alice Rossi. Chicago: University of Chicago Press.

———. 2001d. "Impact of Family Problems on Social Responsibility." Pp. 321–

347 in *Caring and Doing for Others,* ed. Alice Rossi. Chicago: University of Chicago Press.

———. 2001e. "The Interplay of Work and Family and Its Impact on Community Service." Pp. 427–462 in *Caring and Doing for Others,* ed. Alice Rossi. Chicago: University of Chicago Press.

Rossi, Peter, and Eleanor Weber. 1996. "The Social Benefits of Homeownership: Empirical Evidence from National Surveys." *Housing Policy Debate* 7: 1–34.

Rothstein, Bo. 2001. "Social Capital in the Social Democratic Welfare State." *Politics and Society* 29: 206–240.

Rotolo, Thomas. 1999. "Trends in Voluntary Association Participation." *Nonprofit and VoluntarySector Quarterly.* 28: 199–212.

———. 2000. "A Time to Join, a Time to Quit: The Influence of Life Cycle Transitions on Voluntary Association Memberships." *Social Forces* 78: 1133–1161.

Rotolo, Thomas, and John Wilson. 2004. "What Happened to the 'Long Civic Generation?' Explaining Cohort Differences in Volunteerism." *Social Forces* 82: 1091–1121.

———. 2006a. "Substitute or Complement? Spousal Influence on Volunteering." *Journal of Marriage and Family* 68: 305–319.

———. 2006b. "Employment Sector and Volunteering: The Contribution of Nonprofit and Public Sector Workers to the Volunteer Labor Force." *Sociological Quarterly* 47: 21–40.

———. 2007. "Job Segregation among Volunteers." Unpublished paper.

——— (forthcoming). "The Effects of Children and Employment Status on the Volunteer Work of American Women." *Nonprofit and Voluntary Sector Quarterly.*

Roxburgh, Susan. 2002. "Racing through Life: The Distribution of Time Pressures by Roles and Role Resources among Full-Time Workers." *Journal of Family and Economic Issues* 23: 121–145.

Roy, Simon, and Lina Danileviciute. 1999. "Volunteering to Help Others or Find a Job? The Motivations Behind Volunteering Activities and Their Impacts on the Well-Being of Older Canadian Adults." http://www.statcan.ca/english /conferences/economic1999/Roy_e.PDF.

Royce, Anya, and Ricardo Rodriguez. 1999. "From Personal Charity to Organized Giving: Hispanic Institutions and Values of Stewardship and Philanthropy." *New Directions for Philanthropic Fundraising.* 24: 9–29.

Rozario, Philip, Nancy Morrow-Howell, and James Hinterlong. 2004. "Role Enhancement or Role Strain." *Research on Aging* 26: 413–428.

Rubin, Allen, and Irene Thorelli. 1984. "Egoistic Motives and Longevity of Participation by Social Service Volunteers." *Journal of Applied Behavioral Science* 20: 223–235.

Ruiter, Stijn, and Nan Dirk de Graaf. 2006. "National Context, Religiosity and Volunteering." *American Sociological Review* 71: 191–210.

Ruston, Dave. 2003. *Volunteers, Helpers and Socializers: Social Capital and Time Use.* London: Office of National Statistics.

Salamon, Lester. 1997. *Holding the Center: America's Nonprofit Sector at a Crossroads.* New York: Nathan Cummings Foundation.

———. 2002. "The Resilient Sector: The State of Nonprofit America." Pp. 3–64 in *The State of Nonprofit America,* ed. Lester Salamon. Washington, D.C.: Brookings Institute Press.

Salamon, Lester, and Helmut Anheier. 1994. Caring Sector or Caring Society? Discovering the Nonprofit Sector Cross-Nationally. Working Paper of the Johns Hopkins Comparative Nonprofit Sector Project, Baltimore: Center for Civil Society Studies, Johns Hopkins University.

———. 1996. The International Classification of Nonprofit Organizations: ICNPO-Revision 1, 1996. Working Paper of the Johns Hopkins Comparative Nonprofit Sector Project, no. 19, Baltimore: Johns Hopkins Institute for Policy Studies.

———. 1997. "Toward a Common Definition." Pp. 29–50 in *Defining the Nonprofit Sector: A Cross National Analysis,* ed. Lester Salamon and Helmut Anheier. Manchester: Manchester University Press.

Salamon, Lester, Helmut Anheier, Regina List, Stephan Toepler, and S. Wojciech Sokolowski. 1999. *Global Civil Society: Dimensions of the Nonprofit Sector.* Baltimore: Center for Civil Society Studies, Johns Hopkins University.

Salamon, Lester, and Sarah Dewees. 2002. "In Search of the Nonprofit Sector: Improving the State of the Art." *American Behavioral Scientist* 45: 1716–1740.

Salamon, Lester, and S. Wojciech Sokolowski. 2001. Volunteering in Cross-National Perspective. Working Paper of the Johns Hopkins Comparative Nonprofit Sector Project, no. 40, Baltimore: Johns Hopkins Center for Civil Society Studies.

———. 2003. "Institutional Roots of Volunteering: Toward a Macro-Structural Theory of Individual Voluntary Action." Pp. 71–90 in *The Values of Volunteering: A Cross-Cultural Perspective,* ed. Paul Dekker and Loek Halman. New York: Kluwer Academic.

Salamon, Lester, S. Wojciech Sokolowski, and Helmut Anheier. 2000. Social Origins of Civil Society: An Overview. Working Paper of the Johns Hopkins Comparative Nonprofit Sector Project, Baltimore: Center for Civil Society Studies, Johns Hopkins University.

Salamon, Lester, S. Wojciech Sokolowski, and Regina List. 2003. *Global Civil Society: An Overview.* Baltimore: Center for Civil Society Studies, Johns Hopkins University.

Salamon, Sonya. 2003. *Newcomers to Old Towns: Suburbanization of the Heartland.* Chicago: University of Chicago Press.

Sampson, Robert. 1991. "Linking the Micro and Macrolevel Dimensions of Community Social Organization." *Social Forces* 70: 43–64.

Sampson, Robert, and W. Byron Groves. 1989. "Community Structure and Crime: Testing Social Disorganization Theory." *American Journal of Sociology* 94: 774–802.

Sampson, Robert, J. Morenoff, and T. Gannon-Rowley. 2002. "Assessing Neighborhood Effects: Social Processes and New Directions in Research." *Annual Review of Sociology* 28: 443–478.

Sapiro, Virginia. 1984. *The Political Integration of Women*. Urbana: University of Illinois Press.

Saunders, Peter. 1990. *A Nation of Home Owners*. London: Unwin Hyman.

Saxton, Gregory, and Michelle Benson. 2005. "Social Capital and the Growth of the Nonprofit Sector." *Social Science Quarterly* 86: 16–35.

Scales, Peter, and Eugene Roehlkepartain. 2004. "Service to Others: a 'Gateway Asset' for School Success and Healthy Development." In *Growing to Greatness 2004*. Saint Paul, Minn.: National Youth Leadership Council.

Schervish, Paul. 1995. "Gentle as Doves and Wise as Serpents: The Philosophy of Care and the Sociology of Transmission." Pp. 1–20 in *Care and Community in Modern Society*, ed. Paul Schervish, Virginia Hodgkinson and Margaret Gates. San Francisco: Jossey-Bass.

Schervish, Paul, and John Havens. 1997. "Social Participation and Charitable Giving: A Multivariate Analysis." *Voluntas* 8: 235–260.

Schieman, Scott, and Heather Turner. 2001. "When Feeling Other People's Pain Hurts: Psychosocial Resources and the Relationship between Empathy and Depressive Emotions." *Social Psychology Quarterly* 64: 376–389.

Schlesinger, Arthur. 1944. "Biography of a Nation of Joiners." *American Historical Review* 50(1): 1–25.

Schlozman, Kay Lehman. 2000. "Did Working Women Kill the PTA?" *American Prospect* 11: 14–16.

Schlozman, Kay Lehman, Nancy Burns, and Sidney Verba. 1995. "Gender and the Pathways to Participation: The Role of Resources." *Journal of Politics* 56: 267–293.

———. 1999. " 'What Happened at Work Today?': A Multistage Model of Gender, Employment, and Political Participation." *Journal of Politics* 61: 29–53.

Schneider, Barbara, and James Coleman. 1996. *Parents, Their Children, and Schools*. Boulder, Colo.: Westview Press.

Schofer, Evan, and Marion Fourcade-Gourinchas. 2001. "The Structural Contexts of Civic Engagement: Voluntary Association Membership in Comparative Perspective." *American Sociological Review* 66: 806–828.

Schondel, Connie, and Kathryn Boehm. 2000. "Motivational Needs of Adolescent Volunteers." *Adolescence* 35: 335–344.

Schor, Juliet B. 1991. *The Overworked American: The Unexpected Decline of Leisure*. New York: Basic Books.

Schram, Vicki, and Marilyn Dunsing. 1981. "Influences on Married Women's Volunteer Work Participation." *Journal of Consumer Research* 7: 372–379.

Schwadel, Philip. 2002. "Testing the Promise of the Churches: Income Inequality in the Opportunity to Learn Civic Skills in Christian Congregations." *Journal for the Scientific Study of Religion* 41: 565–575.

Schwirian, Kent, and Margaret L. Helfrich. 1988. "Economic Role and Community Involvement of Business Executives." *Sociological Quarterly* 9: 64–72.

Schuman, Howard, and Michael Johnson. 1976. "Attitudes and Behavior." *Annual Review of Sociology* 2: 161–207.

Schuman, Howard, and Jacqueline Scott. 1989. "Generations and Collective Memories." *American Sociological Review* 54: 359–381.

Scott, Ann Firor. 1991. *Natural Allies: Women's Associations in American History.* Urbana: University of Illinois Press.

Secret, Philip, James Johnson, and Audrey Forrest. 1990. "The Impact of Religiosity on Political Participation and Membership in Voluntary Associations among Black and White Americans." *Journal of Black Studies* 21: 87–102.

Segal, Lewis. 1993. "Four Essays on the Supply of Volunteer Labor and Econometrics (Labor Supply)." Ph.D. thesis, Northwestern University.

Segal, Lewis, and Burton Weisbrod. 2002. "Volunteer Labor Sorting Across Industries." *Journal of Policy Analysis and Management* 21: 427–447.

Selbee, L. Kevin, and Paul Reed. 2001. "Patterns of Volunteering Over the Life Cycle." *Canadian Social Trends* 61: 2–6.

Selle, Per. 1999. "The Transformation of the Voluntary Sector in Norway: The Decline of Social Capital?" Pp. 144–166 in *Social Capital and European Democracy*, ed. Jan van Deth, Marco Maraffi, Kenneth Newton, and Paul Whiteley. London: Routledge.

Serow, Robert, Joseph Ciechalski, and Curtis Daye. 1990. "Students as Volunteers." *Urban Education* 25: 157–168.

Sherkat, Darren, and T. Jean Blocker. 1997. "Explaining the Political and Personal Consequences of Protest." *Social Forces* 75: 1049–1070.

Sigelman, Lee, and Susan Welch. 1994. *Black Americans' Views of Racial Inequality: The Dream Deferred.* Cambridge: Cambridge University Press.

Sills, David. 1957. *The Volunteers: Means and Ends in a National Organization.* Glencoe, Ill.: Free Press.

Simon, Bernd, and Bert Klandermans. 2001. "Politicized Collective Identity: A Social Psychological Analysis." *American Psychologist* 56: 319–331.

Simon, Bernd, Stefan Sturmer, and Kerstin Steffens. 2000. "Helping Individuals or Group Members? The Role of Individual and Collective Identification in AIDS Volunteerism." *Personality and Social Psychology Bulletin* 26: 497–506.

Simon, Christopher, and Changhua Wang. 2002. "The Impact of Americorps Service on Volunteer Participants: Results from a Two-Year Study in Four Western States." *Administration and Society* 5: 522–540.

Simpson, Charles. 1996. "A Fraternity of Danger: Volunteer Fire Companies and the Contradictions of Modernization." *American Journal of Economics and Sociology* 55: 17–34.

Skinner, Rebecca, and Chris Chapman. 1999. *Service-Learning and Community*

Service in K-12 Public Schools. Washington, D.C.: National Center for Education Statistics, U.S. Department of Education.

Skocpol, Theda. 2003. *Diminished Democracy: From Membership to Management in American Civic Life.* Norman: University of Oklahoma Press.

Smidt, Corwin. 1999. "Religion and Civic Engagement: A Comparative Analysis." *Annals of the American Academy of Political and Social Science* 565: 176–192.

Smith, Bradford, Sylvia Shue, Jennifer Vest, and Joseph Villareal. 1999. *Philanthropy in Communities of Color.* Bloomington: Indiana University Press.

Smith, Christian, and Robert Faris. 2002. *Religion and American Adolescent Delinquency, Risk Behaviors and Constructive Social Activities.* Chapel Hill, NC: National Study of Youth and Religion.

Smith, David Horton. 1982. "Altruism, Volunteers, and Volunteerism." Pp. 23–44 in *Volunteerism in the Eighties,* ed. John Harman. Washington, D.C.: University Press of America.

———. 1994. "Determinants of Voluntary Association Participation and Volunteering." *Nonprofit and Voluntary Sector Quarterly* 23: 243–263.

———. 2000. *Grassroots Associations.* Thousand Oaks, Calif.: Sage.

Smith, Elizabeth. 1999. "The Effects of Investments in the Social Capital of Youth on Political and Civic Behavior in Young Adulthood: A Longitudinal Analysis." *Political Psychology* 20: 553–580.

Smith, Justin Davis. 1998. *The 1997 National Survey of Volunteering.* London: National Centre for Volunteering.

Smith, Thomas, Beth Young, Yupin Bae, Susan Choy, and Nabeel Alsalam. 1997. *U.S. Department Of Education, National Center for Statistics, the Condition of Education 1997 NCES 97-388.* Washington, D.C.: U.S. Government Printing Office.

Smith, Tom. 1997. "Factors Relating to Misanthropy in Contemporary American Society." *Social Science Research* 26: 170–196.

Smock, Kristina. 2004. *Democracy in Action: Community Organizing and Urban Change.* New York: Columbia University Press.

Snyder, Mark, and E. Gil Clary. 2003. "Volunteerism and the Generative Society." Pp. 221–237 in *The Generative Society: Caring for Future Generations,* ed. Ed. De St. Aubin, Dan McAdams, and Tae-Chang Kim. Washington, D.C.: American Psychological Association.

Snyder, Mark, E. Gil Clary, and Arthus Stukas. 2000. "The Functional Approach to Volunteerism." Pp. 365–393 in *Why We Evaluate,* ed. Gregory Maio and James Olson. Mahwah, N.J.: Lawrence Erlbaum Associates.

Snyder, Mark, and Allen Omoto. 1992. "Who Helps and Why? The Psychology of AIDS Volunteerism." Pp. 213–239 in *Helping and Being Helped,* ed. Shirlynn Spacapan and Stuart Oskamp. Newbury Park, Calif.: Sage.

Snyder, Mark, Allen Omoto, and A. Lauren Crain. 1999. "Punished for Their Good Deeds: Stigmatization of AIDS Volunteers." *American Behavioral Scientist.* 42: 1175–1188.

Sobel, Richard. 1993. "From Occupational Involvement to Political Participation: An Exploratory Analysis." *Political Behavior* 15: 339–353.

Sokolowski, S. Wojciech. 1996. "Show Me the Way to the Next Worthy Deed." *Voluntas* 7: 259–276.

Soo, Kim, and Hong Gong-Soog. 1998. "Volunteer Participation and Time Commitment by Older Americans." *Family and Consumer Sciences Research Journal* 27: 146–167.

Stack, Carol. 1974. *All Our Kin: Strategies for Survival in a Black Community.* New York: Harper & Row.

Staines, Graham. 1980 "Spillover and Compensation: A Review of the Literature on the Relationship between Work and NonWork." *Human Relations* 33: 111–129.

Stall, Susan, and Randy Stoecker. 1998. "Community Organizing or Organizing Community? Gender and the Crafts of Empowerment." *Gender and Society* 12: 729–756.

Stark, Rodney and Roger Finke, 2000. *Acts of Faith: Explaining the Human Side of Religion.* Berkeley: University of California Press.

Statham, Anne, and Patricia Rhoton. 1985. *The Volunteer Work of Mature and Young Women: 1974–1981.* Columbus: Center for Human Resource Research, Ohio State University.

Statistics Bureau, Ministry of Internal Affairs and Communications. 2002. *Survey on Time Use and Leisure Activities.* http://www.stat.go.jp/english/data/shakai/index.htm

St. John, Craig, and Jesse Fuchs. 2002. "The Heartland Responds to Terror: Volunteering After the Bombing of the Murrah Federal Building." *Social Science Quarterly* 83: 397–415.

Stebbins, Robert. 2004. "Introduction." Pp.1–12 in *Volunteering as Leisure/Leisure as Volunteering,* ed. Robert Stebbins. Cambridge, Mass.: CABI Publishing.

Steger, Mary Ann, John Pierce, Brent Steel, and Nicholas Lovrich. 1989. "Political Culture, Postmaterial Values and the New Environmental Paradigm: A Comparative Analysis of Canada and the United States." *Political Behavior* 11: 233–254.

Stein, Michael. 1989. "Gratitude and Attitude: A Note on Emotional Welfare." *Social Psychology Quarterly* 52: 242–248.

Steinberg, Kathryn, Partrick Rooney, and William Chin. 2002. "Measurement of Volunteering: A Methodological Study Using Indiana as a Test Case." *Nonprofit and Voluntary Sector Quarterly* 484–501.

Steinberg, Reva. 1999. "Why Pro Bono Counts." *Practicing CPA* 23: 5.

Steinberg, Ronnie, and Jerry Jacobs. 1994. "Pay Equity in Nonprofit Organizations: Making Women's Work Visible." Pp. 79–120 in *Women and Power in the Nonprofit Sector,* ed. Teresa Odendahl and Michael O'Neill. San Francisco: Jossey-Bass.

Stephan, Paula. 1991. "Relationships among Market Work, Work Aspirations and Volunteering: The Case of Retired Women." *Nonprofit and Voluntary Sector Quarterly*, 20: 225–236.

Stevens, Carolyn. 1997. *On the Margins of Japanese Society: Volunteers and the Welfare of the Urban Underclass*. London: Routledge.

Stewart, Eric, and Rhona Weinstein 1997. "Volunteer Participation in Context: Motivations and Political Efficacy within Three AIDS Organizations." *American Journal of Community Psychology* 25: 809–838.

Stockdill, Brett. 2001. "Forging a Multidimensional Oppositional Consciousness: Lessons from Community-Based AIDS Activism." Pp. 204–237 in *Oppositional Consciousness: The Subjective Roots of Social Protest*, ed. Jane Mansbridge and Aldon Morris. Chicago: University of Chicago Press.

———. 2003. *Activism against Aids*. Boulder, Colo.: Lynne Rienner Publishers.

Stoker, Laura, and M. Kent Jennings. 1995. "Life-Cycle Transitions and Political Participation: The Case of Marriage." *American Political Science Review* 89: 421–433.

Stoll, Michael. 2001. "Race, Neighborhood Poverty, and Participation in Voluntary Associations." *Sociological Forum* 16: 529–557.

Stolle, Dietlind. 2001. "Clubs and Congregations: The Benefits of Joining an Association." Pp.202–244 in *Trust in Society*, ed. Karen Cook. New York: Russell Sage Foundation.

Stolle, Dietlind, and Marc Hooghe. 2002. "The Roots of Social Capital: The Effects of Youth Experience on Participation and Value Patterns in Adult Life." Paper presented at the 98th Annual Meeting of the American Political Science Association, Boston.

Stolle, Dietlind, and Thomas Rochon. 1998. "Are All Associations Alike?" *American Behavioral Scientist* 42: 47–465.

———. 1999. "The Myth of American Exceptionalism: A Three-Nation Comparison of Associational Membership and Social Capital." Pp. 192–210 in *Social Capital and European Democracy*, ed. Jan van Deth, Marco Maraffi, Kenneth Newton, and Paul Whiteley. London: Routledge.

Stone, Leroy, and Andrew Harvey. 2001. "Gender Differences in the Transitions to Total-Work Retirement." Pp. 258–269 in *Retructuring Work and the Life Course*, ed. Victor Marshall, Walter Heinz, Helga Kruger and Anil Verma. Toronto: University of Toronto Press.

Strawbridge, William, Richard Cohen, Sara Shema, and George Kaplan. 1999. "Frequent Attendance at Religious Services and Mortality Over 28 Years." *American Journal of Public Health* 87: 957–961.

Stukas, Arthur, Mark Snyder, and E. Gil Clary. 1999. "The Effects of 'Mandatary Volunteerism' on Intention to Volunteer." *Psychological Science* 10: 59–68.

Sundeen, Richard. 1990. "Family Life Course Status and Volunteer Behavior: Implications for the Single Parent." *Sociological Perspectives* 33: 483–500.

———. 1992. "Differences in Personal Goals and Attitudes among Volunteers." *Nonprofit and Voluntary Sector Quarterly* 21: 271–291.

Sundeen, Richard, and Sally Raskoff. 1994. "Volunteering among Teenagers in the United States." *Nonprofit and Voluntary Sector Quarterly* 23: 383–403.
———. 1995. "Teenage Volunteers and Their Values." *Nonprofit and Voluntary Sector Quarterly* 24: 337–357.
———. 2000. "Ports of Entry and Obstacles: Teenagers' Access to Volunteer Activities." *Nonprofit Management and Leadership* 11: 179–197.
Szinovacz, Maximiliane. 1992. "Social Activities and Retirement Adaptation: Gender and Family Variations." Pp. 236–253 in *Families and Retirement,* ed. Maximiliane Szinovacz, David Ekerdt, and Barbara Vinick. Newbury Park, Calif.: Sage.
Taniguchi, Hiromi. 2006. "Men's and Women's Volunteering: Gender Differences in the Effects of Employment and Family Characteristics." *Nonprofit and Voluntary Sector Quarterly* 35: 83–101.
Taylor, Rebecca. 2004. "Extending Conceptual Boundaries: Work, Voluntary Work and Employment." *Work, Employment and Society* 18: 29–49.
Taylor, Robert. 1988. "Structural Determinants of Religious Participation among Black Americans." *Review of Religious Research* 30: 114–125.
Taylor, Robert, Linda Chatters, Rukmalie Jayakody, and Jeffrey Levin. 1996. "Black and White Differences in Religious Participation: a Multi-Sample Comparison." *Journal for the Scientific Study of Religion* 35: 403–410.
Teske, Nathan. 1997. *Political Activists in America: The Identity Construction Model of Political Participation.* Cambridge: Cambridge University Press.
Thoits, Peggy. 1986. "Multiple Identities: Examining Gender and Marital Status Differences in Distress." *American Sociological Review* 51: 259–272.
Thoits, Peggy, and Lynda Hewitt. 2001. "Volunteer Work and Well-Being." *Journal of Health and Social Behavior* 42: 115–131.
Thompson, Alexander. 1993a. "Volunteers and Their Communities: A Comparative Analysis of Firefighters." *Nonprofit and Voluntary Sector Quarterly* 22: 155–166.
———. 1993b. "Rural Emergency Volunteers and Their Communities: A Demographic Comparison." *Journal of Community Health* 18: 379–393.
———. 1995. "The Sexual Division of Leadership in Volunteer Emergency Medical Service Squads." *Nonprofit Management and Leadership* 6: 55–66.
Tiehen, Laura. 2000. "Has Working More Caused Married Women to Volunteer Less? Evidence from Time Diary Data, 1965 to 1993." *Nonprofit and Voluntary Sector* 4: 505–529.
Tilly, Charles. 2001. "Do Unto Others." Pp. 27–47 in *Political Altruism? Solidarity Movements in International Perspective,* ed. Marco Giugni and Florence Passy. Landham, Md.: Rowman and Littlefield.
Tilly, Chris, and Charles Tilly. 1998. *Work under Capitalism.* Boulder, Colo.: Westview Press.
Toppe, Christopher. 2005. Measuring Volunteering: A Behavioral Approach. Circle Working Paper 42. www.civicyouth.org. Accessed March 8, 2006.

Toppe, Christopher, Arthur Kirsch, and Jocabel Michel. 2002. *Giving and Volunteering in the United States.* Washington, D.C.: The Independent Sector.

Torbert, William, and Malcolm Rogers. 1973. *Being for the Most Part Puppets.* Cambridge: Schenkman.

Torcal, Mariano, and Jose Ramon Montero. 1999. "Facets of Social Capital in New Democracies: The Formation and Consequences of Social Capital in Spain." Pp. 167–191 in *Social Capital and European Democracy,* ed. Jan van Deth, Marco Maraffi, Kenneth Newton, and Paul Whiteley. London: Routledge.

Torney-Purta, Judith, and Jo-Ann Amadeo. 2003. "A Cross-National Analysis of Political and Civic Involvement among Adolescents." *PS: Political Science and Politics* 36: 269–274.

Tossutti, Livianna. 2003. "Does Volunteerism Increase the Political Engagement of Newcomers?" *Canadian Ethnic Studies* 35: 70–85.

Trudeau, K. J., and A. S. Devlin. 1996. "College Students and Community Service: Who, with Whom, and Why?" *Journal of Applied Social Psychology* 26: 1867–1888.

Tsitsos, William. 2003. "Race Differences in Congregational Social Service Activity." *Journal for the Scientific Study of Religion* 42: 205–215.

Turner, Howard. 1992. "Older Volunteers: An Assessment of Two Theories." *Educational Gerontology* 18: 41–55.

Uggen, Christopher, and Jennifer Janikula. 1999. "Volunteerism and Arrest in the Transition to Adulthood." *Social Forces* 78: 331–362.

Umberson, Debra, Meichu Chen, James House, Kristin Hopkins, and Ellen Slaten. 1996. "The Effect of Social Relationships and on Psychological Well-Being: Are Men and Women Really So Different?" *American Sociological Review* 61: 837–857.

U.S. Bureau of Labor Statistics. 2002. *Volunteering in the United States.* Washington, D.C.: Government Printing Office.

——. 2003. *Volunteering in the United States.* Washington, D.C.: Government Printing Office.

——. 2004. *Time-Use Survey.* Washington, D.C.: Government Printing Office.

——. 2005. *Volunteering in the United States.* Washington, D.C.: Government Printing Office.

Uslaner, Eric. 2001. "Volunteering and Social Capital: How Trust and Religion Shape Civic Participation." Pp. 104–117 in *Social Capital and Participation in Everyday Life,* ed. Paul Dekker and Eric Uslaner. London: Routledge.

——. 2002a. *The Moral Foundation of Trust.* Cambridge: Cambridge University Press.

——. 2002b. "Religion and Civic Engagement in Canada and the United States." *Journal for the Scientific Study of Religion* 41: 239–254.

Uslaner, E. M. 2006. Does Diversity Drive Down Trust? FEEM Working Paper No. 69, http://ssrn.com/abstract=903051.

Uslaner, Eric, and Mitchell Brown. 2005. "Inequality, Trust, and Civic Engagement." *American Politics Research* 33: 868–894.

Uslaner, Eric, and Paul Dekker. 2001. "The 'Social' in Social Capital." Pp. 176–187 in *Social Capital and Participation in Everyday Life*, ed. Paul Dekker and Eric Uslaner. London: Routledge.

Utz, Rebecca L., Deborah Carr, Randolph Nesse, and Camille B. Wortman. 2002. "The Effect of Widowhood on Older Adults' Social Participation: An Evaluation of Activity, Disengagement, and Continuity Theories." *Gerontologist* 42: 522–533.

Vaillancourt, Francois. 1994. "To Volunteer or Not: Canada, 1987." *Canadian Journal of Economics* 27: 813–826.

Van Schaik, Ton. 2002. *Social Capital in the European Values Study Surveys.* Paper prepared for the OECD-ONS International Conference on Social Capital Measurement, London.

Van Willigen, Mary. 2000. "Differential Benefits of Volunteering Across the Life Course." *Journal of Gerontology: Social Sciences* 55B: S308–318.

Varese, Federico, and Meir Yaish. 2000. "The Importance of Being Asked: The Rescue of Jews in Nazi Europe." *Rationality and Society* 12: 307–334.

Veenstra, Gerry. 2000. Social Capital, SES and Health: An Individual-Level Analysis." *Social Science and Medicine* 50: 619–629.

Vela-McConnell, James. 1999. *Who Is My Neighbor? Social Affinity in a Modern World*. Albany: State University of New York Press.

Verba, Sidney, Kay Lehman Schlozman, and Henry Brady. 1995. *Voice and Equality: Civic Voluntarism in American Politics*. Cambridge: Harvard University Press.

Vidich, Arthur, and Joseph Bensman. 1960. *Small Town in Mass Society: Class, Power and Religion in a Rural Community*. New York: Anchor Books.

Voicu, Malina, and Bogdan Voicu. 2003. "Volunteering in Romania: A *Rara Avis*." Pp. 143–160 in *The Values of Volunteering: A Cross-Cultural Perspective*, ed. Paul Dekker and Loek Halman. New York: Kluwer Academic.

Wagner, David. 2000. *What's Love Got to Do with It?: A Critical Look at American Charity*. New York: New Press.

Waite, Linda, and Maggie Gallagher. 2000. *The Case for Marriage*. New York: Doubleday.

Wandersman, Abraham, Paul Florin, Robert Friedmann, and Ron Meier. 1987. "Who Participates, Who Does Not, and Why? An Analysis of Voluntary Neighborhood Organizations in the United States and Israel." *Sociological Forum* 2: 534–555.

Warburton, Jeni, and Tim Crosier. 2001. "Are We Too Busy to Volunteer? The Relationship between Time and Volunteering Using the 1997 ABS Time Use Data." *Australian Journal of Social Issues* 36: 295–315.

Warburton, Jeni, Robyne Le Brocque, and Linda Rosenman. 1998. "Older People—the Reserve Army of Volunteers? An Analysis of Volunteerism among Older Australians." *International Journal of Aging and Human Development* 46: 229–246.

Warburton, Jeni, and Allyson Mutch. 2000. "Volunteer Resources." Pp. 32–43 in *Volunteers and Volunteering*, ed. Jeni Warburton and Melanie Oppenheimer. Annandale, Australia: Federation Press.

Warburton, Jeni, and Jennifer Smith. 2003. "Out of the Generosity of Your Heart: Are We Creating Active Citizens through Compulsory Volunteer Programmes for Young People in Australia?" *Social Policy & Administration* 37: 772–786.

Warburton, Jeni, Deborah Terry, Linda Rosenman, and Margaret Shapiro. 2001. "Differences between Older Volunteers and Nonvolunteers." *Research on Aging* 23: 586–605.

Warde, Alan, Gindo Tampulon, Brian Longhurst, Kathryn Ray, Mike Savage, and Mark Tomlinson. 2003. "Trends in Social Capital: Membership of Associations in Great Britain, 1991–1998." *British Journal of Political Science* 33: 515–534.

Warren, Mark. 2004. "What is the Political Role of Nonprofits in a Democracy?" Pp. 37–50 in *In Search of the Nonprofit Sector*, ed. Peter Frumkin and Jonathan Imber. New Brunswick, N.J.: Transaction Publishers.

Weatherington, Elaine, Phyllis Moen, Nina Glasgow, and Karl Pillemer. 2000. "Multiple Roles, Social Integration and Health." Pp. 48–74 in *Social Integration in the Second Half of Life,* ed. Karl Pillemer, Phyllis Moen, Elaine Weatherington, and Nina Glasgow. Baltimore: Johns Hopkins University Press.

Weitzman, Elissa, and Ichiro Kawachi. 2000. "Giving Means Receiving: The Protective Effect of Social Capital on Binge Drinking on College Campuses." *American Journal of Public Health* 2000 90: 1936–1939.

Weschler, Henry, George McDowell, Andrea Davenport, and Sonia Castillo. 1995. "Correlates of College Student Binge Drinking." *American Journal of Public Health* 85: 921–926.

West, Guida, and Rhoda Blumberg. 1990. "Reconstructing Social Protest from a Feminist Perspective." Pp. 3–36 in *Women and Social Protest,* ed. Guida West and Rhoda Blumberg. New York: Oxford University Press.

Wharton, C. 1991. "Why Can't We Be Friends?" Expectations versus Experience in the Volunteer Role." *Journal of Contemporary Ethnography* 20: 79–107.

Wheeler, Judith, Kevin Gorey, and Bernard Greenblatt. 1998. "The Beneficial Effects of Volunteering for Older Adults and the People They Serve." *International Journal of Aging and Human Development* 47: 69–80.

White, R. 1968. "Toward a Theory of Religious Influence." *Pacific Sociological Review* 7: 23–38.

Whiteley, Paul. 1999. "The Origins of Social Capital." Pp. 45–72 in *Social Capital and European Democracy,* ed. Jan van Deth, Marco Maraffi, Kenneth Newton, and Paul Whiteley. London: Routledge.

———. 2004. *A Health Check for British Democracy: What Do We Know*

About Participation and Its Effects in Britain? A Report Arising from the Economic and Social Research Council's Democracy and Participation Research Program. http://www.esrc.ac.uk/esrccontent/ourresearch/democracy _and_participation.asp.

Whittier, Nancy. 1997. "Political Generations, Micro-Cohorts and the Transformation of Social Movements." *American Sociological Review* 62: 760–778.

Whyte, William. 1957. *The Organization Man.* Garden City, N.Y.: Doubleday.

Wilensky, Harold. 1961. "Orderly Careers and Social Participation." *American Sociological Review* 26:521–539.

Wilkinson, Jennifer, and Michael Bittman. 2002. *Volunteering: The Human Face of Democracy. SPRC Discussion Paper No. 114.* Sydney: Social Policy Research Centre, University of New South Wales.

Wilkinson, Jennifer, and Michael Bittman. 2003. *Relatives, Friends and Strangers: The Links between Voluntary Activity, Sociability and Care. SPRC Discussion Paper No. 125.* Sydney: Social Policy Research Centre, University of New South Wales.

Wilson, Carla, Anne Kerslake, and Rachel Smithies. 2001. " 'Lady Bountiful' and the 'Virtual Volunteers': The Changing Face of Social Service Volunteering." *Social Policy Journal of New Zealand* 17: 124–146.

Wilson, James. 1973. *Political Organizations* New York: Basic Books.

Wilson, John, and Thomas Janoski. 1995. "The Contribution of Religion to Volunteer Work." *Sociology of Religion* 56: 137–152.

Wilson, John, and Marc Musick. 1997a. "Who Cares? Toward an Integrated Theory of Volunteer Work." *American Sociological Review* 62: 694–713.

———. 1997b "Work and Volunteering: The Long Arm of the Job." *Social Forces* 76: 251–272.

———. 1998. "The Contribution of Social Resources to Volunteering." *Social Science Quarterly* 79: 799–814.

———. 1999. "Attachment to Volunteering." *Sociological Forum* 14(2): 243–272.

———. 2000. Women's Labor Force Participation and Volunteer Work. Nonprofit Sector Research Fund Working Paper Series, Washington, D.C.: Aspen Institute.

———. 2003. "Doing Well by Doing Good: Volunteering and Occupational Achievement among American Women." *Sociological Quarterly* 44: 433–450.

Wilson, William J. 1980. *The Declining Significance of Race: Blacks and Changing American Institutions.* Chicago: University of Chicago Press.

Wirthlin Group. 1995a. *The Prudential Spirit of Community Adult Survey.* Newark, N.J.: Prudential Insurance Co.

———. 1995b. *The Prudential Spirit of Community Youth Survey.* Newark, N.J.: Prudential Insurance Co.

Wolch, Jennifer. 1990. *The Shadow State: Government and the Voluntary Sector in Transition.* New York: Foundation Center.

Wollebaek, Dag, and Per Selle. 2003a. "The Importance of Passive Membership for Social Capital Formation." Pp. 67–88 in *Generating Social Capital*, ed. Marc Hooghe and Dietlind Stolle. New York: Palgrave MacMillan.

———. 2003b. "Generations and Organizational Change." Pp. 161–178 in *The Values of Volunteering: A Cross-Cultural Perspective*, ed. Paul Dekker and Loek Halman. New York: Kluwer Academic.

Wood, Richard. 1997. "Social Capital and Political Culture: God Meets Politics in the Inner City." *American Behavioral Scientist* 40(5): 595–605.

Woodard, Michael. 1987. "Voluntary Association Membership among Black Americans." *Sociological Quarterly* 28: 285–301.

Woolley, Frances. 1998. *Social Cohesion and Voluntary Activity: Making Connections*. Paper presented at the CSLS Conference on the State of Living Standards and the Quality of Life in Canada, Ottawa.

———. 2003. "Social Cohesion and Voluntary Activity: Making Connections." Pp. 150–181 in *The Economic Implications of Social Cohesion*, ed. Lars Osberg. Toronto: University of Toronto Press.

Wuthnow, Robert. 1991. *Acts of Compassion: Caring for Others and Helping Ourselves*. Princeton: Princeton University Press.

———. 1994a. *God and Mammon in America*. New York: Free Press.

———. 1994b. *Sharing the Journey: Support Groups and America's New Quest for Community*. New York: Free Press

———. 1995. *Learning to Care: Elementary Kindness in an Age of Indifference*. New York: Oxford University Press.

———. 1998. *Loose Connections*. Cambridge: Harvard University Press.

———. 1999. "Mobilizing Civic Engagement: The Changing Impact of Religious Involvement." Pp. 331–363 in *Civic Engagement in American Democracy*, ed. Theda Skocpol and Morris Fiorina. Washington, D.C.: Brookings Institute Press.

———. 2002. "Beyond the Quiet Influence? Possibilities for the Protestant Mainline." Pp. 381–404 in *The Quiet Hand of God: Faith-Based Activism and the Public Role of Mainline Protestantism*, ed. Robert Wuthnow and John Evans. Berkeley: University of California Press.

———. 2004. *Saving America? Faith-Based Services and the Future of Civil Society*. Princeton: Princeton University Press.

Yates, Miranda, and James Youniss. 1998. "Community Service and Political Identity Development in Adolescence." *Journal of Social Issues* 54: 495–512.

Young, Frank, and Nina Glasgow. 1998. "Voluntary Social Participation and Health." *Research on Aging* 20: 339–362.

Youniss, James, Jeffrey McLellan, and Barbara Mazer. 2001. "Voluntary Service, Peer Group Orientation, and Civic Engagement." *Journal of Adolescent Research* 16: 456–468.

Youniss, James, and Miranda Yates. 1999. "Introduction: International Perspectives on the Roots of Civic Identity." Pp. 1–15 in *Roots of Civic Identity: International Perspectives on Community Service and Activism in Youth*, ed. Miranda Yates and James Youniss. Cambridge: Cambridge University Press.

Youniss, James, Miranda Yates, and Y. Su. 1997. "Social Integration: Community Service and Marijuana Use in High School Seniors." *Journal of Adolescent Research* 12: 245–262.

Zappala, Gianni, Ben Parker, and Vanessa Green. 2001. *The 'New Face' of Volunteering in Social Enterprises: The Smith Family Experience [Background Paper No 2]*. Camperdown, NSW, Australia: Smith Family.

Zeldin, Shepherd, and Dimitri Topitzes. 2002. "Neighborhood Experiences, Community Connection, and Positive Beliefs About Adolescents among Urban Adults and Youth." *Journal of Community Psychology* 30: 647–669.

Ziemek, Susanne. 2003. *The Economics of Volunteer Labor Supply: An Application to Countries of a Different Development Level*. New York: Peter Lang.

Zukin, Sharon. 2004. *Point of Purchase: How Shopping Changed American Culture*. New York: Routledge.

Zurcher, Louis A. 1983. *Social Roles: Conformity, Conflict and Creativity*. Beverly Hills, Calif.: Sage.

Zweigenhaft, Richard, Jo Armstrong, Frances Quintis, and Annie Riddick. 1996. "The Motivation and Effectiveness of Hospital Volunteers." *Journal of Social Psychology* 136: 25–34.

Index

Page numbers in *italics* refer to graphs and charts.

ability signaling, 127, 488, 526
abortion, 22, 108
Abrahams, Naomi: on employment, 245; on gender, 187; on identity, 317, 444; on motives, 60; on motives of volunteers, 63
accomplishment, 65
achievement, 56
ACL. *See* Americans' Changing Lives (ACL)
Active Communities Agenda, 394
activism: and attachment, 427; and caring, 524–525; and class distinctions, 141; compared with volunteerism, 12–13, 17–23, 26, 71, 542n10, 543nn11–13; and disillusionment, 448; and education, 122; and gender, 183–184; and identity, 517–521; and interests, 16; and motives, 431–432; peace activists, 131–132, 427, 448; and time volunteered, 169; *See also* advocacy
"activity" theory, 263
Adair, Andrea, 60
adultery, 104
advocacy: and age, 223, 261–262; and classification, 34; and cross-national differences, 353; defined, 11, 20–21; and gender, 183; and generational differences, 376, 377; and income, 493; and inter-state differences, 340; and mobilization, 551n11; and motives, 79; and occupations, 142; and parental status, 249; and profile of the volunteer, 364; and race, 204; and religion, 312, 362, *363*; and social identity, 316; and trust, 47; *See also* activism
advocates of volunteerism, 4
affluence, 52, 333, 364
African American Protestants, 311, 340
African Americans. *See* Blacks
age, 221–237; and activism, 20; and attitudes, 265–266; and barriers to

volunteering, 164; and benefits of volunteerism, 14; and cross-national differences, 367–368; and domains, 223–224, 261–262, 562n5; and education, 123, 125, 252–253, 265; and employment, 259, 506; and free time, 254, 255; and gender, 179–181, 183, 192–193, *194*; and generational differences, 372–378, 572n4, 573n8; and income, 252–253; and job segregation, 416–417; and the life course, 222–223; and mental health, 503–505; and monetary donations, 133, 135; and motives, 74–75, 254–255, 549n14; and personality traits, 48, 52; and preferences of volunteers, 223–224; productive aging, 251–252, 514; and race, 200–201, 204; and rate of volunteerism, 222–223; and recruitment, *130*, 265, 291, *292, 294,* 295, 296; and resources, 111; and schools, 303; and social networks, 223, 251, 254, 255; of societies, 355; successful aging, 265, 497; and tasks, 407; and time volunteered, 168, 545n18; and trust, 46; and voluntary associations, 272; and volunteer histories, 224–225; youth (*see* teenagers; youth and young adult volunteers); *See also* middle age; older volunteers; retirement
Age Concern, 15
agrarian communities, 329
agreeableness, 39, 40, 41, 43, 51
AIDS volunteers: and activism, 21–22, 518, 542n10, 543n 11; and burnout, 452; and generalized reciprocity, 99; and identity, 19; and informal social interaction, 268; and motives, 60, 62, 78–79, 445, 447; and NAMES Project AIDS Memorial Quilt, 551n 11; and satisfaction, 440; and social identity, 316, 317; and stigmatization, 115, 123; and stress, 494; and values, 83

Philanthropic and Nonprofit Studies

Dwight F. Burlingame and David C. Hammack, editors

Thomas Adam, editor. *Philanthropy, Patronage, and Civil Society: Experiences from Germany, Great Britain, and North America*

Albert B. Anderson. *Ethics for Fundraisers*

Peter M. Ascoli. *Julius Rosenwald: The Man Who Built Sears, Roebuck and Advanced the Cause of Black Education in the American South*

Karen J. Blair. *The Torchbearers: Women and Their Amateur Arts Associations in America, 1890-1930*

Eleanor Brilliant. *Private Charity and Public Inquiry: A History of the Filer and Peterson Commissions*

Dwight F. Burlingame, editor. *The Responsibilities of Wealth*

Dwight F. Burlingame and Dennis Young, editors. *Corporate Philanthropy at the Crossroads*

Charles T. Clotfelter and Thomas Ehrlich, editors. *Philanthropy and the Nonprofit Sector in a Changing America*

Ruth Crocker. *Mrs. Russell Sage: Women's Activism and Philanthropy in Gilded Age and Progressive Era America*

Marcos Cueto, editor. *Missionaries of Science: The Rockefeller Foundation and Latin America*

William Damon and Susan Verducci, editors. *Taking Philanthropy Seriously: Beyond Noble Intentions to Responsible Giving*

Gregory Eiselein. *Literature and Humanitarian Reform in the Civil War Era*

David C. Hammack, editor. *Making the Nonprofit Sector in the United States: A Reader*

Jerome L. Himmelstein. *Looking Good and Doing Good: Corporate Philanthropy and Corporate Power*

Warren F. Ilchman, Stanley N. Katz, and Edward L. Queen II, editors. *Philanthropy in the World's Traditions*

Warren F. Ilchman, Alice Stone Ilchman, and Mary Hale Tolar, editors. *The Lucky Few and the Worthy Many: Scholarship Competitions and the World's Future Leaders*

Thomas H. Jeavons. *When the Bottom Line Is Faithfulness: Management of Christian Service Organizations*

Amy A. Kass, editor. *The Perfect Gift*

Ellen Condliffe Lagemann, editor. *Philanthropic Foundations: New Scholarship, New Possibilities*

Daniel C. Levy. *To Export Progress: The Golden Age of University Assistance in the Americas*

Mike W. Martin. *Virtuous Giving: Philanthropy, Voluntary Service, and Caring*

Kathleen D. McCarthy, editor. *Women, Philanthropy, and Civil Society*

Marc A. Musick and John Wilson, editors. *Volunteers: A Social Profile*

Mary J. Oates. *The Catholic Philanthropic Tradition in America*

Robert S. Ogilvie. *Voluntarism, Community Life, and the American Ethic*

J. B. Schneewind, editor. *Giving: Western Ideas of Philanthropy*

William H. Schneider, editor. *Rockefeller Philanthropy and Modern Biomedicine: International Initiatives from World War I to the Cold War*

Bradford Smith, Sylvia Shue, Jennifer Lisa Vest, and Joseph Villarreal. *Philanthropy in Communities of Color*

David Horton Smith, Robert A. Stebbins, and Michael A. Dover, editors. *A Dictionary of Nonprofit Terms and Concepts*

David H. Smith. *Entrusted: The Moral Responsibilities of Trusteeship*

David H. Smith, editor. *Good Intentions: Moral Obstacles and Opportunities*

Jon Van Til. *Growing Civil Society: From Nonprofit Sector to Third Space*

Andrea Walton. *Women and Philanthropy in Education*

Marc A. Musick is Associate Professor of Sociology and a Faculty Research Associate in the Population Research Center at the University of Texas at Austin. He also holds an appointment as an Adjunct Research Associate Professor in the Institute for Social Research at the University of Michigan. His research interests include the causes and consequences of volunteering, religious behavior and belief, and other forms of productive activity. His research has appeared in publications such as *American Sociological Review, Journal of Health and Social Behavior, Journal of Gerontology: Social Sciences, Journal for the Scientific Study of Religion,* and *Social Forces.*

John Wilson is Professor of Sociology at Duke University. He has published many articles on volunteerism and the impact of race, gender, religion, and leisure on volunteering in publications such as *Social Science Quarterly,* and *American Sociological Review.*